Lecture Notes in Computer Science 7304

Commenced Publication in 1973
Founding and Former Series Editors:
Gerhard Goos, Juris Hartmanis, and Jan van Leeuwen

Editorial Board

David Hutchison
  Lancaster University, UK
Takeo Kanade
  Carnegie Mellon University, Pittsburgh, PA, USA
Josef Kittler
  University of Surrey, Guildford, UK
Jon M. Kleinberg
  Cornell University, Ithaca, NY, USA
Alfred Kobsa
  University of California, Irvine, CA, USA
Friedemann Mattern
  ETH Zurich, Switzerland
John C. Mitchell
  Stanford University, CA, USA
Moni Naor
  Weizmann Institute of Science, Rehovot, Israel
Oscar Nierstrasz
  University of Bern, Switzerland
C. Pandu Rangan
  Indian Institute of Technology, Madras, India
Bernhard Steffen
  TU Dortmund University, Germany
Madhu Sudan
  Microsoft Research, Cambridge, MA, USA
Demetri Terzopoulos
  University of California, Los Angeles, CA, USA
Doug Tygar
  University of California, Berkeley, CA, USA
Gerhard Weikum
  Max Planck Institute for Informatics, Saarbruecken, Germany

Carlo A. Furia   Sebastian Nanz (Eds.)

Objects, Models, Components, Patterns

50th International Conference, TOOLS 2012
Prague, Czech Republic, May 29-31, 2012
Proceedings

 Springer

Volume Editors

Carlo A. Furia
Sebastian Nanz
ETH Zurich
Department of Computer Science
Clausiusstr. 59
8092 Zurich
Switzerland
E-mail: {caf, nanz}@inf.ethz.ch

ISSN 0302-9743   e-ISSN 1611-3349
ISBN 978-3-642-30560-3   e-ISBN 978-3-642-30561-0
DOI 10.1007/978-3-642-30561-0
Springer Heidelberg Dordrecht London New York

Library of Congress Control Number: 2012937846

CR Subject Classification (1998): F.3, D.2, D.3, D.1, C.2, D.2.4, D.4

LNCS Sublibrary: SL 2 – Programming and Software Engineering

Typesetting: Camera-ready by author, data conversion by Scientific Publishing Services, Chennai, India

Printed on acid-free paper

Springer is part of Springer Science+Business Media (www.springer.com)

Preface

Started in 1989, the TOOLS conference series has played a major role in the development of object technology and, with its emphasis on practically useful results, has contributed to making it mainstream and ubiquitous. This year's 50th edition of the International Conference on Objects, Models, Components, Patterns (TOOLS Europe 2012) appropriately celebrated this "triumph of objects": object technology is now commonplace.

TOOLS Europe 2012 took place in Prague during May 29–31, 2012. The Program Committee received 77 paper submissions, consisting of 61 regular papers and 16 short and tool demo papers. Each submission was reviewed by three experts. Based on the reviewers' reports and one week of intense discussion among Program Committee members, we selected 24 papers for presentation at the conference. We were impressed by the overall quality of the submissions, which resulted in a strong competition for acceptance and in a final program of excellent standing. We sincerely thank all authors for their hard work and for choosing TOOLS Europe as venue.

Keynote talks by Lionel Briand and Alan Kay completed the scientific program, together with a presentation by Bertrand Meyer – the Conference Chair and a founder of the TOOLS series – on the occasion of the 50th edition. We would like to express our gratitude to these three outstanding speakers for contributing to making TOOLS Europe 2012 a memorable event.

We also thank the Program Committee members and their subreviewers for their timely and thorough reviewing work. This was instrumental, together with a very lively and constructive discussion, in selecting the best contributions and in giving constructive feedback to all submissions. The EasyChair system helped manage the whole process smoothly and efficiently.

The significant number of submissions received, a record for the latest editions of TOOLS, was largely thanks to the extensive publicity work carried out by our Publicity Chair Scott West. The conference would not have been possible without the great work of the local organization team led by Pavel Tvrdík and including Michal Valenta, Jindra Vojíková, and Jan Chrastina from the Czech Technical University in Prague. Claudia Günthart at ETH Zurich helped manage the finances for all TOOLS co-located conferences. The conference also benefited from the financial support of Microsoft Research and the European Association for Programming Languages and Systems, which sponsored the TOOLS 2012 best paper award.

March 2012

Carlo A. Furia
Sebastian Nanz

Organization

Program Committee

Jonathan Aldrich	Carnegie Mellon University, USA
Gilles Barthe	IMDEA Software Institute, Spain
Lorenzo Bettini	University of Turin, Italy
Yuriy Brun	University of Washington, USA
S.C. Cheung	The Hong Kong University of Science and Technology, China
Gordon Fraser	Saarland University, Germany
Carlo A. Furia	ETH Zurich, Switzerland
John Gallagher	Roskilde University, Denmark
Angelo Gargantini	University of Bergamo, Italy
Michael Goedicke	University of Duisburg-Essen, Germany
Susanne Graf	VERIMAG, France
Mark Harman	University College London, UK
Michael Huth	Imperial College London, UK
Yves Le Traon	University of Luxembourg, Luxembourg
Yang Liu	National University of Singapore, Singapore
Tiziana Margaria	University of Potsdam, Germany
Sebastian Nanz	ETH Zurich, Switzerland
Jerzy Nawrocki	Poznan University of Technology, Poland
Nathaniel Nystrom	University of Lugano, Switzerland
Manuel Oriol	University of York, UK
Alessandro Orso	Georgia Institute of Technology, USA
Richard Paige	University of York, UK
Alexander K. Petrenko	Moscow State University, Russia
Grigore Rosu	University of Illinois at Urbana-Champaign, USA
Peter Sestoft	IT University of Copenhagen, Denmark
Andrey Terekhov	St. Petersburg State University, Russia
Zdeněk Troníček	Czech Technical University in Prague, Czech Republic
Naoyasu Ubayashi	Kyushu University, Japan
Antonio Vallecillo	University of Malaga, Spain
Kapil Vaswani	Microsoft Research, Bangalore, India
Tao Xie	North Carolina State University, USA
Amiram Yehudai	Tel Aviv University, Israel
Michal Young	University of Oregon, USA
Jian Zhang	Chinese Academy of Sciences, China
Lu Zhang	Peking University, China

Additional Reviewers

Arcaini, Paolo
Bartel, Alexandre
Barzilay, Ohad
Beschastnikh, Ivan
Bono, Viviana
Bosselmann, Steve
Brooke, Phillip J.
Buzdalov, Denis
Caire, Patrice
Crespo, Juan Manuel
Demange, Delphine
Edwards, George
El Kateb, Donia
Ellison, Chucky
Gil, Yossi
Gorham, Justin
Guangdong, Bai
Haemmerlé, Rémy
Hwang, Jeehyun
Isberner, Malte
Ivanovic, Dragan
Jin, Dongyun
Katz, Shmuel
Klein, Jacques
Kolovos, Dimitrios
Kuhlemann, Martin
Kunz, César
Li, Yueqi
Loreti, Michele
Lucio, Levi

Matragkas, Nikos
Meng, Guozhu
Meredith, Patrick
Naujokat, Stefan
Neubauer, Johannes
Nguyen, Phu
Nistor, Ligia
Nordio, Martin
Novikov, Evgeny
Pandita, Rahul
Radjenovic, Alek
Rojas, Jose Miguel
Scandurra, Patrizia
Serbanuta, Traian
Shakya, Kiran
Shi, Ling
Song, Wei
Stefanescu, Andrei
Steffen, Bernhard
Tolstov, Konstantin
Tyszberowicz, Shmuel
Voelter, Markus
Wei, Jun
Wei, Yi
Wu, Ling
Wu, Rongxin
Xiao, Hao
Xiao, Xusheng
Ye, Chunyang
Zhang, Zhenyu

Table of Contents

Integrating Efficient Model Queries
in State-of-the-Art EMF Tools⋆

Gábor Bergmann, Ábel Hegedüs, Ákos Horváth,
István Ráth, Zoltán Ujhelyi, and Dániel Varró

Budapest University of Technology and Economics,
Department of Measurement and Information Systems,
1117 Budapest, Magyar tudósok krt. 2
{bergmann,hegedusa,ahorvath,rath,ujhelyiz,varro}@mit.bme.hu

Abstract. Model-driven development tools built on industry standard platforms, such as the Eclipse Modeling Framework (EMF), heavily use model queries in various use cases, such as model transformation, well-formedness constraint validation and domain-specific model execution. As these queries are executed rather frequently in interactive modeling applications, they have a significant impact on the runtime performance of the tool, and also on the end user experience. However, due to their complexity, they can also be time consuming to implement and optimize on a case-by-case basis. The aim of the EMF-INCQUERY framework is to address these shortcomings by using declarative queries over EMF models and executing them effectively using a caching mechanism.

In the current paper, we present the new and significantly extended version of the EMF-INCQUERY Framework, with new features and runtime extensions that speed up the development and testing of new queries by both IDE and API improvements.

We demonstrate how our high performance queries can be easily integrated with other EMF tools using an entirely new case study in which EMF-INCQUERY is deeply integrated into the EMF modeling infrastructure to facilitate the incremental evaluation of derived EAttributes and EReferences.

1 Introduction

As model management platforms are gaining more and more industrial attention, the importance of automated model querying techniques is also increasing. Queries form the underpinning of various technologies such as model transformation, code generation, domain-specific behaviour simulation and well-formedness validation that are all essential in state-of-the-art modeling tools and toolchains.

The leading industrial modeling ecosystem, the Eclipse Modeling Framework (EMF [1]), provides different ways for querying the contents of models. These

⋆ This work was partially supported by the SecureChange (ICT-FET-231101) European Research Project, the CERTIMOT (ERC_HU-09-01-2010-0003) Project, the grant TÁMOP (4.2.2.B-10/1–2010-0009) and the János Bolyai Scholarship.

C.A. Furia and S. Nanz (Eds.): TOOLS Europe 2012, LNCS 7304, pp. 1–8, 2012.
© Springer-Verlag Berlin Heidelberg 2012

approaches range from manually coded model traversal to high-level declarative constraint languages such as Eclipse-OCL [2]. However, industrial experience [3] shows strong evidence of scalability problems in complex query evaluation over large EMF models, taken from the various modeling domains; and manual query optimization is time consuming to implement on a case-by-case basis.

In order to overcome this limitation, the EMF-INCQUERY[1] framework [3] proposes to use declaratively specified queries over EMF models, executing them efficiently *without manual coding* using incremental graph pattern matching techniques [4]. The benefits of EMF-INCQUERY with respect to the state-of-the-art of querying EMF models [2,5] include: (i) high performance querying of models in the range of millions of elements, (ii) efficient addressing of instance enumeration and backward navigation (which are both frequently encountered shortcomings of the EMF API); and (iii) a user friendly yet powerful declarative graph pattern based formalism.

In the current tool demonstration paper, we present the next evolutionary step of the EMF-INCQUERY framework, focusing on novel query and execution features. As a complex case study, we illustrate how EMF-INCQUERY can be deeply integrated into the EMF modeling layer to facilitate the efficient evaluation of *derived features* (virtual attributes and references that represent indirectly calculated structural information).

The paper is structured as follows: first, Section 2 gives a brief architectural and feature-oriented overview of EMF-INCQUERY, with a focus on novel contributions. Section 3 shows how incremental queries can be integrated into the EMF modeling layer for the evaluation of derived features. Section 4 gives an overview of related work, and Section 5 concludes the paper.

2   Overview of EMF-INCQUERY

2.1   Model Queries by Graph Patterns

Graph patterns [6] are an expressive formalism that can be used for various purposes in model-driven development, such as defining declarative model transformation rules, capturing general-purpose model queries including model validation constraints, or defining the behavioral semantics of dynamic domain-specific languages [7]. A graph pattern (GP) represents conditions (or constraints) that have to be fulfilled by a part of the instance model. A basic graph pattern consists of *structural constraints* prescribing the existence of nodes and edges of a given type, as well as *expressions* to define *attribute constraints*. A *negative application condition* (NAC) defines cases when the original pattern is *not* valid (even if all other constraints are met), in the form of a negative sub-pattern. A match of a graph pattern is a group of model elements that have the exact same configuration as the pattern, satisfying all the constraints (except for NACs, which must not be satisfied). The specification for the complete query language of the EMF-INCQUERY framework was described in [6], the current tool paper presents its implementation.

---

[1] http://viatra.inf.mit.bme.hu/incquery/new

Example. We illustrate our approach on a simple demonstration domain of *Schools* (encoded in EMF's ECore language as illustrated in Figure 1) that manage *Courses* involving *Teachers*, and enroll their students assigned to *Years* and *SchoolClasses*. Aside from simple EAttributes and EReferences, it also features *derived features* that are marked as volatile and transient, i.e. not stored explicitly in instance models but rather calculated on-demand by hand-written code. Such attributes or references usually represent a (simple) computed view the model and are frequently supported by ad-hoc Java implementations integrated into the EMF model representation.

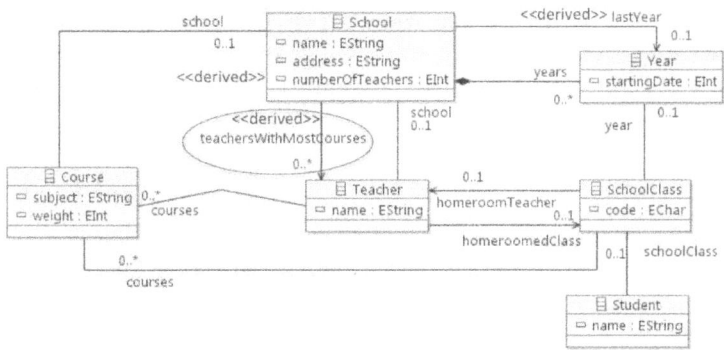

Fig. 1. The domain metamodel of the case study

In this paper, we show how graph patterns and EMF-INCQUERY as the underlying execution engine can be used to ease the specification and automate the efficient evaluation of such features. The graph pattern *teachersWithMostCourses(S, T)* (Figure 2) is used to express the semantics of the *teachersWithMostCourses* derived EReference (connecting *School* and *Teacher* in Figure 1, highlighted with an ellipse), that is to identify those teachers who have the maximum number of *Course* instances assigned (through the *Teachers.courses* reference).

This graph pattern defines the target set of teachers by combining a negative application condition (NAC) and cardinality constraints. It expresses that a teacher T belongs to this set iff there is no other teacher $T2$ whose number of courses M (the actual cardinality, i.e. number of elements connected through the *courses* reference) would be larger than the number of courses N assigned to T.

2.2 Execution of Incremental Queries

The overall development workflow of the EMF-INCQUERY framework focuses on the language tooling for specifying queries and then automatically generating integration code that plugs into any existing EMF-based application. As a

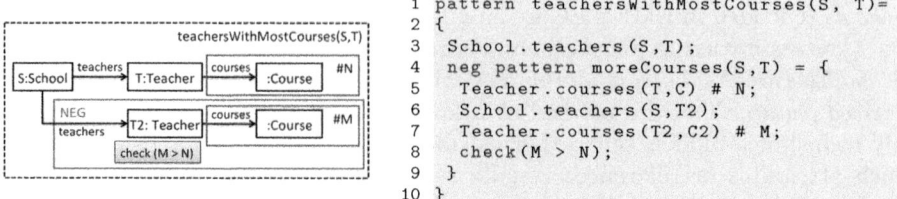

```
 1  pattern teachersWithMostCourses(S, T)=
 2  {
 3    School.teachers(S,T);
 4    neg pattern moreCourses(S,T) = {
 5      Teacher.courses(T,C) # N;
 6      School.teachers(S,T2);
 7      Teacher.courses(T2,C2) # M;
 8      check(M > N);
 9    }
10  }
```

Fig. 2. Graph pattern example in graphical and textual syntax

novelty targeted towards simplification, EMF-INCQUERY now also features an interpretative query execution facility that allows the developer to specify ad-hoc queries directly from Java code, without involving the tooling and the code generator.

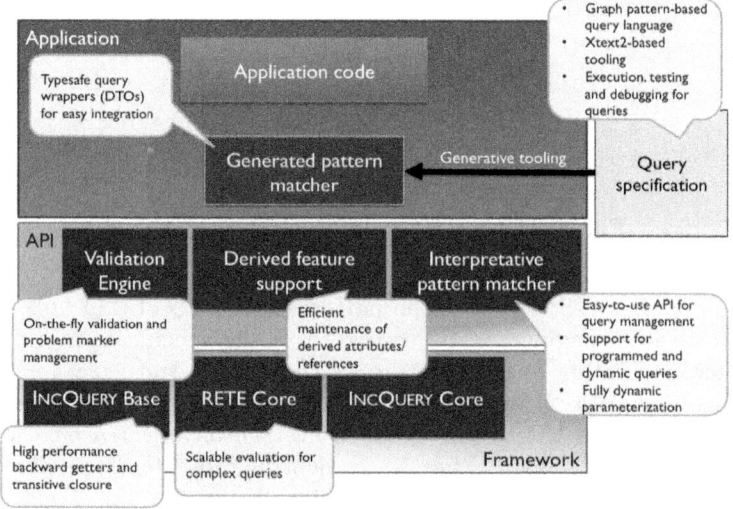

Fig. 3. Overview of the novel EMF-INCQUERY architecture

The overall architecture of and EMF-based application built in EMF-INCQUERY is overviewed in Figure 3. Based on the query specification (supported by an Xtext 2-based [8] editor, featuring syntax highlighting, code completion and well-formedness validation), pattern matcher plugins are generated that can be easily integrated to an existing Eclipse-based application. These plugins access the core functionality of the system through the EMF-INCQUERY API that exposes three key novel services: (1) the *Validation Engine* provides a wrapper to the EMF Validation service, to provide EMF-INCQUERY-based on-the-fly well-formedness validators using standard Eclipse Error Markers;

(2) the *Interpretative pattern matcher* provides an access point to quickly execute ad-hoc queries directly from Java code; (3) the $BASE^2$ component provides frequently used low-level incremental queries such as the instant enumeration of all instance elements belonging to a given EClass, or reverse navigation along unidirectional EReferences. BASE also provides a novel incremental transitive closure query algorithm that can be used to incrementally compute reachability regions.

Benefits. At the core, the incremental evaluation and lifecycle management of queries is facilitated by the RETE engine, originally developed for the VIATRA2 model transformation framework [4]. Using this approach, the query results (the match sets of graph patterns) are cached in memory, and can be instantaneously retrieved when queries are issued. These caches are automatically and incrementally maintained upon model updates, using automatic notifications provided by EMF. There is a slight performance overhead on model manipulation, and a memory cost proportional to the cache size (approx. the size of match sets). These special performance characteristics make incremental techniques suitable for application scenarios such as on-the-fly well-formedness checking, live model transformation and other complex use cases.

3   Integrating Incremental Queries to the EMF Modeling Layer

In this section, we outline how the efficient querying features of the EMF-INCQUERY framework can be integrated to EMF-based applications in a deep and transparent way, through the incremental evaluation and maintenance of derived features. The overall architecture of our approach is shown in Figure 4.

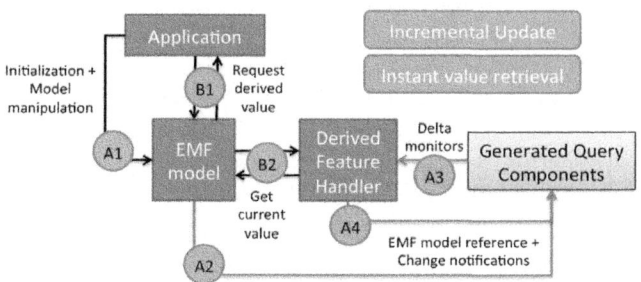

Fig. 4. Overview of the integration architecture

Here, the application accesses both the model and the query results through the standard EMF model access layer (query results are represented as the values of derived attributes or references) – hence, no modification of application source

---
^{2} http://viatra.inf.mit.bme.hu/incquery/base

code is necessary. In the background, *Derived feature handlers* (novel features of the EMF-INCQUERY API) are attached to the EMF .model plugin that integrate the generated query components (pattern matchers). This approach follows the official EMF guidelines of implementing derived features and is identical to how ad-hoc Java code, or OCL expression evaluators are integrated.

Challenges of Using Derived Features in EMF. In using derived features with EMF-based applications, developers may encounter two key challenges. First, depending on the complexity of the semantics of derived features, their evaluation may impose a *severe performance impact* (since complex calculations and extensive model traversal may be necessary for execution). Unfortunately, this scalability issue will affect all other software layers using the .model code, including the user interface, model transformations, well-formedness validators etc. Second, due to the *lack of propagating notifications* for derived features, model changes will not trigger e.g. user interface updates.

Our approach provides a solution for both of these challenges. As the performance characteristics of the EMF-INCQUERY engine have been shown to be practically agnostic of query complexity and model size [3], derived features of complex semantics and inter-dependencies can be used without severe evaluation performance degradation. Additionally, as shown in Figure 4, the update propagation mechanism of the RETE network (*delta monitors*) are connected to the EMF Notification layer so that the application software components are automatically kept up-to-date about the value changes of derived features.

Implementation Details. In our prototype implementation[3], we augmented the architecture outlined above with a code generator that supports the automatic generation of integration code (*derived feature handlers*) based on a simple specification model that encodes the *core semantics* of backing queries, that can either be (i) a reference with a multiplicity of one (mapped to a scalar derived reference value) or * (mapped to an unmodifiable EList as a derived reference value); (ii) the cardinality (match set size) of the backing query (e.g. to support the *School.numberOfTeachers* derived attribute in Figure 1).

The lifecycle of such handler objects is tied to the host EObjects, to enable their garbage collection together with the instance model itself. Additionally, they can be parameterized to use the EMF-INCQUERY engine in the *batch evaluation mode*, which disables incremental update propagation, but may be more efficient overall for rarely used queries, or queries whose incremental maintenance would require too much memory.

4   Related Work

EMF-INCQUERY is not the first tool to apply graph pattern based techniques to EMF [9, 10], but its incremental pattern matching feature is unique.

---

[3] http://viatra.inf.mit.bme.hu/incquery/examples/derivedfeatures

Model Queries over EMF. There are several technologies for providing declarative model queries over EMF. Here we give a brief summary of the mainstream techniques, none of which support incremental behavior.

EMF Model Query 2 [5] provides query primitives for selecting model elements that satisfy a set of conditions; these conditions range from type and attribute checks to enforcing similar condition checks on model elements reachable through references. Unfortunately, the expressive power of Model Query 2 is weaker than first order logic (and thus that of OCL and EMF-INCQUERY). For example, more complex patterns involving circles of references or attribute comparisons between nodes cannot be detected.

EMF Search [11] is a framework for searching over EMF resources, with controllable scope, several extension facilities, and GUI integration. Unfortunately, only simple textual search (for model element name/label) is available by default; advanced search engines can be provided manually in a metamodel-specific way.

OCL Evaluation Approaches. OCL [12] is a standardized navigation-based query language, applicable over a range of modeling formalisms. Taking advantage of the expressive features and wide-spread adoption of OCL, the project Eclipse OCL provides a powerful query interface that evaluates OCL expressions over EMF models. However, backwards navigation along references can still have low performance, and there is no support for incrementality.

Cabot et al. [13] present an advanced three-step optimization algorithm for incremental runtime validation of OCL constraints that ensures that constraints are reevaluated only if changes may induce their violation and only on elements that caused this violation. The approach uses promising optimizations, however, it works only on boolean constraints, and as such it is less expressive than our technique.

An interesting model validator over UML models is presented in [14], which incrementally re-evaluates constraint instances whenever they are affected by changes. During evaluation of the constraint instance, each model access is recorded, triggering a re-evaluation when the recorded parts are changed. This is also an important weakness: the approach is only applicable in environments where read-only access to the model can be easily recorded, unlike EMF. Additionally, the approach is tailored for model validation, and only permits constraints that have a single free variable; therefore, general-purpose model querying is not viable.

5   Conclusions

Previously [3] we presented EMF-INCQUERY as prototype framework for efficiently executing complex queries over EMF models, which adapts incremental technologies [4] for graph pattern matching. In the current paper, we present an evolved tool that includes two key improvements compared to previous versions: (i) an Xtext2-based tooling that fully implements the extended graph pattern language [6] and (ii) a new runtime architecture that features several novel services including the on-the-fly validation engine and the interpretative ad-hoc query evaluator, built on a rewritten core that provides core queries and efficient transitive closures.

The secondary focus of this paper was a novel feature whereby queries can be deeply and transparently integrated into EMF-based applications to facilitate the efficient evaluation of derived features. The two key advantages of this approach are: (i) complexity-agnostic performance characteristics that allow developers to easily integrate derived references and attributes with complex semantics, without a severe scalability impact, even over very large instance models; (ii) transparent and automatic notification propagation that simplifies the integration to already existing user interfaces, model transformations and any other code that uses EMF models.

References

1. The Eclipse Project: Eclipse Modeling Framework, `http://www.eclipse.org/emf`
2. The Eclipse Project: MDT OCL,
   `http://www.eclipse.org/modeling/mdt/?project=ocl`
3. Bergmann, G., Horváth, Á., Ráth, I., Varró, D., Balogh, A., Balogh, Z., Ökrös, A.: Incremental Evaluation of Model Queries over EMF Models. In: Petriu, D.C., Rouquette, N., Haugen, Ø. (eds.) MoDELS 2010. LNCS, vol. 6394, pp. 76–90. Springer, Heidelberg (2010)
4. Bergmann, G., Ökrös, A., Ráth, I., Varró, D., Varró, G.: Incremental pattern matching in the VIATRA model transformation system. In: Karsai, G., Taentzer, G. (eds.) Graph and Model Transformation (GraMoT 2008). ACM (2008)
5. The Eclipse Project: EMF Model Query 2, `http://wiki.eclipse.org/EMF/Query2`
6. Bergmann, G., Ujhelyi, Z., Ráth, I., Varró, D.: A Graph Query Language for EMF Models. In: Cabot, J., Visser, E. (eds.) ICMT 2011. LNCS, vol. 6707, pp. 167–182. Springer, Heidelberg (2011)
7. Syriani, E., Vangheluwe, H.: Programmed Graph Rewriting with DEVS. In: Schürr, A., Nagl, M., Zündorf, A. (eds.) AGTIVE 2007. LNCS, vol. 5088, pp. 136–151. Springer, Heidelberg (2008)
8. The Eclipse Project: Xtext, `http://www.eclipse.org/xtext`
9. Biermann, E.. Ermel, C., Taentzer, G.: Precise Semantics of EMF Model Transformations by Graph Transformation. In: Czarnecki, K., Ober, I., Bruel, J.-M., Uhl, A., Völter, M. (eds.) MoDELS 2008. LNCS, vol. 5301, pp. 53–67. Springer, Heidelberg (2008)
10. Giese, H., Hildebrandt, S., Seibel, A.: Improved flexibility and scalability by interpreting story diagrams. In: Proceedings of GT-VMT 2009. ECEASST, vol. 18 (2009)
11. The Eclipse Project: EMFT Search,
    `http://www.eclipse.org/modeling/emft/?project=search`
12. The Object Management Group: Object Constraint Language, v2.0 (May 2006),
    `http://www.omg.org/spec/OCL/2.0/`
13. Cabot, J., Teniente, E.: Incremental integrity checking of UML/OCL conceptual schemas. J. Syst. Softw. 82(9), 1459–1478 (2009)
14. Groher, I., Reder, A., Egyed, A.: Incremental Consistency Checking of Dynamic Constraints. In: Rosenblum, D.S., Taentzer, G. (eds.) FASE 2010. LNCS, vol. 6013, pp. 203–217. Springer, Heidelberg (2010)

Poporo: A Formal Methods Tool for Fast-Checking of Social Network Privacy Policies*

Néstor Cataño[1], Sorren Hanvey[1], and Camilo Rueda[2]

[1] Carnegie Mellon University - Portugal, Madeira ITI
Campus da Penteada, Funchal, Portugal
{nestor.catano,sorrenhanvey}@m-iti.org
[2] Pontificia Universidad Javeriana, Cali, Colombia
Department of Computer Science
crueda@cic.puj.edu.co

Abstract. The increase in use of Smart mobile devices has allowed for an ever growing market for services providers. These services are increasingly used to connect to users' on-line private information through social networking sites that share and personalise on-line information. This leads to the problem of privacy leaks stemming from an application's non-adherence to a predefined set of privacy policies. This paper presents a formal methods tool to reliably restrict the access to content in on-line social network services. The Poporo tool builds upon a previous work in which we provided a predicate calculus definition for social networking in B that models social-network content, privacy policies, and social-network friendship relations. This paper presents the implementation and the functionality of our Poporo tool through a running example in the domain of social networking sites.

1 Introduction

The popularity of Smart mobile devices has allowed for a new domain of on-line user services. Demands from users for further functionality has prompted service providers and manufactures to adopt a crowd-sourced approach to application development wherein third party developers are allowed to build external applications that implement bespoke functionality. Although this alleviates the burden on the service providers and manufacturers, it raises a number of privacy concerns stemming from the fact that users' information from their on-line profiles are now made available to third parties, who might not adhere to information sharing policies the user might have defined within these profiles.

In this paper, we present our Poporo tool [6] for fast-checking of an application's adherence to a privacy policy that is defined within a social-networking site (SNS). A privacy policy consists of a user defined policy and a set of axioms

---

* Sorren Hanvey and Néestor Cataño have been funded by the Portuguese Research Agency FCT through the R&D Project WeSP, PT/SE/0028/2008.

C.A. Furia and S. Nanz (Eds.): TOOLS Europe 2012, LNCS 7304, pp. 9–16, 2012.

defined by the SNS that specify its most fundamental behaviour. For example, an axiom might state that a user that adds a content to the SNS must be granted all access permissions/privileges over that content.

The Poporo tool relies on a previous work in which we introduced *Matelas*[1], a predicate calculus abstract definition for social networking written in B [5]. Matelas enables the Poporo tool to express privacy policies unambiguously. Poporo further builds upon a previous work in which we defined a sound translation of B machines into JML specifications [8], and from JML specifications into the input language of the Yices SMT prover [7]. JML (Java Modeling Language) is a model-based language for specifying the behaviour of Java classes [12,4]. Yices provides support for checking satisfiability of formulae containing uninterpreted functions [11,10].

2 Preliminaries

2.1 JML

A simple JML specification for a Java class consists of pre- and post-conditions added to its methods and class invariants restricting the possible states of class instances. Specifications for method pre- and post-conditions are embedded as comments immediately before method declarations. JML predicates are first-order logic predicates formed of side-effect free Java boolean expressions and several specification-only JML constructs. JML provides notations for forward and backward logical implications, ==> and <==, for non-equivalence <=!=>, and for logical or and logical and, | | and &&.

requires P. specifies a method pre-condition P, which must be true when the method is called. Predicate P is a valid JML predicate.

ensures Q. specifies a normal method post-condition Q. It says that if the method terminates in a normal state, *i.e.* without throwing an exception, then the predicate Q will hold in that state. Predicate Q is a valid JML predicate.

signals (E e) R. specifies an exceptional method post-condition R. If the method throws an exception e of type E, then the JML predicate R must hold. Predicate R is a valid JML predicate.

2.2 The SMT Solver Yices

Yices is an SMT (Satisfiability Modulo Theories) solver developed at SRI International [11,10]. It provides support for checking satisfiability of formulae containing uninterpreted function symbols with equality, linear real and integer arithmetic, bit-vectors, arrays, recursive data-types, universal and existential quantifiers, lambda expressions, tuples, and records. Hence, given a model in Yices, the solver returns "sat", "unsat", or "unknown", meaning the model satisfiable, unsatisfiable or the solver cannot decide, respectively.

---

[1] Mattress in French.

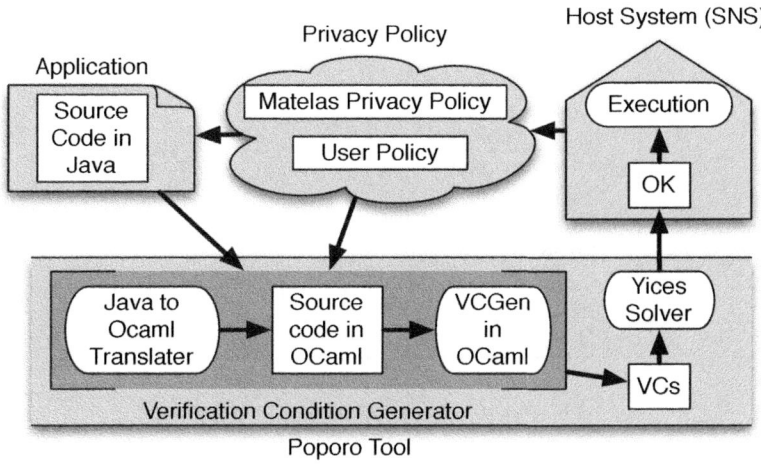

Fig. 1. Poporo Framework

The example below introduces a function foo in Yices. The symbol : : means "it has type", so foo is a function over integers. foo is defined as a `lambda` function that takes an integer y and returns its successor. Variable x is declared and equalised to function foo applied to 1. The Yices `check` instruction checks whether a valuation for x exists that equals foo applied to 1. The Yices model is therefore satisfiable (one needs to take x equals to 2).

```
(define foo::(-> int int))
(assert (= foo (lambda (y::int) (+ y 1))))
(define x::int)
(assert (= (foo 1) x))
(check)
```

3   Poporo Tool Architecture

The Poporo tool [6] works directly on Java programs specified with JML specifications. This allowed us to have a greater control of privacy policies through JML, and enabled us to re-use previous work and tools. Figure 1 shows the architecture of Poporo. The tool relies on a previous work in which we introduced Matelas [5], a predicate calculus definition for social networking written in B, modelling social-network content, privacy policies, social-network friendship relations, and how these affect policies and user content in the network. Matelas' B machine invariants model the privacy policies of a social-networking site (SNS). In addition to this, Matelas implements social-networking operations for creating, publishing and editing content, as well as operations for commenting the "wall". A privacy policy is composed of Matelas' invariants augmented with user defined policies.

$$
\begin{array}{l}
\mathit{transmit\_rc}(ow, rc, pe) \;\; \widehat{=} \\
\quad \textsf{PRE} \\
\quad\quad rc \in rawcontent \land \\
\quad\quad ow \in person \land \\
\quad\quad pe \in person \land \\
\quad\quad ow \neq pe \land pe \mapsto rc \notin content \\
\quad \textsf{THEN} \\
\quad\quad \textsf{ANY } prs \textsf{ WHERE } prs \subseteq person \\
\quad\quad \textsf{THEN} \\
\quad\quad\quad content := content \cup \{pe \mapsto rc\} \cup prs \times \{rc\} \\
\quad \textsf{END} \\
\quad \textsf{END}
\end{array}
$$

Fig. 2. B machine for social networking

Poporo translates Matelas abstract machines into JML abstract class specifications [8], which are then translated into a social-networking *prelude* written in the input language of the Yices SMT solver [7]. Therefore, Matelas' abstract machines are translated into JML abstract classes, machine invariants into JML invariants, machine operations generate JML abstract method specifications with pre-conditions, post-conditions and "frame-conditions". JML provides support for design-by-contract principles. JML logical operators such as ==> (logical implication), && (logical and), and || (logical or) are naturally mapped into predicates imp, and, and or in Yices respectively. The mapping of JML pre- and post-conditions into Yices relies upon the use of lambda expressions that capture the semantics of the JML specifications.

Poporo works directly on the source code of the external Java program. It translates the Java program (a restricted syntax) into an equivalent program written in OCaml. The user defined policy is written in JML and then translated into Yices [7]. The verification condition generator (VCGen) takes the OCaml program and calculates a set of weakest preconditions, one for each program instruction (see Section 4). The verification conditions (VCs) are passed to the Yices SMT solver for satisfiability checking. If all the checks succeed, then the Java program does not breach the user defined policy. The Java program can be composed of assignments, class and method declarations, conditional and looping statements, and method calls. We only allow pre-defined social-networking methods to be called within the Java program, e.g. methods/operations for transmitting and creating content, for uploading content to the network, and for setting content permissions. This ensures that the Java program does not break Matelas' invariants (the privacy policies of the SNS).

4   Expressing Social Networking Privacy Policies in Yices

Figure 2 shows an abstract definition of the operation for publishing content to people in the network as defined in Matelas. The operation *transmit_rc* is used to

```
/*@ public normal_behavior
      requires rawcontent.has(rc) && person.has(ow) && person.has(pe) &&
              !ow.equals(pe) && !content.has(pe,rc);
      ensures (\exists JMLEqualsSet<Integer> prs; prs.isSubset(person);
              content.equals(\old(content.union(
                  JMLEqualsToEqualsRelation.singleton(pe, rc)).union(
                      ModelUtils.cartesian(prs, JMLEqualsSet.singleton(rc))))));
  also public exceptional_behavior
      requires !( rawcontent.has(rc) && person.has(ow) && person.has(pe) &&
                 !ow.equals(pe) && !content.has(pe, rc) );
      signals (Exception) true; @*/
  public abstract void transmit_rc(Integer rc, Integer ow, Integer pe);
```

Fig. 3. A partial JML translation of the social networking machine

publish the raw content *rc* from the page of *ow* (the owner of *rc*) to the page of *pe*. If *transmit_rc* is invoked when its pre-condition (following PRE) is true, the meaning of the operation is the meaning of its substitution (the code following THEN). The operation is not guaranteed to achieve any result if invoked when its pre-condition does not hold. In the definition of *transmit_rc*, *pe* ↦ *rc* represents the pair of elements (*pe, rc*), so that the content *rc* is explicitly transmitted to person *pe*. The construct ANY models unbounded choice substitution: it gives the implementer the opportunity to choose any value for the bound variable *prs* that satisfies the WHERE condition *prs* ⊆ *person*. Set *prs* represents a group of friends of *pe* to whom *rc* should further be transmitted. Figure 3 presents the JML translation of the operation in Figure 2. In the specification of the `transmit_rc` method, the `normal_behavior` case guarantees that if the `requires` clause (pre-condition) is satisfied, no exception will be thrown, only the locations listed in the `assignable` clause can be modified by the method, and the post-state will satisfy the `ensures` clause (post-condition). In an `ensures` clause, expressions in `\old` are evaluated in the pre-state, while all other expressions are evaluated in the post-state. The `exceptional_behavior` case specifies that the method will throw an exception and no locations will be modified if its pre-condition is satisfied.

Poporo maps JML specifications into Yices [7]. For each JML method specification, we define two predicates in Yices implementing the mapping. The first predicate models the pre-condition and the second the post-condition. For instance, the pre-condition of `transmit_rc` is mapped into Yices as the function below, which makes use of predicate `jmlset-is-member` for checking the existence of an element in a set, and the standard Yices function `mk-tuple` for constructing a pair of elements.

```
(define precondition-transmit-rc::
        (-> jmlset jmlset jmlrel (-> int int int bool))
  (lambda(rawcontent::jmlset person::jmlset content::jmlrel)
   (lambda(ow::int rc::int pe::int)
    (and (jmlset-is-member rawcontent-carrier rc)
     (jmlset-is-member rawcontent rc) (jmlset-is-member person-carrier ow)
     (jmlset-is-member person ow) (not (= ow pe))
     (not (jmlrel-is-member content (mk-tuple pe rc)))))))
```

5   Generating Verification Conditions

The verification condition generator takes a program in OCaml (obtained as a translation of external Java program) and calculates a weakest precondition predicate (WP) based on the program instructions [9]. Program instructions can be assignments, conditional, looping statements, or calls to pre-defined methods of the social-network, for which we know their interfaces (their pre- and post-conditions). $WP(SS, Q)$ stands for the weakest condition that must hold before the execution of the program statements SS such that Q holds after their execution. We defined a number of WP rules that account for the verification of external programs, some of which are shown below, where $m.P$ and $m.Q$ are the pre-condition and post-condition of method m respectively, and $result$ is a global variable that keeps the value of the evaluation of the last program expression.

Assg: $WP(x = E, Q) = WP(E, Q[x \backslash result])$
Seq: $WP(S; T, Q) = WP(S, WP(T, Q))$
MCall: $WP(m(y), Q) = m.P \wedge m.Q[x \backslash y] \Rightarrow Q$

The VCGen parses the program statement by statement generating a verification condition VC_i for every statement S_i. VC_i takes the form shown below, where r_i is the pre-condition of instruction S_i and t_i is its post-condition. The consolidated VC is passed to the Yices SMT solver and is checked for satisfiability. This is further illustrated in Section 6. If S_i is a method call (MCall), VC_{i+1} represents the property Q (calculated through WP) the method postcondition t_i must verify. If all the VCs are verified, then the program does not breach the social network privacy policy.

```
(define VCᵢ::bool
   (let ((rᵢ::bool (precondition-Sᵢ prestate-vars))
         (tᵢ::bool (postcondition-Sᵢ prestate-vars poststate-vars)))
      (and rᵢ (implication tᵢ VCᵢ₊₁ ))))
```

$$VC = \bigwedge_{i=1}^{i=N} VC_i$$

6   Running Example

We present an example of a Java program that is verified against a social network privacy policy. The program plugs into a social-network site in which users are allowed to add content to the network and transmit this content to a number of other users. The program is slated for running on a smart mobile device such as a smartphone, and has a number of components for creating a content, accepting the intended recipient, and transmitting content to a specified number of users. The code of the program is implemented by function `main` below. Lines 1 and 2 create two social-network users ow and pe respectively. Line 3 creates a picture rc (a raw content). Line 4 uploads the picture rc to the content page of user ow so that he becomes the owner of the picture. In Line 5, ow transmits the picture rc to user pe.

```
    public class RunningExample {
      public void main(){
1     int ow = create_content();
2     int pe = create_content();
3     int rc = create_rc();
4     upload_rc(ow,rc);
5     transmit_rc(ow,rc,pe);
      }
    }
```

We want to check the main external program against a user defined policy stating that the user pe to whom ow transmits the picture rc is a *colleague* of ow that is not a *superior*. The user policy is encoded in Yices as shown below. VCs are generated for the $WP(\text{main},Q)$ as described in Section 5, where Q is the user defined policy[2], for which Yices answers "sat".

```
(implication
  (jmlrel-is-member visible (mk-tuple rc pe))
  (jmlset-is-member (jmlset-diff (jmlrel-apply colleagues ow)
                                 (jmlrel-apply superior ow) pe)) )
```

7 Related Work

The Mobius infrastructure [3], put forth by G. Barthe and al., targets the verification of embedded frameworks that can run third party applications, which are checked against a privacy policy modeling platform. Mobius builds upon Foundational Proof Carrying Code [1]. It generates VCs directly from the underlying operational semantics so that proof-obligations are more complicated to generate. The Poporo approach based on weakest-precondition calculus simplifies proofs as all Matelas operations have been proven to satisfy the system invariants within the B Model beforehand.

IBM's Enterprise Privacy Authorization Language (EPAL) [2] and the OASIS eXtensible Access Control Markup Language (XACML) [13] are definition languages for privacy policies. These formats of policy specification raise problems in the context of SNS as they are too restrictive, requiring the specification of rules relating each user to each content and they do not provide the flexibility for specifying multiple generalizable policies.

In [14], N. Sadeh and al. present several frameworks to deal with privacy concerns when using location aware services. These frameworks rely on various anonymization techniques. As these techniques primarily rely on altering the content the user is sharing, they are not suitable as a generalized approach towards policy definition.

---

[2] The full output produced by Poporo is available from http://poporo.uma.pt/-~ncatano/Projects/wespfm/Poporo/poporo.php

8   Conclusion

Poporo is an effective tool for identifying possible breaches that might occur when an untested external application is plugged into a social-networking site. Poporo has been continuously refined to become more efficient, e.g. most recursive definitions for functions in Yices were made non-recursive. This improved the time taken by Poporo for verifying external applications. A description of the average processing times for standard processes can be found at http://poporo.uma.pt/~ncatano/Projects/wespfm/Poporo.html.

Poporo accepts plug-in source code that uses a subset of Java as defined in the OCaml VCGen. Future extensions will include Java loops. Extending Poporo to provide support to JML libraries (e.g. for sets) at the user level would allow for the tool to check adherence to a privacy policies defined on-the-fly as opposed to pre-existing policies alone.

References

1. Appel, A.W.: Foundational proof-carrying code. In: LCS (2001)
2. Backes, M., Bagga, W., Karjoth, G., Schunter, M.: Efficient Comparison of Enterprise Privacy Policies. IBM Research, Zurich Research Laboratory (September 2003)
3. Barthe, G., Crégut, P., Grégoire, B., Jensen, T., Pichardie, D.: The MOBIUS Proof Carrying Code Infrastructure. In: de Boer, F.S., Bonsangue, M.M., Graf, S., de Roever, W.-P. (eds.) FMCO 2007. LNCS, vol. 5382, pp. 1–24. Springer, Heidelberg (2008)
4. Breunesse, C., Cataño, N., Huisman, M., Jacobs, B.: Formal methods for smart cards: An experience report. Science of Computer Programming 55(1-3), 53–80 (2005)
5. Cataño, N., Rueda, C.: Matelas: A Predicate Calculus Common Formal Definition for Social Networking. In: Frappier, M., Glässer, U., Khurshid, S., Laleau, R., Reeves, S. (eds.) ABZ 2010. LNCS, vol. 5977, pp. 259–272. Springer, Heidelberg (2010)
6. Cataño, N., Rueda, C., Hanvey, S.: The Poporo tool (2011), http://-poporo.uma.pt/~ncatano/Projects/wespfm/Poporo/poporo.php
7. Cataño, N., Rueda, C., Hanvey, S.: Verification of jml generic types with yices. In: CCC (2011)
8. Cataño, N., Wahls, T., Rueda, C., Rivera, V., Yu, D.: Translating B machines to JML specifications. In: SAC-SVT (to appear, 2012)
9. Dijkstra, E.W.: A Discipline of Programming. Prentice Hall, Inc. (October 1976)
10. Duterte, B., de Moura, L.: The Yices SMT solver. Technical report, Computer Science Laboratory, SRI International (2006)
11. Dutertre, B., de Moura, L.: A Fast Linear-Arithmetic Solver for DPLL(T). In: Ball, T., Jones, R.B. (eds.) CAV 2006. LNCS, vol. 4144, pp. 81–94. Springer, Heidelberg (2006)
12. Leavens, G.T., Baker, A.L., Ruby, C.: Preliminary design of JML: A behavioral interface specification language for Java. ACM SIGSOFT 31(3), 1–38 (2006)
13. Moses, T.: eXtensible Access Control Markup Language (XACML) Version 2.0. OASIS (2005)
14. Sadeh, N., Gandon, F.: Semantic web technologies to reconcile privacy and context awareness. Journal of Web Semantics 1 (2004)

DroidSense: A Mobile Tool to Analyze Software Development Processes by Measuring Team Proximity

Luis Corral, Alberto Sillitti, Giancarlo Succi,
Juri Strumpflohner, and Jelena Vlasenko

Free University of Bozen-Bolzano
Piazza Domenicani 3
39100 Bolzano-Bozen, Italy
luis.corral@stud-inf.unibz.it, {alberto.sillitti,
giancarlo.succi,juri.strumpflohner,jelena.vlasenko}@unibz.it

Abstract. Understanding the dynamics of a software development process is of paramount importance for managers to identify the most important patterns, to predict potential quality and productivity issues, and to plan and implement corrective actions. Currently, major techniques and tools in this area specialize on acquiring and analyzing data using software metrics, leaving unaddressed the issue of modeling the "physical" activities that developers do. In this paper, we present DroidSense, a non-invasive tool that runs on Android-based mobile phones and collects data about developers involvement in Agile software development activities, e.g. Pair Programming, daily stand-ups, or planning game, by measuring their proximity to computers and also other developers. Droid-Sense collects data automatically via Bluetooth signal created by other phones, personal computers, and other devices. We explain detailed design and implementation of the tool. Eventually, to show a possible application of DroidSense we present the results of a case study.

Keywords: Mobile, Bluetooth, Proximity Measurement, Process Analysis, Pair Programming.

1   Introduction

Despite years of research in Software Engineering, the specific actions that people undertake when developing software are often unknown. Understanding the dynamics of a software development process is of paramount importance for managers to identify the most relevant patterns, to predict potential quality and productivity issues, and to plan and implement corrective actions. The job of a software engineer is to deliver high-quality software products at the agreed cost and schedule. For this purpose "he needs to plan his work, do it according to this plan, and strive to produce the highest possible quality" [1]. Project managers, on the other side, need to oversee and control the development process, negotiate with customers, and adjust budget and resources accordingly. To accomplish a successful and continuously improved development process, it is necessary to count on efficient and reliable techniques and tools that collect data and reconstruct the underlying process. Currently, there are

C.A. Furia and S. Nanz (Eds.): TOOLS Europe 2012, LNCS 7304, pp. 17–33, 2012.
© Springer-Verlag Berlin Heidelberg 2012

techniques and tools that gather and analyze data using various approaches, such as software metrics. In this case, the quality of the collected data is of paramount importance for the resulting conclusions. For this purpose, the data can be collected in an automated fashion using non-invasive measurement tools [2]. This also avoids the "context-switch" problem [3], allowing engineers to focus on their actual work without imposing additional procedures related to the process analysis.

However, this leaves unaddressed the issue of modeling the "physical" activities that developers do. In novel software development processes, such as Agile Methods, developers move a lot "physically." They attend daily stand-up meeting, move to work in pairs, interact with an on-site customer, etc. Collecting such information is of high importance because it allows to gather essential information to complement the one coming from software metrics. For instance, it may be of extreme interest to determine whether developers introduce less defects while working in pairs, after meeting a customer or a senior developer.

In this paper, we present DroidSense: a non-invasive tool that runs on Android-based mobile phones and collects data about developers involvement in "physical" software development activities (e.g. Pair Programming, daily stand-ups, or planning game) by measuring their proximity to computers, various hardware devices, and also other developers. DroidSense collects data automatically via Bluetooth signal created by other phones, personal computers, and other devices. We explain in detail the design and implementation of the tool. The usage of DroidSense contributes to the problem of collecting data reliably and non-invasively during physical activities undertaken by software developers. This kind of data can be used to reconstruct and improve a software development process. To evidence possible applications of DroidSense, we present results of a case study.

The rest of this paper is organized as follows: in Section 2 we present background on software goals and software measurements focusing on Agile software development process. In Section 3 we identify related work. In Section 4 we discuss technologies required for proximity analysis and our approach to reproduce a software development process through proximity measurements using Bluetooth and Android. In Section 5 we describe the detailed design of DroidSense. In Section 6 we present a case study. In Section 7 we discuss the obtained results. Then, in Section 8 we identify limitations and discuss future work. Eventually, in Section 9 we draw some conclusions.

2   Measuring Software Development Processes

Measurement activities should be carefully planned in order to get useful and valid results. Thus, before measuring it is necessary to specify the goals that need to be achieved. Then, the identified goals should be decomposed into suitable metrics that allow to achieve these goals. Eventually, after completing the previous steps, the data collection process can be started. The goal-question-metric approach [4] is essential for identification of entities and attributes that are planned to be measured.

Software development comprises different stakeholders that are interested in diverse kinds of perspectives of the process [5]. Managers are interested in the variables like cost, productivity, product quality, and effectiveness of methodologies and tools in order to define costs, build teams of appropriate sizes, and compare a variety of products against each other. On the other side, developers are interested in product and process quality measures to evaluate a project's status and continuously improve the development process.

It is expected from software metrics to deliver relevant information on development processes and products. Along with the general software process and the final outcome, each task should be seen as a sub-activity that yields an intermediate product that can be measured, analyzed, and also improved [6]. Software metrics should be calculated using data provided by a robust collection plan. A defective collection effort may produce faulty metrics that lead to erroneous results. Therefore, data collection processes and tools should be carefully designed and deployed. One approach to assure validity and objectivity of data collection tasks is to execute them without personal bias of an operator [7]. An automatic data collection effort approach helps building a trustworthy measurement system that is less prone to inconsistencies typical for individuals and human-operated measurement instruments.

Examples of tools for non-invasive and automated data collection and analysis coming from software development activities are PROM [8] and Hackystat [9]. These tools allow silent data collection mechanism on developer's performance (i.e., programs used, modified classes, methods, etc.) and permit aggregation of different data sources to compute other metrics. Hence, automated data collection tools help to reduce the complexity related to the technological aspects of metrics collection and facilitate data acquisition without affecting the productivity of a software developers. However, these works also have limitations analyzing the software process itself, especially with regard to automated detection of interaction among participants.

3   Related Work

The idea of measuring proximity is not totally new. Many approaches involving indoor proximity detection use Radio Frequency Identification (RFID) systems that generally consist of two components: so-called tags that are allocated to or carried by individuals and a specialized RFID tag reader that senses for such tags in its proximity. A previous work [10] describes the realization of such a system where authors use RFID tags in a hospital environment, tagging patients, personnel, and medical equipment for data collection and analysis. Given the short-range nature of RFID tag signals, the reader can assume to be in near proximity by purely detecting a given tag.

More sophisticated approach for proximity detection with wireless protocols exploits the so-called "path loss" that is defined as the loss of power of a radio frequency (RF) signal propagating through space. It is expressed in dB or dBm as an abbreviation for the power ratio in decibels of the measured power of the signal referenced to one milliwatt. The path loss depends on the distance between the transmitting and receiving antennas and the line of sight between both of them.

Our work aims at a much less invasive approach that does not require prior setup as needed in RFID systems (i.e., tagging of people). Instead, the objective is to reuse existing tools. Bluetooth fulfills all of the mentioned requirements. It is a widespread technology available on most of today's portable devices such as mobile phones, notebooks, and headsets. It has a suitable maximum wireless range, being larger than infrared or RFID chipsets, but smaller than WiFi, perfectly suitable for information processing of a device's immediate surroundings.

With a different research approach, the main goal of our work is to find mechanisms that allow to infer a person's interaction with respect to other people or devices. The analysis reported on this work converged to studying the Bluetooth protocol and its possibilities for proximity measurement on the Android operating system. This proximity data may be studied against the possibility of acquiring interesting information regarding the software development process. Furthermore, data collection process based on proximity analysis of Bluetooth signals is fully automated, requiring no additional effort or intervention from software engineers, which improves the data quality, guarantees its objectiveness and avoids the "context-switch" problem mentioned in [3]. The proposed mechanism based on proximity data detects when developers work alone and when they do Pair Programming and with whom. Pair Programming is a technique when two developers work together on the same task using one computer and one keyboard. Many advantages of this technique have been identified: [11, 12, 13, 14, 15, 16, 17].

It has been found that the developers working in pairs detect defects already when typing and that the code written by pairs is significantly shorter than the code written by developers working alone. Eventually, developers working in pairs constantly exchange knowledge and are also more satisfied with their work. Still, also negative aspects of this technique were detected. In [14] authors analyzed four software projects. It has been found that Pair Programming does not provide extensive quality benefits and does not result in consistently superior productivity compared to Solo programming. In [18] it has been identified that Pair Programming decreases productivity but also   increases code quality.

4   Implementation Approach and Required Technologies

To provide an adequate environment for the automated collection of proximity information, it is necessary to furnish an application that facilitates a mobile data sampling approach, and communication with a central component responsible for receiving, storing and analyzing the data. To solve this, cellphones offer a natural mobile platform; and a server for data storing and analysis is sufficient.

As explained in Section 3, Bluetooth allows to measure proximity signals based on signal strength. This specification for short-range wireless communication is widely available on current mobile phones. Bluetooth has been designed for low-power consumption, a high level of security, and robustness against interference, making it suitable for small devices with reduced battery capabilities.

Bluetooth is defined by a protocol stack, that consist of a hardware part and a software part. By design, it requires two initialization phases before a connection between devices can be established: First, an initial inquiry followed by a scan phase. The inquiry phase is needed to detect discoverable Bluetooth devices in the sender's neighborhood [19]. Then, after a successful device discovery, a service discovery is carried out to retrieve information about the exposed services and their attributes [20]. After successfully completing these two operations, the Bluetooth devices are paired and then ready to collaborate.

To measure proximity using Bluetooth, we can take advantage of the device discovery features, completing it with the detection of several parameters that the protocol broadcasts. In particular, one of these parameters, called RSSI (Receive Signal Strength Indication), provides strength values measured in dB for power control purposes [21]. Nonetheless, a related value called Inquiry Result with RSSI is additionally retrieved during a device discovery scan. In such a case, since performing scanning only does not implies connection to a device yet, Inquiry Result monitors the received power level and infers an approximation to the RSSI value. Such approximation can be interpreted as a measurement of the distance between the reference device and the sensed one, making it suitable for proximity analysis.

In order to deploy this strategy, we need to count on an operative environment that supports the management of the Bluetooth stack and the associated parameters. The Bluetooth API introduced in Android OS version 2.0 contains the parameters and methods to write applications for Bluetooth usage and management [22], including methods for requesting Bluetooth activation or and initiating discovery, and supporting the retrieval of the selected Inquiry Result with RSSI.

As a development platform, Android's layered architecture includes a Linux Kernel as an abstraction layer between the hardware and the rest of the software stack, a Runtime layer, Libraries that provide the capabilities delivered to the developers, an Application Framework written in Java that consists of open APIs used by the core applications, and User Applications written in Java, that are end-user features [23]. In particular, the open approach of the Application Framework and the User Application layers makes Android as the platform of choice to develop a tool to address the requirements of proximity analysis using Bluetooth.

5   DroidSense Tool

5.1   Software System

The result of the conducted research is a system for the automated collection of data related to the software process by using proximity measurement. The system is composed of a set of tools grouped in a mobile Android client application, and a central server component (Figure 1). The DroidSense client is the point of interaction of the end user with the system, responsible for the data collection, while the server the responsible for receiving, storing, and analyzing the data. Data can be retrieved and visualized using a set of APIs provided by Google.

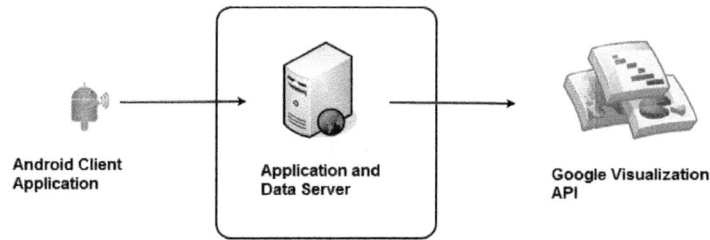

Android Client Application   **Application and Data Server**   **Google Visualization API**

Fig. 1. System architecture

The client application presents all the Bluetooth devices detected in the surroundings with device discovery. Data is retrieved from Bluetooth hardware and processed through the proper APIs. After processing and storing, data is accessed exclusively through the DroidSense Content Provider that has been implemented according to Google's guidelines. This allows to easily abstract the data from the rest of the application logic by exposing content URIs that can be used by DroidSense's own user interface, as well as by potential future extensions to access the data. The main application logic resides in the "Core" component which contains the object model and controller classes responsible for managing the collection and persisting of the discovered devices and RSSI values.

The core contains as well the logic for the automated detection of sessions. These components have been developed by using a test-driven development methodology, aiming for a high degree of test coverage. The according Data Access Object (DAO) layer abstracts the data access, potentially allowing to attach another database in the case of a DroidSense desktop application. The DroidSense services are Android services responsible for initiating the data collection process or data upload. They don't contain any major logic, but rather invoke according operations on the "Core". Finally, the Bluetooth Discovery Action directly attaches to the Android Bluetooth API, performing the device discovery and RSSI retrieval (Figure 2).

To guarantee an accurate measurement, the user should use the client application to calibrate his device on the first use of the application. Calibration consists in placing the phone for a specified time interval at an indicated distance from the Bluetooth adapter of the scanned device. During the process, the average of the obtained values is taken. Based on that average and a constant value, the offset used to determine the RSSI values is calculated.

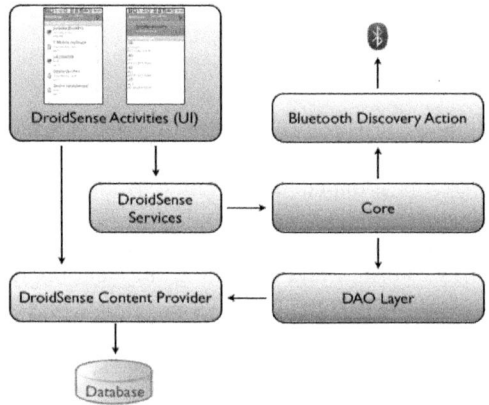

Fig. 2. Client architecture

Bluetooth devices are sensed out, detected and processed in separate entries. Each entry of the device contains the collected proximity raw data, and the time stamp of the discovery (Figure 3). These values are the primitives that will be used throughout the

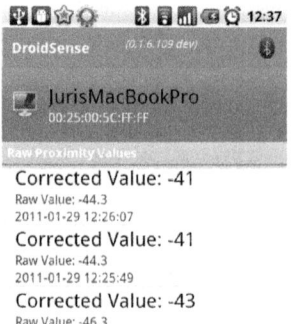

Fig. 3. Device detail showing proximity values

system to evaluate proximity and evaluate time investment for the user. These primitives are subject to an additional evaluation that, based on threshold values, classifies the signal in ranges called "aside", "near", and "far". This taxonomy is utilized further, for the evaluation and categorization of the collected data.

To allow the automated evaluation of the collected proximity information, it is necessary to classify the found devices using predefined tags, associated manually by the user through a DroidSense Tagging Dialog.

- *My device:* Devices that the user owns or is actively using such as his own notebook or personal computer used at work;
- *Team member:* Any other device whose owner is part of the team the user is working in;
- *Work:* Devices whose owners are also co-located, but that do not work in the same team.

Taking advantage of the device classification, a client view allows to retrieve a list of aggregated sessions evaluated on the transmitted proximity data. These results show the total amount of Solo Programming or Pair Programming sessions. By entering the detail of a session, the involved participants are being shown too.

A "Solo Programming" session is where the user is sitting in front of his own computer workstation. For this session to be detected successfully, the retrieved values from the user's workstation need to be in the range of the so-called "aside" proximity, and the device must be of type "Computer", and it must be tagged as "Work" and "My Device" (Figure 4). A "Pair Programming" session can be detected when the scanning device detects two devices in "aside" proximity, a computer tagged as "My Device" and "Work" and a mobile device tagged as "Team Member".

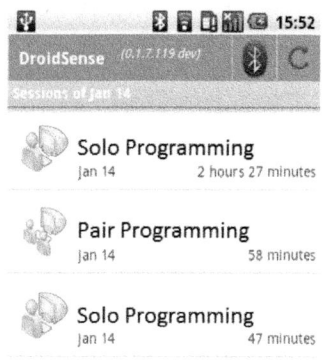

Fig. 4. List of calculated sessions

According to Bluetooth's architecture, DroidSense is able to detect those devices that have been explicitly set to be discoverable by their respective owners. DroidSense primarily acts as a scanner, sensing in fixed time intervals for devices (both DroidSense users or other devices with an active Bluetooth signal) in its range and recording all of the results. At the same time, it may also have the role of being scanned by another DroidSense device.

In Table 1 we present a list of the most relevant values calculated and recorded by DroidSense:

Table 1. Values recorded and stored by DroidSense

Value	Description
Bluetooth MAC address	A unique 48 bit address assigned by the Bluetooth adapter manufacturer.
Display Name	User-defined display name, usually the phone model or hostname for computers.
Device Class	Class of device record containing a major service class, major device class, and minor device class; this helps to categorize, for example, as "Computer" or "Phone".
RSSI value	The received signal strength indicator that is being received by executing an inquiry with RSSI request. This value is used for estimating the distance of the scanned device.
Discovery Timestamp	Each discovered Bluetooth device may have a series of RSSI values associated that have been retrieved during several discovery operations. For the purpose of determining the detection time, DroidSense associates a time stamp with each RSSI record

Completing the system architecture, the DroidSense server is in charge of storing and analyzing the collected values by all of the DroidSense Android clients. It has been implemented on top of J2EE and by using the Spring Application framework. For the web front-end, the Spring Web MVC framework has been used, in conjunction with its JSP view resolver engine and jQuery.

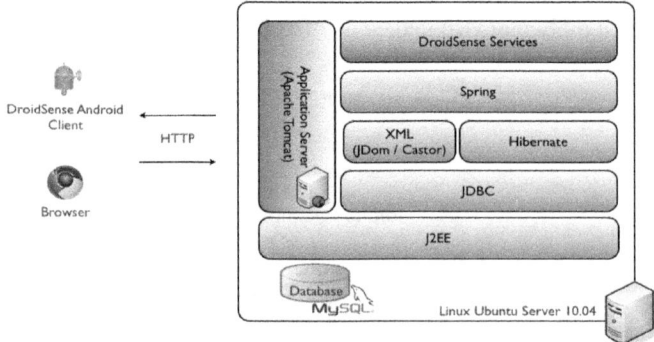

Fig. 5. Server architecture

DroidSense client and server operate relational databases, managed by SQLite and MySQL, respectively, to store the data collected by different clients. The schema of both databases is similar, with slight differences to suit other internal processes and support metric calculations in the server side. The data between the client and server is exchanged over the HTTP protocol. To transmit such data in a structured form, XML-RPC has been used. XML-RPC is a remote procedure call protocol that uses XML to encode the procedure call and HTTP as transport mechanism.

5.2   Data Visualizations

Data visualization reports in DroidSense are the primary mean to present the information gathered by Bluetooth devices; an accurate, concise data delivery represents an enormous help for the correct analysis and interpretation of the software development process. For this purpose a web front-end has been created on the server allowing to specify a set of filter criteria based on which the data are retrieved from the database. The visualization is done by using jQuery and the Google Visualization API. The visualizations that DroidSense currently offers are:

-   *Present devices:* Lists all of the devices that have been detected during the specified day as well as their associated tags (Figure 6).

Fig. 6. Visualization: Present devices

-   *Sessions:* Displays the result of an automated analysis of the proximity data against potential patterns. Currently, DroidSense is able to automatically identify Solo Programming and Pair Programming sessions. This analysis is based on the proximity classification done by DroidSense, incorporating only "aside" values and discriminating other nearby data to avoid any possibility of noise. (Figure 7).

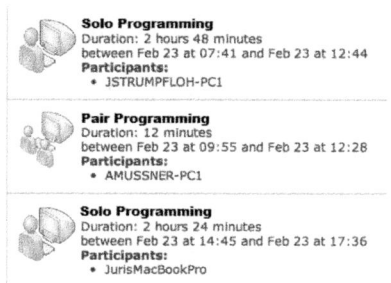

Fig. 7. Visualization: Sessions

-   *Scatterplot:* Shows the actual values collected by the mobile client throughout a day. The view allows to set filters to just show certain devices and provides a basic zoom functionality to only show the values within a defined time interval (Figure 8).

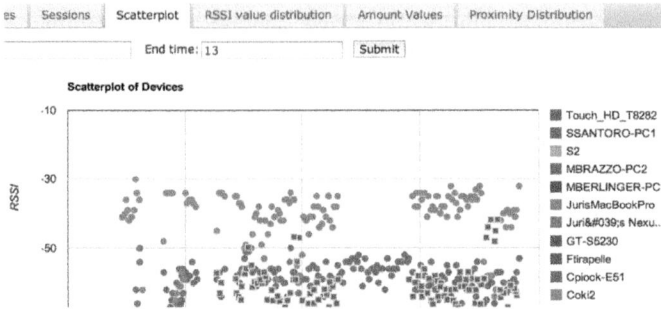

Fig. 8. Visualization:Scatterplot of the collected proximity values

- *RSSI value distribution:* Shows the distribution of the collected proximity values by highlighting the percentage of values indicating "aside", "near", and "far" proximity (Figure 9).

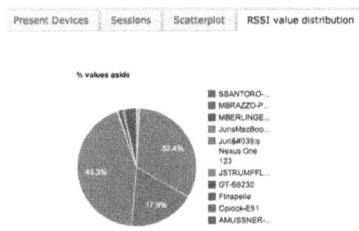

Fig. 9. Visualization: Distribution of the collected proximity values

- *Amount values:* Shows the percentage of the collected proximity values of a device in proportion to the total number of values collected for a day (Figure 10).

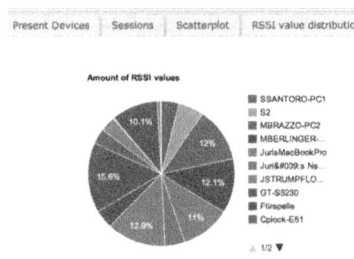

Fig. 10. Visualization: Amount of proximity values

- *Proximity distribution:* Compares the number of collected values of all the devices. Then, for each of them, it highlights the percentage of "aside", "near", and "far" proximity values (Figure 11).

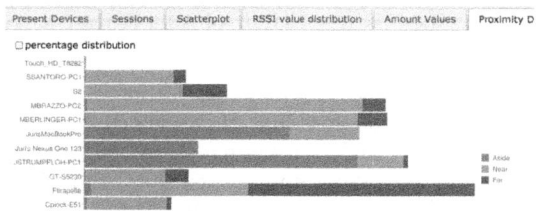

Fig. 11. Visualization: Proximity distribution

- *Session timeline:* Presents the detected sessions for longer periods and visualizes them in a straightforward way that allows for the recognition of patterns in their distribution (Figure 12).

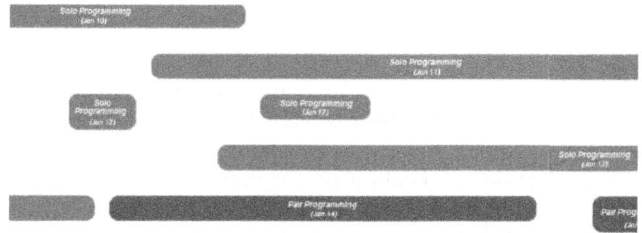

Fig. 12. Visualization: Session timeline for a week

The information provided by visualizations deliver administrative reports such as the number of active users, the way they collaborate, what kind of interactions exist among themselves, and what is the organization of a regular working day (e.g., schedule, activities, meetings, etc.). In Table 2 we present some potential scenarios in which the information coming from DroidSense may provide useful information that can be directly applied to improve software development process:

Table 2. Measurement scenarios for DroidSense

Scenario	Description
Personal process	The software developer is able to understand how much time he dedicates to actual work in front of his computer versus being around, discussing with team members or work mates. Such analysis may be used in the context of a personal software process (PSP).
Historical information	DroidSense data may be used by the developer to help him remember what activities he performed a given day. The visualizations show the proximity to given people/devices at a given time, making it easy to know whether he was in front of his work computer or together with people in a meeting, or even not present in the office at all. This may be especially useful for filling in time sheets or billing hours
Team process	Data may be aggregated so that project managers are able to identify the degree of communication among team members. This may be helpful in determining the necessity of stand-up meetings or to lower the amount of them in case it exceeds the actual time spent doing work at each person's computer.
Detection of Teammates	The user is able to identify which of his teammates is currently in the office by looking at the DroidSense discovered devices.

These measurements contain very valuable information, since it comes directly from developers and may be applied on a constant basis for:

- Delivering an overview of the activities and resources used by the team, outline the time spent by the team on individual and team tasks;
- Identifying work patterns and correlating them with labor productivity (e.g., detecting the impact of Pair Programming sessions on quality and productivity or calculating the amount of time spent on meetings), and
- Providing the means to facilitate teamwork among developers (e.g., by physically reallocating team members identified as frequent collaborators).
- Giving an accurate way to understand the time spent on productive activities.
- Reporting hourly time sheets, calculating the time used on team activities such as Pair Programming sessions, meetings, coaching, etc.

5.3   Privacy

DroidSense ensures data transparency and user privacy implementing the strategy when all data are visible to a user before being processed. The user has the full control over such data. For example, the user can manually delete any collected data and choose to deactivate the data collection mechanism. Moreover, the data transmission process is also manually initiated by the user.

The Android client tool uses notifications for announcing important events or signaling ongoing operations. All of the performed activities can be seen by the user and hence he has the possibility to stop them. No operation executed by the system is performed hidden from the user.

In the offered visualization, the scope of the available information is bounded only to personal data. In this way, the visualization offers the users a powerful tool to understand their own performance, assuring privacy.

6   Application of DroidSense

In order to test the performance of DroidSense we have conducted 3-months long case study in a real working environment. The obtained results evidence that the usage of such tool could be highly beneficial for improving software measurement process.

6.1   Research Design

We have conducted a case study in order to test the performance of DroidSense and also to verify the quality of the collected data. The goal of this study is to show that the proposed tool can be used in a real working environment and that the collected data are suitable for software process analysis and reconstruction.

The first release version of DroidSense has been tested by 11 employes of a large Italian IT Company operating in the e-government sector. Due to confidentiality reasons, the company prefers to remain anonymous and it will be referenced as "the Company." The study covers a time frame of 3 months, from January to March, 2011, and the participation in this study was on the voluntary basis.

Before the beginning of the experiment we provided all the participants with Android-based mobile phones with installed and configured DroidSense software version. Then, we upgraded existing workstations with Bluetooth USB dongles.

Eventually, we have given a brief introductory lecture in order to explain the participants main functionality of DroidSense and how we are going to use the results. We demonstrated how to use the software and asked the participants to carry the issued mobile phones with activated DroidSense all the time with them during their working day. The participants were informed that they were free to stop using the application at any moment.

During the experiment we have collected more than 240,000 proximity values that represent activities of the 11 participants. We have used these data in order to understand if they are valid for reconstructing the whole or at least parts of the software development process. In the next section, we present the obtained results.

6.2 Results

The collected data represent a large time interval. To simplify its understanding, we first provide an example of the collected data with its possible interpretation. The data in the example cover a time frame of 4 hours from 7 to 11 am.

The plot (Figure 13) is generated automatically by the DroidSense server. It visualizes the collected proximity values gathered from the device of *User_1*, and represents user's interaction with its own machine and a machine of *User_2*.

It shows only the proximity values for the two following devices (other values have been removed for the sake of clearness):

- *PC_1*: the machine of user *User_1* (cross points), the user of reference.
- *PC_2*: the machine of user *User_2* (dot points), a teammate of *User_1*.

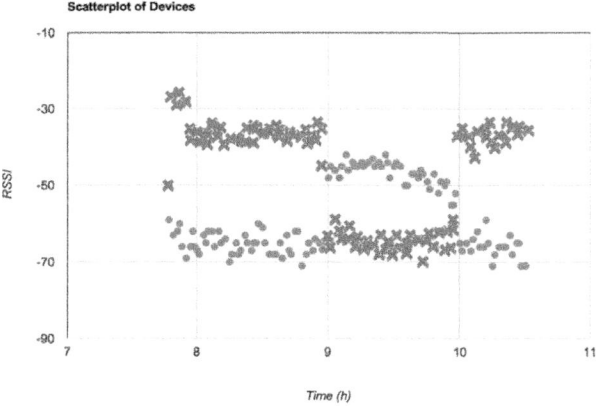

Fig. 13. Raw Values collected at the Company

These data can be interpreted in the following way: *User_1* starts to work at about 07:45 am. First, *User_1* works alone at his machine *PC_1*. *User_1* does not approach the machine of his teammate *PC_2* as it is always located at a distance of 5 to 7 meters. At around 09:00, we notice a change in collected proximity values: the distance between *User_1* and the machines *PC_1* and *PC_2* inverts; this could be interpreted in the following way: *User_1* left his machine *PC_1* and approached the machine *PC_2* of his teammate *User_2*. *User_1* spent about 1 hour at *PC_2*, then returned to his working place.

The DroidSense server analyzes these data and recognizes different working sessions: Solo Programming and Pair Programming (Figure 14). It stores the following values for each session:

– *Session type:* Solo Programming/Pair Programming
– *Timestamp:* Start time/End time of the session
– *Participant:* Machine that is used by an observed user (his own machine or another machine)

Fig. 14. Calculated sessions at the Company

Figure 14 proves that the DroidSense server properly recognizes the Solo Programming and Pair Programming sessions, reflecting the obtained proximity values, shown in Figure 13.

In the end of the study we presented the data to the Company representatives and discussed our results. Data obtained from DroidSense gave new insights into the behavior of the team, considering that outcome data was useful for understanding the interaction process among the team members. The proposed visualization method was acknowledged as suitable for the further analysis on the importance of distribution of people in a collaborative team.

Clearly, this is only one case study. In a long-term strategy and involving more participants, data delivered by DroidSense could certainly be used for deeper purposes on process analysis and process mapping, and also for validation of the quality of the collected data.

7   Discussion

The results presented in the experimental setup at the company show that DroidSense is capable to automatically collect proximity information in a non-invasive, fully transparent approach. Also, by analyzing the collected values, it is able to infer working sessions. Results have been verified for correctness by asking the participants to confirm the information delivered by the system.

The implementation of the system, and feedback from user organizations confirmed that DroidSense is of high value to constantly and accurately collect data from developers with the purpose of process analysis. Additionally, its data aggregation and visualizations mechanisms deliver a powerful interpretation of the collected data, that allows the user organization to understand and improve its development and operative processes on several areas, namely:

- *Process Analysis:* Providing a deeper insight of the organization's software development process, based on factual data, collected in a high-frequency basis.
- *Process Mapping:* Delivering the necessary data to understand the development process, based on individual contributor's behaviors and activities (e.g., personal work, Pair Programming sessions, etc).
- *Team Collaboration:* Helping to streamline and improve organization's internal processes, based on patterns drawn by collaboration among individual contributors.
- *Team Management:* Identifying a realistic composition of teams, based on typical grouping of contributors. This is useful to provide the necessary means to facilitate such collaboration.
- *Automated Data Collection:* Automating parts of the data collection effort: data collection activities previously conducted manually, now are executed automatically, and can be tracked using visualizations.
- *Job Automation:* Automating common tasks. For example, by using certain visualization users have accurate information to voucher hourly work. It is possible as well, to automatically check the attendance in a meeting.

It is important to highlight that the success of the data collection effort relies on how users trust the system. It was explained to developers how DroidSense operates, how data privacy is ensured at all times, and how data aggregations and visualizations are properly bounded to protect user's personal data.

8   Limitations and Future Work

We interviewed the participants of our case study in order to understand their feelings about the experiment and DroidSense. We have discovered that there is a certain need for an enhancement of the tool. It has been detected that DroidSense has a very high battery consumption rate. For a fully charged mobile phone with DroidSense activated the battery needs to be recharged every 10 hours. As a possible solution we plan to move most of the client side computations on the collected data to the server for reducing the work load of the mobile phone. According to the Android Bluetooth Open Source Documentation [24], some future releases may include Bluetooth Low Energy which might potentially optimize Bluetooth's impact on battery consumption.

Another potential problem is the human factor: when DroidSense detects a new device, it is the user who has to tag this devices. There is a always a possibility that instead of tagging the device as a teammate's device, he/she can mistakenly tag it as his device or vice versa. This could lead to an incorrect detection of Solo Programming or Pair Programming sessions.

Eventually, we found that when the users keep their phones on a table results in a higher number and better quality of RSSI values than when they carry them in their pockets. This issue could lead to a wrong conclusion in the proximity estimation. As a possible solution, we plan to implement recommender algorithms on the collected data, allowing DroidSense to automate the tagging of the detected devices based on the data collected from the other users.

9   Conclusions

In software quality management it is vitally important to understand the dynamics of the development process to identify opportunities for optimization as well as to avoid potential problems in quality and productivity. Collecting and analyzing data about the process is an initial yet important step to understand process deficiencies and areas for optimization. The quality of the collected data is of the highest importance for drawing correct conclusions. Therefore, it is necessary to carefully design and implement a data collection strategies that accurately mirror what happens in the measured processes.

This paper presents a new approach to collect data about software development process by leveraging proximity measures via Bluetooth. The results of the study conducted with 11 software developers at a large IT company demonstrate practical usage of DroidSense and validate obtained results of a process analysis. Thus, the collected data provide valuable insights into the developers' behavior during their daily work by automatically detecting their involvement in Solo Programming or Pair Programming sessions.

Using Android Operating System and Bluetooth network technologies allows to deploy DroidSense with no additional costs or setup activities other than those associated with mobile devices. Eventually, data collection process is organized in a non-invasive and automated way, so that the developers are not distracted from their daily activities and only need to carry their mobile devices with DroidSense activated.

References

1. Humphrey, W.S.: Introduction to the personal software process. Addison-Wesley (1997)
2. Sillitti, A., Succi, G., De Panfilis, S.: Managing Non-Invasive Measurement Tools. Journal of Systems Architecture 52(11), 676–683 (2006)
3. Johnson, P.M., Kou, H., Agustin, J.M., Chan, C., Moore, C.A., Miglani, J., Zhen, S., Doane, W.E.: Beyond the Personal Software Process: Metrics collection and analysis for the differently disciplined. In: Proceedings of the 2003 International Conference on Software Engineering, Portland, Oregon, USA, pp. 641–646 (2003)
4. Basili, R.V., Caldiera, G., Rombach, H.D.: The Goal Question Metric Approach (1994)
5. Sillitti, A., Janes, A., Succi, G., Vernazza, T.: Measures for mobile users: an architecture. Journal of Systems Architecture 50(7), 393–405 (2004)
6. Humphrey, W.S.: Characterizing the software process: a maturity framework. IEEE Software 5(2), 73–79 (1988)
7. Fenton, N.E., Pfeeger, S.L.: Software metrics: a rigorous & practical approach, 2nd edn. PWS Publishing Co., Boston (1997)
8. Sillitti, A., Janes, A., Succi, G., Vernazza, T.: Collecting, Integrating and Analyzing Software Metrics and Personal Software Process Data. In: EUROMICRO Conference (2003)
9. Johnson, P.M.: You can't even ask them to push a button: Toward ubiquitous, developer-centric, empirical software engineering. The NSF Workshop for New Visions for Software Design and Productivity: Research and Applications, Nashville, TN, USA (2001)
10. Sanders, D., Mukhi, S., Laskowski, M., Khan, M., Podaima, B., McLeod, R.D.: A Network-Enabled Platform for Reducing Hospital Emergency Department Waiting Times Using an RFID Proximity Location System. In: IEEE 19th International Conference on Systems Engineering, pp. 538–543 (2008)
11. Cockburn, A., Williams, L.: The costs and benefits of pair programming. In: Succi, G., Marchesi, M. (eds.) Extreme Programming Examined. The XP Series, pp. 223–243. Addison-Wesley Longman Publishing Co. (2001)
12. Succi, G., Pedrycz, W., Marchesi, M., Williams, L.: Preliminary analysis of the effects of pair programming on job satisfaction. In: Proceedings of XP 2002 (2002)

13. Heiberg, S., Puus, U., Salumaa, P., Seeba, A.: Pair-Programming Effect on Developers Productivity. In: Marchesi, M., Succi, G. (eds.) XP 2003. LNCS, vol. 2675, pp. 215–224. Springer, Heidelberg (2003)
14. Hulkko, H., Abrahamsson, P.: A multiple case study on the impact of pair programming on product quality. In: Proceedings of the 27th International Conference on Software Engineering, pp. 495–504 (2005)
15. Lui, K.M., Chan, K.C.: Pair programming productivity: Novice-novice vs. expert-expert. International Journal on Human-Computer Studies 64(9), 915–925 (2006)
16. Braught, G., Eby, L.M., Wahls, T.: The effects of pair-programming on individual programming skill. In: Proceedings of SIGCSE 2008, vol. 40 (1), pp. 200–204 (2008)
17. Vanhanen, J., Korpi, H.: Experiences of Using Pair Programming in an Agile Project. In: Proceedings of the 40th Annual International Conference on System Sciences (2007)
18. Canfora, G., Cimitile, A., Garcia, F., Piattini, M., Visaggio, C.A.: Evaluating performances of pair designing in industry. Journal of Systems and Software 80(8), 1317–1327 (2007)
19. Bluetooth SIG. Profles Overview, Bluetooth Special Interest Group, http://www.bluetooth.com/English/Technology/Works/Pages/ Profles_Overview.aspx (retrieved on April 14, 2010)
20. Scott, D., Sharp, R., Madhavapeddy, A., Upton, E.: Using Visual Tags to Bypass Bluetooth Device Discovery. ACM SIGMOBILE Mobile Computing and Communications Review 9, 41–53 (2005)
21. Bluetooth SIG. Core Specification Version 4.0 - Architecture - Radio, Bluetooth Special Interest Group, http://www.bluetooth.com/English/Technology/Works/Pages/ Architecture__Radio.aspx (retrieved on April 14, 2010)
22. Android Developers. Android Application Fundamentals, http://developer.android.com/guide/topics/fundamentals.html (retrieved August 20, 2011)
23. Android Documentation. What is Android? http://developer.android.com/guide/basics/ what-is-android.html (retrieved August 20, 2011)
24. Google Code: Open Bluetooth Low Energy SDK for Android, http://code.google.com/p/broadcom-ble/ (retrieved on January 10, 2011)

TimeSquare:
Treat Your Models with Logical Time[*]

Julien DeAntoni and Frédéric Mallet

Aoste Team-Project
Université Nice Sophia Antipolis
I3S - UMR CNRS 7271, INRIA Sophia Antipolis Méditerranée
2004 route des Lucioles - BP 93
06902 Sophia Antipolis Cedex, France
{julien.deantoni,frederic.mallet}@inria.fr
http://www-sop.inria.fr/aoste/

Abstract. TimeSquare is an Eclipse and model-based environment for
the specification, analysis and verification of causal and temporal constraints. It implements the MARTE Time Model and its specification
language, the Clock Constraint Specification Language (CCSL). Both
MARTE and CCSL heavily rely on logical time, made popular by its use in
distributed systems and synchronous languages. Logical Time provides
a relaxed form of time that is functional, elastic (can be abstracted or
refined) and multiform. TimeSquare is based on the latest model-driven
technology so that more than 60% of its code is automatically generated. It provides an XText-based editor of constraints, a polychronous
clock calculus engine able to process a partial order conforming to the
set of constraints and it supports several simulation policies. It has been
devised to be connected to several back-ends developed as new plugins
to produce timing diagrams, animate UML models, or execute Java code
amongst others.

Keywords: Embedded systems, Polychronous specifications, Logical
Time, Model-Driven Engineering.

1   Introduction

Models abstract away the irrelevant aspects of a system to focus on what is important for a given purpose. Model-driven engineering provides tools and techniques to deal with models. These models are nowadays mainly structural but
can often be refined with a behavioral description. The behavioral description is
usually a specific implementation of externally defined behavioral requirements.
To fully benefit from models right from the requirements we propose to specify
behavioral requirements as logical time constraints directly linked to the model.

---

[*] This work has been partially supported by the RT-SIMEX ANR
project (http://www.rtsimex.org) and the PRESTO ARTEMIS project
(http://www.presto-embedded.eu/).

C.A. Furia and S. Nanz (Eds.): TOOLS Europe 2012, LNCS 7304, pp. 34–41, 2012.

This is done by using the Time Model from MARTE conjointly with its formal companion language CCSL (Clock Constraint Specification Language [1]). This approach is tooled by the TimeSquare framework, which is a set of Eclipse plugins that implement the model-based declarative language CCSL and provide support for the analysis and execution of CCSL specifications.

In this paper, we overview the main functionality of TimeSquare. Our tool, which is itself based on a model-driven approach, allows for the enrichment of models with formal annotations by using semantic models. CCSL concrete syntax is based on Xtext (http://www.eclipse.org/Xtext/) so that the user directly constructs an EMF model while typing. This model can be parsed easily to provide useful information like the clock tree graph that represents the polychronous specification in a graphical way [6]. Keeping the specification as a model enables a better integration with a model-driven approach because the model, the formal language and the solver are in the same technological space. The main benefits is the ability to link specification as well as results directly to the models. The feedback to the user is then greatly improved compared with transformational techniques, which translate a model to an existing formal language. The output of TimeSquare is also an EMF model that defines a specific partial order of events, which represents the trace of the simulation. It is important to notice that a single simulation provides a partial order and consequently captures several possible executions (several total orders). It is possible to subscribe to specific events during the construction of this trace by using the extension point mechanism provided by Eclipse. User-defined or domain-specific backends can be deployed by registering to selected events.

The architecture of TimeSquare is shown in Figure 1. Straight arrows indicate the model flows, whereas dashed arrows represent the links between two models. The trace model is directly linked to CCSL model elements, which in turns are linked to other (EMF) model elements.

The paper organization follows this architecture. Section 2, after a brief overview of CCSL semantics, describes the CCSL concrete syntax and tooling. Section 3 explains how the solver produces the trace model according to the simulation policy. Finally, before concluding, section 3.1 details the back-end mechanism and details some of the main existing back-ends.

2   CCSL Specifications

2.1   Semantics

Contrary to most real-time constraint tools, we use a polychronous time model that allows the duration and time values to be expressed relatively to other clocks, and not only relatively to a common chronometric clock counting physical time. For instance, a duration can be expressed relative to the clock cycle of a given processor core or bus. In many current electronic devices, the clock cycle varies according to the battery level or some other optimization criteria. This kind of time is named logical time and has been used in distributed systems [5,4]

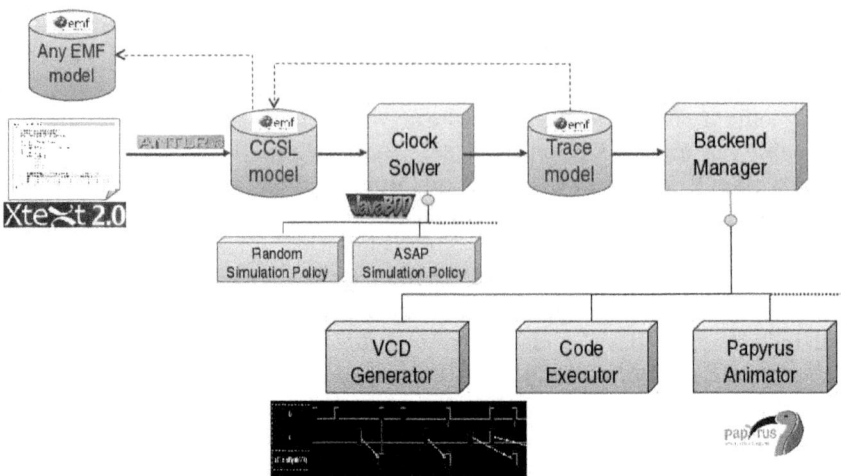

Fig. 1. Big Picture of the TimeSquare Architecture

for its ability to represent (untimed) causalities but also in synchronous language where it has prooved to be meaningful from requirements to implementations [2].

In MARTE, the Time Model relies on logical time. In this context, a *clock* is a totally ordered set of *instants*. A *time structure* is a set of clocks C and a set of relations on instants. I denotes the union of all instants of all clocks within a given time structure. We consider two kinds of relations: *causal* and *temporal* ones. The basic causal relation over I is causality/*dependency*, $i \in I, j \in I, i \preccurlyeq j$ means i causes j or j depends on i, *i.e.*, if j occurs then i also occurs. The three basic temporal relations over I are *precedence* ($\prec$), *coincidence* ($\equiv$), and *exclusion* ($\#$). For any instants i and j in a time structure, $i \prec j$ means that the only acceptable execution traces are those where i occurs strictly before (precedes) j. $i \equiv j$ imposes instants i and j to be coincident, *i.e.*, they must always occur at the same execution step, both or none . $i \# j$ forbids the coincidence of the two instants, *i.e.*, they cannot occur at the same execution step. Note that, some consistency rules must be enforced between causal and temporal relations. $i \preccurlyeq j$ can be refined either as $i \prec j$ or $i \equiv j$, but j can never precede i. Furthermore, we do not assume a global notion of time. Temporality is given by the *precedence* binary relation, which is partial, asymmetric (*i.e.*, antisymmetric and irreflexive) and transitive. The *coincidence* binary relation is an equivalence relation on instants, *i.e.*, reflexive, symmetric and transitive. Specifying a full time structure using only instant relations is not realistic since clocks are usually infinite sets of instants. Thus, CCSL defines a set of relations and expressions between clocks that apply to infinitely many instant relations. Please refer to [1] to learn about CCSL semantics.

2.2   Implementation

The clock constraint specification language (CCSL) complements structural models by formally defining a set of kernel clock constraints, which apply to infinitely many instant relations. The operational semantics of CCSL constraints is defined in a technical report [1]. Some recurrent constraints from a specific domain can be complex. To ease the application of such complex constraints, libraries of user-defined constraints can be built by composing existing constraints. This language and the library mechanism is defined in a metamodel accessible here: http://timesquare.inria.fr/resources/metamodel. This metamodel can be instantiated from two different classes depending on whether the user wants to create a CCSL specification or a library. Because using the ecore reflective editor provided by EMF is not suitable for any user, we created a textual concrete syntax using XText. XText automatically generates a textual editor for a given EMF metamodel and allows for customizing the concrete syntax. Then, when using the textual editor, the corresponding EMF model is automatically built. Amongst other things, direct links to external EMF models are supported. In the CCSL editor, we use such links to map CCSL clocks to EMF model elements such as the UML model elements whose execution is triggered by the CCSL clocks. Such direct links are important to help the user in the specification of constraints and the creation of a coherent specification (completion, detection of errors on the fly, tips, etc). Two kinds of model can be imported in a CCSL specification: external libraries and EMF-based models. If a library is imported, the Xtext editor automatically proposes, as a completion mechanism, the relations and the expressions from the library. It also checks the parameters provided and proposes some changes if a problem is detected. Such customization features are very helpful to build the specification. Figure 2 illustrates a simple CCSL specification being edited with the XText constraint editor.

Fig. 2. A simple CCSL specification in TimeSquare

If an EMF model is imported in a CCSL specification, all the elements from the model that own a "name" property will be accessible and possibly constrained. Figure 3 shows a part of the previous CCSL specification where an import from a

UML model is done. It allows enriching the *Clock* declaration with the structural element from the UML model (here subject to completion). The meaning of the link can also be specified: *i.e.,*, the clock ticks can represent the starting/finishing of a behavior, the sending/reception of a message...

```
ClockConstraintSystem MySpec {
imports {
      import "ccsl:kernel" as kernel ;
      import "model.uml" as aModel;
}
entryBlock main
Block main {
      Clock cl->event1("aModel->Model::"):send
      ⚹ Model::Component_1::Connector1 [Connector]
      ⚹ Model::Component_1::Connector2 [Connector]
      ⚹ Model::Component_1::Connector3 [Connector]
   } ⚹ Model::Component_1::Connector7 [Connector]
      ▫ Model::Component_1::P1 [Port]
      ▫ Model::Component_1::P2 [Port]
      ▫ Model::Component_1::P3 [Port]
      ▫ Model::Component_1::P4 [Port]
```

Fig. 3. Link between a model (UML here) and a CCSL specification, helped by completion

3 Simulation

The formal operational semantics of CCSL constraints makes CCSL specifications executable. A *run* of a time system is an infinite sequence of *steps* (if no deadlocks are found by the solver). During a step, a Boolean decision diagram represents the set of acceptable sets of clocks that can tick. If the CCSL specification contains assertion(s), then the Boolean decision diagram also represents the state of the assertion (violated or not). Assertions never change the clocks that can tick. It has been used in the RT-Simex project to check if a specific execution trace is correct with regards to a CCSL specification [3]. If the CCSL specification is deterministic, there exists a single set; if not, a simulation policy is used to choose amongst the possible solutions. TimeSquare offers several simulation policies (Random, As soon as possible, etc). It is possible for a user to add a new simulation policy by using a specific TimeSquare extension point. The choice of the simulation policy, the number of steps to compute as well as the choices about debugging information are integrated in the existing eclipse configuration mechanism so that a run or a debug (step by step) of a CCSL specification is accessible as in other languages like java.

3.1   Analysis Features and Back-Ends

TimeSquare can be used in various model-driven approaches. Depending on the domain, users are interested in different feedback or analysis of the results. To allow an easy integration of TimeSquare in various domains, we implemented a back-end manager, which enables the easy addition of user-defined back-ends.

The back-end manager receives the status of the clock (it ticks or not) at each simulation step. It also receives the status of relations (causality and coincidence) as well as the status of the assertions (violated or not). By using a specific extension point, a developer can create a back-end that subscribes to some of these events. The registered back-end are then notified when the events they subscribed to occur during the simulation step. We present in the remainder of this section the three main backends: the VCD diagram creator, the papyrus animator and the code executor.

VCD Diagram Creator: VCD is a format defined as part of IEEE1364 and is mainly used in the electronic design domain. It is very close to the UML timing diagram and represents the evolution of each event (Clock) *vs.* time evolution, represented horizontally. It classically represents a total order of events. Because TimeSquare provides a trace which is only partially ordered, the classical VCD features have been extended to graphically represent such a partial order. On Figure 4, a simple VCD is represented. It results from the simulation of the CCSL specification represented on Figure 2 where the c0 clock is hidden to simplify the reading. We can notice the optional presence of two kinds of links between the ticks of the clocks: blue arrows, which represent causalities (loose synchronizations) and red links, which represent coincidences (strong synchronizations). The result is that the partial order is valid as long as the red links are not broken and the blue arrows never go back in time.

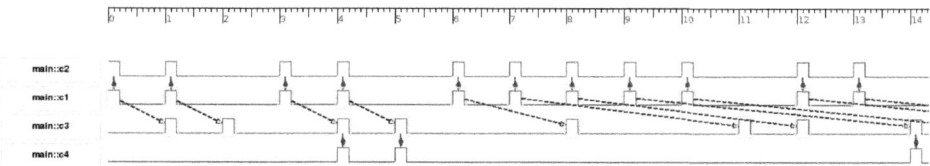

Fig. 4. The extended VCD diagram back-end

Papyrus Diagram Animator: When a CCSL specification is linked to a UML model, the model is often represented graphically in a UML tool. Papyrus (http://www.eclipse.com/Papyrus) is an open source UML tool integrated with eclipse EMF and GMF. The papyrus animator provides a graphical animation of the UML diagrams during the simulation. The kind of graphical animation depends on the "meaning" of the event linked to the UML model (send, reveive, start, etc). This animation provides a very convenient feedback to the user who wants to understand what happens in the model according to the constraints he wrote. Additionally to graphical animation, the Papyrus animator adds *comments* to the UML model elements that represent their activation trace, keeping this way a trace of the simulation directly in the UML model. The Papyrus animator is shown conjointly (and synchronized with) the VCD diagram on Figure 5.

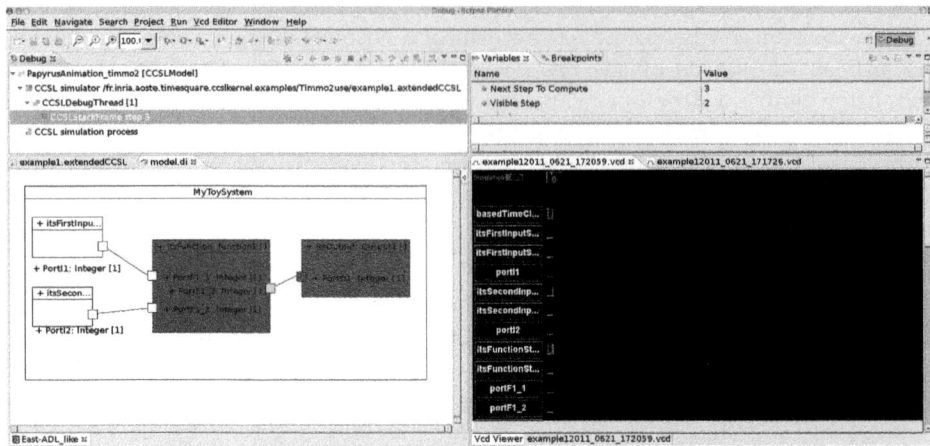

Fig. 5. The animation of a UML model and the associated timing diagram in Time-Square

Code Executor: When a software is prototyped, it can be convenient to run some piece of code in order to provide application specific feedback. For instance we developped a simple digital filter by using UML composite structure in Papyrus and we added constraints on it representing its synchronizations (so that the diagram can be animated conjointly with the VCD diagram). To test our algorithm and ease the debugging of the synchronization in the model, we used the JAVA code executor. It allows the declaration of object and the launch of specific method of these objects when a desired event occurs (tick of a clock, etc). It can be used, as in the digital filter, to represent the data manipulation of the filter and to graphically represent the internal state of the memory. It can also be used to pop-up information windows when an assertion is violated, etc.

Clock Graph: To allow static analysis as, for instance the one described in [6], TimeSquare is able to build statically a clock graph that depicts the synchronous/asynchronous relations between clocks. This specific mechanism is not a back-end *per se* because it does not depend on the dynamics of the model but it is a very useful feature to deal with polychronous specifications. A simple CCSL specification, the corresponding and synchronized EMF model in the outline and the associated clock graph are represented on Figure 6. The vertices are the clocks and the edges are the clock relationships: *sub* denotes a subclocking and therefore a synchronous relationship, whereas $<$ denotes a precedence by nature asynchronous. When two clocks are synchronous, they are merged into a single vertex (as $c1 == c2$). This graph shows that the specification is fully synchronous: $c0$ is the super clock of both $c1$ and $c3$. $c1$ in turns is a super clock of $c4$ and is synchronous with $c2$. It also shows the precedence relationship between $c1$ and $c3$.

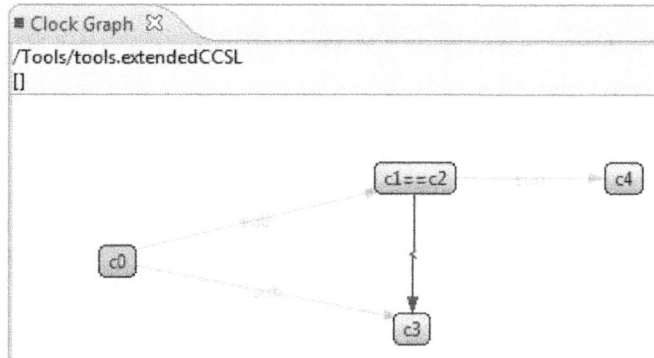

Fig. 6. Clock Graph extracted from a CCSL specification

4   Conclusions

This paper briefly presents TimeSquare. It is a model-based tool well integrated in the Model Driven Development process. Its goal is to ease the use of the formal declarative language CCSL and provides analysis support. Additionally, we wanted to develop it by using model driven technology; in one hand it has helped in the development of our tool and on the other hand it put the tool in the same technological space than the model under development. The main benefit is the direct feedback offered to the users during the simulation. A video demonstration is available from the TimeSquare website (in French): http://timesquare.inria.fr/. Finally, while not presented here, it also supports a form of runtime analysis through the generation of VHDL or Esterel observers.

References

1. André, C.: Syntax and semantics of the clock constraint specification language (ccsl). Research Report 6925, INRIA (May 2009)
2. Benveniste, A., Caspi, P., Edwards, S.A., Halbwachs, N., Le Guernic, P., De Simone, R.: The synchronous languages twelve years later. Proceedings of the IEEE, 64–83 (2003)
3. Deantoni, J., Mallet, F., Thomas, F., Reydet, G., Babau, J.-P., Mraidha, C., Gauthier, L., Rioux, L., Sordon, N.: RT-simex: retro-analysis of execution traces. In: In, K.J., Sullivan, G.-C. (eds.) SIGSOFT FSE, Santa Fe, États-Unis, pp. 377–378 (2010) ISBN 978-1-60558-791-2
4. Fidge, C.: Logical time in distributed computing systems. Computer 24(8), 28–33 (2002)
5. Lamport, L.: Time, clocks, and the ordering of events in a distributed system. Communications of the ACM 21(7), 558–565 (1978)
6. Yu, H., Talpin, J.-P., Besnard, L., Gautier, T., Mallet, F., André, C., de Simone, R.: Polychronous analysis of timing constraints in UML MARTE. In: IEEE Int. W. on Model-Based Engineering for Real-Time Embedded Systems Design, Parador of Carmona, Spain, pp. 145–151 (2010)

Quality Evaluation of Object-Oriented and Standard Mutation Operators Applied to C# Programs

Anna Derezińska and Marcin Rudnik

Institute of Computer Science, Warsaw University of Technology,
Nowowiejska 15/19, 00-665 Warsaw, Poland
A.Derezinska@ii.pw.edu.pl

Abstract. Mutation testing is a kind of fault injection approach that can be used to generate tests or to assess the quality of test sets. For object-oriented languages, like C#, both object-oriented and standard (traditional) mutation operators should be applied. The methods that can contribute to reducing the number of applied operators and lowering the costs of mutation testing were experimentally investigated. We extended the CREAM mutation tool to support selective testing, sampling and clustering of mutants, and combining code coverage with mutation testing. We propose an approach to quality evaluation and present experimental results of mutation operators applied to C# programs.

Keywords: mutation testing, object-oriented mutation operators, C#.

1 Introduction

Mutation testing is a fault-injection technique that can be used for assessment of test set quality and support for test case generation [1]. Once a defined fault is introduced in a program, a mutated program (*mutant*) is created. A program modification is determined by a *mutation operator*. Within this paper we deal with first order mutation, i.e. one mutation operator is applied in one place. If a mutant behavior differs from that of the original program while running against a test case, the mutant is said to be *killed* by this test. The test is effective at killing the mutant. A quality of a test set is a mutation score MS calculated as the ratio between the number of killed mutants over all the generated but not equivalent mutants. An *equivalent* mutant has the same behavior as the original program and therefore cannot be killed by any test.

Mutation testing process is counted as a very cost-demanding testing activity. The cost is determined by the number of generated mutants, the number of tests involved in the process and their ability to test mutants, the number of equivalent mutants and their recognizing, a kind of a mutation tool support, etc.

Important factors of mutation testing are mutation operators that reflect possible faults made by programmers and therefore should deal with different constructs in programming languages. In C# programs, as for any general purpose language, standard (i.e. structural, intra-class or statement-level) operators can be applied, e.g. dealing with logical, arithmetical, relational operators like those defined in Fortran or C. Moreover, object-oriented (or inter-class) operators should also be used. Operators

C.A. Furia and S. Nanz (Eds.): TOOLS Europe 2012, LNCS 7304, pp. 42–57, 2012.

of object-oriented features were primarily defined for the Java language [2-4]. Applicability of those operators was studied for C# programs, and analogous operators of the same or similar scope were proposed [5]. Its set was extended with new operators, for example dealing with exception handling, or devoted to the programming constructs specific to C# but not present in Java, like delegates or properties [6]. Empirical evaluation of object-oriented and other advanced operators in C# programs was conducted on above 13 thousands of mutants [6-11].

However, a quality of object-oriented mutations, both in Java or C#, remains still an open question in the relation to the cost estimation. A problem is, which object-oriented operators we really need, and which of them can be omitted without loosing the ability to qualify a given test set. Should we reduce the cost by selecting operators, random sampling of mutants, or other reduction techniques? These issues were studied for structural languages [12-15] and partially for Java programs [16-18].

According to our experience [6-11], object-oriented operators generate fewer mutants than the standard ones, and are more dependant on the concerned programs. Therefore we extended the CREAM mutation testing tool for C# programs with the facility to carry out experiments into cost reduction techniques. They cover operator selecting, mutant random sampling and clustering [1, 19-22]. Using the tool some experiments on fist-order mutation in C# programs were conducted. They showed that relations between different cost techniques are not necessarily the same as for the standard mutation in C [15]. The main contributions of the paper are:

- Evolution of the mutation testing tool for C# programs, and incorporated processes of an empirical and statistical analysis of mutation results.
- New quality metrics for assessment of a tradeoff between mutation score accuracy and mutation costs in terms of number of mutants and number of tests.
- The first experiments on the selective mutation of C# programs performed and analyzed for 18 object-oriented (OO in short) and 8 standard mutation operators.
- The first general estimation of results for experiments on mutant sampling and clustering for object-oriented mutation.

The paper is organized as follows: Section 2 summarizes briefly the main features of the CREAM mutation testing tool. In Section 3 we give details about selected investigation processes incorporated in the tool and the quality metrics. Section 4 describes an experimental set-up and results of the conducted experiments. Finally, the remaining sections present related work and conclusions.

2   CREAM Mutation Testing Tool for C# Programs

CREAM (CREAtor of Mutants) was the first mutation testing tool supporting object-oriented mutation operators for C# programs [7,8,23]. It is a parser-based tool. A fault defined by a mutation operator is introduced into a parser output after analysis of a C# project. Then the C# source code is reconstructed from the modified syntax tree. It can be compiled, so creating a mutated program that can be run against a test set.

Currently, the next, third version of the tool is ready to use. It was extended to support more mutation operators, to keep-up with new versions of the C# language and cooperate with new tools in order to work on emerging real-word applications. It can create mutants for the whole code or only for the code covered by the test cases, if required. Moreover, it was equipped with a wizard aimed at evaluation of detailed statistics and supporting experimental studies on mutation operator assessment. The most important functionalities of the current version of CREAM are as follows:

1. It supports parser-based generation of first order mutants of C# programs with 18 object-oriented operators and 8 selected standard operators, listed in Tab. 1.
2. It runs mutants against test suites and evaluates test results. Unit tests can be compatible with the NUnit tool [24] or with MSTest (another tool built in Microsoft Visual Studio).
3. It optionally takes into account code coverage results while creating mutants. The coverage data can be delivered by NCover [25] (.xml files), Microsoft Visual Studio (.coverage files) or Tester [9] (.txt files).
4. It optionally stores mutants in the local or remote SVN repository [26] in order to reduce an occupied disk space [9].
5. It automates analysis of generated mutants according to cost reduction techniques: mutation operator selection, mutant sampling and clustering.
6. It evaluates statistics of many experiments, and enables presentation of output data in cooperation with a Data Viewer tool.

Table 1. Mutation operators: standard and object-oriented supported in CREAM v.3

No	Type	Abbreviation	Name
1	Standard	ABS	Absolute Value Insertion
2	Standard	AOR	Arithmetic Operator Replacement (+, -, *, /, %)
3	Standard	ASR	Assignment Operator Replacement (=, +=, -=, /=, *=)
4	Standard	LCR	Logical Connector Replacement (&&, ‖)
5	Standard	LOR	Logical Operator Replacement (&, |, ^)
6	Standard	ROR	Relational Operator Replacement (<, <=, >, >=, ==, !=)
7	Standard	UOI	Unary Operator Insertion (+, -, !, ~)
8	Standard	UOR	Unary Operator Replacement (++, --)
1	Object-oriented	DMC	Delegated Method Change
2	Object-oriented	EHR	Exception Handler Removal
3	Object-oriented	EOA	Reference Assignment and Content Assignment Replacement
4	Object-oriented	EOC	Reference Comparison and Content Comparison Replacement
5	Object-oriented	EXS	Exception Swallowing
6	Object-oriented	IHD	Hiding Variable Deletion
7	Object-oriented	IHI	Hiding Variable Insertion
8	Object-oriented	IOD	Overriding Method Deletion
9	Object-oriented	IOK	Overriding Method Substitution
10	Object-oriented	IOP	Overriding Method Calling Position Change
11	Object-oriented	IPC	Explicit call of a Parent's Constructor Deletion
12	Object-oriented	ISK	Base Keyword Deletion
13	Object-oriented	JID	Ember Variable Initialization deletion
14	Object-oriented	JTD	This Keyword Deletion
15	Object-oriented	OAO	Argument Order Change
16	Object-oriented	OMR	Overloading Method Contents Change
17	Object-oriented	PRM	Property Replacement with Member Field
18	Object-oriented	PRV	Reference Assignment with other Compatible Type

3   Investigation Process of Mutation Operators

In this section we explain the basic setup of an experimental process. The empirical evaluation of mutant features can be considered as several experimental scenarios: three relating to selective mutation, six to mutant sampling, and one to mutant clustering. Mutant sampling refers to random selection of a given % of all mutants or of mutants uniformly distributed for all classes, files, methods, operators or namespaces. The examination of mutation results is done independently for object-oriented operators and standard ones. For the brevity reasons we only describe the general experimental scenario of all types of experiments and the details of selective mutation. The details of sampling and clustering scenarios are omitted [27].

3.1   Generic Scenario of Experiments

A) In the first step, common for all experiments, all mutants of a program under test are generated for a given set of operators. In this case all standard and all object-oriented operators available in CREAM v.3 were used independently (Tab. 1). This original set of all mutants is called M_{All}.

B) Secondly, all mutants are run against a whole set of tests T_{All} considered as a basic, complete set of tests taken into account in the experiments for a given program. Results of all mutants and all tests are stored in a file and can be examined during different experiments, or viewed by a user. Taking into account these results a mutation score can be calculated. Further we refer to this value as to the "original" mutation score $MS_{orig.} = MS (M_{All}, T_{All})$.

C) Next, the subsequent steps (C1-C4) and D are repeated many times in accordance to different parameters specific to each kind of experiments (e.g. numbers of mutation operators, number of kinds of mutant sampling, etc.).

C1) A subset of mutants $M_{C1} \subseteq M_{All}$ is selected according to given criteria of the experiment. This set determines the maximal mutation score generated using all tests $MS_{C1max} = MS (M_{C1}, T_{All})$.

C2) A list L of subsets of T_{All} is created. Usage of any test set in L against M_{C1} gives the mutation score equal to MS_{C1max}. But each test set of L is minimal, i.e. all tests are necessary. All test sets of this kind can be generated using prime implicant of a monotonous Boolean function [27]. The number of all test sets is finite but can be high. Therefore the cardinality of the list L is limited, $|L| \leq TestSetLimit$. It is fixed as a parameter of an experiment that restricts its complexity. $|X|$ is cardinality of set X.

C3) For a set $M_{C3} \subseteq M_{All}$, mutation scores MS_{C3j} are calculated using consecutively each minimal test set in L: $MS_{C3j} = MS(M_{C3}, T_j)$, where $T_j \subseteq T_{All}$, $T_j \in L$, $j=1..|L|$. The considered mutant set M_{C3} depends on the type of the experiment (Sec. 3.2).

C4) The average mutation score $MS_{avg} = (\sum_{j=1..|L|} MS_{C3j})/|L|$ is calculated for all minimal test sets in L. The average number of test sets in L is $NT_{avg} = (\sum_{j=1..|L|} |T_j|)/|L|$.

D) In mutant sampling, calculation of average statistics for many random runs of steps C1-C4 for a given experiment parameter. Basing on data from C4 new average values MS_{avg}, NT_{avg} are calculated over those repeated runs for this parameter.

E) Calculation of final statistics and normalization of results (see Sec. 3.3).

3.2   Experimental Flows on Selective Mutation

In selective mutation, only a subset of mutation operators is used. Considering different policies of operator selection, and determination of minimal test sets and sets of mutants used for evaluation of a final mutation score, three kinds of experiments are supported in CREAM.

Experiment 1. Mutation operators that generate the biggest number of mutants are excluded. Therefore, omitting the fewer number of operators the biggest number of mutants could be not used.

In these experiment, steps C1-C4 are repeated for different numbers of excluded operators ($i = 0..k$, where k is a number of all operators, in this case 8 for standard and 18 for object-oriented ones). In general, for a given value of i it could be the binomial coefficient $C(k,i)$ of various subsets including i operators. But we exclude i operators generating the biggest number of mutants. In almost all cases there was exactly one such subset with i operators, otherwise one such subset was randomly selected.

In step C1, M_{C1} is the subset of M_{All} containing the mutants generated by the operators not excluded in the current experiment run.

In step C3, the mutation scores are calculated for all mutants, i.e. $M_{C3} = M_{All}$.

Step D is not used.

Experiment 2. One mutation operator is excluded. The selection is performed for each mutation operator separately. In this way all mutation operators are examined in accordance to their influence on the mutation score result.

The number of repetition of steps C1-C4 is equal to the number of considered mutation operators. Step D is not used.

In step C1, we determine M_{C1} as the subset of M_{All} containing the mutants generated by the operators not excluded in the current experiment run.

In step C3, $M_{C3} = M_{All}$.

Experiment 3. One mutation operator is excluded, similarly as in the second type of the selective experiment (steps C1 and C2 are the same). But, in this case the mutation scores in step C3 are calculated for the set of mutants M_{C3} generated by the operator excluded in the current experiment run ($M_{C1} \cup M_{C3} = M_{All}$). Step D is not used.

The motivation of this experiment is assessment of an operator quality. A "good" operator is an operator for which no mutants are generated by other operators and are killed by the same tests. A "poor" operator can be counted as a redundant one, tests that kill other mutants can also kill mutants generated by this operator.

3.3   Quality Metrics

The cost of mutation testing process is influenced by different factors, mainly the cost of mutant generation, of running mutants against tests, dealing with equivalent mutants and analyzing test results. Reduction of the cost can cause decrease of mutation score accuracy. Therefore, we proposed metrics to assess a tradeoff concerning the loss of MS accuracy on the one hand and profits of using a smaller number of mutants and smaller number of tests on the other hand. It assists in comparing results for different programs and different experiments.

The quality metric EQ takes into account three variables:

S_{MS} - reflects a loss of Mutation Score adequacy (MS) in an experiment,

Z_T - approximates a profit of a cost decrease due to a reduced number of tests required for killing mutants in an experiment,

Z_M - assesses a profit of a cost decrease due to a reduced number of mutants considered in an experiment.

These variables are calculated as given in Equations (1)-(3).

The first variable S_{MS} is evaluated in a different way in accordance to the experiment type. It is calculated as a ratio of the current average mutation score to the original mutation score if we look for a possible smallest difference to MS_{orig}. Otherwise, if we are interested in the biggest difference, S_{MS} is equal to 1 minus the ratio mentioned in the previous case (Eq. 1). The average mutation score MS_{avg} is calculated for all minimal test sets in step C4 (or in D if applicable).

$$
S_{MS} = \begin{cases} MS_{avg} / MS_{orig} & \text{in } 1^{st} \text{ selective experiment, sampling, clustering} \\ 1 - (MS_{avg} / MS_{orig}) & \text{in } 2^{nd} \text{ and } 3^{rd} \text{ selective experiment} \end{cases} \tag{1}
$$

Variable Z_T is calculated as 1 minus a ratio of an average number of tests for a current experiment divided by the number of all tests considered for a program, if the divident is bigger than zero. Otherwise Z_T is equal to zero (Eq. 2). The average number of tests NT_{avg} is defined in step C4 (or in D if used for many random cases).

$$
Z_T = \begin{cases} 1 - (NT_{avg} / |T_{All}|) & \text{if } NT_{avg} > 0 \\ 0 & \text{otherwise} \end{cases} \tag{2}
$$

Value Z_M is equal to 1 minus a ratio of a mutant number currently taken into account in the experiment ($|M_{Cl}|$ from step C1) to a maximal number of all mutants generated for the program (in the set M_{All}), if the current mutant number is bigger than zero. Otherwise Z_M is set to zero (Eq. 3).

$$
Z_M = \begin{cases} 1 - (|M_{C1}| / |M_{All}|) & \text{if } |M_{C1}| > 0 \\ 0 & \text{otherwise} \end{cases} \tag{3}
$$

Next, the variables obtained for different parameters of an experiment are normalized. The normalization function $NORM(x)$ represents a normalized value of variable x over a set of its values X (Eq. 4).

$$
NORM(x) = (x - MIN(X)) / (MAX(X) - MIN(X)), \text{ where } x \in X \tag{4}
$$

In result, the normalized variable x will be distributed within the <0,1> interval and can be further processed in an comparable way. The normalization is calculated for a set of results determined by experiment parameters. For example, in the second selective experiment on object-oriented operators the set of variables correspond to exclusion of one selected operator. In this case cardinality of the set X equals the number of operators (18).

The quality metric EQ is based on a weighted sum of three components (Eq. 5).

$$EQ(W_{MS,} W_T, W_M) = NORM(W_{MS}*NORM(S_{MS}) + W_T*NORM(Z_T) + W_M*NORM(Z_M)) \qquad (5)$$

The weight coefficients $W_{MS,} W_T, W_M$ state for parameters of the analysis and are determined according to the importance assigned to particular components of the metric. The sum of coefficients must be equal to 1.

The whole metric is also normalized over the set of values calculated for different parameters of an experiment, similarly as the variables.

4   Experiments

In this section we describe the subject programs and their results of mutation testing. Outcomes of experiments on selective mutation are also discussed.

4.1   Investigated Programs

Objects of experiments were three, commonly used open-source programs. They were selected to cover different types of complexity, application domain, and origin.

1. Enterprise Logging [http://entlib.codeplex.com] - a module from the "pattern & practices" library developed by Microsoft. It is used for logging information about code faults.
2. Castle [http://www.castleproject.org] - a project supporting development of advanced applications in .NET. Four modules were used in experiments: Castle.Core, Castle.DynamicProxy2, CastleMicroCernel and Castle.Windsor.
3. Mono Gendarme [http://www.mono-project.com/Gendarme] - a tool for inspection of programs written in Mono and .NET environments. It looks for flaws not detected by a compiler.

The following measures of the programs are summarized in Table 2.

1. *Files* - number of file modules with the source code included in a program.
2. *Statements* - number of statements in a program.
3. *Lines* - number of all lines in a project including comments.
4. *Percent comment lines* - % of lines with comments among all program lines.
5. *Percent documentation lines* - % of lines with documentation among all program lines.
6. *Class, Interfaces, Structs* - number of all such items defined in a program.
7. *Methods per Class* - average number of methods per class (a ratio of the number of all methods to the number of all defined classes, structs and interfaces).
8. *Calls per method* - average number of calls of other methods in a given method.
9. *Statements per method* - average number of statements in a method.
10.   *Maximum complexity* - maximal number of conditional decisions in a method.
11.   *Average complexity* - average number of conditional decisions in methods.
12.   *Depth of inheritance* - maximal number of inheritance levels in a project.

Table 2. Details of tested programs (measured with SourceMonitor [28] and Microsoft Visual Studio)

No	Measure	1.Enterprise Logging		2.Castle		3.Mono Gendarme	
		with tests	without tests	with tests	without tests	with tests	without tests
1	Files	662	497	533	403	291	170
2	Statements	33451	17427	20284	14001	21739	9715
3	Lines	87552	57885	54496	41288	51228	25692
4	% comment lines	8.1	9.1	13.7	13.8	18.9	21.9
5	% document. lines	19.2	29.0	11.4	14.6	9.9	19.5
6	Classes, Interfaces,	991	587	724	493	907	171
7	Methods per class	5.4	5.9	5.0	5.4	3.8	5.1
8	Calls per method	3.1	1.3	2.7	2.2	2.0	2.7
9	Statem. per method	3.3	2.3	3.2	2.9	3.7	7.9
10	Max. complexity	14	14	25	25	53	28
11	Average complex.	1.3	1.5	1.6	1.8	2.0	4.0
12	Depth of inherit.	6	6	4	4	10	3

4.2   Mutant Generation and Execution

The tested programs were distributed with unit tests. For two programs additional test cases were prepared in order to increase their code coverage results (Table 3). The first program has unit tests compatible to MSTest and its code coverage was evaluated using functionality build in Microsoft Visual Studio. Remaining two programs have unit tests for NUnit [24] and were examined with the NCover coverage tool [25].

Table 3. Code coverage results (measured with NCover [25] and Microsoft Visual Studio)

	1. Enterprise Logging	2. Castle	3. Mono Gendarme
	MSTest tests	NUnit tests	NUnit tests
Number of original tests	1148	578	784
Number of additional tests	0	64	115
All test cases	1148	642	899
Line coverage [%]	82	77	87

If demanded, CREAM v3 can generate mutants for these code statements that were covered by tests from a test suit under consideration, when the appropriate coverage data are provided. According to our experiences, if MS was evaluated, it was useless to mutate the code not covered by these tests. Just in case, all possible mutants of the programs discussed in this paper were generated and run against tests. But none of uncovered mutants was killed by any test. Therefore, as generated mutants (column *Gen* in Table 4.) are only counted these mutants that are created by modification of covered code lines. Only this sort of mutants is used further in the calculation of mutation results. Based on the uncovered code we obtained 265 standard and 336 object-oriented mutants for Enterprise Logging, 448 and 367 for Castle and 392, 449 for MonoGardarme, accordingly. These uncovered mutants were discarded.

Table 4 presents mutation results for each standard and object-oriented operator implemented in CREAM v3. The full names of the operators are given in Tab. 1. Columns Kill include numbers of mutants killed using all tests defined in Tab. 2.

Table 4. Mutation results (mutants generated, killed, equivalent, and mutation score in [%])

Opera tor	1. Enterprise Logging				2. Castle				3. Mono Gendarme			
	Gen	Kill	Eq	MS	Gen	Kill	Eq	MS	Gen	Kill	Eq	MS
ABS	114	7	60	13%	102	9	60	23%	116	3	79	8%
AOR	328	322	-	99%	68	19	-	28%	88	67	-	76%
ASR	160	97	-	61%	98	43	-	44%	85	54	-	64%
LCR	34	27	-	79%	196	138	-	70%	417	270	-	65%
LOR	2	0	0	0%	2	0	0	0%	16	14	-	88%
ROR	220	141	-	64%	645	427	-	66%	900	575	-	64%
UOI	795	537	-	68%	1070	842	-	79%	2342	1920	-	83%
UOR	30	20	-	67%	198	133	-	67%	189	106	-	56%
Sum	1683	1151	60	71%	2379	1611	60	70%	4153	3009	79	74%
DMC	0	0	0	-	0	0	0	-	0	0	0	-
EHR	9	6	0	67%	8	3	4	75%	5	5	-	100%
EOA	22	0	21	0%	23	2	13	20%	7	2	1	33%
EOC	98	43	18	54%	494	209	119	56%	536	159	124	39%
EXS	22	1	10	8%	11	3	0	27%	3	0	1	0%
IHD	0	0	0	-	0	0	-	-	0	0	0	-
IHI	1	0	0	0%	0	0	-	-	0	0	0	-
IOD	21	20	-	95%	13	10	-	77%	10	9	-	90%
IOK	20	19	-	95%	13	9	-	69%	10	8	-	80%
IOP	20	7	11	78%	7	2	4	67%	34	22	-	65%
IPC	45	35	-	78%	39	31	-	79%	0	0	-	-
ISK	51	32	-	63%	18	11	-	61%	30	30	-	100%
JID	80	32	24	57%	143	106	-	74%	155	135	-	87%
JTD	458	52	353	50%	48	38	3	84%	17	0	17	0%
OAO	164	115	-	70%	212	117	-	55%	142	66	-	46%
OMR	17	16	-	94%	54	50	-	93%	0	0	-	-
PRM	17	11	1	69%	16	12	-	75%	15	10	-	67%
PRV	296	169	-	57%	109	98	-	90%	34	32	-	94%
Sum	1341	558	438	62%	1208	701	143	66%	998	478	143	56%

CREAM prevents in some cases, especially for OO operators, from creating of equivalent mutants, but still many such mutants can be obtained. Therefore, some not killed mutants were examined manually. First, a preliminary mutation indicator was calculated for each operator and a program (i.e. the number of killed mutants divided be the number of generated mutants). If the indicator was below 50% for an OO operator, or below 40% for a standard one, mutants generated by this operator were examined, whether they are equivalent or not. These thresholds were selected after the empirical evaluation of data. In addition, we checked those mutants that were easily to be verified.

Mutants examined of being equivalent are denoted in Table 4. In column Eq a number of detected equivalent mutants is given ("-" states for not examined mutants).

Finally, a mutation score (column MS) was evaluated, as a ratio of killed mutants to generated but not equivalent mutants.

4.3 Experiments on Selective Mutation

The experiments were conducted according to assumptions given in Sec. 3, and for the limit of minimal test sets *TestSetLimit* equal to 100. The required quality condition is that a decrease of the mutation score accuracy is acceptable while there are considerable benefits in the cost reduction in terms of the lowering of the mutant number and the number of tests required for killing those mutants. The quality metrics EQ given in tables (Tab. 5, 6) were calculated for the weight coefficients W_{MS}, W_T, W_M equal to 0.6, 0.2, 0.2 accordingly, i.e. the mutation score accuracy amounts to 60% in the quality measure whereas efficiency factors to 40% (20% for the number of mutants and 20% for the number of tests).

1st Experiment on Selective Mutation - Exclusion of the Most Popular Operators
The experiment investigates how many mutation operators that generate the biggest number of mutants (and which of them) can be omitted. Selection of less than 8 standard, or less than 8 object-oriented operators to be excluded was unique in all cases (comp. Sec. 3.2). In general, excluding mutation operators that generate the biggest numbers of mutants results in the decrease of the mutation score even for one operator (Table 5.), regardless standard or object-oriented operators were concerned. In the first column a number of excluded operators is given. Columns MS1 include average mutation scores (in %) calculated under these conditions.

Considering potential profits in a reduced number of mutants and tests, the quality metric was calculated ($EQ1$). Selecting the quality value above 90% for object-oriented operators, we obtained different sets of operators to be excluded. The common result for all programs was elimination of two operators EOC and OAO.

In the case of the standard operators, the results for different programs are more similar to each other than for object-oriented ones. A maximal quality value was obtained for one or two excluded operators. Assuming a quality value about 90% the common two operators to be excluded are UOI and ROR .

2nd Experiment on Selective Mutation - Exclusion of One Mutation Operator
In this experiment each time one mutation operator was omitted. Average mutation scores obtained while omitting mutants generated by one of operators are given in Tab. 6 (column MS2 in [%]). Omitting one mutation operator gives in many cases similar results in comparison to all operators (row None, i.e. none operator omitted).

Quality measure $EQ2$ has value close to 100% when an operator attributes to the MS (is a selective one), while values close to 0% when the operator could be omitted. On the contrary to the previous experiment, we look for operators that should not be excluded from the analysis, because it causes observable lowering of a mutation score The following operators give $EQ2$ above 15% for at least one program and could stay: 7 OO operators PRV, OAO, JTD, JID, EOC, IPC, IOP, and 3 standard ones UOI, ROR, LCR. It can be seen that the result partially contradicts the previous experiment.

Table 5. Average results for excluding the most popular mutation operators: mutation score (MS1) and quality metric (EQ1)

| | 1. Enterprise Logging | | | | 2. Castle | | | | 3. Mono Gendarme | | | |
| | MS1 [%] | | EQ1 [%] | | MS1 [%] | | EQ1 [%] | | MS1 [%] | | EQ1 [%] | |
	OO	St	OO	St	OO	St	OO	St	OO	St	OO	St
0	62	71	86	91	66	70	71	84	56	74	87	61
1	57	65	100	100	56	65	86	93	45	67	100	99
2	48	55	91	94	52	63	92	100	34	59	89	100
3	43	48	85	89	51	58	100	97	24	33	70	57
4	39	24	94	60	45	37	91	75	20	24	65	39
5	38	22	99	59	41	28	91	65	18	20	56	32
6	35	13	96	48	35	24	78	61	12	8	33	2
7	33	0	94	0	30	0	67	0	9	7	25	0
8	33		98		29		66		9		25	
9	25		74		25		56		4		5	
10	23		64		24		53		3		0	
11	9		2		17		34		0		0	
12	9		3		15		26		0		0	
13	7		0		8		4		0		0	
14	0		0		7		0		0		0	

3rd Experiment on Selective Mutation - Mutation Operator Quality

This experiment evaluates a quality of each implemented mutation operator. In this case quality metric $EQ3$ of a low value (close to zero) denotes an operator that could be omitted. The operator generates some mutants that are redundant (i.e. tests that kill mutants of other operators are also able to kill those mutants). In the contrast to the previous metric $EQ2$, this metric is less sensitive to the number of generated mutants.

However, it should be noted that this qualification does not take into account the ability to generate equivalent mutants. For example ABS operator has $EQ3$ equal to 100% (is selective and generated necessary mutants), but also generated many equivalent mutants that were distinguished and removed during the preliminary analysis (Sec. 4.2). One of the following operators could be selected: standard ABS, LCR, UOI, ROR, UOR for $EQ3 > 25\%$ and object-oriented EHR, EOC, EXS, OAO, IPC, JTD, PRV for $EQ3 > 50\%$. The obtained values are in many cases different for various programs, which is observable especially for the object oriented operators.

Comparison of Experiment Results. The results based on the above experiments are summarized in Table 7. Program identifiers and types of mutation operators (standard or object-oriented) are denoted in the first column. Number of mutants, number of tests and mutation scores calculated in four cases are compared. In the first, reference case, mutants are generated for all considered operators and all tests are used (columns All). Remaining results (columns Ex1, 2, 3) refer to cases decided on the basis of the above experiments and their quality metrics. If we exclude the most popular operators selected in experiment 1st, or use operators chosen in experiment 2nd, or finally select operators according to *EQ3*, then we would obtain less accurate mutation score but also use fewer mutants and fewer tests, as given in columns Ex1-3, accordingly. The tradeoff of the accuracy and efficiency is visible, but in general the best results are in the last two cases (Ex2, Ex3), i.e. mutation scores close to the maximal ones for the significantly lower numbers of mutants and tests.

Table 6. Results for omitting one mutation operator (MS and quality metrics in [%])

Omitted operator	1. Enterprise Logging			2. Castle			3. Mono Gendarme		
	MS2	EQ2	EQ3	MS2	EQ2	EQ3	MS2	EQ2	EQ3
ABS	70.7	3	87	69.6	0	0	73.9	0	0.7
AOR	70.9	8	12	69.6	1	15	73.9	2	6
ASR	70.7	5	13	69.4	2	12	73.8	2	0.4
LCR	70.7	2	18	68.8	19	54	71.7	30	100
LOR	70.9	0	0	69.6	0	0	73.9	1	0
ROR	70.3	12	19	68.9	24	35	73.3	13	31
UOI	64.4	100	100	65.1	100	100	66.8	100	92
UOR	70.9	0	0	69.4	6	26	73.7	5	20
None	70.9			69.6			73.9		
DMC	61.8	0	0	65.8	0	0	55.9	0	0
EHR	61.3	5	57	65.7	1	34	55.4	4	69
EOA	61.8	0	0	65.8	1	0.2	55.9	0	1
EOC	58.7	50	89	55.0	100	100	44.1	100	100
EXS	61.7	3	85	65.7	3	67	55.9	0	0
IHD	61.8	0	0	65.8	0	0	55.9	0	0
IHI	61.8	0	0	65.8	0	0	55.9	0	0
IOD	61.7	2	6	65.8	0	0	55.9	2	1
IOK	61.7	11	12	65.8	1	1.3	55.9	2	1
IOP	61.8	0	0	65.8	1	41	54.6	16	47
IPC	60.1	17	30	63.6	17	78	55.9	0	0
ISK	61.3	11	21	65.8	1	1.5	55.9	1	5
JID	61.3	15	19	65.1	14	23	53.2	32	33
JTD	60.0	31	49	65.5	5	13	55.9	0	0
OAO	52.1	100	100	63.8	26	41	51.3	41	68
OMR	60.9	10	41	64.9	11	25	55.9	0	0
PRM	61.8	6	2	65.6	3	20	55.8	3	15
PRV	56.6	71	58	65.1	24	33	53.7	15	51
None	61.8			65.8			55.9		

4.4 Threats to Validity

Conclusion validity of the experiments is limited by a number of investigated programs. Three programs were not small, quite representative and of different origin, but may not reflect all programming tendencies in usage of new programming concepts of the C# language. Therefore, for example, no mutants for the DMC operator dealing with delegates were created, which is a specialized concept of C#.

Table 7. Mutation results and benefits for three experiments on mutation operator selection

Prog. Oper.	Mutation Score [%]				Number of mutants				Number of tests			
	All	Ex1	Ex2	Ex3	All	Ex1	Ex2	Ex3	All	Ex1	Ex2	Ex3
1 OO	61.8	42.5	57.1	59.7	903	363	710	711	1148	63	105	115
1 St	70.9	59.2	70.3	70.6	1623	578	1015	1103	1148	47	114	120
2 OO	65.8	52.0	61.6	62.4	1065	478	887	795	642	81	132	135
2 St	69.6	58.0	68.3	69.2	2316	403	1715	1950	642	60	124	143
3 OO	55.9	39.1	55.1	49.7	855	267	777	595	899	78	132	94
3 St	73.9	58.8	71.4	73.3	4074	643	3242	2987	899	157	273	319

Another factor influencing the reasoning behind the experiments is existence of equivalent mutants. The manual analysis significantly lowered this threat, but it cannot guarantee that all equivalent mutants were detected.

Construct validity concerns the quality metrics used for evaluation of experimental results. Their interpretation is in accordance to weight coefficients subjectively selected by the authors. However, they suggest only tendencies in usage of different operators. The data calculated for other coefficients (0.8, 0.1, 0.1) gave analogous results. The final results (Table 7.) are expressed in terms of strict measures, such as mutation score, number of mutants or number of tests.

In order to minimize a threat to external validity, the programs used in experiments were parts of big, commonly used projects. Though, all of them were open-source projects and might have slightly different features than the commercial ones.

5   Related Work

Research on object-oriented mutation operators was conducted on Java and C# programs. Previous experiments on object-oriented operators of C# [5-10] were summarized in [11]. It concerned 29 object-oriented and specialized mutation operators defined for C#, and indicated on the difficulty to generalize results of the object-oriented operators. One operator (e.g. PNC, JID) can generate many mutants for one program, but only few for another program.

Application of object-oriented mutation operators to Java was studied in series of experiments [15-18, 22,29,30] with MuJava [31] that implements the most comprehensive set of 28 object-oriented operators, and MuClipse [32] - the plug-in for Eclipse adopted from MuJava.

An overview of cost reduction techniques, including selective mutation, mutant sampling and clustering can be found in [1,19]. Selective mutation was studied for structural languages [12-14], giving a recommendation of five standard operators in [12] that were also applied in CREAM. Ten operators for C were selected in empirical studies performed using the Proteum tool [13]. Comparison between two approaches: operator-based mutant selection and random mutant selection did not confirm a superiority of the first one [15], but this result only referred to standard operators.

Selectiveness of operators was also investigated for Java programs [16,17]. General conclusions were similar to those of C#. Object-oriented mutants are killed by a lower number of tests than standard mutants, but a significant decrease in the number of mutation operators is no so visible as for standard operators. In [17] it was recommended not to use OAC, PCI, and one of EAM, EMM operators, but those operators were not selected for implementation in CREAM.

Apart from CREAM, only the ILMutator prototype implements 10 object-oriented and C# specific mutation operators [10]. It introduces mutations into Intermediate Language of .NET for programs originated from C#, hence is more time effective in generating mutants than CREAM. Other mutation tools for C# like Nester [33] and PexMutator [34], do not support any object-oriented operators.

A problem of code converge in relation to the ability of killing mutants was addressed in the work of [35]. Uncovered mutants were manually identified as a type of equivalent mutants, whereas CREAM can automatically decide not to generate an uncovered mutant, if appropriate coverage data are provided. In experiments reported in [32] sufficiently high statement coverage (80%) was an initial requirement, but did not directly influence mutant generation. In the contrast to other tools PexMutator is aimed at creating test cases in order to kill mutants. It extends the Pex tool that creates tests in order to obtain the high code coverage.

6   Conclusions

The main lessons learned after investigation of three different open-source C# projects are the following.

The simplest and most beneficial way of mutation cost reduction is introducing mutation only to a covered code. Using tests that cover on average 82% of the code 75% of all mutants were generated giving no loss in the mutation score (MS) accuracy. The conclusion is obvious, but it practically means that coverage and mutation tools should be combined. In CREAM the mutants can be generated for the whole code, or for the fragments covered by a given test set. It is especially important for a project under development, when only parts of the code are currently examined. Though, the cost will be not reduced if the code is covered in 100%.

The remaining results gave no explicit conclusion about the general superiority of one applied cost reduction technique over the other ones. However, it was possible to obtain a small decline of a mutation score (99% of MS_{orig} for standard mutation and 93% for object-oriented) with a significant gain in lowering mutation costs: the number of mutants (81% of standard mutants used, 74% OO mutants) and the number of tests (22% for standard and 14% for OO). We proposed metrics to evaluate a tradeoff between these factors. They could also be used to compare tradeoffs in other mutant selection experiments and adjusted to higher order mutation [18].

In all investigated approaches to mutation operator selection and mutant sampling the MS accuracy of object-oriented mutants was worse (from few to 10%) than the corresponding accuracy of standard mutants. We stated that omitting a selected mutation operator was more beneficial than excluding mutants generated by the most popular operators (about 10% better MS). However, similarly to the previous studies on the object-oriented mutation the detailed results depend on the programs under concern. Especially programs using specialized programming constructs can give different results (e.g. DMC - operator of delegates was not used in these programs).

The same approach to quality evolution was also applied to mutant sampling. The best quality tradeoff was obtained when 35% of mutants where randomly selected for each class giving about 85% of the original MS for the object-oriented mutation and using 10% of tests. In the case of standard operators, 30% of mutants selected for each operator and 15% of tests resulted in 93% of MS_{orig}. In general, the random mutant sampling allows to obtain significant reduction in number of mutants and tests, but the loss of MS accuracy was a bit higher than in the operator selection experiments.

The detailed results of mutant clustering are also behind the scope of this paper. However, in general we obtained 97% of the original MS for object-oriented mutants using 32% of mutants and 17% of tests. Whereas for standard mutations, it was only 91% MS for 19% of mutants and 15% of tests. These results were less promising than the results of clustering for standard mutation in C [21]. Moreover, experiences of clustering are difficult to reproduce to other projects.

The experiments on the cost reduction techniques can be performed on other kinds of C# projects using the wizard built-in the CREAM mutation testing tool.

References

1. Jia, Y., Harman, M.: An Analysis and Survey of the Development of Mutation Testing. IEEE Transactions on Software Engineering 37(5), 649–678 (2011)
2. Chevalley, P.: Applying Mutation Analysis for Object-Oriented Programs Using a Reactive Approach. In: Proc. of the 8th Asia-Pacific Software Engineering Conference, ASPEC, pp. 267–270 (2001)
3. Kim, S., Clark, J., McDermid J.A.: Class Mutation: Mutation Testing for Object-Oriented Programs. In: Conference on Object-Oriented Software Systems, Erfurt, Germany (2000)
4. Ma, Y.-S., Kwon, Y.-R., Offutt, J.: Inter-class Mutation Operators for Java. In: Proc. of International Symposium on Software Reliability Engineering, ISSRE 2002. IEEE Computer Soc. (2002)
5. Derezińska, A.: Advanced Mutation Operators Applicable in C# Programs. In: Sacha, K. (ed.) Software Engineering Techniques: Design for Quality. IFIP, vol. 227, pp. 283–288. Springer, Boston (2006)
6. Derezińska, A.: Quality Assessment of Mutation Operators Dedicated for C# Programs. In: Proc. of the 6th International Conference on Quality Software, QSIC 2006, pp. 227–234. IEEE Soc. Press (2006)
7. Derezińska, A., Szustek, A.: Tool-supported Mutation Approach for Verification of C# Programs. In: Zamojski, W., et al. (eds.) Proc. of International Conference on Dependability of Computer Systems, DepCoS-RELCOMEX 2008, pp. 261–268. IEEE Comp. Soc. (2008)
8. Derezińska, A., Szustek, A.: Object-Oriented Testing Capabilities and Performance Evaluation of the C# Mutation System, In: Szmuc, T., Szpyrka, M., Zendulka, J. (eds.) CEE-SET 2009. LNCS, vol. 7054, pp. 229–242 (2012)
9. Derezińska, A., Sarba, K.: Distributed Environment Integrating Tools for Software Testing. In: Elleithy, K. (ed.) Advanced Techniques in Computing Sciences and Software Engineering, pp. 545–550. Springer, Dordrecht (2009)
10. Derezińska, A., Kowalski, K.: Object-oriented Mutation Applied in Common Intermediate Language Programs Originated from C#. In: Proc. of 4th International Conference Software Testing Verification and Validation Workshops, 6th Workshop on Mutation Analysis, pp. 342–350. IEEE Comp. Soc. (2011)
11. Derezińska, A.: Classification of Operators of C# Language. In: Borzemski, L., et al. (eds.) Information Systems Architecture and Technology, New Developments in Web-Age Information Systems, pp. 261–271. Wrocław University of Technology (2010)

12. Offut, J., Rothermel, G., Zapf, C.: An Experimental Evaluation of Selective Mutation. In: Proc. of 15th International Conference on Software Engineering, pp. 100–107. IEEE Comp. Soc. Press (1993)
13. Barbosa, E.F., Maldonado, J.C., Vincenzi, A.M.R.: Toward the Determination of Sufficient Mutant Operators for C. Journal Software, Testing, Verification, and Reliability 11, 113–136 (2001)
14. Namin, S., Andrews, J.H.: On Sufficiency of Mutants. In: Proc. of 29th International Conference on Software Engineering, ICSE 2007 (2007)
15. Zhang, L., Hou, S.-S., Hu, J.-J., Xie, T., Mei, H.: Is Operator-Based Mutant Selection Superior to Random Mutant Selection? In: Proc. of the 32nd International Conference on Software Engineering, ICSE 2010, pp. 435–444 (2010)
16. Ma, Y.-S., Kwon, Y.-R., Kim, S.-W.: Statistical Investigation on Class Mutation Operators. ETRI Journal 31(2), 140–150 (2009)
17. Hu, J., Li, N., Offutt, J.: An Analysis of OO Mutation Operators. In: Proc. of 4th International Conference Software Testing Verification and Validation Workshops, 6th Workshop on Mutation Analysis, pp. 334–341. IEEE Comp. Soc. (2011)
18. Kaminski, G., Praphamontripong, U., Ammann, P., Offutt, J.: A Logic Mutation Approach to Selective Mutation for Programs and Queries. Information and Software Technology, 1137–1152 (2011)
19. Usaola, M.P., Mateo, P.R.: Mutation Testing Cost Reduction Techniques: a Survey. IEEE Software 27(3), 80–86 (2010)
20. Mathur, A.P., Wong, W.E.: Reducing the Cost of Mutation Testing: An Empirical Study. Journal of Systems and Software 31, 185–196 (1995)
21. Hussain, S.: Mutation Clustering. Ms. Th., King's College London, Strand, London (2008)
22. Ji, C., Chen, Z.Y., Xu, B.W., Zhao, Z.: A Novel Method of Mutation Clustering Based on Domain Analysis. In: Proc. of 21st International Conference on Software Engineering & Knowledge Engineering, SEKE 2009, pp.422–425 (2009)
23. CREAM, http://galera.ii.pw.edu.pl/~adr/CREAM/
24. NUnit, http://www.nunit.org
25. NCover, http://www.ncover.com
26. Subversion svn, http://subversion.tigris.org
27. Derezińska, A., Rudnik, M.: Empirical Evaluation of Cost Reduction Techniques of Mutation Testing for C# Programs, Warsaw Univ. of Tech., Inst. of Computer Science Res. Rap. 1/2012 (2012)
28. Source Monitor, http://www.campwoodsw.com/sourcemonitor.html
29. Lee, H.-J., Ma, Y.-S., Kwon, Y.-R.: Empirical Evaluation of Orthogonality of Class Mutation Operators. In: Proc. of 11th Asia-Pacific Software Engineering Conference. IEEE Comp. Soc. (2004)
30. Ma, Y.-S., Harrold, M.J., Kwon, Y.-R.: Evaluation of Mutation Testing for Object-Oriented Programs. In: Proc. of 28th International Conference on Software Engineering, pp 869–872. IEEE Comp. Soc. Press (2006)
31. Ma, Y.-S., Offutt, J., Kwon, Y.-R.: MuJava: an Automated Class Mutation System. Software Testing, Verification and Reliability 15(2) (June 2005)
32. Smith, B.H., Williams, L.: A Empirical Evaluation of the MuJava Mutation Operators. In: Proc. 3rd International Workshop on Mutation Analysis Mutation 2007 at TAIC.Part 2007, Cumberland Lodge, Windsor UK, pp. 193–202 (September 2007)
33. Nester, http://nester.sourceforge.net/
34. Pexmutator, http://www.pexase.codeplex.com
35. Segura, S., Hierons, R.M., Benavides, D., Ruiz-Cortes, A.: Mutation Testing on an Object-oriented Framework: an Experience Report. Information and Software Technology, 1124–1136 (2011)

101companies: A Community Project on Software Technologies and Software Languages

Jean-Marie Favre[1], Ralf Lämmel[2], Thomas Schmorleiz[2], and Andrei Varanovich[2]

[1] University of Grenoble, France
[2] University of Koblenz-Landau, Germany

Abstract. *101companies* is a community project in computer science (or software science) with the objective of developing a free, structured, wiki-accessible knowledge resource including an open-source repository for different *stakeholders* with interests in **software technologies**, **software languages**, and **technological spaces**; notably: teachers and learners in software engineering or software languages as well as software developers, software technologists, and ontologists. The present paper introduces the *101companies* Project. In fact, the present paper is effectively a call for contributions to the project and a call for applications of the project in research and education.

Keywords: 101companies, Software technologies, Software languages, Technological spaces.

1 Introduction

Today's developers face a myriad of software technologies and software languages. IT industry demands technology-savvy 'polyglot developers' with strong knowledge of entire development ecosystems. Any project of significant size involves a dozen of different technologies and languages, each one with specific concepts and terminology possibly obfuscated by buzzwords. The involved languages are programming languages, modeling languages, technology-specific languages for configuration and metadata, and various other software languages.

How can such stress be relieved? What would help developers so that they are faster at technology and language adoption and more profoundly informed about vocabulary, abstractions, and options? How can research help here? How can education contribute?

Part of the problem is that developers may be framed in a specific technological space [DGD06,KBA02], i.e., a specific context of software development with regard to community and technologies, e.g., 'Javaware with the use of JDBC, DOM, and Swing'.[1] Developers acquire 'silos of knowledge' laboriously. However, developers are expected

---

[1] For the reader's convenience, we quote a more profound and assumably fitting definition of 'technological space' as of [KBA02]: '*A technological space is a working context with a set of associated concepts, body of knowledge, tools, required skills, and possibilities. It is often associated to a given user community with shared know-how, educational support, common literature and even workshop and conference meetings. It is at the same time a zone of established expertise and ongoing research and a repository for abstract and concrete resources.*'

C.A. Furia and S. Nanz (Eds.): TOOLS Europe 2012, LNCS 7304, pp. 58–74, 2012.

to travel technological spaces and to adopt to new technologies and languages rapidly and continuously. This will only be possible once developers obtain convenient access to sufficiently organized, abstract, and connected knowledge resources.

The present paper introduces the community project *101companies*[2], which provides a knowledge resource as motivated before.

Objective of *101companies*. *101companies* is a community project in computer science (or software science) with the objective of developing a free, structured, wiki-accessible knowledge resource including an open-source repository for different *stakeholders* with interests in **software technologies**, **software languages**, and **technological spaces**; notably: teachers and learners in software engineering or software languages as well as software developers, software technologists, and ontologists.

The Notion of Contribution. The project relies on the aggregation, organization, annotation, and analysis of an open-source corpus of *contributions* to an imaginary *Human Resource Management System*: the so-called *101companies* System, which is prescribed by a set of optional *features*. *Contributions* may be *implementations* of system variations and *specifications* thereof. Each contribution should pick a suitable, typically small set of features and demonstrate original and noteworthy aspects of *software technologies* and *software languages* in a focused manner. *Contributions* are grouped in *themes* to better apply to varying stakeholders and objectives. The project also relies on contributions in the broader sense of resources for *software technologies* and *software languages*, or components of an emerging *ontology*.

Connection to Research and Education in Computer Science. The project is interesting from a research perspective because it provides challenges for applying ontologies to software engineering [Ahm08], for developing new forms of models for software technologies, e.g., megamodels [BJV04,SCFC09], and for comparative and yet other forms of software linguistics [FGLP11]. The project is interesting from an education perspective because it directly provides content and structure for different forms of classical education, self-learning, or e-learning. The project supports comparison and cross-referencing for diverse software technologies and software languages across technological spaces. Hence, the project serves a more general scope in software development, when compared to other efforts on program collections and domain-specific software development challenges or benchmarks; see the related work discussion.

Objective of the Paper and Call to Arms. This is the inaugural paper describing the *101companies* Project in terms of identifying the key categories of an emerging ontology, the relevant stakeholders, optional features of the *101companies* System, and a

---

[2] http://101companies.org/ The "companies" postfix in "101companies" refers to the kind of system that is built time again in this project: a system that models companies in terms of some human resources aspects: department structure, employees, salaries. The "101" prefix in "101companies" refers to "101 ways" of building said system. Indeed, there are more than "101 ways" of building a human resource management system with different software technologies and software languages.

model for the structured documentation of implementations of said system. *101com-panies* is an active project, in fact, it is a Research 2.0 effort. Hence, the current paper must be understood as just a snapshot of current affairs. (Most of the paper's content was extracted from the project's current wiki and repository.) The present paper is effectively a call for contributions to the project and a call for applications of the project in research and education.

Road-Map of the Paper §2 illustrates the nature of the *101companies* Project. §3 identifies *key categories* of an emerging ontology for software technologies and software languages as well as project-specific concepts. §4 identifies *stakeholders* of the project. §5 sketches *features* of the *101companies* System. §6 briefly discusses *themes* as a grouping mechanism for contributions to the project. §7 proposes a *document model* for contributions (in fact, *implementations* at this stage). §8 discusses related work. §9 concludes the paper.

2   Illustration

The following illustrations are meant to clarify the nature of the project and the scale that has been reached. These illustrations should not be confused with any sort of (scientific) validation of the project or the existing contributions.

The *101companies* System (or just "the system") is an imaginary *Human Resource Management System (HRMS)* that serves as the "running example" in the *101companies* Project. That is, *contributions* to the project implement or specify or otherwise address a HRMS system for a conceived *company* as a client.

A company consist of (top-level) departments, which in turn may break down hierarchically into further sub-departments. Departments have a manager and other employees. The imaginary system may be used by conceived employees and managers within the conceived company. Employees have a name, an address, and a salary. The system may support various features. For instance, the system could support operations for *totaling all salaries of all employees and cutting them in half*, it could provide a user interface of different kinds, and it could address concerns such as scalability or security. Features of the system are discussed in §5. Figure 1 specifies the basic data model of the system in UML.

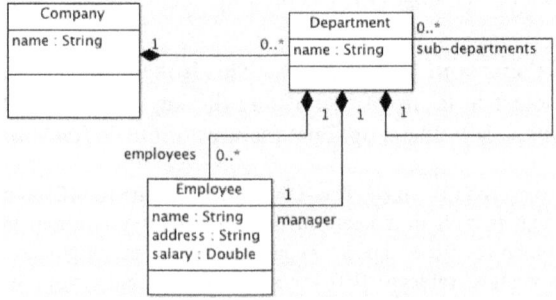

Fig. 1. A UML class diagram serving as an illustrative data model

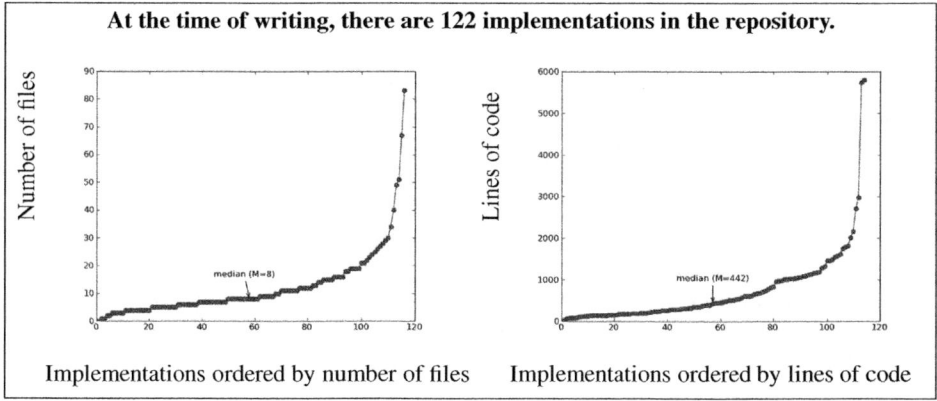

Fig. 2. Illustrative code-level complexity indicators for *101companies* implementations

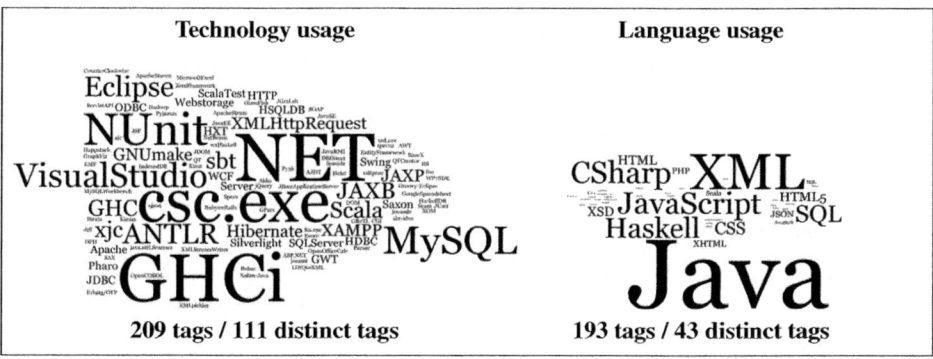

Fig. 3. Illustrative tag clouds regarding usage of technologies and languages by implementations

Figure 2 gives an idea of the varying code-level complexity for the existing implementations of the *101companies* System. (Other forms of contributions are not considered here.) Based on systematic tagging, we count only developer-authored code-like units as opposed to generated code or IDE support files. The plots show the number of files and the lines of code for such units. (Lines of code may include comments.) The number of files hints at 'file-level modularity' of the implementations. As the medians suggest, most implementations are in the range of a few hundred lines of code and less than ten files. The distribution of these numbers is a result of different programming languages, different technologies, different feature sets that are implemented as well as subjective factors due to developer choices. We should emphasize that the plots serve for illustration; they cannot be expected to hint at any proper metric.

Figure 3 gives an idea of the diversity of technology and language usage for the existing implementations. The size of a term in a tag cloud expresses the frequency of usage across all the implementations: the bigger, the more implementations declare to use a technology or a language.

3   Key Categories of the *101companies Ontology*

The ontology classifies all entities that are relevant for the *101companies* Project. The categories (or classes or concepts) are organized in two dimensions. In the first dimension, we distinguish between *general entities* that can be said to exist regardless of the project (such as technologies) versus *project-specific entities* (such as the features of the *101companies* System). In the second dimension, we distinguish between *primary entities* versus *subordinated entities*. While the first dimension is profound, the second dimension is only introduced for convenience of consuming the classification.

The categories for primary, general entities are *Technology* for the deep classification of actual software technologies, *Capability* for the deep classification of capabilities of technologies, *Language* for the deep classification of actual software languages and

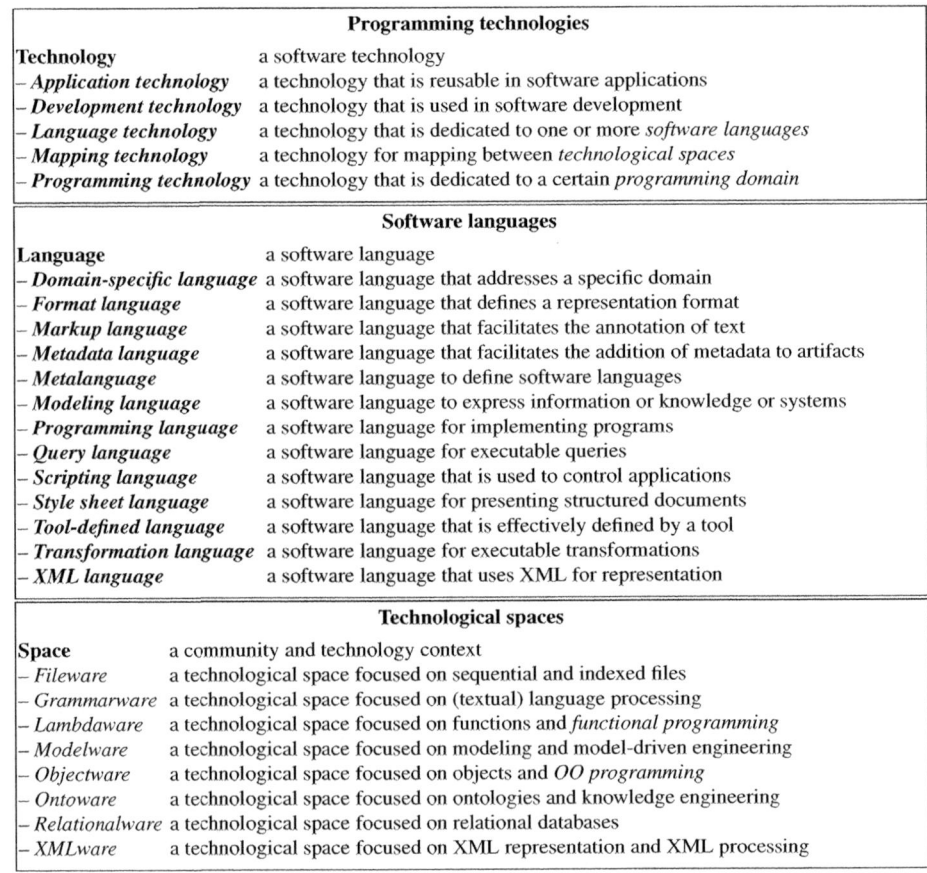

Programming technologies

Technology	a software technology
– *Application technology*	a technology that is reusable in software applications
– *Development technology*	a technology that is used in software development
– *Language technology*	a technology that is dedicated to one or more *software languages*
– *Mapping technology*	a technology for mapping between *technological spaces*
– *Programming technology*	a technology that is dedicated to a certain *programming domain*

Software languages

Language	a software language
– *Domain-specific language*	a software language that addresses a specific domain
– *Format language*	a software language that defines a representation format
– *Markup language*	a software language that facilitates the annotation of text
– *Metadata language*	a software language that facilitates the addition of metadata to artifacts
– *Metalanguage*	a software language to define software languages
– *Modeling language*	a software language to express information or knowledge or systems
– *Programming language*	a software language for implementing programs
– *Query language*	a software language for executable queries
– *Scripting language*	a software language that is used to control applications
– *Style sheet language*	a software language for presenting structured documents
– *Tool-defined language*	a software language that is effectively defined by a tool
– *Transformation language*	a software language for executable transformations
– *XML language*	a software language that uses XML for representation

Technological spaces

Space	a community and technology context
– *Fileware*	a technological space focused on sequential and indexed files
– *Grammarware*	a technological space focused on (textual) language processing
– *Lambdaware*	a technological space focused on functions and *functional programming*
– *Modelware*	a technological space focused on modeling and model-driven engineering
– *Objectware*	a technological space focused on objects and *OO programming*
– *Ontoware*	a technological space focused on ontologies and knowledge engineering
– *Relationalware*	a technological space focused on relational databases
– *XMLware*	a technological space focused on XML representation and XML processing

Fig. 4. The key categories of the *101companies Ontology*

Space for the enumeration of actual technological spaces. When adding a new technology to the ontology, then classifiers from the *Technology* tree are to be applied and the technology may also be associated with capabilities, languages as well as technological spaces. When documenting a *contribution* to the *101companies* Project, the contribution is to be associated with technologies and languages. Classification and association help the *users* of the *101companies* Project to navigate between software technologies, capabilities thereof, software languages, technological spaces, and contributions of the project.

In Figure 4, the categories of technologies and languages are broken down into (only the immediate) subcategories for the classification of such entities; also, actual technological spaces are revealed as members of category *Space*. Specific technologies and languages may be members of multiple subcategories, and they may be associated with multiple technological spaces.

Technologies may be subdivided into *development* or *application technologies* depending on whether they target the developer by providing some kind of tool support or the application by providing some kind of reusable components. For instance, *IDE*s or *tool*s count as development technologies whereas *libraries* or *frameworks* count as application technologies. Classification of technologies may also apply to their possible status of being a *programming technology* in the sense that they serve specific programming domains; consider, for example, *web technology* or *data technology*. Given the central role of *technological spaces*, classification of technologies may also apply to their possible status of being a *mapping technology* across spaces. Finally, some technologies specifically support some software language, giving rise to further classification according to *language technology*; consider, for example, *compilers* or *program generators*. All these categories of technologies may be broken down further into subcategories. Some technologies may be naturally instances of multiple categories. Technologies are further characterized by their *capabilities*.

Technologies are seen as providing *capabilities* to the developers or the systems that use the technology. Examples of capabilities include *logging, serialization, data parallelism*, and *mapping*. Thus, each specific technology is not just classified according to technology subcategories, but it is also to be associated with capabilities. For instance, the *mapping* capability further breaks down into *Object/XML mapping, Object/Relational mapping*, etc. Each specific technology can be indeed associated with several capabilities. For instance, *JAXB* provides the capabilities of both *Object/XML mapping* for *Java* and (XML-based, *open*) *serialization*.

4   Stakeholders of the *101companies Project*

A stakeholder of the *101companies* Project is someone who affects or is affected by the project or could be expected to do so. There are *users* of the project: *learners* subject to self-learning, professional training, etc. who use the project to learn about software technologies and languages as well as *teachers* in university or professional education who use the project to prepare their courses, lectures, etc. Further, there are *contributors* to the project: *developers* of implementations or specifications of the *101companies* System, *authors* of wiki content including classifications of software technologies and

101stakeholder	a stakeholder of the *101companies* Project
– *101contributor*	anyone who contributes to the *101companies* Project
– – *101advisor*	anyone who serves on the advisory board of the project
– – *101author*	anyone who authors content for the wiki of the *101companies* Project
– – *101developer*	anyone who develops a *contribution* to the *101companies* Project
– – *101engineer*	anyone who contributes to the infrastructure of the *101companies* Project
– – *101gatekeeper*	anyone administering wiki and repository of the *101companies* Project
– – *101research20er*	anyone who contributes as a community engineer to the *101companies* Project
– – *101reviewer*	anyone who reviews a *contribution* to the *101companies* Project
– *101researcher*	anyone interested in research on software technologies and languages
– – *101linguist*	anyone researching software linguistics
– – *101ontologist*	anyone researching *ontologies* for software technologies and languages
– *101technologist*	anyone seeking technology adoption through the *101companies* Project
– *101user*	anyone who uses the *101companies* Project
– – *101learner*	anyone who leverages the *101companies* Project for learning
– – *101teacher*	anyone who leverages the *101companies* Project for teaching

Fig. 5. Stakeholders of the *101companies Project*

languages, *community engineers* who manages the project from a Research 2.0 perspective, and yet other kinds of contributors. There are also stakeholders who may be interested in the project more broadly because they are *researchers* in a relevant context (such as ontology engineering or software linguistics) or *technologists* (such as owners of a software technology). Stakeholder roles are non-disjoint. For instance, a technologist may be expected to also serve as an educator (a teacher) as well as a contributor.

The classification tree of stakeholders is shown in Figure 5.

5   Features of the *101companies System*

The term feature should be understood broadly as referring to optional requirements for the imaginary system, e.g., as in the established sense of functional and non-functional requirements. The optionality of features encourages smaller contributions that demonstrate specific aspects of software technologies and software languages. The feature set is not driven by concepts of the human resources domain. Instead, the important consideration for each new feature is that it should be helpful in demonstrating particularities of software technologies and software languages. The feature set is constantly under revision since each additional technology in scope, each new implementation (planned or completed) may trigger additional features or a revision of the classification tree. Some features are left underspecified intentionally so that contributions can apply suitable refinements for the benefit of useful demonstrations. (For instance, there is a *feature Client-server* to constrain design such that an implementation uses a client-server architecture without though specifying precisely client and server.) Ideally, each feature would be demonstrated by several contributions. Some features may not be demonstrated yet at all because they are at the stage of calling for contributions.

101feature	features of the *101companies* System
– *101behavior*	behavior-related features of the *101companies* System
– – Cut	an operation to cut the salaries of all employees in half
– – Depth	an operation to determine the depth of department nesting
– – Export	the behavior to export company data from the system
– – Import	the behavior to import company data into the system
– – Logging	the behavior of logging data access on company data
– – Total	an operation to total the salaries of all employees
– – Visualization	the behavior of visualizing company data in an insightful manner
– *101meta*	features related to reverse/reengineering of implementations
– – API usage analysis	analyse and report *API* usage
– – Complexity metrics	calculate and report structural complexity metrics
– – Coupled transformation	perform a coupled system transformation
– *101quality*	quality-like features of the *101companies* System
– – *101design*	design *qualities* of the *101companies* System
– – – Code generation	leverage code generation for implementation
– – – Data mapping	leverage *mapping* for the data access layer
– – – Reusability	provide reusability for other provided features
– – *101execution*	execution *qualities* of the *101companies* System
– – – Access control	support access control for company data
– – – Client-server	leverage a *client-server architecture*
– – – Persistence	support persistence of company data
– – – Reliability	provide reliability for the system services
– – – Scalability	provide scalability for large data volume or multiple users
– – – Serialization	support serialization of company data
– *101structure*	structure-related features of the *101companies* System
– – Company	the basic tree-based data model for companies
– – Mentoring	an association between employees for mentees and mentors
– – Precedence	a constraint on salaries to decrease with department nesting
– *101ui*	UI-related features of the *101companies* System
– – Attribute editing	provide UI support for editing attributes
– – Intelligent UI	provide intelligent UI support
– – Localization	provide UI support for different languages
– – Navigation	provide a basic UI for the navigation of companies
– – Structural editing	provide UI support for structural editing
– – Touch control	provide UI support for touch control
– – Undo/redo	provide undo/redo capability in the UI
– – Voice control	provide UI support for voice control
– – Web UI	run the system through a *web browser*

Fig. 6. Features of the 101companies system

The classification tree of features is shown in Figure 6. The feature set could be subdivided in a classic manner into functional and non-functional requirements. Instead, a richer categorization is applied here:

– *101structure*: *structure-related features.* There is a feature for the basic, *tree-like* structure of company data. There is another feature for adding mentoring so that

487 feature tags / 25 distinct feature tags across 122 implementations

Fig. 7. Illustrative tag cloud regarding feature frequency for implementations

a *graph-like* structure is needed. Further structure-related features are conceivable, e.g., a *global invariant* for salaries to decrease downwards the company tree.

– *101behavior*: *behavior-related features*. There are features for basic operations to total all salaries in a company or to cut salaries in half. These features exercise the fundamental notions of *aggregation* and *(endogenous) transformation*. Various other operations or behaviors are conceivable, e.g., for *importing/exporting* company data, for computing the depth of the company trees (thereby exercising the notion of a *recursive query*) as well as for *logging* data modifications such as salary changes.

– *101ui*: *UI-related features*. These features are concerned with navigation and editing of companies as well as support for additional UI facets such as voice control, touch control, localization, and intelligence.

– *101quality*: *quality-like features*. Some features are concerned with *execution qualities*, e.g., *scalability*. Other features are concerned with "design qualities", e.g., *code generation*. Most of these features are likely to necessitate the use of a designated software technology such as library, framework, or code generator.

– *101meta*: *features related to reverse/reengineering of implementations*. These features do not directly concern the system itself; instead, they are part of a demonstrated lifecycle of the system.

Figure 7 gives an idea of the distribution of feature coverage by existing contributions (in fact, by implementations). The size of a feature name in the tag cloud expresses the frequency of demonstration across all the implementations: the bigger, the more implementations declare to demonstrate the feature. (The popularity of *Company*, *Total*, and *Cut* is a consequence of the fact that most implementations pick these functional requirements as a lower bar for demonstration. In fact, these basic structural and behavioral features are interesting enough to demonstrate already many programming techniques, mapping concerns, and overall capabilities of software technologies.)

6   Themes of *101companies* Contributions

A theme is an explicitly declared group of *contributions* to the *101companies* Project. Themes are meant to help *users* of the *101companies* Project to efficiently consume knowledge about *contributions*, *software technologies*, *capabilities* thereof, *software languages*, and *technological spaces*. To this end, themes are tailored towards interests of specific stakeholders. Such specificity translates into focus on a certain

Themes with lists of members

Java mapping theme *Java* theme of implementations that travel technological spaces
– antlrObjects   *Object/Text mapping* for *Java* with *ANTLR* for *parsing*
– emf   *Model/Object mapping* for *Ecore* and *Java* with *EMF*
– hibernate   *Object/Relational mapping* for *Java* and *SQL/HQL* with *Hibernate*
– jaxbComposition   *Object/XML mapping* for *Java* and *XSD* with *JAXB*

XML theme   *XML* theme of implementations
– csharpLinqToXml   *in-memory XML processing* in *C#* with *LINQ to XML*
– dom   *in-memory XML processing* in *Java* with *DOM*
– jaxbComposition   *Object/XML mapping* for *Java* and *XSD* with *JAXB*
– sax   *push-based XML parsing* in *Java* with *SAX*
– xmlReader   *pull-based XML parsing* in *C#* with *XmlReader*
– xquery   *XML processing* in *XQuery*
– xslt   *XML processing* in *XSLT*

Haskell theme   *Haskell* theme of implementations
– happstack   *Web programming* in *Haskell* with *Happstack*
– haskell   a basic implementation in *Haskell*
– haskellConcurrent   concurrent programming in *Haskell*
– haskellDB   type-safe *database programming* in *Haskell* with *HaskellDB*
– haskellParser   parsing of concrete textual syntax in *Haskell* with *Parsec*
– hxt   *in-memory XML processing* in *Haskell* with *HXT*
– syb   scrap your boilerplate in *Haskell*
– wxHaskell   GUI programming in *Haskell* with *wxHaskell*

Detailed theme descriptions

XML theme: The theme collects representatives of the most established *XML processing* options. Several of these options rely on *APIs* so that of XML processing is embedded into an existing language such as *C#* or *Java*. More specifically, there are options for *in-memory XML processing, push-based XML parsing*, and *pull-based XML parsing*. In the case of in-memory processing, two options are included: one for the more classic *DOM* approach and another more declarative, query-oriented which is based on *LINQ* in that case. Besides those API-based options, the theme also covers two major styles of XML processing when it is supported directly by languages designated to either querying or transformation. Finally, there is a *mapping*-based option such that an object model is derived from an XML schema such that *de-/serialization* can be used to access XML data through objects and extract XML data from objects.

Java mapping theme: Subject to appropriate bridges, i.e., subject to *mapping* facilities, any programming language can be made to access and process *models, XML*, relational database *tables*, and *text* (concrete syntax) in a type-based (say, schema-aware or metamodel-aware or grammar-aware) manner. The present theme collects corresponding implementations for the programming language *Java*.

Haskell theme: This theme demonstrates *Haskell*'s approach to several programming domains: *concurrent programming, database programming, generic programming, GUI programming, parsing*, and *XML programming*. As a starting point, there is also a simple (a trivial) Haskell-based implementation. Some of the implementations nicely demonstrate some strengths and specifics of Haskell. This is true, for example, for the implementations that illustrate concurrency, XML processing, and *SYB*. Some other implementations are mainly included to provide coverage for important domains without necessarily arguing that the Haskell-based implementation is superior, interesting, or surprising. This is true, for example, for the implementation that demonstrates GUI programming. The selection of theme members was also based on the idea that relatively mature and established options should be demonstrated as opposed to research experiments.

Fig. 8. Some themes of 101implementations

technological space, or a category of technologies, or a certain programming language, etc. For instance, the *Haskell theme* addresses interests of those who want to approach Haskell through the 101companies setup as well as those who want to approach the 101companies setup on the grounds of Haskell knowledge.

Themes should be of a manageable size: 4-10 contributions per theme. Accordingly, the composition of a theme needs to be selective in identifying theme members. For instance, the *XML theme* covers presumably all fundamental approaches to XML processing, but it leaves out variations in terms of APIs and languages. Such variations can still be discovered easily by users because contributions are richly tagged and cross-referenced.

Some themes of implementations are sketched in Figure 8.

7   A Document Model for *101companies* Implementations

An implementation of the *101companies* System can only be useful for the *stakeholders* of the *101companies* Project, if it is appropriately documented. Such documentation associates the implementation with metadata based on the *101companies* Ontology and

---

Intent: *Object/XML mapping* for *Java* and *XSD* with *JAXB*

Motivation: *XML* import and export is supported for a Java-based implementation by means of O/X mapping. The primary data model for companies is an XML schema. The schema compiler *xjc* of *JAXB* is used to generate Java classes from the schema. In this manner, operations on an XML representation of companies can be implemented in near-to-regular OO fashion while using a problem-specific object model. In different terms, one can carry out *XML processing* while essentially staying in the technological space of *objectware*. It is insightful to compare XML schema and schema-derived classes. The XML schema is defined in a manner that the resulting object model systematically leverages *object composition* and no *class inheritance*. In fact, the schema-derived classes are very similar to a regular OO design; see *implementation javaComposition*. It is important to note that the operations on companies are not implemented as *instance methods* since this would imply modification of schema-derived classes—unless advanced modularization mechanisms were leveraged. Instead, the operations are implemented as *static methods* in non-schema-derived classes.

		Features
Technologies	**Languages**	– Company
	– *XML*	– Total
– *JAXB*	– *XSD*	– Cut
– *xjc* (part of JAXB)	– *Java*	– Import
– *Eclipse*	– *JAXB annotations*	– Export
– *GNU make*	– *xjc POJOs*	– Data mapping
		– Code generation

Fig. 9. Documentation of the *implementation jaxbComposition* (part I/III)

Illustration: The following XML schema fragment shows the element declaration for departments:

```
<xs:element name="department">
 <xs:complexType>
  <xs:sequence>
   <xs:element ref="name"/>
   <xs:element name="manager" type="employee"/>
   <xs:element ref="department" maxOccurs="unbounded" minOccurs="0"/>
   <xs:element name="employee"
        type="employee" maxOccurs="unbounded" minOccurs="0"/>
  </xs:sequence>
 </xs:complexType>
</xs:element>
```

That is, department elements line up children elements for name, manager, sub-departments, and employees. There is an XSD type *employee* which is used in two local element declarations: one for managers; another one for regular employees. The schema-derived class for departments looks as follows:

```
@XmlAccessorType(XmlAccessType.FIELD)
@XmlType(name = "",
 propOrder = { "name", "manager", "department", "employee" })
@XmlRootElement(name = "department")
public class Department {
    @XmlElement(required = true)
    protected String name;
    @XmlElement(required = true)
    protected Employee manager;
    protected List<Department> department;
    protected List<Employee> employee;
    // Getters and setters omitted
}
```

This class essentially models *POJO*s for departments in a way similar to regular OO programming. However, the schema compiler injects a number of *annotations* into the schema-derived classes so that sufficient information is tracked for serialization, and, in fact, XML Schema-based *validation*. For instance, the fields for name and manager are annotated with *required=true*, thereby expressing that a valid department object must specify a name and a manager. On top of the schema-derived classes, the operation *cut* can be implemented with *static methods* as follows:

```
public class Cut {
  public static void cut(Company c) {
    for (Department d : c.getDepartment())
      cut(d);
  }
  public static void cut(Department d) {
    cut(d.getManager());
    for (Department s : d.getDepartment())
      cut(s);
    for (Employee e : d.getEmployee())
      cut(e);
  }
  public static void cut(Employee e) {
    e.setSalary(e.getSalary() / 2);
  }
}
```

Fig. 10. Documentation of the *implementation jaxbComposition* (part II/III)

describes important aspects of the implementation in free (English) text. There is the following document model; "?" is used to mark an optional section; all other sections are mandatory:

Architecture: *Company.xsd* is the schema for *schema-first mapping*. *Makefile* shows how to (trivially) invoke the schema compiler *xjc* of *JAXB*. Package *org.softlang.company* hosts all schema-derived classes and interfaces. Package *org.softlang.features* hosts implementations for *feature Total* and *feature Cut* as well as some boilerplate code for importing and exporting XML documents. Package *org.softlang.tests* hosts JUnit tests.

Usage:

- The implementation is provided as an Eclipse project.
- The schema-derived classes are included into the repository.
- Hence, open the project with Eclipse; this will also build the project.
- There are JUnit tests available in package *org.softlang.tests*.
- If you want to regenerate classes from the scheme, see the *Makefile*.

Hint: if you need to add schema files to a project so that XML files are automatically validated on the grounds of their namespace, as it is useful for the schema Company.xsd, which is part of the present implementation, then you need to add the files via Eclipse preferences → XML → XML catalog.

Fig. 11. Documentation of the *implementation jaxbComposition* (part III/III)

- *Intent*: an extended title for overall classification and association
- *Motivation*: the demonstration value of an implementation
- *Status*?: maturity status of an implementation
- *Technologies*: a list of used technologies
- *Languages*: a list of used languages
- *Features*: a list of implemented features
- *Illustration*?: a code snippet-based summary of the implementation
- *Architecture*?: a short description of the architecture
- *Usage*: advice on building, testing, and running an implementation
- *Issues*?: a list of issues to be aware of and to be fixed eventually
- *Contributors*: a list of contributors and their roles
- *Acknowledgments*?: any credits not yet covered by the contributors section

The *Motivation* section is critical in making an implementation useful for *users* of the *101companies* Project. The section should answer these questions: What does the implementation demonstrate in terms of software technologies, capabilities thereof, software languages, and other concepts in software development? What does the implementation contribute to the corpus, when compared to other implementations; that is, how does it complement or vary other implementations?

The *Usage* section is supposed to help users with building, testing, and running implementations. Easy to follow steps should be provided for the users. This is particularly important when a given implementation requires technology-specific steps. The *Architecture* section describes the architecture of the implementation, where different notions of architecture may apply, e.g., package- or file-level architecture as well as linguistic architecture based on megamodels.

For instance, figures 9–11 show the documentation of *implementation jaxbComposition*: an implementation with the intent of demonstrating "*Object/XML mapping* for *Java* and *XSD* with *JAXB*". Hence, the intent points out a capability of JAXB that is demonstrated by the implementation. The text of the motivation section makes good use of references to the *101companies* Ontology (as indicated by the terms in italics). Finally, consider the software languages exercised by the implementation; there are straightforward languages such as Java, XML, and XSD; there are also very technology-specific languages: the annotation or metadata language used by JAXB and the Java subset for POJOs that are generated by JAXB's class generation tool xjc. In this manner, we obtain a 'semantically rich' documentation, thereby facilitating navigation and understanding.

8   Related Work

In the communities of modeling, metamodeling, software languages, and elsewhere, the notion of *technological spaces* [KBA02,DGD06] has been recognized as being helpful in identifying and communicating commonalities and differences for grammarware, XMLware, modelware, objectware, and relationalware. The *101companies* Project is an unprecedented, advanced, technical effort to illustrate the variation points and technology options that are linked to the notion of technological spaces.

Let us compare the *101companies* Project with *programming chrestomathies*, i.e., collections of program examples, possibly in different languages, which are used to demonstrate the specifics of programming languages, their implementations, paradigms, and platforms. In the simplest case, a chrestomathy may exercise the 'Hello World!' example. In more advanced cases, chrestomathies demonstrate 'stacks' or even 'product portfolios' by vendors; see, e.g., chrestomathies for Microsoft[3] or Oracle/Sun[4]. Suites of performance benchmarks account for a specific category of programming chrestomathies. Such suites consist of source code of programs that are suitable to challenge performance of language implementations systematically. The results can be compared across different implementations of a language or across different languages. For instance, The *Computer Language Benchmarks Game* (CLBG)[5] is a widely used repository of such comparisons across a wide range of programming languages.

As a concise approach to the comparison of some related programming chrestomathies with the *101companies* Project, we offer the following matrix whose rows are concerned with aspects that relate to the objectives of the *101companies* Project and its stakeholders.

To summarize, no existing chrestomathy specifically targets technology comparison. The *101companies* Project also stands out in being repository-based, ontology-driven, class room-tested, in using structured documentation, and in being focused on technological spaces. Overall, the *101companies* Project must not be reduced to an effort for

---

[3] http://archive.msdn.microsoft.com/ContosoAutoOBA
[4] https://wikis.oracle.com/display/code/Home
[5] http://shootout.alioth.debian.org/

Table 1. Comparison of programming chrestomathies and the *101companies* Project

Aspect	101companies	Java Pet Store[6]	99 Bottles of Beer[7]	Rosetta Code[8]	CLBG
Focus	Technologies	Java platform	Task	Tasks	Algorithms
Scope of comparison	Implementations	-	Languages	Languages	Languages
Technological spaces	covered	limited	ignored	limited	ignored
Ontology-driven	yes	no	no	no	no
Class room-tested	yes	yes(?)	no	no	no
Source code	GitHub	Zip archive	Website	Website	Website

the collection of program samples; the role of documentation, cross-referencing, and underlying ontology must not be underestimated. Also, software languages other than programming languages play an important role.

There are also generalized benchmarks or 'challenges' that go beyond the notion of program collections with the focus on performance. These generalized benchmarks usually involve elements of expressiveness (perhaps in combination with performance). Such benchmarks exist in various areas of programming languages, databases, and software engineering, and they are usually focused on the evaluation of technologies and approaches in a more specific domain, e.g.: [RJJ+08]—a generic programming benchmark for Haskell libraries; STBenchmark [ATV08]—a benchmark for mapping systems for schemas such as relational database schemas; [RG10]—a contest for graph-transformation tools; the Semantic Web Services Challenge [MKS12]—a challenge dedicated to taming the complexity of service orchestration and service discovery.

The *101companies* Ontology is meant to help managing knowledge about programming technologies and it relates in this regard to other applications of ontologies to knowledge management [CJB99,SSSS01]. For instance, the work of [RFD+08] describes the semi-automatic derivation of an ontology for domain-specific programming concepts—as they are supported, for example, by APIs for XML or GUI programming. Such ontologies may feed into a more comprehensive ontology of programming technologies. There is also related work on the use of ontologies in teaching, e.g., [SG05,KYNM06], which may help in advancing the *101companies* Project in becoming more accessible for its stakeholders. In §6, we presented the notion of theme as a related ontological tool in organizing implementations.

9 Concluding Remarks

101companies may become to the specialized community of 'polyglot developers and technological space travelers' what *Wikipedia* is to the 'general population'. *101companies* combines a wiki, an open source repository, an ontology, and further abstractions under development. At the given stage, the aggregated corpus of contributions, the associated documentation, and the emerging ontology already constitute several man-years

---

[6] http://java.sun.com/developer/releases/petstore
[7] http://www.99-bottles-of-beer.net/
[8] http://rosettacode.org/

of qualified software language engineer's time. There are problems of quality and coverage, which require strong community involvement and the project's ability to manage such involvement. New forms of modeling and data integration (e.g., based on RDF, or, in fact, Linked Data) are currently investigated to get to the next level of sophistication.

An important direction for future work concerns Web 2.0 and Research 2.0. That is, at the point of writing, *101companies* is relatively conservative in terms of the process for submitting, maintaining, and annotating contributions to the project. For instance, content authors must register on the designated wiki, and no other means are provided to affect the semi-structured content for contributions, technologies, and languages. We are in urgent need of having Web 2.0 community features. In this context, we invision that data acquisition from developers or other stakeholders as well as automated data mining from source code and wiki content should enable interesting empirical research on software technologies and software languages. At the next level of sophistication, we expect *101companies* to possibly serve as a *Research 2.0* infrastructure.

A short or midterm target for the project is to prove itself useful in classical undergraduate education (that is, in Master's courses, and advanced Bachelor's courses at universities) and in innovative graduate education and research (e.g., in summer schools on software development). Some experiences have been gathered by the authors[9], but it remains to broadly export the utility of *101companies*. As of writing, discussions are underway to build new *101companies*-supported themes (see §6), if not courses, for example, for the domains of parallel programming, security, and embedded systems.

Acknowledgments. The authors are grateful to all those people who contributed *101companies* implementations, wiki content, and insight as well as energy to the project. We want to mention Sebastian Jackel and Tobias Zimmer specifically. A number of hackathons (at GTTSE 2011 and in Koblenz in summer 2011) have helped to mature the project. The authors are particularly grateful to Dragan Gasevic who was inspiring and instrumental in launching the project in summer 2010.

References

Ahm08.   Ahmed, E.: Use of Ontologies in Software Engineering. In: Proceedings of the 17th International Conference on Software Engineering and Data Engineering (SEDE 2008), pp. 145–150. ISCA (2008)

ATV08.   Alexe, B., Tan, W.-C., Velegrakis, Y.: STBenchmark: towards a benchmark for mapping systems. Proc. VLDB Endow. 1, 230–244 (2008)

BJV04.   Bezivin, J., Jouault, F., Valduriez, P.: On the Need for Megamodels. In: Proceedings of Workshop on Best Practices for Model-Driven Software Development at the 19th Annual ACM Conference on Object-Oriented Programming, Systems, Languages, and Applications (2004)

CJB99.   Chandrasekaran, B., Josephson, J.R., Richard Benjamins, V.: What Are Ontologies, and Why Do We Need Them? IEEE Intelligent Systems 14, 20–26 (1999)

DGD06.   Djuric, D., Gasevic, D., Devedzic, V.: The Tao of Modeling Spaces. Journal of Object Technology 5(8), 125–147 (2006)

---

[9] http://softlang.wikidot.com/course:ptt

FGLP11.   Favre, J.-M., Gasevic, D., Lämmel, R., Pek, E.: Empirical Language Analysis in Soft-
          ware Linguistics. In: Malloy, B., Staab, S., van den Brand, M. (eds.) SLE 2010. LNCS,
          vol. 6563, pp. 316–326. Springer, Heidelberg (2011)
KBA02.   Kurtev, I., Bézivin, J., Aksit, M.: Technological Spaces: an Initial Appraisal. In:
          CoopIS, DOA 2002 Federated Conferences, Industrial track (2002)
KYNM06.   Kasai, T., Yamaguchi, H., Nagano, K., Mizoguchi, R.: Building an ontology of IT
          education goals. International Journal of Continuing Engineering Education and Life
          Long Learning 16, 1–17 (2006)
MKS12.   Margaria, T., Kubczak, C., Steffen, B.: The XMDD Approach to the Semantic Web
          Services Challenge. In: Brian Blake, M., Cabral, L., Knig-Ries, B., Kster, U., Her-
          ausgeber, D.M. (eds.) Semantic Web Services: Advancement through Evaluation.
          Springer. Heidelberg (to appear, 2012)
RFD⁺08.   Ratiu, D., Feilkas, M., Deissenboeck, F., Jürjens, J., Marinescu, R.: Towards a Repos-
          itory of Common Programming Technologies Knowledge. In: Proc. of the Int. Work-
          shop on Semantic Technologies in System Maintenance, STSM (2008)
RG10.   Rensink, A., Van Gorp, P.: Graph transformation tool contest 2008. STTT 12(3-4),
          171–181 (2010)
RJJ⁺08.   Rodriguez, A., Jeuring, J., Jansson, P., Gerdes, A., Kiselyov, O., Oliveira, B.C.D.S.:
          Comparing libraries for generic programming in Haskell. In: Proceedings of the 1st
          ACM SIGPLAN Symposium on Haskell, Haskell 2008, pp. 111–122. ACM (2008)
SCFC09.   Sottet, J.-S., Calvary, G., Favre, J.-M., Coutaz, J.: Megamodeling and Metamodel-
          Driven Engineering for Plastic User Interfaces: MEGA-UI. In: Human-Centered Soft-
          ware Engineering, pp. 173–200 (2009)
SG05.   Sosnovsky, S., Gavrilova, T.: Development of Educational Ontology for C-
          Programming. In: Proceedings of the XI-th International Conference Knowledge-
          Dialogue-Solution, vol. 1, pp. 127–132. FOI ITHEA (2005)
SSSS01.   Staab, S., Studer, R., Schnurr, H.-P., Sure, Y.: Knowledge processes and ontologies.
          IEEE Intelligent Systems 16(1), 26–34 (2001)

An Object-Oriented Application Framework for the Development of Real-Time Systems

Francesco Fiamberti, Daniela Micucci, and Francesco Tisato

University of Milano - Bicocca, Viale Sarca 336, Milan, Italy
{fiamberti,micucci,tisato}@disco.unimib.it

Abstract. The paper presents an object-oriented application framework that supports the development of real-time systems. The framework consists of a set of architectural abstractions that allow time-related aspects to be explicitly treated as first-class objects at the application level. Both the temporal behavior of an application and the way the application deals with information placed in a temporal context can be modeled by means of such abstractions, thus narrowing the semantic gap between specification and implementation. Moreover, the framework carefully separates behavioral policies from implementation details improving portability and simplifying the realization of adaptive systems.

Keywords: real-time, object-orientation, application framework, architectural abstractions.

1 Introduction

Time is a key element in real-time systems as their correctness depends on *when* activities are performed [15]. Key elements in specific application domains are usually captured and modeled by means of architectural abstractions [6]. In particular, the design of real-time systems should be supported by a set of architectural abstractions that model the temporal behavior of the system with concepts including *time* and *speed*. Surprisingly, time and speed seldom emerge as basic abstractions. The lack of such abstractions leads to the development of tricky code that heavily depends on platform mechanisms, intermixes design choices and implementation details, can be hardly tested and maintained.

Many recent developments focus on the representation and on the analysis of time-related issues. MARTE [11], for example, is a UML profile that adds capabilities to UML for the design of real-time and embedded systems. AADL [13] is an analysis and design language that not only allows a representation of the software architecture to be defined, but also the syntax and semantics, so that the representation can be verified and validated [10]. Both the approaches, however, only provide modeling capabilities but no embedded tools to directly implement the system. The same holds for [12], which exploits MARTE (the logical time concept) and the CCSL language (Clock Constraint Specification Language) [9] to specify the causal and temporal characteristics of the software as well as the hardware parts of the system.

C.A. Furia and S. Nanz (Eds.): TOOLS Europe 2012, LNCS 7304, pp. 75–90, 2012.
© Springer-Verlag Berlin Heidelberg 2012

Languages like Giotto [4] and SIGNAL [3] extend existing paradigms to include time-related issues. However, such issues are managed at compile time, preventing the system temporal behavior from being adaptive. Similar to Giotto, PTIDES (Programming Temporally Integrated Distributed Embedded Systems) [16] is a programming model for distributed embedded systems based on a global, consistent notion of time. Finally, [8] proposes a modular modeling methodology to specify the timing behavior of real-time distributed component-based applications. It allows building models of resources and of software components, which are reusable and independent from the applications that use them.

It is widely known that object-oriented frameworks promote reuse and reduce design effort [5]. This is demonstrated by the wide range of application frameworks that have been proposed for many different application domains. Surprisingly, there is relatively little work on application frameworks for the design of real-time systems. An example is SESAG [5], an object-oriented application framework for real-time systems. SESAG proposes five components in the design of real-time systems, but neglects an explicit representation of time-related concepts. The same holds for SIMOO-RT [1], which is an object-oriented framework designed to support the whole development cycle of real-time industrial automation systems. It is based on the concept of distributed active objects, which are autonomous execution entities that have their own thread of control, and that interact with each other by means of remote methods invocation. Other frameworks have been proposed for specific domains: [14], for example, is a an object oriented framework for GPGPU-based image processing.

The key idea behind our proposal is that time should be a full-fledged first-class concept, which directly turns into basic architectural abstractions supported by a running machine [2]. The abstractions are reified by mechanisms that an application can directly exploit to dynamically adapt its own policies by relying on time-related knowledge both about the domain and its own behavior. According to the principle of separation of concerns, the abstractions capture three well distinguished concepts: *time sensitivity, time consciousness* and *time observability*. A *time sensitive* activity is driven by events that are assumed to model the flow of time (for example, it periodically samples incoming data). A *time conscious* activity reasons about facts placed in a temporal context, no matter when the computation is realized (for example, it performs off-line statistics on timestamped historical data). A *time observer* activity observes "what time it is" (for example, it observes the current time to timestamp the generated data). *Performers* are entities that accomplish time sensitive activities. Performers may be further classified: a *time conscious performer* is a performer whose time sensitive activity is also time conscious, a *time observer performer* is a performer whose time sensitive activity is also time observer. A full-fledged *time-aware* system is a collection of performers that are time conscious, time observer and/or a combination of the two.

The identified time-related concepts turn into an object-oriented application framework that provides the base classes to easily define domain-dependant performers, the running machine that supports the real-time execution of the performers, a set of scheduling algorithms and a simple configuration schema to specify the initial system configuration. The framework has been developed in the Java language, thus it is suitable to build soft real-time systems.

The paper is organized as follows: Section 2 presents key concepts related to time; Section 3 illustrates how the identified abstractions are realized by the object-oriented application framework; Section 4 presents some experimental results; finally, Section 5 presents conclusions and outlines future work.

2   Basic Concepts

2.1   Core Concepts

Time sensitivity implies the generation of events modeling the flowing of the time. As sketched in Figure 1, a *timer* is a source of *ticks*, which are periodic events that are assumed to denote the flowing of the time. A timer ticks *time sensitive entities*, that is, entities that must be periodically activated. Timers are hierarchically arranged in a tree. A *virtual timer* is a timer with an associated *reference* timer and whose *period* is the number of ticks it receives from its reference timer for each tick it generates. In other words, a virtual timer is a time sensitive entity that, in turn, behaves like a timer: it counts the events generated by its reference timer and ticks the time sensitive entities it controls when the count equals its period. The root of the hierarchy is a *ground timer*, which is an autonomous source of ticks. The period of a ground timer can be interpreted as the elapsed time between two ticks expressed in terms of an arbitrary "real" reference time. The *absolute period* of a virtual timer is the number of ground ticks for each tick of the virtual timer.

Time consciousness implies the temporal contextualization of facts. As sketched in Figure 1, a *timeline* models the time as a numbered sequence of atomic time grains. A *grain* is an elementary unit of time, identified by the *index* of its position in the timeline. A *time interval* is a sequence of contiguous time grains. A *fact* is a predicate about a subject. A *timed fact* is a fact that is valid inside a time interval defined over a timeline. Timelines are arranged in a tree. A *virtual timeline* is a timeline whose grains (*virtual grains*) have a *duration* that can be expressed as a time interval in an associated *reference* timeline. The *ground timeline* is the root of the hierarchy (i.e., it does not have a reference timeline). Grains of the reference timeline (*ground grains*) have a duration that can be interpreted as an elementary time interval in an arbitrary ground reference time (e.g., the "real" time from the application viewpoint).

Finally, *time observability* implies to be aware about the current time. As sketched in Figure 1, a *clock* associates a timer with a timeline. It defines the duration of the grains of the timeline according to the period of the timer. It also defines the concepts of *past* and *future* in the associated timeline by counting the ticks generated by its timer. If c is the current *count* of the clock, the grains with *index* less than c belong to the past of the timeline and the grains with *index* greater than c belong to the future of the timeline. *Present time* corresponds to the grain whose *index* is c.

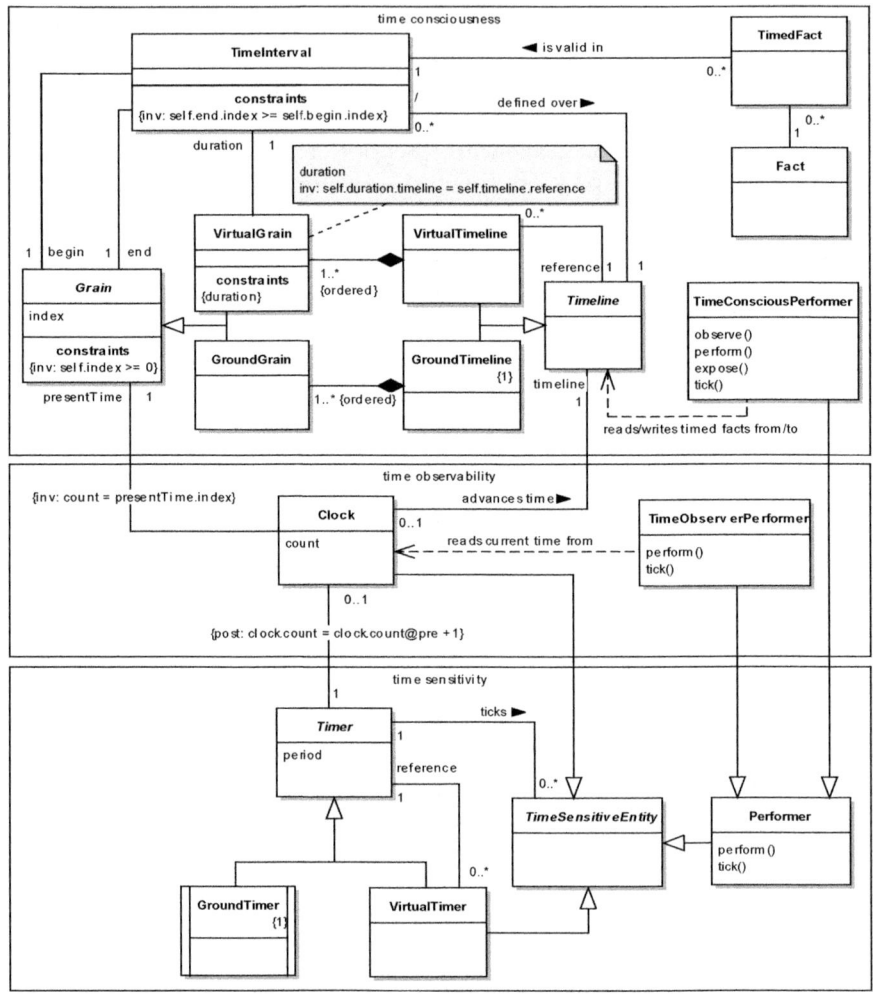

Fig. 1. Core concepts

2.2   Performers

Performers are entities that accomplish domain-dependant time sensitive activities, thus they are time sensitive entities (see Figure 1). It follows that their activation is triggered by the ticks of a timer. The performer activity is reified by the *perform* operation, whose duration must be less than or equal to the period of the ticking timer to fulfill real-time constraints.

As depicted in Figure 2, two states characterize a performer: *waiting* and *running*. When its ticking timer ticks, the performer passes in the *running* state, which implies the execution of its *perform* operation. When this operation is completed, the performer passes in the *waiting* state.

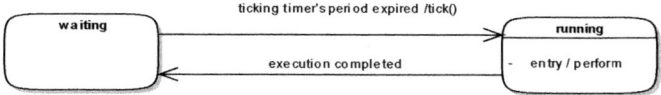

Fig. 2. Performer states

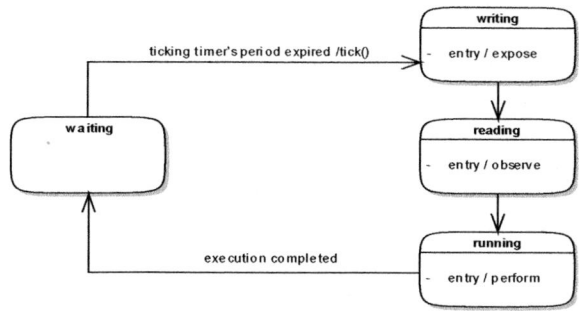

Fig. 3. Time conscious performer states

Performers can be further classified. A *time conscious performer* reads and writes timed facts from or to one or more timelines. A *time observer performer* reads one or more clocks to get their current times. The states of a time observer performer are the same as the ones of a pure time sensitive performer. Different is the case of time conscious performers, since they deal with timelines. A time conscious performer is expected to read facts, to perform some operations (possibly on the read facts) and to write new facts. However, the duration of the *perform* operation is in general not negligible and can be shorter than the duration of the grain. Because time is discrete and what happens inside a grain is not observable, facts cannot be written directly at the end of the *perform* operation. Thus, a performer must read facts at the beginning of a grain and can write facts only at the end of the grain. Because the end of a grain is the same as the beginning of the next one, writing facts at the end of a grain is equivalent to writing them at the beginning of the next grain. Therefore, a time conscious performer writes facts at the beginning of the next grain. This behavior is depicted in Figure 3. The *expose* operation writes timed facts to timelines, whereas the *observe* operation reads timed facts from timelines.

3   The Application Framework

3.1   Performers

As sketched in Figure 4, the `Performer` interface reifies the *performer* as defined in Subsection 2.2. Since the duration of the *perform* operation may not be negligible and several performers may be competing for computing resources, some mechanisms are required to explicitly manage preemption. For example, the framework running machine (detailed in Subsection 3.3) must be able to suspend the execution of a performer because another performer has been given higher priority according to the used scheduling policy. At the aim, the `Performer` interface defines the `suspend` method that suspends the execution of the performer and the `execute` method that starts/resumes its execution. Moreover, the interface defines the `getDuration` method that returns the duration of the performer execution, required for schedulability checks (see Subsection 3.5).

Two kinds of performers have been specified, shown in Figure 4: threaded and state machine-based. Threaded performers (`ThreadedPerformer` class) have been designed to provide full preemptive behavior: the `perform` method reifies the *perform* operation and it is executed in a separate thread, which is resumed or suspended by the framework running machine by means of the `resume` and `suspend` methods respectively, whose implementations are based on methods of the Java `Thread` class. Notice that the preemption mechanism is completely controlled by the framework running machine rather than by the Java virtual machine, because at every moment at most one among the performer threads is left in the runnable state. Only the low-level context-switch management between a thread that has been explicitly suspended and a thread that has been started or resumed is delegated to the Java virtual machine. Even though the methods `suspend` and `resume` of the Java `Thread` class are deadlock-prone, they can be used under the assumption that all the performers use timelines as the only shared resources. This may result in a limitation, but the proposed one is a prototype implementation aimed at validating the main ideas.

State machine-based performers (`StateMachinePerformer` class) have been designed for use with cooperative preemption: the *perform* operation is reified by an ordered set of methods (denoted `step`n, where n is a positive discrete number) whose executions can be assumed to be of negligible duration with respect to the typical time scales of the system. Every time the performer is given control of a processing resource, a single step is invoked synchronously. At the end of the step, the performer relinquishes the control of the resource, thus allowing the framework running machine to select the next performer to execute.

Observing Figure 4, it is possible to notice that all the methods are stereotyped *system*. This stereotype means that the methods are designed to be used by the framework running machine only, to prevent an improper use that would result in an uncorrect behavior of the system. On the contrary, the *user* stereotype (see for example Figure 5) means that the developer can safely use the method when designing the `perform` or `step`n methods of the performer.

Following the performer classification introduced in Subsection 2.2, the `TimeConsciousPerformer` and `TimeObserverPerformer` interfaces have been defined as sketched in Figure 5. Such interfaces define all the methods a time conscious and a time observer performer respectively require. Since the Java language does not support multiple inheritance, it was necessary to use interfaces and to implement the defined methods in delegate classes (respectively, `TimeConsciousPerformerDelegate` and `TimeObserverPerformerDelegate`).

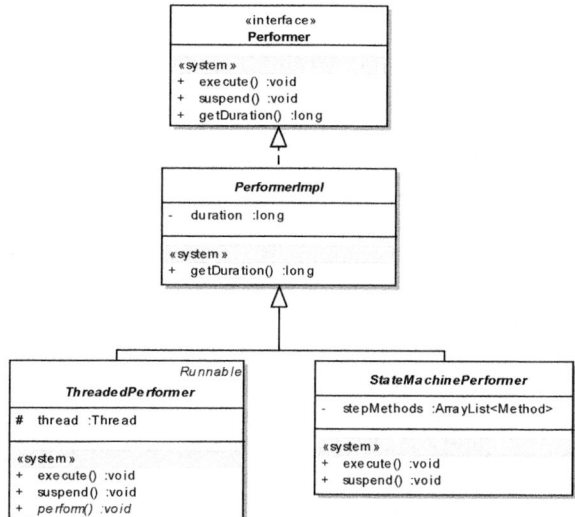

Fig. 4. Performer types for preemption

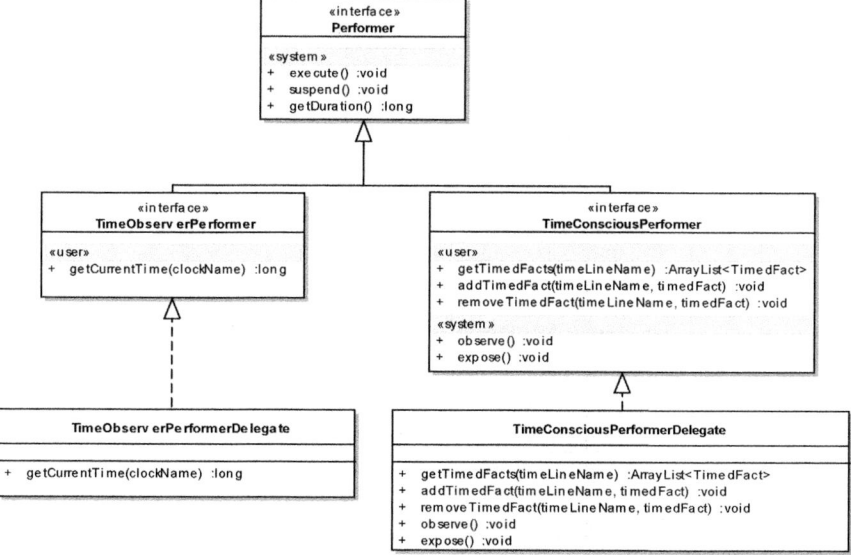

Fig. 5. Performer classification

Dealing with time conscious performers, the `TimeConsciousPerformer` inter-face defines the methods a developer can use to manage timed facts on time-lines. In particular, the `getTimedFacts`, `addTimedFacts` and `removeTimedFacts` methods read, write and delete timed facts from timelines respectively. It is im-portant to note that these methods work on local copies of timelines. Such copies

are synchronized with the "real" timelines by means of the *system* methods
`expose` and `observe` (reifying the homonymous operations described in Subsection 2.2) at the beginning of every grain. This ensures that all the performers
that are ticked at the same time have the same picture of the timelines independently from the order of execution. Finally, the `TimeObserverPerformer`
interface defines the single method `getCurrentTime`, which a developer can use
to read a clock's current time.

The framework provides a set of basic predefined classes that the developer
can subclass to build real-time systems. If the system only requires performers,
for every threaded performer the developer has to override the `perform` method,
whereas for every state machine-based performer all the needed `stepn` method
must be implemented. If a full time-aware system is required, the framework
provides all the classes needed to define time conscious, time observer and the
combination of the two typologies, both for threaded and state machine-based
performers. Figure 6 shows such classes (highlighted in gray) in the threaded
case. Again, the developer is only expected to implement the `perform` method
for threaded performers, or the `stepn` methods for state machine-based ones.

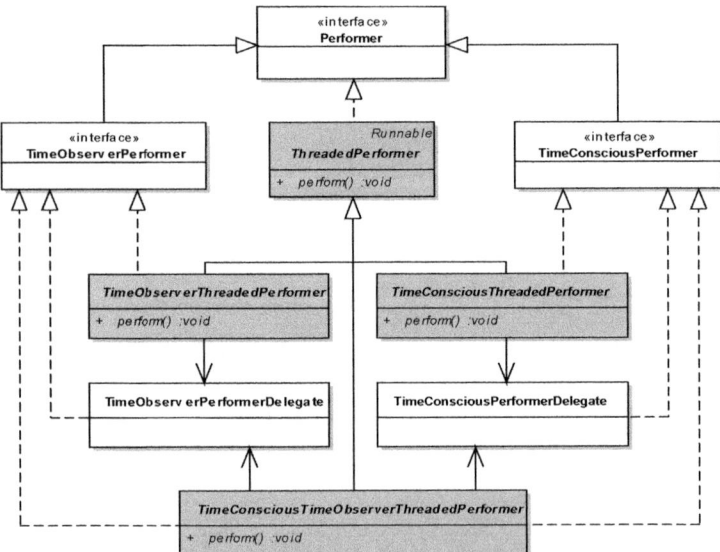

Fig. 6. Predefined performer classes

3.2 Core Classes

Classes sketched in Figure 7 reify the concepts presented in Subsection 2.1,
except for the `Performer` interface described in the previous subsection.

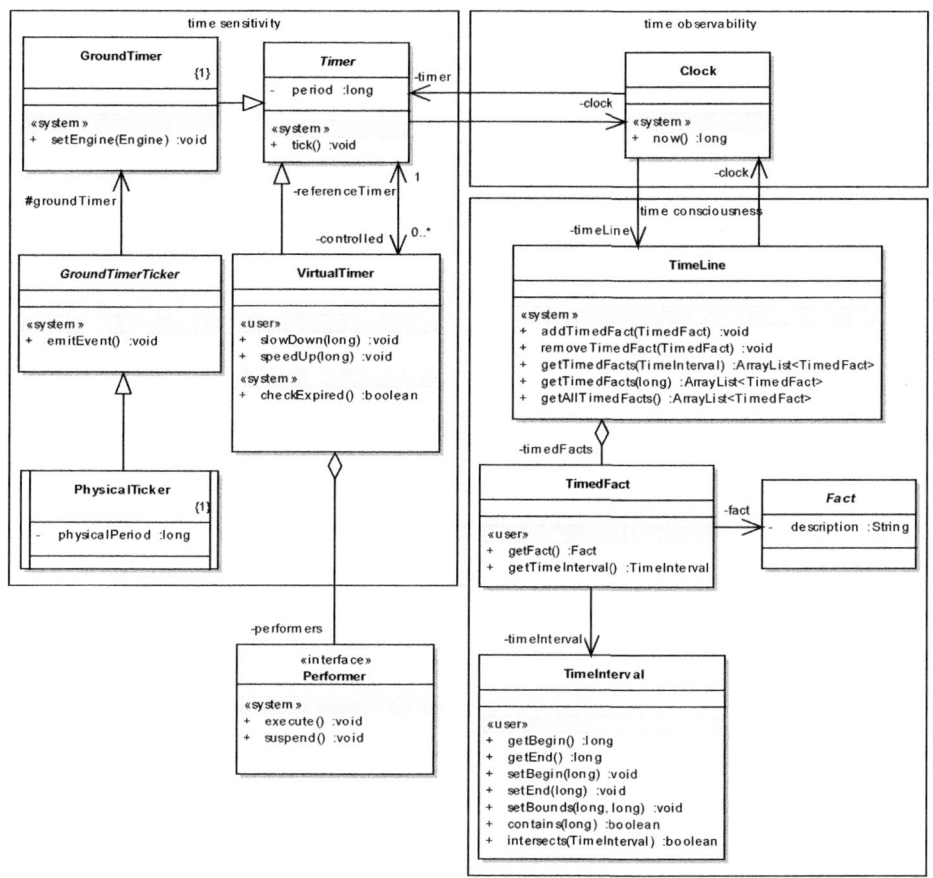

Fig. 7. Framework core classes

Dealing with time sensitivity, the `GroundTimerTicker` is an abstract class modeling a source of periodic events for the `GroundTimer` (i.e., the ground timer as defined in Subsection 2.1). A special kind of ticker is the `PhysicalTicker`, an autonomous source of ticks that models the "real" reference time: it ticks the `GroundTimer` when its `physicalPeriod` (expressed in milliseconds) elapses. Another possible implementation of `GroundTimerTicker` may consist in a user interface that provides controls to realize a step-by-step execution (simulated time). It is important to note that the `GroundTimerTicker` is the only (possible) connection with the "real" external time, which guarantees reproducibility of the temporal system behavior in a testing environment.

The `Timer` class models the timer concept as specified in Subsection 2.1. The `GroundTimer` reifies the ground timer, being the root of the virtual timers hierarchy. The `VirtualTimer` class reifies the virtual timer. Each `VirtualTimer` has one reference timer only and each `Timer` may have several controlled timers. The `tick` method of a timer counts the number of received ticks and ticks the controlled timers when the count equals the period. The `VirtualTimer` class makes available to developers the `slowDown` and `speedUp` methods to respectively slow down or speed up virtual timers. A period variation implies a modification of the activation speed of all the time sensitive entities ticked by the timer. A period variation of a virtual timer VT_i produces a corresponding variation of the absolute periods of all the virtual timers in the subtree whose root is VT_i. Thus, it indirectly modifies the activation speeds of all the time sensitive entities ticked by the timers belonging to the subtree. Moreover, the `VirtualTimer` class maintains the list of the performers that it periodically ticks.

Dealing with time consciousness, the `TimeLine` class reifies a timeline. Its methods handle timed facts on timelines. For this reason, they must be only used by the framework running machine, allowing the performers to share a consistent view of the timelines. Grains as defined in Subsection 2.1 are reified by long values. The remaining classes model facts, time intervals and timed facts.

Finally, the `Clock` class enables time observability by realizing the concept of current time over a timeline: it binds a `Timer` with a `TimeLine`. Its `now` method returns the current time of the clock.

3.3   The Framework Running Machine

The running machine is the core of the framework in charge of executing performers. Main classes are sketched in Figure 8.

The `Engine` class models the entity that triggers the execution of performers by means of its `execute` method (detailed in Subsection 3.4). It is a time sensitive entity periodically ticked by the `GroundTimer`. In details, the engine is responsible both of ordering the ticked performers in a queue and of executing them. The ordering and execution of performers are not encapsulated inside the `Engine` class, but they are delegated to the `SchedulingPolicy` and `Dispatcher` classes respectively. This way, when building a time-aware system, the developer may specify the preferred scheduling policy and the way in which the performers are actually executed, which heavily depends on the available resources (e.g., the number of CPU cores). The actual implementation of the framework includes three specializations of the `SchedulingPolicy`, providing the following scheduling policies: *Rate Monotonic*, *First Come First Served* and *Earliest Deadline First*. Each class properly overrides the `reorder` method whose aim is to reorder the ticked performers. On the contrary, the framework provides one dispatcher only, denoted `SingleCoreDispatcher`, designed to manage the execution of one performer at a time on a single-core configuration. Its `dispatch` method suspends the running performer (`suspend` method) and executes (`execute` method) the one that has been given highest priority by the scheduling policy.

3.4   Dynamics

Time sensitivity implies the generation of events at each unit of the "real" reference time and the corresponding update of the timer hierarchy. As sketched in Figure 9, the `PhysicalTicker` ticks the `GroundTimer` when its physical period

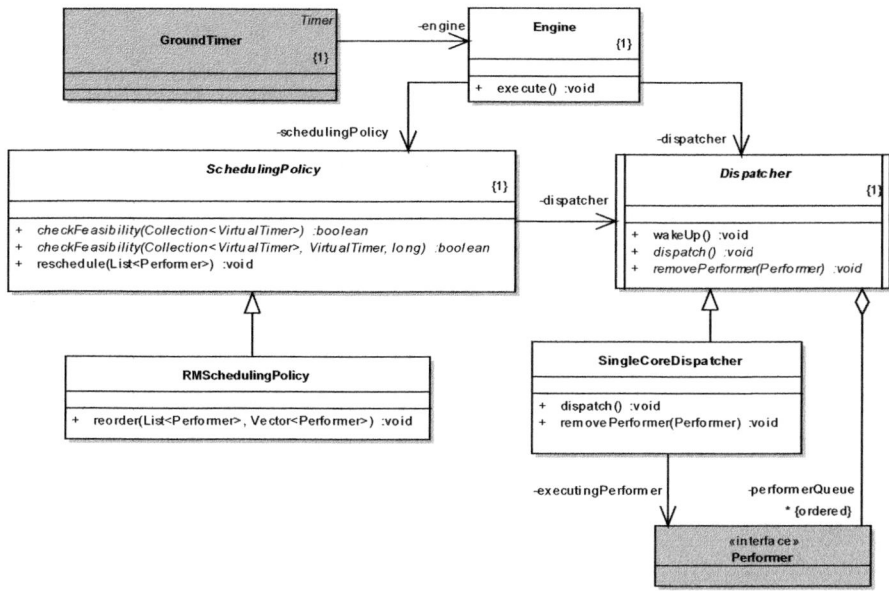

Fig. 8. Running machine

expires. The `GroundTimer` ticks its controlled virtual timers when its counter equals its period. In turn, each ticked `VirtualTimer` ticks its controlled virtual timers every time its period expires and marks itself as expired. The update process goes on until the leaves of the timer hierarchy have been reached. At the end of the update process, the `GroundTimer` invokes the `execute` method of the `Engine` that, as described later, ultimately executes the ticked performers. At the end of the `execute` method, the ticker is ready to emit the next event. If the ticker is an instance of `PhysicalTicker`, its thread suspends (`sleep` call) until the time at which the next event must be emitted.

Going back to the `Engine`'s execute method (detailed in Figure 10), it:

1. Retrieves the expired timers
2. Gets the list of the performers ticked by each expired timer
3. Writes timed facts to timelines by calling the `expose` method of every ticked time conscious performer
4. Reads timed facts from timelines and synchronizes them with the performers' internal copies by calling the `observe` method of each ticked time conscious performer
5. Synchronously invokes the `reschedule` method of the `SchedulingPolicy`, to add the performers to the `performerQueue` (Figure 8) according to the chosen scheduling policy
6. Wakes up the `Dispatcher` by means of an asynchronous call to the `wakeUp` method

It is remarkable that both kinds of performers (threaded or state machine-based) are dealt with in the same way by the framework running machine.

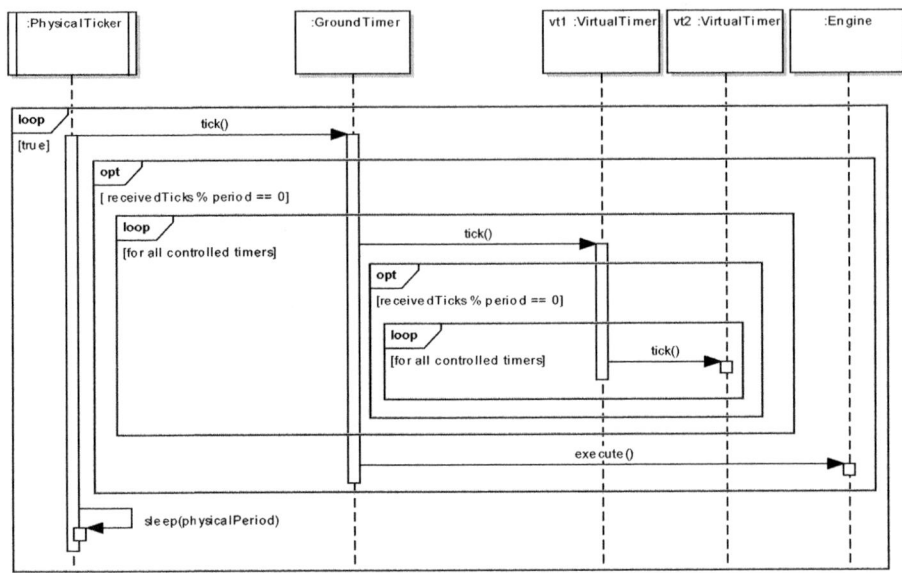

Fig. 9. Timer update

3.5   System Start-Up

The framework provides an easy way to configure a time-aware application by means of an XML file, where the developer can specify the timers, clocks, time-lines and performers and their relations, the required scheduling policy and, basing on computing resources, the dispatcher type.

When the system is started, the framework reads the configuration file and instantiates all the specified objects with the required associations. Moreover, if the durations of performer executions are provided, the framework performs a schedulability check (if supported by the chosen scheduling policy). This analysis makes the developer aware of the actual schedulability of the built system when sufficient conditions are met. If the schedulability check is not performed (because no sufficient conditions are known for the chosen scheduling policy or because the check has been explicitly disabled in order to allow the system to execute even if it did not pass the check), the framework supports anyway the execution. In this case, an exception is thrown when a deadline is missed. Finally, the framework starts the system execution.

The schedulability check is also performed at every attempt to modify a virtual timer's period by means of a call to speedUp or slowDown. This is particularly useful to ensure that schedulability is always preserved even in temporally adaptive systems.

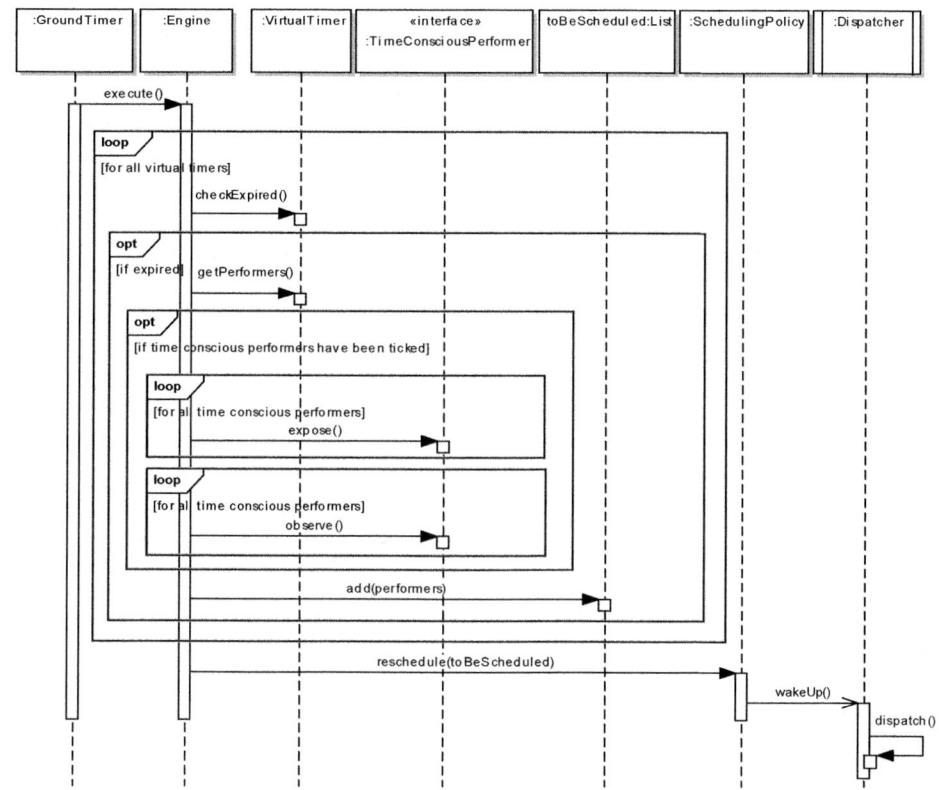

Fig. 10. Running machine behavior

4   Experimental Results

In order to check the functional correctness of the framework, we considered a test set of performers and implemented it using several scheduling algorithms. Threaded performers have been used, because this provides full preemption and therefore the closest resemblance to the standard approach used in hard real-time operating systems. Moreover, we used simple time-sensitive performers, as properties related to time observation or consciousness are not of interest for this kind of experimentation.

The algorithms we tested are: First Come First Served (FCFS), Rate Monotonic (RM) and Earliest Deadline First (EDF). For the sake of simplicity, deadlines are assumed to be equal to the corresponding periods. The performers we considered have the following properties:

- T_1 with period $P_1 = 4$ s and duration $d_1 = 1$ s
- T_2 with period $P_2 = 7$ s and duration $d_2 = 4$ s

This choice of periods and durations fulfills the sufficient conditions for schedulability with RM and EDF [7], and is found to be schedulable with FCFS too. Figures 11a, 11b and 11c show the results of the tests run with the three scheduling algorithms. In all the cases, the system has been let run for 60 s, with a ground timer period of 1 and a physical period for the ground timer ticker of 1 s. The relevant performer events (start, finish and context switches) have been logged to a file and later reloaded for plotting. In the figures, dark gray and light gray rectangles denote execution slices of T_1 and T_2 respectively. Note that the logging of the low-level behavior related to preemption was very easy because, even though the framework implementation uses standard Java threads, it does not rely on the virtual machine thread management, but threads are controlled directly by the framework by means of the methods provided by the Thread class.

As an example of a more detailed analysis of the behavior of the scheduling algorithm, Figure 12 shows the expanded view of the scheduling sequence for a short time interval in the EDF case. In that figure, the arrows denote the ticks of the virtual timers ticking the two performers. This view allows checking the correctness of the scheduling according to the EDF algorithm in a simpler way:

1. At $t = 0$ both timers tick. The absolute deadline for the corresponding execution of T_1 is represented by the instant of the next tick of its ticking timer, that is, $t = 4$. Similarly, the deadline for T_2 is $t = 7$. Because the latter deadline is farther in the future than the former, T_1 is selected for execution

2. At $t = 1$, T_1 ends its execution and the dispatcher selects T_2 for execution. T_2 continues to run past $t = 2$ and $t = 3$, being the only performer in the execution queue

3. At $t = 4$, a tick by the ticking timer puts T_1 into the execution queue, with deadline at $t = 8$. However, since the deadline for T_2 is at $t = 7$, T_2 continues its execution until the end, at $t = 5$. Now T_1 can run, ending at $t = 6$

4. At $t = 7$ a new tick by the timer causes the beginning of the execution of T_2, which is the only performer in the queue, with deadline $t = 14$

5. At $t = 8$, T_1 is woken up again, with deadline $t = 12$. Because such a deadline is closer than the one for T_2, the execution of T_2 is stopped and T_1 is let run

6. At the end of T_1's execution, at $t = 9$, the suspended execution of T_2 is resumed until its end at $t = 12$, when a new execution of T_1 is started

The results show that the framework correctly deals with the given set of performers and the chosen scheduling algorithm. Moreover, some typical features of the three considered algorithms can be easily recognized. As for the RM algorithm, the execution of the performer with shorter period (which thus gets the highest priority) is exactly regular (no jitter). The EDF algorithm produces greater jitter for both performers, but it guarantees schedulability also for performer sets presenting higher CPU loads [7]. Finally, the FCFS algorithm shows no preemption at all, as expected.

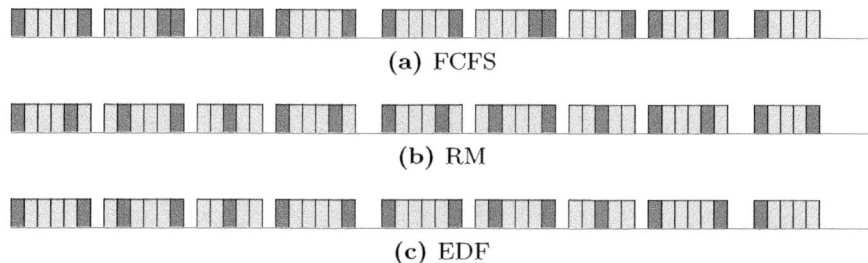

(a) FCFS

(b) RM

(c) EDF

Fig. 11. Diagram of scheduling behavior using different algorithms

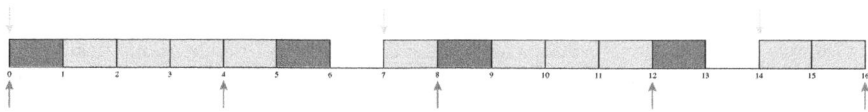

Fig. 12. More detailed diagram of scheduling behavior using the EDF algorithm

5   Conclusions and Future Directions

The paper presented an object-oriented application framework that supports the design of real-time systems. The framework is based on a set of architectural abstractions that model the temporal behavior of a system, allowing time-related aspects to be explicitly treated as first-class concepts at the application level.

The framework provides a set of base classes that the developer will specialize to code the domain-dependant behavior of the system. Moreover, the framework internally supports the mechanisms for the proper temporal execution of the system. Finally, the framework also provides an easy way to configure a time-aware system by means of an XML file. This allows developers to concentrate only on domain-related issues, because the temporal synchronization of activities is completely managed by the framework.

Moreover, since the framework allows time-related aspects to be explicitly treated as first-class objects, time-related concepts can be observed and partially controlled. In particular, the execution speed of the activities can be dynamically varied to meet fluctuating temporal constraints, thus promoting the realization of time-aware adaptive systems.

The actual implementation of the framework in based on the Java language and experimental results demonstrated that the framework correctly (from a temporal point of view) manages the scheduling of a set of performers with different period and duration. Even though this Java implementation cannot always be used to build actual real-time systems, this framework can help dramatically for debugging.

In view of the achieved results, we are planning to implement the architecture on a microcontroller, which would allow testing its usefulness for the development of bare-metal, hard real-time systems.

In the same way, we are evaluating to implement the architecture as an intermediate layer to be used on top of an existing underlying real-time operating system, to simplify the construction of time-aware applications.

References

1. Becker, L.B., Pereira, C.E.: SIMOO-RT-an object-oriented framework for the development of real-time industrial automation systems. IEEE Transactions on Robotics and Automation 18(4), 421–430 (2002)
2. Fiamberti, F., Micucci, D., Tisato, F.: An architecture for time-aware systems. In: 2011 IEEE 16th Conference on Emerging Technologies & Factory Automation (ETFA), pp. 1–4. IEEE (2011)
3. Gamatié, A., Gautier, T., Guernic, P.L., Talpin, J.P.: Polychronous design of embedded real-time applications. ACM Trans. Softw. Eng. Methodol. 16(2) (2007)
4. Henzinger, T., Horowitz, B., Kirsch, C.: Giotto: a time-triggered language for embedded programming. Proceedings of the IEEE 91(1), 84–99 (2003)
5. Hsiung, P.A., Lee, T.Y., Fu, J.M., See, W.B.: Sesag: an object-oriented application framework for real-time systems: Research articles. Softw. Pract. Exper. 35, 899–921 (2005)
6. Kristensen, B.: Architectural abstractions and language mechanisms. In: Proceedings of 1996 Asia-Pacific Software Engineering Conference, pp. 288–299 (1996)
7. Liu, C.L., Layland, J.W.: Scheduling algorithms for multiprogramming in a hard-real-time environment. J. ACM 20, 46–61 (1973)
8. Lopez, P., Medina, J., Drake, J.: Real-time modelling of distributed component-based applications. In: 32nd EUROMICRO Conference on Software Engineering and Advanced Applications, SEAA 2006, pp. 92–99 (2006)
9. Mallet, F.: Clock constraint specification language: specifying clock constraints with UML/MARTE. Innovations in Systems and Software Engineering 4(3), 309–314 (2008)
10. de Niz, D.: Diagrams and Languages for Model-Based Software Engineering of Embedded Systems: UML and AADL, http://www.aadl.info/aadl/documents/UML_AADL_Comparison.pdf
11. OMG: MARTE Modeling and Analysis of Real-Time and Embedded systems (2009), http://www.omg.org/spec/MARTE/1.0/PDF/
12. Peraldi-Frati, M., DeAntoni, J.: Scheduling multi clock real time systems: From requirements to implementation. In: 14th IEEE International Symposium on Object/Component/Service-Oriented Real-Time Distributed Computing (ISORC 2011), pp. 50–57 (2011)
13. SAE: AADL Architecture Analysis and Design Language (2009), http://www.aadl.info
14. Seiller, N., Singhal, N., Park, I.K.: Object oriented framework for real-time image processing on gpu. In: 17th IEEE International Conference on Image Processing (ICIP 2010), pp. 4477–4480 (2010)
15. Stankovic, J.: Misconceptions about real-time computing: a serious problem for next-generation systems. Computer 21(10), 10–19 (1988)
16. Zhao, Y., Liu, J., Lee, E.A.: A programming model for Time-Synchronized distributed Real-Time systems. In: 13th IEEE Real Time and Embedded Technology and Applications Symposium, RTAS 2007, pp. 259–268. IEEE (2007)

Measuring Test Case Similarity to Support Test Suite Understanding

Michaela Greiler, Arie van Deursen, and Andy Zaidman

Delft University of Technology, The Netherlands
{m.s.greiler,arie.vandeursen,a.e.zaidman}@tudelft.nl

Abstract. In order to support test suite understanding, we investigate whether we can automatically derive relations between test cases. In particular, we search for trace-based similarities between (high-level) end-to-end tests on the one hand and fine grained unit tests on the other. Our approach uses the shared word count metric to determine similarity. We evaluate our approach in two case studies and show which relations between end-to-end and unit tests are found by our approach, and how this information can be used to support test suite understanding.

1 Introduction

Modern software development practice dictates early and frequent (automated) testing. While automated test suites are helpful from a (continuous) integration and regression testing perspective, they lead to a substantial amount of test code [16]. Like production code, test code needs to be maintained, understood, and adjusted upon changes to production code or requirements [8,10,13].

In light of the necessity of understanding and maintaining test suites, which can become very costly due to the large amounts of test code, it is our stance that tool support can reduce the burden put on the software and test engineers. The V-model from Figure 1 shows that different levels of tests validate different types of software artifacts, with each level contributing to the large amount of test code. Figure 1 also shows that, ideally, requirements can be *traced* all the way to source code, making it easier to perform *impact analysis*, i.e., determining what the impact of a changing requirement is on the source code. The right side of the V-model however, the test side, does not have similar tool support.

In this paper we propose to support engineers by helping them to understand relationships between different types of test suites. As an example, an automated test suite can include "end-to-end" tests, exercising an application from the user-interface down to the database, covering functionality that is meaningful to the end user.[1] The test suite will typically also include dedicated unit tests, aimed at exercising a very specific piece of behavior of a particular class. Suppose now a requirement changes, entailing a modification to the end-to-end test, which unit tests should the software engineer change as well? And vice-versa, if a unit test is changed, should this be reflected in an end-to-end test as well?

---

[1] We deliberately did not use the term acceptance test, as it is commonly associated with tests executed by the customers/users.

C.A. Furia and S. Nanz (Eds.): TOOLS Europe 2012, LNCS 7304, pp. 91–107, 2012.
© Springer-Verlag Berlin Heidelberg 2012

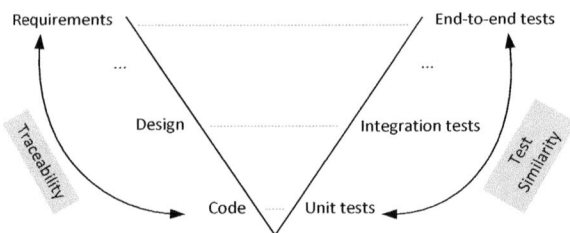

Fig. 1. The V-model for testing

Our goal is to develop an automated technique for establishing relations between test cases, in order to assist developers in their (test suite) maintenance activities. To reach this goal, we employ *dynamic analysis* [4]. We collect call traces from test executions, and use these to compute a *similarity* value based on the shared word count metric. The resulting technique, which we call *test connection mining*, can be used to establish connections between test cases at different levels. An implementation of our technique is available via a framework called the *Test Similarity Correlator*.

We evaluate the approach in two case studies, by elaborating on the usefulness of the approach to improve the understanding. We analyze how measuring similarity based test relations can help to (1) find relevant tests by showing test relationships, (2) understand the functionality of a test by describing high-level test cases with related unit test cases and (3) reveal blank spots in the investigated unit test suites.

This paper is structured as follows: in Section 2, we discuss our test execution tracing approach. In Section 3, we describe the similarity metrics we use to compare traces. Subsequently, we describe our approach and its implementation (Section 3) as well as the set-up of our case studies (Section 4). The two case studies are covered in Sections 5 and 6. We conclude with discussion, related work, and a summary of our contributions in Sections 7–9.

2   Tracing and Trace Reduction

Test connection mining first of all requires obtaining execution traces with relevant information of manageable size. This section describes the specific execution trace we use and the trace reduction techniques we apply.

2.1   Tracing Test Executions

Before the test run, the production and test code are instrumented. Subsequently, during the test run we obtain an execution trace comprised of various types of *events*: (1) *test execution* events represent the execution of a test method, (2) *set-up and tear-down* events mark the execution of a method which is either used for test set-up or tear-down, (3) *method execution* events signalling the execution of a public method within the code under test and (4) *exception thrown* events indicating that an exception has been thrown.

For the similarity measurements it is important to be able to distinguish between production and test code. Otherwise, executions of test helper methods will appear in the trace and render the test cases as less related. Due to the common practice to put the test code in a separate package (e.g., test.jpacman), we simply filter executions of methods belonging to test code out during instrumentation. If test and production code are within the same packages, test classes can be annotated and correctly addressed during instrumentation.

2.2   Handling Mocks and Stubs

When mocks or stubs are used, care has to be taken to correctly trace calls to mocked classes and map these calls to the corresponding original class.

A first issue is that using mocking frameworks can have the effect that an automatically created mock-object is not part of the instrumented package. For example, by using the JMock[2] library interfaces and classes defined to be mocked are automatically wrapped in a proxy class which is located in the same package as the class directing the mocking operation, which will usually be the test class or a helper class within the test package. Because we do not trace executions of methods defined in the test package, these classes have to be addressed specifically. We do so by keeping track of a list of mocked types.

Mocking also plays a role for tracing the production code, as the mocked and unmocked classes have to be mapped to allow identifying their similarity. Therefore, we have to indicate that a method on a mockable object has been invoked. To that end, we check whether the runtime type of the target is contained in the list of mocked classes. If yes, we further investigate whether the method intercepted is part of the mockable type, since a class implementing a mockable interface can have additional methods. Therefore, we derive recursively, via reflection, the set of methods belonging to this type including all methods defined by it and its (potential) super-types. Only if the method intercepted is an actual method of the mockable type, we discovered a mockery execution. As such, we add it to the trace and mark it with a *mockery mark*.

Finally, we need to neutralize those mock and stub calls. As illustrated in Listing 1.1, an execution of a method of a mocked type can be traced as the execution of an inner class within the (test) class defining the mock operation. As this differs from the trace events left behind by the execution of a method of the actual type, we render them as similar, by using the *mockery marks* set during tracing. Note also the actual type might differ from the mocked type by being the implementation of a type or extending a common type. We inspect the trace and replace all executions of methods of an actual type, as well as the executions of the mocked type by their common (super) type. For example, the traces in Listing 1.1 would be mapped to "void Sniper.join()".

---

[2] http://www.jmock.org

Listing 1.1. Trace differences with or without mocking

```
//Execution of method join of the mocked interface Sniper
void TestClass.$Proxy1.join()
```

```
//Execution of method join of class AuctionSniper implementing Sniper
void AuctionSniper.join()
```

2.3   Trace Reduction

Trace reduction techniques are important in order to reduce the size of traces to improve performance and scalability, and to help reveal the key functionality of the test case, e.g., by reducing common functionality or noise [3]. We adopt the following five reduction techniques before starting our analysis:

Language based Reduction. The traces are reduced to only public method executions and do not comprise any private or protected methods. Furthermore, only the production code is fully traced; for the test code only test method execution events are traced to be able to separate individual test cases from an entire test run.

Set-up and Tear-Down Reduction. As set-up and tear-down methods do not explicitly contribute to the specific focus of a unit test, and are usually shared by each test case within a test class, all method executions taking place during set-up or tear-down are removed.

Shared Word Reduction. This trace reduction focuses on helping identify the core functionality of a test case, by removing trace events that are omnipresent in almost all test traces (defined by a variable threshold).

Complement Reduction. This reduction focuses on reducing the trace size by removing calls within the trace of interest that are not existing in any of the test traces to compare to. Although, after such a reduction target traces will be calculated as more similar to the source trace, the reduction itself does not influence the information perceived useful for ranking the target traces with respect to each other.

Unique Set of Calls. This technique reduces all trace events within a trace to a unique set of events. Because information such as order and position of events are not preserved this reduction is only useful for similarity measurements that do not take such information into account.

3   Determining Similarity Measurements

The second step involved in test connection mining consists of computing trace similarities. In particular, we compute the similarity between a source trace te (e.g., from an end-to-end test) and a target trace tu (e.g., from a unit test).

As similarity metrics we compared (1) shared word count [14], (2) Levenshtein distance [12] and (3) pattern matching based on the Knuth-Morris-Pratt algorithm [12]. From an initial experiment we observed that all three metrics provided similar results, which is why we continue with the shared word count in the remainder of this paper.

The shared word count measurement [14] assesses the number of tracing events that two test execution traces have in common. The similarity between a source trace and a target trace is calculated as the number of tracing events comprised in both test traces.

3.1 Relevancy Support Based on Occurrence

Some tests are related to other tests, because they test common functionality. Using this piece of knowledge, we can improve our results, by marking these more general tests as less important. Vice versa, by giving a test appearing less often a high impact, results with more specific functionality are ranked higher. We do so by multiplying the similarity measurement for a specific trace tu with the total number of test cases it has been compared to, and dividing this by the number of times the trace appeared as a result. We also use the average similarity of test case tu_i to rank similar results. For example, if target test cases tu_1 and tu_2 have the same similarity with te, than the test case with the smaller average similarity among all te_j is ranked first.

3.2 Implementation

We implemented the various trace reduction techniques and similarity measurements presented in this paper in a Java based framework called *Test Similarity Correlator*.[3] Our tool offers an API to steer customized test similarity measurements, varying in trace reduction, thresholds and similarity calculations.

To instrument the test execution we use the AspectJ[4] framework. We offer three different annotations to facilitate tracing of execution of test-methods, set-up and tear-down methods. *Test Similarity Correlator* comprises several aspects, addressing join points to weave in our tracing advices, including the aspect to address code generated by the mocking library JMock.

4   Set-Up for Case Studies

4.1 Research Questions

To evaluate the usefulness of test connection mining, we conducted an explorative study based on two case studies. In these case studies, we aim at answering the following questions:

RQ1 How do the associations found by test connection mining relate to associations a human expert would establish?
RQ2 Are the associations found useful for a typical test suite understanding task, i.e., getting familiar with the test suite of a foreign system?
RQ3 How does mocking influence the similarity measurements?
RQ4 What are the performance characteristics, both in time and in space, of the analysis conducted?

---

[3] http://swerl.tudelft.nl/bin/view/Main/TestSimilarityCorrelator
[4] http://www.eclipse.org/aspectj

To answer these questions, we select a subject system that is shipped with both a functional test suite as well as a unit test suite. We manually compile a *conceptual mapping* between unit and functional test cases, and compare these to the mappings found through test connection mining automatically.

The first case study is used to assess RQ1 and RQ4, whereby in the second case study we focus on RQ2 and RQ3.

4.2   Technique Customization

The specific trace reduction configuration (see Section 2) we use in the case studies consists of the following steps.

Before calculating the trace similarity, traces are reduced by using the *Set-up and Tear-Down* reduction, followed by the *Shared Word*, and the *Complement* reductions. The order of the reduction is important and influences the ranking of the results. For example, if all unit test cases call a method "quit()" as part of their tear down method, but only one unit test actually uses this method during test execution, the application of first the *Shared Word* reduction and then the *Set-up and Tear-Down* reduction would eliminate this call from the trace. The *Shared Word* reduction technique can be customized by a threshold influencing how many traces must comprise a trace event before it is removed.

For similarity measurements based on shared word count, which does not take the order of events into account, the traces are further reduced to their unique set of events.

5   Case Study I: JPacman

As first subject system we use JPacman,[5] a simple game written in Java inspired by Pacman, used for educational purposes at Delft University of Technology since 2003. Key characteristics of JPacman are listed in Figure 2.

JPacman follows the model-view-controller architecture. Each class in the model package comes with a (JUnit) unit test class, which together comprise 73 unit test cases. The test suite makes use of several test patterns described by Binder [1], using state machines, decision tables, and patterns such as *polymorphic server test* (reusing superclass test suites at the subclass level). This results in a line coverage of 90% in the model package, as measured by Cobertura.[6]

Code size (lines)	4,000
Test code size (lines)	2,000
No of classes	26
No of test classes	16
No of unit tests	73
No of functional tests	14

Fig. 2. JPacman characteristics

```
Given [context]
    And [some more context]...
When  [event]
Then  [outcome]
    And [another outcome]...
```

Fig. 3. JPacman Test Scenarios

---

[5] Version 4.4.4, dated October 2011. JPacman can be obtained for research and educational purposes from its author, 2nd author of this paper.

[6] http://cobertura.sourceforge.net/

The functional test suite is directly derived from a set of JPacman user scenarios written in *behavior-driven development*[7] style. These scenarios are of the form given in Listing 3. There are 14 such scenarios, each of which is translated into a JUnit test case. The resulting functional test cases exercise around 80% of the user interface code and around 90% of the model code.

5.1   Obtaining the Conceptual Mapping

JPacman's main developer created a conceptual mapping in advance. The key criterion to identify a relation between an end-to-end test t and a unit test u was the question whether the behavior of u is important in order to understand the behavior of t. The conceptual mapping contains both *positive* incidences (important connections to be established) and *negative* ones (unlikely connections that would be confusing). In most end-to-end (ETE — numbered from *ETE01* to *ETE14*) test cases, we had at least 5 positive and 9 negative connections.

While the mapping obtained can be considered a useful baseline, it should be noted that it is *incomplete*: it only identifies clearly connected and clearly disconnected test pairs. The remaining tests are categorized as *undecided*. Furthermore, we tried to be as specific as possible: relations to "infrastructure" unit test cases relevant to many end-to-end tests were not included.

5.2   RQ1: Comparison to Conceptual Mapping

We used a spreadsheet containing 14×73 matrices to study the differences between the conceptual mapping as well as the ones obtained through our automated analysis. Due to size restrictions, we can not show all results of the measurements[8]. Besides saving space, showing the top 5 results is also realistic from a practical point of view, because in practice a user of the tool would also look primarily at the highest ranked results. In Table 1 we show for each end-to-end test the 5 most similar unit tests based on the shared word count metric. A ranking is indicated as *optimal* in case it is marked as highly related in the conceptual mapping and it is ranked high (i.e. top match). Incidences marked as related by the expert which are high ranked are evaluated as *good*. Results of the category undecided are subjected to additional manual analysis: the results are indicated as *ok* only if the relation is strong enough to be justified, and labeled as *nok* otherwise. Unrelated results ranked highly, as well as (highly) related results ranked low, are also evaluated as *nok*.

The overall impression is that the automated analysis provides a useful approximation of the manually obtained mapping. Looking at all the results for each end-to-end test case, we found that:

- For all but one end-to-end test (i.e. *ETE02*), the top match is ranked as the first or second automatically calculated result.

---

[7] http://dannorth.net/whats-in-a-story/
[8] The complete results are available at
   http://swerl.tudelft.nl/twiki/pub/Main/TestSimilarityCorrelator/
   similarityResults.zip

Table 1. Top 5 ranked unit tests per end-to-end test for JPacman

Test Case (no.)	match	Test Case (no.)	match	Test Case (no.)	match
1 Move to empty cell & undo		**2 Move beyond border**		**3 Move to wall**	
MovePlayer (23)	optimal	FoodMove (44)	ok	DxDyImpossibleMove (15)	optimal
UndoEmptyMove (17)	optimal	FoodMoveUndo (39)	ok	SimpleMove (22)	good
UndoDxDy (18)	optimal	UndoFoodMove (19)	ok	DieAndUndo (26)	optimal
UndoFoodMove (19)	ok	PlayerWins (24)	ok	DieAndRestart (25)	optimal
Apply (38)	optimal	wonSneakPaths (35)	ok	MovePlayer (23)	good
4 Eat food & undo		**5 Win and restart**		**6 Get killed and restart**	
FoodMoveUndo (39)	optimal	SetUp (12)	ok	DieAndRestart (25)	optimal
UndoFoodMove (19)	optimal	PlayerWins (24)	optimal	PlayerWins (24)	ok
UndoFood (47)	optimal	FoodMoveUndo (39)	good	wonSneakPaths (35)	ok
FoodMove (44)	optimal	FoodMove (44)	optimal	Updates (37)	ok
MovePlayer (23)	good	DxDyPossibleMove (14)	ok	UndoFoodMove (19)	ok
7 Monster to empty cell		**8 Monster beyond border**		**9 Monster to wall**	
16 UndoMonsterMove	optimal	Wall (70)	optimal	EmptyCell (69)	optimal
MoveMonster (28)	optimal	MonsterPlayer (73)	ok	MonsterFood (72)	ok
Updates (37)	ok	MonsterFood (72)	ok	MonsterPlayer (73)	ok
OutOfBorder (68)	ok	EmptyCell (69)	optimal	Wall (70)	optimal
FoodMove (71)	ok	MonsterKillsPlayer (27)	ok	MonsterKillsPlayer (27)	ok
10 Monster to food		**11 Monster to player**		**12 Suspend**	
MoveMonster (28)	optimal	MonsterPlayer (73)	optimal	SuspendRestart (29)	optimal
Updates (37)	ok	70 Wall	ok	Start (21)	good
Apply (66)	good	MonsterFood (72)	ok	SneakPlaying (33)	ok
FoodMoveUndo (67)	optimal	EmptyCell (69)	good	SuspendUndo (30)	optimal
FoodMove (71)	ok	MonsterKillsPlayer (27)	optimal	SneakHalted (36)	good
13 Die and Undo		**14 Smoke**			
DieAndUndo (26)	optimal	SetUp (12)	good		
MovePlayer (23)	good	PlayerWins (24)	optimal		
wonSneakPaths (35)	ok	FoodMoveUndo (39)	ok		
SimpleMove (22)	ok	wonSneakPaths (35)	ok		
DieAndRestart (25)	optimal	FoodMove (44)	ok		

- Within the top 10 results only one unit test case marked unrelated is listed.
- All remaining results ranked within the top 10 (i.e. from the undecided category) are sufficiently related to the end-to-end tests to justify investigation.
- No relations are missing as all test cases marked as relevant by the expert have been identified as related. Thereby, 80% of all test cases marked as related have been ranked within the upper half of the results *showing similarity* and within the top 30% of overall results.
- 92% of all tests marked as unrelated correctly map to *no similarity* by the measurements. The remaining unrelated tests revealed weak connections and have been ranked in the bottom half of the results, except for one test (14).

Correct Identifications. *Top matches.* The top two results of the measurements in most cases also contain the top match for an end-to-end test case. For example, the end-to-end test involving a keyboard event to move the player to the right and then undoing that move (*ETE01*), is connected to a unit test actually moving the player. As another example, *ETE03* attempts to move through a wall (which is impossible), and is connected to a unit test addressing the correct positioning of the Pacman's mouth after attempting an impossible move. As dying is a type of an impossible state, connections to dying are also correct.

Moving Monsters vs. Players. Some groups of test cases are moving players (i.e. 44, 45, 46), whereas other tests (72, 73, 74) are moving monsters. In the conceptual mapping, tests moving players are related to ETE tests 1-6, and marked as unrelated for ETE tests 7-11, whereby tests moving players are related the opposite way. These relations respectively non-relations are correctly identified by the measurements, except for test case 74, which we will outline below.

Surprises. *Moving Monsters.* According to the expert, a group of tests (72, 73, 74) all move monsters, and should lead to similar rankings. Surprisingly, one test (74) performs differently from the rest, and also differs from the conceptual mapping. After investigation, it became apparent that this test is not as focused as expected and desired by the expert. The test even concludes with a method which is never followed by an assertion statement. This investigation revealed a clear "test smell" and pointed the expert to a place in need of a refactoring.

Sneak paths. A surprising connection is provided for the "monster to player" test (*ETE11*), which is connected to "wonSneakPaths" (35). This relates to unit tests aimed at testing for *sneak paths* in state machines, following Binder's test approach for state machines [1]. A sneak path is an illegal transition, and the JPacman sneak path test cases verify that illegal ⟨state, event⟩ pairs do not lead to a state change. To do so, the test case brings the application in the desired state (e.g., *Playing*, or *Died*), and then attempts to trigger a state change.

The process of bringing the application in a given state, however, may bear similarity with other test cases. For example in unit test 35, the player first wins. Then multiple steps, such as the player getting caught by a monster or the player running into a monster, are triggered which should not change the state from "won" to "lost" anymore. As this triggers the player to die or being killed, this sneak path test case shows up as being related not only to end-to-end tests triggering winning situations. A better separation of set-up logic (bringing the application in the right state) and executing the method-under-test would help reveal more focused associations.

Deviations. *Moving beyond border.* ETE02 is the only test which does not map to a top match within the first 5 results. The first top matches are found from rank 7 onwards. Reasons for this behavior are that *ETE02* is one of the smallest end-to-end tests involving a move, and that testing the behavior for "beyond border" covers branches that only lead to different data, not different calls made. All 5 high ranked results correctly involve doing a move. After investigation of the results, the expert reports that the unit test cases indicated as related in the conceptual mapping do a bit more than only a move (e.g. an undo operation), which is why our approach gives these unit tests a lower rank.

Move to Wall. ETE03 contains the only unrelated connection within the top 10 results: on rank 9 is the "possible move" test. On the other hand, counterpart test "impossible move" is a top match.

Disparate test sizes. The main deviations (tests marked as unrelated being ranked higher than tests marked as related) are due to extreme size differences in unit tests. The expert easily relates narrow focused tests, whereby the automatic approach, by design of the shared word count, gives preference to broader tests (which share more events). A prime example is the "wonSneakPaths" test, which is related to many end-to-end tests as it triggers a broad range of functionality. The more equal the amount of functionality tested by the unit test cases is, the better the results revealed by the automatic approach.

Additional Lessons Learned. *API violations.* The smoke test (*ETE14*) consists of a series of events applied to JPacman. As such, it is fairly heterogeneous, doing many different things. This makes it hard to come up with a reasonable positive mapping to unit tests. On the other hand, some unit test cases are not relevant to *any* end-to-end test, including the "smoke test". As an example, tests 57, 58 and 59 deal with using the API in a wrong way, which should generate an appropriate exception. Seeing that these test cases are not related to the smoke test gives confidence that such violations are not possible at a higher level.

Human vs. automated mapping. Fine-grained deviations between tests, like state and specific object instantiations, have been used by the expert to relate tests to each other. For example, for the expert the determining events for relating unit test cases involving moving to end-to-end tests have been the actual actors (objects). The automated approach is able to differentiate similar to an expert between objects. On the other hand, the importance of states for human mappings is not equally reflected by the automated approach as it assigns every event the same importance. Identifying and prioritizing states before the similarity calculation is performed could improve the approximation to the "human" conceptual mapping. As we will see in the second case study, if tests are small and focused, the impact of state changes reflects well in the similarity measurements.

5.3   RQ4: Performance Characteristics

Since JPacman is the larger case study, we will answer RQ4 here. The traces obtained for both case studies are relatively small: the smallest one is 1kb and comprises 2 trace events, the largest being 62Kb and 700 trace events (after applying trace reduction). Similarity calculations within this dimension are computed within 10 seconds for the whole test suite. Even the results for the smoke test of JPacman, comprising approximately 60,000 trace events (4Mb) before reduction, are almost instantly ready after applying trace reduction techniques.

6   Case Study II: Auction Sniper

The second case study revolves around a system developed in strict test-driven development (TDD) manner called Auction Sniper. Its test suite also makes heavy use of mocking techniques in order to isolate unit tests. In contrast to the first case study, where we compare the test relations with a conceptual mapping of an expert, in this case study we investigate the usefulness of the technique to help an outsider understand test relations (RQ2). In addition, we investigate how our technique can cope with the influence of mocking techniques (RQ3).

Auction Sniper is an application which allows to automatically bid in auctions. Auction Sniper watches different auctions and increases the bid in case a higher bid of another bidder arrived until the auction closes or a certain limit has been reached. This system is used as an example in the book "Growing Object-Oriented Software, Guided by Tests" by Freeman et al. [6] to describe TDD techniques. The software and the related tests are explained in detail in this book and are publicly available[9]. The system comprises approximately 2,000 lines of code. The test suite has 1,240 lines of code, which constitute 37 unit tests, 6 end-to-end tests and 2 integration tests.

6.1   Obtaining an Initial Understanding

We analyzed the book and derived an initial understanding of the relations between end-to-end tests and unit tests. The authors always start with an end-to-end test, which kick-starts each development circle for a new functionality, whereby the authors explain each end-to-end test "should have just enough new requirements to force a manageable increase in functionality" [6]. Then, the scaffold implementation of the new functionality follows. Prior to implementation of detailed functionality, the authors develop and explain the necessary unit tests.

Based on this iterative development, we map each unit test case developed within the cycle of an end-to-end (ETE) test as related to this ETE test. We refine this first mapping by identifying the differences of the ETE test cases based on their code. We mapped some unit tests not covered in the book based on their name. In the following we summarize the functionality of the six ETE tests. All unit test case names are given in Table 4 which can be helpful during comprehension of the presented results.

The End-to-End Tests. ETE tests 01 to 06 are actually enhancements of each other, involving a lot of common functionality. The main steps are: 1. An auction sells an item, 2. An auction sniper joins this auction. 3. Then, the auction closes, 4. Finally, the auction sniper shows the outcome of an auction.

In addition, test cases 02 to 05 place actual bids. Only test case 06 deviates from the rest, as it does not close the auction and sends an invalid message. Another main difference between the test cases is the state in which the sniper is when the auction closes. In *ETE01* the sniper is in the state "joining" when the auction closes, which results in a lost auction. In *ETE02* the sniper makes a bid, but loses in the "bidding" state. In *ETE03* the sniper makes a higher bid, and wins in the "winning" state. *ETE04* simply tests that a sniper can bid on two items. The functionality of *ETE03* and *ETE04* is so similar that we will treat them as one test subsequently. In *ETE05* the sniper is already in "losing" state before the auction closes, because of a stop price. *ETE06* tests failure reporting. The test sends an invalid message to the auction and causes the application to throw and handle an error, but leaves the auction unclosed.

6.2   RQ2: Suitability of Measurements for Understanding Test Relations

After measuring the similarity of the tests, we investigate each unit test via code inspection, and assess the ranking and the mapping, which results in the final

---

[9] `https://github.com/sf105/goos-code`

Listing 1.2. Test case: *hasEnoughColumns*

```
@Test public void
isWonWhenAuctionClosesWhileWinning() {
  assertEquals(SniperState.LOST, SniperState.JOINING.whenAuctionClosed());
  assertEquals(SniperState.LOST, SniperState.BIDDING.whenAuctionClosed());
  assertEquals(SniperState.WON, SniperState.WINNING.whenAuctionClosed()); }
```

conceptual mapping illustrated in Table 4. Based on this detailed investigation we finally assess the rankings of the similarity measurements. Below we outline correct identifications, surprises and deviations of the measurements with our initial understanding by sketching groups of unit tests. We will see that the automatic mapping reflects the final mapping derived after in-depth investigation very accurately, and is thus useful for supporting an outsider in understanding the test suite and its relations. The rankings and assessments for the best 5 results are illustrated in Table 2. For test case *ETE06* we present the top 10 results to illustrate the effect of the relevancy support (see Table 3). A ranking is indicated as *optimal* only in case it is highly related and ranked within the top first results. Otherwise, results highly related, or results related are indicated as okay (i.e., *ok*) in case they are within the first 5 results. On the other hand, in case of a related result, which is not highly related, but is ranked before the highly related ones, it is marked as not okay (i.e., *nok*).

Correct Identifications. *Report Close of Auction.* Unit test cases 02, 08, and 09 revolve around reporting the closing of an auction, and are thus indeed related to all ETE tests except to *ETE06*. Nevertheless, each of them provokes a different state of the sniper when the auction closed event takes place. Therefore, the mapping should be the strongest for *ETE01* with test 02, *ETE02* with test 08, *ETE3/04* with test 11, and *ETE05* with test 09. The measurements for these relations accurately reflect those subtle differences.

Notifies Bid Details. Tests 33 and 34 are related to all of the ETE tests, except for *ETE01*, which does not make a bid. As *ETE02* exclusively focuses on bidding, the relation is correctly identified as the strongest for this test. For other tests they appear on ranks 6 and 7.

Mapping per Focus. Test case 03 which only bids correctly achieves the highest rank for test *ETE02*. Test case 10, related to winning an auction, maps to *ETE03/04*. Tests 05, 06 and 09, which address losing before the auction is closed are also correctly identified as highest-ranking results for *ETE05*. Test cases 35-37, and 12-15 are testing the reporting of a failing auction. They are correctly ranked as highly related to *ETE06*. *ETE06* is a good example to demonstrate the impact of the *relevancy support based on occurrence*, described in Section 3.1. Test cases 33 and 34 share more steps with *ETE06* than for example test cases 35 and 37. Both achieve just a similarity ranking of 0.2. Nevertheless, tests 35 and 37 reflect much stronger the focus of *ETE06*. Because 35 and 37 are never indicated as related to any other ETE test, the *relevancy support* pushes them to the top results. The new ranking of, for example test 35, is calculated as its

Table 2. Top 5 similarity rankings for ETE01 to ETE05

ETE 01				ETE 02				ETE 03 & 04				ETE 05			
test	sim	avg	match	test	sim	avg	match	test	sim	avg	match	test	sim	avg	match
02	1.20	1.73	optimal	03	0.55	1.95	optimal	11	0.64	3.15	optimal	05	0.55	1.95	optimal
09	0.67	2.50	ok	08	0.55	2.88	optimal	06	0.55	2.13	ok	06	0.55	2.13	optimal
08	0.67	2.88	ok	11	0.45	3.15	nok	08	0.45	2.88	ok	09	0.55	2.50	optimal
11	0.67	3.15	ok	33	0.44	1.85	ok	10	0.44	1.57	ok	08	0.45	2.88	ok
20	0.50	0.61	ok	34	0.44	1.85	ok	15	0.44	1.77	ok	11	0.45	3.15	ok

similarity divided by the number of times it has been ranked as a result among all tests (i.e., 0.2 divided by 1/6).

Surprises. *Winning and State Transitions.* A surprise was the ranking of test case 20 "isWonWhenAuctionClosesWhileWinning" within the results of *ETE01*, as the name suggests it is rather related to winning (i.e., *ETE03/04*). Inspecting the code, illustrated in Listing 1.2, reveals that the name is misleading as it tests different auction outcomes. Two times the auction is lost, contrary to the name, and it also triggers the rarely addressed state of *ETE01* (i.e., "joining" when the auction is closed). Test case 18 also triggers the transition between each stage and therefore should have a low relation to each of the test cases.

Not bidding, bidding and losing. Test cases 05 and 06, contrary to their name suggestions, do place bids and lose and are therefore also related to other test cases than *ETE06*. Actually only test case 32 does not make a bid, which is correctly mapped to *ETE01* and gets low ratings for the other tests. Since test case 06 also reaches the winning state before losing, the indicated relation to *ETE03/04* in understandable.

Defects and a Failing Auction. We expected test cases 21, 22 to be related to *ETE06*. But, tests 21 and 22 create a different failure as they put the system in a faulty state and assert a specific exception to be thrown. Such a behavior is not triggered in the end-to-end test, and consequently the non-appearance of those test cases for any ETE is correct.

Deviations. *Reporting winning.* Test case 11, which reports that an auction has been won after closing is ranked as the third result for *ETE02* even though this end-to-end test addresses losing. The common events, such as starting an auction, bidding for an item and closing an auction dominate the ranking.

Additional Lessons Learned. *Common functionality.* Some functionality is common to all tests. For example, tests of the class *"SniperTablesModelTest"* check the rendering of the user interface. Tests 01, 16, and 17 trigger common functionality such as adding a sniper and listeners. Such trace events are reduced and can yield to empty test cases. Traces reduced to empty traces are marked as common functionality in the ranking.

6.3   RQ3: Handling Mocking

The test suite of Auction Sniper makes heavy use of the mocking library JMock. Without explicitly addressing mocked types during the analysis test cases in-

Table 3. Similarity rankings for ETE06 with and without support

ETE 06						
test	sim	avg	match	test	sim_s	avg	match
12	0.50	1.59	optimal	13	1.20	0.20	optimal
15	0.50	1.77	optimal	35	1.20	0.20	optimal
14	0.40	1.22	optimal	36	1.20	0.20	optimal
33	0.40	1.85	ok	37	0.60	0.10	optimal
34	0.40	1.85	ok	12	0.60	1.59	optimal
03	0.40	1.95	ok	15	0.60	1.77	optimal
05	0.40	1.95	ok	14	0.48	1.22	optimal
06	0.40	2.13	ok	33	0.48	1.85	ok
10	0.30	1.57	nok	34	0.48	1.85	ok
08	0.30	2.88	nok	03	0.48	1.95	ok

volving mocked classes are ranked very low or as unrelated even though they are highly related. For example, without the mockery aspect test case 35 is not linked to test *ETE06* as the runtime types differ. By addressing mockery classes as described in Section 2.2 we can correctly identify test relations.

7   Discussion

Lessons Learned and Limitations. *Separation of Set-up and Tear-down.* Consistent usage of set-up and tear-down methods improves the similarity results, as it helps in revealing the core functionality and focus of test cases. Test suites which a priori do not use set-up and tear-down methods to structure their test might yield less accurate results.

Performance. The performance of the approach is an important criterion especially if the size and complexity of the system under study increases. During our two case studies, we experienced no performance issues with the systems under study. For larger systems further trace reduction techniques might become necessary [3]. On the other hand, performance depends more on the size of the traces (i.e., amount of functionality covered by a test), than on the number of tests. Test case size is independent of the complexity and size of the systems.

Future Work. *Assertions.* At this stage, our technique does not address the meaning of assertions. As future work, we would like to investigate how the meaning of assertions can influence the ranking of a test case.

Test suite quality inspection. The discovered relations do not only help to see similarity of test cases, they also help to assess the quality of the test suite and discover areas for improvement, e.g., identifying unit test cases that do too much, or identifying behavior which is not addressed by any end-to-end test.

User study. We aim to further investigate the usefulness of our tool through a user study that allows actual developers and testers to work with it.

Threats to Validity. Concerning *external validity*, our case studies address relatively small Java systems. Scalability to larger case studies is a key concern that we aim to address in our future work, making use of case studies from the Eclipse plug-in domain we used in earlier studies (Mylyn, EGit) [8].

Table 4. Final conceptual mapping of end-to-end tests to unit tests

Test Case Name	Test Case	Relation
sniperJoinsAuctionUntilAuctionCloses – ETE01		
notifiesAuctionClosedWhenCloseMessageReceived	≡ 32	highly related
reportsLostWhenAuctionClosesImmediately	≡ 02	highly related
isWonWhenAuctionClosesWhileWinning	≡ 20	related
reportAuctionClosesX	≡ 08, 09, 11	related
sniperMakesAHigherBidButLoses – ETE02		
reportsLostIfAuctionClosesWhenBidding	≡ 08	highly related
bidsHigherAndReportsBiddingWhenNewPriceArrives	≡ 03	highly related
doesNotBidAndReportsLosingIfSubsequentPriceIsAboveStopPrice	≡ 05	related
doesNotBidAndReportsLosingIfPriceAfterWinningIsAboveStopPrice	≡ 06	related
reportAuctionClosesX	≈ 09, 11	related
sniperWinsAnAuctionByBiddingHigher – ETE03 and sniperBidsForMultipleItems – ETE04		
reportsWonIfAuctionClosesWhenWinning	≡ 11	highly related
reportsIsWinningWhenCurrentPriceComesFromSniper	≡ 10	highly related
doesNotBidAndReportsLosingIfPriceAfterWinningIsAboveStopPrice	≡ 06	related
reportAuctionClosesX	≡ 08, 09	related
sniperLosesAnAuctionWhenThePriceIsTooHigh – ETE05		
reportsLostIfAuctionClosesWhenLosing	≡ 09	highly related
doesNotBidAndReportsLosingIfSubsequentPriceIsAboveStopPrice	≡ 05	highly related
doesNotBidAndReportsLosingIfPriceAfterWinningIsAboveStopPrice	≡ 06	highly related
doesNotBidAndReportsLosingIfFirstPriceIsAboveStopPrice	≡ 04	highly related
continuesToBeLosingOnceStopPriceHasBeenReached	≡ 07	highly related
(reportAuctionClosesX)	≡ 08, 11	related
sniperReportsInvalidAuctionMessageAndStopsRespondingToEvents – ETE06		
notifiesAuctionFailedWhenBadMessageReceived	≡ 35	highly related
notifiesAuctionFailedWhenEventTypeMissing	≡ 36	highly related
writesMessageTranslationFailureToLog	≡ 37	highly related
reportsFailedIfAuctionFailsWhenBidding	≡ 12	highly related
reportsFailedIfAuctionFailsImmediately	≡ 13	highly related
reportsFailedIfAuctionFailsWhenLosing	≡ 14	highly related
reportsFailedIfAuctionFailsWhenWinning	≡ 15	highly related
ETE 01 – 06		
transitionsBetweenStates	≡ 18	related
ETE 02 – 06		
bidsHigherAndReportsBiddingWhenNewPriceArrives	≡ 03	related
ETE 02 - 05		
notifiesBidDetailsWhenCurrentPriceMessageReceivedFromOtherBidder	≡ 33	related
notifiesBidDetailsWhenCurrentPriceMessageReceivedFromSniper	≡ 34	related
Common functionality and UI		
UI related tests (e.g. test of class SniperTablesModelTest)	≡ 23 – 31	related
Listeners and common states	≡ 01, 16, 17	related
Functionality not addressed by any ETE		
defectIfAuctionClosesWhenWon	≡ 21	unrelated
defectIfAuctionClosesWhenLost	≡ 22	unrelated

With respect to *internal validity*, the main threat consists of the manually obtained conceptual mapping. Creating such a mapping is inherently subjective, as illustrated by the process we applied to the Auction Sniper case study.

In order to reduce *threats to reliability* and to improve repeatability, both our tool and the systems under study are available to other researchers.

8   Related Work

An initial catalogue of *test smells* negatively affecting understanding was presented by Van Deursen et al., together with a set of corresponding refactorings [5]. Later, a thorough treatment of the topic of refactoring test code was provided by Meszaros [10]. Van Rompaey et al. continued this line of work by studying automated analysis of these smells [13].

Tools for assisting in the understanding of test suites have been proposed by Cornelissen et al., who present a visualization of test suites as sequence diagrams [2]. Greiler et al. propose higher level visualizations, aimed at assisting developers in seeing plug-in interactions addressed by their test suites [8].

Galli et al. have developed a tool to order broken unit tests [7]. It is their aim to create a hierarchical relation between broken unit tests, so that the most specific unit test that fails can be inspected first. In essence, their technique allows to steer and optimize the debugging process.

Rothermel and Harrold discuss safe regression testing techniques in [11]; regression test selection techniques try to find those tests that are directly responsible for testing the changed parts of a program and subsequently only run these tests. Hurdugaci and Zaidman operationalize this in the IDE for unit tests [9].

Yoo et al. cluster test cases based on their similarity to support experts in test case prioritisation, which outperforms coverage-based prioritisation [15].

9   Conclusion

In this paper we showed how a combination of *dynamic analysis* and the shared word count metric can be used to establish relations between end-to-end and unit tests in order to assist developers in their (test suite) maintenance activities.

We evaluated our *test connection mining* techniques in two case studies, by elaborating the usefulness of the approach to improve understanding. We saw that after using the proposed trace reduction techniques our approach produces accurate test mappings, which can help to 1) identify relevant tests, 2) understand the functionality of a test by describing high-level test cases with related unit test cases and 3) reveal blank spots in the investigated unit test suites.

Contributions. The contributions of this paper are 1) tracing and trace reduction techniques tailored for handling test code, including test specific events such as set-up, tear-down and mocking 2) an assessment of the usefulness of the rankings based on two case studies, 3) the development of a *Test Similarity Correlator*, a framework for mining test connections.

References

1. Binder, R.V.: Testing Object-Oriented Systems: Models, Patterns, and Tools. Addison-Wesley Professional (October 1999)
2. Cornelissen, B., van Deursen, A., Moonen, L., Zaidman, A.: Visualizing testsuites to aid in software understanding. In: Proc. of the European Conference on Software Maintenance and Reengineering (CSMR), pp. 213–222. IEEE CS (2007)
3. Cornelissen, B., Moonen, L., Zaidman, A.: An assessment methodology for trace reduction techniques. In: Proc. Int'l Conf. Software Maintenance (ICSM), pp. 107–116. IEEE CS (2008)

4. Cornelissen, B., Zaidman, A., van Deursen, A., Moonen, L., Koschke, R.: A systematic survey of program comprehension through dynamic analysis. IEEE Transactions on Software Engineering 35(5), 684–702 (2009)
5. van Deursen, A., Moonen, L., van Den Bergh, A., Kok, G.: Refactoring test code. In: Extreme Programming Perspectives, pp. 141–152. Addison Wesley (2002)
6. Freeman, S., Pryce, N.: Growing Object-Oriented Software, Guided by Tests, 1st edn. Addison-Wesley Professional (2009)
7. Galli, M., Lanza, M., Nierstrasz, O., Wuyts, R.: Ordering broken unit tests for focused debugging. In: Int'l Conf. Softw. Maintenance (ICSM), pp. 114–123. IEEE (2004)
8. Greiler, M., Groß, H.G., van Deursen, A.: Understanding plug-in test suites from an extensibility perspective. In: Proceedings Working Conference on Reverse Engineering (WCRE), pp. 67–76. IEEE CS (2010)
9. Hurdugaci, V., Zaidman, A.: Aiding developers to maintain developer tests. In: Conf. Softw. Maintenance and Reengineering (CSMR), pp. 11–20. IEEE CS (2012)
10. Meszaros, G.: xUnit Test Patterns: Refactoring Test Code. Addison-Wesley (2007)
11. Rothermel, G., Harrold, M.: Empirical studies of a safe regression test selection technique. IEEE Transactions on Software Engineering 24(6), 401–419 (1998)
12. Stephen, G.A.: String searching algorithms. World Scientific Publishing Co. (1994)
13. Van Rompaey, B., Du Bois, B., Demeyer, S., Rieger, M.: On the detection of test smells: A metrics-based approach for general fixture and eager test. IEEE Transactions on Software Engineering 33(12), 800–817 (2007)
14. Weiss, S., Indurkhya, N., Zhang, T., Damerau, F.: Text Mining: Predictive Methods for Analyzing Unstructured Information. Springer (2004)
15. Yoo, S., Harman, M., Tonella, P., Susi, A.: Clustering test cases to achieve effective and scalable prioritisation incorporating expert knowledge. In: Proceedings of the Eighteenth International Symposium on Software Testing and Analysis, ISSTA 2009, pp. 201–212. ACM, New York (2009)
16. Zaidman, A., Van Rompaey, B., van Deursen, A., Demeyer, S.: Studying the co-evolution of production and test code in open source and industrial developer test processes through repository mining. Empir. Softw. Eng. 16(3), 325–364 (2011)

Enhancing OSGi with Explicit, Vendor Independent Extra-Functional Properties*

Kamil Ježek, Premek Brada, and Lukáš Holý

Department of Computer Science and Engineering
University of West Bohemia
Univerzitni 8, 30614 Pilsen, Czech Republic
{kjezek,brada,lholy}@kiv.zcu.cz

Abstract. Current industry and research organisations invest considerable effort to adopt component based programming which is promising rapid development process. Several issues, however, hinder its wider adoption. One of them is the practical use of extra-functional properties (EFPs) that research community aims at integrating to component composition but for which industrial applications are still rare. When extra-functional properties are not considered or mis-interpreted, inconsistencies in application performance, security, reliability, etc. can result at run-time. As a possible solution we have proposed a general extra-functional properties system called EFFCC. In this paper we show how it can be applied to an industrial component model, namely the OSGi framework. This work analyses OSGi from the extra-functional properties viewpoint and shows how it can be enhanced by EFPs, expressed as OSGi capabilities. The proposed benefits of the presented approach are seamless integration of such properties into an existing framework and consistency of their interpretation among different vendors. This should support easier adoption of extra-functional properties in practice.

Keywords: Component, Extra-functional, Compatibility, Binding, OSGi.

1 Introduction

With today's need for large and complex software, industry and the research community invest considerable effort to component based programming. Despite partial success, several issues remain unsolved. One of the important ones concerns the usage of extra-functional properties (EFPs) that should improve compatibility verifications of the components.

On the one hand, EFPs and their use in component models are an area of active research. On the other hand, practically used industrial models such as

---

* The work was partially supported by the UWB grant SGS-2010-028 Advanced Computer and Information Systems and by the Czech Science Foundation project 103/11/1489 Methods of development and verification of component-based applications using natural language specifications.

C.A. Furia and S. Nanz (Eds.): TOOLS Europe 2012, LNCS 7304, pp. 108–123, 2012.

OSGi or Spring only slowly adopt systematic EFP support. One of the reasons may be wide misunderstanding of what EFPs are [9] that eventually leads to only a partial and non-systematic EFPs adoption in practice. As a suggested solution, a general mechanism consolidating EFPs understanding among different vendors as well as different applications, called EFFCC[1], has been proposed in our previous work[2] [13]. In this paper, the application of the mechanism to OSGi as a demonstration of its abilities is presented.

Dealing with the discrepancies in EFP terminology, the following generic definition will be used within this paper while other possible options of EFP understanding will be omitted:

> An extra-functional property holds any information, explicitly provided by a software system, to specify a characteristic of the system apart from its genuine functionality to enrich client's understanding of usage of the system supported by technical [computational] means.

This paper first overviews other related approaches in Section 2. Then, a summary of the current OSGi specification and its abilities to express EFPs (according to the given definition) is provided in Section 3. Finally, Section 4 introduces the application of EFPs in OSGi using the EFFCC mechanism [13] and discusses pros and cons of the approach.

2   Related Work

EFP systems have been addressed from several directions and a lot of approaches have been proposed. For instance, one group of approaches proposes independent descriptions of EFPs [7,1,17,11,18]. While this group splits the EFP description from their application, a different group concerns modelling of the EFPs as a part of a software design [16]. These groups treat EFPs rather independently. On the other hand, comprehensive component models exists which take EFPs natively into account [2,27].

Concerning EFP specification, one of the approaches is to employ an ordinary programming code. Examples are: NoFun [7] describes EFPs in a general manner first, then the definitions are applicable to software systems; CQML [1] uses named *Quality Characteristic* with their constraints assigned in *Quality Statement* and put into *Quality Profile* on a component; CQML+ [26] is an extension of CQML allowing to define dependencies of components on runtime environment. These dependencies also allow to express Deployment Contracts [17]. There also exist a lot of specialized languages: TADL [18] for security and safety, HQML [11] for web-development, or SLAng for service-level agreement [15].

QML/CS deals with EFPs in terms of a language as well as formal approach. A system is modelled using Temporal Logic of Actions (TLA+) [16] that specifies

---

[1] Extra-functional properties Featured Compatibility Checks.
[2] Project hosted at: http://assembla.com/spaces/efps

a system as states with traces among the states. The system is called feasible (fulfilling requirements) if the combination of intrinsic, resource and container models implies the extrinsic ones. Other approaches cover component models and frameworks with native EFP support.

Palladio [2] comprises a software architecture simulator, which focuses on performance, reliability, maintainability, and cost for the architecture realization prediction. All of these can be analysed in the Palladio Component Model allowing to make the balance among EFP to achieve desired trade-offs. It is able to accomplish a model-to-model transformation of an architectural model to a stochastic process algebra automatically and then evaluate the algebraical expressions analytically. It uses extended UML State Diagrams to model states of a system with performance characteristics on the diagram edges. Palladio allows deriving the right software architecture design, on the other hand stochastic probabilities and models settings rely on correct human estimation.

Procom [27] defines Attributable elements that consist of a type and one or more values. The ability to store multiple values for one attribute comes from the Procom's concept of refining attributes during the development process. The values consist of data, metadata and conditions under which each attribute is valid. Data is a generic structure which can be specialized into simple data types or a reference to an object. It also enables attribute compositions to get an attribute for the composite component as well as defining the attribute value for composite component explicitly. User is able to select the attributes by versions or configuration filters. The selection may comprise a number of conditions combining AND/OR operators, attribute metadata and Latest, Timestamp, and Versionname keywords. As a result, Procom can define EFPs for different deployment runtime and compose complex properties.

SOFA 2.0 [5] has components and connectors and the key abstraction is metamodelling using MOF [21]. SOFA's concepts such as automatic reconfiguration, behaviour specifications or dynamic evaluation of an architecture at runtime extends a simple functionality and it may be understood as extra-functionality.

Further, specialised component models are: Robocop [19,3] dealing with realtime characteristics for portable or embedded devices; PECOS [8,20] using Petri Nets to model timing and synchronising behaviour of a system. Developers separately model behaviour of each component and the components are composed using a scheduler to coordinate the composition of Petri Nets.

An issue also being solved is modelling of EFPs. For instance, the OMG group standardized a UML profile [22] covering the quality of services, or MARTE [23] for real-time and embedded systems. Furthermore, UML Profiles for NoFun [4] or CQML [1] have been developed.

On the other side, widely used industrial frameworks OSGi (detailed in Section 3), Spring [28], EJB [6] use advanced features such as localisation, transaction, user privileges, synchronisation, composition specification (e.g. @Qualifier annotation in Spring allows to specialise candidates to the Dependency Injection) that may be understand as EFPs. However, they still do not provide a systematic EFP approach.

3   Overview of Extra-Functionality in OSGi

The OSGi specification [25] is an approach to modularised Java-based applications adopting several aspects of component based programming as it has been stated by Szyperski [29]. In a nutshell, a component is a Java .jar file (possibly) developed by third parties and independently deployable to its runtime.

OSGi introduces the concept of Bundles as the components. The bundles encapsulate main communication mean, services, in a form of Java classes implementing Java interfaces. Each bundle explicitly exports and imports its packages and explicitly registers and obtains services. The package and service based communication is the main concept and other extensive means such as remote service calls will be omitted here. OSGi runtime then accesses only these packages and services while other ones are hidden. The hiding is technically realised by using separate classloaders for each bundle. This considerably distinguishes OSGi bundles from the standard Java .jar files where only coarse-grained accessibility modifiers (`public`, `private` or `protected`) are provided.

The OSGi specification allows to express restrictions that influences binding of the packages as well as the service lookup. Although they are not called EFPs in the OSGi specification, they may be understood as EFPs.

It is worth mentioning OSGi supports e.g. security concerning signed .jar files, certificates or Remote services calls. Although it goes behind genuine services' function, this work concerns only the properties extending the binding process.

3.1   Motivation: Components Enriched with EFPs

This section shows an example component application enriched with EFPs. The example has been inspired by the Nokia adaptation of the web browser product line [12]. In Nokia's project, components to develop a variety of browsers have been designed. The components follow a structure of web browsers presented in [10] a subset of which is shown in Fig. 1. For simplicity, only the sub-part rendering web pages loaded via the Internet is shown. Following Fig. 1, `RenderingEngine` loads raw HTTP data via the `Networking` interface and renders HTML pages using `CSS`, `HTML` and `JS` components. The `UI` interface accesses platform dependent libraries to draw User Interface primitives. Finally, the pages are provided by the `RenderingQuery` interface. Their consequent processing is omitted here.

Fig. 1 furthermore shows some EFPs (shown as UML notes) expressing selected web browser characteristics. The EFPs concern several disjunctive domain dependent areas. A first domain covers performance (a network speed and a speed to process HTML, CSS and JavaScript), a second domain covers different operating systems (a user interface library – `ui_library` and dynamic HTML support – `dhtml` – depending on graphical libraries provided by the operating system) and the last one covers domain constant characteristics (JavaScript, CSS and HTML versions).

Section 3.2 will show ability and limitation of expressing such properties in current OSGi while Section 4 will show our approach aiming at avoided the detected limitations.

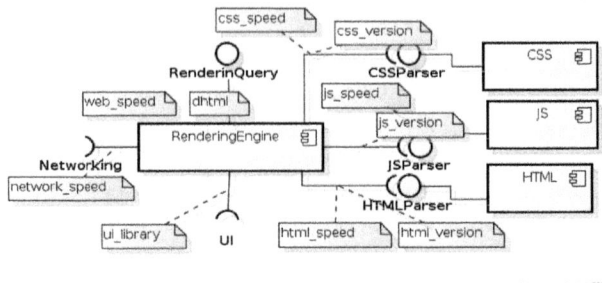

Fig. 1. Example Web Browser Components

3.2 OSGi Parameters, Attributes and Filters

The following parts of this section show four OSGi aspects that have been localised as allowing to express certain EFPs.

Parametrised Exports and Imports. OSGi binding process matches exported and imported packages that consist of a name and a set of parameters. For instance, a bundle implementing operations on HTML pages for a web browser may declare the following package export:

```
Bundle-Name: HTML
Export-Package: cz.zcu.kiv.web.html;version=1.3,html_version=5.0
```

A bundle rendering the web pages requires the `html` package to parse the web pages:

```
Bundle-Name: RenderingEngine
Import-Package: cz.zcu.kiv.web.html;version=1.3;
   resolution:=optional,html_version=5.0
```

A variety of built-in as well as user defined parameters may be used. In this example, `version` and `resolution` are built-in parameters while `html_version` is a user-defined one. Specialising fine-grained binding constraints, `html_version` has been used to define a HTML version these bundles provide/require.

Although these parameters may express EFPs, OSGi lacks their common understanding. Some parameters have a specialised meaning, however, the meaning is defined only in the OSGi text specification with no technical support. User defined parameters are only ad-hoc definitions. Hence, it is a question of how these parameters may be used across different vendors. For instance, if one vendor provides the `html_version` parameter, a different vendor does not have to even know of the existence of the parameter.

Provided and Required Capabilities. In contrary to the packages' parameters, the capabilities are attributes and filters counter elements. The attributes are typed name-value pairs while filters are LDAP conditions over the attributes.

In addition, the capabilities are bound to name spaces that are supposed to explicitly assign them with semantics.

For instance, a bundle from the web browser domain responsible for drawing user interfaces may require some graphical libraries:

```
Bundle-Name: UIBackand
Require-Capability: osgi.ee;
   filter:="(|(ui_library=GTK)(ui_library=Qt))"
```

The example shows an LDAP filter that constraints `ui_library` to either GTK or Qt libraries. The Execution Environment name space (`osgi.ee`) is an OSGi predefined one, however, users may also use their own ones.

Provided capabilities are set as OSGi runtime parameters or by other bundles. Using the latter case, a bundle may provide the `ui_library` (a different name space signals it is not a Runtime Environment attribute):

```
Bundle-Name: UILibrary
Provide-Capability: cz.zcu.kiv.web.ui;ui_library=Qt
```

A set of predefined name spaces exists[3] as well as any user defined one may be created. Despite the name spaces aim at providing the parameters with semantic, it still lacks of common understanding. There is no technical mean to distribute existing name spaces across vendors.

Parametrised Services. Each bundle may register a service and the registration may contain a set of attributes. An LDAP filter may be then used to obtain the service according to the attributes used in its registration. This principle is equivalent to the capabilities.

OSGi API is called within the bundles' source code to register and get the services. This approach is awkward because a developer of one bundle should have to study the source code of another bundle to find out which parameters are actually used.

A way to register and get a `Networking` service stating its *Network speed* attribute may look as follows:

```
Hashtable ht = new HashTable();
ht.put("network_speed", 10);
bundleContext.registerService(Networking.class, this, ht);
```

It is assumed that `bundleContext` is a reference to the `BundleContext` class specified in OSGi. The different bundle may obtain it according to a filter condition:

```
Collection<ServiceReferences<Networking>> services = bundleContext
   .getServiceReferences(Networking.class,
      "(network_speed >= 10)");
```

---

[3] Current list is available at http://www.osgi.org/headers (2011).

Notice that apart from the capabilities, there is no name space definition. Together with different concepts to express import/export parameters, filters used for capabilities and non-transparent usage of parametrised services, this brings yet another ambiguity to the concept.

Parametrised Declarative Services. Introduction of Declarative Services to OSGi specification aims at avoiding drawbacks of Services mentioned above. The registration concept has been replaced by Dependency Injection defined in XML files distributed with bundles.

Although the explicit publication of Declarative Services outside the source code is considerable improvement, the attribute-filter concept remains unchanged. The XML files contain specific elements to express the attributes and filters described in the OSGi Service Compendium [24].

4   Our Approach: Explicit Extra-Functional Properties in OSGi

Although OSGi contains variety of properties that may be considered as EFPs, it has been already mentioned its approach is weak in terms of semantics, general understanding, exchange and evaluation of EFPs. In this section a novel approach aimed at these deficiencies will be presented. The approach uses a general extra-functional properties framework called EFFCC [13] applied to OSGi.

In nutshell, EFFCC is the implementation of a general extra-functional properties support consisting of remotely accessible EFPs storage, tools to apply the EFPs to components and an embeddable evaluator. The EFPs storage is implemented as a JEE[4] Server and the tools are Java desktop applications described in our previous work [13]. The embeddable evaluator provides a generic evaluation mechanism also implemented in Java that is included into existing Java-based component frameworks via a set of extension points.

Fig. 2 overviews the main usage concept: describing the image from left to right, independent (worldwide) vendors develop their components accessing common EFPs storage first. Another vendor then uses the components to assembly an application verifying the components are compatible for the assembly.

Another EFFCC novelty is the split of component development and deployment phases in which different process of EFPs work-flow is used. First, the EFPs are loaded from the repository (using the tool) via the Internet and applied to components in the development phase. The EFPs are copied from the repository and mirrored on the components which furthermore causes the components may be used in the off-line mode without the Internet connection in the assembly or deployment phase.

Main advantage of this solution lies in the repository that unifies EFPs and thus improves EFPs' understanding among the vendors. Apart from any kind of written documentation, the EFP understanding is here supported by a technical mean instantly available to general usage.

---

[4] Java Enterprise Edition.

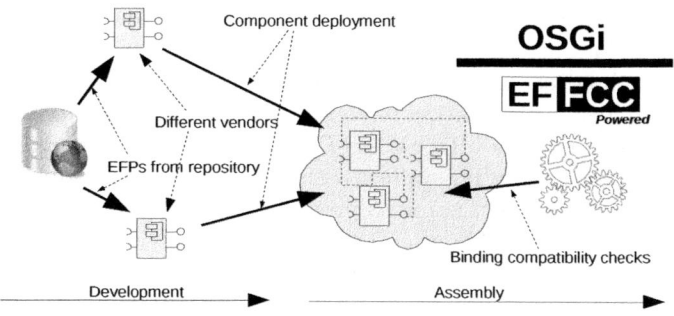

Fig. 2. Development Process with EFFCC on OSGi

As a result, this concept should prevent misunderstanding and improve consolidation of EFPs used among components provided by different vendors and integrated to a final application. As it will be shown later, the repository is capable of holding more detailed information about EFPs than e.g. the OSGi name spaces.

In this work, EFFCC is embedded to OSGi enriching its binding process explicitly considering the binding parameters, attributes and filters as EFPs. The main idea, which will be detailed later in this work, is that the OSGi binding integrates data from the EFP repository unifying their semantics.

The EFFCC mechanism uses approach that splits component model dependent and independent part. The independent part holds the most logic related to EFPs' operations in an abstracted form while the dependent part is a light-weighted layer customising the abstract form to the concrete component model implementation. A benefit is that a common logic may be re-used among multiple component models while a little of additional code must be written to apply the approach to a concrete component model. A detailed description of the independent part, abstract EFPs' definitions and the evaluator algorithm have been already given in our previous work [13] while this work details the application of the component model dependent part, in particular to OSGi.

4.1   Structure of the EFP Data

Although the abstract EFP definitions have been already formalised in [14], a short overview will be provided here to support the fluency of the text. The repository stores EFPs as tuples $e = (n, E_d, \gamma, V, M)$ where tuple elements respectively represent: n the name of the property, $E_d = \{e_i \mid i = 1 \cdots N, N > 0\}$ a set of properties deriving (composing) this property, $\gamma : V \times V \to \mathbb{Z}$ a gamma function comparing two property values, V data type and M extensible set of meta informations.

The repository itself is named Global Registry and formalised as: $GR = (id, name, \{e_i \mid i = 1 \cdots N, N > 0\})$. It means the repository has a unique identifier (id) a human readable name ($name$) and it lists the EFPs. One Global Registry represents one domain of usage and it is furthermore segmented to a set of sub-domains for different area-of-usage. Each such a sub-domain is called Local Registry formalised as: $LR = (id, GR, name, \{LR_i \mid i = 1 \cdots N, N > 0\}, S, D)$ holding a unique identifier (id), a reference to its Global Registry (GR), a name ($name$), a set of other Local Registries (LR_i) that this Local Registry aggregates.

S and D are sets holding values assigned for this particular sub-domain. Shortly, the S set assigns a name to property values giving them semantic and rounding their precision while the D set assigns formulas evaluating the derived properties from the deriving ones. Due to the space constrains, detail formalisation is not provided here and may be found in [14].

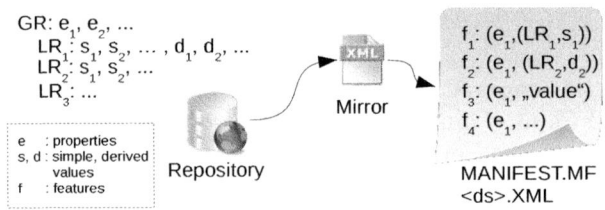

Fig. 3. A Mirrored Repository Assigned to a Bundle

4.2   Specifying EFPs as OSGi Attributes

The application of this EFP mechanism in OSGi is shown in Fig. 3. Its realisation stores the component model independent EFP data as an XML file distributed together with each bundle. In addition, this EFP data are linked to a bundle in the manifest file format or the declarative service XML descriptor via the existing means described in Section 3. It creates a set of all possible assignments $F \times E \times V_A$ where F is a set of all component features (e.g. Bundle packages or services), E is a set of properties from current GR ($e \in E \in GR$) and V_A is a set of assigned values that includes a value from LR, directly assigned value of the V type or a computed value.

The advantage of this solution is that the EFP data are written in a manner similar to the existing OSGi attributes and filters. In addition, a more precise semantic is stored in the unified XML file. While the OSGi resolving process treats these EFPs as standard attributes and filters, the EFP mechanism triggered in the resolving process evaluates also these additional data, resulting in more precise compatibility checks.

OSGi EFP Attributes. Designing a new concept of EFPs, still compatible with current OSGi attributes, lead to the following proposed structure of the EFP attributes:

```
<gr-id>.<efp>=<lr-id>.<value>
```

Here `efp` is a string name of an EFP and `gr-id` is a unique identifier of Global Registry this property is defined for. Furthermore, `lr-id` is a unique identifier of Local Registry and `value` is a value assigned to the EFP. The value form will differ depending on a Registry used. If the `lr-id` is omitted, the EFP has a value assigned that is valid among the domain Global Registry it has been created for. In this case, either a concrete value or a computing formula may be used. It is proposed to use a string representation of concrete values and string representation of formulas evaluating computed values.

If the `lr-id` prefix is used, the value is related to Local Registry (sub-domain of Global Registry) and a named value or a formula deriving a derived property may be used. It is proposed to use a string name for the named values (e.g. "small", "slow", "high", "fast") directly to represent named intervals assigned in respective Local Registry and the literal `"computed"` for the deriving rules. The deriving rules itself will be stored in the XML file.

For instance, two attributes may be defined as: `1.network_speed=1.fast` and `1.html_version=[4.0..5.0]` where $fast = [10..100]$ Mb/s is an interval stored in XML and $[4.0..5.0]$ is a directly assigned interval. A small drawback of this solution may be that the named values are not known without looking into related XML files. However, it is assumed users will access the data via the provided tools and thus do not need to access manifest files manually.

EFP Attribute Data Type. A task related to EFP attributes is their evaluation. Original OSGi specification allows to define a data type of the value (e.g. Long, Double, String, Version, using a colon syntax) that in essence denotes the comparing method to be used. User defined types may be also used. Hence, the writing `:EFP` (e.g. `1.html_version:EFP=[4.0..5.0]`) causes the values to be bound to the new EFP data type and OSGi tries to load a respective class named `EFP`. This class is implemented in EFFCC as an adapter which delegates the evaluation to the EFP system, concretely to the respective gamma function defined for each EFP and stored in the XML file. Since not all OSGi implementations currently handle the data type concept[5], a temporal solution is to store all EFP-related attributes in a separate file distributed along the manifest file.

The attributes defined this way may be used in all OSGi parts mentioned in Section 3 (exported packages, provided capabilities and registered services). One exception is that the parameters on exported packages do not allow to define the data type. These parameters use only string comparison. This is a restriction inherited from older OSGi specification which cannot be overcome for compatibility reasons. On the other hand, the parametrised package export/import may be replaced by capability wiring allowing full attributes/filter evaluation. For instance, a provided/required capabilities' pair may look like:

```
Provided-Capability: osgi.wiring.package;
  (osgi.wiring.package=cz.zcu.kiv.web.html,
    1.html_version=[4.0..5.0]
```

---

[5] Apache Felix for example, which is used in our experiments.

```
Required-Capability: osgi.wiring.package;
  (&(osgi.wiring.package=cz.zcu.kiv.web.html)
    (1.html_version=4.0))
```

This notation expresses package export and import. It is also worth pointing out that the study of the Apache Felix OSGi implementation have also shown a tendency to internally express export/import packages as these wiring capabilities. Therefore, there is a chance this approach may be a recommended practise in the future while export/import package headers may be marked as obsolete.

4.3   EFP Queries as OSGi Filters

Having the attributes defined according to rules mentioned in previous section, the OSGi filters may be used the same way as it is described in the OSGi specification. When OSGi applies the filters, it compares values required by the filter with the values of provided attributes. As long as the provided attributes are defined together with a Bundle, EFFCC loads them and a filter is evaluated delegating each value comparing to the EFFCC implementation (described in Section 4.5).

For instance, a filter may be defined as: (1.network_speed>=1.slow) to filter a network service with at least a "slow" connection where the value $slow = [1..10]Mb/s$ will be loaded from the XML file when the filter is being evaluated.

As a result, the filters are used transparently without explicitly considering EFPs while EFFCC running behind treats the values as extra-functional ones. The main advantage is that OSGi implementation is enriched with EFPs providing better semantic than OSGi standard means, however, modification to neither OSGi specification nor implementation is required.

4.4   An Example: EFPs in XML Mirror and OSGi Manifest

Section 3.1 showing a few OSGi bundles will be in this section completed by the example of the EFP data assigned to the bundles.

Fig. 4 depicts a shortened version of the EFP XML repository and attributes plus filters referring to these EFPs. The XML contains definitions of EFPs originating from one Global Registry (the gr element) and several disjunctive Local Registries (the lr element).

The example shows two Local Registries with IDs 463 and 464 designed for different performance platforms and Local Registry with ID 465 for a concrete operating system. It is assumed these values are understood as the most typical ones for respective platforms. Hence, deployment of such components may use compatibility verifications according to these platforms. This may look as a weakness because this approach requires measurement of all components in all assumed platforms. On the other hand, vendors should test their products for all the platforms to ensure quality and this approach provides a technical mean to express and publish component measurement results together with the component.

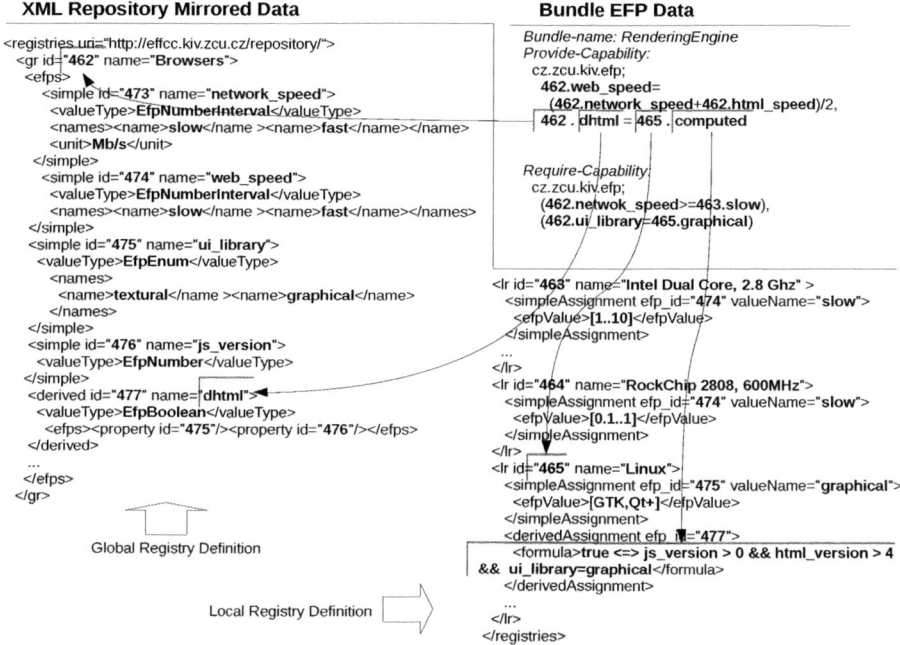

Fig. 4. Example EFPs Applied in OSGi

The case-study furthermore shows several kind of assignable values: (1) `web_speed` is specialised using a mathematical function, (2) `dhtml` has a value assigned for which computation is expressed as a logical formula in Local Registry with ID 465, and (3) `network_speed` is used in a filter referencing the value `slow` from Local Registry ID 463. The last type of value – directly assigned – is not used in the example.

4.5   EFP Evaluation Connected to OSGi Binding

A crucial moment to integrate EFFCC to OSGi is to invoke the evaluation of EFPs at the moment OSGi performs binding of bundle features (e.g. packages or capabilities) or bundles service lookup. OSGi version 4.3 have brought the concept of hooks that may be used to observe and modify the bundles' binding in their life-cycle. A hook is an implementation of a specific interface with a set of call-back methods invoked once a particular operation is performed. According to features described in Section 3 two hooks have been implemented to bridge OSGi binding and EFP evaluation.

The first hook implements the `ResolverHook` interface with a method:

```
void filterMatches(BundleRequirement requirement,
  Collection<BundleCapability> candidates)
```

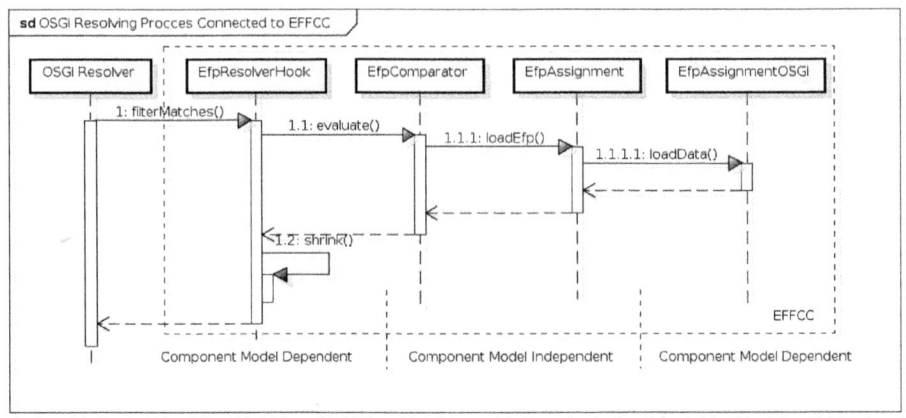

Fig. 5. EFFCC Connected to OSGi Resolver Process

This method is called every time the framework is to bind one feature to another one. The first method argument is a requirement that can be fulfilled by capabilities in the second argument. Concrete implementation may remove an item from the capabilities collection to prevent the binding.

This is the moment at which EFFCC evaluation is called. The sequence of calls is depicted in Fig. 5. Once the `filterMatches` method is called, EFFCC adaptor to OSGi (`EfpResolverHook`) invokes `EfpComparator` that consequently loads EFP data from a bundle using `EfpAssignment`. The data are evaluated and a result is returned to the hook. If the matched EFPs are incompatible, the capabilities collection is shrunk which excludes the capability from the binding.

The only implementation necessary to adapt EFFCC to OSGi have been the `EfpResolverHook` class and an EfpAssignment sub-module (`EfpAssignmentOSGi`) loading the EFP data from the OSGi bundles. All other parts are component model independent and re-usable among variety of different systems. It is also important to highlight that the amount of program code written in `EfpResolverHook` and `EfpAssignmentOSGi` is considerably smaller comparing to the code used in other EFFCC modules. As a result, a noticeable strength of this approach is that it requires only a little code to be implemented while most logic have been already pre-prepared.

The other hook implements the `FindHook` interface. This hook covers service dynamism and it is invoked every time a bundle tries to get a service from its bundle context or a declarative service is to be injected. The only method of the hook is:

```
void find(BundleContext context, String name, String filter,
    boolean allServices, Collection<ServiceReference<?>> references);
```

The implementation of this hook may filter the service references, returning a shrunk collection of available references. The work-flow is similar to that presented for the Resolver Hook: once the EFFCC implementation of `FindHook` receives a request for a service, the EFFCC modules are invoked to load and compare EFP data. If the EFP data are incompatible, the respective service reference is removed from the `references` collection preventing a bundle to obtain it. Because of the similarity with the Resolver Hook process, a detailed sequence diagram is not provided here.

To sum up, the implementation of the mentioned two hooks covers both static binding of bundle features stated in the manifest file and dynamic finding of services among bundles. Therefore, static features (export/import packages, capabilities) as well as dynamic features (services, declarative services) from Section 3 are covered which fulfils the main goal of this work.

5   Conclusion

This paper has pointed out a discrepancy in the use of extra-functional properties in research and industrial component models caused among other reasons by a weak standardisation of properties' understanding. OSGi has been selected as one of the industrial models and discussion of its possibilities to express EFPs have been provided. The discussion has shown that OSGi is capable of defining certain EFPs, however, their semantic is weak.

The main contribution of this paper is the demonstration of how an existing component model may be enriched with a strong EFP support. It has been demonstrated that our previously proposed mechanism that consolidates EFP understanding among vendors and component models can be used to enhance OSGi with better EFP support. Thanks to the design of the mechanism which separates the component model dependent and independent parts, we could reuse the latter part in full. The former part consists of a semantic rich EFP definitions stored in unified XML format.

In this particular work, two extensions to OSGi have been proposed. First, OSGi parameters, attributes and filters are used to link independent EFP definitions with concrete OSGi bundle features. Secondly, this work uses the concept of OSGi hooks that invokes EFP evaluation as bundles are being resolved or bundle services are being found. Comparing to plain OSGi, this new approach adds better EFP semantics with EFPs consolidated among multiple vendors since EFPs come from the common repository. The means to express EFPs for different applications are also provided using a layered structure of the repository where each layer targets a concrete application.

References

1. Aagedal, J.Ø.: Quality of Service Support in Development of Distributed Systems. Ph.D. thesis, University of Oslo (2001)
2. Becker, S., Koziolek, H., Reussner, R.: The Palladio component model for model-driven performance prediction. Journal of Systems and Software 82(1), 3–22 (2009), special Issue: Software Performance - Modeling and Analysis

3. Bondarev, E., Chaudron, M.R., de With, P.H.: Compositional performance analysis of component-based systems on heterogeneous multiprocessor platforms. In: Proceedings of Euromicro Conference on Software Engineering and Advanced Applications, pp. 81–91. IEEE Computer Society (2006)

4. Botella, P., Burgues, X., Franch, X., Huerta, M., Salazaruml, G.: Modeling non-functional requirements. In: Proceedings of Jornadas de Ingenieria de Requisitos Aplicada JIRA 2001 (2001)

5. Bures, T., Hnetynka, P., Plasil, F.: SOFA 2.0: Balancing advanced features in a hierarchical component model. In: Software Engineering Research, Management and Applications, pp. 40–48. IEEE Computer Society (2006)

6. EJB: Enterprise JavaBeans, Version 3.0. EJB Core Contracts and Requirements. Sun Microsystems (May 2006), JSR220 Final Release

7. Franch, X.: Systematic formulation of non-functional characteristics of software. In: Proceedings of International Conference on Requirements Engineering (ICRE), pp. 174–181. IEEE Computer Society (1998)

8. Genssler, T., Christoph, A., Schulz, B., Winter, M., Stich, C.M., Zeidler, C., Müller, P., Stelter, A., Nierstrasz, O., Ducasse, S., Arevalo, G., Wuyts, R., Liang, P., Schönhage, B., van den Born, R.: PECOS in a nutshell. Pecos Handbook (September 2002)

9. Glinz, M.: On non-functional requirements. In: Requirements Engineering Conference, pp. 21–26. IEEE Computer Society, Los Alamitos (2007)

10. Grosskurth, A., Godfrey, M.W.: A reference architecture for web browsers. In: Proceedings of the 21st IEEE International Conference on Software Maintenance, pp. 661–664. IEEE Computer Society, Washington, DC (2005)

11. Gu, X., Nahrstedt, K., Yuan, W., Wichadakul, D., Xu, D.: An XML-based quality of service enabling language for the web. Journal of Visual Language and Computing, Special Issue on Multimedia Language for the Web 13, 61–95 (2001)

12. Jaaksi, A.: Developing mobile browsers in a product line. IEEE Software 19, 73–80 (2002)

13. Ježek, K., Brada, P.: Correct matching of components with extra-functional properties - a framework applicable to a variety of component models. In: Evaluation of Novel Approaches to Software Engineering (ENASE). SciTePress (2011) ISBN: 978-989-8425-65-2

14. Ježek, K., Brada, P.: Formalisation of a Generic Extra-functional Properties Framework. In: Evaluation of Novel Approaches to Software Engineering. CCIS. Springer, Heidelberg (to be published, 2012)

15. Lamanna, D.D., Skene, J., Emmerich, W.: Slang: A language for defining service level agreements. In: IEEE International Workshop of Future Trends of Distributed Computing Systems, p. 100. IEEE Computer Society (2003)

16. Lamport, L.: Specifying Systems, The TLA+ Language and Tools for Hardware and Software Engineers. Addison-Wesley (2002)

17. Lau, K.-K., Ukis, V.: Defining and Checking Deployment Contracts for Software Components. In: Gorton, I., Heineman, G.T., Crnković, I., Schmidt, H.W., Stafford, J.A., Ren, X.-M., Wallnau, K. (eds.) CBSE 2006. LNCS, vol. 4063, pp. 1–16. Springer, Heidelberg (2006)

18. Mohammad, M., Alagar, V.S.: TADL - An Architecture Description Language for Trustworthy Component-Based Systems. In: Morrison, R., Balasubramaniam, D., Falkner, K. (eds.) ECSA 2008. LNCS, vol. 5292, pp. 290–297. Springer, Heidelberg (2008)

19. Muskens, J., Chaudron, M.R.V., Lukkien, J.J.: A Component Framework for Consumer Electronics Middleware. In: Atkinson, C., Bunse, C., Gross, H.-G., Peper, C. (eds.) Component-Based Software Development for Embedded Systems. LNCS, vol. 3778, pp. 164–184. Springer, Heidelberg (2005)
20. Nierstrasz, O., Arévalo, G., Ducasse, S., Wuyts, R., Gao, X.-X., Müller, P.O., Zeidler, C., Genssler, T., van den Born, R.: A Component Model for Field Devices. In: Bishop, J.M. (ed.) CD 2002. LNCS, vol. 2370, pp. 200–209. Springer, Heidelberg (2002)
21. OMG: MOF 2.0 core. OMG Document ptc/06-01-01 (January 2006)
22. OMG: UML profile for modeling quality of service and fault tolerance characteristics and mechanism specification 1.1. Tech. rep., OMG - Object Management Group (2008), formal/2008-04-05
23. OMG: UML Profile for MARTE: Modeling and Analysis of Real-Time Embedded Systems. OMG (2009), formal/2009-11-02,
http://www.omg.org/spec/MARTE/1.0/PDF (2010)
24. OSGi: OSGi Service Platform Service Compendium 4.2. The OSGi Alliance (2009), http://www.osgi.org/Download/Release4V42 (2011)
25. OSGi: OSGi Service Platform Core Specification 4.3. OSGi Aliance (2011), http://www.osgi.org/
26. Röttger, S., Zschaler, S.: CQML+: Enhancements to CQML. In: Bruel, J.M. (ed.) Proc. 1st Int'l Workshop on Quality of Service in Component-Based Software Engineering, Toulouse, France, pp. 43–56. Cépaduès-Éditions (June 2003)
27. Sentilles, S., Štěpán, P., Carlson, J., Crnković, I.: Integration of Extra-Functional Properties in Component Models. In: Lewis, G.A., Poernomo, I., Hofmeister, C. (eds.) CBSE 2009. LNCS, vol. 5582, pp. 173–190. Springer, Heidelberg (2009)
28. Spring Comunity: Spring Framework, ver.3, Reference Documentation. SpringSource, ver. 3 edn. (2010), http://static.springsource.org/spring/-docs/3.0.x/spring-framework-reference/html/
29. Szyperski, C., Gruntz, D., Murer, S.: Component Software - Beyond Object-Oriented Programming, 2nd edn., 624 pages. Addison-Wesley / ACM Press (2002) ISBN-13: 978-0201745726

Efficient Method Lookup Customization for Smalltalk

Jan Vraný[1], Jan Kurš[1], and Claus Gittinger[2]

[1] Software Engineering Group,
Czech Technical University in Prague,
Thákurova 9, Prague, Czech Republic
{jan.vrany,kursjan}@fit.cvut.cz
[2] eXept Software A.G.
Zeppelinstrasse 4, Bönnigheim, Germany
cg@exept.de

Abstract. Programming languages are still evolving, and programming languages and language features are being designed and implemented every year. Since
it is not a trivial task to provide a runtime system for a new language, existing
runtime systems such as the Java Virtual Machine or the Common Language
Runtime are used to host the new language.

However, most of the high-performance runtime systems were designed for
a specific language with a specific semantics. Therefore, if the new language
semantics differs from the semantics hard-coded in a runtime system, it has to be
emulated on top of features supported by the runtime.

The emulation causes performance overhead.

To overcome the limitations of an emulation, a runtime system may provide
a meta-object protocol to alter the runtime semantics. The protocol should fulfill
opposing goals: it should be flexible, easy to use, fast and easy to implement at
the same time.

We propose a simple meta-object protocol for customization of a method
lookup in Smalltalk. A programmer may define his own custom method lookup
routine in Smalltalk and let the runtime system to call it when needed. Therefore there is no need to modify the runtime system itself. Our solution provides
reasonable performance thanks to low-level support in a runtime system, nevertheless the changes to the runtime system are small and local. At the same time, it
provides the flexibility to implement a wide range of features present in modern
programming languages.

The presented approach has been implemented and validated on a Smalltalk
virtual machine.

1 Introduction

Many new programming, scripting and domain specific languages are created every
year. In the past, each of the languages came up with its own runtime system – there is
the Java Virtual Machine for Java, the Common Language Runtime for .NET languages
and runtime systems for Perl, Python and Ruby.

Unfortunately, the implementation of a high-quality runtime system for a new language is challenging. Modern and high-performance runtime systems are complex machines providing memory management, thread management, performance optimization

C.A. Furia and S. Nanz (Eds.): TOOLS Europe 2012, LNCS 7304, pp. 124–139, 2012.

and other features. Therefore, the current trend is to reuse an existing runtime system, such as the Java Virtual Machine (JVM) or the Common Language Runtime (CLR) to host the new language. For example, there have been over 300 languages implemented on top of the JVM [12], and many languages have been implemented on top of the CLR (IronPython, IronRuby or IKVM.NET to name some of them) or the Parrot VM[1].

Unfortunately, most of the high-performance runtime systems were designed with a particular semantics. Part of the hosted language where the semantics differs must be emulated on top of facilities provided by the runtime. A method lookup algorithm is one place where languages differ.

Despite many tricks which can be employed to improve the performance of an emulated method lookup, the performance is worse in comparison with a direct support in the underlying runtime system.

Microsoft provides a Dynamic Language Runtime (DLR) framework [4] built on top of the CLR. The DLR is an universal and flexible framework that does not require any changes in the underlying CLR. As discussed later, a disadvantage of the DLR is that it does not provide sufficient performance. In the JVM, there is a new instruction called invokedynamic in version 7 implemented within a scope of a JSR 292 [8]. Although the invokedynamic provides an excellent performance, the use of the new instruction means that an existing code cannot be customized without recompilation.

In this paper we present a simple meta-object protocol [9] for customization of a method lookup in the Smalltalk environment. A user-provided method lookup routine implemented in Smalltalk can be set for an arbitrary class. This user method lookup routine is then called by the Smalltalk runtime system. We validated our solution on Smalltalk/X, yet we are not aware of any obstacles preventing implementation in an arbitrary Smalltalk runtime system. The proposed meta-object protocol (MOP) allows the extension of an existing Smalltalk language or the implementation of a new language with a wide range of different lookup algorithms.

To get a better performance, our solution relies on a support in the underlying runtime system. However, the changes to the runtime system are kept as small as possible to facilitate the implementation of the proposed solution.

The contributions of this paper are (i) a design and an implementation of a simple, flexible and fast meta-object protocol for Smalltalk runtime systems and (ii) a validation of the presented approach on a language extension (selector namespaces) and a language implementation (Ruby) in Smalltalk/X.

The paper is organized as follows: Section 2 provides motivation and describes the problem in more detail. Section 3 describes our solution – a meta-object protocol (MOP) for a method lookup. Section 4 presents examples of using the MOP and validates its design. Section 6 discusses implementation issues, section 5 presents results of performance benchmarks. Section 7 discusses related work, and finally section 8 concludes and discusses directions of future research.

---

[1] http://parrot.org

2   Problem Description

Current runtime systems (or virtual machines – we will use these terms as synonyms) are complex systems providing high performance execution of high-level languages. Since most of the runtime systems were designed to support only one language, they lack a sufficient meta object protocol (MOP). In the following section we will present some examples, in which existing runtime systems fail to provide required flexibility.

2.1   Motivation

Selector Namespaces. Many object-oriented languages including Smalltalk, Ruby and C# provide class extensions – a mechanism to add or override a method for a class already present in the system and defined in a module other than the extending one. Because any module may extend a class in another module, naming conflicts are likely to occur. Selector namespaces provide a mechanism to solve such name clashes. A selector namespace defines a namespace for methods: multiple methods with same name but in a different namespace may coexist in the same class. A selector namespace may import other namespaces. During a method lookup, a class is first searched for a method in the same namespace as the sending method's namespace. If no method is found, the search continues in an imported namespace, if any.

Although selector namespaces can provide useful functionality and can solve some problems of the class extensions, we are not aware of any runtime system supporting selector namespaces. The only exception is the Smalltalk/X [1], which utilizes the meta-object protocol proposed in this paper.

SmallRuby. SMALLRUBY[2] is an implementation of the Ruby programming language built on top of the Smalltalk/X virtual machine [1]. One of the goals of SMALLRUBY is to provide a fast Ruby implementation with a seamless integration into the Smalltalk development platform. Because of the scripting nature of Ruby, it provides some useful language shortcuts including default argument values, variadic arguments, optional block arguments and mixin inheritance [3]. All these features are directly supported by Ruby's original runtime system.

Smalltalk/X VM lacks a direct support for these features, because they are missing in the Smalltalk language for which the VM has been designed.

Classboxes. Classbox [2] is a module system supporting local class refinements. Within a classbox, classes, methods and variables may be defined. Each class, method and variable belongs precisely to one classbox, namely the one in which it is originally defined. A classbox may import classes from other classboxes making them visible in the importing classbox. Any class visible within a classbox may be imported by another classbox *i.e.,* imports are transitive.

Classboxes were implemented for Java on the JVM and for Smalltalk on the Squeak VM. The implementation of classboxes requires a method lookup refinement, but neither of the VMs provides a direct support. Therefore, the implementations are based on a reflection and a bytecode manipulation. A runtime system with a customized method lookup can make the implementation simpler and more straightforward.

---

[2] https://swing.fit.cvut.cz/projects/smallruby

2.2   Problems

In the previous section we motivated a flexible meta-object protocol. Modern runtime systems use various techniques, such as inline caches, a just-in time (JIT) compilation or inlining to get a better performance during execution. But the optimization makes systems hard to modify. A flexible meta-object protocol design has to consider an implementation effort and a performance impact. Therefore, the design of a meta-object protocol must balance between flexibility, implementation and performance.

2.3   Requirements

We identified the following requirements for the meta-object protocol, which we kept in mind during the design of the MOP.

Simplicity. The meta-object protocol should be easy to use and easy to implement. The meta-object protocol should provide an interface in the user-level code. Simultaneously, the meta-object protocol should minimize the implementation impact on the runtime system.

Flexibility. Implementors of new languages should have as much freedom in design as possible. Therefore, the meta-object protocol should provide enough flexibility to support features such as multiple dispatch, selector namespaces, classboxes, mixins, variadic arguments and others.

To support multiple languages on top of a single virtual machine, the MOP should allow programmers to specify different lookup algorithms for different classes.

Efficiency. The performance of the runtime system without the meta-object protocol should be comparable to the runtime system with the meta-object protocol. Modern runtime systems use low-level techniques – inline caches, polymorphic inline caches, method inlining and just-in-time compilation to improve the performance. The meta-object protocol should be compatible with these techniques.

Compatibility. This requirement comes from practice. Many lines of code have been already written and verified and they must run on an MOP-enabled runtime system. Selector namespaces, for example, require an extension of the existing lookup semantics. The meta-object protocol should allow the implementation of selector namespaces without having to change existing code.

3   Method Lookup Customization

3.1   Customization in a Nutshell

The main idea is to move the method lookup outside the VM to the user-level code. It makes changing the method lookup semantics simple. The VM is instructed to call the user code whenever a method is looked up. Figure 1 shows the whole method invocation process. Consider a code that sends an #asURL message to a string. A VM routine responsible for sending messages (step 1) asks the VM lookup routine for a method that will be dispatched (step 2). The VM lookup routine eventually calls a user-level

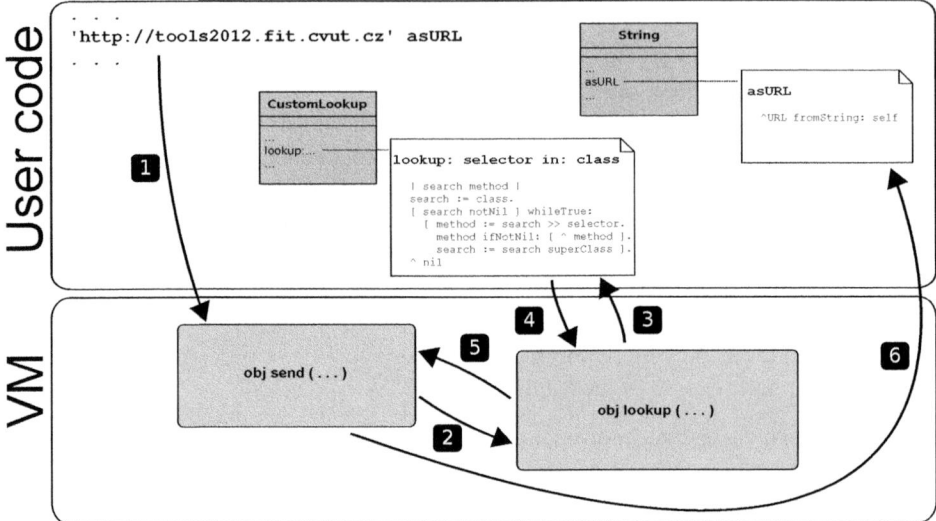

Fig. 1. Method invocation in MOP-enable VM

code with a method lookup (step 3). A proper method is looked up, returned to the VM send routine (steps 4,5) and dispatched (step 6).

In an object oriented world a common approach to realize a callback is to provide an object that implements a method with a predefined signature. In accordance with this approach we call the object a *lookup object*. A lookup object is responsible for looking up a method based on a receiver, a sender, a given method name and arguments.

Figure 2 shows a standard Smalltalk method lookup implemented using the method lookup MOP. It iterates a class hierarchy, starting with the initial search class, and searches for a method with the given selector (line 7). If the method is found, it is returned to the VM and dispatched (line 10). If no method is found along the inheritance hierarchy, a nil is returned indicating that the method with the given selector is not found (line 12). The VM may be instructed to remember the result of the lookup to avoid subsequent, possibly costly, invocations of the custom method lookup routine (line 9). Caching and cache effects are discussed later in section 3.3. Line 13 installs the custom method lookup routine into the class XMLNode, so all instance methods of the XMLNode will be looked up by the custom lookup.

3.2   Virtual Machine Support

In traditional virtual machines a method lookup is performed by the virtual machine as a part of the message send operation. In our solution, the method lookup routine is extended to allow method lookup customization. It consists of two phases.

- **Lookup-Object Lookup.** Within a lookup phase, a sending method and receiver's class are searched for a *lookup object*. When the sending method or the receiver class acquires the lookup object, the method lookup semantics is in possession of the lookup object attached to the sending method or to the receiver. Semantics specified by sending method takes priority over receiver-specified semantics.

- **Lookup.** Once the lookup object is determined (by the *lookup-object lookup* phase), the VM asks for a method, passing a method name, a receiver's class, arguments and other information required for the method lookup. The result of the lookup will be either a method to execute or `nil`. The `nil` means that the message is not understood by the receiver.

MOP-Enabled Lookup Routine. Figure 3 shows the meta-object protocol-aware method lookup VM routine. We will use pseudo-C to distinguish VM code from user level code, which is in Smalltalk. Whenever the method must be looked up, the virtual machine uses this routine to determine which method should be executed. If there is no custom lookup object set, *i.e.,* the `lookup_lookup` method returns `nil`, a lookup hard-coded in the virtual machine is used (Figure 3, line 11). Otherwise, a custom method lookup routine is invoked to determine which method to execute.

Contrary to traditional method lookup routines as found in common virtual machines, our MOP-enabled lookup routine takes three more arguments: a method that issued the message send (`sending_method`), an array of actual arguments, and a cache object representing the inline cache. The first two extra arguments allow us to implement lookup algorithms where the result depends on the sender or on the arguments. The cache object can be used to avoid subsequent lookups. We will discuss method caching later in section 3.3. The extra arguments are present for method execution in Smalltalk/X and in most of the common virtual machines, so they do not bring significant implementation overhead.

Lookup-Object Lookup Phase. The lookup object is used to specify a customized method lookup algorithm.

The *lookup-object lookup* algorithm is shown in Figure 4. The first step of the lookup object lookup process (line 3) gives us the possibility to override the method lookup on a per-sending method basis. Searching for the lookup object within the class hierarchy (lines 5-8) gives us a possibility to define the lookup object at one place without having to deal with subclasses that may be dynamically loaded or created later.

```
1  StdLookup»lookupMethodForSelector: sel directedTo: searchCls
2    from: sendingMethod arguments: args cache: cache
3
4    | class method |
5    class ← searchCls.
6    [ class notNil ] whileTrue:
7      method ← class compiledMethodAt: sel.
8      method ifNotNil:
9        [cache bindTo: method.
10        ↑ method].
11      class ← class superclass].
12    ↑ nil.
13  XMLNode setLookupObject: StdLookup new.
```

Fig. 2. An example of a custom method lookup

```
1  Method method_lookup (String selector, Class search_class,
2      Method sending_method, Object[] args, Cache cache )
3  {
4      Object lookup;
5      Method method;
6      lookup = lookup_lookup(sending_method,receiver_class );
7      if (lookup != nil) {
8          method = lookup_custom(lookup,selector,receiver_class,sending_method,
9              args,cache);
10     } else {
11         method = lookup_vm(selector,receiver_class,sending_method);
12     }
13     return method;
14 }
```

Fig. 3. Method lookup routine hard-coded to the virtual machine

Line number 3 in Figure 4 is not essential. The lookup on a per-sending method basis can be achieved if each receiver checks the sender. Nevertheless, we use it in our protocol, because it is minor modification and it might help with the implementation of some features.

The reader may raise the objection that since the sending method always takes precedence, it might override the receiver's class lookup. Since the lookup objects are accessible through the reflection API, a method-specified lookup object can communicate with the lookup object of the receiver's class and decide which lookup routine will be used.

```
1  Object lookup_lookup ( Method sending_method, Class receiver_class )
2  {
3      if (sending_method.lookup != nil) return sending_method.lookup
4      Class current_class = receiver_class;
5      while (current_class != nil) {
6          if (current_class.lookup != nil) return current_class.lookup;
7          current_class = current_class.superclass;
8      }
9      return nil;
10 }
```

Fig. 4. Lookup object lookup algorithm

Lookup Phase. The *lookup* phase takes the *lookup-object* determined in the *lookup-object lookup* phase and invokes a custom method lookup routine by sending a "lookup" message to the lookup-object. The lookup routine is shown in Figure 5. During the custom lookup, other messages might be sent. It may happen that one of the messages uses the custom lookup as well. In that case, a message sent from the custom method lookup routine may lead to another custom method lookup routine invocation and to the endless recursive loop. To prevent such a situation, a thread-local stack of the activated lookup objects is maintained (lines 6 and 8). If a recursive activation is detected (by examining the lookup object stack), a built-in lookup routine is used. This mechanism enables setting a lookup object on the root of a class hierarchy, and to some extent, it allows programmers to use the customized lookup even for the lookup objects.

The solution with a stack of activated lookups might be replaced by a more straight-forward approach. The thread-local boolean variable can be used to signal whether the lookup is performed from the lookup object or not. If the lookup is initiated from the lookup object, the lookup_vm routine is called by default. In this approach, the lookup object is not allowed to use a customized method lookup.

```
1  Method lookup_custom (Object lookup, String selector, Class search_class,
2      Method sending_method, Object[] args, Cache cache )
3  {
4      Method method;
5      if ( ! is_recursive_lookup(lookup) ) {
6          push_lookup(lookup);
7          method = send(lookup,"lookup",selector,search_class,
8              sending_method,args,cache);
9          pop_lookup();
10     } else {
11         method = lookup_vm(selector,search_class,sending_method);
12     }
13     return method;
14 }
```

Fig. 5. A Lookup routine that calls a user-defined method lookup

3.3   Caching of Method Lookup Results

Most VM implementations use caching strategies to reduce or eliminate the perfor-mance penalties of the dynamic method lookup algorithm. For instance, Smalltalk/X uses a three-layer cache hierarchy, consisting of (i) inline cache, (ii) polymorphic in-line cache and (iii) global selector cache. The inline caches remember the code-pointer of the last lookup at the call site as described in [5] and [13]. These caches reduce message-send overhead to a single direct or indirect function call instruction followed by a check of the receiver class in the called method (a compare and branch). For a hit (i.e. the send is to an instance of the same class as cached), the dynamic overhead consists of a function call, followed by a compare and an untaken conditional branch.

For a miss, a polymorphic inline cache is consulted. It provides code addresses for a small (<20) number of receiver classes organized as the least-recently-used cache of recently called targets [7].

Finally, if the inline cache fails to provide a target address, the VM built-in lookup method is invoked which performs a full search, fills the polymorphic inline cache and/or the inline cache cache slots for the next call, and passes a control to the target method. This built-in full lookup uses a global selector cache[3], but its effect is actually marginal.

---

[3] Note, that for MOP-enabled VM the global selector cache must use triplet {receiver's class, selector, sending method } as a key.

The key point is that the result of a full lookup (either of the built-in lookup or the custom lookup method) is placed into the inline cache or polymorphic inline cache as usual. Therefore, the performance penalties of the MOP as compared to the built-in lookup are only seen in the cache miss situations. In typical programs, inline cache hit rates are above 95 The relatively slow MOP performance is hardly noticed. The case of a very polymorphic code, such as iterating all objects in a system or a very deep inheritance hierarchy when the polymorphic inline cache overflows [6] is when the performance slowdown appears.

Inline cache, polymorphic inline cache and global selector caching significantly improve method invocation performance by avoiding a full method lookup in most cases. However, they can be used only for those method lookup algorithms whose result is effect-free and depends only on a receiver class and a selector. To allow method lookup algorithms that do not fit into the above limitations, an implementor may instruct the VM not to cache the result. The cache object passed to a custom method lookup routine is used for this purpose. If the custom method lookup routine does not explicitly bind the cache to a result, the result of the method lookup is not cached and the subsequent message send results in another invocation of the custom method lookup. Caches are flushed as usual – when a class or method is added or removed or explicitly flushed.

The proposed MOP does not suggest more flexible changes in VM caches because of the implementation effort. It does not suggest more flexible caching mechanism on a higher level, which is easier to implement, because it cannot provide sufficient performance – as shown in section 5. The limitation of the traditional VM caches can be partly overcome, albeit with a performance penalty, which we discuss in the following section.

3.4   Multiple-Dispatch and Other Non-single-Dispatch Lookup Algorithms

Although almost all widely used programming languages use a single-dispatch, some languages use more interesting lookup algorithms. For example, CLOS [10] or Groovy[4], use a multiple-dispatch – a method lookup where the dispatched method depends on a selector and runtime types of a receiver and arguments. In a Classboxes-enabled environment, the dispatched method also depends on a classbox associated with the given execution thread. In theory, a method lookup may depend on an arbitrary context.

Such dispatch algorithms can be handled using the proposed MOP as long as a result of the lookup is not cached. As mentioned before, commonly used caching mechanisms, such as a global selector table and inline caches cache the lookup result only on a per-receiver type basis.

To avoid caching while using our MOP, the custom method lookup routine should simply return a method without binding the cache. This way, the custom method lookup routine is invoked upon each message send.

Naturally invocation of the custom method lookup routine over and over significantly affects the overall performance. To improve the performance, the lookup routine may generate an intermediate method that does additional resolution and caching on the object level. This approach is a trade-off between the implementation effort (changes

---

[4] http://groovy.codehaus.org/

in the VM caching mechanism) and flexibility (allowing multiple dispatch and other non-single dispatch lookup algorithms).

4   Validation

We defined the requirements of the meta-object protocol in section 2.3. The user of MOP can easily redefine the lookup semantics by specifying an algorithm in a user-level code. To facilitate the implementation of our protocol, we changed only the lookup routine.

Since our solution does not change the bytecode and since our protocol provides a default implementation of the lookup algorithm, the backward compatibility is ensured. In this section, we will validate the flexibility requirements; the performance will be discussed in section 5.

Selector Namespaces. Selector namespaces defines a new lookup algorithm different from a method lookup algorithm used in a standard Smalltalk environment. Methods are not looked up only by a name but also by a namespace of a sending method. In systems that does not allow for customization of method lookup, the required lookup would be emulated on the user-level. This emulation requires considerably more effort to implement, and the resulting code is much slower.

Figure 6 shows a selector namespace aware lookup method for Smalltalk/X using proposed MOP. For backward compatibility, if no method is found in a given or in an imported namespaces, the search continues in a nil namespace, which means that the method is in no namespace, and thus visible in every selector namespace.

SmallRuby. We re-implemented the lookup algorithm to account for variadic arguments, mixins, block arguments and default argument values as mentioned in section 2.1 using the proposed MOP. We used selector namespaces (described in section 4) to deal with a situation in which multiple versions of a method must coexist in a single class.

Prior to describing the custom lookup method used in SMALLRUBY, we have to explain the difference between a *function name* and a *selector*. The *function name* is the name of the Ruby function or method as written in the source code. The *selector* is an identifier of a method used by the VM. The selector reflects the number of given arguments. In Smalltalk, there is no difference between the function name and the selector. Due to Ruby's default argument values, variadic arguments and optional blocks, a single Ruby method with one function name may match multiple selectors.

SMALLRUBY's lookup method is shown as Figure 7.

First, it searches the given class for a method that exactly matches the selector, taking the inheritance and mixed modules into account (lines 6 − 9). If no method is found, it searches the classes again for a method with the given function name. If a method is found, a new placeholder method is compiled dynamically and installed into the receiver's class for future use and returned.

```
 1  lookupMethodForSelector: selector directedTo: initialSearchClass
 2     from: sendingMethd arguments: args cache: cache
 3
 4     | sendingNs queue seen namespaces methods method |
 5
 6     sendingNs ← sendingMthd nameSpace.
 7     namespaces ← Array with: sendingNs.
 8     seen ← Set new.
 9     [namespaces notEmpty] whileTrue:
10        [|imports |
11        namespaces ← queue removeFirst.
12        imports ← Set new.
13        methods ← self lookupMethodsForSelector: selector
14           directedTo: initialSearchClass
15           inNamespaces: namespaces.
16        methods size > 0 ifTrue:
17           [methods size == 1
18              ifTrue: [method ← methods anyOne].
19              ifFalse: [method ← self ambiguousMessage: selector].
20           cache bindTo: method.
21           ↑ method].
22        namespaces do: [ :namespace | imports addAll: namespace imports].
23        namespaces ← imports].
24
25     methods ← self lookupMethodsForSelector: selector
26        directedTo: initialSearchClass.
27     methods size == 1 ifTrue:
28        [method ← methods anyOne.
29        cache bindTo: method.
30        ↑ method].
31     ↑ nil
```

Fig. 6. A selector namespace aware lookup method

5   Performance Benchmarks

5.1   Performance of Method Lookup MOP

A natural question to raise concerns about actual performance overhead of the MOP. To measure an actual overhead, a set of benchmarks was run in Smalltalk/X in four different configurations.

STD VM – a standard, unmodified Smalltalk/X virtual machine without the MOP support. The method lookup algorithm is hard-coded in the virtual machine. This configuration serves as a reference.

MOP VM, no lookup object – an MOP-enabled VM with no lookup object set for any class. This configuration shows the overhead of the MOP-enabled VM lookup routine.

```
 1  lookupMethodForSelector: selector directedTo: searchClass
 2    from: sendingMethod arguments: args cache: cache
 3
 4    | fname method |
 5    method ← self lookupMethodForSelector:selector directedTo:searchClass.
 6    method ifNotNil:[cache bindTo: method. ↑ method].
 7
 8    fname ← selector asRubyFunctionName.
 9    method ← self lookupMethodForName: fname directedTo: searchClass.
10    method ifNotNil:
11      [method ← Ruby::Compiler new
12            compileProxyForSelector: selector
13            method: method inClass: searchClass.
14      cache bindTo: method.
15      ↑ method].
16    ↑ nil.
```

Fig. 7. SMALLRUBY's method lookup implementation

MOP VM, std. lookup object (C optimized) – an MOP-enabled VM with a user-defined lookup object set on an `Object` class (it is the worst case as the custom
lookup is performed for every message send to arbitrary object). The custom lookup
object implements a standard Smalltalk lookup. The actual implementation of the
method lookup is optimized at the C level and uses a global selector cache. This
configuration shows the overhead of the MOP when the hand-optimized custom
method lookup is used.

MOP VM, std. lookup object (pure Smalltalk) – an MOP-enabled virtual machine
with a custom lookup object set on an `Object` class. The actual implementation
of the custom method lookup is written purely in Smalltalk and does not use any
caching. This configuration shows the worst case: a custom method lookup algorithm is used for every message send and the implementation of the method lookup
is not optimized at all.

STD VM, callsite simulator – a standard unmodified Smalltalk/X virtual machine without the MOP support. This configuration uses an approach similar to the DLR. A
custom lookup is encoded by special compiler instrumenting and emulating on the
object level. Results of the lookup are cached in a polymorphic inline cache-like
structure.

Benchmarks consist of:

Unimorphic sends – a micro-benchmark that performs 1 000 000 message sends sending the same message to an instance of the same class.

Polymorphic sends x – a micro-benchmark that performs 1 000 000 message sends
sending the same message each time to an instance of different classes. The x stands
for the total number of unique classes. Tests were run for $x \in \{2, 4, 20, 512\}$.

Web application – a macro-benchmark that measures the time required to process
an HTTP request made to a simple web application written in the AidaWeb framework and running on the Swazoo HTTP server (both are written purely in Smalltalk).
The computer used for this experiment is Intel Core 2 Duo 2.00GHz, 3GB RAM, running Linux 2.6.31 and Smalltalk/X 6.2.1β.

Figure 8 shows the slowdown ratio for each benchmark compared to the results obtained by running the benchmark on the standard unmodified VM[5].

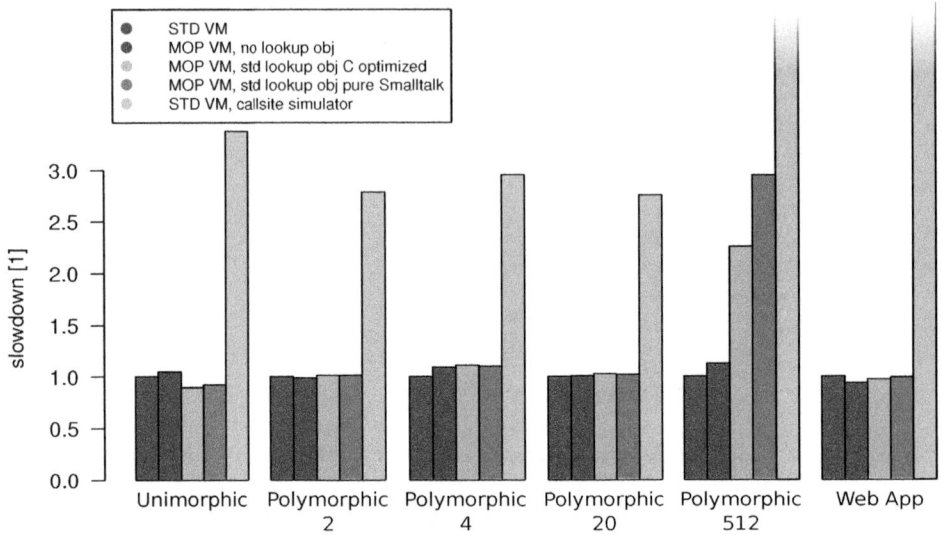

Fig. 8. Performance benchmarks of an MOP-enabled VM

Unimorphic and Polymorphic Sends Up to 20 Classes. The results show that the MOP does not impose noticeable runtime overhead. This is due to the use of the inline caches and polymorphic inline caches – the method is looked only for the very first message send for each unique class. In 1 000 000 sends, the overhead of Smalltalk lookup method is hardly noticeable. The time variations are within the precision of the measurement.

Polymorphic sends 512. This scenario represents a super-polymorphic code, which has 512 different receiver classes and therefore overflows the capacity of a polymorphic inline cache. The capacity of the polymorphic inline cache in Smalltalk/X is 21. Therefore, the polymorphic inline cache fails each time and the full method lookup is performed. Since the class hierarchy is flat and the method is always found in the receiver's class, the overhead is caused just by dispatching back to the Smalltalk code which involves a relatively expensive context manipulation.

Web Application. A web application using a web framework and an HTTP server represents a typical code. The vast majority of polymorphic message sends fit into a polymorphic inline cache and thus the runtime overhead of an MOP lookup is negligible.

The benchmarks show that the overhead introduced by the MOP is hardly noticeable in cases where inline caches or polymorphic inline caches are used. This property holds for the vast majority of the code.

The callsite simulator configuration shows that emulation of a custom lookup on the object level is roughly 3 times slower than the cached lookup. The Web Application

---

[5] A complete benchmark description, code and results can be found at
`https://swing.fit.cvut.cz/wiki/supplementarymaterials/`
`TOOLS2012a`

benchmark was not run in the callsite simulator configuration because it required us to instrument the whole system, including basic classes, which is not technically possible in Smalltalk/X, to get proper numbers. The Polymorphic 512 benchmark with a custom method lookup routine is magnitude slower than a VM built-in lookup.

5.2   Performance Comparison of DLR, and `Invokedynamic`

As discussed before, the VM-level caching mechanism is essential for a high-performance execution. As a proof of our statement we provide results of a measurement in which we compared the performance of user-level caches and VM-level caches. We run a program with the same semantics, first time written in Java and second time written in C#. We measured the time of a native message send and the time of a message sends with a customized method lookup (using invokedynamic or DLR)[6]. The DLR uses the user-level caches and the Java 7 (using the invokedynamic instruction) uses VM-level caches.

The results for unimorphic sends (one receiver) and for polymorphic sends (with 2, 4 and 16 receivers) are in Table 1. The dynamic invocation in Java is only 4 This has fundamental impact on performance, considering that unimorphic sends are the most common sends. In case of polymorphic code, the invokedynamic is the slower the higher is a level of polymorphism, for highly polymorphic codes, it is comparable with the DLR. But the highly polymorphic code is rather unusual in standard programs.

Table 1. A slowdown of a dynamic invocation compared to a native invocation for the particular level of polymorphism

Level of polymorphism	Java 7	DLR
Unimorphic	1.04	13.02
Polymorphic 2	3.32	12.81
Polymorphic 4	3.51	12.75
Polymorphic 16	7.60	16.37

6   Discussion

Implementation Implications. Only the method lookup routine must be changed to add the proposed MOP support into an existing Smalltalk implementation (or into any other similar virtual machine). This has several important consequences. First, the rest of the virtual machine responsible for a code execution, such as a bytecode interpreter or a JIT compiler, remains unchanged. Second, every method invocation can be customized, which makes modifications to existing languages significantly easier. For example, a selector namespaces can be implemented just by implementing a proper custom lookup routine and by attaching the routine to a root of a class hierarchy. Once accomplished, every object in a system understands selector namespaces.

Method Inlining. The inline caches and the polymorphic inline caches significantly improve performance.

---

[6] A complete benchmark description, code and results can be found at
https://swing.fit.cvut.cz/wiki/supplementarymaterials/
TOOLS2012a

Advanced compilers go even further and generate more optimized code by inlining a target method into a code of a sending method, eliminating the overhead connected with the method execution. The proposed MOP does not impose any difficulties for inlining compilers. Before inlining, the inlined method must be looked up with the method lookup routine. The only change is to update the compiler to use the MOP-enabled method lookup routine. In most cases the inlining compiler exploits data in inline caches and polymorphic inline caches.

7 Related Work

JSR 292: Invoke Dynamic. JSR 292: Invoke Dynamic introduces a new, general mechanism for method calls into the Java Virtual Machine. A new bytecode instruction – the invokedynamic – with a few supporting objects allows language implementors to intercept method calls at the call site and provide their own method lookup logic [11].

Whereas the JSR 292 provides support for other languages on top of the JVM, our MOP allows the modification of the native language itself, *i.e.,* the language the runtime system was designed for. Both the JSR 292 and the described MOP can be used to provide a user-specific method lookup algorithm without a performance loss. In both cases, a user has to explicitly mark objects with a user-defined lookup and the lookup itself can be implemented as a normal Smalltalk or Java code without a changing the virtual machine itself. However, the proposed MOP differs from the JSR 292 in two ways. Firstly, since the JSR 292 uses a new instruction, a code that uses a custom lookup should be compiled specially. However, our MOP allows lookup customization without recompilation. Secondly, the JSR 292 allows only a call site interception of a method lookup, whereas our protocol allows both call site and (possibly at the same time) a receiver site interception.

To illustrate the limitations of JSR 292, consider a hypothetical implementation of traits using the invokedynamic. Then, consider an object o of a class that uses a trait to reuse an implementation of hashCode() and equals() methods. When the object o is added into a HashSet collection, the instance of the HashSet sends the hashCode() to the o. To get the proper method called, *i.e.,* the method from a trait, the JSR 232 requires all the methods of the HashSet to be recompiled with the invokedynamic[7]. Using the described MOP, the only change required is to attach a trait-aware method lookup to the class of the o.

Dynamic Language Runtime. A Dynamic Language Runtime (DLR) is .NET library that facilitates the implementation of dynamic languages for the .NET platform. The scope and purpose of the DLR are similar to those of the JSR 292 and also to those of the described MOP.

The difference is that the DLR requires no special support in a runtime system, whereas the described MOP relies on the runtime support because of performance reasons. The DLR emulates all the semantics on the object level. Despite all the optimizations done by a JIT compiler, a method dispatch encoded by the DLR is on order of magnitude slower than method dispatch directly supported by the CLR.

---

[7] Which is impossible anyway due to limitations and "security features" of JVM.

8 Conclusion

In this paper we have motivated the need for a virtual machine with a meta-object protocol that customizes a method lookup and we have presented such a protocol. We have validated the protocol by implementing selector namespaces. We have also shown that the possibility to control the method lookup is very useful for porting existing languages (Ruby in our case) to a new platform (Smalltalk/X in our case).

We plan to extend the meta-object protocol at the object level and provide mechanisms to combine multiple custom lookups that are not aware of each other.

Another interesting direction would be to explore how to decouple the VM from class objects and their internal layout which now has to be known to the VM.

Acknowledgement. We would like to gratefully thank to Alexandre Bergel, Stéphane Ducasse for valuable discussions we had, and Oscar Nierstrasz and Jorge Ressia and for their precious comments.

References

1. Smalltalk/X (August 2010),
   http://www.exept.de/en/products/smalltalk-x/stx-overview
2. Bergel, A., Ducasse, S., Nierstrasz, O., Wuyts, R.: Classboxes: Controlling visibility of class extensions. Computer Languages, Systems and Structures 31(3-4), 107–126 (2005)
3. Bracha, G., Cook, W.: Mixin-based inheritance. In: Proceedings OOPSLA/ECOOP 1990. ACM SIGPLAN Notices, vol. 25, pp. 303–311 (October 1990)
4. Chiles, B., Turner, A.: Dynamic Language Runtime (August 2010),
   http://dlr.codeplex.com/wikipage?title=Docs%20and%20specs
5. Peter Deutsch, L., Schiffman, A.M.: Efficient implementation of the Smalltalk-80 system. In: Proceedings POPL 1984, Salt Lake City, Utah (January 1984)
6. Gittinger, C.: Smalltalk/X Programmers Reference Manual - Smalltalk Performance Myths and Facts, http://live.exept.de/doc/online/english/programming/STspeed.html
7. Hölzle, U., Chambers, C., Ungar, D.: Optimizing Dynamically-typed Object-oriented Languages with Polymorphic Inline Caches. In: America, P. (ed.) ECOOP 1991. LNCS, vol. 512, pp. 21–38. Springer, Heidelberg (1991)
8. JSR-000292 Supporting Dynamically Typed Languages on the Java Platform (August 2010),
   http://jcp.org/aboutJava/communityprocess/edr/jsr292/index.html
9. Kiczales, G., des Rivières, J., Bobrow, D.G.: The Art of the Metaobject Protocol. MIT Press (1991)
10. Lawless, J.A., Milner, M.M.: Understanding Clos the Common Lisp Object System. Digital Press (1989)
11. Rose, J.R.: Bytecodes meet combinators: Invokedynamic on the jvm. In: VMIL 2009: Proceedings of the Third Workshop on Virtual Machines and Intermediate Languages, pp. 1–11. ACM, New York (2009)
12. Tolksdorf, R.: Programming languages for the java virtual machine (August 2010),
    http://www.is-research.de/info/vmlanguages/
13. Ungar, D.M.: The Design and Evaluation of A High Performance Smalltalk System. PhD thesis, EECS Department, University of California, Berkeley (February 1986)

Fake Run-Time Selection
of Template Arguments in C++

Daniel Langr[1], Pavel Tvrdík[1], Tomáš Dytrych[2], and Jerry P. Draayer[2]

[1] Czech Technical University in Prague
Department of Computer Systems, Faculty of Information Technology
Thákurova 9, 160 00, Praha, Czech Republic
[2] Louisiana State University
Department of Physics and Astronomy
Baton Rouge, LA 70803, USA

Abstract. C++ does not support run-time resolution of template type arguments. To circumvent this restriction, we can instantiate a template for all possible combinations of type arguments at compile time and then select the proper instance at run time by evaluation of some provided conditions. However, for templates with multiple type parameters such a solution may easily result in a branching code bloat. We present a template metaprogramming algorithm called for_id that allows the user to select the proper template instance at run time with theoretical minimum sustained complexity of the branching code.

Keywords: C++, run-time selection, template arguments, template metaprogramming, type sequences.

1   Introduction

C++ templates allow to define a piece of code for which we specify data types later as template arguments. According to the C++ Standard [15], template arguments must be known at compile time. However, consider the following situations where we might want to postpone the choice of template arguments to run time:

Run-Time Choice of Floating-Point Precision: Many pieces of nowadays scientific and engineering software allow to choose the floating-point precision at compile time, see for instance [3, 13, 14, 16, 22]. If we then want to alternate single-precision and double-precision computations, we need either to recompile programs frequently or to maintain both versions simultaneously.

Minimization of Memory Requirements: Indexes pointing into arrays of different sizes constitute essential parts of data structures in scientific and engineering software. Let us have an array of size ξ whose elements are indexed from 0 to $\xi - 1$. The minimum number of bits of unsigned integer data type that is capable to index such an array on a 64-bit computer is then

$$b(\xi) = \min\{\eta \in \{8, 16, 32, 64\} : \xi \leq 2^\eta\}. \tag{1}$$

C.A. Furia and S. Nanz (Eds.): TOOLS Europe 2012, LNCS 7304, pp. 140–154, 2012.

In some software, such as PETSc [3], users can choose between 32-bit and 64-bit data types for indexes. However, the choice has to be done at compile time and the same data type is then used for all indexes independently of the actual size of indexed arrays.

Reading Data from Binary Files: The program might not know particular data types until it opens the file at run time. For instance, when reading files based on the HDF5 file format [20], we can find out information about the types of stored data sets in the form of numerical constants.

Let us now define the problem we want to address.

Problem 1. Assumptions:

1. Suppose f is a function object[1] with a templated function call operator. We will call the number of its template parameters the *dimension* of the problem and denote it by d.

2. Let us have d finite sequences of data types $\mathcal{T}_1, \ldots, \mathcal{T}_d$, where

$$\mathcal{T}_i = \{t_i^k : k = 1, \ldots, n_i\}.$$

3. Let us further have d sequences of mutually exclusive Boolean conditions $\mathcal{C}_1, \ldots, \mathcal{C}_d$, where

$$\mathcal{C}_i = \{c_i^k : k = 1, \ldots, n_i - 1\},$$

that cannot be evaluated until run time (for every $\mathcal{C}_i$, at most one condition can be true at a given time).

We now want to *apply* the function object f, that is, to call

f.operator()<$t_1, \ldots, t_d$>();

such that

$$t_i = \begin{cases} t_i^k & \text{if there exists } k \in \{1, \ldots, n_i - 1\} \text{ such that } c_i^k \text{ is true,} \\ t_i^{n_i} & \text{otherwise.} \end{cases}$$

□

A simple one-dimensional example of Problem 1 is a run-time selection of floating point precision for some algorithm via program's command line option:

Example 1. Suppose a function object called `algorithm` defined as follows:

```
struct {
  template <typename T> void operator()() { ... /* some code */ }
} algorithm;
```

Let $\mathcal{T}_1 = \{\texttt{float}, \texttt{double}\}$ and $\mathcal{C}_1 = \{\texttt{strcmp(argv[1], "1")}\}$.

□

---

[1] A *function object*, or simply a *functor*, is an object of a class that overloads the *function call operator*. See, for example, Prata [17] or Stroustrup [18] for more details.

That is, we want to invoke `algorithm.operator()<double>()` if the value of the first command line options is "1", and `algorithm.operator()<float>()` otherwise. The obvious solution is to branch the code according to the provided condition as follows:

```
if (strcmp(argv[1], "1"))   algorithm.operator()<float>();
else                        algorithm.operator()<double>();
```

Generally, for Problem 1, we may define the solution based on code branching as follows.

Solution 1.

```
if (c₁¹ && c₂¹ && ··· && c_d¹)        f.operator()<t₁¹,t₂¹,...,t_d¹>();
else if (c₁¹ && c₂¹ && ··· && c_d²)   f.operator()<t₁¹,t₂¹,...,t_d²>();
···
else                                   f.operator()<t₁^{n₁},t₂^{n₂},...,t_d^{n_d}>();
```

The drawback of this solution is obvious—the complexity of the branching code grows combinatorially (recall that we need the templated function call operator to be instantiated for all possible combinations of data types). That is, it yields the total number of branches $\mathcal{N}_\Pi = \prod_{i=1}^d n_i$.

The theoretical minimum for the number of branches is $\mathcal{N}_\Sigma = \sum_{i=1}^d n_i$, because all conditions must be evaluated in the worst case scenario. Such a minimum would be achieved by the following *imaginary* code:

```
???? t₁;
if (c₁¹)            t₁ = t₁¹;
else if (c₁²)       t₁ = t₁²;
···
else if (c₁^{n₁-1}) t₁ = t₁^{n₁-1};
else                t₁ = t₁^{n₁};

··· // similarly for the remaining dimensions

f.operator()<t₁,...,t_d>();
```

Unfortunately, such a code is not valid, because C++ does not allow to assign types[2].

In this paper, we present a solution of Problem 1 that achieves the theoretical minimum of required code branches $\mathcal{N}_\Sigma$. Its application to Example 1 may look simply like:

```
typedef boost::mpl::vector<float, double> fp_types;
···
int fp_id = (strcmp(argv[1], "1")) ? 0 : 1;
for_id<fp_types>(algorithm, fp_id);
```

---

[2] Using `typedefs` instead of assignment would not help here, because even though most C++ compilers do accept `typedefs` in a function body, such type definitions would not propagate from inside the code branches.

This solution is based on template metaprogramming [2,4,12,21] and sequences of types from Boost Metaprogramming Library (MPL) [1]. Although we cannot choose template arguments at run time, we can choose positions (ids) of desired data types inside type sequences. Based on these ids, the presented `for_id` algorithm invokes a proper template instance[3]. Since both approaches are syntactically similar, we refer to our solution as *fake* run-time selection of template arguments.

The rest of the paper is organized as follows. In Section 2, the previous work related to our problem is presented and analyzed. Section 3 covers design and implementation of the proposed `for_id` algorithm. In Section 4, experiments are described and their results are presented and discussed. Section 5 summarizes the properties of the `for_id` algorithm and describes its usage in an existing high performance computing (HPC) code.

2   Related Work

C++ templates and template metaprogramming have always been intended to be utilized primarily at compile time. Boost MPL [1] is a widely-used general-purpose metaprogramming library advertised as *"high-level C++ template metaprogramming framework of compile-time algorithms, sequences and metafunctions"* [19]. There are many compile-time algorithms inside Boost MPL, but there is only one run-time algorithm called `for_each`. The call `boost::mpl::for_each<seq>(f)` applies the function object f (calls its function call operator) to every element of the type sequence `seq` at run time. There are two significant differences between Boost MPL's `for_each` and our `for_id`:

1. `for_each` applies the function object to all elements in the type sequence. `for_id` applies the function object to a single element only—the one that is identified by its position (id).
2. `for_each` is one-dimensional, that is, it can operate only on a single type sequence. `for_id` is multi-dimensional and we designed it with no imposed limit of the number of dimensions (type sequences). This limit is given solely by the compiler.

Generic Image Library (GIL) [6] allows to design generic algorithms for different types of images that are not known until run time. According to the actual image properties, such as the color space or bit depth, a proper template instance of the algorithm is invoked at run time. However, this functionality is tightly coupled with GIL and is not presented as an independent metaprogramming algorithm for general-purpose usage. Some implementation details are described in the paper of Bourdev and Järvi [7], but for deeper understanding of their solution, we need to study undocumented functions and class templates from GIL's source code.

---

[3] In fact, `for_id` is an ordinary C++ templated function (not a metafunction). However, its functionality matches the category that is called *algorithms* in Boost MPL.

3 Design and Implementation

3.1 Notation

To prevent code listings from being too long, we use the following notation rules in the further text:

1. We omit inclusion directives for all necessary header files.
2. We omit the `boost::` and `boost::mpl::` prefixes, as well as the `::type` and `::value` suffixes for all Boost entities. For example, we simply write `next<B1>` instead of `boost::mpl::next<B1>::type`.
3. We omit the `typename` keyword. For example, we simply write
   `template<S1, B1 = begin<S2> >` instead of
   `template <typename S1, typename B1 = typename begin<S1> >`.
4. We use the τ symbol for MPL iterators such that `deref<`τ_i^k`>` is equal to t_i^k, and $\tau_i^{n_i+1}$ denotes `end<`$\mathcal{T}_i$`>`.

By the symbol *id* we denote a zero-based index into a type sequence. We say that *id* is *valid* for the sequence S if it belongs to $\{0, \ldots, \texttt{size<S>} - 1\}$.

3.2 Initial Step

Let us first define a metafunction `pos` that returns a zero-based index of a type within a type sequence (that is, `pos <`$\mathcal{T}_i, t_i^k$`>` is equal to to $k - 1$).

```
template <S,T> struct pos : distance<begin<S>, find<S,T> > { };
```

Our initial solution of one-dimensional Problem 1 is then:

```
template <S1, B1=begin<S1>, E1=end<S1> > struct for_id_impl_1 {      // (1)
 template <T> static void execute(T& f, int id1) {                   // (2)
  if (pos<S1, deref<B1> > == id1)                                    // (3)
   f.template operator()<deref<B1> >();                              // (4)
  else if (1 == distance<B1,E1>) throw std::invalid_argument("");    // (5)
  else for_id_impl_1<S1, next<B1>, E1>::execute(f, id1)              // (6)
} };
template <S1, E1> struct for_id_impl_1<S1, E1, E1> {                 // (7)
 template <T> static void execute(T& f, int id1) { } };
```

It iterates over the type sequence S1 either until the position of the actual type matches the desired *id*, or until the end of the sequence is reached. In the former case, the function object is applied. In the latter case, an exception is thrown. The partial specialization (7) is never reached at run time, however, it is needed to stop the recursive instantiation at compile time.

Let us go back to our Example 1 where $\mathcal{T}_1 = \{\texttt{float}, \texttt{double}\}$. What happens when we now call `for_id_impl_1<`$\mathcal{T}_1$`>::execute(algorithm, id1)` and id1 is 1?

1. At code line (1), the default arguments are resolved resulting in $<\mathcal{T}_1, \tau_1^1, \tau_1^3>$.
2. At code line (2), the `execute` function is invoked, wherein id1 is equal to 1 and `pos<`$\mathcal{T}_1, t_1^1$`>` is equal to 0.

3. The condition at code line (3) is hence not satisfied. At the same time, the condition at code line (5) is not satisfied as well, because $\texttt{distance}<\tau_1^1, \tau_1^3>$ is 2. Hence, the following command is executed: $\texttt{for\_id\_impl\_1}<\mathcal{T}_1, \tau_1^2, \tau_1^3>\texttt{::execute(algorithm,1)}$.

4. The condition at code line (3) is now satisfied, because both $\texttt{pos}<\mathcal{T}_1, t_1^2>$ and $\texttt{id1}$ are equal to 1. Since $\texttt{deref}<\tau_1^2>$ is equal to t_1^2 which is $\texttt{double}$, the following command is executed: $\texttt{algorithm.template operator()}<\texttt{double}>()$.

This is exactly what we wanted, that is, to select the $\texttt{<double>}$ instance of the function call operator of $\texttt{algorithm}$ by a run-time parameter $\texttt{id1}$ (zero-based index of $\texttt{double}$ in $\mathcal{T}_1$ is 1).

What would happen if $\texttt{id1}$ would be invalid—for example, would be equal to 10? Up to the point 3. in the previous list the behavior would be the same. However, then it would run differently:

4′. The condition at code line (3) is not satisfied, because $\texttt{id1}$ is equal to 10 and $\texttt{pos}<\mathcal{T}_1, t_1^2>$ is equal to 1. However, the condition at line (5) is now satisfied, since $\texttt{distance}<\tau_1^2, \tau_1^3>$ is 1. We are already at the end of $\mathcal{T}_1$ and there are no more types to iterate over. Hence, the exception that indicates the wrong $\texttt{id1}$ argument is thrown.

3.3   Extension to Multiple Dimensions

The following solution for two dimensions is based on the same idea of iterating over type sequences—we just have two of them and for each one a separate *id*.

```
template <S1, S2, B1=begin<S1>, B2=begin<S2>, E1=end<S1>,
         E2=end<S2>, T1=deref<B1> > struct for_id_impl_2 {        // (1)
 template <T> static void execute(T& f, int id1, int id2) {
   if (pos<S1, deref<B1> > == id1)                                // (2)
    for_id_impl_2<S1,S2,E1,B2,E1,E2,deref<B1> >::execute(f,id1,id2);
   else if (1 == distance<B1,E1>) throw std::invalid_argument("");
   else for_id_impl_2<S1,S2,next<B1>,B2,E1,E2,T1>::execute(f,id1,id2);
} };
template <S1, S2, B2, E1, E2, T1>
struct for_id_impl_2<S1,S2,E1,B2,E1,E2,T1> {                      // (3)
 template <T> static void execute(T& f, int id1, int id2) {
   if (pos<S2, deref<B2> > == id2)                                // (4)
    f.template operator()<T1,deref<B2> >();
   else if (1 == distance<B2,E2>) throw std::invalid_argument("");
   else for_id_impl_2<S1,S2,E1,next<B2>,E1,E2,T1>::execute(f,id1,id2);
} };
template <S1, S2, E1, E2, T1>
struct for_id_impl_2<S1,S2,E1,E2,E1,E2,T1> {
 template <T> static void execute(T& f, int id1, int id2) { } };
```

In the primary template at code line (1), the program iterates over the first type sequence S1. However, when the desired type is found, that is, when the condition at code line (2) is satisfied, the function object cannot be applied, because the second type is not yet known. Instead, the resolved type is stored into the template parameter T1 and the process proceeds to the second dimension. This is done by setting B1 to E1, which causes the transition to the partial specialization defined at code line (3). This partial specialization iterates over the second type sequence and when id2 is matched at code line (4), the function object may be finally applied, since all data types are now known.

Extension to three and more dimensions can be done by following the same pattern. However, this approach has the quadratic complexity of the number of definitions. For the dimension d, we need $d + 1$ definitions—a primary template and d partial specializations. So, if we want to support all dimensions from 1 to some d_{max}, we finally need $d_{max}(d_{max} + 3)/2 = O(d_{max}^2)$ definitions, which is not optimal.

3.4   The Optimal Solution

We present here the solution that needs only $2d_{max} + 1 = O(d_{max})$ definitions. It primarily uses only $d_{max}+1$ definitions that are common for all $d \in \{1, \ldots, d_{max}\}$. For $d_{max} = 2$ these definitions are the following:

```
template <int D, S1, S2=vector<>, B1=begin<S1>, B2=begin<S2>, E1=end<S1>,
E2=end<S2>, T1=deref<B1>, T2=deref<B2> > struct for_id_impl {
 template <T> static void execute(T& f, int id1, int id2 = 0) {
  if (pos<S1, deref<B1> > == id1)
   if (1 == D) executor<D, deref<B1>, T2>::execute(f);        // (1)
        // f.template operator()<deref<B1> >();               // (2)
    else for_id_impl<D,S1,S2,E1,B2,E1,E2,deref<B1>>::execute(f,id1,id2);
   else if (1 == distance<B1,E1>) throw std::invalid_argument("");// (3)
   else for_id_impl<D,S1,S2,next<B1>,B2,E1,E2,T1>::execute(f,id1);
} };
template <D, S1, S2, B2, E1, E2, T1, T2>
struct for_id_impl<D,S1,S2,E1,B2,E1,E2,T1,T2> {
 template <T> static void execute(T& f, int id1, int id2 = 0) {
  if (pos<S2, deref<B2> > == id2)
   executor<D, T1, deref<B2> >::execute(f);                   // (4)
// f.template operator()<T1, deref<B2> >();                   // (5)
   else if (1 == distance<B2,E2>) throw std::invalid_argument("");// (6)
   else for_id_impl<D,S1,S2,E1,next<B2>,E1,E2,T1>::execute(f,id1,id2);
} };
template <D, S1, S2, E1, E2, T1, T2>
struct for_id_impl<D,S1,S2,E1,E2,E1,E2,T1,T2> {                 // (7)
 template <T> static void execute(T& f, int id1, int id2 = 0) { } };
```

The idea of iterating over type sequences and moving to the next dimension after resolving the actual one is preserved. Comparing for_id_impl with the previously defined template for_id_impl_2, we may find the following differences as essential:

1. The D template parameter was introduced that is equal to the number of dimensions d of the actual problem.

2. The S2 template parameter and the id2 function parameter have default values, because they are useless for one-dimensional problems and we do not want to force the user to specify some meaningless values for them.
3. The condition at code line (1) was introduced, because when the type is resolved for a particular dimension, we need to select the further action according to the number of dimensions of the problem. At code line (1), when the first type is already known, we need either
   (a) to apply the function object for one-dimensional problems (D is 1),
   (b) or move to the next dimension for two-dimensional (generally more-than-one-dimensional) problems.
   At code line (4), we further see that no such condition is needed, because the executor structure is defined only for D equal to 1 or 2.
4. Unfortunately, within this new solution, we cannot apply the function object directly inside for_id_impl::execute, as is suggested by the comments at code lines (2) and (5). The reason is that for a two-dimensional problem, we suppose a function object with a templated function call operator that has exactly two template parameters. However, in such a case, the call f.template operator()<deref<B1> >() at code line (2) would trigger a compilation error, because no such one-parameter version of the function call operator exists. We have solved this problem by delegation of the application of the function object to a helper structure called executor that is defined as follows:

```
template <int D, T1, T2> struct executor;
template <T1, T2> struct executor<1, T1, T2> {
   template <T> static void execute(T& obj) {
     obj.template operator()<T1>(); } };
template <T1, T2> struct executor<2, T1, T2> {
   template <T> static void execute(T& obj) {
     obj.template operator()<T1, T2>(); } };
```

As in Section 3.3, the extension to three and more dimensions is straightforward. For each supported dimension, we need to define one particular specialization of for_id_impl and one of executor. Totally, we hence need $2d_{max} + 1$ definitions.

It might seem that this new solution introduces some overhead comparing with the one in Sections 3.2 and 3.3, because there is too much code branching. However, we need to realize that the conditions at code lines (1), (3) and (6) may be evaluated at compile time and an efficient compiler will not propagate the branching into the resulting machine code.

3.5   Wrapping Up

Although for_id_impl already solves Problem 1, we can make things more comfortable by introducing the following wrappers:

```
template <S1, T> void for_id(T& f, int id1) {
    for_id_impl<1, S1>::execute(f, id1); }
template <S1, S2, T> void for_id(T& f, int id1, int id2) {
    for_id_impl<2, S1, S2>::execute(f, id1, id2); }
```

which allows to write simply `for_id<seq>(f,id)` instead of `for_id_impl<1,seq>::execute(f,id)`.

3.6 Summary

With `for_id`, we may write the solution of Problem 1 as follows.

Solution 2.

```
int id₁;
if  (c₁¹)              id₁= 0;
else if (c₁²)          id₁= 1;
...
else if (c₁ⁿ¹⁻¹)       id₁= n₁ − 2;
else                   id₁= n₁ − 1;

... // similarly for the remaining dimensions
for_id <𝒯₁,...,𝒯_d>(f, id₁,..., id_d);
```

□

This solution hence achieves the minimal number of code branches $\mathcal{N}_\Sigma$.

4 Experimental Results

4.1 Test Program

To evaluate `for_id`, we have developed a program for computing the dominant eigenvalue of a real symmetric matrix that is obtained from a file based on the Matrix Market file format [5]. The file name is specified as a program's command line option, therefore, the number of matrix rows (columns) and the number of nonzero elements are not known until run time. Within the program, the matrix is stored in the memory in the *coordinate storage sparse format* using the following data structure:

```
struct Matrix { uint64_t n, z; void *i, *j, *a; } m;
```

where

- n is the number of matrix rows;
- z is the number of matrix nonzero elements;
- i, j and a are arrays containing *row indexes*, *column indexes*, and *values* of matrix nonzero elements, respectively.

The body of the `main` function of the program looks like:

```
std::ifstream ifs(argv[1]);                                    // ( 1)
while ('%' == ifs.peek()) ifs.ignore(1024, '\n');              // ( 2)
ifs >> m.n >> m.n >> m.z;                                      // ( 3)
uint64_t q = boost::lexical_cast<uint64_t>(argv[2]);           // ( 4)
MatrixReader mr(m, ifs);                                       // ( 5)
```

```
...                                                            // ( 6)
double lambda;                                                 // ( 7)
PowerMethod pm(m, q, lambda);                                  // ( 8)
...                                                            // ( 9)
std::cout << "Lambda: " << lambda << "\n";                     // (10)
```

It consists of the following steps:

1. The file input stream `ifs` for the matrix file is opened (1).
2. The header and the comments are skipped (2).
3. The number of rows and the number of nonzero elements are read (3).
4. The required number of iterations for the power method is got from the second command line option (4).
5. The `mr` function object is defined (5) that is responsible for allocating arrays `m.i`, `m.j`, `m.a` and for filling their values. (The application of `mr` (6), as well as of `pm` (9), will be described later.)
6. The variable `lambda` for storing the resulting eigenvalue is defined (7).
7. The `pm` function object is defined that is responsible for computing the eigenvalue and deallocating the arrays (8).
8. The computed eigenvalue is printed out (10).

Since we wanted to evaluate the `for_id` algorithm, we created the following instances (cases) of the program:

	C_{16}^f	C_{32}^f	C_{16}^d	C_{32}^d	C_*^*
floating-point type	float	float	double	double	resolved by `for_id`
indexing type	uint16_t	uint32_t	uint16_t	uint32_t	resolved by `for_id`

In C_{16}^f–C_{32}^d, the function call operators at code lines (6) and (9) are invoked directly, which corresponds to the classical approach where data types are resolved at compile time. For example, in the case C_{16}^f, it looks as follows:

```
mr.operator()<float, uint16_t>();                             // (6)
```

However, in the case C_*^*, the `for_id` algorithm was utilized as follows:

```
for_id<fp_types, ind_types>(mr, fp_id, ind_id);               // (6)
```

where:

1. `fp_types` and `ind_types` are type sequences defined as

   ```
   typedef boost::mpl::vector<float, double> fp_types;
   typedef boost::mpl::vector<
       uint8_t, uint16_t, uint32_t, uint64_t> ind_types;
   ```

2. the floating-point type *id* was selected by the third command line option:

   ```
   int fp_id = (strcmp(argv[3], "1")) ? 0 : 1;
   ```

3. the indexing type *id* was selected as[4]:

```
int                        ind_id = 3;
if        (m.n <= (1UL <<  8)) ind_id = 0;
else if (m.n <= (1UL << 16)) ind_id = 1;
else if (m.n <= (1UL << 32)) ind_id = 2;
```

Moreover, we distinguish two sub-cases of C_*^*—C_*^f and C_*^d for *single* and *double* precision computation selected at run time, respectively.

Finally, we used the following definitions of the MatrixReader and Power-Method classes:

```
class MatrixReader { public:
  MatrixReader(Matrix& m, std::ifstream& ifs) : m_(m), ifs_(ifs) { }
  template <typename F, typename I> void operator()() {
    I* i = new I[m_.z]; I* j = new I[m_.z]; F* a = new F[m_.z];
    for (uint64_t k = 0; k < m_.z; ++k) {
      ifs_ >> i[k] >> j[k] >> a[k]; i[k]--; j[k]--; }
    m_.i = (void*)i; m_.j = (void*)j; m_.a = (void*)a;
  }
  private: Matrix& m_; std::ifstream& ifs_; };

class PowerMethod { public:
  PowerMethod(Matrix& m, uint64_t q, double& lambda)
    : m_(m), q_(q), lambda_(lambda) { }
  template <typename F, typename I> void operator()() {
    I* i = (I*)m_.i; I* j = (I*)m_.j; F* a = (F*)m_.a;
    std::vector<F> x(m_.n, 1.0), y(m_.n);
    F lambda = 0.0;
    do {
      ... // single iteration of the power method
    } while (--q_ > 0);
    lambda_ = (double)lambda;
    delete[] i; delete[] j; delete[] a;
  }
  private: Matrix& m_; uint64_t q_; double& lambda_; };
```

Note, that:

1. We used the power method for computing the dominant eigenvalue.
2. We used void pointers for storing data whose types are not known until run time.
3. We used *pass-by-value* and *pass-by-reference* constructor arguments to pass data *to* and *from* the function objects, respectively.

4.2   Results and Discussion

For all measurements, we used GNU C++ compiler version 4.4.4.

We first compared the compilation time—the results are presented in Table 1. When the program was built completely, the compilation time of C_*^* was of

---

[4] The rows and columns indexes are integer numbers between 0 and m.n − 1, thus, we need an unsigned integer data type of width $b(m.n)$ bits (1).

Table 1. Compilation time of the test program in seconds; average results of 10 measurements

	C_{16}^f	C_*^*
preprocessing, compiling, linking	0.93	1.17
compiling only	0.76	0.94

Table 2. Sizes of the compiled files in kilobytes

	C_{16}^f	C_*^*
executable file	53.2	97.6
object file	104.7	211.1

25 percent higher compared to C_{16}^f. When the program was compiled only, the increase was 31 percent.

Next, we compared the sizes of output files—the results are presented in Table 2. The executable file size of C_*^* is of 83 percent higher compared to C_{16}^f.

For comparison of the memory requirements of the program instances, we used three real symmetric matrices from the collection [8]; their names and characteristics are contained in Table 3. We measured the memory size of the matrix and vector data structures and compared them separately for single and double precision computations—the results are shown in Fig. 1. It is clear that the program instances based on for_id always require the minimum amount of memory, because an optimal data type is used for indexes (if we included program instances using the uint64_t data type into our measurements, this advantage would be even more significant).

Lastly, we measured the computational overhead of the for_id algorithm. We used the clock_gettime POSIX function to get the actual time values in nanoseconds at three places:

1. just before the code line (9) in the main function,
2. at the beginning of the function call operator of the PowerMethod class,
3. just after the code line (9) in the main function.

The difference of the first and the second time values is equal to the time overhead of the *invocation* of the pm's function call operator. The difference of the first and the third time values is equal to the duration of the *application* of the pm's function call operator, that is, the whole run of the power method. The statistical information for the performed measurements are summarized in Table 4. It is clear that the time overhead introduced by the for_id algorithm is relatively high—the invocation of the function call operator takes 2.5 times longer than in the cases when this operator is called directly. However, in the context of the whole program run, this overhead is insignificant, since it is of five orders of magnitude lower than the duration of a single power method iteration.

Table 3. Characteristics of matrices used for experiments

	nos1	thread	ldoor
number of rows	237	$29.7 \cdot 10^3$	$952.2 \cdot 10^3$
number of nonzero elements	627	$2.3 \cdot 10^6$	$23.7 \cdot 10^6$

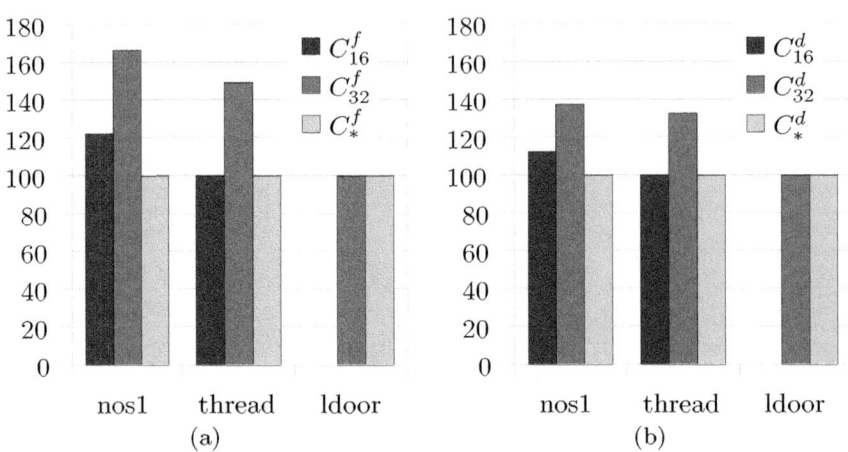

Fig. 1. Comparison of program's memory requirements of the matrix and vector data structures in percents for different matrices and for computations in *single* (a) and *double* (b) floating-point precision

Table 4. Time differences for the pm's function call operator in nanoseconds. Statistical information was gathered from 200 measurements with the thread matrix. The number of iterations of the power method was set to 10.

		C_{16}^f	C_{32}^d	C_*^f
	mean value	191.1	191.0	477.9
invocation	median	186.0	187.0	470.0
	standard deviation	23.0	25.1	43.1
	mean value	$6.1 \cdot 10^8$	$6.1 \cdot 10^8$	$6.1 \cdot 10^8$
application	median	$6.1 \cdot 10^8$	$6.1 \cdot 10^8$	$6.1 \cdot 10^8$
	standard deviation	$6.9 \cdot 10^6$	$7.7 \cdot 10^6$	$6.6 \cdot 10^6$

5   Conclusions

The contribution of this paper is a new method that allows users to select data types for a piece of templated C++ code at run time with the minimal sustained complexity of code branching. The only requirement for such a piece of code is that it has to be in a form of a templated fuction call operator of some function object. The following conclusions can be drawn from the results of the performed experiments:

- The use of for_id allows users to select the floating-point precision for computations at run time without the need of program recompilation.
- The use of for_id allows the best utilization of the computer memory for data structures that contain indexes.
- The use of for_id results in a longer compilation time.
- The use of for_id results in a bigger executable file, that is, in a bigger program's code segment.
- The use of for_id imposes a run-time overhead into the application of the function object.

The drawbacks seemingly prevail over the advantages. However, we need to realize that in typical real-world situations these drawbacks will be insignificant, since:

- Programs are usually compiled only once and then executed multiple times, and/or their compilation time is usually much smaller than their execution time.
- The size of the code segments of running program instances are usually much smaller than the size of their data segments.
- The execution time of the templated code is usually of several orders of magnitude longer than the run-time overhead of its invocation.

The purpose of our rather artificial test program was to evaluate the for_id algorithm. However, we have also successfully integrated for_id into an existing HPC code, namely the code that solves *symmetry-adapted no-core shell model* problems [9–11]. These problems are extremely memory-demanding and the limit for the size of the problem that can be solved on a particular HPC system is given rather by the amount of available memory than by the computational power of its processors. Inside the code, we have utilized for_id for many different tasks, including a sparse matrix-vector multiplication or a parallel file input/output of sparse matrices.

The use of for_id allows to eliminate wasting of data memory for applications that use many different data structures containing arrays of indexes. In addition, it also allows to compile such applications only once even if the types of indexes of submitted data and/or the floating-point precision of computations vary for various runs. This may be especially useful for HPC programs that run on massively parallel supercomputers. Another example where for_id might be useful as well is the implementation of generic image algorithms as used inside GIL (see Section 2).

Acknowledgements. This work was supported by the Czech Science Foundation under Grant No. P202/12/2011, by the U.S. National Science Foundation under Grant No. OCI-0904874, and by the U.S. Department of Energy under Grant No. DOE-0904874.

References

1. Abrahams, D., Gurtovoy, A.: C++ Template Metaprogramming: Concepts, Tools, and Techniques from Boost and Beyond. C++ in Depth Series. Addison-Wesley Professional (2004)
2. Alexandrescu, A.: Modern C++ Design: Generic Programming and Design Patterns Applied. Addison-Wesley Longman Publishing Co., Inc., Boston (2001)
3. Balay, S., Brown, J., Buschelman, K., Eijkhout, V., Gropp, W.D., Kaushik, D., Knepley, M.G., McInnes, L.C., Smith, B.F., Zhang, H.: PETSc Users Manual. Tech. Rep. ANL-95/11 - Revision 3.2, Argonne National Laboratory (2010)
4. Barton, J.J., Nackman, L.R.: Scientific and Engineering C++: An Introduction with Advanced Techniques and Examples, 1st edn. Addison-Wesley Longman Publishing Co., Inc., Boston (1994)
5. Boisvert, R.F., Pozo, R., Remington, K.: The Matrix Market Exchange Formats: Initial Design. Tech. Rep. NISTIR 5935, National Institute of Standards and Technology (December 1996)
6. Bourdev, L., Jin, H.: Generic Image Library, http://opensource.adobe.com/gil (accessed December 2011)
7. Bourdev, L., Järvi, J.: Efficient run-time dispatching in generic programming with minimal code bloat. Science of Computer Programming 76(4), 243–257 (2011)
8. Davis, T.A., Hu, Y.F.: The University of Florida Sparse Matrix Collection. ACM Transactions on Mathematical Software 38(1) (November 2011)
9. Dytrych, T., Sviratcheva, K.D., Bahri, C., Draayer, J.P., Vary, J.P.: Dominant role of symplectic symmetry in ab initio no-core shell model results for light nuclei. Physical Review C 76(1), 014315 (2007)
10. Dytrych, T., Sviratcheva, K.D., Bahri, C., Draayer, J.P., Vary, J.P.: Evidence for symplectic symmetry in ab initio no-core shell model results for light nuclei. Physical Review Letters 98, 162503 (2007)
11. Dytrych, T., Sviratcheva, K.D., Draayer, J.P., Bahri, C., Vary, J.P.: Ab initio symplectic no-core shell model. Journal of Physics G: Nuclear and Particle Physics 35(12), 123101 (2008)
12. Gennaro, D.D.: Advanced C++ Metaprogramming. CreateSpace (2011)
13. Guennebaud, G., Jacob, B., et al.: Eigen, version 3.0.1 (2010), http://eigen.tuxfamily.org (accessed July 2011)
14. Heroux, M.A., Willenbring, J.M.: Trilinos users guide. Tech. Rep. SAND2003-2952, Sandia National Laboratories (2003)
15. ISO/IEC 14882:2003: Programming languages: C++ (2003)
16. OpenFOAM User Guide, Version 2.0.0 (2011)
17. Prata, S.: Primer Plus, 4th edn. Sams, Indianapolis, IN, USA (2001)
18. Stroustrup, B.: The C++ Programming Language: Special Edition, 3 edn. Addison-Wesley Professional (February 2000), http://www.worldcat.org/isbn/0201700735
19. The Boost MPL Library, http://www.boost.org/doc/libs/1_48_0/libs/mpl/doc/index.html (accessed December 12, 2012)
20. The HDF Group. Hierarchical data format version 5 (2000-2010), http://www.hdfgroup.org/HDF5/ (accessed March 27, 2011)
21. Vandevoorde, D., Josuttis, N.M.: C++ Templates—The Complete Guide. Addison-Wesley (2002)
22. Vuduc, R., Demmel, J.W., Yelick, K.A.: OSKI: A library of automatically tuned sparse matrix kernels. Journal of Physics: Conference Series 16(1), 521–530 (2005)

Supporting Compile-Time Debugging
and Precise Error Reporting in Meta-programs

Yannis Lilis[1] and Anthony Savidis[1, 2]

[1] Institute of Computer Science, FORTH
[2] Department of Computer Science, University of Crete
{lilis,as}@ics.forth.gr

Abstract. Compile-time meta-programming is an advanced language feature enabling to mix programs with definitions that are executed at compile-time and may generate source code to be put in their place. Such definitions are called meta-programs and their actual evaluation constitutes a compilation stage. As meta-programs are also programs, programmers should be supported in handling compile-time and runtime errors, something introducing challenges to the entire tool chain along two lines. Firstly, the source point of a compile error may well be the outcome of a series of compilation stages, thus never appearing within the original program. Effectively, the latter requires a compiler to track down the error chain across all involved stages so as to provide a meaningful, descriptive and precise error report. Secondly, every compilation stage is instantiated by the execution of the respective staged program. Thus, typical full-fledged source-level debugging for any particular stage should be facilitated during the compilation process. Existing implementations suffer in both terms, overall providing poor error messages, while lacking the required support to debug meta-programs of any staging depth. In this paper we firstly outline an implementation of a meta-programming system offering all mentioned facilities. Then, we detail the required amendments to the compilation process. Finally, we discuss the necessary interoperation points between the compiler and the tool-chain (IDE).

Keywords: Meta-programs, compile-time meta-programming, staged languages, source-level debugging, error messages.

1 Introduction

The term meta-programming is generally used to denote programs that generate other programs and was originally related to the existence of a macro system like the *C Preprocessor* (CPP) [1] or the *Lisp* macro system [2] that would allow program fragments to be built up at compile-time. Lexical systems like the CPP are recognized as being inadequate for meta-programming as they operate on raw text, unaware of any context information, while most languages do not share Lisp's syntactic minimalism to provide an equally powerful facility with seamless integration. In modern languages, meta-programming is closely coupled with functions that operate on some abstract syntactic form, like an abstract syntax tree (AST), and can be

C.A. Furia and S. Nanz (Eds.): TOOLS Europe 2012, LNCS 7304, pp. 155–170, 2012.
© Springer-Verlag Berlin Heidelberg 2012

invoked during compile-time to change existing code or produce and inject additional code in the source being compiled. Such functions are called meta-functions and they as a whole constitute the meta-program. The compilation of a program that contains a meta-program requires it to be executed at compile-time to produce a possibly changed source file. If the resulting source contains additional meta-programs they are executed in the same way until we reach a final source with no meta-programs that will be compiled into the final executable. This iterative process may involve multiple steps of meta-program evaluations called *compilation stages*. Languages that support such a compilation scheme are called *multi-stage languages* ([3], [4]) with *MetaML* [5] and *MetaOCaml* [6] being two typical examples. Multi-stage programs are essentially programs whose source code is finalized through a sequence of evaluations defined in the program itself. They use special annotations to explicitly specify the order of their computations, with respect to the compilation stage they appear in. These annotations are called *staging annotations*. Staging annotations however are not limited to multi-stage languages. For example, *C++* [7] is a two-stage language where the first stage is the interpretation of the templates (denoted by the < > tags) and the second stage is the compilation of the non-template code.

Meta-programming can help achieve various benefits [8], the most typical of which is performance. It provides a mechanism for writing general purpose programs without suffering any overhead due to generality; rather than writing a generic but inefficient program, one writes a program generator that generates an efficient solution from a specification. Additionally, by using partial evaluation it is possible to identify and perform many computations at compile time based on a-priori information about some of the program's input, thus minimizing the runtime overhead. Another application is the reasoning about object-programs. It is possible to analyze properties of an object-program that can be used to improve performance, or provide object program validation. Finally, meta-programming can achieve code reusability at a macroscopic scale by implementing parameterized proven design practices (design patterns) and instantiating them based on the given parameters.

Context. As with normal programs, when writing meta-programs errors are bound to happen, so it is important to have the proper tools to understand the origin of the error and finally resolve it. In normal programs, there are two main error categories: compilation and execution errors. Compilation errors are generally resolved easily as compilers can identify exactly where something went wrong and why. On the other hand, execution errors involve runtime state that may be different between executions and is not directly visible to the programmer, making them harder to resolve. Fortunately, debuggers can provide the required information by allowing inspection of runtime values and call stack, tracing the program execution, and adding breakpoints, thus significantly aiding the error resolution process.

Problem. The same principles regarding errors and their management apply for meta-programs as well. However, both meta-program compilation and execution may involve code that was never part of the original program. This means that compilation errors are not that easy to deal with anymore as the error provided no longer reflects code that the programmer can see and understand. Moreover, meta-program execution errors are even harder to face since there is no actual source that can be used for debugging. It becomes obvious that error handling in meta-programs requires more sophisticated tools, without which the programmer's ability to write, understand and maintain meta-programs may be severely hindered. Clearly, compilation errors due to staging should encompass sufficient information to identify their cause while stage execution errors should be detectable using typical source-level debugging.

Contributions. In this paper, we discuss the implementation details of a meta-programming system addressing the previous issues based on:

- Generating source files for compilation stages and their outputs (original source transformations) and incorporating them into the project manager of the IDE, associated with the source being built. These files become part of the workspace and can be used for code review, error reporting and source-level debugging.
- Maintaining the chain of all source locations involved in the generation of an erroneous code segment to provide precise error reports. This chain includes the original source as well as the generated compilation stage source files and their outputs and can be easily traversed within the IDE to resolve any error.
- Mapping original source breakpoints to breakpoints for some compilation stage and using its generated source to provide compile-time source-level debugging.

We then detail the amendments required to support such functionality. Finally, we discuss the necessary contact sites between the compiler and the tool-chain.

2   Related Work

Our work targets the field of meta-programming in compiled languages and focuses on the delivery of an integrated system able to support debugging of meta-programs being executed at compile-time as well as provide precise and meaningful messages for compilation errors originating within meta-code. In this context, the topics directly relevant to our work are compile-time debugging and error reporting.

2.1   Compile-Time Debugging of Stages

C++ [7] support for meta-programming is based on its template system that is essentially a functional language interpreted at compile time [9], [10]. There are *C++* debuggers (e.g. *Microsoft Visual Studio Debugger, GDB*) that allow source level debugging of templates, but only in the sense of tracing the execution of the template instantiation code and matching it to the source containing the template definition. However, there is no way to debug the template interpretation during compilation. A step towards this end is *Templight* [11], a debugging framework that uses code instrumentation to produce warning messages during compilation and provide a trace of the template instantiation. Nevertheless, it is an external debugging framework not integrated into any development environment and relies on the compiler generating enough information when it meets the instrumented code. Finally, there is no programmer intervention; the system provides tracing but not interactive debugging.

D [12] is a statically typed multi-paradigm language that supports meta-programming by combining templates, compile time function execution, and string mixins (text code injected into the source). *Descent* [13] is an *Eclipse* plug-in for code written in *D* and provides an experimental compile-time debugging facility that supports simple templates and compile-time functions. However, the debugging process does not involve the normal execution engine of the language; instead it relies on a custom language interpreter for both execution and debugging functionality.

Nemerle [14] is a statically typed object oriented language, in the *Java / C#* vein that supports meta-programming through its macro system. *Nemerle* and its IDE, *Nemerle Studio*, provide support for debugging macro invocations during compile time. *Nemerle* macros are actually compiler plug-ins that have to be implemented in separate files and modules and are loaded during the compilation of any other file that invokes them. Since they are dynamically linked libraries with executable code, it is possible to debug them by debugging the compiler itself; when a macro is invoked, the code corresponding to its body is executed and can be typically debugged. Nevertheless, the development model posed, requiring each macro to be in a separate file and module, is restrictive and the macro debugging process is rather cumbersome.

There are a lot more compiled languages, both functional and imperative, that support meta-programming. Some examples include *MetaOCaml* [6], *Template Haskell* [15], *Dylan* [16], *Metalua* [17] and *Converge* [18]. However, none of them provide any support for debugging meta-programs during compilation.

2.2   Compile-Error Reporting

To our knowledge, most compiled languages that support meta-programming provide very limited error reporting for compilation errors originating from generated code. Typically, the error is reported directly at the generated code with no further information about its origin or the context of its occurrence. Below we examine some of the few cases that offer a more sophisticated error reporting mechanism.

C++ compilers (e.g. *Microsoft Visual Studio Debugger, GDB*) provide fairly descriptive messages regarding compilation errors occurring within template instantiations. Using these messages provided, the programmer may follow the instantiation chain that begins with the code of the initial instantiation that caused the error (typically user code) and ends with the code of the instantiation that actually triggered the error (probably library code). Essentially, these error messages represent the execution stack of the template interpreter. While potentially informative and able to provide accurate information to experienced programmers, template error messages are quite cryptic for average programmers and require significant effort to locate the actual error. Unfortunately, this is the common case for nontrivial meta-programs and applies especially to libraries with multiple template instantiations (e.g. *Boost* [10]).

Converge [18] provides some error reporting facilities related to meta-programming by keeping the original source, line and column information for quoted-code and retaining it at splice locations (injections into the program AST). For runtime errors, this approach works fine but is limited by the single source code location that can be associated with a given virtual machine instruction, not allowing for a complete trace of the error. For compile-time errors, *Converge* can track down the source information of the quasi-quotes and associated insertions (i.e. any AST creation) to provide a detailed message. However, it fails to provide information about the splice locations, which actually involve staging execution. This means that any error originating in generated code cannot be properly traced back to the code that actually produced it. Finally, any compile error reported is presented only with respect to the original source, thus providing no actual context regarding the temporary module (i.e. computation stage) being executed to perform the splice.

3   Meta-programming System

Our meta-programming system[1] is based on the *Delta* programming language [19] and its IDE, *Sparrow* [20]. To support meta-programming facilities, several extensions were made to the language itself as well as to its compiler and IDE.

3.1   Language Extensions

To support multi-stage meta-programming, *Delta* has been extended with staging annotations similar to the ones of *MetaOCaml* [21].

- *Quasi-quotes* (written <<...>>) can be inserted around almost any language element to enclose its syntactic form into an AST. This annotation provides the easiest way to create language values containing code segments.
- *Escape* (written ~(expr)) can be used on an expression within quasi-quotes to escape the syntactic form and interpret the expression normally. It allows combining existing AST values in the AST being constructed by the quasi-quotes.
- *Inline* (written !(expr)) can be used on an expression to evaluate it at translation time and inject its value directly into the source code. For the injection to be valid the expression must evaluate to an AST or AST convertible value and it is performed by properly incorporating the evaluated AST into the main source AST.
- *Execute* (written &stmt) can be used to execute a statement at translation time. An addition to the original *MetaOCaml* annotations, it differs from *inline* as it does not modify the source. It is used for computations not expressible through expressions (e.g. loops) but also to generate code available only during compilation.

The following program is a simple example of compile-time meta-programming illustrating the staging annotations used in *Delta* (trivially adopted from [21]). Function *ExpandPower* creates the AST of its *x* argument being multiplied by itself *n* times, while function *MakePower* creates the AST of a specialized power function.

---

[1] The system is fully functional and its complete source code is available for public download through our Subversion repository https://139.91.186.186/svn/sparrow /branches/meta using a guest account (username: 'guest' and empty password).

```
&function ExpandPower (x, n) {
    if (n == 0) return <<1>>;
    else if (n == 1) return x;
    else return <<~x * ~(ExpandPower(x, n - 1))>>;
}
&function MakePower (n) {
    return << (
        function (x) { return ~(ExpandPower(<<x>>, n)); }
    )>>;
}
power3 = !(MakePower(3)); //(function(x){return x*x*x;};)
std::print("2^3 = ", power3(2));
```

3.2 Compiler Extensions

The *quasi-quotes* and *escape* annotations are used to create and combine code segments and involve no staging computation on their own. Staging occurs due to the existence of the *inline* and *execute* annotations, which are therefore also referred to as *staging tags*. Essentially this means that any program containing these staging tags cannot be compiled until all of them are translated first. However, staging tags can be nested or their evaluation may introduce additional staging tags, so the whole compilation process requires multiple translation and execution stages (Fig. 1). To support this scheme, we extend the compilation process using the following steps:

1. Parse the original source program to produce the *main AST*.
2. If no staging tags exist in the main AST go to step 8.
3. Traverse the main AST collecting the nodes for the next compilation stage.
4. Assemble the collected nodes to create the *compilation stage AST*.
5. Normally compile the compilation stage AST to executable code.
6. Execute the produced code updating the main AST in the process.
7. Go to step 2.
8. Normally compile the main AST (final AST) to executable code.

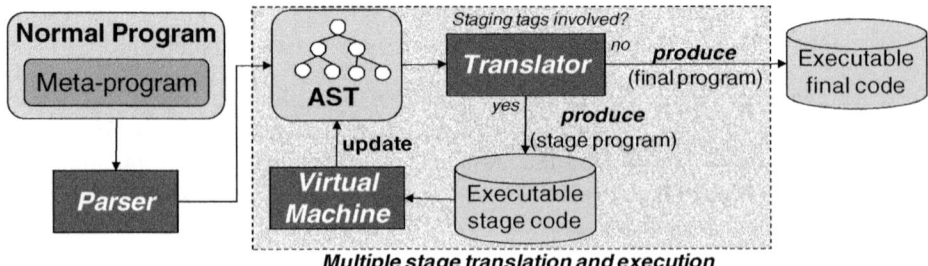

Fig. 1. High level overview of a multi-stage compilation process

Each compilation stage takes place in steps 3-6. The node collection in step 3 relies on the two following properties: (i) nested staging tags should always be evaluated at an earlier stage than outer ones; and (ii) staging tags of the same nesting level should be evaluated within the same stage. This practically means that the staging tags selected for a given compilation stage are the innermost. After assembling the nodes to create the compilation stage AST (step 4), we normally compile it to executable code (step 5). This normal compilation is possible since, by construction, the assembled AST contains no staging tags. Then we continue with the code execution (step 6), during which the original source *inline* tags that were translated to virtual machine instructions will modify the source by injecting code into the main AST. After the execution, the main AST is fully updated and ready for either the next stage (step 7), or – if no more staging tags exist – the final compilation (step 8).

3.3   IDE Support for Meta-programming

Meta-programming especially for multiple stages is a quite demanding task, so our system aims to facilitate the development of meta-programs as much as possible[2].

Since the transformations of the original source code performed by the various compilation stages are performed internally by the compiler and are therefore transparent to programmers, special attention is given to providing them with meaningful, descriptive and precise error reports in case some compilation stage raises a compilation error. Such error reports provide the full error chain across all stages involved in the generation of the erroneous code. Within *Sparrow*, programmers may easily navigate back and forth across this error chain. This feature is a significant aid in tracking the origin of the error and ultimately resolving it.

Additionally, every compilation stage is instantiated by the execution of the respective staged program. As such, it should be subject to typical source-level debugging even though its execution occurs during the compilation process. *Sparrow* provides such functionality supporting typical debugging facilities such as expression evaluation, watches, call stack, breakpoints and tracing. Fig. 2 illustrates a compile-time debugging session highlighting the following points:

1. Breakpoints are initially set within a meta-function in the original source file.
2. The source file is built with debugging enabled. This launches the compiler for the build and attaches the debugger to it for any staged program execution.
3. During compilation, the IDE is notified about any compilation stage sources.
4. Stage sources are added in the workspace associated with the source being built.
5. A breakpoint is hit, so execution is stopped at its location.
6. The source corresponding to the breakpoint hit is opened within the editor to allow further debugging operations such as tracing, variable inspection, etc.
7. The breakpoints in the generated stage source (including the one hit) were automatically generated based on the breakpoints set in the original source file.
8. The execution call stack is available for navigation across active function calls.
9. It is possible to inspect variables containing code segments as AST values.

---

[2] A video showing an overview of all meta-programming related features of our system is available from: http://www.ics.forth.gr/hci/files/plang/metaprogramming.avi

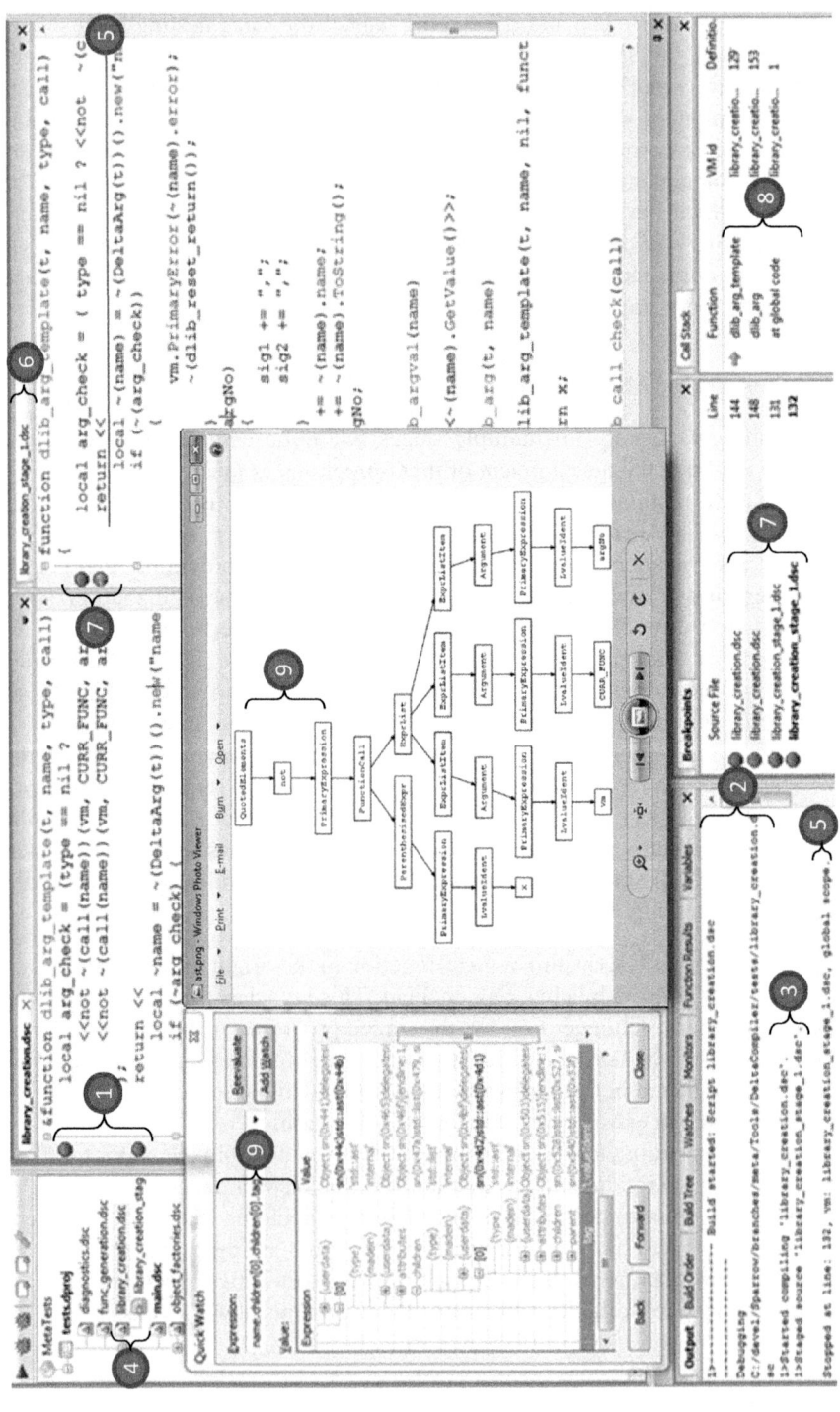

Fig. 2. A compile-time debugging session in Sparrow. Highlighted items 1-9 are discussed within text.

The compilation stage sources as well as their output (main AST transformation stages) are actually created and inserted into the workspace even when performing a non-debugged build. This allows programmers to review the assembled and the generated code of each stage along with the effect it has on the final program even after the build is completed, thus allowing for a better understanding of their code. Fig. 3 highlights this functionality showing all sources related to the power example.

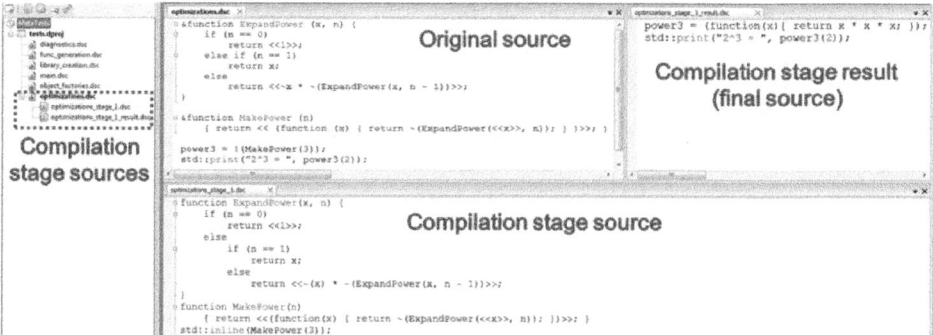

Fig. 3. Reviewing the compilation sources in Sparrow: Project manager view (*left*), original source file (*middle*), compilation stage source (*bottom*), compilation stage result (*middle right*)

4   Compiler Amendments

4.1   Storing the Source Code of Every Stage and Its Output

The ASTs assembled for each compilation stage are temporary and only used for code generation. To support reporting compile errors for stage sources or applying source-level debugging during their execution, these ASTs can be further utilized to create source files containing the code they represent, a process known as *unparsing*. These files are meant for programmers, so their code must span across multiple lines and be properly indented. For better visualization, we also consider that any code segment present in the initial source should keep its original form as an unparsed version may be significantly different (different indentation, empty lines, comments, etc), and the one written by the programmer is clearly user-friendlier. To support this efficiently, AST nodes contain their starting and ending character positions in the original source to retrieve their text segments (direct association of each node with its text would be far too resource demanding). This way, the unparsing algorithm will combine original and generated text segments to produce a complete source for each compilation stage.

To obtain the source code for a specific compilation stage, we apply the unparsing algorithm on its AST and store the result using some naming convention, for example adding a suffix along with the current stage number. To allow programmers to review not only the compilation stages, but also the code they generate and the modifications they perform on the main AST, we also unparse the updated main AST after the successful execution of each compilation stage. Essentially, this means that for an execution involving *n* compilation stages, there will be $2 \cdot n$ source files generated. The final program being compiled into executable code is actually the output of the last compilation stage, so it will also be available as the last generated source (Fig. 4).

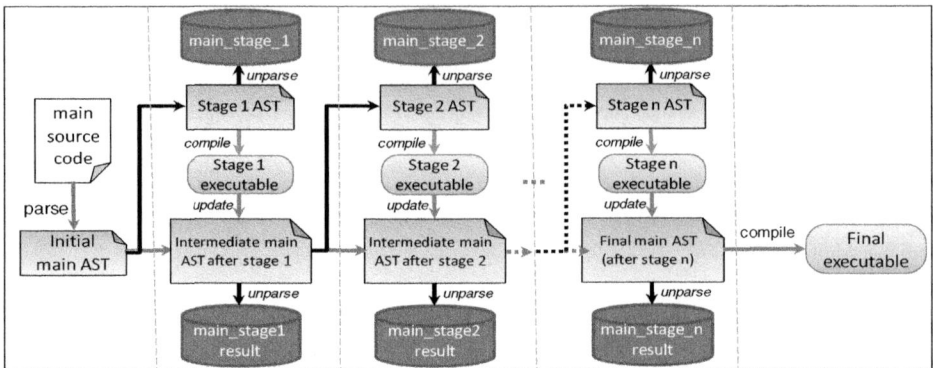

Fig. 4. Storing the source code of all compilation stages and their outputs

4.2   Tracking the Compile-Error Chain across Stages and Outputs

Any compilation stage (and the final program) is the outcome of a series of previous compilation stages and may never appear in the original source. As a result, to provide a meaningful and precise report for compile errors, the compiler has to track down the error chain across all involved stages and combine all relevant information in a descriptive message. To provide such functionality, each AST node is enriched with information about its origin, thus creating a list of associated source references. The source references for each node are created using the following rules:

1. Nodes created by the initial source parsing have no source reference.
2. When assembling nodes for a compilation stage, a source reference is created, pointing to the current source location of the node present in the main AST.
3. When updating the main AST, the source locations of the modified nodes are mapped to the latest stage source, creating the corresponding source reference.

Rules 1 and 3 along with the fact that the main AST can be modified only through the execution of the compilation stages guarantee that the main AST nodes will always either be a part of the original source or be generated by some previous stage and have a source reference to it. Furthermore, rule 2 and the fact that compilation stages are created using only nodes from the main AST guarantee the same property for all compilation stages as well. This means that any AST being compiled, either for some compilation stage or the final program, will incorporate for each of its nodes the entire trajectory of the compilation stages involved in their generation. Fig. 5 provides a sample visualization of this information upon the occurrence of an error.

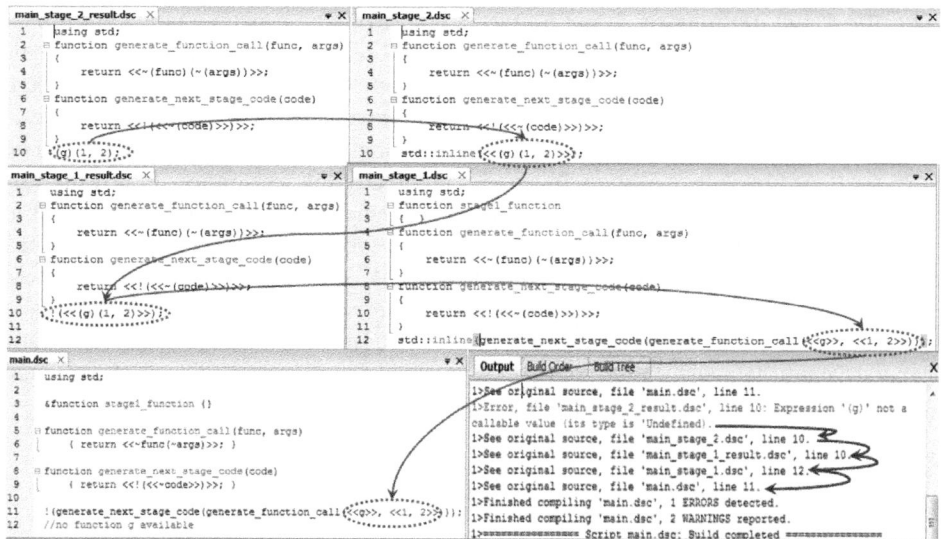

Fig. 5. Precise error reporting for compilation stages using the entire chain of generated sources

4.3   Compile-Time Source-Level Debugging of Stages

In order to support compile-time debugging, we need to provide the source code for each compilation stage and support breakpoints both before and during debug sessions. We continue by firstly discussing the general case of debugging dynamic source code and the way we improved it when it comes to stages.

General Case: Debugging Dynamic Source Code. Debugging in the absence of a respective source file is common when either the source code is stored in a buffer or only its respective syntax tree is available for translation, usually both resulting from a computation. Clearly, this is a more general case compared to the need of source-level debugging for stages where no explicit source files are available too.

The latter is already handled in the Delta language through the reflection infrastructure as follows: The source text is incorporated into the debug information of the generated binary. Once the binary is loaded for execution, the source text from the debug information is extracted by the debugger backend and is posted to the debugger frontend when a breakpoint is hit in a statement of such dynamic source code. Then, the frontend opens an editor for the dynamic source code enabling users review it and also add or remove breakpoints as needed.

Apparently, before the initial creation of the dynamic source file, there is no way to introduce respective breakpoints. At a first glance it seems that the latter applies to stages as well, since their source code is also dynamically produced. Thus, an initial meta-compilation round is required so that the stage sources become available.

In this context, as we discuss below, we have implemented a method improving the debugging of stage source code by enabling the insertion of stage breakpoints directly on the main source file even before meta-compilation.

Specific Case: Debugging Stage Source Code. Prior to a meta-compilation round, there are no stage sources available and no breakpoints associated with their execution. The only available breakpoints concern the original source being compiled, but we can translate them to breakpoints for the dynamically generated stage sources.

As discussed, every node of the syntax tree belonging to a compilation stage can be directly traced-back across all earlier stages involved in its generation. Following this generation chain we can always reach the original source, as even nodes introduced in some particular stage will have been created recursively by code originating from the initial source. Essentially, there is a direct mapping of a compilation stage node to a node of the original source. By also keeping the reverse mapping, we can associate any node of the original source to a list of compilation stage nodes (a single node may generate multiple ones). In the same sense, we can associate each line of the original source with the compilation stage source lines that they actually generate.

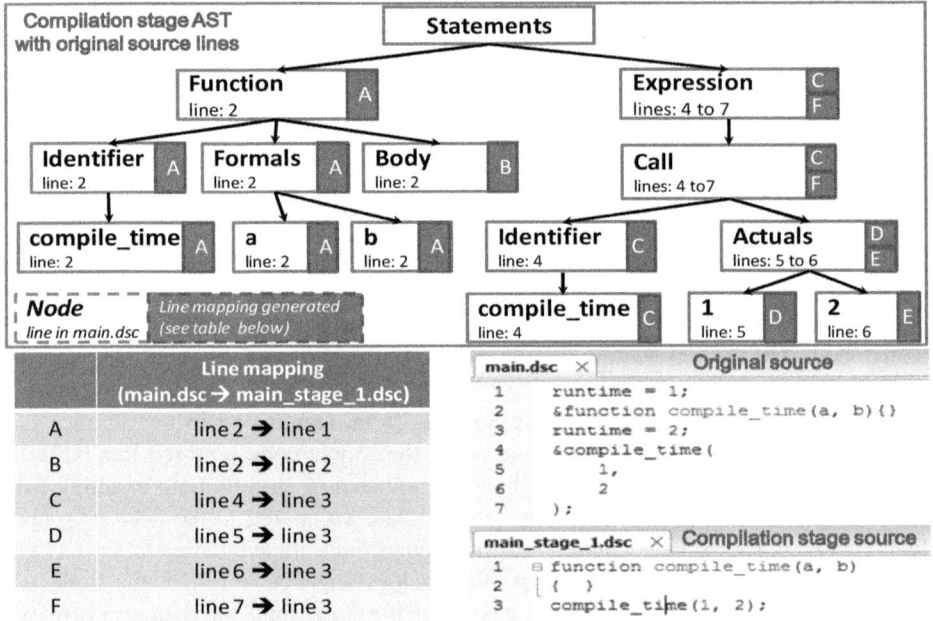

Fig. 6. Extracting line mappings for a compilation stage: The assembled stage AST (*top*), the original source and the compilation stage source (*bottom right*) and the line mappings generated by each AST node (*next to each of the AST nodes, referring to elements of the bottom left table*)

To achieve this, we extend the unparsing process earlier discussed to associate each node line of the AST being traversed to the current line of the source being generated, taking into account the lines introduced by the unparsing implementation (Fig. 6). Finally, we can use this association to transform breakpoints intended for the original source into breakpoints for the compilation stage sources.

The line mappings are not unique, so a single original source breakpoint may generate multiple stage source breakpoints (e.g. a multi-line function) and multiple source breakpoints may generate the same stage source breakpoint (e.g. a complex multi-line expression that generates a single line of code). Nevertheless, this is the expected functionality supposing that code modifications occur directly at the original source line. For instance, an expression generating a function can be seen as substituting itself with a single line containing the function definition. A breakpoint set on the single line function would be hit during the execution of any statement within the function; likewise, the breakpoint of the original source will generate breakpoints for all lines the function expands to, achieving the same functionality.

5   Contact Sites between the Compiler and the Tool-Chain

5.1   Debugger

In order to support proper debugging of the compilation stages, there are two main additions required related to the debugger. The first one is regarding the expression evaluator and the need to inspect runtime values that represent code segments and the second one relates to the handling of breakpoints for the compilation stage sources.

The execution of a compilation stage typically targets the modification of the original source being compiled by adding, removing or editing code segments expressed in ASTs. In order to properly debug such operations, it should be possible to inspect such runtime values and browse through their contents. For example, the programmer should be able to inspect any specific node attribute (e.g. type, name, value, etc) as well as other related tree nodes (e.g. children, parent). The inspection facility can be delivered using typical tree views or custom tree visualization (Fig. 7).

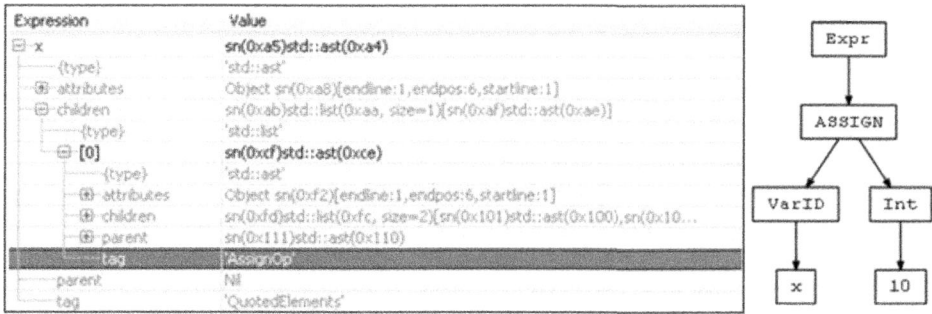

Fig. 7. Inspecting code segments expressed in AST form: using an expression tree view (*left, Sparrow IDE Zen debugger*) and using a graphical tree visualizer (*right, GVEdit for Graphviz*)

Being able to specify stop points for a program execution is a vital debugging facility, so it is important to support adding breakpoints for the execution of any compilation stage. However, the compilation stage sources are dynamically produced during compilation, so it is not possible for the programmer to add breakpoints to them prior to their creation and execution. When launching the compiler, the IDE uses the debugger frontend to collect the breakpoints for the original source and passes them to the compiler to later map them to breakpoints for the compilation stage sources. During compilation, after performing the requested breakpoint mappings, the compiler has to notify the debugger backend about the new breakpoints. Instead of sending the breakpoints back to the IDE to propagate them to the debugger frontend that would in turn have to communicate them to the backend, it is much simpler and efficient to allow the execution system itself (i.e. the compiler) issue breakpoints directly to the debugger running within it (Fig. 8). The only additional requirement is the notification of the debugger frontend for the new breakpoints. Since these breakpoints are essentially transient, the frontend can simply keep track of them during the execution of each compilation stage and discard them after it is completed.

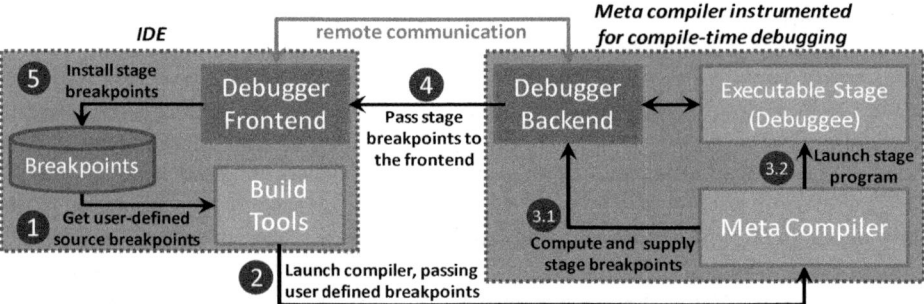

Fig. 8. Components involved in the generation of compilation stage breakpoints based on original source breakpoints. Arrows indicate the information flow among the components.

5.2   IDE

The compiler can be seen as a service invoked by the IDE during the build process. As such, the IDE may provide actions to be performed for specific events like compilation errors, or generation of stage sources. If the compiler is implemented as a separate executable spawned by the IDE, the communication channel between them is typically a memory pipe using standard text input and output facilities. This requires establishing a protocol for communicating the compiler events to the IDE using some text representation. For example, to notify the IDE about the existence of the stage sources, the compiler may use a special message containing resource identifiers for them (e.g. file paths). The IDE can then retrieve these files and use them to provide the sources required for the debugging process but also to maintain a reference point of internal compilation resources externalized to the programmer.

Since the IDE typically incorporates the debugger frontend, another requirement for supporting the compilation-time debugging is the ability to launch the debugger during compilation and to properly orchestrate any other facilities previously targeted only for build or debug sessions. Essentially, IDEs provide different tools during a build session (e.g. error messages, build output, etc.) and during a debug session (e.g. call stack, watches, active threads and processes, loaded modules, etc.), while usually applying different visual configurations for each activity. Compile-time debugging involves both a build and a debug session, so it is important to combine the provided facilities in a way that maintains a familiar working environment for the programmer.

6   Conclusion

In this paper we focused on providing error handling facilities in the context of meta-programming. Since meta-programs are essentially programs, proper handling is required to resolve errors occurring both during their compilation and execution. However, existing implementations provide poor error messages and lack the required support to debug meta-programs of any staging depth.

Towards this direction, we implemented a meta-programming system that features: (i) precise reports for errors occurring at compilation stages or the final program using a series of source references across the entire code generation chain; and (ii) full-fledged source-level debugging for any stage during the compilation process. To support these features, we based our implementation on the following three axes: (i) source files are generated for both compilation stages and their outputs and are incorporated into the IDE's project manager associated with the source being built; (ii) the chain of all source locations involved in generating an erroneous code segment is utilized to provide precise error reports and (iii) original source breakpoints are mapped to breakpoints for compilation stages. These features are not tightly coupled with meta-programming, so we plan to further investigate their application to other program transformation approaches like aspect-oriented programming.

To evaluate the effectiveness of our system we created a suite of meta-programs containing various errors. We then assembled two groups of programmers of similar experience and skill level and asked them to resolve the errors. One group worked with the support of our system, while the other worked without it. Results showed that the group using our system resolved the errors significantly faster. Users also noted that our debugging features allowed them to handle even complex errors quite easily.

Finally, we provided a detailed overview of the amendments required to the compilation process and tool-chain to support such functionality. We focused on an untyped language, but the same approach can also be used with typed languages. The only difference is that in our case, type errors result into stage execution errors, while a type system could detect them at the stage compilation. This however, is a typical trade-off between typed and untyped languages not related to meta-programming. All in all, apart from the meta-programming system we built for the Delta language, we believe that our work can provide a basis for extending other meta-programming systems with similar features, arguably improving the meta-programming experience.

References

1. Kernighan, B.W., Ritchie, D.M.: The C programming language. Prentice-Hall, Englewood Cliffs (1988)
2. Bawden, A.: Quasiquotation in Lisp. In: Danvy, O. (ed.) Proceedings of the Workshop on Partial Evaluation and Semantics-Based Program Manipulation, San Antonio, pp. 88–99. University of Aarhus, Dept. of Computer Science. Invited talk (1999)

3. Martel, M., Sheard, T.: Introduction to multi-stage programming using MetaML. Technical report, OGI, Portland, OR, 211, 213 (September 1997)
4. Taha, W., Sheard, T.: Multi-stage programming with explicit annotations. In: Proceedings of the Symposium on Partial Evaluation and Semantic-Based Program Manipulation (PEPM), Amsterdam, pp. 203–217. ACM Press (1997)
5. Sheard, T.: Using MetaML: A Staged Programming Language. In: Launchbury, J., Sheard, T., Meijer, E. (eds.) AFP 1996. LNCS, vol. 1129, pp. 207–239. Springer, Heidelberg (1996)
6. MetaOCaml: A compiled, type-safe multi-stage programming language (2003), http://www.metaocaml.org/ (accessed September 13, 2011)
7. Stroustrup, B.: The C++ Programming Language Special Edition. Addison-Wesley (2000)
8. Sheard, T.: Accomplishments and Research Challenges in Meta-programming. In: Taha, W. (ed.) SAIG 2001. LNCS, vol. 2196, pp. 2–44. Springer, Heidelberg (2001)
9. Veldhuizen, T.: Using C++ template metaprograms. C++ Report 7(4), 36–43 (1995)
10. Abrahams, D., Gurtovoy, A.: C++ Template Metaprogramming: Concepts, Tools, and Techniques from Boost and Beyond. Addison-Wesley Professional (2004)
11. Porkolab, Z., Mihalicza, J., Sipos, A.: Debugging C++ template metaprograms. In: Proc. of GPCE 2006, pp. 255–264. ACM (2006)
12. Alexandrescu, A.: The D Programming Language. Addison-Wesley Professional (2010)
13. Descent: An Eclipse plugin providing an IDE for the D programming language, http://www.dsource.org/projects/descent (accessed September 13, 2011)
14. Skalski, K., Moskal, M., Olszta, P.: Meta-programming in Nemerle (2004), http://nemerle.org/metaprogramming.pdf (accessed September 13, 2011)
15. Sheard, T., Jones, S.P.: Template meta-programming for Haskell. In: Proceedings of the Haskell Workshop 2002. ACM (2002)
16. Bachrach, J., Playford, K.: D-expressions: Lisp power, dylan style (1999), http://www.ai.mit.edu/people/jrb/Projects/dexprs.pdf (accessed September 13, 2011)
17. Fleutot, F.: Man Metalua (April 2007), http://metalua.luaforge.net/metalua-manual.html
18. Tratt, L.: Compile-time meta-programming in a dynamically typed OO language. In: Proceedings Dynamic Languages Symposium, pp. 49–64 (October 2005)
19. Savidis, A.: Dynamic Imperative Languages for Runtime Extensible Semantics and Polymorphic Meta-Programming. In: Guelfi, N., Savidis, A. (eds.) RISE 2005. LNCS, vol. 3943, pp. 113–128. Springer, Heidelberg (2006)
20. Savidis, A., Bourdenas, T., Georgalis, J.: An Adaptable Circular Meta-IDE for a Dynamic Programming Language. In: Proceedings of the 4th International Workshop on Rapid Integration of Software Engineering Techniques (RISE 2007), Luxemburg, November 26-27, pp. 99–114 (2007)
21. Taha, W.: A Gentle Introduction to Multi-stage Programming. In: Lengauer, C., Batory, D., Blum, A., Vetta, A. (eds.) Domain-Specific Program Generation. LNCS, vol. 3016, pp. 30–50. Springer, Heidelberg (2004)

Identifying a Unifying Mechanism for the Implementation of Concurrency Abstractions on Multi-language Virtual Machines

Stefan Marr and Theo D'Hondt

Software Languages Lab, Vrije Universiteit Brussel
Pleinlaan 2, 1050 Elsene, Belgium
{stefan.marr,tjdhondt}@vub.ac.be

Abstract. Supporting all known abstractions for concurrent and parallel programming in a virtual machines (VM) is a futile undertaking, but it is required to give programmers appropriate tools and performance. Instead of supporting all abstractions directly, VMs need a unifying mechanism similar to INVOKEDYNAMIC for JVMs.

Our survey of parallel and concurrent programming concepts identifies concurrency abstractions as the ones benefiting most from support in a VM. Currently, their semantics is often weakened, reducing their engineering benefits. They require a mechanism to define flexible language guarantees.

Based on this survey, we define an ownership-based meta-object protocol as candidate for VM support. We demonstrate its expressiveness by implementing actor semantics, software transactional memory, agents, CSP, and active objects. While the performance of our prototype confirms the need for VM support, it also shows that the chosen mechanism is appropriate to express a wide range of concurrency abstractions in a unified way.

Keywords: Virtual Machines, Language Support, Abstraction, Parallelism, Concurrency.

1 The Right Tool for the Job

Implementing parallel and concurrent systems has been argued to be a complex undertaking that requires the right tools for the job, perhaps more than other problems software engineering encountered so far. Instead of searching for a non-existing *silver bullet* approach, we argue that language designers need to be supported in building domain-specific concurrency abstractions.

Let us consider the implementation of a typical desktop application. A mail application combines several components that interact and have different potentials to utilize computational resources. The user interface component is traditionally implemented with an event-loop to react to user input. In a concurrent setting, it is also desirable to enforce encapsulation like in an actor model, since encapsulation simplifies reasoning about the interaction with other components.

C.A. Furia and S. Nanz (Eds.): TOOLS Europe 2012, LNCS 7304, pp. 171–186, 2012.

Another part of the application is the data storage for emails and address book information. This part traditionally interacts with with a database. The natural way to implement this component is to use a software transactional memory (STM) system that extends the transaction semantics of the database into the application. This allow a unified reasoning when for instance a new mail is received from the network component and needs to be stored in the database.

A third part is a search engine that allows the user to find emails and address book entries. Such an engine can typically exploit data-parallel approaches like map/reduce or parallel collection operations for performance.

However, supporting the various different approaches to parallel and concurrent programming on top of the same platform comes with the challenge to identify basic commonalities that allow to abstract from the particularities of specific constructs and languages. Today's high-level language virtual machines (VMs) do not provide intrinsic support for more than one specific approach [17]. While some approaches like Fork/Join [14], Concurrent Collections [3] or PLINQ can be implemented as libraries without losing any semantics or performance, approaches like the actor model are typically implemented as an approximation losing for instance the engineering benefits of encapsulation [11].

We approach this problem with a survey of the various concepts of parallel and concurrent programming to identify concepts that are relevant for a multi-language virtual machine (short: VM). Based on this survey, we define an ownership-based meta-object protocol and evaluate its suitability to implemented the identified concepts. Furthermore, we briefly evaluate the performance properties of our prototype and discuss related work which could be used to realize an implementation with optimal performance characteristics.

2   A Survey of Parallel and Concurrent Programming Concepts

The goal of this survey is to *identify concepts* that are relevant for a multi-language VM. To that end, we first select questions that enable us to categorize the concepts by relevance. Afterwards, we detail our approach to identify the concepts and finally, we present the findings and discuss our conclusions.

2.1   Survey Questions

When concepts are considered for inclusion in a VM, one of the main goals is to avoid unnecessary complexity. From that follows, that a new concept only needs to be added to a VM if it cannot be implemented reasonably in terms of a library on top of the VM. Thus, our first question is:

LIB. Can this concept be implemented in terms of a library?

Interpreting the question very broadly, we consider whether some variation of the concept can be implemented. Typically, such a library implementation can either suffer from losing semantic guarantees, or it has to take performance drawbacks into account. Common examples are implementations of the actor model on top of the JVM or CLR [11].

To account for that variation, we need the following two questions:

SEM. Does this concept require runtime support to guarantee its semantics?

PERF. Would runtime support enable significant performance improvements compared with a pure library solution?

To answer SEM, we also consider interactions of different languages on top of a VM. This is relevant since common language guarantees are enforced by a compiler but do not carry over to the level of the VM. One example is the semantics of single-assignment variables, which is typically not transferred to the bytecode level of a VM. Similarly, we considered for PERF that knowledge about full language semantics often enables better optimizations. For instance, the knowledge about immutability enables constant folding, and taking the semantics of critical sections into account enables optimizations like lock elision.

The last categorization criterion is whether the concept is prior art:

PA. Is the concept already supported by a VM like the JVM or CLR?

2.2 Selecting Subjects and Identifying Concepts

To identify concepts, we rely foremost on the overview given by two surveys [2,25] as our main subjects. They give a broad foundation but are dated. To ensure that the most common concepts are included, we survey also a number of languages used in research or industry and select research papers from recent years to cover current trends. The full list of *subjects* is given in Tab. 1.

Table 1. Survey Subjects: Languages and Papers

Active Objects [13]	Charm++	Fortress	Occam-pi	Simple Java
Ada	Cilk	Go	OpenCL	Skillicorn&Talia [25]
Aida [15]	Clojure	Io	OpenMP	Sly
Alice	CoBoxes [23]	JCSP	Orleans [4]	StreamIT
AmbientTalk	Concurrent Haskell	Java Views [5]	Oz	Swing
Ateji PX	Concurrent ML	Join Java	PAM [22]	UPC
Axum	Concurrent Objects	Linda [7]	Reactive Objects [20]	X10
Briot et al. [2]	Concurrent Pascal	MPI	SCOOP [19]	XC
C#	Erlang	MapReduce [16]	STM [24]	
Chapel	Fortran 2008	MultiLisp [9]	Simple C/C++	

Starting with the two surveys, we *identify* for each subject the basic concepts and mechanisms introduced in the paper or provided by the language. For languages, we regard the language-level as well as possible implementation-level concepts. Note that the identified concepts necessarily abstract from specific details that vary between the different subjects. Thus, we do not regard every minor variation of a concept separately. However, this leaves room for different interpretations of our survey questions. For subjects like C/C++ and Java, we regard the *simple* core language and standard libraries. Interesting libraries or extensions available for their eco systems are considered as separate subjects.

2.3   Results

The analysis of the subjects given in Tab. 1 resulted in 82 identified concepts. Since most of them are accepted concepts in the literature, we will only discuss the results with regard to our questions in this paper. As mentioned earlier, some concept variations have been considered together as a single concept. For example, the distinct concepts of monitors and semaphores, have been regarded as part of *locks* in this survey. Similarly, *parallel bulk operations* is included and also covers *parallel loops* because of their similarity and closely related implementation strategies. Thus, Tab. 2a and 2b include 60 concepts and their respective survey results.

Table 2a. *Survey Results:* Prior Art and Library Solutions

Prior Art	PA	LIB	SEM	PERF		PA	LIB	SEM	PERF
Atomic Primitives	X	-	-	X	Co-routines	X	-	-	X
Condition Variables	X	X	-	X	Critical Sections	X	X	-	X
Global Address Spaces	X	X	-	X	Green Threads	X	-	-	-
Immutability	X	-	X	X	Join	X	-	-	-
Locks	X	X	-	X	Memory Model	X	-	X	X
Method Invocation	X	-	-	X	Race-And-Repair	X	X	-	-
Thread Pools	X	X	-	-	Thread-local Variables	X	X	-	X
Threads	X	X	-	-	Volatiles	X	-	X	-
Wrapper Objects	X	X	-	X					

Library Solutions	PA	LIB	SEM	PERF		PA	LIB	SEM	PERF
APGAS	-	X	-	-	Agents	-	X	-	-
Atoms	-	X	-	-	Concurrent Objects	-	X	-	-
Event-Loop	-	X	-	-	Events	-	X	-	-
Far-References	-	X	-	-	Fork/Join	-	X	-	-
Futures	-	X	-	-	Guards	-	X	-	-
Message Queue	-	X	-	-	One-sided Communication	-	X	-	-
PGAS	-	X	-	-	Parallel Bulk Operations	-	X	-	-
Reducers	-	X	-	-	Single Blocks	-	X	-	-
State Reconciliation	-	X	-	-					

Table 2b. *Survey Results:* Runtime Support Required

Runtime Support Required	PA	LIB	SEM	PERF		PA	LIB	SEM	PERF
Active Objects	-	X	X	-	Actors	-	X	X	X
Asynchronous Invocation	-	X	X	X	Axum-Domains	-	X	X	-
Barriers	-	X	-	X	By-Value	-	X	X	X
Channels	-	X	X	X	Clocks	-	X	-	X
Data Movement	-	-	-	X	Data Streams	-	X	X	X
Implicit Parallelism	-	X	-	X	Isolation	-	X	X	X
Locality	-	-	-	X	Map/Reduce	-	X	X	-
Message sends	-	X	X	X	Mirrors	-	X	-	X
No-Intercession	-	X	X	X	Ownership	-	-	-	X
Persistent Data Structures	-	X	X	-	Replication	-	X	X	-
Side-Effect Free	-	-	X	X	Speculative Execution	-	-	X	X
Transactions	-	X	X	X	Tuple Spaces	-	X	X	-
Vats	-	X	X	X	Vector Operations	-	X	-	X

As Tab. 2a shows, about half of the concepts are either already available in JVM and CLR or can be implemented in terms of a library without sacrificing semantics or performance aspects. We will discuss only the remaining 26.

With 18, the majority of the concepts requiring runtime support (Tab. 2b) suffer from weaker semantics. Most of these concepts are usually realized either with enforcement on a compiler level or require correct construction by the programmer. However, a compiler cannot enforce guarantees on a VM if they are not present in the bytecode intermediate language. Thus, a Java program can mutate a supposedly immutable object of another language. An example is the semantics of final fields in Java, which can be changed via reflection, and thus, are not truly constant. Persistent data structures and tuple spaces are examples that rely on the notion of immutable values to provide a consistent framework for reasoning. Similarly, E's vats, AmbientTalk's actors, and Axum's domains restrict mutation to an owner. While a reference can be obtained to an object owned by another actor or vat, they can only be mutated within the owner's context. These concepts also share the property that method invocation on such objects need to be done asynchronously in the context of the owning entity and under the scheduling regime of the entity. This applies to active objects, too.

The other concepts, like barriers, clocks, data movement, locality, and vector operations, will benefit from adaptive optimizations of a just-in-time compiler, which is aware of their semantics, or require information of the underlying hardware that is normally not exposed by the VM. Implicit parallelism and speculative execution can be considered as adaptive optimizations, too. However, they imply likely a significantly higher complexity.

2.4   Conclusions and Requirements

We conclude from our survey that approaching the semantics of concurrency constructs is the most promising angle to take when improving support for parallel and concurrent languages. Performance is another important but to specific problem. The concepts discussed here do not lend themselves towards more generally applicable optimizations. Instead, such optimizations would likely be specific to a single concept. Thus, from the set of concepts that will benefit from semantic enforcement, we distill the following requirements for a VM:

Managed Mutation. Many concept impose rules for when and how state can be modified. Thus mutation must be manageable in a flexible manner.
Managed Execution. Similarly, the activation of methods on an object is typically also regulated and needs to be adaptable.
Ownership. One recurring notion is that mutation and execution are regulated based and relative to an owning entity. Thus, ownership needs to be supported in a manner that enables adaptable mutation and execution rules.
Leveled Reflection. Many use cases of reflective meta-programming still need to follow the concurrency-related language semantics to be safe. Thus, there is a need to distinguish between restricted language-level reflection, and unrestricted meta-level reflection.
Enforceability. These rules need to be enforceable across different concurrency models. Thus, if a reference to an object belonging to an actor is obtained, everything done with it must obey the rules of the actor language.

3   An Ownership-Based MOP to Express Concurrency Abstractions

Based on the described requirements we define a meta-object protocol (MOP) [12] that is based on the notion of ownership. First, we describe its semantics, then given an example how it can enforce immutability, and finally, we are going to detail the implementation approach for our Smalltalk-based prototype.

3.1   Design of the MOP

Following the stated requirements, we base our approach on the notions of object ownership, state access, and execution. The owner of an object, here called *domain*, defines the semantics of operations on all objects it owns. The semantics it defines regard *reading* of object fields, *writing* of object fields, and *invocation* of methods on objects. A thread of execution is executing in a domain, but as objects may change their owners, threads can change the domains they execute in. In addition, the thread has a flag that defines whether it is executing on the base level, where the domain semantics are enforced, or on the meta level without enforcement. See Fig. 1 for an overview.

Depending on the VM, a domain also needs to regard globally accessible resources that may lie beyond its scope but that can have impact on the execution. That typically includes *lexical* globals and primitive operations of a VM that cannot be regarded otherwise. Thus, the following conceptual semantics are associate with the MOP.

A **Domain** owns objects, and every object has an owner. It defines the concurrency semantics for owned objects. This satisfies the *ownership* requirement.

A **Thread** is the unit of execution. It executes either in the base level, enforcing the semantics of domains (incl. reflective operations), or it executes on the meta level without enforcement (execLevel). This satisfies the *leveled reflection* requirement. Furthermore, a thread *runs in* the context of a domain. The newThread operation enables the domain to control the number of threads executing at the same time. execInContext enables an existing thread to change the execution domain for the duration of the execution of method. This is necessary for the *managed execution* requirement.

All **Read/Write** operations of object fields are delegated to readField and writeField of the owner. The domain can then decide based on the given object

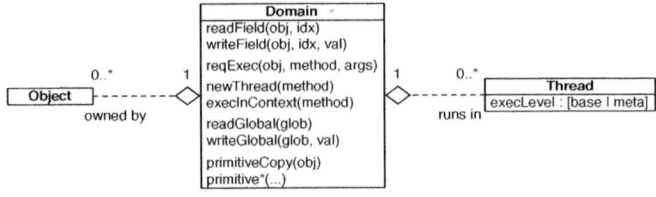

Fig. 1. Ownership-based Meta-object Protocol Supported by the Domain Object

and the slot index, as well as other execution state, what action needs to be taken. This satisfies the *managed mutation* requirement.

Request Execution (`reqExec`) is used for all method invocations enabling the domain to decide based on the given object, the method to be executed, its arguments, and other execution state, how the invocation is to be handled. This satisfies, together with the execution context of a thread, the *managed execution* requirement.

External Resources, i.e., globally shared variables and primitives need to be handled by the domain if they otherwise break semantics. To that end, the domain includes `readGlobal/writeGlobal` which enables for instance to give globals a semantic local to the domain. Furthermore, it includes `primitive*` operations, as for instance `primitiveCopy` to override the semantics of VM primitives. The direct use of `primitiveCopy` would allow to copy arbitrary objects without regarding domain semantics. This and all of the above allow us to satisfy the *enforceability* requirement.

3.2   Example: Enforcing Immutability

Fig. 2 gives a sequence diagram of how immutability could be enforced based on our approach. The `JavaThread` starts running in the meta level and then directly starts to execute application code in the base level. At some point, it invokes `setFoo` on an immutable object. In our model, this invocation goes first as a request for execution to the domain owning the immutable object. The domain code executes itself on the meta level. Since immutability does not interfere with method execution semantics, the request is granted, and `setFoo` is invoked on the object. The invocation is executed in the base level to enforce the desired semantics, which then results in a request to the domain to write a field in the object. For this immutable object, the request is denied and instead an exception is raised to notify the `JavaThread` which executes the code. The mutation would also be denied if `JavaThread` would use reflection while executing in the base level, since the reflective operations also pass by the domain.

Section 4.1 discusses a longer example, showing how to implement Clojure's agents based on the MOP.

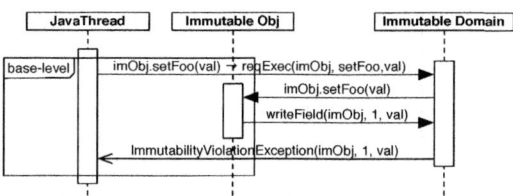

Fig. 2. Example of Immutability Enforcement based on the MOP

3.3   Implementation Strategy

Our prototype is implemented in Smalltalk applying the implementation strategy presented by Renggli and Nierstrasz for an STM [21]. Similar to their solution, we enforce the use of our MOP by transforming Smalltalk bytecode. Thereby, we abstract from a particular language that compiles to bytecode. Our transformations change reads and writes of instance variables as well as globals to the corresponding MOP operations discussed earlier. Message sends are adapted similarly to request execution on the owning domain.

To keep meta and base level apart, selectors in base-level message sends are prefixed. This prefixing also separates the actual compiled methods for meta and base level. The unmodified version of the bytecode executes on the meta level, while the transformed code executes on the base level. Instead of relying on the conceptual `execLevel` flag in a thread, we explicitly enter and exit the base level. Entry points are marked by sending `#enter:` to a block. The compiler transforms all blocks that statically receive the enter message, i.e., lexically in the form of `[foo doSomething] enter: domain`. To exit the base-level code, certain methods are not transformed. To mark such exit points methods can be annotated with `<doNotTransform>`. VM primitives are handled by annotating their Smalltalk representation with `<replacement: #selector>`.

The owner of an object is expressed by a new slot for the domain in all classes that support it. For some classes the VM make special assumptions and does not allow adding slots. One example is the `Array` class. Here we provide an adapted subclass with the slot and ensure it is used instead of `Array`.

4   Evaluation

To evaluate our approach, we present Clojure's agents[1] as a detailed example and then discuss the expressiveness and performance of our approach. The expressiveness is assessed by demonstrating that a number of concurrency models can be implemented straightforwardly. Furthermore, we comparing how our abstraction fairs compared to ad-hoc implementations. For the performance evaluation, we use an actor implementation as well as an STM system. Both have been implemented in an ad-hoc version and in a version based on our MOP to compare the performance of the two approaches. Note that Sec. 3.1 already evaluated how the MOP satisfies the requirements derived from our survey.

4.1   By Example: Clojure's Agents

Since the discussion was so-far theoretical, we will look into one concurrency construct more closely. Clojure's agents provide an abstraction for *event-loop* concurrency. An agent represents a resource with a mutable state. However, the state is modified only by the agent itself. The agent receives *update functions* asynchronously. An update function takes the old state and produces a new

---

[1] http://clojure.org/agents

state. The execution is done in a dedicated thread, so that at most one update function can be active for a given agent at any time. Furthermore, other threads will always read a consistent state of the agent at any time. However, while Clojure encourages the use of immutable data structures, it is not enforcing it. Thus, in practice the assumed guarantees can be violated. See Lst. 1.1 for a simplified implementation. The complete implementation is slightly longer and takes 8 methods with a total of 31 lines of code (LOC) (cf. Tab. 3).

```
Object < #Agent instanceVariables: 'mailbox state'.

Agent >> await [ mailbox waitUntilEmpty ]
Agent >> read  [ ^ state ]

Agent >> send: anUpdateBlock [ mailbox nextPut: anUpdateBlock ]

Agent >> send: anUpdateBlock with: args [
        self send: [:old | anUpdateBlock value: old value: args ] ]

Agent >> initialize [
        mailbox := SharedQueue new.
        [true whileTrue: [ self processIncomingMessages ]] fork ]

Agent >> processIncomingMessages [
        | updateBlock |
        updateBlock := mailbox waitForFirst.
        state       := updateBlock value: state.
        mailbox removeFirst ]
```

Listing 1.1. Agent implementation in Smalltalk

Like in Clojure, Lst. 1.1 does not guarantee any execution semantics. Since Smalltalk does not have private methods, #processIncomingMessages could even be called from another thread and violate the assumption that only one update function is executed at a time.

To enforce the expected guarantee, we now define AgentDomain in Lst. 1.2. Since Agent and AgentDomain implement the concurrency semantics, all methods need to be annotated with <doNotTransform>, including the ones in Lst. 1.1. With this annotation, we make sure that our implementation code is executed on the meta level. The domain then defines the #requestExecutionOf:on:... methods to ensure that the main constraint of having a single thread of execution for agent methods is obeyed.

```
Domain < #AgentDomain instanceVariables: 'agent'

AgentDomain >> agent: anAgent [ agent := anAgent ]

AgentDomain >> requestExecutionOf: aSelector on: anObject [
        <doNotTransform>
        "Rules are only enforced on the agent itself"
        anObject = agent           ifFalse: [ ^anObject perform: aSelector].
        (aSelector = #read or:      [ "White-listed methods"
         aSelector = #await or:     [
         aSelector = #shutdown     ]]) ifTrue: [ ^agent perform: normSel     ].
        Error signal: 'Access denied'. "Everything else is an error"]

AgentDomain >> requestExecutionOf: aSel on: obj with: par1 [
        <doNotTransform>
        obj = agent       ifFalse: [ ^obj perform: aSel with: par1. ].
        (aSel = #send:) ifTrue: [ ^agent send: par1              ].
```

Table 3. Agent Implementation Metrics

Class	#M	LOC	#BC		With Immutability	#M	LOC	#BC
Agent	8	31	77		Agent	8	41	100
					AgentDomain	4	34	132
With Guarantees					ImmutableDomain	6	17	25
Agent	8	39	85		#M: number of methods			
AgentDomain	4	34	132		#BC: number of bytecodes			

```
      Error signal: 'Access denied'. "Else: an error"]

AgentDomain >> requestExecutionOf: aSel on: obj with: p1 with: p2 [
    <doNotTransform>
    obj = agent            ifFalse: [ ^obj perform: aSel with: p1 with: p2].
    (aSel = #send:with:) ifTrue:  [ ^agent send: p1 with: p2          ].
    Error signal: 'Access denied'. "Else: an error"]
```

Listing 1.2. AgentDomain to enforce desired guarantees

As already demonstrated in Sec. 3.2, it becomes also simple to add the guarantee that an agent state only refers to immutable data structures. The implementation of `ImmutableDomain` changes the semantics of all operations that write to object fields. Thus, for instance `writeField` throws an error as in Fig. 2. The agent itself will ask the `ImmutableDomain` to adopt the new state after an update function is completed. This guarantees that the immutability cannot be violated while executing code on the base/language level. Tab. 3 shows that the necessary adaptations are minimal to provide this extra guarantee.

4.2 Subjects

LRSTM is the STM implementation by Renggli and Nierstrasz [21]. We reimplemented the compiler transformations to use the same Smalltalk and libraries as for our MOP to allow a comparison of the systems. Since the MOP is implemented using the ideas of the LRSTM implementation, the resulting systems are very similar. The STM algorithm tracks read and write operations, by keeping read- and write-logs. It uses the read-log to detect conflicts during the commit phase and when no conflicts are detected, it will apply the writes atomically.

AmbientTalkST is a framework to build applications using actor semantics similar to E [18] and AmbientTalk [28]. We call it a framework, since it requires care to set up the actors correctly to enforce the desired semantics. We have not implemented a full language with its own syntax, parser, and compiler, which would take care of these details implicitly. However, the framework uses stratified proxies [1,27] to guarantee actor semantics. Since the proxies are stratified, the guarantees are also given for reflective operations.

Actors refer to objects owned by other objects only via far-references which in return enforce that all messages sent to them will be reified and put into the inbox of an actor. The actor will process the messages one at a time. The far-reference implementation makes sure that parameters and return values are encapsulated in far-references as necessary to avoid introducing shared state. This implementation approach is different from our MOP-based one, but reflects more closely how AmbientTalk enforces its language guarantees.

Additional Concurrency Abstractions. To demonstrate the expressiveness of our abstraction, we implemented also as already discussed Clojure's agents. Furthermore, we implemented the Active Object pattern [13] and CSP+π, a minimal version of occam-π's semantics.

4.3   Expressiveness

Appropriate abstractions allow a concise description of a problem. Thus, we compare implementation metrics to assess the impact of using our abstraction instead of ad-hoc approaches. The used metrics are *number of classes, number of methods, LOC,* and *number of bytecodes.* Number of methods includes necessary extensions and changed methods in system classes. LOC refers to the length of a method including comments but excluding blank lines. Since LOC varies based on coding conventions and comments, we also list the number of bytecodes of all methods.

Table 4. Metrics for Ad-hoc and MOP-based Implementations

	#Classes	#Methods	LOC	#Bytecodes
Agents (ad-hoc, without enforcement)	1	8	31	77
Agents (MOP, with enforcement)	2	12	73	217
LRSTM (ad-hoc)	8	151	886	2411
LRSTM (MOP)	7	69	167	452
AmbientTalkST (ad-hoc)	6	37	163	390
AmbientTalkST (MOP)	2	26	115	213
Active Objects (MOP)	3	15	73	148
CSP+π (MOP)	5	16	39	61
MOP base system	5	170	1068	2767
AmbientTalkST (MOP*)	2	38	213	638
MOP base system*	5	206	1163	3016

* including duplicated code for variadic argument emulation

As the results in Tab 4 show, the concurrency constructs and their guarantees can be expressed concisely. As pointed out in Sec. 4.1, the 31 LOC of the ad-hoc agent implementation do not include any enforcement, while the additional 42 LOC of the MOP-based one include the domain and its guarantee enforcement. The more than 80% reduction of LOC for the MOP-based LRSTM comes mostly from avoiding the need for a custom bytecode transformation, which is already included in the MOP base system. The MOP-based AmbientTalkST implementation is with 115 LOC also slightly more concise than the ad-hoc version with 163 LOC. The MOP further enables the implementation of active objects in 73 LOC, and a minimal CSP in 39 LOC, both enforcing their full semantics.

Note that Smalltalk does not support variadic methods, which currently results in replicating code for the handler of method execution requests. We duplicate the code for 0 to n parameters manually, which could be avoided with a template or macro mechanism. For completeness, we also give the numbers including the duplicated code for variadic methods.

The MOP base system is with 170 methods and 1068 LOC still manageable. This core provides the main mechanisms for the unified reusable abstraction of our MOP and simplifies the implementation of concurrency constructs.

4.4   Performance

We assess the overhead of our prototype by comparing the performance of the ad-hoc with the MOP-based implementations by using AmbientTalkST and LRSTM. We concentrate on AmbientTalkST and LRSTM, because these two provide in both implementations the same semantics, while the other concurrency constructs do not enforce their semantics in the ad-hoc implementation. Furthermore, since our prototype is meant to demonstrate the expressiveness of our MOP-based approach, we will concentrate on kernel benchmarks to get a first impression of the performance impact. Thus, we use adapted versions of four kernel benchmarks from the *Computer Language Benchmarks Game*[2] for general assessment. Additional microbenchmarks then allow to assess which part of the MOP influences performance most.

Our methodology is derived from the advice of Georges et al. [8]. All benchmarks are executed 100 times on the CogVM. We measure steady-state performance to account for the just-in-time compiler. The used machine runs OS X 10.6 with Intel Xeon E5520 processors. The benchmarks use only a single core to avoid noise in the measurements.

Fig. 3 depicts the results as a box plot. It shows the performance ratio of ad-hoc/MOP-based. Ideally, the implementations would perform on-par, i. e., would be at the dashed ideal line with a value of 1. However, the benchmarks show that the ad-hoc implementation of AmbientTalkST outperforms MOP-based one for all but one kernel benchmark. The microbenchmarks point out that the MOP has an impact on all method invocations and array as well as instance variable accesses. The implementation of asynchronous (remote) message sends to other actors is however more efficient. This explains also the behavior observed for the FannkuchRedux kernel, which has almost no instance variable accesses, but a high amount of inter-actor message sends. While the proxy-based solution of the ad-hoc implementation has a higher overhead on remote sends to other actors, it does not incur any cost for local sends and variable accesses.

The LRSTM kernel benchmarks show an overhead of 26–34% for the MOP-based solution. Here the impact of the message sends overhead is smaller since the performance impact of array and instance variable access is not as high as for the AmbientTalkST implementation, since LRSTM already modifies them.

---

[2] http://shootout.alioth.debian.org/

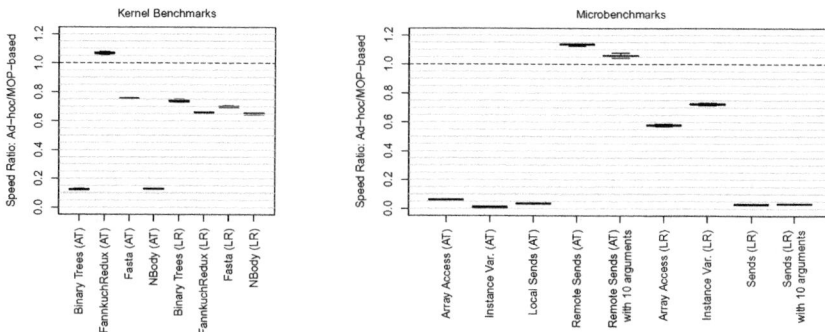

Fig. 3. Boxplot of Speed Ratio Ad-hoc/MOP-based for AmbientTalkST (AT) and LRSTM (LR): The ideal line (dashed) is at 1. While higher means better, everything below indicates that the MOP-based implementations are slower than the ad-hoc ones.

While our prototypical implementation is able to enforce the desired semantics, it comes with a high performance cost. Therefore, we will discuss in the next section how our approach could be implemented in a VM.

5   Discussion and Performance Perspectives

While performance is an issue, the current MOP also has limitations since it only regards the owner of an object as the entity defining the semantics for interaction. This approach does not offer any mechanism to control the interaction of different semantics. Thus, they need to be defined directly as part of the concurrency model for all possible combination with other concurrency models. However, for instance the possible interaction between actor-like models and STM systems cover a wide design space that needs to be carefully considered to achieve appropriate semantics.

Other types of guarantees, for instance deadlock freedom, are also problematic. Deadlock freedom is usually guaranteed by providing only non-blocking operations in a language. Thus, it is not clear how such a guarantee could be given in a system that provides arbitrary blocking mechanisms to other languages.

Our prototypical implementation does not yet rely on runtime support. However, we expect to be able to reduce the overhead to an acceptable level by applying the following techniques. Most promising seems to be the implementation techniques used by Hoffman et al. [10]. They use the hardware memory protection support to enable the isolation of program components in an otherwise shared memory model. It could be used to reduce the performance overhead for a wide set of concurrency models, too. Especially actor-like and CSP-like models could benefit from a protection model where local operations do not impose any overhead. While memory protection is relevant for field accesses, the overhead of customized semantics of method invocation mechanisms is also significant. This could be solved with the INVOKEDYNAMIC infrastructure [26] included in current JVMs. Furthermore, tracing compilers [6] are known to enable the elimination of expensive guarding checks to ensure semantics effectively.

6   Related Work

Classic MOPs were an inspiration for our approach. However, the CLOS [12] and also current Smalltalk MOPs [29] are based on the notion of classes or metaclasses that define the semantics of their subclasses. In contrast to that, our model is based on ownership. Thus, a domain defines the concurrency semantics for its objects and is orthogonal to the classic classification-based schemes.

Our survey is based on two surveys [2,25] and thus closely related to them. However, we are not aware on any survey or approach that enables a runtime system to directly support the semantics of multiple concurrency models.

As mentioned in Sec. 5 the work of Hoffmann et al. [10] is closely related in the field of VMs. They enable the isolation of components enabling the enforcement of memory access constraints inside an application. As argued, this is a promising technique to approach the performance implications of our approach.

The prototype implementation of our approach is closely related, and inspired by the work of Renggli and Nierstrasz [21]. While they use it to implement an STM, we use the same ideas to enable our MOP which in return allows use to enforce different language semantics. A similar transformation based approach was also used to implement an STM for Java [30].

7   Conclusion

Our survey showed that most parallel constructs can be provided in terms of libraries without sacrificing neither performance nor semantics. Concurrency constructs however, often suffer from either the loss of semantic integrity or a high performance penalty when implemented in terms of libraries. Based on this survey we identified the requirements for the support of such concurrency mechanisms in a multi-language virtual machine. A VM needs a mechanism to managed mutation/execution with regard to ownership, as well as support for leveled reflection to guarantee enforceability of language semantics.

Based on these requirements, we designed an ownership-based MOP and demonstrated that it is a *unifying mechanism* to enforce the semantics for a wide range of concurrency models in a concise manner. The main concepts of the MOP are reification of field accesses, message sends, and object ownership. The distinction between language-level and meta-level reflection enables us further to guarantee concurrency semantics even when meta-programming is used.

The performance of our bytecode-transformation-based prototype shows that the performance impact is significant and actual VM support is required to achieve acceptable performance. However, it also shows the unifying potential of the MOP. It enabled us to implement active objects, actors, agents, CSP, and STM in less than 500 LOC in total. With the example of agents, we were also able to demonstrate how a concurrency abstraction can be easily extended to provide desirable engineering properties.

For our future work, we identified a number of promising techniques that can be used to implement our MOP more efficiently as part of a VM.

Acknowledgments. Stefan Marr is supported by a doctoral scholarship of the Institute for the Promotion of Innovation through Science and Technology in Flanders (IWT-Vlaanderen), Belgium.

References

1. Bracha, G., Ungar, D.: Mirrors: design principles for meta-level facilities of object-oriented programming languages. In: Proc. of OOPSLA 2004, pp. 331–344. ACM (2004)
2. Briot, J.P., Guerraoui, R., Lohr, K.P.: Concurrency and distribution in object-oriented programming. ACM Computing Surveys 30(3), 291–329 (1998)
3. Budimlic, Z., Chandramowlishwaran, A., Knobe, K., Lowney, G., Sarkar, V., Treggiari, L.: Multi-core implementations of the concurrent collections programming model. In: The 14th Workshop on Compilers for Parallel Computing (January 2009)
4. Bykov, S., Geller, A., Kliot, G., Larus, J.R., Pandya, R., Thelin, J.: Orleans: Cloud computing for everyone. In: Proc. of SOCC 2011, pp. 16:1–16:14. ACM (2011)
5. Demsky, B., Lam, P.: Views: object-inspired concurrency control. In: Proc. of ICSE 2010 (2010)
6. Gal, A., Probst, C.W., Franz, M.: Hotpathvm: An effective jit compiler for resource-constrained devices. In: Proc. of VEE 2006, pp. 144–153. ACM (2006)
7. Gelernter, D.: Generative communication in linda. ACM TOPLAS 7, 80–112 (1985)
8. Georges, A., Buytaert, D., Eeckhout, L.: Statistically rigorous java performance evaluation. SIGPLAN Not. 42(10), 57–76 (2007)
9. Halstead Jr., R.H.: Multilisp: a language for concurrent symbolic computation. ACM Trans. Program. Lang. Syst. 7, 501–538 (1985)
10. Hoffman, K.J., Metzger, H., Eugster, P.: Ribbons: A partially shared memory programming model. SIGPLAN Not. 46, 289–306 (2011)
11. Karmani, R.K., Shali, A., Agha, G.: Actor frameworks for the jvm platform: A comparative analysis. In: Proc. of PPPJ 2009, pp. 11–20. ACM (2009)
12. Kiczales, G., des Rivières, J., Bobrow, D.G.: The Art of the Metaobject Protocol. MIT (1991)
13. Lavender, R.G., Schmidt, D.C.: Active object: An object behavioral pattern for concurrent programming. In: Pattern Languages of Program Design 2, pp. 483–499. Addison-Wesley Longman Publishing Co., Inc. (1996)
14. Lea, D.: A java fork/join framework. In: JAVA 2000: Proceedings of the ACM 2000 Conference on Java Grande, pp. 36–43. ACM (2000)
15. Lublinerman, R., Zhao, J., Budimlić, Z., Chaudhuri, S., Sarkar, V.: Delegated isolation. SIGPLAN Not. 46, 885–902 (2011)
16. Lämmel, R.: Google's mapreduce programming model - revisited. SCP 70(1), 1–30 (2008)
17. Marr, S., Haupt, M., D'Hondt, T.: Intermediate language design of high-level language virtual machines: Towards comprehensive concurrency support. In: Proc. VMIL 2009 Workshop, pp. 3:1–3:2. ACM (October 2009) (extended abstract)

18. Miller, M.S., Tribble, E.D., Shapiro, J.S.: Concurrency Among Strangers: Programming in E as Plan Coordination. In: De Nicola, R., Sangiorgi, D. (eds.) TGC 2005. LNCS, vol. 3705, pp. 195–229. Springer, Heidelberg (2005)
19. Morandi, B., Bauer, S.S., Meyer, B.: SCOOP – A Contract-Based Concurrent Object-Oriented Programming Model. In: Müller, P. (ed.) LASER Summer School 2007/2008. LNCS, vol. 6029, pp. 41–90. Springer, Heidelberg (2010)
20. Nordlander, J., Jones, M.P., Carlsson, M., Kieburtz, R.B., Black, A.P.: Reactive objects. In: Symposium on Object-Oriented Real-Time Distributed Computing, pp. 155–158 (2002)
21. Renggli, L., Nierstrasz, O.: Transactional memory for smalltalk. In: ICDL 2007: Proceedings of the 2007 International Conference on Dynamic Languages, pp. 207–221. ACM (2007)
22. Scholliers, C., Tanter, E., De Meuter, W.: Parallel actor monitors. In: 14th Brazilian Symposium on Programming Languages (2010)
23. Schäfer, J., Poetzsch-Heffter, A.: JCoBox: Generalizing Active Objects to Concurrent Components. In: D'Hondt, T. (ed.) ECOOP 2010. LNCS, vol. 6183, pp. 275–299. Springer, Heidelberg (2010)
24. Shavit, N., Touitou, D.: Software transactional memory. In: Proc. of PODC 1995. ACM (1995)
25. Skillicorn, D.B., Talia, D.: Models and languages for parallel computation. ACM CSUR 30, 123–169 (1998)
26. Thalinger, C., Rose, J.: Optimizing invokedynamic. In: Proc. of PPPJ 2010, pp. 1–9. ACM (2010)
27. Van Cutsem, T., Miller, M.S.: Proxies: Design principles for robust object-oriented intercession apis. In: Proc. of DLS 2010, pp. 59–72. ACM (October 2010)
28. Van Cutsem, T., Mostinckx, S., Gonzalez Boix, E., Dedecker, J., De Meuter, W.: Ambienttalk: Object-oriented event-driven programming in mobile ad hoc networks. In: Proc. of SCCC 2007, pp. 3–12. IEEE CS (2007)
29. Verwaest, T., Bruni, C., Lungu, M., Nierstrasz, O.: Flexible object layouts: Enabling lightweight language extensions by intercepting slot access. In: Proc. of OOPSLA 2011, pp. 959–972 (2011)
30. Ziarek, L., Welc, A., Adl-Tabatabai, A.-R., Menon, V., Shpeisman, T., Jia, L.: A Uniform Transactional Execution Environment for Java. In: Ryan, M. (ed.) ECOOP 2008. LNCS, vol. 5142, pp. 129–154. Springer, Heidelberg (2008)

Verification of Snapshotable Trees Using Access Permissions and Typestate

Hannes Mehnert[1] and Jonathan Aldrich[2]

[1] IT University of Copenhagen, 2300 København, Danmark
hame@itu.dk
[2] School of Computer Science, Carnegie Mellon University, Pittsburgh, USA
aldrich@cs.cmu.edu

Abstract. We use access permissions and typestate to specify and verify a Java library that implements snapshotable search trees, as well as some client code. We formalize our approach in the Plural tool, a sound modular typestate checking tool. We describe the challenges to verifying snapshotable trees in Plural, give an abstract interface specification against which we verify the client code, provide a concrete specification for an implementation and describe proof patterns we found. We also relate this verification approach to other techniques used to verify this data structure.

1 Introduction

In this paper we use access permission and typestate to formally verify snapshotable search trees in Plural [4, Chapter 6]. Snapshotable trees have been proposed as a verification challenge [10], because they contain abstract separation and internal sharing: the implementation uses sharing, while the user sees each tree and snapshot separately. The complete verified code is available at http://www.itu.dk/people/hame/SnapTree.java.

We only verify API compliance rather than full functional correctness in this paper. The protocol of the data structure is verified, rather than the tree content. The protocol is intricate, with internal sharing that is hidden from the client. The tree content could be modeled as a set, but in Plural no reasoning about sets is implemented.

We will first recapitulate the snapshotable tree verification challenge [10], typestate, and access permissions. Then we will briefly describe Plural and introduce our solution to the challenge.

To our knowledge this is the first formal verification of a tree data structure using access permissions and typestate. The verification of the Composite pattern [6], which consists of a tree data structure, used non-formalized extensions of Plural and was not formalized in Plural.

Snapshotable Search Trees. A snapshotable search tree is an ordered binary tree with the additional method `snapshot`, which returns a handle to a read-only persistent view of the tree. Both the tree and the snapshot implement the same

C.A. Furia and S. Nanz (Eds.): TOOLS Europe 2012, LNCS 7304, pp. 187–201, 2012.

interface ITree. While the client can think of a tree and a snapshot as disjoint, the actual implementation requires that snapshot be computed in constant time. This is achieved by sharing the nodes between the tree and its snapshots. If a new node is inserted into the tree, the nodes are lazily duplicated (copy on write).

There are two implementation strategies, *path copy persistence* and *node copy persistence* [8]. While the former duplicates the entire path from the root node to the freshly inserted node, the latter has an additional handle in each node, which is used for the first mutation of the node.

```
public interface ITree extends Iterable<Integer> {
    public boolean contains(int x);
    public boolean add(int x);
    public ITree snapshot();
    public Iterator<Integer> iterator();
}
```

The methods of the ITree interface have the following effects:

- contains return true if the given item is in the tree, otherwise false.
- add inserts the given item into the tree. If the item was already present, this method does not have any effect and its return value is false, otherwise true.
- snapshot returns a readonly view of the current tree. Taking a snapshot of a snapshot is not supported.
- iterator returns an iterator of the tree's (or snapshot's) items.

We consider only iterators over snapshots for the remainder of the paper. There is no limit to the number of iterators over a snapshot. Iterators over a snapshot are valid even if the original tree is mutated.

Our client code uses this behaviour, and iterates over the snapshot while mutating the original tree:

```
void client (ITree t) {
    t.add(2); t.add(1); t.add(3);
    ITree s = t.snapshot();
    Iterator<Integer> it = s.iterator();
    while (it.hasNext()) {
        int x = it.next();
        t.add(x * 3);
    }
}
```

The client code adds some elements to a ITree, creates a snapshot, and iterates over the snapshot while it adds more items to the underlying tree. The client code is computationally equivalent to the original challenge [10], we do not introduce an unnecessary boolean variable for the loop condition.

Typestate. Typestate systems [12] were developed to enhance reliability of software. A developer specifies the API usage protocol (a finite state machine) directly in the code. These protocols are statically checked. Empirical results [2] have shown that API protocol definitions occur three times more often than definitions of generics in object-oriented (Java) code. In Plaid, an upcoming programming language, typestate is a first-class citizen [13] and has been incorporated into the type system.

A motivating example for typestate is the *File* class, shown in Figure 1. Reading a file is only valid if it is open, thus the abstract *File* class has two states, *Opened* and *Closed*, and the method read is only defined in the *Opened* state. The method open (only defined in the *Closed* state) transitions the object from the *Closed* to the *Opened* state (indicated by >>), and vice versa for close.

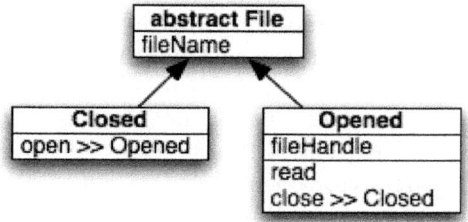

Fig. 1. Typestate example

This prevents common usage violations, like trying to read a closed file or opening a file multiple times.

Access Permissions. A developer can annotate references with alias information [1] by using access permissions [4]. Access permissions are used for controlling the flow of linear objects. In the presented system there are five different permissions: exclusive access (*unique*), exclusive write access with others possibly having read access (*full*), shared write access (*share*), read-only access with others possibly having write access (*pure*) and immutable access in which no others can write either (*immutable*).

Boyland et al [7] presented fractions to reason about permissions. This allow us to split and join permissions: for example a *unique* permission can be split into a *full* and a *pure*, which can later be merged back together.

Plural. The Plural[1] tool does sound and modular typestate checking; it employs fractional permissions to provide flexible alias control.

---

[1] https://code.google.com/p/pluralism/

Plural was implemented as a plugin for Eclipse, on top of the Crystal framework[2]. It consists of a static dataflow analysis which tracks constraints about permissions in a lattice and infers local permissions.

A developer can annotate each interface with abstract states, specified by name. Interface methods can be annotated with pre- and postconditions (required and ensured permissions and states).

Each class can be annotated with concrete states, which consist of a name and an invariant: a linear logic formula consisting of the access permission to a field in a specific state, or the (boolean or non-null) value of a field.

In a formula the standard linear logic conjunctions are available: *implies* ($\multimap$, written =>), *and* ($\otimes$, written *), *or* ($\oplus$, written +) and external choice (&).

Each state can be a refinement of another state; a state can be refined multiple times. We use this to refine the default *alive* state.

In order to access the fields of an object, the object must be unpacked, allowing temporary violations of the object's state invariants. Special care has to be taken to not unpack the same object multiple times (by using different aliases and permissions thereof), because this leads to unsoundness. Plural enforces the restriction that only a single object can be unpacked at a time. Before a method is called, all objects must be packed. Plural makes an exception to this rule for objects with unique permission, which is obviously sound since there cannot be any aliases to these objects.

Overview. In Section 2 the interface specification and client code verification will be shown. Section 3 describes some proof patterns used in the verification of the actual implementation. In Section 4 we will describe related work and in Section 5 we conclude and present future work.

Our study is based on Plural, and indeed we observed certain low-level tool-specific artifacts (discussed in the conclusion) and the Plural-specific "ghost method" proof pattern. The main focus of this paper, however, including all other specification and proof patterns in Sections 2–3, is a high-level application of typestate and permission concepts to verify the tree and its clients. This may provide insights useful in other settings based on permissions [1,7] and/or typestate [12,13].

2   Interface Specification and Client Code Verification

The verification challenge is to give an abstract specification that does not expose implementation details, is usable by a client, and for each state an invariant can be specified by an implementor to verify her implementation.

We will first describe the specification of the interface ITree and Iterator, and afterwards we will show the verification of the client code using those specifications.

---

[2] https://code.google.com/p/crystalsaf/

2.1 Interface ITree

We specify the interface ITree by having two disjoint typestates, *Tree* and *Snapshot*, which keep track whether the object is a tree or a snapshot of a tree. The marker=true annotation ensures that the state cannot change during the lifetime of an object. Both states refine the default state *alive*.

```
@States(refined="alive", value={"Tree", "Snapshot"}, marker=true)
interface ITree extends Iterable<Integer> {
  @Pure
  public boolean contains(int item);
  @Full(requires="Tree", ensures="Tree")
  public boolean add(int item);
  @Full(requires="Tree", ensures="Tree")
  @ResultPure(ensures="Snapshot")
  public ITree snapshot();
  @Pure(requires="Snapshot", ensures="Snapshot")
  @ResultUnique
  @Capture(param="underlying")
  public TreeIterator iterator();
}
```

The annotations are intuitive: the method contains requires a *pure* permission in any typestate, and returns the very same permission. The method add requires a *full* permission in the *Tree* state; the method snapshot requires a *full* permission in the *Tree* state and the return value has a *pure* permission in the *Snapshot* state. The iterator method requires a *pure* permission in the *Snapshot* state, whereas the resulting iterator will have a *unique* permission. The Capture annotation indicates that this is captured by the returned TreeIterator object.

The access permissions and typestates formalize the informal constraints presented in the description of the ITree interface in Section 1.

2.2 Interface Iterator

Iterators have been specified previously in Plural [3], we include the specification for self-containedness of this paper. We follow similar ideas (namely a non-empty and empty state), whereas our implementation is different (see Section 3.5).

There are three states defined for an iterator, *NonEmpty*, *Empty* and *Impossible*, all refine *alive*. The last one is only for specifying the remove method which throws an exception in our implementation.

The method next requires *unique* permission to a *NonEmpty* iterator. The hasNext method requires *immutable* permission and if it returns true, the object is in the *NonEmpty* state, if false is returned, it is in the *Empty* state.

The need for a *unique* permission is due to recursive calls and Plural's restriction of having only a single unpacked object, mentioned in Section 1. We will discuss this in more detail when we show the iterator implementation in

Section 3.5. This is a marginal drawback, since in practice iterators are used on the stack rather than shared via the heap.

This specification actually enforces that *hasNext* is called before each call to *next*, because otherwise the iterator is not known to be in the *NonEmpty* state.

```
@States(refined="alive", value={"NonEmpty", "Empty", "Impossible"})
interface TreeIterator extends Iterator<Integer> {
  @Unique(requires="NonEmpty")
  public Integer next();
  @Imm
  @TrueIndicates("NonEmpty")
  @FalseIndicates("Empty")
  public boolean hasNext();
  @Unique(requires="Impossible")
  public void remove();
}
```

2.3   Client Code Verification

The client code needs only a single annotation, that it has *full* permission in the *Tree* state of the given argument.

```
class ClientCode {
  @Perm(requires="full(#0) in Tree")
  void client (ITree t) {
    t.add(2); t.add(1); t.add(3);
    ITree s = t.snapshot();
    TreeIterator it = s.iterator();
    while (it.hasNext()) {
      int x = it.next();
      t.add(x * 3);
    }
  }
}
```

The method `client` adds the elements 1, 2 and 3 to the tree (line 4), creates a snapshot s (line 5) and an iterator it over the snapshot (line 6). The body of the while loop (lines 8 and 9) adds more elements to the original tree (line 9).

In this section we have demonstrated that the client code preserves the required permissions and states, using the given specification for the ITree and Iterator interfaces.

3   Proof Patterns and Verification of the Implementation

We have verified the A1B1 implementation [10], which does not implement rebalancing and uses path copy persistence: when a snapshot is present, the complete path from the root down to the newly inserted node is copied in a call to add. This ensures that add does not mutate any node that is shared between the snapshot and the tree.

The specifications of field getters, field setters, and constructors are omitted in the paper: they are straightforward, a field getter requires an *immutable* permission, a field setter a *full* permission and the constructor ensures a *unique* permission.

The SnapTree class, which implements the ITree interface, contains two boolean fields, isSnapshot and hasSnapshot, and a field root, which contains a handle to the root node.

3.1 Formula Guarded by a Boolean Variable and Implication

The invariant for *Snapshot* is straightforward. It contains an *immutable* permission to the root in the *PartOfASnapshot* state; the isSnapshot field is true, and the hasSnapshot field is false.

The field isSnapshot is used in the invariant to distinguish between the *Tree* and *Snapshot* states.

For the *Tree* invariant we distinguish between two cases: either there is a snapshot present, or there is no snapshot present. In the former case the invariant contains an *immutable* permission to the root node in the *PartOfASnapshot* state. This ensures the no node is mutated. In the latter case the invariant contains a *unique* permission to the root node in the *NotPartOfASnapshot* state.

To implement this conditional we use a proof pattern: the permission is guarded by an implication whose left hand side tests a boolean program variable. The variable hasSnapshot is compared to true (or false), and on the right hand side of the implication we have an *immutable* (or *unique*, respectively) permission to the root node in the *PartOfASnapshot* (or *NotPartOfASnapshot*) state.

```
@ClassStates({
  @State(name="Snapshot", inv="immutable(root) in PartOfASnapshot *
    isSnapshot == true * hasSnapshot == false")
  @State(name="Tree", inv="isSnapshot == false *
    (hasSnapshot == true => immutable(root) in PartOfASnapshot) *
    (hasSnapshot == false => unique(root) in NotPartOfASnapshot)"),
})
```

This distinction between the two cases is natural and follows from the program implementation.

3.2 Specification of a Recursive Structure

This implementation either contains a completely immutable tree (if snapshots are present) or a mutable tree. This is specified by the invariants of the states of the node class. Two states are defined, and both refine *alive*: either the node is part of a snapshot (*PartOfASnapshot*) or not part of a snapshot (*NotPartOfAS-napshot*). The invariant recursively contains *immutable* (or *unique*) permissions

in the *PartOfASnapshot* (or *NotPartOfASnapshot*, respectively) state for the
left and right children.

```
@Refine({
  @States(refined="alive",
          value={"PartOfASnapshot","NotPartOfASnapshot"}),
})
@ClassStates({
  @State(name="PartOfASnapshot",
         inv="immutable(left) in PartOfASnapshot *
              immutable(rght) in PartOfASnapshot"),
  @State(name="NotPartOfASnapshot",
         inv="unique(left) in NotPartOfASnapshot *
              unique(rght) in NotPartOfASnapshot")
})
```

The base case for the recursion is that both the left and the right child are null.
Plural assumes the possibility that these might be null by default.

3.3   Conditional Composition of Implementations

The method add behaves differently for a mutable tree and an immutable one.
The add method in the SnapTree checks in which case the tree is and calls
the correct method, either a mutating or a functional insert. In both cases the
precondition and postcondition are a *full* permission to an object in the *Tree*
state. The annotation use=Use.FIELDS specifies that this has to be unpacked
in the method body, which is required to access the fields.

The implementation first checks whether root is null and instantiates a new
Node object if that is the case. Otherwise the boolean field hasSnapshot is tested
to determine whether a mutating insert (addM) or a functional insert (addF)
should be done. The proof goes through because the test is the same as in the
invariant of the *Tree* state, thus one guard is false, its implication is eliminated,
and the other guarded formula is used.

```
@Full(use=Use.FIELDS, requires="Tree", ensures="Tree")
public boolean add (int i) {
  assert(isSnapshot == false);
  if (root == null) {
    setRoot(new Node(i));
    return true;
  } else
    if (hasSnapshot) {
      RefBool x = new RefBool();
      setRoot(root.addF(i, x));
      return x.getValue();
    } else {
```

```
        RefBool x = new RefBool();
        root.addM(i, x);
        return x.getValue();
    }
}
```

The implementation of addF requires an *immutable* permission of the node in the *PartOfASnapshot* state, and ensures an *immutable* permission in the *PartOfASnapshot* state for the returned object. It recurses down the tree to find the location at which to insert the given value, and if the value was inserted, it duplicates the entire path (which is on the call stack). It uses some helper methods to get and set fields.

```
@Perm(requires="immutable(this) in PartOfASnapshot",
      ensures="immutable(result) in PartOfASnapshot")
public Node addF (int i, RefBool x) {
  Node node = this;
  if (item > i) {
    Node lef = getLeft();
    Node newL = null;
    if (lef == null) {
      newL = new Node(i);
      x.setValue(true);
    } else
      newL = lef.addF(i, x);
    if (x.getValue()) {
      Node r = getRight();
      node = new Node(newL, item, r);
    }
  } else if (i > item) {
    Node rig = getRight();
    Node newR = null;
    if (rig == null) {
      newR = new Node(i);
      x.setValue(true);
    } else
      newR = rig.addF(i, x);
    if (x.getValue()) {
      Node l = getLeft();
      node = new Node(l, item, newR);
    }
  }
  return node;
}
```

The implementation of addM also searches for the correct place by calling itself recursively, and assigns a freshly instantiated Node object to that place.

```
@Unique(use=Use.DISP_FIELDS,
        requires="NotPartOfASnapshot",
        ensures="NotPartOfASnapshot")
public void addM (int i, RefBool x) {
  if (item > i)
    if (left == null) {
      left = new Node(i);
      x.setValue(true);
    } else
      left.addM(i, x);
  else if (i > item)
    if (rght == null) {
      rght = new Node(i);
      x.setValue(true);
    } else
      rght.addM(i, x);
}
```

3.4   Dropping Privileges (Ghost Method)

The method snapshot requires a *full* permission to this in the *Tree* state. The
!fr annotation is equivalent to use=Use.FIELDS, but can be used in the more
general Perm annotation.

The implementation of snapshot needs to drop the permissions to all nodes,
because they are now shared with the tree and the snapshot. This is achieved in
the snapall method.

```
@Perm(requires="full(this!fr) in Tree",
      ensures="pure(result) in Snapshot * full(this!fr) in Tree")
public ITree snapshot() {
  assert(!isSnapshot);
  if (hasSnapshot)
    return new SnapTree(root);
  else {
    Node r = root;
    r.snapall();
    hasSnapshot = true;
    return new SnapTree(r);
  }
}
```

The method snapall drops the privileges recursively by traversing the tree. It is
implemented in the Node class. It does not have any observable computational
effect, but it is required because we must drop the permissions for the entire tree
and Plural only allows this to occur as each node is unpacked going down the
tree. In order to verify it with Plural, we need to specifically assign null to the
left/right sibling if it is already null (to associate a bottom permission).

```
@Perm(requires="unique(this!fr) in NotPartOfASnapshot",
      ensures="immutable(this!fr) in PartOfASnapshot")
public void snapall () {
  if (left != null)
    left.snapall();
  else
    left = null;
  if (rght != null)
    rght.snapall();
  else
    rght = null;
}
```

Although the specific technique used here is specialized for Plural, note that an analogous mechanism would be required to convince any tool that the permissions and/or typestates are dropped recursively.

3.5 Iterator

The iterator implementation uses a field `context`, which contains a stack of nodes that have not yet been yielded to the client. This is initially filled recursively with the left path, and whenever an item is popped from the stack, the left path of its right subtree is pushed onto the stack. The Stack class is annotated with a proper specification, but its implementation is not verified (especially that `pop` returns an object in the *PartOfASnapshot* typestate).

```
@Perm(requires="immutable(this) in Snapshot",
      ensures="unique(result)")
public TreeIterator iterator() {
  Node r = this.getRoot();
  TreeIteratorImpl it = new TreeIteratorImpl(this);
  it.pushLeftPath(r);
  return it;
}
```

The concrete class specifies an invariant only for the top-level `alive` state:

```
@ClassStates({
  @State(name="alive",
         inv="immutable(tree) in Snapshot * unique(context) in alive")
})
```

The method `pushLeftPath` calls itself recursively with the left child to push the entire left path onto the stack. It requires a *unique* permission to `this` in order to unpack `this`, access the `context` field, and call a method on the `context` object while `this` remains unpacked. As mentioned in Section 1, for soundness reasons, leaving an object unpacked during a method call is only possible in Plural if there is a *unique* permission to the unpacked object.

```
@Perm(requires="unique(this!fr) in alive * immutable(#0) in PartOfASnapshot",
      ensures="unique(this!fr) in alive * immutable(#0) in PartOfASnapshot")
public void pushLeftPath(Node node) {
  if (node != null) {
    context.push(node);
    pushLeftPath(node.getLeft());
  }
}
```

The `hasNext` method is simply a check whether the stack is non-empty.

```
@TrueIndicates("NonEmpty")
@FalseIndicates("Empty")
@Imm(use=Use.FIELDS)
public boolean hasNext() {
  return !context.empty();
}
```

The method `next` pops the first element of the stack and pushes the left path of the right child onto the stack. In contrast to the original implementation [10], a guard if `hasNext()` is true around lines 4-7 is not needed, because Plural verifies that `next` is only called on a non-empty iterator.

```
@Unique(use=Use.DISP_FIELDS, requires="NonEmpty")
public Integer next() {
  Integer result;
  Node node = context.pop();
  result = node.getItem();
  if (node.getRight() != null)
    pushLeftPath(node.getRight());
  return result;
}
```

Here a *unique* permission is required in order to call `pushLeftPath`.

In this section we described proof patterns used in the verification of the path copy persistence implementation of snapshotable trees. The complete implementation has been automatically verified with Plural.

4   Related Work

The Composite pattern, which is a tree data structure, has been verified using typestate and access permissions [6]. This work differed in multiple aspects: first of all it was not formalized in a tool, then it relied on extensions, like multiple unpacking and equations using pointers, which were not proven to be sound. Also, the verification challenge is different: the Composite pattern exposes all nodes to a user using a *share* permission, and preserves an invariant upwards the tree, namely the number of children of the subtree rooted in each node. This leads to a specification with several typestates in the different dimensions of each node, which fractions are cleverly distributed to allow for bottom-up updates of the count.

A prior iterator verification [3] is similar to our specification, but the implementation of the iterator is completely different. In this paper we present an iterator which shares its content with the snapshot and holds only some elements on the stack, pushing more onto the stack on demand.

Snapshotable trees have been verified using a higher-order separation logic [10]. This approach verified full functional correctness, while this paper can only prove correct API usage: add and snapshot are always called on the tree, and by having *immutable* permission to the contents of a snapshot, we can verify that it will not be modified. Also, our work verifies that an iterator is always taken on a snapshot, not the original tree, and that next is never called on an empty iterator.

We use automation in the proof, which requires only a moderate number of annotations to the source code. The higher-order separation logic proof requires roughly 5000 lines of proof script, while the code and annotations for this paper are together under 400 lines; this is less than 2 lines of annotation for every line of source code.

An unpublished verification of snapshotable trees in Dafny [9], done by Rustan Leino, is similar to the Plural approach. Both are automated systems using a first-order logic. In Dafny functional correctness can be proven. The advantage of Plural is that already existing code written in a widely deployed programming language (Java) can be analyzed, whereas Dafny specifies its own programming language. Dafny uses implicit framing and also relies on annotations by the user, whereas Plural is based on linear logic (access permissions) and typestates. Dafny does not support inheritance, thus no abstract specification is provided.

5   Conclusion and Further Work

There exist several extensions to the access permission system which support verifying full functional correctness: Object propositions [11] combine access permissions with first-order formulae; but there is currently no implementation available. Symplar [5] combines access permissions with JML, thus access permissions are used to reason about aliasing, and JML formulae for full functional correctness.

In order to verify iterators over the tree (vs. its snapshots) we would need to change the *unique* permission of the nodes to *full* in order to share them between the tree and the iterator. Because the proof relies on method calls while a *unique* object is unpacked, we would have to modify Plural in order to achieve this.

There are also more advanced implementations of snapshotable trees [8], namely rebalancing - for which we would need to have partly *unique* and partly *immutable* permissions to the nodes in the tree. An important observation is that rebalancing involves only freshly allocated nodes in the path copy persistence implementation. Thus, we would need to carefully write the code such that Plural can derive this observation.

The node copy persistence implementation is more challenging: parts of a node are immutable while other parts are mutable. Here orthogonal dimensions of state, which are implemented in Plural, might become useful.

To conclude this paper, we successfully verified a snapshotable tree implementation and client code in Plural. In order to achieve that we had to rewrite parts of the reference implementation [10], mainly by adding explicit getter and setter methods, which is good object-oriented style.

An interesting method was add, which in the reference implementation calls addRecursive, which handles all cases at once: whether a snapshot is present (functional insertion) or no snapshots are present (mutating insert). In the higher-order separation logic proof this leads to three different specifications for addRecursive, one for each separate case. In automated tools (Plural and Dafny), it is easier to implement and verify two methods for those two cases, due to size of invariants and automated reasoning. Evidence for this is also provided by Rustan Leino, who implemented insertion in a clean-room setting from the beginning as two different methods. The reference implementation is clearly more compact, but it is arguable which implementation is clearer or more in the object-oriented spirit.

We modified the client code slightly by removing an additional temporary boolean variable, because we found that Plural's inference of boolean values works better this way. The original challenge used a boolean variable because their semantics does not allow for statements (heap access) in the loop condition, but only expressions (stack access).

While doing this proof we found several proof patterns for Plural: using implications instead of multiple typestates, inserting explicit return statements to help Plural with automation, writing explicit alternatives for conditionals, moving methods into the specific class that concerns them because static methods are not as well supported, avoiding choice conjuncts, and assigning null explicitly so that Plural can associate a bottom permission with the field. To get the proof through, we had to write the method snapall, which does not have any observable computational effect, but reassigns fields which were null to null.

We consider Plural to be a helpful static analysis tool which prevents runtime bugs: it issues an error when add is called on a snapshot or when a snapshot of a snapshot is taken.

One bug in Plural has been found (while (lc == true) leads to infinite recursion), which silently crashed Plural, making it appear that the code was proven. This has subsequently been fixed by the author of Plural.

Many thanks to Kevin Bierhoff for helping with specifications and best practices in Plural. The second author was funded by NSF grant CCF-1116907.

References

1. Baker, H.G.: "use-once" variables and linear objects: storage management, reflection and multi-threading. SIGPLAN Not. 30, 45–52 (1995)
2. Beckman, N.E., Kim, D., Aldrich, J.: An Empirical Study of Object Protocols in the Wild. In: Mezini, M. (ed.) ECOOP 2011. LNCS, vol. 6813, pp. 2–26. Springer, Heidelberg (2011)

3. Bierhoff, K.: Iterator specification with typestates. In: Proceedings of the 2006 Conference on Specification and Verification of Component-Based Systems, SAVCBS 2006, pp. 79–82 (2006)
4. Bierhoff, K.: Api protocol compliance in object-oriented software. Tech. Rep. CMU-ISR-09-108, CMU ISR SCS (2009)
5. Bierhoff, K.: Automated program verification made symplar. In: Proc. of Onward! 2011 (2011)
6. Bierhoff, K., Aldrich, J.: Permissions to specify the composite design pattern. In: Proc. of SAVCBS 2008 (2008)
7. Boyland, J.: Checking Interference with Fractional Permissions. In: Cousot, R. (ed.) SAS 2003. LNCS, vol. 2694, pp. 55–72. Springer, Heidelberg (2003)
8. Driscoll, J., Sarnak, N., Sleator, D., Tarjan, R.: Making data structures persistent. Journal of Computer and Systems Sciences 38(1), 86–124 (1989)
9. Leino, K.R.M.: Dafny: An Automatic Program Verifier for Functional Correctness. In: Clarke, E.M., Voronkov, A. (eds.) LPAR-16 2010. LNCS, vol. 6355, pp. 348–370. Springer, Heidelberg (2010)
10. Mehnert, H., Sieczkowski, F., Birkedal, L., Sestoft, P.: Formalized Verification of Snapshotable Trees: Separation and Sharing. In: Joshi, R., Müller, P., Podelski, A. (eds.) VSTTE 2012. LNCS, vol. 7152, pp. 179–195. Springer, Heidelberg (2012)
11. Nistor, L., Aldrich, J.: Verifying object-oriented code using object propositions. In: Proc. of IWACO (2011)
12. Strom, R.E., Yemini, S.: Typestate: A programming language concept for enhancing software reliability. IEEE Transactions on Software Engineering (1998)
13. Sunshine, J., Naden, K., Stork, S., Aldrich, J., Tanter, É.: First-class state change in plaid. In: OOPSLA 2011 (2011)

Multiparty Session C: Safe Parallel Programming with Message Optimisation

Nicholas Ng[1], Nobuko Yoshida[1], and Kohei Honda[2]

[1] Imperial College London
[2] Queen Mary, University of London

Abstract. This paper presents a new efficient programming toolchain for message-passing parallel algorithms which can fully ensure, for any typable programs and for any execution path, deadlock-freedom, communication safety and global progress through a static checking. The methodology is embodied as a multiparty session-based programming environment for C and its runtime libraries, which we call Session C. Programming starts from specifying a *global protocol* for a target parallel algorithm, using a protocol description language. From this global protocol, the projection algorithm generates *endpoint protocols*, based on which each endpoint C program is designed and implemented with a small number of concise session primitives. The endpoint protocol can further be refined to a more optimised protocol through subtyping for asynchronous communication, preserving original safety guarantees. The underlying theory can ensure that the complexity of the toolchain stays in polynomial time against the size of programs. We apply this framework to representative parallel algorithms with complex communication topologies. The benchmark results show that Session C performs competitively against MPI.

1 Introduction

High-performance computing based on message-passing is one of the highly scalable frameworks for executing parallel algorithms with a wide range of hardware configurations starting from a small LAN to a large cluster to supercomputers. It is, however, hard to implement message-passing applications correctly, partly because they rely on not only local calculation at each endpoint, but also on global message exchange among all endpoints: if the message-passing part of a program is wrongly implemented, then the result of the calculation is either unavailable (e.g. by deadlock) or wrong (e.g. by receiving some values at wrong timings or as wrong types), even if all local calculations are correct.

One of the root causes of errors in communications programming is the lack of conformance to an assumed protocol among endpoint programs. Typical examples (written as MPI commands [27]) are a circular wait such as `MPI_Send(to2)` from process 1, `MPI_Recv(from3)` from process 2 and `MPI_Send(to1)` from process 3; and a communication mismatch such as `MPI_Recv(from2)` followed by `MPI_Send(to3)` from process 1, `MPI_Recv(from3)` followed by `MPI_Send(to1)` from process 2 and

C.A. Furia and S. Nanz (Eds.): TOOLS Europe 2012, LNCS 7304, pp. 202–218, 2012.
© Springer-Verlag Berlin Heidelberg 2012

MPI_Recv(from1) followed by MPI_Send(to2) from process 3. To avoid such deadlocks, one might permute the order of messages using asynchronous sending such as Isend followed by Recv, but it is often forgotten to write a required synchronisation (Wait). These are simple errors often illustrated in the textbooks [14,15], but still appeared in many programs including large scale MPI applications, e.g [24]. Such communication errors are often hard to detect except by runtime analysis. Even if detected, hard to locate and fix the bug because the issue comes from distributed processes. Testing in general does not offer full safety assurance as it relies on executing a particular sequence of events and actions.

This paper proposes a new programming framework for message-passing parallel algorithms centring on explicit, formal description of *global protocols*, and examines its effectiveness through an implementation of a toolchain for C. All validations in the toolchain are done statically and are efficient, with a polynomial-time bound with respect to the size of the program and global protocol. The framework is based on theory of multiparty session types [3,10,18], and it supports a full guarantee of deadlock-freedom, type-safety, communication-safety and global progress for any well-typed programs. Global protocols serve as a guidance for a programmer to write safe programs, representing a type abstraction of expressive communication structures (such as sequencing, choice, broadcast, synchronisation and recursion). The toolchain uses a language Scribble [16,31] for describing the multiparty session types in a Java-like syntax.

```
protocol Simple(role P1, role P2, role P3) {
    int   from P1 to P2;
    char  from P3 to P1;
    float from P2 to P3;
}
```

A simple example of a protocol in Scribble which corrects the first erroneous MPI program (a wait cycle) is given on the left. For endpoint code development, the programmer uses the *endpoint protocol* generated by the projection algorithm in the toolchain. For example, the above global protocol is projected to P2 to obtain int from P1; float to P3;, which gives a template for developing a safe code for P2 as well as a basis of static verification. Since we start from a correct protocol, if endpoint programs conform to the induced endpoint protocols, it automatically ensures deadlock-free, well-matched interactions.

Overview of the Toolchain. A Session C program is developed in a top-down approach. Fig. 1 (l.h.s.) shows the relationships between the four layers (i–iv) that make up a complete Session C program. A Session C programmer first designs a global protocol (i) using Scribble (explained in § 2.1). A Session C program is a collection of individual programs (iv) in which each of the programs implements a participant (called *endpoint*) of the communication. We first extract the endpoint protocol from the global protocol by *projection* (ii). The projection takes the global protocol G and an endpoint (say Alice), and extracts only the interaction that involves Alice (T_{Alice}). Step (iii) describes a key element of our toolchain, the *protocol refinement*. T'_{Alice} is an endpoint protocol refined from the original T_{Alice}. This allows the programmer to write a more refined program P_{Alice} (which conforms to T'_{Alice}) than a program following the original T_{Alice}. Session C supports the *asynchronous message optimisation* [25, 26], the reordering of messages for minimising a waiting time as a refinement, through its

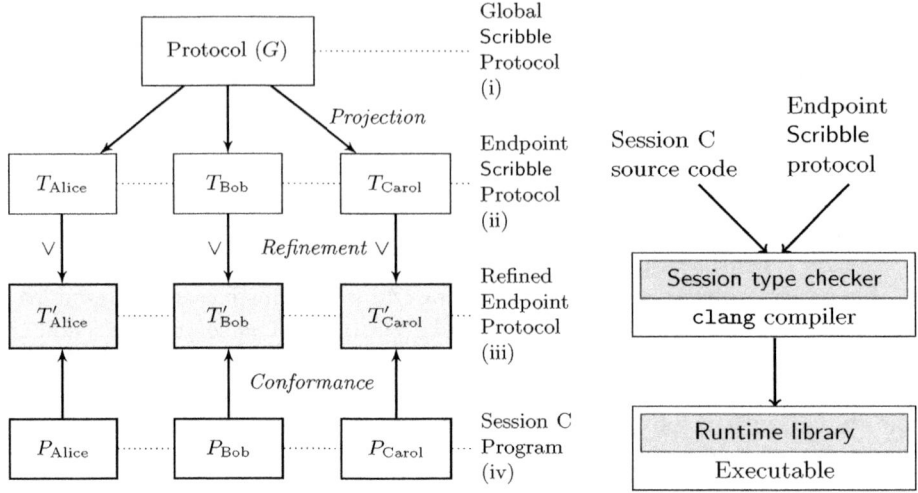

Fig. 1. Session C programming framework (l.h.s.) and architecture (r.h.s.)

subtyping checker (§ 3.2). Once P_{Alice} conforms T'_{Alice} such that $T'_{\text{Alice}} < T_{\text{Alice}}$ (T'_{Alice} is more refined), then P_{Alice} automatically enjoys safety and progress in its interactions with P_{Bob} and P_{Carol}.

Programming Environment. The programming environment of Session C is made up of two main components, the *session type checker* and the *runtime library* (§ 2.2). Fig. 1 (r.h.s.) shows the architecture. The session type checker takes an endpoint protocol (T_{Alice}) and a source code P_{Alice} as an input from the user. The endpoint protocol is generated from the global protocol G through the projection algorithm. The session type checker validates the source code against its endpoint protocol. When the program is optimised, it generates T'_{Alice} from P_{Alice} and checks if $T'_{\text{Alice}} < T_{\text{Alice}}$ (§ 3.2). The API provides a simple but expressive interface for session-based communications programming.

Contributions

1. A toolchain for developing and executing message-passing parallel algorithms based on a formal and explicit description of interaction protocols (§ 2.1), with an automatic safety guarantee. All algorithms used in the toolchain are polynomial-time bounded (§ 3.2).
2. The first multiparty session-based programming environment for a low-level language, Session C, built from expressive session constructs supporting collective operations (§ 2), together with the associated runtime library.
3. A session type checker for Session C, which is the first to offer automatic, full formal assurance of communication deadlock-freedom (i.e. for any possible control path and interleaving) for a large class of message-passing parallel programs (§ 3.1), supporting messaging optimisations through the incorporation of the asynchronous subtyping [25, 26] (§ 3.2).

4. The practical validation of our methodology through the implementations of typical message-passing parallel algorithms, leading to concise and clear programs (§ 4). The benchmark results show that representative parallel algorithms in Session C are executed competitively against their counterparts in MPI (the overhead is on average 1%) (§ 5).

All code and details of benchmark results are available from [13].

2   Protocols and Programming in Session C

2.1   Scribble, A Protocol Description Language

Our toolchain uses Scribble [16, 31], a developer-friendly notation for specifying application-level communication protocols based on the theory of multiparty session types [3, 10, 18]. Scribble's development tool [31] supports parsing, well-formedness checking and endpoint projection, with bindings to multiple programming languages. We briefly introduce its syntax.

```
1   /* Protocol: Monte Carlo Pi estimation. */
2   import int;
3   protocol MonteCarloPi(role Master, role Worker0, role Worker1) {
4     // number of simulations to do in each worker
5     int from Master to Others; // broadcast
6     rec LOOP {
7       from Others to Master { Yes: No: }; // gather
8       LOOP; }
9   }
```

Above listing shows a simple Scribble global protocol for Monte Carlo π estimation. The algorithm uses random sampling to estimate the value of π. A Scribble protocol begins with the preamble, in Line 1, consisting of a message type declaration after the keyword import. Then the protocol definition is given starting from, in Line 2, the keyword protocol, followed by the protocol name, MonteCarloPi, and its parameters which are the roles to be played by participants. Then the description of a conversation structure follows. Line 4 says that the Master should send an integer (which specifies the number of tries) to Others, i.e. to all other roles than Master, i.e. to the workers. Line 5 declares a recursion named loop. In Line 6, (after each worker locally generates a random point on a square and tests if the point is in the quarter of a circle, i.e. the shaded area in the right figure above. Master is informed by Others (workers) whether the test was a hit, by choosing Yes or No. Regardless, Line 7 recurs.

The description of interaction in Lines 4-8 is generic, catering for any number of workers. Here we use *collective roles* in Scribble, where a single role can denote multiple participants. We introduce two collectives roles, All (for "every role") and Others (for "all other roles"). Using them, we can accurately represent the protocols for MPI collective operations as:

- MPI_Bcast (broadcast) from A: from A to Others.
- MPI_Reduce to A, a gather operation: from Others to A.

- `MPI_Barrier` with `A` as a gather point, for which we use consecutive interactions: `from Others to A; from A to Others`.
- `MPI_Alltoall`, a scatter-gather operation: `from All to Others`.

These collective roles can be used as a source and/or a target as far as it is not ambiguous (e.g. `from Others to Others`) and it does not induce a self-circular communication (e.g. `from All to All`). Each `All` is macro-expanded for each endpoint when projecting a global protocol, whereas `Others` is preserved after projection and is linked to programming constructs, as we shall discuss later.

Global protocol	Endpoint protocol
U `from myrole to role1,..,  rolen/Others`	U `to role1,..,  rolen/Others`
U `from role1,..,  myrole,..,  rolen/Others to role`	U `to role`
U `from role1,..,  rolen/Others to myrole`	U `from role1,..,rolen/Others`
U `from role to role1,..,  myrole,..,  rolen/Others`	U `from role`
U `from All to Others`	U `to Others;` U `from Others`
`from myrole to role {` $l_1 : T_1 \cdots l_n : T_n$ `}`	`to role {` $l_1 : T_1' \cdots l_n : T_n'$ `}`
`from role to myrole {` $l_1 : T_1 \cdots l_n : T_n$ `}`	`from role {` $l_1 : T_1' \cdots l_n : T_n'$ `}`
`from All to Others {` $l_1 : T_1 \cdots l_n : T_n$ `}`	`to Others {` $l_1 : T_1' \cdots l_n : T_n'$ `};`
	`from Others {` $l_1 : T_1' \cdots l_n : T_n'$ `}`
`repeat from myrole to role {` T `}`	`repeat to role {` T' `}`
`repeat from role to myrole {` T `}`	`repeat from role {` T' `}`
`rec X {` T `}`	`rec X {` T' `}`

We present a summary of the Scribble syntax for global and local protocols in above table, which also shows how the former is projected to the latter. In each line, the left-hand side gives a syntax of a global protocol, while the right-hand side gives its projection onto participant `myrole`. U is a payload type; T and T' are global and endpoint types; and l is a label for branching. T and T' can be empty, denoting termination. Line 1 indicates two cases, one "U `from myrole to role1,..,  rolen`", which is a multicast from `myrole` to n other roles; and "U `from myrole to Others`", which is a multicast from `myrole` to all others. Similarly for Lines 2-4. The right-hand side views the left-hand global interaction from the viewpoint of `myrole`. In Line 5, "`from All to Others`" means "every role sends to the remaining roles". Hence, for `myrole`, it means (1) it is sending to all others, i.e. broadcast; and then (2) receiving from all others, i.e. reduce.

```
/* Endpoint Scribble for Master */      /* Endpoint Scribble for Worker0 */
import int;                             import int;
protocol MonteCarloPi at Master         protocol MonteCarloPi at Worker0
   (role Worker0, role Worker1){            (role Master, role Worker1) {
  int to Others;                           int from Master;
  rec LOOP {                               rec LOOP {
    from Worker0, Worker1 { Yes: No: }       to Master { Yes: No: }
  LOOP; }                                  LOOP; }
}                                        }
```

As a concrete example of projection acting on the whole protocol, the endpoint protocols resulting from the projection of the Monte Carlo simulation example onto `Master` and `Worker0`, respectively, are given in the above listings.

2.2 Session C: Programming and Runtime

Session C offers a high-level interface for safe communications programming based on a small collection of primitives from the session type theory. These primitives are supported by a runtime whose implementation currently uses the ØMQ (ZeroMQ) [37] socket library, which provides efficient messaging over multiple transports including local in/inter-process communication, TCP and PGM (Pragmatic General Multicast).

A Session C program is a C program that calls the session runtime library. The following code implements Master whose endpoint protocol is given in the previous subsection. In the **main** function, join_session (Line 7) indicates the start of a session, whose arguments (from the command line arguments argc and argv) are a session handle of type session * and the location of the endpoint Scribble file. join_session establishes connections to other participating processes in the session, according to a connection configuration information such as the host/port for each participant, automatically generated from the global protocol. Next, the lookup function get_role returns the participant identifier of type role *. Then we have a series of session operations such as send_*type* or recv_*type* (discussed below). Lines 15-18 expand the choice from Others in the protocol into individual choices.

```
1   /* Session C implementation for Master */
2   #include <libsess.h>
3   ...
4   int main(int argc, char *argv[])
5   { // variable declaration ...
6     session *s;
7     join_session(&argc, &argv, &s, "MCPi_Master.spr");
8     const role *Worker0 = s->get_role(s, "Worker0");
9     const role *Worker1 = s->get_role(s, "Worker1");
10
11    int count = 100;
12    msend_int(100, _Others(s));
13
14    while (count-- > 0) {
15      switch(inbranch(Worker0, &rcvd))
16        { case Yes: hits++; break; case No: break; }
17      switch(inbranch(Worker1, &rcvd))
18        { case Yes: hits++; break; case No: break; }
19    }
20    printf("Pi: %.5f\n", (4*hits)/(2*100.0));
21    end_session(s);
22  }
```

Finally an end_session cleans up the session. Any session operation before join_session or after end_session is invalid because they do not belong to any session.

Programming Communications in Session C. We now outline communication primitives of Session C. In addition to the standard send/receive primitives, our library includes a primitive for multicast sending and its reverse. msend sends the same value to all receivers, and mrecv receives values (not necessarily identical but of the same type) from multiple senders, as we illustrate below.

The table above lists these primitives as well as control primitives we illustrate next, in correspondence with the Scribble protocol construct introduced in the § 2.1. The first six lines are for message passing. Each function name mentions a type explicitly, as in send_*datatype*, following MPI and to ensure type-safety

Scribble endpoint	Session C runtime interface
`int to Bob`	`send_int(role *r, int val);`
`string from Bob`	`recv_string(role *r, char *str);`
`int to role1,..,rolen`	`msend_int(int val, int roles_count,...);`
`string from role1,..,rolen`	`mrecv_string(char *str, int roles_count,...);`
`int to Others`	`msend_int(int val, _Others(sess));`
`string from Others/role1,..,rolen`	`mrecv_string(char *str, _Others(sess));`
`repeat to Bob { ... }`	`while(outwhile(int cond,int roles_cnt,...)){..}`
`repeat from Bob { ... }`	`while(inwhile(int roles_cnt, ...)){..}`
`rec { ... }`	ordinary `while` loop or `for` loop
`to Bob { LABEL0: ... }`	`outbranch(role *r, const int label);`
`from Bob { LABEL0: ... }`	`inbranch(role *r, int *label);`

under the lack of strong typing in C. We support `char`, `int`, `float`, `double`, `string` (C-string, contiguous NULL-terminated array of `char`), `int_array` (contiguous array of `int`), `float_array` (contiguous array of `float`), and `double_array` (contiguous array of `double`). These types are sufficient for implementing most parallel algorithms; for composite types that are not in the runtime library, the programmer can choose to combine existing primitives, or augment the library with marshalling and unmarshalling of the composite type, to allow type checking.

In Lines 3/4 of the table, `msend` and `mrecv` specify the number of roles (a roles count) of the targets/sources, respectively. Lines 5/6 show how the programmer can specify `Others` in `msend` and `mrecv`: the roles count and roles list are replaced by a macro `_Others(s)` with the session handle as the argument.

Structuring Message Flows: Branching and Iteration. Branching (choice) in Session C is declared explicitly by the use of `outbranch` and `inbranch`. Different branches may have different communication behaviours, and the deciding participant needs to inform the other participant which branch is chosen. The passive participant will then react accordingly.

```
if (i>3) {
  outbranch(Bob, BR_LABEL0);
  send_int(Bob, 42);
} else {
  outbranch(Bob, BR_LABEL1);
  recv_int(Bob, &val);
}
```

```
switch (inbranch(Alice, &rcvd_label)) {
  case BR_LABEL0:
    recv_int(Alice, &val);
    break;
  case BR_LABEL1:
    send_int(Alice, 42);
    break;}
```

Above, the branching is initiated by a call to `outbranch` in the then-block or else-block of an if-statement. On the receiving side of the branch, the program first calls `inbranch` to receive the branch label. A switch-case statement should then be used to run the segment of code which corresponds to the branching label.

For iteration, two methods are provided: *local* and *communicating iterations*. *Local iteration* is a standard statement such as `while`-statements, with session operations occurring inside. *Communicating iteration* is a distributed version of loop, where, at each iteration, the loop condition is computed by the process calling `outwhile` and is communicated to processes calling `inwhile`. This while loop is designed to support multicast, so that a single `outwhile` can control multiple processes. This is useful in a number of parallel iterative parallel algorithms, which the loop continues until certain conditions (e.g. convergence) are reached and cannot be determined statically.

```
// Master process (Alice)              // Slave process (Bob)
while (outwhile(i++<3, 1, Bob))        while (inwhile(1, Alice))
  recv_int(Bob, &value);                 send_int(Alice, 42);
```

Above, `Alice` issues an `outwhile` with condition `i++<3` which will be evaluated in each iteration. `outwhile` then sends the result of the evaluation (i.e. 1 or 0) to `Bob` and also uses that as the local `while` loop condition. Then `Bob` receives the result of the condition evaluation from `Alice` by the `inwhile` call, and uses as the local `while` loop condition. Both processes execute the body of the loop, where `Bob` sends an integer to `Alice`. This repeats until `i++<3` evaluates to `0`, then both processes exit the while loop.

3   Type Checking and Message Optimisation

3.1   Session Type Checker

The session type checker for an endpoint program is implemented as a `clang` C compiler plugin. The `clang` compiler is the full-featured C/C++/Objective-C compiler frontend of the LLVM (Low-Level Virtual Machine) project [22]. LLVM is a collection of modular and reusable individual libraries for building compiler toolchains. The modular approach of the project allows easy mix-and-match of individual components of a compiler to build source code analysis and transformation tools. Our session type checker is built as such a tool, utilising the parser and various AST-related frontend modules from the `clang` compiler.

Endpoint Type Checking. verifies that the source code conforms to the corresponding endpoint protocol in Scribble. The type checker operates by ensuring that the linear usage of the communication primitives conforms to a given Scribble protocol, based on the correspondence between Scribble and Session C constructs given in the table in § 2.2. The following example shows how Scribble statements are matched against Session C communication primitives.

We quickly outline how the type checker works, which also gives the background for §3.2 later. First, the Scribble endpoint protocol is parsed into an internal tree representation. For brevity, hereafter we refer to it as *session tree*. Except for recursion (which itself is *not* a communication), each node of a session tree consists of (1) the target role, (2) the type of the node (e.g. send, receive, choice, etc.) and (3) the datatype, if relevant (e.g. `int`, `string`, etc.). For example, a Scribble endpoint type statement "`int to Worker;`" becomes a node {role: Worker, type: send, datatype: int}.

The type checking is done by *inferring* the session typing of each program and matching the resulting session tree against the one from the endpoint protocol. The type inference is efficiently done by extracting session communication operations from the source code.[1] A session tree is then constructed from this session typing. For example, a runtime function call, `send_int(Worker, result)` will be represented by a node {role: Worker, type: send, datatype: int}.

We can now move to the final process of session type checking in Session C. After their construction, the session trees from both Scribble endpoint protocol and the program are *normalised*, removing unused dummy nodes, branches without session operations and iteration nodes without children, thus compacting the trees to a canonical form. We then compare these two normalised session trees, and verify that they are in the asynchronous subtyping relation (illustrated in § 3.2) up to minimisation.

3.2   Asynchronous Message Optimisation

This subsection illustrates one of the key contributions of our toolchain, the type checking in the presence of *asynchronous message optimisation*. Parallel programs often make use of parallel pipelines to overlap computation and communication. The overlapping can reduce stall time due to blocking wait in the asynchronous communication model, as far as the overlapping does not interfere with data dependencies.

Stage I	Stage II	Stage III		Stage I	Stage II	Stage III
send——→recv						
	send——→recv			send	send	send
‑ ‑ ‑→recv		send‑ ‑ ‑→		recv	recv	recv

Above (left) shows a native but immediately safe ring pipeline and (right) an efficient parallel pipeline, which needs only two steps to complete instead of three, since Stage I does not need to wait for data from Stage III. However, this parallel pipeline is hard to type check against a naturally specified global type (which would be based on the left figure where interactions take place one by one), because of the permuted communication operations – we cannot match the **send** against the **recv**, because they criss-cross. But these two figures are equivalent under the asynchronous communication model with non-blocking send and blocking receive.

```
while (i++ < N) { /* StageII */        while (i++ < N) { /* Optimised StageII */
  recv_int(StageI, &rcvd);               send_int(StageIII, result);
  send_int(StageIII, result);            compute(result);
  compute(result);                       recv_int(StageI, &rcvd);
  result = rcvd;                          result = rcvd;
}                                      }
```

To see this point concretely, the above listing juxtaposes an unoptimised and optimised implementation of the Stage II. Both programs communicate values

---

[1] Because C allows unrestricted type conversion by casting, we use the datatype explicitly mentioned in communication functions as the type of an argument rather than the type of its expression. For example, `send_int(Bob, 3.14)` says that sending 3.14 as int is the intention of the programmer, which is safe if the receiver is intended to receive an integer.

correctly despite the different order of communication statements. Note compute is positioned after a send, so that compute can be carried out while the data is being sent in the background, taking advantage of non-blocking sends.

The use of parallel pipelines is omnipresent in message-passing parallel algorithms. To type-check them, we apply the asynchronous subtyping theory [25,26], which allows the following deadlock-free permutations:

1. Permuting Receive-Send to Send-Receive in the same or different channels;
2. Permuting order of Send-Send if they are in difference channels;
3. Permuting order of Receive-Receive if they are in different channels

Note that if we permute in the different direction from (1) (i.e. Send-Receive to Receive-Send), it causes a deadlock. E.g. in the efficient pipeline described above, if send-recv is permuted to recv-send in the Stage I, it causes a deadlock between the Stage I and II.

We give the subtyping rules against Scribble endpoint protocols below, taking the iso-recursive approach [25], where T is an endpoint type: where use the

$$\frac{-}{T < T}\lfloor\text{ID}\rfloor \quad \frac{\forall i.\ T_i < T_i'}{\text{from/to role}\ \{l_1: T_1 \cdots l_n: T_n\} < \text{from/to role}\ \{l_1: T_1' \cdots l_n: T_n'\}}\lfloor\text{BRA}\rfloor$$

$$\frac{T_1 < C[T_2] \quad U' \text{ to role}' \notin C \quad \forall \text{role}'.\ U' \text{ from role}' \notin C}{U \text{ from role}; T_1 < C[U \text{ from role}; T_2]}\lfloor\text{RECV}\rfloor$$

$$\frac{T_1 < C[T_2] \quad U' \text{ from/to role} \notin C}{U \text{ to role}; T_1 < C[U \text{ to role}; T_2]}\lfloor\text{SEND}\rfloor \quad \frac{T_1 < T_2}{\text{rec } \mathtt{X}\,\{T_1\} < \text{rec } \mathtt{X}\,\{T_2\}}\lfloor\text{REC}\rfloor$$

type context C defined as:

$$C ::= [] \mid U \text{ from role}; C \mid U \text{ to role}; C$$

The subtyping algorithm in Session C conforms to the rules listed above (which come from [25]) and is their practical refinement, which we describe below:

1. ($\lfloor\text{RECV}\rfloor$) For each receive statement, search for a matching receive for the same channel in the source code until a receive statement is found or search failed. Send and other statements in different channels can be skipped over.
2. ($\lfloor\text{SEND}\rfloor$) For each send statement, search for a matching send for the same channel in the source code until a receive statement is found or search failed. Sends can only be permuted between statements in different channels, so overtaking a receive operation is disallowed.
3. We apply the permutation described above on consecutive statements within rec and repeat blocks following the iso-recursive approach [25], which is more suitable for languages such as C and Java.

Finally, we check that all nodes in the source code and protocol session type trees have been visited.

We end this section by identifying the time-complexity of the present toolchain. It uses well-formedness checking of a global protocol and its projection, which are both polynomial-time bound w.r.t. the size of the global type [8, 10]. The asynchronous subtype-checker as given above is polynomial against the size of a local type based on the arguments from [8, 25, 26]. Type inferences for session typed processes are polynomial [10, 18, 26]. We conclude:

Remark 1. The complexity of the whole toolchain is polynomial time-bounded against the size of a global type and a program.

Thus the toolchain is in principle efficient. Further, a careful examination of each algorithm suggests they tend to perform linearly with a small factor in normal cases (e.g. unless deeply nested permutations are carried out for optimisations). Our usage experience confirms this observation.

4   Parallel Algorithms

In this section we demonstrate the effectiveness of Session C for clear, structured and safe message-passing parallel programming, through two algorithms which exemplify complex optimisations and communication topologies. For other implementations of representative parallel algorithms [11, 15, 23], see [13].

4.1   N-Body Simulation: Asynchronous Optimisation for Pipelines

The parallel N-body algorithm forms a circular pipeline. Such a ring topology [2] is used in many parallel algorithms such as LU matrix decomposition [6]. The N-body problem involves finding the motion, according to classical mechanics, of a system of particles given their masses, initial positions and velocities. Parallelisation is achieved by partitioning the particle set among a set of m worker processes. Each worker is responsible for a partition of all particles.

```
protocol Nbody /* Global protocol */
    (role Head, role Body, role Tail) {
  rec NrOfSteps {
    rec SubCompute {
      particles from Head to Body;
      particles from Body to Tail;
      particles from Tail to Head;
      SubCompute; }
    NrOfSteps; }
}
```

Above shows the global protocol with 3 workers, Head, Body and Tail. The simulation is repeated for a number of steps (rec NrOfSteps). In each step, the resultant forces of particles held by a worker are computed against all particles held by others. We arrange our workers in a ring pipeline and perform a series of sub-computations (rec SubCompute) to propagate the particles to all workers, each involving receiving particles from a neighbouring worker and sending particles received in the previous sub-computation to the next worker.

All of the endpoint protocols inherit the two nested rec blocks from the global protocol. In the body block of rec SubCompute, the order of send and receive are different in Head and Body. As discussed in §3.2, Session C allows permuting the order of send and receive for optimisations under the asynchronous

```
protocol Nbody at Body /*endpoint*/   /* Implementation of Body worker */
   (role Head, role Tail) {           while (iterations++ < NR_OF_ITERATIONS) {
   rec NrOfIters {                      while (rounds++ < NR_OF_NODES) {
     rec SubCompute {                     send_particles(Tail, tmp_parts);//permuted
       particles from Head;               // Update veclocities
       particles to Tail;                 compute_forces(particles, tmp_parts,...);
       SubCompute;}                        recv_particles(Head, &tmp_parts);
                                        } // Update positions by reeceived velocities
     NrOfIters;}                        compute_positions(particles, pvs, ... );
}                                     }
```

subtyping, so that we can type-check this program. Using the endpoint protocols as specification, we can implement the workers. The code on the right implements the Body worker which is typable by our session type checker, despite the difference in order of send and receive from its endpoint Scribble.

4.2   Linear Equation Solver: A Wraparound Mesh Topology

The aim of the linear equation algorithm is finding a x such that $Ax = b$, where A is an $n \times n$ matrix and x and b are vectors of length n. We use the parallel Jacobi algorithm [1], which decomposes A into a diagonal component D and a remainder R, $A = D + R$. The algorithm iterates until the normalised difference between successive iterations is less than a predefined error.

```
/* Global protocol */
protocol Solver (role Master, ...) {
  rec Iter {
    rec Pipe {
      double_array from Master to Last;
      double_array from Last to East;
      double_array from East ro Master;
      // Other communication in pipeline
      Pipe;}
    // Distribute X vector from diagonal
    double_array from Master to SouthWest;
    double_array from Master to West;
    // Distribution of other columns
    Iter;}
}
```

Our parallel implementation of this algorithm uses p^2 processors in a $p \times p$ wraparound mesh topology to solve an $n \times n$ system matrix. The matrix is partitioned into submatrix blocks of size n^2/p^2, assigned to each of the processors. Above shows the global protocol and the dataflow of the linear equation solver implementation with 9 workers.

An endpoint protocol is listed below on the left. The overall iteration of the algorithm is controlled by a rec Iter block. In each iteration, the computed values are put into a horizontal pipeline, as shown on the right to compute the sums. The resultant X vector is then calculated by the diagonal node to other workers in the mesh for the next iteration. The corresponding code is given on the right. The asyn-

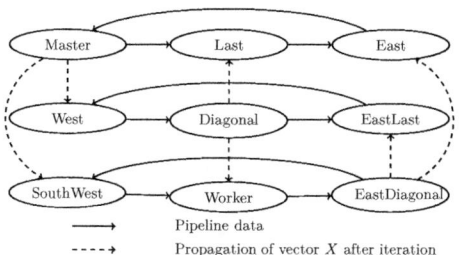

→   Pipeline data
----→ Propagation of vector X after iteration

chronous message optimisation is again applied to the horizontal pipeline in order to overlap communications and computations.

```
protocol Solver at Diagonal          while (!iter_completed)) {
   (role West, role EastLast,           computeProducts(partsum, blkA, newXVec, ...);
    role Last, role Worker) {           computeSums(sum, partsum, ...);
  rec Iter {                            pipe = 0;
    rec Pipe {                          while (pipe++ < columns) {
      double_array from West;             send_double_array(EastLast, partsum, blkDim);
                                          computeSums(sum, partsum, blkDim);
      double_array to EastLast;           recv_double_array(West, partsum, &length);
      Pipe;                             }
    }                                   // calculate X vector
    double_array to Last, Worker;       copyXVector(newXVec, oldXVec, ...);
    Iter;                               computeDivisions(newXVector, sum, ...);
  }                                     msend_double_array(newXVec, Last, Worker, ...);
}                                     }
```

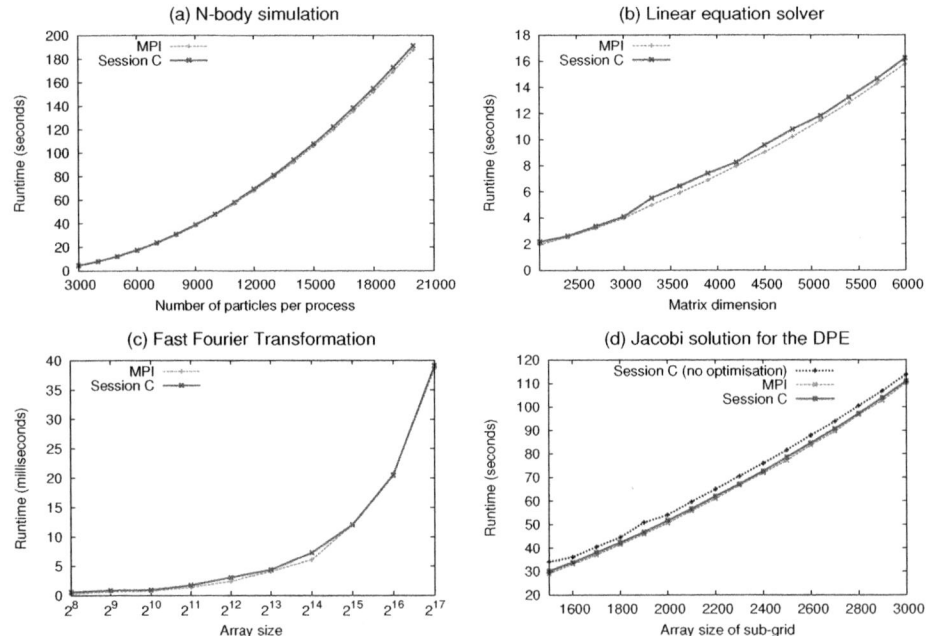

Fig. 2. Benchmark results

5   Performance Evaluation

This section presents performance results for the four algorithms which feature different topologies and communication structures. The first three benchmarks were taken on workstations with Intel Core i7-2600 processors with 8GB RAM running Ubuntu Linux 11.04; the Jacobi solution benchmarks were taken on a high performance cluster with nodes containing AMD PhenomX49650 processor with 8GB RAM running CentOS 5.6, connected by a dedicated Gigabit Ethernet switch. Each benchmark was run 5 times and the reported runtime is the average of all 5 runs. For the MPI versions, OpenMPI 1.4.3 were used. Both use gcc 4.4.3 to compile with the optimisation level -03.

N-body Simulation. Our results are compared against MPI. Both versions use a ring pipeline to propagate the particles, and the two implementations share the same computational component by linking the same compiled object code for the `compute` functions. Our implementations were benchmarked with 3 workers and 1000 iterations on a set of input particles in the two-dimensional space. The results in Fig. 2(a) show that Session C's execution time is within 3% of the MPI implementation.

Linear Equation Solver. Fig. 2(b) shows that the MPI linear equation solver is faster than Session C implementation by 1–3%, with the ratio decreasing as the matrix size increases, suggesting the communication overhead is low, if any. The MPI implementation uses `MPI_Bcast` to broadcast the results of each iteration to all nodes in the column, while Session C explicitly distributes the results.

FFT (Fast Fourier Transform) Butterfly Algorithm. We use a 8 node FFT butterfly. As seen from Fig. 2(c), Session C demonstrates a competitive performance compared to MPI implementation, again with the difference in ratio decreasing as the array size gets larger. The algorithm takes advantage of asynchronous optimisation for the butterfly message exchanges.

Jacobi Solution for the Discrete Poisson Equation. Fig. 2(d) shows the benchmark results of the implementation of Jacobi solution. We benchmarked an optimised Jacobi solution implemented in Session C against a version without asynchronous message optimisation and found that the optimisation improved the performance by up to 8%. The result of this optimisation is very close (within 1%) to that of our reference implementation in MPI, demonstrating the effectiveness of the asynchronous optimisation.

6   Related Works and Further Topics

Due to space limitations, we leave comparisons with other session-based languages and HPC/PGAS languages to [29].

Deadlock Detection in MPI. ISP [34] is a dynamic verifier which applies model-checking techniques to identify potential communication deadlocks in MPI (by "communication deadlock" we mean deadlocks due to communication mismatch/circularity, rather than local computation, e.g. divergent loop). Their tool uses a fixed test harness. In order to reduce the state space of possible thread interleavings of an execution, the tool exploits an independence between thread actions. Later in [35], they improved its scheduling policy to gain efficiency of the verification. TASS [32] is another model checking-based tool for a deadlock analysis in MPI. It constructs an abstract model of a given MPI program and uses symbolic execution to evaluate the model for finding deadlocks.

Our session type-based approach differs from these approaches in that it offers a full deadlock-free guarantee for communications by type-checked programs, without being restricted to external test sets or extracted models from program code, as well as offering a low-cost static checking. We believe a communication protocol is an abstraction which a developer of a message-passing parallel algorithm is anyway aware of. Session C encourages programmers to make this abstraction explicit, and offers primitives and a type checker for well-structured and formally safe message-passing parallel programs.

Formally-Founded Communication-Based HPC Languages. Pilot [5] is a parallel programming layer on top of standard MPI, aiming to simplify complex MPI primitives based on CSP. The communication is synchronous and channels are untyped to allow a reuse for different types. They have a runtime analysis for some deadlock patterns. Occam-pi [30] is a system-level efficient concurrent language with channel-based communication based on CSP and the π-calculus. It offers various locking and barrier abstractions, but do not support deadlock-free analysis. Heap-Hop [33] is a verification tool for C based on dual contracts and Separation Logic. It can detect a deadlock based on contract specifications, but treats only *binary* (two parties) communications. Our work differs in that we centre on multiparty session-based abstractions for structured communications programming combined with a full formal assurance for communication safety.

Our previous work [29] applied Session Java (SJ) [19,20], Java enhanced with session types, to parallel algorithms. SJ treats only *binary* session types [17] and cannot guarantee deadlock freedom and global progress between more than two processes. To ensure these properties, the tool in [29] has to run an additional topology verification on the top of the session type-checking. Session C offers a significant speed-up (60%) compared to SJ as well as MPI for Java [28].

Optimisation in MPI. Techniques for improving performance of MPI include building libraries for efficient transmission of data, e.g. [7] or MPI-aware optimising compilers, e.g. [12]. Most optimisations share a common theme to utilise computation and communication overlap to reduce the negative impact of the communication overhead. Our asynchronous message optimisation is one such instance to facilitate communication-computation overlap. Unlike Session C, existing works do not offer a similar framework, where a type-theoretic basis gives a formal safety assurance for optimised code.

Further Topics. To fulfill its full potential as a session-based programming framework for parallel algorithms, we are planning several extensions of Session C, including the support of parametrised [36] and multirole multiparty session types [9] in Scribble, Session C and its tool chain for a fully generic protocol descriptions and programming (e.g. with respect to the number of workers in the examples in §2); synthesis of global protocols for better development lifecycle; and adding design-by-contracts [4] for fine-grained logical verification. We also intend to combine some features of Cyclone [21] in extending our framework to ensure stronger safety properties in addition to communication safety.

Acknowledgements. We thank Gary Brown for his fantastic work in the Scribble project, the members of Mobility Reading Group and Custom Computing Group for discussions, and reviewers for valuable comments. The work is partially supported by EPSRC EP/F003757/01 and EP/G015635/01.

References

1. Jacobi and Gauss-Seidel Iteration,
   http://math.fullerton.edu/mathews/n2003/GaussSeidelMod.html
2. N-body algorithm using pipeline,
   http://www.mcs.anl.gov/research/projects/mpi/usingmpi/examples/advmsg/nbodypipe_c.htm
3. Bettini, L., Coppo, M., D'Antoni, L., De Luca, M., Dezani-Ciancaglini, M., Yoshida, N.: Global Progress in Dynamically Interleaved Multiparty Sessions. In: van Breugel, F., Chechik, M. (eds.) CONCUR 2008. LNCS, vol. 5201, pp. 418–433. Springer, Heidelberg (2008)
4. Bocchi, L., Honda, K., Tuosto, E., Yoshida, N.: A Theory of Design-by-Contract for Distributed Multiparty Interactions. In: Gastin, P., Laroussinie, F. (eds.) CONCUR 2010. LNCS, vol. 6269, pp. 162–176. Springer, Heidelberg (2010)
5. Carter, J., Gardner, W.B., Grewal, G.: The Pilot approach to cluster programming in C. In: IPDPSW, pp. 1–8. IEEE (2010)
6. Casanova, H., Legrand, A., Robert, Y.: Parallel Algorithms. Chapman & Hall (July 2008)
7. Danalis, A., et al.: MPI-aware compiler optimizations for improving communication-computation overlap. In: ICS 2009, pp. 316–325 (2009)
8. Deniélou, P.M., Yoshida, N.: Buffered Communication Analysis in Distributed Multiparty Sessions. In: Gastin, P., Laroussinie, F. (eds.) CONCUR 2010. LNCS, vol. 6269, pp. 343–357. Springer, Heidelberg (2010)
9. Deniélou, P.M., Yoshida, N.: Dynamic multirole session types. In: POPL, pp. 435–446. ACM (2011)
10. Deniélou, P.M., Yoshida, N.: Multiparty Session Types Meet Communicating Automata. In: Seidl, H. (ed.) Programming Languages and Systems. LNCS, vol. 7211, pp. 194–213. Springer, Heidelberg (2012)
11. Dwarf Mine homepage, http://view.eecs.berkeley.edu/wiki/Dwarf_Mine
12. Friedley, A., Lumsdaine, A.: Communication Optimization Beyond MPI. In: IPDPSW and Phd Forum. IEEE (2011)
13. Online Appendix, http://www.doc.ic.ac.uk/~cn06/pub/2012/sessionc/
14. Grama, A., Karypis, G., Kumar, V., Gupta, A.: Introduction to Parallel Computing, 2nd edn. Addison Wesley (January 2003)
15. Gropp, W., Lusk, E., Skjellum, A.: Using MPI: Portable Parallel Programming with the Message-Passing Interface. MIT Press (1999)
16. Honda, K., Mukhamedov, A., Brown, G., Chen, T.-C., Yoshida, N.: Scribbling Interactions with a Formal Foundation. In: Natarajan, R., Ojo, A. (eds.) ICDCIT 2011. LNCS, vol. 6536, pp. 55–75. Springer, Heidelberg (2011)
17. Honda, K., Vasconcelos, V.T., Kubo, M.: Language Primitives and Type Discipline for Structured Communication-Based Programming. In: Hankin, C. (ed.) ESOP 1998. LNCS, vol. 1381, pp. 122–138. Springer, Heidelberg (1998)
18. Honda, K., Yoshida, N., Carbone, M.: Multiparty asynchronous session types. In: POPL 2008, vol. 5201, p. 273 (2008)
19. Hu, R., Kouzapas, D., Pernet, O., Yoshida, N., Honda, K.: Type-Safe Eventful Sessions in Java. In: D'Hondt, T. (ed.) ECOOP 2010. LNCS, vol. 6183, pp. 329–353. Springer, Heidelberg (2010)
20. Hu, R., Yoshida, N., Honda, K.: Session-Based Distributed Programming in Java. In: Ryan, M. (ed.) ECOOP 2008. LNCS, vol. 5142, pp. 516–541. Springer, Heidelberg (2008)

21. Jim, T., Morrisett, G., Grossman, D., Hicks, M., Cheney, J., Wang, Y.: Cyclone: A Safe Dialect of C. In: Usenix Annual Technical Conference, Monterey, CA (2002)
22. Lattner, C., Adve, V.S.: LLVM: A Compilation Framework for Lifelong Program Analysis & Transformation. In: CGO 2004, pp. 75–88 (2004)
23. Leighton, F.T.: Introduction to parallel algorithms and architectures: arrays, trees, hypercubes. Morgan Kaufmann (1991)
24. Metis and parmetis, glaros.dtc.umn.edu/gkhome/views/metis
25. Mostrous, D.: Session Types in Concurrent Calculi: Higher-Order Processes and Objects. Ph.D. thesis, Imperial College London (2009)
26. Mostrous, D., Yoshida, N., Honda, K.: Global Principal Typing in Partially Commutative Asynchronous Sessions. In: Castagna, G. (ed.) ESOP 2009. LNCS, vol. 5502, pp. 316–332. Springer, Heidelberg (2009)
27. Message Passing Interface, http://www.mcs.anl.gov/research/projects/mpi/
28. MPJ Express homepage, http://mpj-express.org/
29. Ng, N., Yoshida, N., Pernet, O., Hu, R., Kryftis, Y.: Safe Parallel Programming with Session Java. In: De Meuter, W., Roman, G.-C. (eds.) COORDINATION 2011. LNCS, vol. 6721, pp. 110–126. Springer, Heidelberg (2011)
30. Occam-pi homepage, http://www.occam-pi.org/
31. Scribble homepage, http://www.jboss.org/scribble
32. Siegel, S.F., Zirkel, T.K.: Automatic formal verification of MPI-based parallel programs. In: PPoPP 2011, p. 309. ACM Press (February 2011)
33. Villard, J.: Heaps and Hops. Ph.D. thesis, ENS Cachan (2011)
34. Vo, A., Vakkalanka, S., DeLisi, M., Gopalakrishnan, G., Kirby, R.M., Thakur, R.: Formal verification of practical MPI programs. In: PPoPP 2009, pp. 261–270 (2009)
35. Vo, A., et al.: A Scalable and Distributed Dynamic Formal Verifier for MPI Programs. In: SC 2010, pp. 1–10. IEEE (2010)
36. Yoshida, N., Deniélou, P.-M., Bejleri, A., Hu, R.: Parameterised Multiparty Session Types. In: Ong, L. (ed.) FOSSACS 2010. LNCS, vol. 6014, pp. 128–145. Springer, Heidelberg (2010)
37. ZeroMQ homepage, http://www.zeromq.org/

Non-interference on UML State-Charts*

Martín Ochoa[1,2], Jan Jürjens[1], and Jorge Cuéllar[2]

[1] Siemens AG, Germany
[2] TU Dortmund, Germany
{martin.ochoa,jan.jurjens}@cs.tu-dortmund.de,
jorge.cuellar@siemens.com

Abstract. Non-interference is a semantically well-defined property that allows one to reason about the security of systems with respect to information flow policies for groups of users. Many of the security problems of implementations could be already spotted at design time if information flow would be a concern in early phases of software development. In this paper we propose a methodology for automatically verifying the interaction of objects whose behaviour is described by deterministic UML State-charts with respect to information flow policies, based on the so-called unwinding theorem. We have extended this theorem to cope with the particularities of state-charts: the use of variables, guards, actions and hierarchical states and derived results about its compositionality. In order to validate our approach, we report on an implementation of our enhanced unwinding techniques and applications to scenarios from the Smart Metering domain.

1 Introduction

Secure Information Flow analysis is a fine-grained methodology for studying the confidentiality and integrity of systems. This kind of analysis (first introduced by Goguen and Meseguer [12] in 1982) is mathematically defined over the inputs and outputs visible to groups of users. Its main advantage over other security analyses is that it allows to pin down subtle flows of information that are difficult to spot when focusing merely on analysing security mechanisms (such as access control mechanisms). Although information flow properties assume perfect access control to guarantee that different groups of users do not see certain inputs and outputs of other users directly, this is a reasonable assumption: attackers usually exploit the information that is shared by victims through common interfaces instead of trying to break directly the access control mechanisms. In words of Anderson [6] "(...) in practice, security is compromised most often not by breaking dedicated mechanisms such as encryption or security protocols, but by exploiting weaknesses in the way they are being used".

---

* This research was partially supported by the MoDelSec Project of the DFG Priority Programme 1496 "'Reliably Secure Software Systems – RS³'" and the EU project NESSoS (FP7 256890).

C.A. Furia and S. Nanz (Eds.): TOOLS Europe 2012, LNCS 7304, pp. 219–235, 2012.
© Springer-Verlag Berlin Heidelberg 2012

In the past decades different information flow properties have been proposed for coping with different system models such as non-deterministic systems, distributed systems and imperative programming languages. At the abstract level results about compositionality and refinement have been published for many security properties, for example [18,19,24]. In the 'Language Based' realm (i.e. analysis of source code) mature tools for information flow analysis on annotated code exist, like [1,11,2]. All of these are indeed promising steps towards the industrial application of the fine-grained analysis offered by the property-centric point of view of Information Flow. Nevertheless, it seems that production environments are still far from adopting these techniques.

In this paper we propose a light-weight, automatic strategy for checking non-interference on a deterministic fragment of UML state-charts. Our aim is to make a formally sound step towards the usability of these techniques based in the so-called *unwinding* theorem, that provides sufficient conditions for non-interference. We have extended previous work on unwinding to cope with the complexity of UML state-charts: the use variables for keeping history of the state, guards for transitions, hierarchical states and actions. Moreover, we aim at verifying systems where object interaction plays a fundamental role. In order to achieve this, we discuss sufficient conditions for deciding on the composition of the behaviour of already verified components. This is a key factor in the scalability of our approach, which is also an important criterion for the success of verification in realistic settings.

In order to validate our theoretical results, we report on a prototypical machine implementation that automatically verifies models where our unwinding theorem is applicable. We apply this implementation to examples motivated by a case study from the Smart Grid domain. Since unwinding conditions are only sufficient conditions, some secure models might be rejected. However it is important to show that non-trivial secure models are actually accepted and verified. The case study allows to discuss and validate the utility of our approach.

The rest of the paper is organized as follows: Sect. 2 discusses some preliminaries about non-interference and Harel state-charts and sets the notation for the rest of the paper. Sect. 3 is the central section of the paper, were the verification strategy is described. In Sect. 4 we discuss the notion of composition used for reasoning about interacting objects and the composition theorem. In Sect. 5 we illustrate our approach on examples from the Smart Metering domain. Sect. 6 reports on related work and we conclude in Sect. 7.

2   Preliminaries

In this section we recall some definitions and set the notation for the rest of the paper. Starting with the original definition of non-interference by [12] many other subtle information flow properties have been proposed for dealing with non-determinism and distributed systems. In this paper we will nevertheless use the original definition, because our focus will be the analysis of deterministic automata.

2.1 Non-interference

Assume a system is a deterministic black-box transforming sequences of input events I into sequences of output events O by means of a semantic function:

$$[\,] : I \to O$$

We further assume there are two types of users : *high* users H and *low* users [1] L. The sets of input and output events can be divided into the events a high or low user is allowed to see. Lists of input and output events can then be filtered according to the type of user allowed to see them by the purging functions $\cdot|_H$ and $\cdot|_L$. Non-interference is the property :

$$\forall \vec{\imath}\ [\vec{\imath}\,]|_L = [\vec{\imath}\,|_L]|_L \tag{1}$$

In other words, the output seen by the lower users is independent of the input by higher users, up to the point that is not even noticeable whether the high users perform any action on the system.

Some authors (for example [17]) use the equivalent definition:

$$\forall \vec{\imath_1}, \vec{\imath_2}\ \ \vec{\imath_1}|_L = \vec{\imath_2}|_L \Rightarrow [\vec{\imath_1}]|_L = [\vec{\imath_2}]|_L \tag{2}$$

which corresponds to the intuition that two runs where the high user perform different actions are equivalent to low users. A stronger version of this property is usually used in the language-based information flow analysis domain [14,7,10].

2.2 State-Charts

In order to model the function $[\cdot]$ of the last subsection, consider *Mealy machines* [20]. Syntactically, a Mealy machine can be represented by a directed graph with annotated transitions of the form α/β, meaning that the input event α triggers the output event β. Formally, a Mealy machine M is defined as a 6-tuple $(S, s_0, \Sigma, \Gamma, T, G)$ where S is a finite set of states, s_0 is an initial state, Σ is finite input alphabet, Γ is a finite output alphabet, $T : S \times \Sigma \to S$ is a transition function defined over states and input symbols and $G : S \times \Sigma \to \Gamma$ is an output function defined over states and input symbols. A Mealy machine induces thus a semantics $[\cdot]$ by $[(\sigma_1, \sigma_2, \ldots, \sigma_n)] = G(s_0, \sigma_1) :: \cdots :: G(s_n, \sigma_n)$ where $s_n = T(\ldots T(T(s_0, \sigma_1), \sigma_2) \ldots, \sigma_n)$ and $::$ denotes concatenation. Notice that the functions T and G are naturally induced by the graph representation. In the following we will assume that if an input is not defined in a given state, the machine enters in a state where no further inputs are processed and no outputs are produced.

---

[1] For simplicity of exposition and historical reasons we will discuss about high and low users in the rest of the paper. However the definition can be extended to an arbitrary partition of groups of users. Also we will restrict to analysing non-interference from high with respect to low (no-down-flows, usually associated to confidentiality), to analyse the converse (i.e. integrity) one can just switch L for H.

If we further divide the input and output events into high an low events, we can apply the definition of non-interference to a Mealy machine.

Example 1. Consider the system defined by the state-machine:

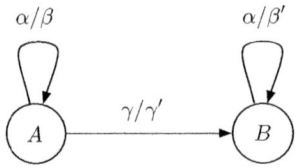

where $\alpha, \beta, \beta' \in L$ and $\gamma, \gamma' \in H$. Then non-interference does not hold since $[(\gamma, \alpha)]|_L = \beta' \neq [(\gamma, \alpha)|_L]|_L = [\alpha]|_L = \beta$.

To deal with the so-called 'state-explosion' problem, that arises when the number of states and transitions increases due to the specification of complex behaviours, other formalisms have been proposed that include the notion of sub and super-states. More prominently Harel [15] proposed the notion of *statechart* that has been used as the basis for UML. This is basically an extension to Mealy machines that allows the following:

- *Hierarchical States:* Single states can contain sub-states and transitions among the sub-states up to arbitrary depth. Let A be a super state containing finitely many sub-states A_i. Then an external state B can have a transition directly to s or to a sub-state A_i. In the first case the transition is to be interpreted as to go to the initial sub-state of s. In the second case it simply goes to s_i. This allows to modularize certain common behaviours into super-states, improving considerably the presentation of complex state charts.
- *Clustering:* To graphically summarize events that trigger a transition to the same state in a group of states, a transition with event γ going out of a super-state A to state B stands for a transition from each sub-state of A with event α to B.
- *Orthogonality and Concurrency:* In some cases, processes within the system are orthogonal between each other, in the sense that they could be described with two separate state-charts with disjoint inputs. Thus, Harel state-charts allow multiple sub-state-charts to be modelled as concurrent processes within the same state-chart, compressing notably the notation, since for each two independent Mealy machines with n and m states respectively, $n \cdot m$ states are needed to represent them in a single machine.

Thus formally, a Harel state-chart can be seen as a set (to represent the concurrent processes) of 6-tuples $(S_i, s_0^i, \Sigma_i, \Gamma_i, T_i, G_i)$ where S_i is as a finite set of super-states and s_0^i is an initial super-state. A super-state is defined as a either a state or a state-chart, such that for every super-state there are only finitely many nested state-charts. T_i and G_i are then similar as in the Mealy machine case, where for a given state T_i depends also on the transitions defined at higher hierarchical states (if any).

Example 2. The following state-chart:

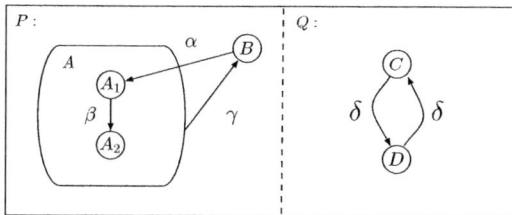

contains a (sub) state-chart P containing a superstate with clustering running concurrently with (sub) state-chart Q.

Notice that all these extensions are syntactic sugar for improving the graphical representation: any deterministic Harel state-chart can be represented by a Mealy-Machine with equivalent semantics, and therefore we can use the same definition of non-interference given in the previous subsection for reasoning about the security of Harel State-charts.

3 Extending Unwinding for UML State-Charts

Verifying system designs for non-interference is a computationally difficult task, because the definition uses universal quantifiers on inputs and outputs: to verify accurately an arbitrary system implies running and comparing all possible input sequences. Therefore, in order to achieve a trade-off between security and efficiency, one usually needs to sacrifice some precision on the verification. In this section we discuss how to obtain sufficient conditions for the non-interference analysis on UML state-charts by extending traditional unwinding theorems for finite state machines. We will first introduce the fragment of the UML state-charts considered and discuss briefly the unwinding theorem. Then we report on our extension for UML state-charts.

3.1 UML State-Charts à la UMLsec

UML has adopted an extension of Harel state-charts to represent the behaviour of classes. It allows a list of *actions* as a consequence of an event, including calling methods, updating variables and outputting values. In this paper we will restrict to a fragment of UML state-charts defined as follows :

- Input events labelling transitions can be either methods of the associated class with concrete parameters or with variables to represent calls with different parameters or global system events (like the tics of a system clock).
- Actions associated to an input event can be either outputting an event (written return event) or a variable assignment, where the variables are attributes of the associated class or parameters of the input.
- Guards are decidable conditions on the input parameters or the values of the attributes.

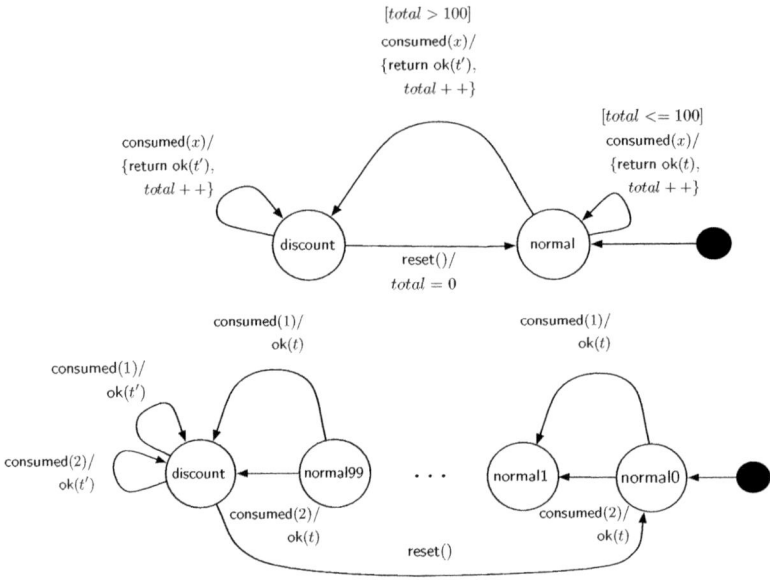

Fig. 1. A model of the smart metering payment processing system as an UML state-chart and a semantically equivalent Mealy Machine for x in range [1..2] in the parameters of consumed

We will restrict to the sub-set of deterministic UML State-charts as defined above. This is similar to the UML state-charts as defined in [17], with the fundamental difference that there state-charts can be non-deterministic, resulting in a more complex semantics. The semantics of the deterministic fragment defined above can be seen as an extension of the Harel state-chart semantics (based on their Mealy machine translation), where the guards and variables are syntactic sugar for describing the history of the state and where parametrized method calls stand for as many transitions as the respective guard allows.

More precisely: a transition labelled with a parametric input stands for multiple transitions, one for each concrete value of the parameter. Transitions where the actions perform variable assignation stand for multiple transitions with distinct targets (one for each possible value of the assignation). Guards with condition C represent the fact that in states where C hold then that particular labelled transition is present, and not present in states where C does not hold. For an example of a UML state-chart and its semantically equivalent Mealy machine see Fig. 1. We will discuss this example in detail in Sect. 5.

3.2   Unwinding

Unwinding theorems were first proposed by Goguen and Meseguer [13]. They provide sufficient conditions for non-interference that are amenable to verify since they rely on local conditions of pairs of states. The idea is that if there exists a reflexive relation R of the states in an input/output state machine M for a policy dividing events in high H and low L such that:

- R is locally consistent: given a state s and $s' = T(s, h)$ the state resulting after a transition triggered by an event $h \in H$ then $(s, s') \in R$.
- R is step-consistent: for all inputs i, if $(s_1, s_2) \in R$ then $(T(s_1, i), T(s_2, i)) \in R$ where $T(s_1, i)$ and $T(s_2, i)$ are the states resulting from the transition triggered by i in s and t.
- R is output-consistent: if $(s_1, s_2) \in R$ then the output of an event $l \in L$ in s_1 is equal to the output of l in s_2.

then non-interference holds on M for the H and L partition. For a proof see for example [13,26].

Example. In example 1, (A, B) must be in R because of locality. However, R is not output consistent and therefore non-interference cannot be established.

3.3 Unwinding for UML Statecharts

There are two main difficulties for extending the unwinding theorems from Mealy machines to the subset of UML state-charts as described in Sect. 3.1: a) The graphical syntactic sugar of Harel state-charts and b) the use of variables and guards for keeping history of the state and for parametrizing inputs. One possibility to verify UML state-charts would be to remove all syntactic sugar, unfold a semantically equivalent Mealy machine and then find an unwinding relation satisfying the conditions described in the previous subsection. This would be however computationally quite expensive in general: the purpose of the UML state-chart notation is to avoid state and transition explosion. We have extended the unwinding theorem accordingly for coping soundly with these differences in the notation in an efficient way. Intuitively, we statically analyse guarded transitions with actions by simultaneously extending an unwinding relation and a tainted set associated to each state. Tainting keeps track of variables whose value is directly or indirectly dependent on high inputs, in the spirit of language based information flow analysis. This information allows to soundly decide on the output consistency of the relation.

In the following when we refer to a state, we mean a state that does not contain further nested sub-states. When we refer to the transitions going out of a state s, we mean all transitions going out of all the super states containing s. Without loss of generality we will analyse concurrent state-charts separately: by definition (Sec. 2) two concurrent Harel state-charts have disjoint inputs, and we further assume they also do not share variables in their UML representation.

Let R' be a relation over the states of a UML state-chart U, H a subset of the inputs of U and tainted(s_i) a set associated to each state s_i, such that:

Local Consistency. For a label on the transition t_1 from s_1 to s_2 of the form

$$[C_1] \ \alpha(y_1) \ / \ \{\text{return } \beta_1, \ x_1 := E_1\} \tag{3}$$

then s_1 is in relation with the initial sub-state of s_2 if there exists a parameter a such that $\alpha(a) \in H$. Moreover $x_1 \in \mathsf{tainted}(s_2)$ and $\mathsf{tainted}(s_2) \supseteq \mathsf{tainted}(s_1)$.

Step Consistency. If $(s_1, s_2) \in R'$ then for every transition t_1 of the form (3) with target s'_1 originating from s_1 and every transition t_2:

$$[C_2]\ \alpha(y_2)\ /\ \{\mathsf{return}\ \beta_2,\ x_2 := E_2\} \tag{4}$$

with target s'_2 originating from s_2 then it follows $(s'_1, s'_2) \in R'$. Moreover, if $\alpha(a) \in H$ for some a or there is a variable $z_i \in \mathsf{tainted}(s_i)$ such that $z_i \in C_i$ or $z_i \in E_i$ then $x_i \in \mathsf{tainted}(s'_i)$ and $\mathsf{tainted}(s'_i) \supseteq \mathsf{tainted}(s_i)$.

Output Consistency. If $(s_1, s_2) \in R'$ with t_1 of form (3) with a such that $\alpha(a) \in L$ we distinguish two cases:

- If there exists x such that $x \in \mathsf{tainted}(s_1)$ and $x \in C_1$ then for all t_2 in s_2 of form (4) it must follow $\beta_1 = \beta_2$.
- Otherwise: if there exists t_2 of form (4) in s_2 such that $C_1 = C_2$ then $\beta_1 = \beta_2$. If no such t_2 exists, then for all other t'_2 in s_2 of form (4) it holds $\beta_1 = \beta_2$.

Moreover there exists no variable x such that $x \in \mathsf{tainted}(s_i)$ and $x \in \beta_i$.

Theorem 1. *If U admits a relation R' as defined above then it respects non-interference.*

Proof. It suffices to show is that the relation R induced by R' on the unfolded Mealy machine M of U is an unwinding relation. A state in M can be seen as a pair $(s, \overrightarrow{v})$ where s is an identifier for a state in U and $\overrightarrow{v}$ is a vector of concrete values $v_1, \ldots, v_n$ for the variables $x_1, \ldots, x_n$ used in U. R is defined thus as $((s_1, \overrightarrow{v}), (s_2, \overrightarrow{w})) \in R \Leftrightarrow (s_1, s_2) \in R'$. Is easy to see that R satisfies local consistency, because R' covers all possible transitions induced by high inputs. Step consistency also holds on R by construction of R'. The extended definition of output consistency is similar to the original one, except for a) it is forbidden to output an expression depending on a tainted variable and b) the output consistency relation is relaxed in case an output is guarded by a condition not depending on tainted variables. It is not hard to see that a) is a necessary condition. Now consider $(s_1, s_2) \in R'$ and w.l.o.g. belonging to the same connected graph of U. Moreover consider a condition C depending on variables $X' = x'_1, \cdots, x'_n$ such that $x'_j \notin \mathsf{tainted}(s_i)$. By the definition of R' there exist ancestors p_1 and p_2 (of s_1 and s_2 respectively) such that there is a high transition between p_1 and p_2 and by definition of tainting this transition does not change the value of any variable in X'. For any input η changing the state of p_1 and p_2 to p'_1 and p'_2 respectively then if $\eta \in H$ then the valuation of X' remains unaltered. If $\eta \in L$ triggers an action changing the value of a variable in X' then the transition was triggered on a condition depending on variables in X'. By hypothesis variables in X' had the same value on p_1 and p_2, and therefore η changes the valuation in both states equivalently. The same reasoning can be done inductively obtaining that the values of X' in s_1 and s_2 depend on the values of X' in p_1 and

side-effects triggered by low inputs exclusively. Therefore if C holds in $(s_1, \overrightarrow{v})$ for a given input trace starting on p_1, then it must also hold in $(s_2, \overrightarrow{w})$ for an equivalent trace on the low inputs that reaches s_2.

Notice that it would be also sound to simply compare all outputs in s_1 and s_2, but this would be too coarse for practical uses, where usually a condition an its negation are defined as guards for the same input on a given state, as we will see in Sect. 5. It suffices to compare the outputs guarded by C and not both the outputs of C and those of $\neg C$, because in the unfolded Mealy machine the states where $\neg C$ holds are not necessarily in the minimal unwinding relation.

4   Object Interaction

As discussed in Sect. 3.1 UML state-charts are commonly used to represent the behaviour of a class. In the previous section we have discussed unwinding theorems that can be used to decide on the security of single, monolithic state-charts. To reason about the security of a system that is built upon interacting objects, we would need to obtain composed state-charts out of the state-charts defining the single object's behaviour. It would be however desirable to have sufficient conditions that allow to reason on information flow policies on the single components mainly for achieving scalability. In this section we discuss the notion of composition we will use and present sufficient conditions that guarantee that a composition respects non-interference for a given policy.

4.1   Composition

We will follow [17] by reasoning at the instance level: we will assume that the behaviour described by a state-chart is that of an instantiated object [2]. The notion of composition we will use is based on message passing between state-charts: the output messages generated by a state-chart A can be input messages for a state-chart B but not vice-versa. This corresponds formally to a special case of parallel composition as defined for example in [8,21] where we restrict the feedback only to occur in one direction. In other words we do not allow call-backs, which are related to recursive method calls. This is indeed a difficult topic on its own, since subtleties on the semantics play a fundamental role (as discussed for example in [28]), and goes outside the scope of this paper. Nevertheless, the composition notion defined here is useful to reason about the security of non-trivial object interaction, as we will see in Sect. 5, and has nice preservation properties for non-interference.

More precisely, let classes A and B with inputs I_A and I_B respectively and outputs O_A and O_B. A and B are composable if $O_A \cap I_B \neq \emptyset$ and $O_B \cap I_A = \emptyset$. The resulting composed object has inputs $I = I_A \cup (I_B \setminus O_A)$ and outputs $O = O_B \cup (O_A \setminus I_B)$. Semantically, $A \otimes B$ is defined by the product of the states in A and B where the states with at least one output $o \in O_A$ such that $o \in I_B$

---

[2] Therefore if we want to reason about different instantiations of an object we would need to define as many classes as desired objects.

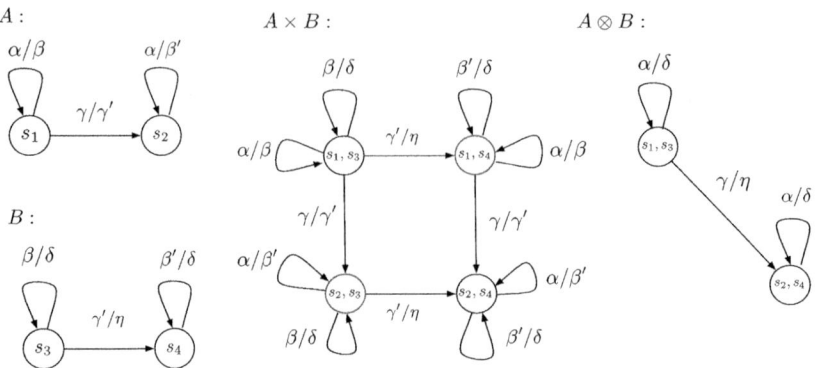

Fig. 2. State-chart U_B and its composition with the state-chart U_A

cannot be processed by B are discarded, because synchronisation cannot take place. This is similar to the notion parallel composition in CCS [21]. The outputs of transitions of A matching inputs of B in every state are then replaced by the induced outputs in B.

Example 3. Consider the state-charts A and B of Fig. 2. Although in principle there exists four possible states in the product state-chart $A \times B$ we discard the states where an output of A that is in the interface of B cannot be processed by B.

4.2   Compositionality and Non-interference

In general, for scalability reasons, it is desirable that verification results on single components can be re-used efficiently for deciding on their composition. In our setting this means, for a given partition of the set of inputs $I = I|_H \cup I|_L$ and outputs $O = O|_H \cup O|_L$ of the composition $A \otimes B$ there exists sufficient conditions on A and B such that this composition respects non-interference. This is notably not the case in general for information flow properties [18]. However, in our case we can derive a positive result in this sense. We first observe that given a policy on a composition $A \otimes B$, the events on $I_B \cap O_A$ remained unspecified since they are not part of the interface of the composition. Although formally possible, it is not sound from a security point of view to mark events from $I_B \cap O_A$ as high in one component and low in the other (or vice-versa), and therefore we will exclude that possibility in the following.

Theorem 2. *Let $I = I|_H \cup I|_L$ and $O = O|_H \cup O|_L$ a partition of the input and output alphabets of $A \otimes B$. If non-interference holds for an extension of the policy in I and O to the unspecified events in $I_B \cap O_A$ in A and B, then non-interference holds on $A \otimes B$.*

Proof. First consider the case where $O_A = I_B$ (sequential composition). If there exists a sequence $\overrightarrow{i}$ of inputs of $A \otimes B$ such that $[\overrightarrow{i}]_{A \otimes B}|_L \neq [\overrightarrow{i}|_L]_{A \otimes B}|_L$.

Then, because of sequentiality and subsequent application of non-interference of B followed by non interference of A and of B again:

$$[\overrightarrow{i}]_{A \otimes B}|_L \overset{S}{=} [[\overrightarrow{i}]_A]_B|_L \overset{B}{=} [[\overrightarrow{i}]_A|_L]_B|_L \overset{A}{=} [[\overrightarrow{i}|_L]_A|_L]_B|_L \overset{B}{=} [[\overrightarrow{i}|_L]_A]_B|_L \qquad (5)$$

now observe that:

$$[\overrightarrow{i}|_L]_{A \otimes B}|_L \overset{S}{=} [[\overrightarrow{i}|_L]_A]_B|_L \qquad (6)$$

but by hypothesis (5) $\neq$ (6), contradiction.

The other cases follow easily by observing that whenever an input i_B of B is not an output of A then A can be extended by adding a single non connected stated with a transition i'_B/i_B, thus returning to the sequential case and without harming the sufficient conditions (and similarly when output o_A is not an input to B).

Notice that the hypothesis of Theorem 2 although sufficient, are not necessary: in fact, the Example 3 has a component A violating non-interference for $H = \{\gamma, \gamma'\}$, but the composition $A \otimes B$ respects it for $H = \{\gamma, \eta\}$.

5   Validation

In this section we report on experiments made to implement the enhanced unwinding technique and the compositionality theorem and applications to examples from our case study.

5.1   Tool Support

There are two basic strategies to construct the relation R' on a given state-chart. One possibility is to proceed top down: first put in relation all the states that respect output consistency and then check for local consistency and step consistency. It is however not clear how to proceed from there if the relationship does not respect the unwinding conditions. We have opted to construct it bottom up: first, put every state in relation with itself. Then we compute all relationships due to local consistency, and subsequently for each pair, we enlarge R' by step consistency. When constructing R' we do a preliminary tainting analysis that could be imprecise in presence of loops. This was enough to evaluate our examples, where tainting occurs only in one step (a more accurate tainting analysis are matter of current work). Finally we check for output consistency. If output consistency does not hold, there exists no unwinding relationship, because there exists no minimal one.

We have prototypically implemented the algorithm described in Sect. 3 in Haskell [3] because of its compact and elegant syntax. A state-chart is represented as a pair of list of nodes and list of transitions where the nodes contain the tainting set and a list of 5-tuples:

```
type Node = (Label,Tainted)
type Transition = (Condition, Input, Output, Origin, Target)
type StateChart = (Nodes,Transitions)
```

For example, to check for output consistency of a pair in R' with respect to a set of low inputs low we have implemented the following code:

```
compareLowOutput :: StateChart -> Low -> (Node,Node) -> Bool
compareLowOutput (nodes,transitions) low (x,y) =
                ( null[(tran1,tran2) | (tran1,tran2) <-lowTransitions,
                (getInputMethod tran1 == getInputMethod tran2),
                (getReturn tran1 /= getReturn tran2)] )
        where lowTransitions = (getLowTransitions transitions low x y)
```

where getLowTransitions is defined as the filtering function including the exception based on the tainting analysis.

5.2   Case Study

Smart grids use information and communication technology (ICT) to optimize the transmission and distribution of electricity from suppliers to consumers, allowing smart generation and bidirectional power flows – depending on where generation takes place. With ICT the Smart Grid enables financial, informational, and electrical transactions among consumers, grid assets, and other authorized users[22]. The Smart Grid integrates all actors of the energy market, including the customers, into a system which supports, for instance, smart consumption in cars and the transformation of incoming power in buildings into heat, light, warm water or electricity with minimal human intervention. Smart grid represents a potentially huge market for the electronics industry [27]. The importance of the smart grid for the society is due to the expectation that it will help optimize the use of renewable energy sources [25] and minimize the collective environmental footprint [9]. Two basic reasons why the attack surface is increasing with the new technologies are: a) The Smart Grid will increase the amount of private sensitive customer data available to the utility and third-party partners and b) Introducing new data interfaces to the grid through meters, collectors, and other smart devices create new entry points for attackers.

Among other requirements, confidentiality and privacy of user data is an important security issue. There are many privacy issues, related to the use of sensitive personally identifiable information (PII) related to the consumption of energy, the location of the electric car, etc. This data must be kept secure from unauthorized access, and the measurement process is subject to strict lawful requirements in terms of accuracy, dependability and security, see in particular the European Union directive [4]. See also [16] for a current version of proposed technologies to solve this power systems management and associated information exchange issues. In the following we will model two scenarios in this domain (for details see [23]).

Scenario 1. Consider the behaviour described in Fig. 1. This models an energy provider that processes the amount energy a user x consumes, described by the event consumed(x) (x is a positive integer, the user's ID) representing one unit of energy consumed. After one unit is consumed, a confirmation ok(t) with the price t of the consumption is sent to the user. If all consumers of a given region consume more than 100 units, the price of the unit drops from t to t'. Now, assuming that a given user with id 1 is not supposed to know about the consume of other users, we would like to check whether this requirement holds for this system. By setting the events {consumed(x) | $x \neq 1$} as high, we can check whether the unwinding conditions hold automatically via our Haskell implementation. In this case, the model is rejected because of output inconsistency. Because unwinding only provides an approximation, it would still be possible that the system is secure. However, by just seeing a difference in the reported price in two consumptions (given that he does not consume himself more than 100 units), the low user could infer bounds on the number of consumptions of his neighbours. A possibility to obtain a positive security guarantee is to modify the model as follows: a discount is given if a *single* user consumes more than 100 units. By modelling two concurrent machines, one accepting only the inputs of the low user and the other from high, we can positively prove the security of the model.

Scenario 2. In this scenario an electric vehicle buys power from a given provider at an agreed price. It does so at a public recharging station. For convenience, the car will automatically stop the recharging when the total consumption exceeds a given value (for example 10 €) or when the battery capacity k is reached. The behaviour of the single components and their composed model is depicted in Fig. 3, where for illustrative purposes also the composition is spelled out. To fulfil privacy requirements of both users and companies, it is desirable that the recharging stations do not learn the single unit price of the energy sold to the vehicle. In other words, we want to treat the events setPrice(x), readPrice and getPrice as confidential for the charging station. All other events are public. We use then Theorem 2 and proceed to verify the single components. In this case, the behaviour of object V violates non-interference, so we cannot use the compositionality result for $P \otimes V \otimes C$. However, if the recharging policy is modified by not being dependent on the price, thus replacing $[t = 10/p]$ with $[t = k]$, then we can verify the composed model automatically, because all components respect the information flow policy.

6   Related Work

Starting with the work of Goguen and Meseguer [12], many information-flow properties have appeared for specific system models and to capture different notions of security. Rushby discusses unwinding theorems in a more modern notation [26] along with transitive and intransitive information flow policies. General Unwinding theorems for a wide range of information flow properties have also been suggested by Mantel in [13]. Mantel has also unified most of these

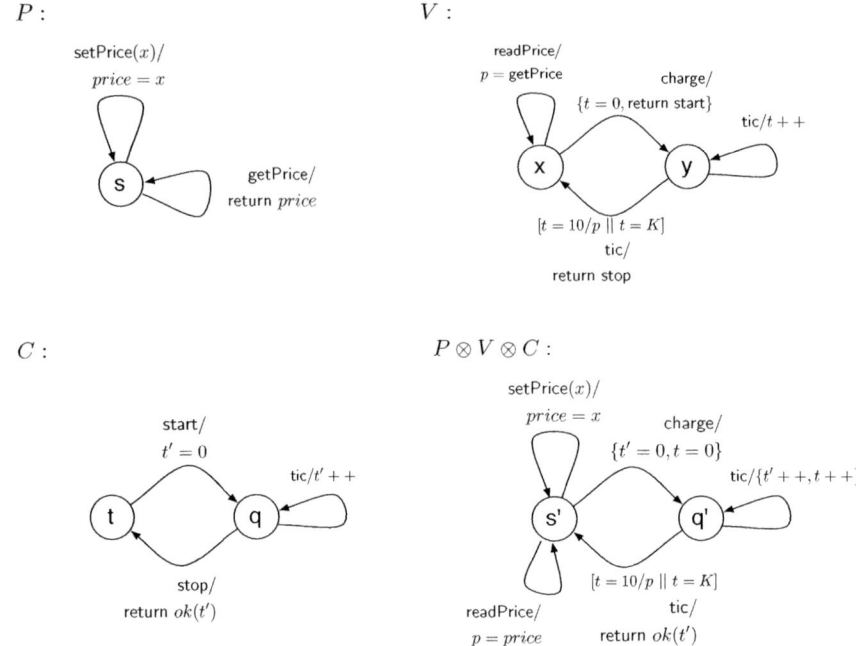

Fig. 3. Single components and composition of the Provider P, the Vehicle V and the Charging station C

properties into a common framework, the Modular Assembly Kit for Security MAKS [19], also deriving new unwinding theorems. This work is also probably the best reference for a discussion on the different properties proposed for abstract non-deterministic and distributed system designs.

In the Language-based world, different static approaches have been suggested for verifying information-flow properties, prominently type-based systems like Volpano-Smith [29] or more recently Barthe et al. [7]. Also works based on abstract interpretation and analysis of Program Dependency Graphs [10,14] give approximations to non-interference for JavaCard-bytecode and Java respectively. Tools for information flow analysis on annotated code using these techniques are for example Jif [1], JOANA [11] and STAN [2]. Works in the language-based domain, in particular program slicing and tainting, are related with our analysis. However the non-interference property analysed at the code level is generally a stronger property tailored for a non reactive system model, where inputs at the initial program state determine all outputs in all subsequent states.

Jürjens [17] defined a stereotype for non-interference on non-deterministic state-charts that is equivalent to the notion used in this paper for the deterministic case, but no verification strategy or compositionality results are discussed. In [5] Alghathbar et al. model flows of information with UML Sequence diagrams and Horn clauses. However their focus is on high-level information flow policies where only actors and the messages their exchange are modelled, and no explicit relation between the information control rules and a semantic property is given.

7 Conclusions

We have presented an efficient verification strategy for state-charts that is sound with respect to classical non-interference. Our technique is fully automatic and can help to narrow the gap between theory and practice for information-flow in secure-software development in industrial context, by applying our results to a non-trivial subset of UML Statecharts, extending previous work in the area. On a technical level, we have shown how to link unwinding theorems defined in input/output state-machines with verification techniques related to the imperative programming language domain.

In order to validate our approach we have modelled interesting aspects of a Smart Metering scenario where subtle information flows related to confidentiality can be captured by non-interference. These examples show that although approximate, our unwinding theorems are fine-grained enough to verify non-trivial state-charts. We have also prototypically implemented the construction and the verification of the newly defined unwinding relation and unwinding conditions. This implementation allowed us to verify the examples of the case study and discuss about the practical efficiency of the procedure.

There are many directions in which this work could be extended. On the one hand, extensions to other information flow properties for non-deterministic state-machines are interesting to study in the context of UML. On the other hand, a more fine-grained approximation using automatic theorem provers or SMT solvers for evaluating expressions could improve the precision of our analysis. Moreover, studying the preservation of non-interference on code generated from secure UML specifications (refinement) constitutes also a necessary step towards industrial acceptance of these verification techniques.

Acknowledgments. The authors would like to thank David von Oheimb and Arnaud Fontaine for useful comments made to an early draft of this paper and Andrei Popescu, Kurt Stenzel and Henning Sudbrock among other researchers from the German Research Foundation RS^3 Priority Programme for interesting discussions on the verification of information flow properties.

References

1. Jif: Java + Information Flow, http://www.cs.cornell.edu/jif/
2. STAN: Information flow analysis for small embedded systems,
   http://stan-project.gforge.inria.fr/
3. The Haskell Programming Language, http://www.haskell.org/
4. The European Parliament and Council. Measuring instruments directive (2004/22/ec). Official Journal of the EU (2004)

5. Alghathbar, K., Farkas, C., Wijesekera, D.: Securing UML information flow using flowUML. Journal of Research and Practice in Information Technology, pp. 229–238. INSTICC Press (2006)

6. Anderson, R.J.: Security engineering - a guide to building dependable distributed systems, 2nd edn. Wiley (2008)

7. Barthe, G., Pichardie, D., Rezk, T.: A Certified Lightweight Non-interference Java Bytecode Verifier. In: De Nicola, R. (ed.) ESOP 2007. LNCS, vol. 4421, pp. 125–140. Springer, Heidelberg (2007)

8. Broy, M.: A logical basis for component-oriented software and systems engineering. Comput. J. 53, 1758–1782 (2010)

9. Das, D., Kreikebaum, F., Divan, D., Lambert, F.: Reducing transmission investment to meet renewable portfolio standards using smart wires. In: 2010 IEEE PES Transmission and Distribution Conference and Exposition: Smart Solutions for a Changing World (2010)

10. Ghindici, D., Grimaud, G., Simplot-Ryl, I.: Embedding verifiable information flow analysis. In: Proc. Annual Conference on Privacy, Security and Trust, Toronto, Canada, pp. 343–352 (November 2006)

11. Giffhorn, D., Hammer, C.: Precise Analysis of Java Programs using JOANA (Tool Demonstration). In: 8th IEEE International Working Conference on Source Code Analysis and Manipulation, pp. 267–268 (September 2008)

12. Goguen, J.A., Meseguer, J.: Security policies and security models. In: IEEE Symposium on Security and Privacy, pp. 11–20 (1982)

13. Goguen, J.A., Meseguer, J.: Unwinding and inference control. In: IEEE Symposium on Security and Privacy (1984)

14. Hammer, C.: Information flow control for Java based on path conditions in dependence graphs. In: IEEE International Symposium on Secure Software Engineering (2006)

15. Harel, D.: Statecharts: A visual formalism for complex systems (1987)

16. International Electrotechnical Commission (IEC). IEC 62351 Parts 1-8, Information Security for Power System Control Operations

17. Jürjens, J.: Secure Systems Development with UML. Springer (2005)

18. Mantel, H.: On the composition of secure systems. In: Proceedings of IEEE Symposium on Security and Privacy, pp. 88–101 (2002)

19. Mantel, H.: A Uniform Framework for the Formal Specification and Verification of Information Flow Security. PhD thesis, Universität des Saarlandes, Saarbrücken, Germany (2003)

20. Mealy, G.H.: A method for synthesizing sequential circuits. Bell System Technical Journal 34(5), 1045–1079 (1955)

21. Milner, R.: A Calculus of Communicating Systems. Springer-Verlag New York, Inc., Secaucus (1982)

22. National Energy Technology Laboratory. A vision for the smart grid. Report (June 2009), http://www.netl.doe.gov/moderngrid/

23. Network of Excellence on Engineering Secure Future Internet Software Services and Systems (Nessos). Deliverable 11.2 (2011)

24. von Oheimb, D.: Information Flow Control Revisited: Noninfluence = Noninterference + Nonleakage. In: Samarati, P., Ryan, P.Y.A., Gollmann, D., Molva, R. (eds.) ESORICS 2004. LNCS, vol. 3193, pp. 225–243. Springer, Heidelberg (2004)

25. Potter, C.W., Archambault, A., Westrick, K.: Building a smarter smart grid through better renewable energy information. In: 2009 IEEE/PES Power Systems Conference and Exposition, PSCE 2009 (2009)

26. Rushby, J.: Noninterference, transitivity and channel-control security policies. Technical report (1992)
27. Schneiderman, R.: Smart grid represents a potentially huge market for the electronics industry. IEEE Signal Processing Magazine 27(5), 8–15 (2010)
28. Tenzer, J., Stevens, P.: On modelling recursive calls and callbacks with two variants of unified modelling language state diagrams. Form. Asp. Comput. 18, 397–420 (2006)
29. Volpano, D., Irvine, C., Smith, G.: A sound type system for secure flow analysis. J. Comput. Secur. 4, 167–187 (1996)

Representing Uniqueness Constraints
in Object-Relational Mapping
The Natural Entity Framework

Mark J. Olah, David Mohr, and Darko Stefanovic

Department of Computer Science, University of New Mexico
1 University of New Mexico, Albuquerque, NM, USA 87131
{mjo,dmohr,darko}@cs.unm.edu

Abstract. Object-oriented languages model data as transient objects, while relational databases store data persistently using a relational data model. The process of making objects persistent by storing their state as relational tuples is called *object-relational mapping* (ORM). This process is nuanced and complex as there are many fundamental differences between the relational model and the object model. In this work we address the difficulties in representing entity identity and uniqueness consistently, efficiently, and succinctly in ORM. We introduce the *natural entity* framework, which: (1) provides a strong concept of value-based persistent object identity; (2) allows the programmer to simultaneously specify natural and surrogate key constraints consistently in the object and relational representations; (3) provides object constructors and initializers that disambiguate the semantics of persistent object creation and retrieval; and (4) automates the mapping of inheritance hierarchies that respect natural key constraints and allows for efficient polymorphic queries and associations.

1 Introduction

In an object-oriented (OO) language, data are represented as objects, but objects are transient—they do not persist beyond a particular process or between subsequent executions of a program. To make the data persistent and accessible for concurrent processes in a structured form, an *object-relational mapping (ORM)* can be used to store objects as tuples in a relational database.[1] An ORM is a method for translating between a data model expressed as a class hierarchy and a data model expressed as a relational schema. ORM software packages allow a program to create, read, update, delete, and query objects stored persistently in a relational database using object and class methods of an OO programming language.

Designing an ORM presents many challenges because the object data model and the relational data model differ profoundly in how they represent, store, and access data. We focus in this work on just one facet of the mapping between the models: the concept of *identity and uniqueness*. Both data models are used to abstractly represent sets of

---

[1] There are other possibilities, beyond the scope of this paper, such as using a persistent object store and a programming language that supports persistence natively. Without going into the merits of different approaches, we concentrate on ORM because of its widespread use.

C.A. Furia and S. Nanz (Eds.): TOOLS Europe 2012, LNCS 7304, pp. 236–251, 2012.
© Springer-Verlag Berlin Heidelberg 2012

physical or conceptual entities. An entity has multiple properties; the values of these properties may affect entity identity and entity uniqueness. However, the concepts of identity and uniqueness have different semantics in the object model and in the relational model [8].

In relational models uniqueness is a value-based notion defined by relational keys. A *key* is a minimal set of attributes (columns) of a relation that uniquely identifies a particular tuple (row). It can be a *surrogate key*, an artificial value introduced solely to distinguish tuples; or it can be a *natural key*, consisting of attributes that correspond to meaningful, real-world, properties of the entities. The attributes in a natural key represent those properties of an entity that define its identity and uniqueness in the context of the application and are well known to the users of the entity. A natural key is a concise description that can be used to query for the existence of a specific individual entity. Every relation must specify a *primary key*, which is used as the default identifier for a tuple. For practical reasons this is often a surrogate key. However, when a natural key exists, it often makes sense to declare its existence as well by enforcing a uniqueness constraint on the natural key attributes. This prevents the database from maintaining two copies of data that represent the same entity. Additionally, declaring a natural key results in the database maintaining an index on the natural key attributes, which allows queries involving the natural key to be optimized [6].

In contrast, in object models value and identity are independent. While an OO execution environment enforces the uniqueness of object identities, this imposes no constraints on the values of objects. Hence, when real-world entities are represented by objects, there can be many distinct objects having the same values for a set of natural attributes and thus representing the same entity. There are no mechanisms to prevent this error-prone duplication of entity representations, and typically no universal mechanism to query for the existence of an object based on its value.

This fundamental difference in how uniqueness and identity are defined in relational databases and in OO programming languages leads to problems when data representing real-world entities are made persistent with a relational database, but are operated on as in-memory objects. If there are multiple in-memory objects all denoting the same entity, which object represents the true current state of that entity, and which one corresponds to the database's current state, i.e., the tuple representing the entity? This question becomes even more confusing when there are multiple execution contexts operating on entities concurrently.

Our real-world motivation for developing the natural entity framework comes from the experience of writing scientific computing simulations, which are distributed, concurrent applications with persistent state. Some of our examples will be drawn from this field; similar modeling and representation problems are encountered in the business world and in web-based applications.

To properly model the concept of entity uniqueness and identity at both the object and the relational level, we propose a new framework of constraints and semantics for object construction and interactions that can be enforced in modern ORM systems and strongly object-oriented languages. Our *natural entity* framework provides a base class `NaturalEntity` with the functionality described in this paper. Natural entities are persistent objects in an OO execution environment that directly enforce value-based uniqueness constraints on natural attribute values. Other ORMs allow natural keys and uniqueness constraints to be declared on the relational model, but they do not enforce these constraints on the object model, or in the inheritance hierarchy. Making these constraints explicit allows persistent objects to more directly represent the semantics of relational tuples used to store their state. This simplifies the programmer's conceptual model and reduces potential problems with concurrency, entity identity, and uniqueness.

In contrast to creating regular objects, there is overhead when checking for value-based uniqueness, but this overhead is not higher than manual enforcement of uniqueness. The proposed natural entities are otherwise normal objects that exist alongside, and interact with, other objects, and they can be queried and used polymorphically. Hence, the natural entity framework does not reduce the expressiveness of the OO language, and a programmer is free to represent entities using persistent objects that do not enforce uniqueness constraints, or using regular non-persistent objects. However, only through the use of the natural entity framework can the programmer maintain the value-based uniqueness constraints for in-memory objects.

The primary contribution of the natural entity framework is that it allows the ORM to manage and enforce value-based object identity and uniqueness on in-memory objects. These value-based constraints match the constraints imposed by natural keys on the relations that store the persistent state of the natural entities. Thus the object model for natural entities is modified to more closely match the relational model.

This provides several advantages: (1) natural entities have a strong concept of value-based identity and uniqueness, accessible through object attributes and methods that prevent multiple in-memory objects from representing the same conceptual entity (Sec. 3); (2) the ORM can use an identity map to provide fast value-based queries for in-memory objects and a uniqueness constraint to provide fast queries for archived objects (Sec. 4); (3) natural entities have constructor methods that automatically manage the uniqueness constraints for in-memory objects and disambiguate object construction from object retrieval (Sec. 5); and, (4) natural entities inheritance hierarchies can be mapped automatically to a relational schema that uses the appropriate constraints and relations to maintain natural key uniqueness constraints and to allow polymorphic queries (Sec. 6).

Given these features, the natural entity framework provides functionality that is lacking in modern ORM systems and presents an abstraction that is easy to understand and implement, allowing the programmer to spend more time on solving the actual problems at hand. We found this to be the case in our work on scientific simulations, and we offer this description in the belief that the framework will be broadly applicable.

2   Background

To be specific about how the concept of uniqueness constraints is implemented, here we summarize the terminology used for relational models and OO programming languages.

2.1   Relational Model

A *relation* is a tuple of attributes denoted $R = R(A_1, \ldots, A_n)$. The attributes come from some domain $\mathbf{A}$, and each attribute A_i has a type τ_i, (written $A_i : \tau_i$), where $\tau_i \in \mathbf{T}$ for some set **T** of basic types. For brevity we omit type signatures where they are not essential to the discussion. A *relation instance* is a set of tuples from the domain $(A_1 \times \ldots \times A_n)$ that represents the current factual state of the relation. When it is not otherwise confusing, the term *relation* is used to describe both the relation's schema (attributes, types, and constraints) and its time-varying instances (the tuples and their values). In the concrete context of a relational database, a relation specifies the names and types of the columns of a table, and an instance specifies a set of table rows and their values.

A non-empty set $k \subset \{A_1, \ldots A_n\}$ is a key of relation $R(A_1, \ldots A_n)$ if for any instance of the relation, the value of the attributes in k uniquely determines a tuple and no proper subset of k is also a key. Thus, a key is a minimal set of attributes that can be used to define the identity of a tuple. A relation may have many keys. A key is *simple* if it consists of a single attribute, otherwise it is *compound*. Each table must have a *primary key*, which is used as the canonical set of attributes for identifying a row for the purpose of database operations and references between tuples of relations. Primary key attributes are underlined in the notation for a relation to highlight their role (e.g., $R(\underline{A_1}, \underline{A_2}, A_3)$ has a primary key $\{A_1, A_2\}$.) Associations between relations are expressed with a *foreign key constraint* that restricts a set of attributes to values that come from the relational instance state of a separate set of attributes that form a key [3].

A *relational schema* is a set $\mathbb{R} = \{R_1, \ldots, R_m\}$ of relations along with constraints. A relational database provides a set of types and mechanisms to define relational schemas over those types. It maintains instances for each relation that obey all the restrictions and allows queries to create, read, update, and delete tuples.

2.2 Object Model

An *object* lives in memory and has identity, type, state, and behavior. An object's state is given by the values of a collection of named attributes that come from a set of types $\mathbf{T'}$.[2] In strongly object-oriented languages, objects have a concept of identity independent of their attribute values or addressability [9]. This allows references to objects to be tested if they refer to the same object, and hence forms a definition for object uniqueness.

An object's type is some class C. A class creates objects: it defines names and types for each attribute, and the set of *methods* that operate on the state of an object. These methods define the behavior of the object. An object that belongs to a class is said to be an *instance* of that class.

Inheritance. A set of classes $\mathbb{C} = \{C_1, \ldots, C_k\}$ is called a *class schema*. Classes have a concept of inheritance. If C_i inherits from C_j, we write $C_i <: C_j$, and the class C_i inherits all of the attributes and methods of C_j. The inheritance relation is reflexive, transitive, and antisymmetric, and so defines a partial ordering on the class schema, called the *inheritance hierarchy*. This relation represents specialization as objects of class C_i now can represent all the state and behavior of C_j, but can also add or modify attributes and methods. Thus, if $C_i <: C_j$ and o is an instance of C_i, then o is also an instance of C_j. This property is called *polymorphism* and allows objects to act as an instance of any class more general than their own.

---

[2] The set of OO types $\mathbf{T'}$ may, but does not necessarily, intersect with the set of types $\mathbf{T}$ used in the relational schema. They will almost certainly not be identical.

The maximal elements in the hierarchy are called the *base classes*. In many languages multiple inheritance is possible, so a class can inherit directly from more than one class. Multiple inheritance is not a focus of this paper, though the implications are briefly considered. In a single inheritance class schema, the inheritance hierarchy is not a general lattice, but a forest of *inheritance trees*, each rooted at a single base class. For single inheritance hierarchies we can uniquely define the super relation $\text{Super}(C_i) = C_j$ if $C_i <: C_j$ and $C_i <: C_k <: C_j$ implies $C_k = C_i$ or $C_k = C_j$. In other words, the super relation determines the smallest class larger than a given class, called the immediate superclass. Conversely, C_i is said to be a subclass of C_j.

A class can be *abstract* or *concrete*. There cannot be objects belonging to an abstract class, only to concrete classes. Abstract classes are only used to be inherited from by other classes.

2.3   Object-Relational Mapping

The object and relational models are general enough to apply to most modern OO languages and relational databases, hence they form a good basis for describing how objects can be mapped to relations. An ORM is a mapping from a class schema $\mathbb{C}$ to a relational schema $\mathbb{R}$ that provides a correspondence between objects in $\mathbb{C}$ and tuples (or sets of tuples) from relations in $\mathbb{R}$.

In this mapping attributes of an object with type $t_1 \in \mathbf{T}'$ are mapped to one or more tuple element with type(s) $\tau_i \in \mathbf{T}$. Since the types available in a programming language (subtly) differ from those available in databases, this mapping of types is a necessity, and may not be 1-to-1. However, for most uses the type differences have no practical effect, and we leave exploring the implications for value-based identity as future work.

3   Object Identity and Uniqueness

The central issue addressed by the natural entity framework is consistently representing real-world entities that possess a concept of uniqueness described succinctly by the values of one or more well known (natural) attributes, i.e., a natural key.

Identity in OO Languages. Like objects in the natural world, objects in a programming language have concepts of identity and uniqueness. Many OO programming languages (Python, Smalltalk, Java, Ruby, etc.) have a strong concept of object uniqueness in that each object has an associated immutable internal id(entifier), distinct from the references used to access it [9]. Such an id is called a *surrogate object id* since it has no relation to the value or meaning of the object. It merely serves to define the identity of the object and allows comparing the identity to those of other objects, as there is a bijection from object ids to objects [14].

Identity in Relational Databases. Identity in relational databases is a value-based property determined by a designated primary key. The primary keys should be unique, immutable, and non-null. The database maintains a uniqueness constraint on the primary key, preventing duplicate tuples, and uses an index to quickly select tuples by their primary key or detect violations of the uniqueness constraint. The primary key is also used to define foreign key relationships.

Because of all these important requirements placed on the primary key, it often makes sense to use a surrogate key as the primary key, even when there is a well-known natural key. There are many good reasons to prefer surrogate keys as primary keys, most of which arise from the fact that using surrogate keys allows the relational schema to decouple identity and value [4]. This allows more flexibility when the relational model needs to be updated or refactored [1]. Other benefits arise due to the fact that surrogate keys are simple (consist of a singleton attribute) and are typically small integral types. Natural keys in contrast are often compound and may include strings and other types that require more space as foreign keys. Since the primary key is always used to represent entity relationships through foreign key constraints, having a small, simple primary key reduces space usage and simplifies join operations. Simple integral keys are also often faster for use in selects against the primary key. For these reasons, ORMs often use surrogate primary keys by default [5].

However, natural keys are still useful and have some desirable characteristics. Declaring a natural key communicates to the database that the relational model has a logical uniqueness constraint on the natural key attributes and prevents a single conceptual entity from being represented by more than one tuple. Additionally, the database can then maintain a uniqueness constraint and index on the natural key. The presence of an index allows clients to quickly retrieve objects by their natural key-values, or determine that no such object exists. This can lead to distinct performance advantages for natural keys in some situations [11].

3.1 Identity in the Natural Entity Framework

The natural entity framework, like other ORM tools, must reconcile the semantics of object identity in OO languages and tuple identity in relational databases. Our goal is to enforce the uniqueness of entity representation across both data models as determined by natural key attributes, but we simultaneously want to support polymorphic queries, efficient entity relationships, and flexibility for refactoring databases.

To achieve these objectives, the natural entity framework enforces the simultaneous use of surrogate primary keys and auxiliary natural keys. This dual-key representation achieves advantages of both surrogate and natural keys. In particular, our surrogate keys are unique within each inheritance hierarchy rooted at the `NaturalEntity` class. This uniformity of primary keys allows us to use a single top level relation to define a primary key for every object belonging to the class hierarchy. This makes polymorphic queries and associations much more efficient and uniform than they could be with natural keys. Indeed, without a uniform key for the entire inheritance tree, representing polymorphic associations would become problematic as there would be no single foreign key constraint that could be used to represent an association. Hence, surrogate primary keys are necessary for polymorphism and flexibility, but they do not fulfill the need for maintaining value-based uniqueness. This is achieved by the auxiliary natural keys. These keys require a separate index, which comes at the cost of storage space and maintenance time. However, this index is exactly what ensures the logical value-based uniqueness of natural entities, and it is heavily used by constructors (Sec. 5) and other common queries against the natural key, thus it is both necessary and useful.

4   Management of Persistent States and Concurrency

Building on the concepts of object and relational identity, an ORM must have a way to track and manage the identity of in-memory objects. Unlike transient objects, which have a limited scope and lifetime, persistent objects must maintain their identity permanently and consistently across concurrent processes. To simplify the tracking of persistent objects and their modifications, modern ORM packages provide the concept of a *session manager*. The natural entity framework relies on a session manager to manage the persistent state of in-memory persistent objects and enforce the uniqueness constraints for natural entities.

Our principal contribution is to provide additional constructor methods which make explicit the assumptions about the state of a persistent object when it is created and prevent the user from violating the value-based uniqueness constraints.

4.1   Transactions

The session manager has transactional semantics and manages a set of persistent objects by implementing the *unit of work* concept [5]. It tracks object creation, modification, and deletion. The session manager delegates large parts of this work to the database by using transactions. This ensures a consistent database state, even when objects are modified concurrently by other processes. It follows that the concurrency guarantees are largely provided by the transaction. The session manager supplies methods to control the global transactional state for an execution context. The begin() method starts a transaction and is implicitly called as needed if no transaction is currently in progress. The flush() method sends pending modifications to the database, but does not end the transaction. The commit() method commits a transaction, and this implies a flush operation if there are still pending changes. Finally, the rollback() method undoes all database changes made during the transaction.

4.2   Object States

From the perspective of an OO execution environment, reasoning about persistent objects is much more complicated than standard transient objects because the data representing the object can be stored in memory, in one or more relations in the RDBMs, and/or in the memory of other concurrent processes. The session manager acts as the single point of persistence management for an OO execution environment. It determines how a persistent object relates to its external relational state in the database. Any object of a class that derives from a persistent base class, such as NaturalEntity, will be understood by the session manager to be in one of the following six states:

- *Transient* – The object is not managed as persistent by the session, while a corresponding tuple with the same natural key in the database may or may not exist; there is no operational connection with any persistent object.

- *Pending* – The object does not yet have a permanent record but has been successfully added to the session and will be added to the database when the session state is flushed to the database. Until the object is successfully flushed it has not yet been assigned a primary key.
- *Persistent Clean* – The object has a primary key and a corresponding representation in the database. No persistently managed attributes have changed values, so no updates need to be sent to the database.
- *Persistent Dirty* – The same as a persistent clean object, except the value of one or more of the persistently maintained attributes has been changed, so that an SQL update operation is needed to save the state of the object. Copies of this object in other sessions do not know about the changes and may have made conflicting changes of their own.
- *Expired* – The object's state is no longer valid because it was created in a session that has been committed or rolled back, so its state needs to be reloaded from the database. This reloading is done transparently by the session manager when necessary.
- *Archived* – The object is not part of the store but is persistently stored in the database. Strictly speaking, this is not a state of an object, since no corresponding object exists in the session, but conceptually the tuple in database represents an object that is not currently loaded.

It is important to remember that the identity of a persistent object is provided by the natural key, and maintained through transactions and the constraint imposed by the database key. In case of conflicting concurrent transactions, e.g., simultaneous inserts or deletes, one of the concurrent processes will be prevented from committing its changes by an exception. In Fig. 1 we show the effect of various operations on the persistent state of an object, but omit the expired state and other effects that occur at transaction boundaries. The effect of commits is to expire all pending and persistent objects and the session manager updates any identity maps of persistent objects accordingly (Sec. 5.1).

5 Object Creation

Maintaining a value-based uniqueness constraint for persistent objects causes difficulties with object creation. Normally, the programming environment's concept of object identity is all that determines object uniqueness. When an object constructor is called, a new object with a unique object id is always created, and an initializer method is called. However, natural entity classes with value-based uniqueness constraints necessitate different semantics. First, the constructor must be given the values for each of the natural key attributes since they must not be null. Given the natural key value, the constructor is presented with several possibilities: (1) an object with those values already exists in memory so we are not allowed to create a new object with a new object id and the same natural key values; (2) an object with those values exists in an archived state, so it must be loaded from the database; or, (3) there is no persistent or in-memory object with the given natural key, so a new object should be created and added to the database.

Such a constructor requires a natural-keyed dictionary of in-memory persistent objects, i.e., an identity map (Sec. 5.1), and a mechanism to query for the existence of

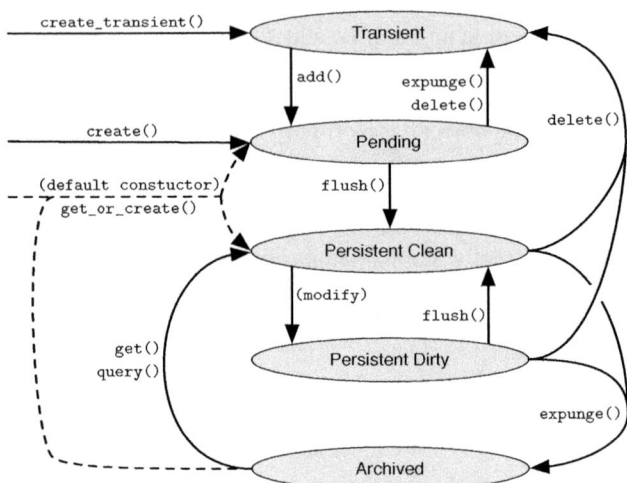

Fig. 1. Persistent object states and effect of constructors and session commands within a single transaction context. The effects of transaction boundaries and the expired state are omitted for clarity.

archived objects. Both of these can be provided efficiently by the session manger, but they nevertheless impose a significant cost, especially when the round trip time for remote database queries is involved. Unfortunately, such queries are necessary if we wish to maintain the consistency constraints; allowing the constructor to make new objects without regard to the natural key values would result in duplicate objects in memory. Furthermore, the cost of frequent queries can be reduced by allowing the caching of natural keys or prefetching of objects (particularly when the database transaction isolation prevents non-repeatable reads). When queries are necessary they can be handled efficiently because of the unique index maintained on the natural key attributes.

Together all of these considerations impose a significant change to the semantics of object creation, and can lead to conceptual problems for programmers. The natural entity framework addresses this conceptual ambiguity by providing additional constructor methods with different semantics. These constructors allow programmers to explicitly state their intentions or assumptions when creating an object.

- get() - A constructor that takes the natural key and returns the object uniquely identified by that key, either by returning a reference to an in-memory object representing that entity, or by loading an archived object from the database and returning it in the persistent clean state. If no such object exists, an exception is raised.
- create() - A constructor that takes the natural key and returns a newly created object in the pending state, but only if no persistent object with the same natural key exists in memory or in the archived state. An exception is raised if the object already exists.

- `get_or_create()` - A constructor with the combined semantics of the `get()` and `create()`. It takes the natural key and either returns an existing persistent object, or returns a newly created object in the pending state. This is the default constructor.
- `create_transient()` - A constructor with normal transient object semantics that always returns a new object in the transient state. It can take arbitrary arguments and ignores the uniqueness constraints.

The `get_or_create()` constructor does whatever it takes to get a reference to the unique object that has the provided natural key. It will find that object if it is in memory and return a reference, or it will look in the database for an archived version and return it, and if no such persistent object exists, it will construct a new object and make it persistent by moving it to the pending state. In our application domain we found that the `get_or_create()` has the appropriate semantics in the vast majority of situations, and therefore we have made it the default constructor, which results in particularly succinct code (e.g., in Python `var=ClassName(...)`).

The `create()` and `get()` constructors are used in cases where the existence or non-existence of a particular `NaturalEntity` object represent a logical error, and the programmer would like an exception to be raised so that the error is not silently ignored.

Finally the `create_transient()` constructor has several uses when the normal semantics of the natural entity construction are too rigid. Unlike the other constructors, `create_transient()` does not need to be given the natural key, and does not use any database connections or in-memory identity maps. This is useful for testing object behavior without using a database. Transient objects are also useful when the user does not wish to immediately pay the cost of the database query to check for archived objects. Furthermore, they support situations where not all of the natural key attributes are immediately available, but it makes sense to partially construct a `NaturalEntity` object, and then finish filling in the natural key attributes later. This is often the case in GUI or web-based applications where objects are built up sequentially by user actions. A transient object can be made persistent by using the `add()` method, which will check that all natural key attributes are specified and will raise an exception if the object already exists.

5.1 Identity Map

When the (non-transient) constructors are called, they are provided with the complete natural key for the desired object. If an object with that natural key already exists in memory in the pending, expired, persistent clean, or persistent dirty states, it would be incorrect to construct and return a new object. Instead we must return a reference to the in-memory object. The ORM's session manager is able to track the persistent state of objects, but it also needs a way to look up objects by their natural key. This is a common requirement for ORMs, which Fowler calls the *identity map* pattern [5]. The purpose of an identity map is simply to map database keys to in-memory objects. When working with persistent objects, sometimes different parts of the code need access to the same data object without understanding whether that object is already in memory. The solution is to keep a global registry (or identity map) of in-memory objects keyed by their primary key. Normally, this identity map is stored in the session manager object, and it is used for internal ORM lookups of foreign key mappings. However, when primary keys are surrogates, it is awkward for a user to make use of this identity map, because the surrogates by definition are meaningless and often obscured from the user. It is much more common for a user to query using natural key attributes, and the constructors must be able to do this efficiently for in-memory objects. Hence, the natural entity system implements an auxiliary identity map, keyed on the natural key attributes. The identity map only stores in-memory persistent objects, i.e., transient objects are excluded. If an object is removed from the persistent store with the `delete()` method, it becomes transient. Thus, a constructor will not return a reference to a deleted object, even if that object is still in memory.

5.2 Initialization

Since the `NaturalEntity` constructors have multiple possible mechanisms for retrieving or creating objects, the concept of initialization also needs to be refined. For natural entities there are three distinct ways a new in-memory object could be created and require initialization: (1) it could be created as a transient object; (2) it could be retrieved from an archived state in the database; or, (3) it could be created as a new persistent object in the pending state. (In the case where the constructor already found the object in memory through the identity map, no initialization is needed.) The `NaturalEntity` class provides three different initializers that will be called by the constructor in each of the three cases.

- `initialize()` – This method is called when a new persistent object is created. The object will be in the pending state and the object's (immutable) natural key attributes will have been set to the values provided to the constructor.
- `reinitialize()` – This method is called when an archived object is brought into memory by a constructor. The object will be in the persistent clean state and all persisted attributes (including the natural key attributes) will have been set by the ORM system.
- `initialize_transient()` – This method is called if and only if the object is constructed with the `create_transient()` method. The object will be in the transient state, and any supplied natural key attributes will have been set, but those omitted by the user (which is permitted for transient objects) will have no default value.

5.3 Object Creation Semantics in Other ORMs

The multiple constructors of the natural entity framework represent a departure from the normal mechanism of persistent object creation presented by modern ORMs. In many modern ORM systems, all objects are initially created as transients, and only after a call to an `add()` method are they moved to a pending (or equivalent) state [13,10]. The difficulty with this mechanism is that it does not allow the ORM to directly manage value-based object uniqueness. If an object with identical natural key already exists in the database, then the next time the session state is flushed, an exception will be raised when the database prevents the SQL INSERT command from violating the uniqueness constraint on the natural key. This failure mode can be eliminated by always first querying for a particular natural key before attempting to create and add an object with that key. This common ORM idiom is often required in code manipulating objects with natural keys. The constructors available for `NaturalEntity` classes make the assumptions of the programmer explicit, succinct, and less error-prone. Instead of remembering to first check if an object already exists before creating it, a programmer can just create a `NaturalEntity` object by passing the natural key to the constructor, and the system will automatically do the right thing; i.e. return the unique object with given natural key. Thus any the overhead of the natural entity constructors is comparable to what would be required by any other implementation that wishes to protect against failures due to duplicate objects.

6   Mapping Natural Entity Inheritance Hierarchies

All natural entity classes must inherit from the `NaturalEntity` class, thus we must map all the classes in each inheritance subtree rooted at `NaturalEntity` into a relational schema. The natural entity system supports flexible mapping of hierarchies to relations, which allows polymorphic queries and associations, as well as different natural keys for separate subtrees of the inheritance hierarchy. The user only needs to supply minimal information about the desired inheritance mapping strategy and the ORM can automatically construct the appropriate tables and constraints. As an example we consider a distributed computer simulation system with two inheritance hierarchies, an abstract `Experiment` class with two concrete subclasses and an abstract `Measurement` class also with two concrete classes (Fig. 2). An `Experiment` has a one-to-many relationship with measurements, so each `Measurement` has a foreign key to the `Experiment` hierarchy's primary key—a polymorphic association. We examine natural keys in the relation further in Sec. 6.2.

6.1   Inheritance Mapping Strategies

The relational data model has no built-in concept of inheritance, but support for inheritance and polymorphism can be enforced by appropriately structuring the relational schema and queries. There are three standard methods for mapping inheritance hierarchies to a relational schema [5]: (1) the *single table* strategy maps all classes in an inheritance hierarchy to a single table; (2) the *class table* strategy maps each class to its own table; and (3) the *concrete table* strategy maps only concrete classes to tables.

The single and class table strategies are particularly useful for polymorphic queries and associations as for every class in the hierarchy they store the class name (i.e., the type) and a surrogate object id in a single top level table. Concrete table inheritance lacks these properties and is not considered further.

Single and class table strategies are distinguished by the technique they use to represent the differing attributes for classes in the hierarchy. Single table inheritance has a single relation which includes all attributes of all classes in the hierarchy. It allows polymorphism by permitting attributes to be null for objects that do not include them. In contrast, class table inheritance only includes non-inherited attributes in each class table. It permits polymorphic queries by using joins on the primary surrogate key to retrieve attribute values from all the relations that store an object's state. These differences lead to quantifiable performance and space trade-offs [7]. Modern ORMs allow

(a)

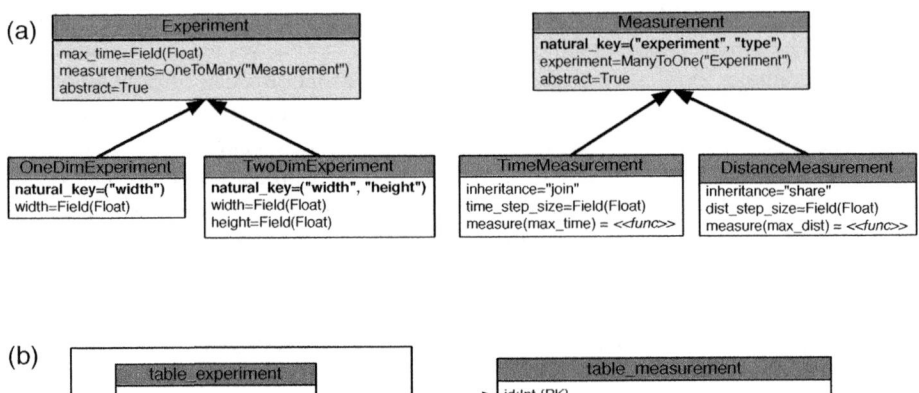

(b)

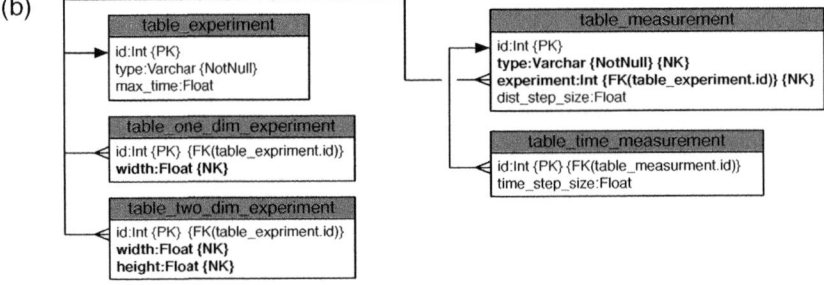

Fig. 2. (a) A simple example of a class schema with two inheritance hierarchies, abstract classes, multiple natural key bases, polymorphic associations, and both shared and joined inheritance mappings. The text in each class entry is close to the actual amount of code needed to specify this hierarchy. We use syntax that is similar to our Python-based reference implementation of the natural entity framework. (b) The relational schema generated by the natural entity framework from the class schema in (a). The foreign key constraints are shown.

the user to specify a mixture of these strategies within a single inheritance hierarchy [2]. When mixing strategies, the single table approach is called *shared* or horizontal mapping, while the class-table approach is called *joined* or vertical mapping [12]. Shared table inheritance works best when the cost of additional join operations needed to load rows is a limiting factor, or when a portion of the class hierarchy shares almost all of the same persistent attributes. Joined table inheritance works best when database space is constrained, or in portions of the hierarchy where few persistent attributes are shared between classes.

In the natural entity framework each class in a hierarchy only needs to specify if it will use the shared or joined inheritance strategy and the ORM can automatically derive the relational schema.

6.2   Natural Keys and Inheritance

Every concrete class that derives from `NaturalEntity` must define or inherit a natural key, so that the constructor can enforce the value-based uniqueness constraint. Abstract classes need not define a natural key, and any class that has no natural key must be declared as abstract.

Because of the option to use joined inheritance, an individual object can have its attributes stored in several relations, but there is always a relation that stores the attributes declared specifically in a class. This is the *primary relation* of the class.

Consider a class C that defines a natural key and that has no superclass which also defines a natural key (i.e., it has only abstract superclasses). The natural key results in a uniqueness constraint which is implemented by the database. A constraint can typically only be defined on attributes in a single table and not on joined tables. It follows that exactly one of the relations representing C must enforce this constraint. None of C's superclasses could have a natural key constraint, as enforcing a uniqueness constraint on $Super(C)$'s primary relation would prevent other subclasses of $Super(C)$ from defining different natural keys. Hence, the natural key constraint for C must be enforced in C's primary relation. This implies that all C's natural key attributes must be defined in C and cannot be inherited, or they would not be present in C's primary relation. Finally, note that any subclass of C will inherit C's natural key attributes, and because these attributes have a uniqueness constraint defined on the relation that stores them, the subclass must also inherit the natural key from C.

Therefore in any inheritance chain, i.e., starting at a concrete class and following the super relation to a base class, there is exactly one class that declares a natural key. Such a class is called a *natural key base*, as all classes that inherit from the natural key base share the same natural key constraint and store their natural key attributes in the primary relation of the natural key base. Furthermore, a natural key base, must use the joined inheritance mapping strategy, because if C is a natural key base, $Super(C)$ does not have a natural key, and so the natural key attributes and uniqueness constraint must be defined in a separate relation from $Super(C)$'s primary relation.

Hence, when mapping a class hierarchy to a relational schema, the mapping will require: (1) a single table for the root class to store the primary key and object type; (2) a table for each natural key base (unless the class is also the root); and (3) a table for each class that uses joined inheritance (unless the class is a natural key root or the base class).

Full-fledged multiple inheritance does not fit into the semantic model of object identity in this paper. However, the concept of mixins (additional abstract base classes) is easily supported, because a mixin does not define entity identity or uniqueness.

6.3   Type as a Natural Key Attribute

A natural key base will pass on its natural key to all of its subclasses, and thus only one object of *any* derived class may have a given natural key value. Sometimes this is too restrictive a condition on the classes. Because the natural key distinguishes objects based on their value, but not their type, it restricts cases where objects have identical values but different behavior because their respective classes have different methods.

For example, consider the class structure of the distributed simulation system in Fig. 2. The Measurement class defines a simple natural key as a foreign key relationship to the Experiment it measures. An experiment should be able to include both a TimeMeasurement and DistanceMeasurement instance. However, because these objects have the same natural key this becomes impossible. The two measurement subclasses have the same attributes, but the meaning of the attributes differs due to different method implementations. Thus, it can make sense to have more than one measurement object with the same natural key, provided they belong to different classes. This can be accomplished by adding the implicit type attribute to the natural key base's primary relation and thus adding the type to the uniqueness constraint. This allows multiple Measurements to belong to a single Experiment, provided they are from different classes.

In the natural entity framework the type can optionally be declared to be part of the natural key of a class to allow this distinction when it is required. The type attribute is automatically managed by the ORM, since it is always present as an attribute of any object in the OO programming language.

7   Conclusion

The natural entity framework provides an OO interface for programming with objects that have a strongly enforced concept of value-based uniqueness. These semantics require restrictions on object creation, initialization, inheritance, and relational structure.

The constructor methods of natural entities provide a consistent interface that distinguishes the different mechanisms by which a persistent class may be created and initialized. These constructors prevent the ORM from representing the same conceptual entity with different in-memory objects by ensuring that the value-based natural key constraints are maintained for all natural entity objects in the execution environment.

Enforcing value-based object identity changes the semantics of object models in the context of OO languages. However, these constraints only apply to objects from classes that inherit from NaturalEntity. Thus natural entities can coexist with objects of other less-strict persistent classes, as well as normal transient objects. Hence the natural entity framework makes it easier for a programmer to reason about object uniqueness for those entities which require it, but does not otherwise constrain the expressiveness of programs or programming languages. This level of flexibility makes a performance evaluation or validation of the framework complicated, as the natural entity framework will only be used in applications that benefit from value-based uniqueness constraints, and hence the specific application context is essential to the performance characteristics. In future work, we will quantify the performance of the Natural Entity framework under different application workloads and degrees of concurrency. Our own experience tells us that many applications have classes of persistent objects that logically require value-based uniqueness, and easily enforcing these constraints has been an invaluable tool in writing correct scientific software.

The natural entity framework can be implemented in any OO language that supports a strong concept of object identity. It relies on the facilities and abstractions provided by modern ORMs. Object and class introspection, and the ability to instrument object construction and destruction are helpful features in making the implementation easy to use. Our reference implementation in Python is built on top of the SQLAlchemy ORM, and the Elixir extension.

Acknowledgments. We thank the conference reviewers for their incisive and detailed comments. This material is based upon work supported by the National Science Foundation under grants 0829896 and 1028238.

References

1. Ambler, S.W.: Agile Database Techniques. Wiley, Indianapolis (2003)
2. Cabibbo, L., Carosi, A.: Managing Inheritance Hierarchies in Object/Relational Mapping Tools. In: Pastor, Ó., Falcão e Cunha, J. (eds.) CAiSE 2005. LNCS, vol. 3520, pp. 135–150. Springer, Heidelberg (2005)
3. Codd, E.F.: A relational model of data for large shared data banks. Communications of the ACM 13(6), 377–387 (1970)
4. Codd, E.F.: Extending the database relational model to capture more meaning. ACM Trans. Database Syst. 4(4), 397–434 (1979)
5. Fowler, M.: Patterns of Enterprise Application Architecture. Addison-Wesley, Boston (2003)
6. Helman, P.: The Science of Database Management. Richard D. Irwin Inc., Burr Ride, IL (1994)
7. Holder, S., Buchan, J., MacDonell, S.G.: Towards a Metrics Suite for Object-Relational Mappings. In: Kutsche, R.-D., Milanovic, N. (eds.) MBSDI 2008. CCIS, vol. 8, pp. 43–54. Springer, Heidelberg (2008)
8. Ireland, C., Bowers, D., Newton, M., Waugh, K.: A classification of object-relational impedance mismatch. In: Proceedings of the 2009 First International Conference on Advances in Databases, Knowledge, and Data Applications, pp. 36–43. IEEE Computer Society (2009)
9. Khoshafian, S., Copeland, G.P.: Object identity. In: OOPSLA 1986, pp. 406–416 (1986)
10. Kowark, T., Hirschfeld, R., Haupt, M.: Object-relational mapping with SqueakSave. In: Proceedings of the International Workshop on Smalltalk Technologies, IWST 2009, pp. 87–100. ACM (2009)
11. Link, S., Lukovic, I., Mogin, P.: Performance evaluation of natural and surrogate key database architectures. Tech. rep., Victoria University of Wellington, Wellington, NZ (2010)
12. Mork, P., Bernstein, P.A., Melnik, S.: Teaching a Schema Translator to Produce O/R Views. In: Parent, C., Schewe, K.-D., Storey, V.C., Thalheim, B. (eds.) ER 2007. LNCS, vol. 4801, pp. 102–119. Springer, Heidelberg (2007)
13. O'Neil, E.J.: Object/relational mapping 2008: Hibernate and the entity data model (EDM). In: Proceedings of the 2008 ACM SIGMOD International Conference on Management of Data, pp. 1351–1356. ACM (2008)
14. Wieringa, R., de Jonge, W.: Object identifiers, keys, and surrogates– object identifiers revisited. Theory and Practice of Object Systems 1(2), 101–114 (1995)

Detection of Seed Methods
for Quantification of Feature Confinement

Andrzej Olszak[1], Eric Bouwers[2,3],
Bo Nørregaard Jørgensen[1], and Joost Visser[2]

[1] University of Southern Denmark, Odense, Denmark
{ao,bnj}@mmmi.sdu.dk
[2] Software Improvement Group, Amsterdam, The Netherlands
{e.bouwers,j.visser}@sig.eu
[3] Delft University of Technology, Delft, The Netherlands
E.M.Bouwers@tudelft.nl

Abstract. The way features are implemented in source code has a significant influence on multiple quality aspects of a software system. Hence, it is important to regularly evaluate the quality of feature confinement. Unfortunately, existing approaches to such measurement rely on expert judgement for tracing links between features and source code which hinders the ability to perform cost-efficient and consistent evaluations over time or on a large portfolio of systems.

In this paper, we propose an approach to automating measurement of feature confinement by detecting the methods which play a central role in implementations of features, the so-called *seed methods*, and using them as starting points for a static slicing algorithm. We show that this approach achieves the same level of performance compared to the use of manually identified seed methods. Furthermore we illustrate the scalability of the approach by tracking the evolution of feature scattering and tangling in an open-source project over a period of ten years.

1 Introduction

Structural organization of software has a major influence on locality of changes during software evolution [9]. One of the important types of such changes are those concerned with extending and modifying the implemented functionality, i.e. *features*, of a system. To minimize the effort of performing such changes, it is important to control the confinement of features in the structural units of source code, so that they remain properly localized and separated from one another [6].

Therefore, it is important to incorporate the quantification of feature confinement into the quality assessment of software systems. A number of metrics for this purpose have already been defined based on the concepts of *scattering* and *tangling* [11]. Scattering describes the delocalization of concerns over units of source code, whereas tangling describes the simultaneous occurrence in the same units of source code. We refer to these two properties jointly as *feature confinement*.

C.A. Furia and S. Nanz (Eds.): TOOLS Europe 2012, LNCS 7304, pp. 252–268, 2012.
© Springer-Verlag Berlin Heidelberg 2012

In order to measure these properties a link between features and source code of a software system needs to be defined. While a number of approaches for doing this exist, they are not fully automated because they rely on an association between units of source code and human-originated specifications of features defined by experts. This lack of automation prevents the cost-efficient evaluation of feature confinement on a large-scale.

To define a consistent, scalable and objective association between source code units and feature specifications this paper proposes an approach for the automatic detection of so-called *seed methods* of features. The approach detects such seed methods using the popularity of method names and the sizes of the static call-graph slices they yield.

The static slices produced from the identified seed methods do not provide an association between specific features and source code units (i.e., units 'x' and 'y' are involved in the implementation of feature "a"), but rather identify functional related code units in a system. These groups are used as a basis for quantification of feature confinement on the system level, e.g., forty percent of the units are involved in the implementation of twenty percent of the function groups of the system. We believe such quantifications to be useful in several quality assurance scenario's such as the tracking of feature confinement over time as well as determining those systems in a portfolio which implement the best/worst level of feature confinement.

We evaluate our approach on a group of open-source systems by comparing the coverage of source code achieved by slices produced from the automatically detected seed methods with that of the slices produced from manually-chosen seed methods. After applying our approach to a population of systems, we demonstrate its applicability to automatic measurement of multiple revisions of a single system by measuring system-level scattering and tangling in 27 revisions of an open-source project released over a period of 10 years.

2   Related Work

Quantifying feature confinement Brcina and Riebisch [5] propose two metrics for assessing the confinement of features in architectural designs. The first one, *scattering indicator*, is designed to quantify the delocalization of features over architectural components of a system. The second metric, *tangling indicator*, captures the degree of reuse of architectural components among multiple features. For both of these metrics, the authors provide a list of problem resolution actions that can be applied to address the problems detected by the metrics.

Eaddy et al. [6] introduced and validated a suite of metrics for quantifying the degree to which a concern is scattered across components and separated within a component. The defined metrics include *concentration* of a concern in a component, *degree of scattering* of a concern over components, *dedication* of a component to a concern and *degree of focus* of a component. Furthermore, the authors provide a set of guidelines for manually identifying concerns in source code, a prerequisite to a practical application of any concern-oriented metrics.

Wong et al. [14] defined three metrics for quantifying *closeness between program components and features*. These metrics capture the *disparity* between a program component and a feature, the *concentration* of a feature in a program component, and the *dedication* of a program component to a feature. To support practical application of their metrics, the authors propose a dynamic-analysis approach for establishing traceability links between features and source code using an execution slice-based technique that identifies regions of source code invoked when a particular feature-triggering program parameter is supplied.

Locating Features in Source Code. The problem of feature location can be seen as an instance of the more general problem of *concern location*. In this context, Marin et al. [7] have proposed a semi-automatic approach to identify crosscutting concerns in existing source code, based on analysis of call relations between methods. This is done by identifying the methods with the highest fan-in values, filtering them, and using the results as *candidate seed* methods of concerns. These candidate seeds are then manually inspected to confirm their usefulness and associate them with the semantics of a particular concern they implement.

Similarly to Marin et al. [7], the majority of approaches to *feature location* employ the notions of seed methods and control flow. One of the first works associating features with control flow was the *software recoinnaissance* approach of Wilde and Scully [13]. Their approach is a dynamic feature location technique that uses run-time tracing of test execution. Wilde et al. propose that feature specifications are investigated in order to define a set of feature-exhibiting and non-exhibiting execution scenarios. Individual execution scenarios are implemented as a suite of dedicated test cases that, when executed on an instrumented program, produce a set of traceability links between features and source code.

Salah and Mancoridis [10] proposed a different approach to encoding the feature-triggering scenarios. Their approach, called *marked traces*, requires one to manually exercise features through a program's user interface. Prior to executing a feature-triggering scenario, a dedicated execution tracing agent is to be manually enabled and supplied with a name of the feature being exercised. Effectively, this approach removes the need for identifying starting-point methods in source code and the need for the up-front effort of implementing appropriate feature-triggering test cases. Though this is achieved at the price of manual scenario execution.

Similarly to Salah and Mancoridis, Olszak and Jørgensen [8] proposed an approach based on user-driven execution of features. However, they reduce the burden of manual activation and deactivation of a tracing agent by introducing the notion of so-called feature-entry points. Feature-entry points are methods analogous to the ones that need to be invoked by test cases in software reconnaissance - the methods through which control flow enters feature implementations. The approach presented in [8] requires a programmer to annotate such methods in the source code. Using this information, the tracing agent is able to activate itself and track the execution of individual features triggered by a user.

Feasibility of using designated methods as starting points for static, as opposed to dynamic, analysis was demonstrated by Walkinshaw et al. [12]. They developed a feature location technique based on slicing a static call-graph according to user-supplied landmarks and barriers. There, landmarks are manually identified as the "methods that contribute to the feature that is under consideration and will be invoked in each execution", whereas barriers are the methods irrelevant to a feature. These two types of methods serve as starting points and constraints for a static slicing algorithm. This static mode of operation improves the overall level of automation by removing the need for designing and executing feature-exhibiting scenarios.

3   Problem Statement

Following the methodology of Basili et al. [4], we define the goal of our study to be to *automatically quantify the confinement of functional concerns* to *provide a high-level indication of this confinement* for the purpose of *automated evaluation of the confinement of functional concerns* from point of view of *software quality evaluators* in the context of *evolutionary and large-scale portfolio analysis*.

Surveying the related work, three important steps in the quantification of the confinement of functional concerns arise:

– Identification of entry points to functional concerns of an application
– Identification of those parts of the application that are being executed when the application's functionality is invoked by a user
– Usage of this information to calculate metrics of feature confinement to compare multiple systems or to analyze the evolution of a single system

In order to quantify confinement of functional concerns on a large scale, these steps need to be automated. Fortunately, Walkinshaw et al. [12] showed the feasibility of using static analysis to identify the parts of the application that are involved in the implementation of a functional concern. There, so-called "landmark"-methods representing starting point of feature implementations are used as seed nodes for static slicing of inter-method call graphs. Unfortunately, the lists of suitable landmarks still have to be established manually.

A close examination of the literature does not provide a solution for automatic identification of methods serving as starting points of functional concern implementations. These starting points, which we call "seed methods", play a key role in identifying functionally related code units, since they are the methods through which the control flow enters functionality-specific parts of a program's source code. By defining an approach to automatically detect those methods, the quantification of the confinement of functional concerns can be fully automated.

4   Detection of Seed Methods

To detect methods that play central roles within the implementation of a software system's functionality (i.e., seed methods), the total set of the system's methods needs to be filtered. The filtering approach proposed in this paper is explained

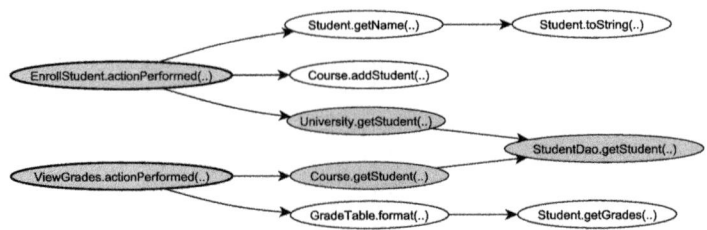

Fig. 1. Call graph of an example program

using the example in Fig. 1 which represents a call-graph of the methods in a small Java system. Note that the use of Java in the examples is only for explanatory purposes, the heuristic is not limited to only this language.

A simple heuristic for filtering the methods is to keep only those methods which are not called from within the system itself, assuming that these methods are used either as call-backs from the interface or are exposed as part of an API of a library. Within Fig. 1 this would lead to identifying the "actionPerformed"-methods as the seed methods.

Unfortunately, this heuristic does not perform well. First of all, for programs defined with a command-line interface the only method that is kept is the static "Main"-method that starts the program. Even though this method is an important part of the system the functional concern of starting an application too general to be considered an important part of a specific application. Secondly, when a system implements an internal event dispatching mechanism, the interesting methods are likely called directly from within the system by the dispatching infrastructure and thus not found by the heuristic.

A second heuristic for filtering is counting the names of all methods within a system and identify names which occur proportionally more often then other names. Note that in this situation the short-name of the methods i.e., *toString* or *getStudent*) instead of the full-name (i.e., *Student.toString* or *Course.getStudent*) should be counted since the latter name uniquely identifies a method within a system, and thus the number of methods with this name is always one.

The assumption behind this approach is that, due to polymorphic mechanisms and programming conventions, the methods with the same name but a different implementation implement variations of a functional concern specific to this system. Given the example in Fig. 1 the method "actionPerformed" is implemented multiple times since this method is enforced by a generic interface provided by the Swing GUI framework to handle actions taken by the user. Similarly, the "getStudent"-method is implemented, either because of polymorphism or a convention, by both "Course" and "University" classes.

Unfortunately, straight-forward application of this heuristic is problematic because this heuristic also identifies those methods which offer generic functionality for objects, such as the "toString"-method, as well as getters and setters for common properties such as names and id's. This last category of methods should not be considered as seed methods, since getters and setters typically do not implement complete functional concerns.

To filter out these uninteresting methods we take into account the number of methods needed to implement a specific method. This is done by counting the number of distinct methods called by the specific method, and then recursively counting the distinct methods used by those methods. Our assumption is that a higher number of methods used in the implementation of a method corresponds to a method which implements more sophisticated functionality. By only keeping those methods which are a) implemented proportionally more often and b) which use many other methods in their implementation we expect to discover the interesting seed methods within a system.

4.1 Heuristic Formalization

For the formalization of the heuristic we model a software system S as a directed graph $D = (V, E)$. The set of vertexes V are methods defined in the software product, and the set of edges E are calls modeled as a pair (x, y) from one method x (the source) to another method y (the destination). Let FN and SN be the sets of full names and short names, a vertex $v \in V$ is a record containing a full name and a short name, i.e., $v = (fn, sn)$ where $fn \in FN$ and $sn \in SN$.

For the first part of the heuristic the sets of vertexes that have the same short-name need to be defined. Using the function $shortname((fn, sn)) = sn$, which retrieves the short name component (sn) from a given vertex $v \in V$. The set of vertexes V_{sn} is the set of vertexes $v \in V$ that have sn as short name, defined as $V_{sn} = \{v \mid shortname(v) = sn\}$.

For the second part of the heuristic we want to compute the vertexes that are transitively connected to a given vertex. For this we define two functions. First a function $connected : V \times V \mapsto 2$ which distinguishes the vertexes that are directly connected by a given edge $e \in E$. For two vertexes $v_1, v_2 \in V$, $connected$ will yield $True$ if $\exists_{e \in E}$ such that $e = (v_1, v_2)$ and $False$ in all other cases. Secondly, a function $connected^+ : V \times V \mapsto 2$ is defined as the transitive closure of function $connected$. Given these functions, the set V_v consisting of vertexes that are transitively connected to vertex $v \in V$ can be defined as $V_v = \{v \mid connected^+(v)\}$.

Given this formalization the heuristic can be defined in three functions. First, a function to calculate the normalized frequency of methods with a certain short name:

Definition 1. $freq(sn) = \frac{|V_{sn}|}{|V|}$

Second, a function to calculate the average number of methods needed to implement the methods with a given short name:

Definition 2. $depth(sn) = \sum_{v \in V_{sn}} \frac{|V_v|}{|V|}$

Note that the results of both of these functions fall into the range $[0, 1]$, which ensures that values calculated from different systems can be compared if desired.

Lastly, to calculate the score for each short name the values of the two functions need to be combined. Ideally, the aggregation function prevents compensation, i.e., a high value on one approach should not overly compensate a low value

Table 1. Normalized scores for the methods as shown in Fig. 1

ShortName	freq	depth	score
actionPerformed	0.20	0.45	0.09
getStudent	0.30	0.06	0.02
getName	0.10	0.10	0.01
format	0.10	0.10	0.01
addStudent	0.10	0.00	0.00
toString	0.10	0.00	0.00
getGrades	0.10	0.00	0.00

on the other approach. Given this property, two simple aggregation functions can be chosen: the minimum and the product. For our heuristic the product is used to ensure a higher level of discriminative power, the total score for a given short name thus becomes:

Definition 3. $score(sn) = freq(sn) \times depth(sn)$

Applying the heuristic to the example in Fig. 1 provides us with the scores in Table 1, note that the scores are normalized against the total number of methods defined within the system. The "actionPerformed"-methods receive the highest score because these methods occur twice in the system and the average number of methods needed to implement them is 4.5. The methods called "getStudent" are second in rank, occurring three times in the system and needing on average 0.66 methods to be implemented.

4.2 Automated Quantification of Feature Confinement

As explained in Section 3, the calculation of feature-confinement metrics requires two steps; identification of seed methods and identification of those parts of the system that are executed when a seed method is executed.

For the first step the score function, as defined above, can be used to identify the δ most interesting methods. For practical reasons we use the $\delta = 10$ best methods as seed methods throughout the rest of this paper. Nevertheless, the optimality of this value and the potential context-dependency of the δ parameter needs to be investigated in the future.

The second step required for measuring feature confinement is to identify which parts of the application are executed when a seed method is executed. This is done by statically slicing the call-graph of the system under review. Using the terminology defined above we execute the method $connected^+$ for a seed method and obtain a set of methods in return. This set, which we call a *static trace*, represents a group of functionally related code units.

5   Evaluation of the Approach

The evaluation of the proposed approach is two-fold. First, in Section 6, we *validate* the proposed heuristic for detecting seed methods by comparing it to a structured manual approach. This is done by comparing the regions of source

Table 2. Subject systems used in the study

Program	Version	KLOC	Type
ArgoUML	0.32.2	40	Application
Checkstyle	5.3	60	Library
GanttProject	2.0.10	50	Application
Gephi	0.8	120	Application
JHotDraw	7.6	80	Framework
k9mail	3.9	40	Mobile application
Mylyn	3.5.1	185	Application
NetBeans RCP	7.0	400	Framework
OpenMeetings	1.6.2	400	Web application
Roller	5.0	60	Web application
Log4J	1.2.16	20	Library
Spring	2.5.6	100	Framework/Container
Hibernate	3.3.2	105	Library
Glassfish	2.1	1110	Container

code covered by the static traces produced by both approaches. Our hypothesis is that the traces stemming from seed methods found by our heuristic cover the same amount and the same regions of code as the traces stemming from manually-identified seed methods.

Secondly, in Section 7, we apply the proposed approach to measuring the evolution of feature confinement in an open-source project. The goal of this study is to evaluate the applicability of the measurements produced by our approach for enriching the analysis of long-term evolution of scattering and tangling of features. This is done by interpreting the fluctuations of the quality of feature confinement over time, in order to generate informed hypotheses about the nature of the performed evolutionary changes.

6   Validation

To validate the heuristic for identifying seed methods the following steps are taken. First, a set of subject programs is chosen (Section 6.1). For each of the programs, we manually identify a ground-truth set of seed methods enforced by the respective interfacing technologies and libraries being used (Section 6.2). This data is then used to compute static traces, whose aggregated source code coverage allows us to reason about the completeness of the constructed ground-truth. Then, the aggregated coverage of ground-truth slices is compared against aggregated coverage of traces generated by the heuristic (Section 6.3). Based on this, we evaluate whether our approach covers similar amounts and similar regions of source code as the manually-established ground truth.

Please note, that the design of this validation experiment deviates from the traditional designs of evaluating the accuracy of concern location approaches. There, false positives and false negatives are usually computed by comparing results of an approach to ground truth on *per-feature* basis. Such an approach is valid for assessing the accuracy of locating features associated with particular semantics, but unfortunately is inapplicable in our case, since our approach aims at system-level application and identifies groups of functionally related code units without attaching semantics.

Table 3. Correlation of subjects with technologies and their ground-truth seed methods

Technology	seed methods	ArgoUML	CheckStyle	GanttProject	Gephi	JHotDraw	k9mail	Mylyn	NetBeans RCP	OpenMeetings	Roller	Log4J	Spring	Hibernate	Glassfish
JDK	run, call, main	✓	✓	✓	✓	✓	✓	✓	✓	✓	✓	✓	✓	✓	✓
Swing	actionPerformed, stateChanged, keyTyped, keyPressed, mouseClicked, mousePressed	✓	✓	✓	✓	✓			✓						
Eclipse/SWT	handleEvent, keyPressed, mouseDown, mouseDoubleClick, widgetSelected, widgetDefaultSelected, runWithEvent, run, start, execute							✓							
Servlet	doGet, doPost										✓				
Android	onCreate, onOptionItemSelected, onClick, onLongClick, onKey, onKeyDown, onTouch, onStartCommand, startService						✓								
Spring	handle, handleRequest, onSubmit, start, initApplicationContext									✓			✓		
Struts	execute, invoke, intercept										✓				
Log4J	getLogger, log											✓			
Hibernate	buildSessionFactory, openSession, update, save, delete, createQuery, load, beginTransaction, commit, rollback													✓	
Glassfish	start, execute, load														✓

6.1   Subject Systems

The evaluation experiment is performed on a set of 14 open-source Java programs summarized in Table 2. The chosen population is intentionally diversified in order to observe how our approach deals with discovering seed methods in not only stand-alone applications but also libraries, frameworks, web applications and application containers. Thereby, we aim at validating the ability of our approach to detect seed methods that are triggered not only by GUI events, but also by command-line parameters, calls to API methods, HTTP requests, etc.

6.2   Ground-Truth

The ground truth in our experiment is formed by manually identifying seed methods in the subject programs. In order to make our classification of methods objective and consistent across all experimental subjects, we use the following procedure that is based on the observation that libraries and frameworks, which are used for interfacing with an environment tend to enforce a reactive mode of implementing functionality and standardize the names of methods for doing so.

For instance, the Swing Java GUI framework defines a set of methods, such as *actionPerformed, onClick*, etc., that are meant to be implemented by a client application and are called by Swing upon the reception of a given event from a user. Such methods, exhibiting individual functional concerns in response to external events, are used as ground-truth seed methods in our experiment. We reckon that such chosen methods could also be appropriate candidates for execution by *software recoinnaissance's* test-cases [13], annotating as feature-entry-points [8], marking as landmark methods [12], or starting points for static analysis [15].

Table 4. Percentage of LOC covered for both approaches

Program	Ground truth	Intersection	Approach
ArgoUML	81,5 %	79,3 %	82,2 %
Checkstyle	51,8 %	48,6 %	73,6 %
GanttProject	93,9 %	93,6 %	96,1 %
Gephi	90,7 %	89,2 %	92,0 %
JHotDraw	87,3 %	85,9 %	88,9 %
k9mail	97,1 %	97,0 %	97,0 %
Mylyn	80,7 %	78,1 %	81,9 %
NetBeans RCP	81,5 %	79,9 %	89,0 %
OpenMeetings	75,9 %	73,6 %	79,5 %
Roller	80,7 %	79,8 %	83,6 %
Log4J	90,1 %	86,3 %	88,6 %
Spring	69,3 %	66,5 %	76,9 %
Hibernate	84,1 %	82,1 %	84,9 %
Glassfish	71,4 %	70,5 %	78,8 %

Based on the mentioned observation, we manually identified interfacing technologies used by the subject programs. This was done based on static dependencies found in source code. For each of the discovered technologies, we identified methods that are intended to be implemented/overridden by client programs in order to provide a client's functionality. We identified such methods by surveying the available official documentation of the investigated libraries. The summary results of this process are listed in Table 3.

6.3   Results

For each of the subject programs, the seed methods of its interfacing technologies served as a starting point for static call-graph slices. Their *aggregated coverage*, being the union of these slices, was used as the ground-truth. The aggregated coverage percentages of both the ground truth and the proposed heuristic are shown in Table 4. In the "Ground truth" column the percentage of code covered by the static-slices originating from the ground truth is shown. The "Approach" column shows the percentage of code covered by the static-slices originating from the methods found by our heuristic. In the "Intersection" column the percentage of code covered by intersection of both result-sets is shown.

We can observe that for most systems the ground-truth coverages remain over 75% of the LOC, which suggests a high degree of completeness of the established ground truth. The only exceptions here are Checkstyle, Spring and Glassfish that are covered in 51,8%, 69,3% and 71,4% respectively. The result of Checkstyle seems to suggest incompleteness of the used ground truth. However, a closer look reveals that there exist four other systems that managed to achieve over 75% coverage based on exactly the same set of seed methods as Checkstyle. As we discuss later, this particular result of Checkstyle had a different cause.

Comparison of columns one and three indicates that aggregated coverage generated by our approach surpasses that of the ground truth for all the systems but k9mail. While the differences for most of the systems appear negligible (below 5% LOC), there are four notable exceptions, namely Checkstyle with difference of 21,8%, Spring with 7,6%, NetBeans RCP with 7,5% and Glassfish with 7,4%.

Interestingly, three of these systems are also the ones that exhibit the lowest ground-truth coverage.

A closer investigation of the reasons for the difference of 21,8% for Checkstyle revealed that the results generated by our approach contained a number of methods that we can categorize as non-technology-originated seed methods. For instance, the methods *process, processFiltered, verify, traverse* and *createChecker*, were found to yield slices containing the highest numbers of classes. These methods constitute important domain-specific abstractions that were established by Checkstyle's developers for implementing functionality, instead of relying on the general-purpose abstractions provided by the JDK or by Swing. Similarly, we found a similar pattern in other subjects, i.e. *afterPropertiesSet, invoke, postProcessBeforeInitialization* and *find* in Spring, or *execute, addNotify* and *propertyChange* in the NetBeans RCP.

Comparison of the columns one and two shows that the proposed heuristic manages to cover most of the regions of source code covered by the manually extracted ground truth, with the average loss of only 2,5% LOC. While this result is something that is expected for the highest sets of coverages (e.g. for the intersection of two result-sets achieving 95% coverage, the maximum possible loss is 5%), it is especially significant in the context of the lowest-scoring ground-truth values, i.e., Checkstyle (for which the maximum possible loss is 26,4%) and Spring (for which the maximum possible loss is 23,1%). This indicates that our approach not only covers as much source code as the manually-established ground truth, but that it also identifies largely the same regions of source code, thus providing analogous input to measuring feature confinement.

Lastly, the aggregated coverage obtained by our approach does not appear to be influenced by size or type of systems. Nevertheless, a sample larger than the one used in our experiment would be needed to confirming the lack of such causalities at a satisfying level of statistical significance.

7   Evolutionary Application

In this section, we apply our approach to evaluating the quality of features confinement in an evolving program. We do this by automatically measuring long-term evolutionary trends of confinement metrics in the release history of Checkstyle[1], a library for detecting violations of coding style in Java source code. The units of functionality in Checkstyle library, and whose historical quality we intend to assess using feature-oriented metrics, are the individual *detectors* for various types of style violations, as well as the core infrastructure of the library responsible of parsing source code, reporting results, etc. In this investigation, we measure 27 major releases of the library since version 1.0 until version 5.4.

7.1   Measuring Feature Confinement

The existing literature proposes and demonstrates the usefulness of a number of diverse metrics for measuring this *confinement*, e.g., [14,6,5]. A common theme

---

[1] http://checkstyle.sourceforge.net/

that tends to re-appear in many works is formulating measures for quantifying *locality of features* in structural units of source code (i.e. packages, classes or methods) and for quantifying *overlap of features* in terms of structural units. Having this in mind, for the purpose of this work we use the most elementary and intuitive formulations of metrics for capturing these properties. The two metrics used here are called *scattering* and *tangling* and they are based on simply counting the number of related classes or features. They are defined as follows:

- Scattering: denotes the delocalization of a functional concern over computational units of a program. In this work, we measure scattering for each seed method as the total number of classes that appear in its static trace.
- Tangling: denotes the interweaving of functional concerns in a structural unit of a program. In this work, we measure tangling for each class as the number of seed methods in whose static traces a given class appears.

The metrics chosen to quantify feature confinement are not directly calculated on the system level, but rather on the level of a single trace (scattering) or on the level of the class (tangling). In order to come to a system level measurement the values of the measurements on the lower level need to be aggregated. To compare a variety of systems in a consistent manner the aggregation needs to be done in such a way that the influence of other factors, for example the size of the system or the number of concerns evaluated, do not influence the aggregated measurement.

7.2 Aggregation of Confinement Metrics

Alves et al. [2] proposed an aggregation strategy based on benchmarking with these characteristics which has been applied successfully [3]. In this aggregation strategy a repository of systems is used to derive thresholds for categorizing unit of measurement in system (i.e., the class or the trace) into one of four categories. By summing up the size of all entities in the four categories a system-level profile is calculated, which in turn is used to derive a system-level rating [1].

The resulting rating, normally on a scale of one to five, indicates how the profile of a specific system compares to the profiles of the systems within the *benchmark* used for calibrating the profile-rating. For example, a rating of 1 indicates that almost all systems in the benchmark have a better profile, while a rating of 4 means that most systems in the benchmark have a lower profile.

The repository used to calibrate the rating for both scattering and tangling consists of industry software systems previously analyzed by the Software Improvement Group (SIG), an independent advisory firm that employs a standardized process for evaluating software systems of their clients [3]. These industry systems were supplemented by open source systems previously analyzed by SIG's research department.

The repository consists of 55 Java systems, of which 11 systems are open source. These systems differ greatly in application domain (banking, logistics, development tools, applications) and cover a wide range of sizes, starting from 2 KLOC up until almost 950 KLOC (median 63 KLOC).

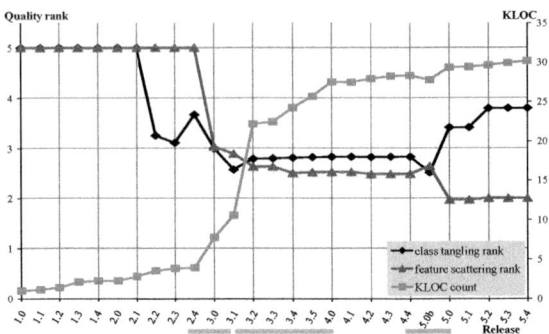

Fig. 2. Evolution of Checkstyle

7.3   Results

Fig. 2 shows a plot of the measured evolutionary trends of Checkstyle. The figure shows the values of KLOC metrics and the *ranking values* of scattering and tangling for each release. Please note that as a result of benchmarking, the quality rankings have to be interpreted inversely to the metrics they originate from - e.g. a high quality rank of scattering means low scattering of features.

The evolutionary trends plotted in Fig. 2 indicate that feature-oriented quality, represented by ranks of scattering and tangling tends to degrade over time. In the following, we investigate three periods marked in Fig. 2 that exhibit particularly interesting changes of the measured ranks.

Versions 2.4 – 3.1: a significant degradation of both scattering and tangling quality ranks is observed. The observed degradation was initiated by changes done in release *3.0*, where one of the major changes was a restructuring to a "completely new architecture based around pluggable module"[2]. This restructuring involved factoring-out a common infrastructure from existing detectors. Doing so was bound to increase the number of classes that features are scattered over, and create a number of infrastructural classes meant to be reused by multiple features, thus contributing to tangling.

Further degradation continued in release *3.1*. According to Checkstyle's change log, the crosscutting introduction of severity levels to all detectors forces all of the detectors to depend on an additional class. This significantly contributes to the increase of tangling and scattering of features because before this introduction most of the detectors were confined to a single class.

Versions 3.1 – 4.0: a rapid extension of Checkstyle's size is observed. In contrast with the previous period, the feature-oriented quality of the program remains stable. Version *3.2* is the version in which the program's size doubled, while the tangling rank slightly improved and the scattering rank declined. Based on the change log, this is caused by the addition of multiple fairly well separated J2EE-rule detectors. As discussed later, this hypothesis is supported by observed

---

[2] http://checkstyle.sourceforge.net/releasenotes.html

reverse changes in tangling and scattering ranks in version *5.0b*, where these detectors are removed.

One of the most interesting characteristics of the *3.1 – 4.0* period is the observed preservation of feature-oriented quality despite a nearly twofold growth of the program's size. This suggests that the new architecture established in *3.0* and adjusted in *3.1* proved appropriate for modularizing the forthcoming feature-oriented extensions. The established underlying infrastructure appears to provide all the services needed by features and the new features are made confined to approximately the same number of classes as the already-existing features.

Versions 4.4 – 5.0: An interesting shift in feature-oriented quality is observed in this period. Firstly, a slight improvement of the scattering rank and a degradation of the tangling rank is observed in the release *5.0b*. Together with the decrease of program's size, these changes suggest a removal of a number of fairly separated features. The program's change log supports this hypothesis, as it reports removal of all the J2EE-rule detectors. It needs to be noted that the observed magnitude of degradation of the tangling rank and improvement of scattering rank is approximately equal to their respective changes in the release *3.2*, where the J2EE-rule detectors were originally added.

Secondly, a significant improvement of the tangling rank and a significant degradation of the scattering rank is observed in release *5.0*. According to the change log, the most likely reason is the "Major change to FileSetCheck architecture to move the functionality of open/reporting of files into Checker", which "reduces the logic required in each implementation of FileSetCheck". In other words, by freeing individual detectors from explicitly calling "open/reporting", the programmers managed to reduce the tangling among them. At the same time, the ten newly-introduced complex detectors caused a visible degradation of the scattering rank.

8   Discussion

The results presented in Section 6 show that seed methods automatically identified by our approach yield static slices that capture largely the same regions of source code as a manually-established ground truth. Moreover, the heuristic improves on the ground-truth coverage results by identifying non-technology-originated seed methods that reflect important domain-specific functional abstractions. Given these observations, we conclude that the seed methods computed by our approach are adequate substitutes to manually identified seed methods for the purpose of system-level quantification of feature confinement.

The application of our approach presented in Section 7 shows that the automated measurement of the evolution of scattering and tangling properties provides a valuable perspective on the evolution of an existing software system. We demonstrated how to interpret these metrics in the context of Checkstyle's change log by generating informed hypotheses about the impact of the individual changes on the feature-oriented quality of the program. While the generated hypotheses need additional validation, they provide a sound and firm starting point for evaluating the evolutionary quality of feature confinement.

Algorithm Parameters. As explained in Section 4.2, the parameter δ is used to limit the number of best-ranked methods to be chosen as seed methods. Theoretically, such a value should preserve all the methods that contribute significantly to aggregated program coverage, whereas all the remaining methods should be filtered out. Even though the chosen δ seems to be correct for our current case-study (i.e., adding more methods to the list of seed methods did not increase the program coverage substantially), more work is needed to determine the optimal value of δ. Additionally, it is important to investigate whether a single optimal value of δ can be found for a portfolio of programs, or whether each program needs an individually-chosen δ value.

Limitations. One of the limitations of the performed experiments is the lack of a direct comparison against outputs of existing feature location approaches. Ideally, a correlation study of system-level scattering and tangling metrics contrasting our approach with the existing ones could be conducted. However, such a study requires a significant number of data points, being software systems, to achieve a satisfactory level of statistical confidence. While in the case of our approach this data can be generated automatically, to the best of our knowledge no sufficiently large data sets exist for existing feature location approaches.

In our evolutionary investigation, the differences among the sets of identified seed methods for subsequent versions of Checkstyle could have influenced our results. We observed this behavior when new types of detectors using new seed methods were added. While such a flux of the sets of seed methods reflects the evolution of how feature implementations change over time, it may turn out problematic with respect to comparability of measurements across versions. As a means of addressing this threat to validity we used the metric aggregation discussed earlier. Additionally, we confirmed that even tough the set of seed methods changed over time the coverage remained between 68% and 75%.

Lastly, because only open-source Java systems where used in the evaluations, the results cannot be generalized to systems with different characteristics (i.e., systems using a different programming paradigm). However, since the heuristic is largely technology agnostic, it remains possible to validate the approach using a more diverse set of systems.

9   Conclusion

Cost-efficiency of applying feature-oriented measurement is constrained by lack of automation of measurement collection procedures. This hinders applicability of feature-oriented metrics in large-scale and evolutionary scenarios. As a result, it remains difficult to assess quality of feature implementations, control it over time, and thoroughly validate new feature-oriented metrics.

In this paper we have proposed an approach for the automated measurement of system-level feature confinement, based on statically slicing the call-graph of a software system starting from a set of seed methods. The contributions of this paper are:

- The definition of a heuristic to automatically detect seed methods in software systems, based on popularity of method names and size of the static call-graph slices they yield.
- The validation of the heuristic by comparing the performance of static slices produced by our approach against slices produced from a set of manually selected seed methods.
- A demonstration of the practical applicability of the proposed approach in a case-study of measuring feature confinement over time.

References

1. Alves, T.L., Correia, J., Visser, J.: Benchmark-based aggregation of metrics to ratings. In: Proceedings of the IWSM/MENSURA 2011, The Joint Conference of the 21th International Workshop on Software Measurement (IWSM) and the 6th International Conference on Software Process and Product Measurement, Mensura (2011)
2. Alves, T.L., Ypma, C., Visser, J.: Deriving metric thresholds from benchmark data. In: Proceedings of the 2010 IEEE International Conference on Software Maintenance, ICSM 2010, pp. 1–10. IEEE Computer Society, Washington, DC (2010)
3. Baggen, R., Schill, K., Visser, J.: Standardized code quality benchmarking for improving software maintainability. In: 4th International Workshop on Software Quality and Maintainability (SQM 2010), Madrid, Spain, March 15 (2010)
4. Basili, V.R., Caldiera, G., Rombach, H.D.: The goal question metric approach. In: Encyclopedia of Software Engineering. Wiley (1994)
5. Brcina, R., Riebisch, M.: Architecting for evolvability by means of traceability and features. In: 23rd IEEE/ACM International Conference on Automated Software Engineering - Workshops, ASE Workshops 2008, pp. 72–81 (September 2008)
6. Eaddy, M., Zimmermann, T., Sherwood, K.D., Garg, V., Murphy, G.C., Nagappan, N., Aho, A.V.: Do crosscutting concerns cause defects? IEEE Transactions on Software Engineering 34, 497–515 (2008)
7. Marin, M., van Deursen, A., Moonen, L.: Identifying crosscutting concerns using fan-in analysis. ACM Transactions on Software Engineering and Methodology 17, 3:1–3:37 (2007)
8. Olszak, A., Jørgensen, B.N.: Remodularizing java programs for improved locality of feature implementations in source code. Science of Computer Programming (2010) (in press, corrected proof)
9. Parnas, D.L.: On the criteria to be used in decomposing systems into modules. Communications of the ACM 15, 1053–1058 (1972)
10. Salah, M., Mancoridis, S.: A hierarchy of dynamic software views: From object-interactions to feature-interactions. In: Proceedings of the 20th IEEE International Conference on Software Maintenance, pp. 72–81. IEEE Computer Society, Washington, DC (2004)
11. Turner, C.R., Fuggetta, A., Lavazza, L., Wolf, A.L.: A conceptual basis for feature engineering. Journal of Systems and Software 49, 3–15 (1999)
12. Walkinshaw, N., Roper, M., Wood, M.: Feature location and extraction using landmarks and barriers. In: IEEE International Conference on Software Maintenance (ICSM 2007), pp. 54–63 (October 2007)

13. Wilde, N., Scully, M.C.: Software reconnaissance: mapping program features to code. Journal of Software Maintenance 7, 49–62 (1995)
14. Wong, W.E., Gokhale, S.S., Horgan, J.R.: Quantifying the closeness between program components and features. Journal of Systems and Software 54, 87–98 (2000)
15. Zhao, W., Zhang, L., Liu, Y., Sun, J., Yang, F.: Sniafl: Towards a static noninteractive approach to feature location. ACM Transactions on Software Engineering and Methodology 15, 195–226 (2006)

Assisted Behavior Driven Development Using Natural Language Processing

Mathias Soeken[1], Robert Wille[1], and Rolf Drechsler[1,2]

[1] Institute of Computer Science, University of Bremen
Group of Computer Architecture, D-28359 Bremen, Germany
{msoeken,rwille,drechsle}@informatik.uni-bremen.de
[2] Cyber-Physical Systems
DFKI GmbH, D-28359 Bremen, Germany
rolf.drechsler@dfki.de

Abstract. In *Behavior Driven Development* (BDD), acceptance tests provide the starting point for the software design flow and serve as a basis for the communication between designers and stakeholders. In this agile software development technique, acceptance tests are written in natural language in order to ensure a common understanding between all members of the project. As a consequence, mapping the sentences to actual source code is the first step of the design flow, which is usually done manually.

However, the scenarios described by the acceptance tests provide enough information in order to *automatize* the extraction of both the structure of the implementation and the test cases. In this work, we propose an assisted flow for BDD where the user enters into a dialog with the computer which suggests code pieces extracted from the sentences. For this purpose, natural language processing techniques are exploited. This allows for a semi-automatic transformation from acceptance tests to source code stubs and thus provides a first step towards an automatization of BDD.

1 Introduction

Historically, software testing has been a post-processing step in the classical waterfall model. After the actual software has been created, usually a team of test engineers writes test cases (e.g. *unit tests*) in order to validate the correctness of the implemented code. In the movement of agile software engineering, the test effort is already incorporated at an earlier point in the development process. In particular, *Test Driven Development* (TDD) [1] employs so-called *acceptance tests* as the starting point for the development process. These acceptance tests represent all scenarios which have to be realized by the final system. While the test cases fail initially before any code has been written, the desired software system is considered complete (*accepted*) if all acceptance tests pass.

It has to be noted that acceptance tests are different from unit tests and are not meant as an alternative. While unit tests check the correct implementation of single atomic components in the software, acceptance tests check a scenario of the

C.A. Furia and S. Nanz (Eds.): TOOLS Europe 2012, LNCS 7304, pp. 269–287, 2012.
© Springer-Verlag Berlin Heidelberg 2012

system as a whole without considering *how* the system is actually implemented. As a result, it is often summarized that a unit test validates that the software does the *thing* right, whereas an acceptance tests checks whether the software does the *right* thing [2]. Consequently unit tests are generally written by the developers and the stakeholders will not take notice of them, whereas acceptance tests are written by the stakeholders and are discussed with the developers as part of the specification.

Recently, *Behavior Driven Development* (BDD) has been proposed [3] as a result of problems that arose with TDD when applying agile software practices. A major obstacle for programmers has often been to find a good starting point or to determine which facets need to be tested and which not. As a result, it has been noticed that the language used for describing the tests, i.e. class names and operation names, plays an important role both for writing test cases and for finding bugs in case of a failing test. Inspired by [4], for this purpose BDD uses *natural language* as a ubiquitous communication mean to describe the acceptance tests by means of scenarios. In fact, the natural language ensures a common understanding of the system to be developed between all members of the project – particularly between the designers and the stakeholders.

Based on the scenarios which are described by the acceptance tests, the designers map the sentences to actual code by implementing the test cases and code skeletons in the first step. Usually, this is a manual and thus time-consuming and error-prone process. However, all the information that is necessary to perform these steps is in principle already included in the natural description.

In this work, we propose a methodology which assists the designer in these first steps by semi-automatically extracting design information from the sentences using natural language processing techniques. We propose a design flow where the user enters into a dialog with the computer. In an interactive manner, the program processes sentence by sentence and suggests to create code blocks such as classes, attributes, and operations. The user can then accept or refuse these suggestions. Furthermore, the suggestions by the computer can be revised which leads to a training of the computer program and a better understanding of following sentences.

Using this new design flow, the following advantages arise.

- Having only scenarios described in natural language, the first steps towards writing the overall structure of the whole system can be cumbersome. However, analyzing the scenarios step by step assisted by a computer program allows for a smoother start into the design process.
- Descriptions in natural language bear the risk of misunderstandings, e.g. due to ambiguities. These risks can be minimized when the description is parsed by natural language processing techniques, because what a computer program might misunderstand is also likely to be misunderstood by another designer or stakeholder.
- Unlike previous work (cf. Sect. 6) where the result of the text processing is given after the whole text has been parsed, our approach provides the user with feedback after every sentence being parsed. As a result, the user can retrace the decisions of the tool and intervene if necessary.

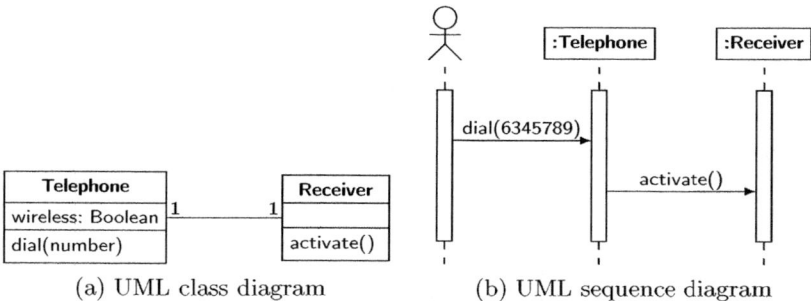

(a) UML class diagram   (b) UML sequence diagram

Fig. 1. UML class and sequence diagram

For the implementation of the proposed approach, we enhance the *Cucumber* tool [2]. The sentences of each scenario are parsed and are transformed into actual code required for the subsequent implementation of the system. Furthermore, also user interactions are written in natural language as pre-defined background scenarios inside the *Cucumber* tool, which lead to a seamless user experience.

We have evaluated our approach in a case study where we have used a candy machine whose specification is provided by means of six use case scenarios in natural language. Using only a few user interactions, it is possible to generate the whole class diagram and test cases with the assistance of the computer. As a consequence, the proposed flow allows for a semi-automatic transformation from acceptance tests to source code stubs and thus provides a first step towards an automatization of BDD.

The paper is structured as follows. The necessary background of methodologies used in this work is provided in the next section. Section 3 illustrates the general idea while Sect. 4 gives a more detailed insight into the extraction techniques. The results of the case study are presented in Sect. 5. Furthermore, Sect. 6 discusses related work and conclusions are drawn in Sect. 7.

2   Preliminaries

In this work, the *Unified Modeling Language* (UML) is applied to represent the code skeletons and test cases which are semi-automatically derived from natural language. Besides that, we are also exploiting language processing tools. To keep the paper self-contained, the underlying concepts of UML and the applied tools are briefly reviewed in the following.

2.1   Unified Modeling Language

In this section, we briefly review the basic UML concepts which are considered in this work. A detailed overview of the UML is provided in [5].

Class Diagrams. A UML *class diagram* is used to represent the structure of a system. The main component of a class diagram is a *class* that describes an atomic entity of the model. A class itself consists of *attributes* and *operations*. Attributes describe the information which is stored by the class (e.g. member variables). Operations define possible actions that can be executed e.g. in order to modify the values of attributes. Classes can be set into relation via *associations*. The type of a relation is expressed by *multiplicities* that are added to each association-end.

Example 1. Figure 1(a) shows a UML class diagram specifying a simple telephone. The class diagram consists of the two classes *Telephone* and *Receiver*. The class *Telephone* has an attribute *wireless* of type *Boolean*. The receiver is related to the telephone which is expressed by an association. As expressed by the multiplicities, each telephone has one receiver and vice versa. Both classes have an operation, i.e. the telephone can dial a number and the receiver can be activated.

Sequence Diagrams. The dynamic flow caused by operation calls can be visualized by sequence diagrams. Sequence diagrams offer the possibility to represent particular scenarios based on the model provided by the class diagram. Hence, several sequence diagrams exist for a given class diagram. In the sequence diagram, instances of the classes, i.e. objects, are extended by *life lines* that express the time of creation and destruction in the scenario. Arrows indicate operations that are called on an object, and are drawn from the caller to the callee. Besides objects also actors from the outside environment can be part of the sequence diagram.

Example 2. A sequence diagram is depicted in Fig. 1(b). In that scenario, first a number is dialed from an actor in the outside environment, before the telephone activates the receiver.

In this work, class diagrams and sequence diagrams are applied to represent the semi-automatically determined code skeletons and test cases, respectively.

2.2 Stanford Parser

The Stanford Parser is an open source software compilation published by the Stanford Natural Language Processing (NLP) Group [6]. It parses sentences in different languages and returns a *phrase structure tree* (PST) representing the semantic structure of the sentence. A PST is an acyclic tree with one root vertex representing a given sentence. Non-terminal and terminal vertices (i.e. leafs) represent the grammatical structure and the atomic words of this sentence, respectively. A simple PST for the sentence "The small child sings a song" is given by means of Fig. 2(a). As can be seen all leafs are connected to distinct vertices that classify the *tag* of the respective word, e.g. nouns and verbs. These word tags are further grouped and connected by other vertices labeled with a tag classifying a part of the sentence, e.g. as noun parts or verb parts. The classifier tags are abbreviated in the PST, however, in Fig. 2(a) the full classifier is annotated

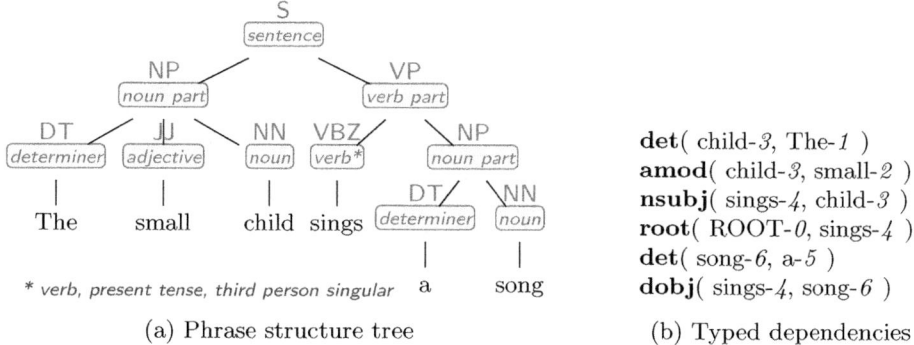

Fig. 2. Application of the Stanford Parser

to the vertices. For details on how a PST is extracted from a sentence, the reader is referred to [7].

Besides the PST, the Stanford Parser also provides *typed dependencies* [8] which are very helpful in natural language processing. Typed dependencies are tuples which describe the semantic correlation between words in the sentence. Figure 2(b) lists all typed dependencies for the sentence considered in Fig. 2(a). For example, the nouns are assigned their articles using the **det** relation. Note that the numbers after the word refer to the position in the text, which is necessary if a word occurs more than once in a sentence. Two further important relations are **nsubj** and **dobj** that allow for the extraction of the typical *subject-verb-object* form. In this case it connects the verb *sings* with both its subject and object.

In this work, the Stanford Parser is applied to process the structure of the sentences describing a scenario.

2.3 WordNet

WordNet [9], developed by the Princeton University, is a large lexical database of English that is designed for use under program control. It groups nouns, verbs, adjectives, and adverbs into sets of cognitive synonyms, each representing a lexicalized concept. Each word in the database can have several *senses* that describe different meanings of the word. In total, WordNet consists of more than 90,000 different word senses, and more than 166,000 pairs that connect different senses with a semantic meaning.

Further, each sense is assigned a small description text which makes the precise meaning of the word in that context obvious. Frequency counts provide an indication of how often the word is used in common practice. The database does not only distinguish between the word forms noun, verb, adjective, and adverb, but further categorizes each word into sub-domains. Those categories are e.g. *artifact, person,* or *quantity* for a noun.

In this work, WordNet is applied to determine the semantics of the sentences describing a scenario.

3   General Idea and Proposed Approach

As outlined in Sect. 1, behavior driven development puts acceptance tests to be realized in the focus of the design flow. These acceptance tests are provided as scenarios written in natural language. The typical BDD design process, as it is applied today, involves the steps illustrated by means of Fig. 3:

1. Write a *scenario* describing a certain behavior in natural language.
2. Write a *step definition* for each sentence (i.e. for each step) in the scenario which connects the natural language to actual code. Since the sentences in a scenario are written in natural language, they have to be implemented as code by the designer. For this purpose, step definitions are written that consist of a regular expression and a block of code. Whenever a step matches a regular expression, the respective code block of that step definition is executed.
3. Write a *code skeleton* such that the code inside the step definition is compilable.
4. *Implement* the operations in the code skeleton such that the scenario passes.

Example 3. Figure 4 shows an example of the BDD flow as it is employed in the *Cucumber* tool [2]. Here, one scenario is provided and eventually implemented in Ruby [10]. An example of a scenario is given in Fig. 4(a) describing the process of initiating a telephone call. For the first sentence, a step definition is created using Ruby as depicted in Fig. 4(b). Inside the step definition code, it is written what should be executed when the step is processed by the *Cucumber* tool. However, the class *Telephone* as well as the operation *pickUp* do not exist yet. Thus, a code skeleton is manually generated in the next step as shown in Fig. 4(c). Then, the step definition compiles. Finally, as illustrated in Fig. 4(d), the code skeleton is implemented in the last step. After this procedure has been applied to all remaining sentences, the whole scenario passes representing a complete implementation of this scenario.

So far, all steps are performed manually. Obviously, the scenario is the starting point for the BDD flow and thus always needs to be created manually. However, when observing the design flow as depicted in Fig. 3, the following conclusion can be drawn. The creation of the step definition and the provision of a code skeleton can in fact be automatized, since the sentences given in the scenario often provide enough information for an automatic determination of these components. For example:

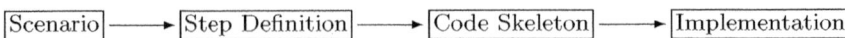

Fig. 3. Behavior Driven Development flow

Scenario: *Placing a call*

    * Ada picks up the receiver from the telephone

    * She dials the number 6-345-789

    * The telephone places a call

(a) Scenario

```
Given /^Ada picks up the receiver from the telephone$/ do
  @telephone = Telephone.new
  @receiver = @telephone.pickUp
end
```

(b) Step Definition

```
                                    class Telephone
                                      attr_reader :receiver

                                      def initialize
class Telephone                         @receiver = Receiver.new
  def pickUp                            end
  end
end                                     def pickUp
                                          @receiver
class Receiver                          end
end                                   end
```

        (c) Code Skeleton   (d) Implementation

Fig. 4. BDD example

- Regular nouns in sentences usually are realized as objects in the system, and therefore, they can automatically be represented by classes.
- Proper nouns usually represent actors from the outside environment who interact with the system.
- Adjectives in sentences usually provide further information about the respective objects. Thus, they can automatically be represented by attributes of classes.
- Verbs in sentences usually describe actions in a scenario, and can therefore automatically be represented by operations of classes. Additionally, they provide information when an operation is called and by whom.

In this work, we propose a BDD methodology which exploits such information in order to semi-automatically generate step definitions and code skeletons from scenarios given in natural language. For this purpose, we are making use of UML class diagrams and UML sequence diagrams that are proper abstractions of code skeletons and step definitions, respectively, from which the required pieces for the BDD flow can easily be generated. In the following, the general idea is briefly illustrated in Figs. 5 and 6 by means of the telephone scenario given in Fig. 4.

First the creation of a class diagram, i.e. a code skeleton, is considered. Using only the first sentence in Fig. 5 for example, the following information can automatically be extracted:

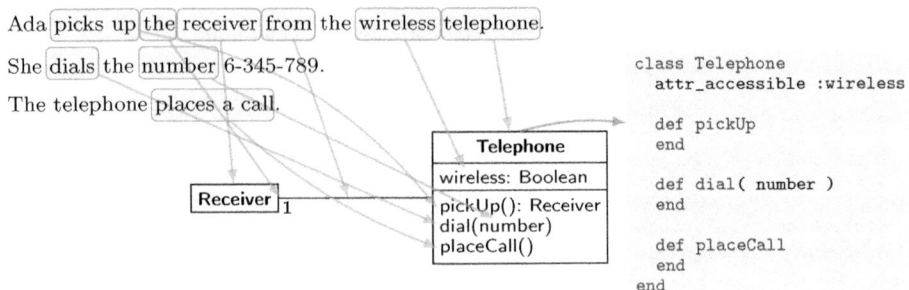

Fig. 5. Extracting class diagrams from scenarios for the generation of code skeletons

- The sentence contains three nouns. Since Ada is a proper noun, it is treated as an actor and not as a component of the system. Accordingly, classes are only created for receiver and telephone.
- The adjective wireless can be identified as related to telephone and thus is extracted as attribute for the respective class.
- The verb pick up is specified to be an operation of telephone.
- The preposition from indicates a relationship between the receiver and the telephone. Since the sentence states "*the* receiver from the wireless telephone" it can be concluded that a telephone can only have one receiver, in contrast to "*a* receiver from the wireless telephone" which would indicate more than one receiver.

Further information can be determined from the remaining two sentences. The fragments dials and places a call indicate further operations of the telephone. The phone number after number can be detected as a parameter for the *dial* operation. This eventually leads to the class diagram shown in Fig. 5, which can be used to generate the code skeleton in the desired language.

Moreover, the order of the sentences and their actions described in it provide the basis to automatically determine a test case. This is done by automatically creating a step definition for each sentence in the scenario. From the first sentence, it is known that Ada, i.e. an actor, invokes the pick up operation. The noun She in the second sentence refers again to Ada. Thus it can be concluded that the same actor invokes dial with the parameter 6-345-789 in the next step. The last sentence states that at the end of this scenario the telephone invokes the operation place a call. All steps can be summarized in a sequence diagram which can be used to generate step definitions in the desired language as depicted in Fig. 6.

As illustrated by this example, step definitions and code skeletons can automatically be generated even if the scenario is provided in natural language. We are aware that sentences in natural language might be ambiguous or incomplete and thus a fully automatic determination would not always lead to the desired

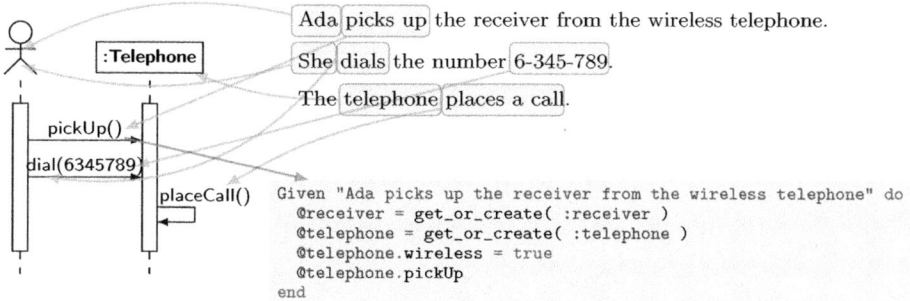

Fig. 6. Extracting sequence diagrams from scenarios for the generation of step definitions

result. However, as discussed in detail in the next section, the application of today's language processing tools in combination with ontologies already shows very good results. In addition, we propose an interactive flow where the designer enters into a dialog with the computer. In this flow, the computer is guiding the designer through the scenario while creating the UML diagrams step by step. During this process, the designer can refuse the automatically generated structures or provide the program with further information which cannot be extracted from the sentence or the ontology. In some cases this can even lead to a rephrasing of sentences in the scenario, e.g. in the presence of ambiguities. Then, the proposed approach also advances the design understanding within the development. If a sentence is misunderstood by the computer program, the same may also apply to other designers.

Overall, an approach is presented which significantly increases the efficiency of behavior driven development. As illustrated in Fig. 7, instead of manually creating step definitions and code skeletons, automatically generated suggestions from the proposed method just have to be revised or confirmed. The generated code skeleton is then used as the basis for the implementation, which remains the only non-automatic step. A further advantage of the new flow is that this implementation can immediately be validated against the scenario as also the step definitions have been generated automatically.

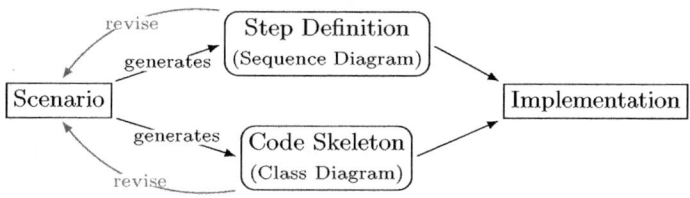

Fig. 7. Proposed flow

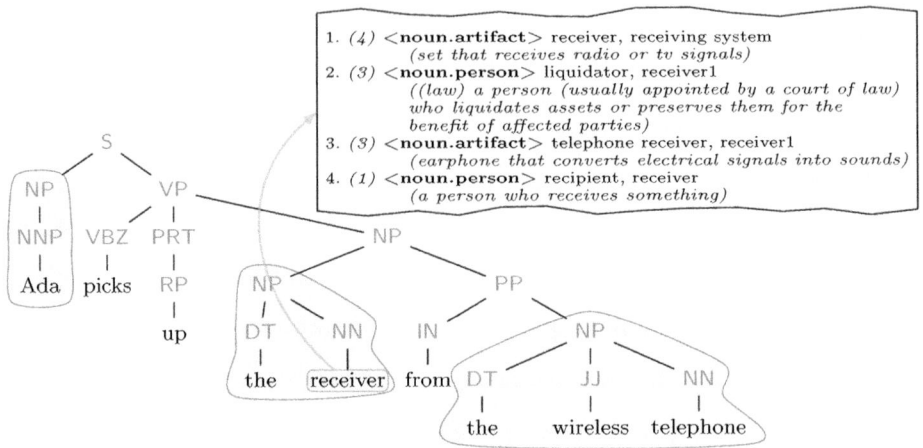

Fig. 8. Extraction of nouns using a PST and the WordNet dictionary

4   Semi-automatic Extraction of Information

As described above, the core of the proposed approach is the semi-automatic determination of UML class and sequence diagrams from a given scenario in natural language. Language processing tools and ontologies are exploited for this purpose. This section provides details on how the required information is extracted from the given scenarios. The determination of classes, attributes, and operations as well as their arrangement in a UML class diagram is initially described. Afterwards, the extraction of the actors of the system and the order of their actions are described which lead to the desired sequence diagram.

4.1   Classes

Components of the system to be implemented will be represented as classes in a UML class diagram. In order to extract these classes, the sentences provided by the scenario are parsed by the Stanford Parser reviewed in Sect. 2.2. This leads to the PST from which parts of the sentence related to a noun are extracted. Initially all *noun parts* (labeled NP in the PST) are extracted, i.e. nouns together with possible adjectives and articles. Afterwards, they are subdivided into *proper nouns* (labeled NNP in the PST) and *nouns* (labeled NN in the PST). Proper nouns are ignored – they represent actors and are required later in order to create the sequence diagram. All remaining nouns are further considered by the WordNet dictionary (cf. Sect. 2.3) in order to check whether they represent further actors of the system or actual components for which classes have to be created.

Example 4. Figure 8 shows the PST for the sentence "Ada picks up the receiver from the wireless telephone". This sentence is composed of three noun parts from which Ada is discarded since it is a proper noun. For the remaining two nouns,

Background:		Phrase	Meaning
* Consider coin.		Consider *noun.*	Considers *noun* as a class
Scenario:		*noun* is a person.	Considers *noun* as an actor
		Ignore *noun.*	Does not consider *noun* nei-
* Bob picks up a coin.			ther as class nor as an actor

(a) Example scenario with background   (b) Possible phrases for interaction

Fig. 9. User interaction for nouns

a further check is performed using WordNet. In case of |receiver|, this exemplary leads to the *lexical file information* as given in the page excerpt in the upper part of Fig. 8. The four entries are ordered by their *frequency counts* providing an indication about the commonly used semantic of this word. As can be seen, |receiver| might been used as a person (denoted by *noun.person*) which would imply an actor of the system and no creation of a class. However, since its use as an object (denoted by *noun.artifact*) has a higher frequency count, this semantic is chosen, i.e. |receiver| is considered a component and thus a respective class is created. The same check is applied to |telephone|.

User Interaction. Although the automatic classification of nouns and thus the creation of classes works very well for many cases, two problems may occur: (1) the frequency counts of WordNet lead to a wrong decision or (2) the considered word cannot be classified using WordNet. In both cases, the user has to intervene.

A trivial approach is a simple modification of the resulting class diagram by the user, e.g. the removal of a class when it was wrongly interpreted as component. Besides that, also an interactive learning scheme can be applied. The latter has been seamlessly implemented into the *Cucumber* BDD flow [2] where scenarios are usually grouped as *features*. Each feature additionally can be enriched by a *background* section which is processed prior to each scenario. We use *pre-defined* background steps for providing additional information (again in natural language) that help the automatic approach to correctly retrieve the meaning of a word or to assume a context of a scenario. The following example illustrates the principle.

Example 5. Consider the sentence "Bob picks up a coin". The word |coin| is specified as a *noun.possession* by WordNet and therefore cannot be classified as class or actor. Thus in order to set the context the designer can additionally provide more background as shown in the *Cucumber* feature illustrated in Fig. 9(a). Due to the phrase "Consider coin", the background of |coin| is clearly set to a component, i.e. a class is generated for it.

Other background phrases that can be used are given in Fig. 9(b). By applying a phrase, the approach automatically learns additional information which can later be applied in other scenarios as well.

4.2   Attributes

The determination of the noun parts as illustrated in Fig. 8 does not only enable the extraction of classes, but also of their corresponding attributes. For this purpose, all vertices representing adjectives are extracted (labeled JJ in the PST) and are simply connected to the corresponding class. By default Boolean attributes are assumed. If the adjective additionally is prefixed by adverbs such as *very*, *slightly*, or *almost*, an integer attribute is assumed instead of the Boolean type. These cases are explicitly emphasized by the proposed approach. The designer may transform this classification later, e.g. to an enumerated type.

Example 6. Consider the noun part the wireless telephone in the example from Fig. 8. From the corresponding noun, a class with the name *Telephone* is extracted. Additionally, the class is enriched by a Boolean attribute *wireless* due to the adjective.

Further attributes can be extracted from other constructs of the sentence. As an example, consider the phrase "the product 12". The word 12 is classified as *cardinal number* (labeled CD in the PST). If this appears after a noun in a noun part, it is implied that the respective class has an attribute *id* of type integer. This also works with floating point numbers. A similar rule applies for sentence parts set in quotes. For example, consider the phrase "the song "Wonderful Tonight"". In this case it does not make sense to treat the words in quotes as normal words – wonderful and tonight should clearly not be considered as adjective and noun, respectively. Instead the whole quote is extracted from the sentence before parsing and it is stored that the word song can have an additional identifier. This finally leads to an attribute *name* of type string.

User Interaction. All information that is automatically extracted from the sentences in the scenarios as described above can also be provided explicitly by pre-defined sentences in the background section. The sentence "A *noun* can be *adjective*" adds an attribute *adjective* of type Boolean to the class representing *noun*. In a similar manner, for the sentence "A *noun* has an id" or "A *noun* has a name", attributes *id* of type integer or *name* of type string, respectively, are added to the class. In contrast, the consideration of certain attributes can be omitted by the sentences "A *noun* cannot be *adjective*", "A *noun* has no id", and "A *noun* has no name".

Further, enumeration types can be added to a class explicitly by the sentence "The *name* of a *noun* can be *value*, . . . , or *value*". In this case, an attribute *name* is added to the class representing *noun* providing an enumeration for each value.

Example 7. Consider again the sentence "Ada picks up the receiver from the wireless telephone". By default the tool extracts an attribute *wireless* of type Boolean. When adding the sentence "The type of a telephone is wireless or wired" to the background section, an enumeration named *type* is added as an attribute to the class *Telephone* having the two values *wired* and *wireless*. In this case, the adjective wireless is not extracted for the class *Telephone* as it already appears as a value in the enumeration.

1 **nsubj**(picks-*2*, Ada-*1*)
2 **root**(ROOT-*0*, picks-*2*)
3 **prt**(picks-*2*, up-*3*)
4 **det**(receiver-*5*, the-*4*)
5 **dobj**(picks-*2*, receiver-*5*)
6 **det**(telephone-*9*, the-*7*)
7 **amod**(telephone-*9*, wireless-*8*)
8 **prep_from**(receiver-*5*, telephone-*9*)

Fig. 10. Typed dependencies for sentence from Fig. 8

4.3 Operations

As outlined in Sect. 3, verbs are usually a good indicator of an operation to be extracted from a sentence. However, in order to assign a verb and, therefore, an operation to the corresponding class, the PST alone is not sufficient. For example, in the sentence "Ada picks up the receiver from the wireless telephone" it is not obvious whether the operation pick up belongs to the receiver or the telephone. As a solution, we additionally make use of the typed dependencies in the sentence (cf. Sect. 2.2). This allows for relating the verb to its subject and object in the typical *subject-verb-object* (SVO) phrase. Thus, the first step consists of extracting the SVO relation in the sentence. In a next step, it is determined whether the subject or the object in the sentence is the class to which the operation should be assigned. If one of the nouns (subject or object) has been identified as an actor and the other one as a class, then this decision is easy. In other cases, user interaction might be required. The following example illustrates the principle.

Example 8. Consider again the sentence in Fig. 8. The verb picks in the sentence is easily identified in the PST by searching for a vertex labeled VBZ (verb, present tense). The typed dependencies for the same sentence are given by means of Fig. 10. With the relations **nsubj** (Line 1, nominal subject) and **dobj** (Line 5, direct object), the SVO relation *Ada-picks-receiver* can be determined. The relation **prt** (Line 3, phrasal verb particle) allows for completing the verb to *picks up* which results in the operation name *pickUp*. Note that the base form of the verb *picks* can be identified using a WordNet query. Using this information, the operation *pickUp* is added to the class *Receiver*, since *Ada* is already classified as an actor.

However, as already depicted in Fig. 5, this is not the right decision. It makes more sense that *pickUp* is an operation of the telephone that returns a receiver. The information for taking this decision is, however, already included in the typed dependencies. This is due to the preposition on the word receiver, which is indicated by the relation **prep_from** (Line 8, prepositional modifier). Further, this relation returns the correct link to the word telephone. Since *Telephone* also has been classified as a class, the operation *pickUp* is added to this class. Further, due to the preposition, *Receiver* can be identified as return type for that operation.

User Interaction. If operations should not be generated for a class, the user can write the sentence "A *noun* does not *verb*". Note that the noun should be the noun representing the class name the operation is assigned. If for example the operation *pickUp* should not be added to the class *Telephone*, the user would add "A telephone does not pick up" as a step to the background section. This seems inconvenient at first glance, since Ada is picking up the receiver in the sentence. However, those decisions are usually taken after seeing the result of the automatic translation.

4.4   Generation of Step Definitions

After the class diagram has been created, the same actors and classes with their attributes and operations can be used to generate the step definitions. While the scenarios serve as the outline in which the steps are executed, the step definitions describe the actual code that has to be executed in that step.

For this purpose, consider again the sentence "Ada picks up the receiver from the wireless telephone". The automatically generated step definition is illustrated in Fig. 6. First, for each class extracted from the sentence a respective object is created. This is done by making use of the factory design pattern [11]. In particular, two cases may occur, i.e. either a new object has to be created or the step refers to a possibly already existing object. The functions *create* and *get_or_create* are made available for these two cases. The article of the noun can be used to determine which function to choose, which is described in detail in the remainder of the section. Besides that, attribute values are assigned and operations are transformed into respective operation calls on the objects.

The Role of Articles in Test Cases. The article in front of a noun can be used to determine whether a new object has to be created or whether the noun references a possibly existing object. This is illustrated by the following example.

Example 9. Consider the following two sentences.

"A telephone starts ringing. A telephone stops ringing"

This scenario indicates that possibly two telephones are involved, one that starts ringing and one that stops ringing. If, however, the scenario was specified as

"A telephone starts ringing. *The* telephone stops ringing",

it is obvious that the telephone in the second sentence is the same one as in the first sentence.

In the generation of test cases, we apply the following rule. For nouns with an undetermined article, always a new instance is generated, i.e. the factory function *create* is used. Otherwise, for nouns with an determined article, it is first tried to find the latest created instance for the respective type. If this is not possible, an instance is generated. This behavior is implemented in the factory function *get_or_create*.

Scenarios:
– Customer pays with exact change
– Customer pays and gets money back
– Customer chooses product without paying
– Machine has no change
– Machine cannot provide desired product
– Employee fills up the machine

Scenario: *Customer pays with exact change*
1. A hungry customer approaches the candy machine
2. The candy machine shows the message "Ready"
3. The customer chooses product 12 by using the keypad
4. The candy machine shows the message "1,20 Dollar"
5. The customer provides the exact price to the machine
6. The candy machine returns a piece of product 12
7. The candy machine is ready for the next customer

Fig. 11. Use case scenarios for a candy machine

A similar effect is noticeable when names are used for the actors. Then, the nouns *She* or *He* have to be assigned accordingly.

Example 10. Consider the following scenario.

"Ada and Bob play soccer. She is the goal keeper. He shoots the ball."

In this scenario, *She* refers to Ada, and *He* refers to Bob.

To automatically determine the relation of words such as *She*, *He* and also *her* or *his*, the first names of the actors have to be assigned a gender. WordNet is not capable of doing this. However, probably other dictionaries suitable for that purpose can be used for this problem. In the meanwhile, we make use of user interaction in form of background steps such as "Ada is a woman" or "Bob is a man".

5 Case Study

We implemented the approach on top of the *Cucumber* tool [2] in Ruby and applied it to semi-automatically design a simple candy machine specified by six acceptance tests. These acceptance tests, provided by means of scenarios, are summarized in the left-hand side of Fig. 11. Due to page limitations, we cannot provide and discuss all scenarios in detail. As a consequence, we demonstrate the usage of the proposed approach for the first scenario (provided in the right-hand side of Fig. 11) only. For this purpose, the output of the approach as well as the resulting parts for the class diagram are sketched for each sentence in the following. The overall class diagram is created as union of all parts.

A hungry customer approaches the candy machine.	CandyMachine
Customer has been detected as actor.	
Detected class *CandyMachine* without attributes.	approach()
Detected operation *approach* for class *CandyMachine*.	

The first sentence was correctly processed by the approach, i.e. customer was correctly identified as an actor and candy machine as a component leading to the creation of a class. The two words candy and machine have correctly been identified as compound noun, since both belong to the same noun part (NN) in the PST. Further, the automatic approach has originally created an operation *approach* for the corresponding verb in the sentence. However, in the role of the designer, we decided not to use this operation in our class. For this purpose, a sentence "A candy machine does not approach" has been added to the background section in the feature description for the *Cucumber* tool.

The candy machine shows the message "Ready".
Detected class *CandyMachine* without attributes.
I do not know how to categorize *message* as actor or class. I know it as *communication*. Do you mean message as in a communication (usually brief) that is written or spoken or signaled; "he sent a three-word message"?

In the second sentence, the approach was not able to determine whether or not a class should be created for the noun message. It is neither classified as *person* nor *artifact* in the WordNet database, but as *communication*. The approach informs the user about that and also prints out the corresponding WordNet information. Based on that, the user can take a decision. In the considered case, a class should be created for message. This is achieved by adding the sentence "Consider message" to the background section. Processing the sentences again including this additional information leads to the following result:

The candy machine shows the message "Ready".	CandyMachine	Message
Detected class *CandyMachine* without attributes.		name: String
Detected class *Message* with attribute *name*.	show(m: Message)	
Detected operation *show* with parameter *message* for class *CandyMachine*.		

Now, everything has been detected correctly. The class *Message* automatically gets the attribute *name* because of the identifier "Ready" in the sentence.

The customer chooses product 12 by using the keypad.	KeyPad	Product
Customer has been detected as actor.	choose(p: Product)	id: Integer
Detected class *Product* with attribute *id*.		
Detected class *Keypad* without attributes.		
Detected operation *choose* with parameter *product* for class *Keypad*.		

In the third sentence, the operation *choose* is added to the class *KeyPad* because of the preposition in the sentence. Since the object in the sentence is product, the operation gets a respective parameter. An attribute *id* is added to the class *Product* due to the number after the noun.

The fourth sentence "The candy machine shows the message "1,20 Dollar"" is equivalent to the second sentence in the scenario when considering structure extraction. In fact, the sentences will even generate the same step definition, since the Cucumber tool automatically extracts regular expressions for words in quotes.

In the fifth sentence, the user has to manually interact since the word price cannot be classified precisely. After it has been added as considered to the background section, the tool proceeds as follows:

The customer provides the exact price to the candy machine.	CandyMachine	Price
Customer has been detected as actor. Detected class *Price* with attributes *exact*. Detected class *CandyMachine* without attributes. Detected operation *provide* with parameter *price* for class *CandyMachine*.	provide(p: Price)	exact: Boolean

Since the adjective ⌐exact⌐ is associated to the noun ⌐price⌐, it appears as an attribute for the class *Price*.

In a similar fashion, the remaining sentences and scenarios have been processed. Eventually, this led to a class diagram that consists of 6 classes with 3 attributes and 7 operations. In total, 9 sentences were added to the background section for a total of 40 sentences in 6 scenarios. Analogously, 18 step definitions have been created which cover all sentences in all scenarios and allow the execution of the acceptance tests.

Overall, step definitions and code skeletons of a complete system, the considered candy machine, have been semi-automatically generated by the proposed approach. For this purpose, each sentence was iteratively processed. In case of uncertainties, the user entered into a dialog with the computer. Compared to an entirely manual flow, this represents a significant improvement considering that the designer is automatically served with several options which she/he can easily refine.

6   Related Work

The proposed approach is a significant step towards an automatization of BDD. In doing so, our solution aligns with other approaches aiming at that goal – in particular in the domain of UML. As an example, the work presented in [12] extracts UML class diagram from specifications in natural language which, afterwards are used to generate code skeletons. The authors make use of a structure similar to the PST, but not of typed dependencies and not of a lexical database for classification. Further, the input language must be written in simple English and follow a certain sentence structure. User interaction is not intended in this approach.

The tool named *REBUILDER UML* [13] uses natural language as constituents for object oriented data modelling by using an approach based on case-based reasoning. However, only class diagrams are supported by this operation. Similarly, the tool *LOLITA* [14] generates an object model from a text in natural language. However, the tool only identifies objects from text and cannot further distinguish between other elements such as classes, attributes, and operations.

Class diagrams can also be extracted from natural language text using the tool *CM-BUILDER* [15]. Also, here dynamic aspects are not considered. Furthermore, the specification is considered as a whole which impedes user interaction and the result is always the complete class diagram such that subsequent modifications are cumbersome.

In [16] a method for generating executable test benches from a textual requirements specification is proposed. For this purpose, a subset of the English language called *textual normal form* has been designed that can be transformed into UML class diagrams which can be translated into classification trees according the *Classification Tree Method for Embedded Systems* (CTM/ES) [17]. These classification trees are finally used to generate the resulting executable test benches which can be utilized in a formal verification environment. However, besides that a different domain is addressed in this approach, the designer is limited to a restricted subset of the English language.

7 Conclusions

In this work, we proposed an assisted flow for BDD where the user enters into a dialog with the computer in order to semi-automatically generate step definitions and code-skeletons from a given scenario. For this purpose, natural language processing tools are exploited. A case study illustrated the application. Instead of going through the established BDD steps manually, the designer is automatically served with options which easily can be refined.

The proposed approach is a significant step towards an automatization of BDD. Moreover, while the case study focuses on acceptance test within the BDD scheme, the results of the proposed approach also motivate a consideration of general natural language system specifications. The proposed methodology provides a basis for further work in this direction.

Acknowledgments. This work was supported by the German Research Foundation (DFG) (DR 287/23-1).

References

1. Beck, K.: Test Driven Development. By Example. Addison-Wesley Longman, Amsterdam (2003)
2. Wynne, M., Hellesøy, A.: The Cucumber Book: Behaviour-Driven Development for Testers and Developers. The Pragmatic Bookshelf (January 2012)
3. North, D.: Behavior Modification: The evolution of behavior-driven development. Better Software 8(3) (March 2006)
4. Evans, E.J.: Domain-Driven-Design: Tackling Complexity in the Heart of Software. Addison-Wesley Longman, Amsterdam (2003)
5. Rumbaugh, J., Jacobson, I., Booch, G.: The Unified Modeling Language reference manual. Addison-Wesley Longman, Essex (1999)
6. Jurafsky, D., Martin, J.H.: Speech and Language Processing. Pearson Prentice Hall (2008)
7. Klein, D., Manning, C.D.: Accurate Unlexicalized Parsing. In: Annual Meeting of the Association for Computational Linguistics, pp. 423–430 (July 2003)
8. de Marneffe, M.C., MacCartney, B., Manning, C.D.: Generating Typed Dependency Parses from Phrase Structure Parses. In: Int'l Conf. on Language Ressources and Evaluation, pp. 449–454 (May 2006)

9. Miller, G.A.: WordNet: A Lexical Database for English. Communications of the ACM 38(11), 39–41 (1995)
10. Flanagan, D., Matsumoto, Y.: The Ruby Programming Language. O'Reilly Media (January 2008)
11. Gamma, E., Helm, R., Johnson, R., Vlissides, J.: Design Patterns: Elements of Reusable Object-Oriented Software. Addison-Wesley Professional, Amsterdam (1994)
12. Bajwa, I.S., Samad, A., Mumtaz, S.: Object Oriented Software Modeling Using NLP Based Knowledge Extraction. European Journal of Scientific Research 35(1) (January 2009)
13. Oliviera, A., Seco, N., Gomes, P.: A CBR Approach to Text to Class Diagram Translation. In: TCBR Workshop at the European Conf. on Case-Based Reasoning (September 2006)
14. Mich, L., Garigliano, R.: A Linguistic Approach to the Development of Object Oriented Systems using the NL System LOLITA. In: Bertino, E., Urban, S. (eds.) ISOOMS 1994. LNCS, vol. 858, pp. 371–386. Springer, Heidelberg (1994)
15. Harmain, H.M., Gaizauskas, R.J.: CM-Builder: A Natural Language-Based CASE Tool for Object-Oriented Analysis. Journal of Automated Software Engineering 10(2), 157–181 (2003)
16. Müeller, W., Bol, A., Krupp, A., Lundkvist, O.: Generation of Executable Test-benches from Natural Language Requirement Specifications for Embedded Real-Time Systems. In: Hinchey, M., Kleinjohann, B., Kleinjohann, L., Lindsay, P.A., Rammig, F.J., Timmis, J., Wolf, M. (eds.) DIPES 2010. IFIP AICT, vol. 329, pp. 78–89. Springer, Heidelberg (2010)
17. Grochtmann, M., Grimm, K.: Classification trees for partition testing. Software Testing, Verification and Reliability 3(2), 63–82 (1993)

Learning to Classify Bug Reports into Components

Ashish Sureka

Indraprastha Institute of Information Technology (IIIT-D)
New Delhi, India
ashish@iiitd.ac.in

Abstract. Bug reports in widely used defect tracking systems contains standard and mandatory fields like product name, component name, version number and operating system. Such fields provide important information required by developers during bug fixing. Previous research shows that bug reporters often assign incorrect values for such fields which cause problems and delays in bug fixing. We conduct an empirical study on the issue of incorrect component assignments or component reassignments in bug reports. We perform a case study on open-source Eclipse and Mozilla projects and report results on various aspects such as the percentage of reassignments, distribution across number of assignments until closure of a bug and time difference between creation and reassignment event. We perform a series of experiments using a machine learning framework for two prediction tasks: categorizing a given bug report into a pre-defined list of components and predicting whether a given bug report will be reassigned. Experimental results demonstrate correlation between terms present in bug reports (textual documents) and components which can be used as linguistic indicators for the task of component prediction. We study component reassignment graphs and reassignment probabilities and investigate their usefulness for the task of component reassignment prediction.

Keywords: Mining Software Repositories (MSR), Empirical Software Engineering and Measurements (ESEM), Automated Software Engineering (ASE).

1 Research Motivation and Aim

Quality of bug reports submitted to defect tracking systems is a topic that has attracted a lot of research attention recently. Previous studies reveals that the quality of information present in a bug report influences its resolution time and has impact on the productivity of the development team [1][2][3][10][12]. Bettenburg et al. and Zimmerman et al. investigate quality of bug reports and mention that bug reports are often poorly written and provide *inadequate* and *incorrect* information. This naturally results in delays during problem identification and bug fixing. They conduct a survey with Apache, Eclipse and Mozilla project developers and present several factors impacting the quality of bug reports [2][12].

C.A. Furia and S. Nanz (Eds.): TOOLS Europe 2012, LNCS 7304, pp. 288–303, 2012.
© Springer-Verlag Berlin Heidelberg 2012

The difference between inadequate and incorrect information in bug reports is import to this work. Not providing important information such as steps-to-reproduce and stack-traces is one kind of quality issue. This is an issue of missing or inadequate information. However, bug reports contain certain mandatory and standard fields like product name, component name, version number, platform and operating system. Prior studies reports that bug reporters often provide incorrect values for such mandatory and standard fields. This is a different kind of issue (pertaining to incorrect information rather than missing or inadequate information) which is of interest to the work presented in this paper. For example, accidently providing incorrect information such as an incorrect operating system is a typical problem in bug reporting [12]. Zimmerman at al. mention that several bug reports in Eclipse project were submitted for "Windows" but later reassigned to "Linux". Their study also reveals that for bug reporters locating a *component* in which a bug occurs is often difficult and impossible to provide [12].

The focus of this work is to investigate the phenomenon of incorrect information in standard fields and in particular study the phenomenon of *incorrect component assignment*. An interesting result of the survey conducted by Zimmerman et al. reveals that information like product name, component name, version number and operating system are important items used by developers during bug fixing and more importantly it causes them problems and delays in bug fixing if such information is wrongly provided [12].

Zimmermann et al. perform an experiment using Eclipse bug reports to construct a decision tree that correlates input features extracted from bug reports (bug severity, operating system, affected component, bug priority, version number, reporter name and platform) and the location of the fix. Their study reports three out of the seven input features influenced the location of a defect. They demonstrate that the input feature with the most impact in determining the defect location is *component name* (due to the direct mapping between source code and component name). They found that the next most influential feature is the version number [13]. Breu et al. analyze frequently asked questions by users and developers in bug reports [5]. They observe that often bugs are submitted to incorrect components or even projects. For example, some of the actual questions used in their paper are: "Is dom the correct component?", "Can you verify that this is a reconciler problem?" "Should I move this bug report to JCore-code assist?" Breu et al. mention that 5 out of the 94 questions (around 5-6%) they analyzed on bug triaging were pertaining to component correction [5]. The research performed by Breu et al. shows that bug reporters often mention incorrect components and developers ask questions to bug reporters for clarification resulting in delays. The research presented in this work is motivated by the following facts.

1. Mandatory fields like *component name* are important indicators for determining the location of a defect in the source code.

2. Bug reporters often provide *incorrect* information for standard fields like *component name*.

3. Wrong information for fields like component name can cause delays and problems to developers in bug fixing.

The specific *research aim* of the work presented in this paper is the following:

1. To perform empirical analysis and measurements on component reassignments phenomenon by mining data archived in defect tracking systems.
2. To investigate the usefulness of machine learning based techniques (text classifiers) and framework for the task of automatically classifying the correct component for bug reports.
3. To investigate the usefulness of machine learning based techniques for the task of predicting if a component reassignment event will occur or not given the initial component assigned by the bug reporter.
4. To study component reassignment graphs and component reassignment probability and investigate their usefulness in improving the accuracy of correct component prediction.

2   Related Work and Research Contributions

Previous research shows that identifying the most competent developer to fix a given bug report is a challenging task and is error prone [4][7][8][11]. The work done on the topic of bug tossing (reassignment of bug reports to various developers) is most closely related to the research study presented in this paper. Recently several researchers have looked into the phenomenon of bug tossing and proposed several techniques (based on machine learning and tossing graphs) to perform automatic triaging and reduce the percentage of bug tossing events [4][7][8][11]. We briefly review closely related work and list some of the key differences between prior study and the work presented in this paper.

To the best of our knowledge and literature study, the initial work on the top of bug tossing was performed by Jeong et al [11]. Jeong et al. introduced the idea of deriving bug tossing graphs from historical data and employ a graph model based on Markov chains to better assign developers to bug reports. Their study reveals that tossing increases the time-to-correction for a bug and show that a significant percentage (about 40%) of bugs (Eclipse and Mozilla project) have been tossed (reassigned to a different developer) at-least once [11]. Bhattacharya et al propose a method (an extension to prior triaging approaches) to reduce tossing path lengths and validate their approach on popular open-source projects like Eclipse and Mozilla [4]. Chen et al. presents an approach that computes textual similarity between bug reports using a vector space model and uses this information in conjunction with tossing graphs to improve bug assignments [7]. Guo et al. mention that bug report reassignments is a commonly occurring phenomenon during the bug fixing process and yet has rarely been studies. They present a large-scale quantitative and qualitative analysis (in Microsoft Windows Vista operating system project) on the topic of reasons for the software bug report reassignments [8].

The key difference between previous work and this study is that while previous work focuses on *developer reassignment* or tossing, our research focuses on *component reassignment*. While there has been work done in the area of *bug report quality* [1][2][3][10][12] and *bug tossing* (reassignment of a bug report to developers) [4][9][11], we identify a *research gap* and a phenomenon which is not yet explored in-depth in the literature on Mining Software Repositories. The problem of incorrect assignment of component field (crucial information for bug fixing) in a bug report is not yet studied closely and the objective of our research is to improve our understanding and throw light on this relatively unexplored phenomenon. In context to existing work, this paper makes the following *unique contributions*:

1. This paper is the *first* focused empirical study on the topic of *incorrect assignment* of *component* in bug reports. We perform experiments on bug report data downloaded from Eclipse and Mozilla (popular open-source projects) and report measurement results.
2. We perform a series of experiments using a *machine learning framework* for the task of predicting the correct component for a given bug report and report classification accuracy results.
3. We perform a series of experiments using a machine learning framework for the task of predicting if a component reassignment event will occur or not given the initial component assigned by the bug reporter.
4. We study *component reassignment graphs* and *component reassignment probabilities* and present our insights.

3   Empirical Analysis

3.1   Experimental Dataset

We perform empirical analysis on publicly available dataset from two popular open-source projects (Eclipse and Mozilla) so that our results can be replicated and used for benchmarking or comparisons. Table 1 presents the details of the experimental dataset obtained by downloading and parsing (XML and HTML files) bug reports from Bugzilla (the issue tracking system used by Eclipse[1] and Mozilla[2] Project) defect tracking systems. The experimental dataset consists of 28618 fixed bug reports from Eclipse project and 16268 bug reports from Mozilla project. Table 1 shows the number of distinct products and components for Eclipse and Mozilla projects. For example, JDT (Java development tools) and Platform (Eclipse platform) are products within Eclipse and APT and Core are components within the JDT product. Table 1 displays the number of distinct reporter, versions and assigned-to in the evaluation dataset. For example, the number of distinct products and components for the Eclipse dataset (28618 fixed bug reports) are 98 and 507 respectively.

---

[1] https://bugs.eclipse.org/bugs/
[2] https://bugzilla.mozilla.org/

Table 1. Experimental dataset details (open-source Eclipse and Mozilla projects)

	Eclipse	Mozilla
From Bug ID	200000	400000
To Bug ID	250000	450000
From Date (Reported)	Aug/2007	Oct/2007
To Date (Reported)	Oct/2008	Aug/2008
Fixed Bugs	28618	16268
Distinct Component	507	449
Distinct Product	98	44
Distinct Assigned To	1078	789
Distinct Version	140	70
Distinct Reporter	3439	2229

3.2   Statistics on Reassignment Events

Bug reports consists of fields like component, product, assignee and version which can be re-assigned after reporting or initial assignment. Guo et al. present a large-scale quantitative and qualitative analysis of the bug reassignment process in the Microsoft Windows Vista operating system project and categorized five primary reasons for reassignments of assignee fields: finding the root cause, determining ownership, poor bug report quality, hard to determine proper fix, and workload balancing [8]. We perform statistical analysis on the evaluation dataset to compute percentage of reassignment on four fields: component, product, assignee and version.

Tables 2 and 3 displays data on the percentage of fixed bug reports in the experimental dataset that have undergone component, product, assignee and version reassignments (the values are computed by extracting relevant information from the bug history available in Bugzilla defecting tracking system). The data in Tables 2 and 3 is presented in a format that enables comparison and contrast between percentage of reassignment across four fields (component, product, assignee and version). Empirical results in Table 2 reveals that the percentage of bug reports in Eclipse undergoing component reassignment is 15.75% (average of 98 products) and 39.63% for the EMF product (one of the products within Eclipse). As shown in Table 3, the percentage of bug reports in Mozilla project (average of 44 products) undergoing component reassignment is 24.21% which is much higher than the corresponding value in Eclipse. Based on the experimental results, we draw a conclusion that there is a significant percentage (15.75% for Eclipse project, 24.21% for Mozilla project) of fixed bug reports for which a component reassignment activity is performed (and hence we believe an interesting topic for scientific investigation).

We performed a manual inspection of bug reports in the valuation dataset and noticed a phenomenon wherein component, product, assignee and version reassignment happens multiple times. We conducted empirical analysis to compute the number of times component, product, assignee and version reassignments

Table 2. [*Eclipse Project*] NUM: number of bug reports (BRs), PER: % of BRs in the experimental dataset, %CR: % of BRs having component reassignment event, %PR: % of BRs having product reassignment event, %AR: % of BRs having assignee reassignment event, %VR: % of BRs having version reassignment event.

Product	NUM	PER	%CR	%PR	%AR	%VR
BIRT	2879	10.06	22.17	0.35	**94.34**	1.36
Community	1168	4.08	4.63	1.29	26.45	0.60
EMF	857	2.99	**39.63**	1.64	25.56	**37.81**
Equinox	1771	6.18	13.88	4.69	61.16	2.66
JDT	1449	5.06	18.88	**5.32**	79.92	4.56
PDE	1242	4.33	8.94	4.51	85.67	2.02
Platform	3083	10.77	13.92	5.23	77.36	4.38
Web Tools	116	0.40	13.80	1.63	37.07	1.63
All [**98**]	28618	100	15.75	6.77	61.77	9.88

Table 3. [*Mozilla Project*] Table 2 defines labels NUM, PER, %CR, %PR, %AR and %VR

Product	NUM	PER	%CR	%PR	%AR	%VR
addons	768	4.72	15.76	3.52	64.98	10.29
Calendar	658	4.04	11.71	1.07	74.02	17.63
Core	3952	24.29	25.26	17.34	64.00	11.11
Firefox	1811	11.13	**40.87**	3.48	55.22	**28.00**
Localiz.	837	5.14	11.59	6.82	24.14	1.08
mozilla.org	2396	14.72	32.06	11.02	**80.22**	11.27
Toolkit	734	4.51	20.58	**63.22**	70.71	25.21
All [**44**]	16268	100	24.21	16.45	61.97	15.62

happens during the lifetime (from creation to close) of each fixed bug in our experimental dataset (refer to Table 4. The data in Table 4 (Left: Eclipse Project, Right: Mozilla Project) reveals the exact percentages of fixed bug reports on which the reassignment activities (enabling comparison and contrast across four fields: component, product, assignee and version) are performed more than once. Table 4 indicates that for Eclipse project, 47.69% of bug reports in the evaluation dataset had one assignee reassignment event and 14.08% of the bug reports had more than one assignee reassignment event. For Mozilla project, 5.79% of the bug reports in the evaluation dataset had more than one component reassignment event. Based on the empirical results displayed in Table 4, we draw a conclusion that multiple reassignment (during the life-cycle of a bug report) of component, product, assignee and version is a phenomenon which is present in open-source projects like Eclipse and Mozilla. An interesting result is that amongst the four fields, assignee field is most frequently reassigned and component field is next (in terms of the percentage of reassignment activities) after assignee field.

We perform a manual inspection of the developer comments (online discussion

Table 4. [*Left: Eclipse Project, Right: Mozilla Project*] Distribution of bug reports across number of times (0,1,2,3, $\geq$ 4) a component, product, assignee and version reassignment event takes place within the lifetime of a fixed bug report

	0	1	2	3	$\geq$4
Component	84.25	13.25	1.96	0.36	0.18
Product	93.23	6.42	0.27	0.06	0.02
Assignee	38.23	47.69	9.51	3.10	1.47
Version	90.12	8.57	1.20	0.06	0.05

	0	1	2	3	$\geq$4
Component	75.79	18.42	4.56	0.86	0.37
Product	83.55	14.53	1.64	0.21	0.07
Assignee	38.03	50.19	7.49	2.95	1.34
Version	84.38	14.16	1.11	0.28	0.07

forum in Bugzilla) to understand the reason for component reassignment in bug reports. Table 5 displays some of the developer comments (entered in threaded discussion) throwing light on component reassignment phenomenon. The comments in Table 5 shows that indentifying the correct component is non-trivial and developers often make mistake in component assignment. As shown Table 5, bug reporters and developers are sometimes not sure of the correct component, often assign bug reports to wrong component and later perform reassignments and discuss (through online forums in Bugzilla) amongst the team to identify the correct component for a given bug report.

We measure the difference between the creation timestamp of the bug report and the timestamp for component and product reassignment events. Table 6 shows the minimum, maximum, lower and upper quartile values for the time difference (in hours) for fixed bug reports in the Eclipse and Mozilla experimental dataset. The median value for the Eclipse project (component reassignment) is 340 and the median value for the Mozilla project is 157. The numbers clearly indicate that component reassignment (or correction) is not immediate and the time difference between reporting time and first reassignment or between subsequent reassignments (for example, between first reassignment and second reassignment) is significant. Hence we believe that automated techniques that can guide developers for the task of correct component assignment aimed at reducing the percentage of reassignment events and time between reassignments can be useful for practitioners involved in the bug fixing process. Figure 1 shows differences phases in the life-cycle of an Eclipse bug report (BUGID 202407). As shown in Figure, the bug is reported at timestamp $T1$ (by developer Alex) and undergoes a component (from Data Access to Connectivity), product (BIRT to Data Tools) and version (2.2.0 to unspecified) reassignment event at timestamp $T2$. At timestamp $T3$, the bug report undergoes assignee reassignment (from birt-dataaccess-inbox to ichan) and version reassignment (from unspecified to 1.5). Component reassignment again happens at timestamp $T4$ (Connectivity to Open Data Access) and finally the bug report is fixed at $T5$ (by developer Ichan) and closed at $T6$ (by developer Bfitzpat). Figure 1 (depicting the bug history and actions perform on Eclipse BUGID 202407) indicates that component, product, version and assignee at the time of bug reporting was not correct as a result of which it undergoes reassignments. The component reassignment happens twice and states at timestamp $T2$, $T3$ and $T4$ are result of reassignments.

Table 5. Illustrative examples of developer comments (on the issue of component reassignment) in Bugzilla threaded discussions

Eclipse		Mozilla	
BUGID	**Comment**	**BUGID**	**Comment**
200513	Not sure if this is us or SWT.	433562	Then this is an addons.mozilla.org bug, not a download manager bug. I've already moved the bug to the proper component.
200849	This is probably the wrong component. We're looking to add a section to the help at help.eclipse.org.	432653	It's a "Provider:GDATA" problem and no "Calendar View" one
200889	I believe this has been incorrectly assigned to the ATNA component	432131	Probably not a theme issue, but I have no idea where to look for the real cause. Might be widget, might be something else.
202384	Bug was categorized as JDT/APT - I don't think it has anything to do with either. I'll attempt to recategorize it.	431665	Definitely a TE bug. the component where this bug now lives.
202893	I notice that this is assigned to User Assistance. Paul, do you think that the bug is in UA code or in Platform UI code?	431451	This should go to Server ops.

3.3   Automatic Component Assignment Using Linguistic Features

One of the research objectives of the work presented in this paper is to derive a statistical and probabilistic model from historical data to predict the correct component for a given bug report. We frame the problem of automatic component assignment as a text classification problem. The input to the classifier is a bug report (title and description) and the output is one of the category (or Top-K categories) from a pre-defined finite number of discrete categories or classes (software components). Every bug report is assigned to only one component (no cross-cutting categorization) and hence the output categories (in the text classification framework) are both exhaustive and mutually exclusive. Every bug report is assigned to exactly one of the pre-defined class. We leverage LingPipe[3] which implements several types of text classifiers and conduct a series of classification experiments.

We perform experiments to investigate the extent to which two different classifiers (TFIDF and DLM) implemented in LingPipe can be used to automatically predict the correct component of a bug report based on the title and textual description [6] provided in the bug report. TFIDF (term-frequency (TF) and inverse document frequency (IDF)) classifier belongs to the class of discriminative classifiers whereas DLM (Dynamic Language Model) is a language model classifier. We frame the task of inducing a classifier as a supervised learning task

---

[3] http://alias-i.com/lingpipe/

Table 6. Minimum, maximum, lower and upper quartile values for the time difference (in hours) between the bug creation timestamp and the component (CM) or Product (PC) reassignment timestamp for fixed bug reports in the Eclipse (EC) and Mozilla (MZ) experimental dataset

	EC-CM	EC-PD	MZ-CM	MZ-PD
Max	30506	30506	27628	29961
3rd Quart	7069	13873	5421	6540
Median	340	5203	157	1721
1st Quart	14	50	4	17
Min	0	0	0	0

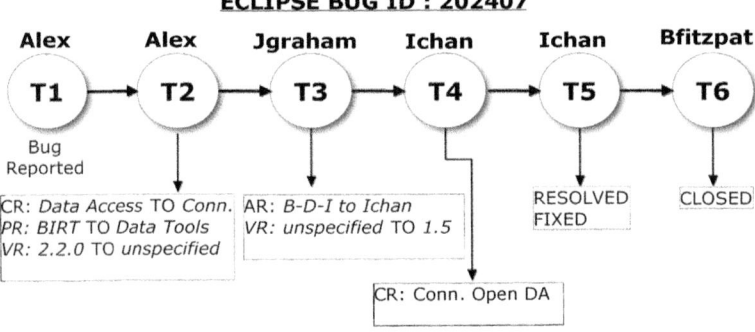

Fig. 1. Lifecycle of Eclipse BUGID 202407 showing PR (product reassignment), CR (component reassignment), AR (assignee reassignment) and VR (version reassignment)

(inferring a function or the classifier) which requires the experimental dataset to be divided into two sets: training (for learning a classifier) and test dataset (for evaluating the performance of the classifier). For TFIDF classifier, linguistic features from bug reports are extracted using the *IndoEuropeanTokenizerFactory* implemented in LingPipe. For the DLM classifier, we train a character based language models and set the size of the NGRAM to be 6 characters.

We divide the experimental dataset into training (bug reports from 20000 to 230000 for Eclipse and bug reports from 400000 to 430000 for Mozilla) and test dataset (bug reports from 23001 to 250000 for Eclipse and bug reports from 430001 to 450000 for Mozilla) and derived a predictive model for 12 products (number of components for each product is displayed in Tables 7 and 8). The ground-truth (correct component for each fixed bug report) is already available as all the bug reports in the evaluation dataset are fixed and closed. Tables 7 and 8 displays accuracy result for two classifiers (default settings of TF/IDF classifier and Dynamic Language Model classifier implemented in LingPipe text processing toolkit). We report Top N accuracy (considered a hit if the actual component is amongst the Top N component predictions) results and the performance results in Table 7 and 8 indicate that word-level and character-level features in

Table 7. Top N (N = 1,2,3,4 and 5) accuracy results (component prediction) for two machine learning (ML) classifiers (TFIDF and DLM) on *Eclipse* project dataset (COMP: Number of components, TRAIN: size of training dataset, TEST: size of test dataset)

PROD.	CMP	TRAIN	TEST	ML	TOP 1	TOP 2	TOP 3	TOP 4	TOP 5
Community	26	737	431	TFIDF	48.95%	65.88%	73.53%	79.09%	83.96%
				DLM	42.45%	56.37%	68.20%	74.69%	79.56%
Platform	17	2027	1056	TFIDF	46.68%	65.24%	76.50%	82.27%	85.86%
				DLM	54.07%	72.06%	78.49%	82.08%	84.44%
BIRT	12	1837	1042	TFIDF	56.33%	75.61%	83.95%	89.80%	93.63%
				DLM	62.18%	78.01%	85.78%	90.09%	93.06%
Equinox	9	1207	564	TFIDF	69.32%	87.05%	92.54%	96.08%	98.03%
				DLM	68.79%	84.92%	92.18%	95.90%	97.49%
JDT	6	969	480	TFIDF	60.62%	82.29%	94.16%	98.32%	99.80%
				DLM	62.29%	81.66%	92.91%	98.53%	99.58%
PDE	5	762	480	TFIDF	68.33%	85.41%	94.78%	98.11%	100%
				DLM	73.95%	86.03%	94.98%	97.06%	100%

free-form textual reports can be used as discriminatory signals for the task of automatic component classification. As shown in Table 7 (Eclipse project), the Top 1 accuracy for the DLM multi-class classifier varies from a minimum of 42.45% (26 mutually exclusive classes) to a maximum of 73.95% (5 mutually exclusive classes). Table 8 (Mozilla project) reveals that the Top 5 accuracy of the TFIDF classifier varies from a minimum of 63.86% (91 components) to a maximum of 91.88% (24 components). We perform empirical analysis to discover correlation or association between terms in bug reports and the components. The purpose is to understand and uncover the discriminatory terms used by the machine learning classifiers (such as the TFIDF classifier) to perform the text categorization task. We represent bug reports as bag of terms (generated by converting the sequence of characters into tokens using a tokenizer) and generate the distribution of words for each category or class. We compute the most frequent terms for each category and compute the probability of each term given a category. If the probability of a term in one specific category is high (i.e., the term is frequent or prevalent) and low in other categories then the term is a good discriminatory feature for the purpose of performing text classification.

We investigate the JDT product (Eclipse project) consisting of six components: APT, CORE, DEBUG, DOC, TEXT and UI. We compute the probability of each unique term in the training dataset corpus in each of the six categories. We observe that *java*, *eclipse*, *org*, *jdt* and *core* are frequent terms in all the six categories and hence are not discriminatory. However, we notice that there are certain terms which are discriminatory for a specific class. Table 9 reveals that the probability of the terms *type* or *junit* is 25 times more in class APT than in class DOC. The probability of the terms *jface* and *text* is significantly higher in TEXT component in contrast to other component. As indicated in Table 9, the probability of the term *kit* is very high in the DOC category in comparison to

Table 8. Top N (N = 1,2,3,4 and 5) accuracy results (component prediction) for two machine learning (ML) classifiers (TFIDF and DLM) on *Mozilla* project dataset (COMP: Number of components, TRAIN: size of training dataset, TEST: size of test dataset)

PROD.	CMP	TRAIN	TEST	ML	TOP 1	TOP 2	TOP 3	TOP 4	TOP 5
Core	91	2814	1138	TFIDF	38.57%	50.78%	56.84%	60.79%	63.86%
				DLM	36.11%	45.51%	50.95%	55.25%	57.79%
Toolkit	26	522	212	TFIDF	43.80%	62.37%	68.56%	75.70%	80.46%
				DLM	34.76%	50.47%	58.09%	64.75%	71.89%
Firefox	25	1415	396	TFIDF	50.75%	68.67%	77.50%	82.80%	85.57%
				DLM	53.53%	63.37%	70.94%	77.00%	80.53%
Mozilla.org	24	1321	1075	TFIDF	53.76%	75.89%	84.63%	89.28%	91.88%
				DLM	61.20%	80.45%	88.82%	91.14%	92.16%
Calendar	19	433	225	TFIDF	40.44%	59.55%	66.66%	76.43%	80.87%
				DLM	40.44%	56.44%	71.10%	79.54%	84.42%
addons.mozilla	16	495	273	TFIDF	55.67%	69.95%	80.20%	85.69%	90.45%
				DLM	58.97%	72.88%	82.77%	85.33%	87.52%

other categories. Terms *debug* and *lib* are common in bug reports belonging to the DEBUG component. The data in Table 9 clearly shows that certain terms are more common in bug reports belonging to one class in contrast to other classes. We perform similar experiments on Equinox product (consisting of nine components) of Eclipse platform (TFIDF classifier Top 1 accuracy is 69.32% and DLM classifier Top 1 accuracy is 68.79%) and observed correlation between certain terms and specific classes. We observe that terms *eclipse*, *org*, *equinox* and *java* are frequent in majority of the classes and hence do not have discriminatory power. We discover that terms *password* and *auth* are discriminatory for the SECURITY component. Term *site* is discriminatory for the component P2. Terms *framework* and *launcher* are frequent in bug reports belonging to the component FRAMEWORK in contrast to other components.

3.4   Component Reassignment Prediction

We perform experiments to examine the degree to which the derived statistical model (for automatic component categorization) can be used to make predictions for the task of predicting if an incoming bug report will be component reassigned or not. We apply the induced predictive model on a given bug report and compare the predictions with the initial component assigned by the bug reporter. If the best category (for computing Top 1 accuracy) does not match the initial component then we predict a component reassignment event. Similarly, for computing Top 2 accuracy we consider top two component predictions. We perform a series of experiments (for which the ground-truth is already available) and report the accuracy results of our predictor. The empirical results displayed in Table 10 indicate that Top 1 prediction accuracy (Eclipse project) of the proposed solution varies from 45.24% to 73.95%. Table 10 provide details

Table 9. Few examples of discriminatory features (terms) or important words discovered from the experimental dataset (Eclipse Project: JDT Product) to demonstrate correlation between terms and categories (components))

	TERM	APT	CORE	DEBUG	DOC	TEXT	UI
1	file	2.541689	1.219373	2.11113	1.580986	1	1.601105
2	type	25.42729	43.36233	13.08619	1	15.81292	18.3523
3	junit	25.42729	10.38253	4.005976	1	1.83097	14.06563
4	compile	10.66306	104.6105	1.869455	1	8.156138	8.171464
5	swt	1	44.14341	70.65426	1.219162	185.2767	96.19375
6	workbench	1	38.39945	40.04826	6.095812	108.1626	70.71629
7	debug	2.956659	7.652804	94.66307	1.201549	1	4.02394
8	lib	4.927765	5.765812	283.9892	6.007745	1	2.414364
9	lang	10.66306	25.38921	41.92921	1	14.1484	16.20897
10	doc	1	2.021024	6.837509	45.10901	1.420522	1.469854
11	kit	9.401176	1	21.42688	286.539	9.538987	1.535373
12	jface	1	37.33575	28.97801	1.219162	81.37564	59.28409
13	text	1	26.69879	12.69823	1.219162	70.41732	30.21366
14	display	1	22.01852	38.09469	3.657487	65.54696	54.05795
15	action	1	14.99812	14.6518	1.219162	46.47137	40.01268

results across two projects (Eclipse and Mozilla), 12 products and two classifiers (TF/IDF and Dynamic Language Model with NGRAM size = 6).

3.5   Component Reassignment Graphs

We conduct a series of experiments to understand component reassignment phenomenon from the perspective of network analysis. While the research goal of the work presented in Section 3.3 is to investigate the extent to which linguistic or textual features (sequence of characters, words, terms) present in bug reports can be used as discriminatory features for automatic component assignment, the goal of the work presented in this section is to view the component reassignment events as a graph or network and uncover patterns that can be used for the task of automatic component assignment. The proposal to construct component reassignment graph is based on our intuition and insight that there are some components which are more prone to reassignment and there is a correlation between certain components assigned by the bug reporter and the component to which the bug report is finally reassigned. We explain our idea using a concrete example (Figures 2) derived from Eclipse project experimental dataset. The bug report history contains information about initial component assignment (by the bug reporter) and subsequent component reassignments (if any) by the traiger or developers. We create a graph (called as the component reassignment graph) where nodes represent components and an arc from one node to another represents reassignment from one component to another. Thus the nodes represent components and arcs or links represent component reassignment relationship.

Table 10. [*Eclipse (ECL) and Mozilla (MZL)* Project] Accuracy results for the task of predicting if a component will be reassigned or not)

ECL PROD.	ML	TOP 1	TOP 2	MZL PROD.	ML	TOP 1	TOP 2
Core	TFIDF	52.19%	62.03%	Community	TFIDF	51.27%	67.28%
	DLM	50.52%	57.46%		DLM	45.24%	57.54%
Toolkit	TFIDF	54.76%	70.47%	Platform	TFIDF	52.55%	66.00%
	DLM	48.09%	60.00%		DLM	59.94%	72.72%
Firefox	TFIDF	59.09%	74.24%	BIRT	TFIDF	63.53%	73.32%
	DLM	60.35%	67.92%		DLM	67.75%	74.28%
Mozilla.org	TFIDF	59.34%	76.83%	Equinox	TFIDF	73.22%	89.00%
	DLM	63.62%	76.83%		DLM	72.34%	86.87%
Calendar	TFIDF	46.22%	62.22%	JDT	TFIDF	66.25%	75.00%
	DLM	44.88%	58.66%		DLM	68.12%	76.04%
addons.mozilla.org	TFIDF	65.56%	75.82%	PDE	TFIDF	68.54%	82.29%
	DLM	68.86%	77.28%		DLM	73.95%	83.12%

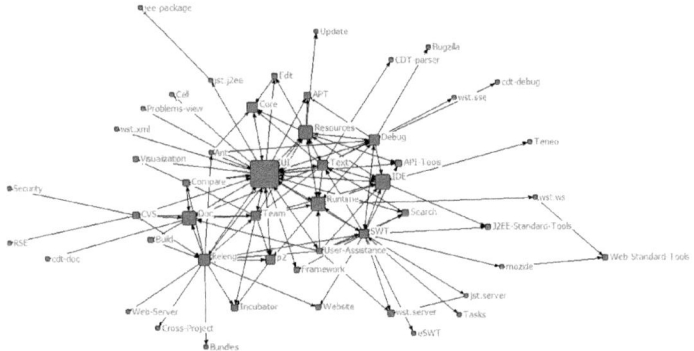

Fig. 2. A component reassignment graph (Eclipse project and Product Platform). The size of the node is proportional to the node's in-degree.

Figure 2 is a component reassignment graphs drawn using UCINET[4]) revealing the degree of reassignment relationship between components for a specific product (Eclipse Project and Product Platform).

Figures 2 is a directed graphs in which the out-degree (degree also referred to as valency) of a node (or a vertex) represents the number of times the component has been removed and the in-degree of a node represents the number of times the component (represented by the node) is added. In Figure 2, the size of the node is proportional to the node's in-degree. Figure 2 reveals that the in-degree (represented by the size of the node) for components like UI, IDE, Runtime, Doc and Resources is higher in contrast to other components. Table 11 shows that the reassignment relationship between pair of components varies and we believe

---

[4] http://www.analytictech.com/ucinet/

Table 11. Illustrative examples of number of times a component is removed (REM) and a different component is added or assigned (ADD) for Eclipse project and Platform product

	ADD	REM	NUM		ADD	REM	NUM
1	SWT	UI	59	7	Releng	P2	13
2	User Ast.	UI	41	8	SWT	IDE	11
3	UI	SWT	40	9	Team	UI	10
4	Text	UI	22	10	UI	Debug	10
5	SWT	Text	18	11	UI	Resources	10
6	Debug	UI	17	12	UI	Test	9

Table 12. Illustrative list of components (Eclipse, Platform) in increasing order of reassignment probability [P(RSN)]

Component	Incorrect	Correct	Total	P(RSN)
Compare	3	76	79	0.0379
Ant	2	38	40	0.05
Team	6	105	111	0.0540
Debug	19	168	187	0.1016
CVS	8	56	64	0.125
UI	208	967	1175	0.1770
Text	34	94	128	0.2656
Resources	24	60	84	0.2857
Runtime	24	23	47	0.5106
Website	12	2	14	0.8571

that this useful knowledge can be learned from historical data and can be used for making future predictions on automatic component reassignments. Table 12 is an Illustrative list of components (Eclipse Project, Platform Product) in increasing order of reassignment probability $P(RSN)$. Reassignment probability is the probability that the component will be reassigned or not and is computed as the ratio of two values: number of times the initially reported component is accurately classified (correct and no reassignment happens) to the number of the times the initially reported component is incorrectly classified (as a result of which a component reassignment event happens).

Figure 3 illustrates the architecture diagram for a system that combines a content-based (such as a TFIDF or a DLM based textual classifier) predictor with a link-based (component reassignment graph derived from historical data) predictor to make recommendation on the correct component or whether the assigned component will be reassigned or not. We perform experiments on Eclipse project data and observe that several times content-based classifier results in false positives (predicts a component to be reassigned when it should not be reassigned) outcomes. We believe that showing a score denoting the reassignment probability of component and the probability of a reassigning relationship with top k components can be useful to the developer.

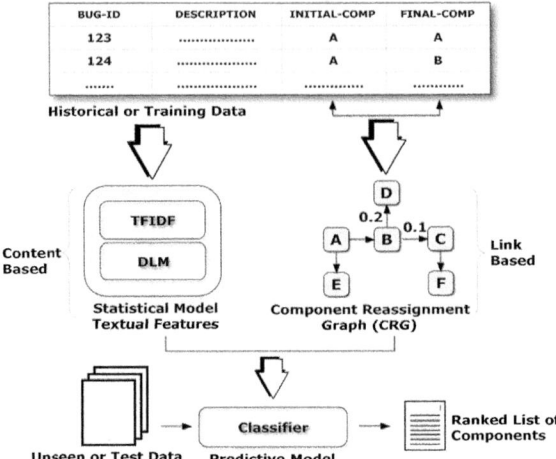

Fig. 3. Architecture diagram for the proposed automatic component reassignment system based on textual (terms present in bug reports) and link-based (derived from reassignment relationship) features

4   Summary

Empirical evidences demonstrate the presence of a phenomenon in which the initial component assigned by the bug reporter is later on reassigned during the life-cycle of a bug report. The study presented in this paper shows presence of correlation between terms in bug reports and components which can be exploited for the task of predicting the correct component of a bug report. We investigate the usefulness of machine learning based techniques for the task of predicting if a component reassignment event will occur or not given the initial component assigned by the bug reporter. Insights on component reassignment graphs and component reassignment probability are presented.

Acknowledgement. The work presented in this paper is partially supported by the Department of Science and Technology (DST, India) FAST grant awarded to the author. The author would like to acknowledge Sangeeta for her help in conducting experiments.

References

1. Bettenburg, N., Just, S., Schröter, A., Weiss, C., Premraj, R., Zimmermann, T.: What makes a good bug report? In: International Symposium on Foundations of software Engineering, SIGSOFT 2008/FSE-16, pp. 308–318. ACM, New York (2008)

2. Bettenburg, N., Just, S., Schröter, A., Weiss, C., Premraj, R., Zimmermann, T.: Quality of bug reports in eclipse. In: OOPSLA Workshop on Eclipse Technology eXchange. ACM Press, New York (2007)
3. Bettenburg, N., Premraj, R., Zimmermann, T., Kim, S.: Extracting structural information from bug reports. In: Working Conference on Mining Software Repositories, MSR 2008, pp. 27–30. ACM, New York (2008)
4. Bhattacharya, P., Neamtiu, I.: Fine-grained incremental learning and multi-feature tossing graphs to improve bug triaging. In: Inter. Conference on Software Maintenance, ICSM 2010, pp. 1–10. IEEE Computer Society, Washington, DC (2010)
5. Breu, S., Premraj, R., Sillito, J., Zimmermann, T.: Frequently asked questions in bug reports. Technical Report 2009-924-03, University of Calgary (March 2009)
6. Carpenter, B., Baldwin, B.: Natural Language Processing with LingPipe 4, draft edition. LingPipe Publishing, New York (2011)
7. Chen, L., Wang, X., Liu, C.: An approach to improving bug assignment with bug tossing graphs and bug similarities. JSW Journal of Software 6(3), 421–427 (2011)
8. Guo, P.J., Zimmermann, T., Nagappan, N., Murphy, B.: "not my bug!" and other reasons for software bug report reassignments. In: Computer Supported Cooperative Work, CSCW 2011, pp. 395–404. ACM, New York (2011)
9. Guo, P.J., Zimmermann, T., Nagappan, N., Murphy, B.: "Not My Bug!" and Other Reasons for Software Bug Report Reassignments. In: ACM Conference on Computer Supported Cooperative Work (2011)
10. Hooimeijer, P., Weimer, W.: Modeling bug report quality. In: IEEE/ACM International Conference on Automated Software Engineering, ASE 2007, pp. 34–43. ACM, New York (2007)
11. Jeong, G., Kim, S., Zimmermann, T.: Improving bug triage with bug tossing graphs. In: European Software Engineering Conference and the ACM SIGSOFT Symposium on the Foundations of Software Engineering, ESEC/FSE 2009, pp. 111–120. ACM, New York (2009)
12. Zimmermann, T., Premraj, R., Bettenburg, N., Just, S., Schröter, A., Weiss, C.: What makes a good bug report? IEEE Transactions on Software Engineering 36(5), 618–643 (2010)
13. Zimmermann, T., Premraj, R., Sillito, J., Breu, S.: Improving bug tracking systems. In: Companion to the 31th International Conference on Software Engineering (May 2009)

Incremental Dynamic Updates
with First-Class Contexts

Erwann Wernli, Mircea Lungu, and Oscar Nierstrasz

Software Composition Group
University of Bern, Switzerland
http://scg.unibe.ch

Abstract. Highly available software systems occasionally need to be updated while avoiding downtime. Dynamic software updates reduce downtime, but still require the system to reach a quiescent state in which a global update can be performed. This can be difficult for multi-threaded systems. We present a novel approach to dynamic updates using first-class contexts, called *Theseus*. First-class contexts make global updates unnecessary: existing threads run to termination in an old context, while new threads start in a new, updated context; consistency between contexts is ensured with the help of bidirectional transformations. We show how first-class contexts offer a practical and flexible approach to incremental dynamic updates, with acceptable overhead.

Keywords: dynamic language, dynamic software update, reflection.

1 Introduction

Real software systems must be regularly updated to keep up with changing requirements. Downtime may not be tolerable for highly available systems, which must then be updated dynamically, *e.g.*, web servers. The key challenge for dynamically updating such systems is to ensure consistency and correctness while maximizing availability.

The most popular scheme for dynamic updates is to interrupt the application to perform a global update of both the code and the state of the program [19,26,25]. Such updates are inherently unsafe if performed at an arbitrary point in time: running threads might run both old and new code in an incoherent manner while old methods on the stack might presume type signatures that are no longer valid, possibly leading to run-time type errors. Quiescent global update points must be selected to ensure safe updates, but such points may be difficult to reach for multi-threaded systems [18,26]. More generally, a global update might not be possible due to the nature of the change, for example it would fail to update anonymous connections to an FTP server that mandates authentication after the update: the missing information cannot be provided *a posteriori* [19].

Instead of global updates, we propose *incremental* updates. During an incremental update, clients might see different versions of the system until the update

C.A. Furia and S. Nanz (Eds.): TOOLS Europe 2012, LNCS 7304, pp. 304–319, 2012.

eventually completes. Each version is represented by a first-class *context*, which can be manipulated reflectively and enables the update scheme to be tailored to the nature of the application. For instance, the update of a web application can be rolled out on a per-thread, or per-session basis. In the latter case, visitors always see a consistent version of the application. Such a scheme would not be possible with a global update: one would need to wait until all existing sessions have expired before starting new ones. The overall consistency of the data is maintained by running bidirectional transformations to synchronize the representations of objects shared across contexts. We show that the number of such shared objects is significantly smaller than the number of objects local to a context, and that this strategy fits well with the nature of the event-based systems we are interested in.

We introduced first-class contexts in a previous workshop paper [27], but this original proof-of-concept suffered from several practical limitations. In contrast to our earlier work, we support now class versioning, garbage collection and lazy transformations, and we rely on program transformations rather than changes to the virtual machine. Bidirectional transformations have been used to cope with version mismatches in other settings (namely C systems [4], databases [5], and type theory [7]). However, neither of these approaches modeled context explicitly, nor did they tackle object-oriented systems in their full complexity, taking into consideration type safety, performance, concurrency and garbage collection. The main contribution of this paper is to demonstrate that first-class contexts offer a practical means to dynamically update software.

First, we present our *Theseus* approach informally with the help of a running example in section 2. We present our model in detail in section 3 and our implementation in section 4. We validate our approach in section 5 and demonstrate that it is practical. We put our approach into perspective in section 6 and we compare it with related work in section 7 before we conclude in section 8.

2   Running Example

To illustrate our approach let us consider the implementation of one of several available Smalltalk web servers[1]. Its architecture is simple; a web server listens to a port, and dispatches requests to so-called services that accept requests and produce responses. For the sake of our running example, let us assume that the server keeps count of the total number of requests that have been served. Figure 1 illustrates the relevant classes.

2.1   The Problem with Updates

Let us consider the evolution of the Response API, which introduces chunked data transfer[2], also depicted in Figure 1. Assume that instead of sending "Hello

---

[1] See http://www.squeaksource.com/WebClient.html (The name is misleading since the project contains both an HTTP client *and* server).

[2] See version 75 of the project.

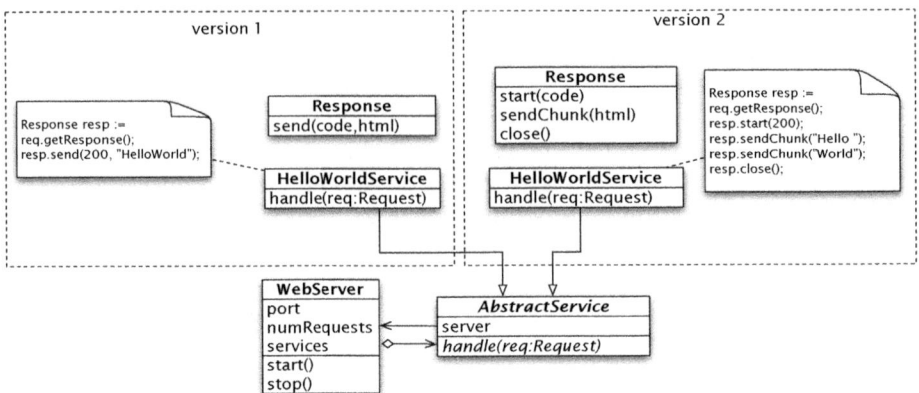

Fig. 1. Design of the web server and a simple behavioral update

World" over the wire we need to produce a sensible answer that takes some time. Installing such an update *globally* raises several challenges. First, both the HelloWorldService and Response classes must be installed together: *How can we install multiple related classes atomically?*

Second, the methods impacted by the update can be modified or added only when no request is being served: *When can we guarantee that the installation will not interfere with the processing of ongoing requests?*

Rather than performing a global update, it would be more appealing to do an *incremental* update, where ongoing requests continue to be processed according to the old code, and new requests are served using the new code. Note that the granularity of the increment might differ depending on the update. We could imagine that the modification of a check-out process spanning multiple pages would imply that the increment be the web session rather than the web request. Our solution to enable incremental updates is to reify the execution *context* into a first-class entity.

Not only the *behavior* but also the *structure* of classes can also change. Fields can be added or removed, and the type of a field can change. As a matter of fact, in a subsequent version of the project[3], the author added a field siteUrl to the WebServer class. Unfortunately, the server is an object shared between multiple requests, and each service holds a reference back to the server. If the object structure is updated globally while different versions of the code run to serve requests, old versions of methods might access fields at the wrong index. While the problem for field addition can be solved easily by ensuring new fields are added at the end, we need to consider type changes as well. For instance, one could imagine that in the future newest versions will store the siteUrl as an HttpUrl rather than a String. Therefore, the general problem remains: *How can we ensure consistent access to objects whose structure (position or type of fields) has changed?*

---

[3] See version 82 of the project.

Our solution to ensure consistent access is to keep one representation of the object per context and to synchronize the representations using bidirectional transformations. Once there is no reference any longer to a context, it is garbage-collected and the corresponding representations of objects as well.

2.2   Lifecycle of an Incremental Update

Let us consider the addition of the field `siteUrl` in the `WebServer` class in more detail. The following steps describe how an *incremental* update can be installed with Theseus[4], the implementation of our approach, while avoiding the problems presented above.

First, the application must be adapted so that we can "push" an update to the system and activate it. Here is how one would typically adapt an event-based server system, such as a web server.

0. *Preparation.* First, a global variable `latestContext` is added to track the latest execution context to be used. Second, an administrative page is added to the web server where an administrator can push updates to the system; the uploaded code will be loaded dynamically. Third, the main loop that listens to incoming requests is modified so that when a new thread is spawned to handle the incoming request, the latest execution context is used. Fourth, the thread that listens to incoming connections in a loop is modified so that it is restarted periodically in the latest context. Note that the listening socket can be passed to the new thread without ever being closed.

After these preliminary modifications the system can be started, and now it supports dynamic updates. The life cycle of an update would be as follows:

1. *Bootstrap.* After the system bootstraps, the application runs in a default context named the *Root* context. The global variable `latestContext` is initialized to refer to the *Root* context. At this stage only one context exists and the system is similar to a non-contextual system.
2. *Offline evolution.* During development, the field `siteUrl` is added to `WebServer` and other related changes are installed.
3. *Update preparation.* The developer creates a class called `UpdatedContext`, which specifies the variations in the program to be rolled out dynamically. This is done by implementing a bidirectional transformation that converts the program state between the *Root* context and the *Updated* context. Objects will be transformed one at a time. By default, the identity transformation is assumed, and only a custom transformation for the `WebServer` class is necessary in our case.
4. *Update push.* Using the administrative web interface, the developer uploads the class `UpdatedContext` as well as the other classes that will be required by the context. The application loads the code dynamically. It detects that one

---

[4] In reference to Theseus' paradox: if every part of a ship is replaced, is it still the same ship?

class is a context and instantiates it. Contexts are related to each other by a ancestor-successor relationship. The ancestor of the newly created context is the active context. The global variable `latestContext` is updated to refer to the newly created instance of the *Updated* context.

5. *Update activation.* When a new incoming request is accepted, the application spawns a new thread to serve the request in the `latestContext` (which is now the *Updated* context) while existing threads terminate in the *Root* context.

6. *Incremental update.* When the web server is accessed in the *Updated* context for the first time, the new version of the class is dynamically loaded, and the instance is *migrated*. Migration is called when the object is accessed from a different context for the first time. In our case, this results in the fields `port` and `services` being copied, and the field `siteUrl` being initialized with a default value. Fields can be accessed safely from either the *Root* or *Updated* context, as each context has its own representation of the object. To ensure that the count of requests processed so far, `numRequests`, remains consistent in both contexts, bidirectional transformations between the representations are used. They are executed *lazily*: writing a new value in a field in one context only invalidates the representation of the object in the other context. The representation in the other context will be *synchronized* only when it is accessed again. Synchronization is called lazily when changes happen to objects that have already been migrated.

7. *Garbage collection.* Eventually the listener thread is restarted, and all requests in the old context terminate. A context only holds weakly onto its ancestor so when no code runs in the old context any longer, the context is finalized. The finalization forces the migration of all objects in the old context that have not been migrated yet. The old context and its object representations can then be garbage-collected. It must be noted that at the conceptual level, all objects in memory are migrated. In practice, only objects that are shared between contexts need to be migrated.

3   First-Class Context

Our approach relies on a simple, yet fundamental, language change: the state of an object is contextual. We assume, without loss of generality, throughout the rest of the paper that at most two contexts exist at a time, which we refer to as the "old" and "new" contexts. Clearly, the model could be generalized to support any number of co-existing contexts.

3.1   User-Defined Update Strategy

Contexts are first-class entities in our system. Programmers have complete control over the dynamic update of objects and classes. Contexts are ordinary instances of the class `Context`, shown in Figure 2. A context is responsible for maintaining the consistency of the representations of the objects belonging to it. A context must implement methods `Context.migrate{To|From}` and `Context.`

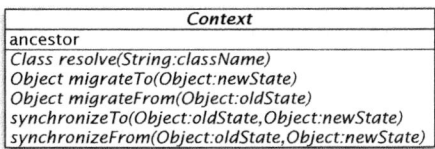

Fig. 2. The `Context` class

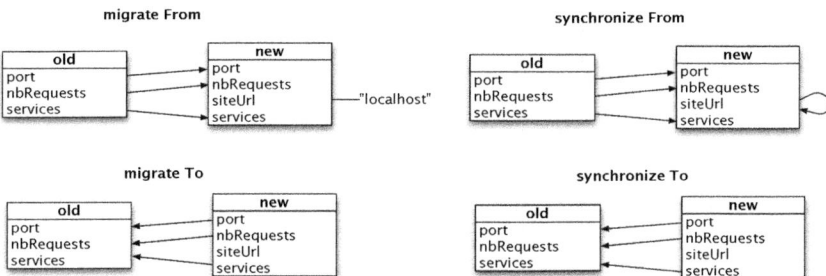

Fig. 3. The effects of the various methods that class `Context` mandates. Note that the arrow means a field copy operation and the method always applies to the new context.

`synchronize{To|From}` to define the update strategy. We call "transformation" either the migration or the synchronization of the representations.

Each context has an ancestor. Since the contexts are loaded dynamically in an unanticipated fashion the update strategy is encoded in the newest context and expressed in terms of its ancestor, never in terms of its successor. Methods `Context.*From` assume the old representation is up-to-date, and transform the representation *from* the old context to the newest context; methods `Context.*To` assume the new representation is up-to-date, and update the representation from the new context *to* the old context. The *Root* context is the only context that does not encode any transformation and has no ancestor. User-defined contexts should default to the identity transformation for objects with no structural changes.

Figure 3 exemplifies the differences between the four methods using the running example. Methods `Context.migrate{To|From}` are responsible for creating the representation of an object upon the first access in the given context. In our case, the migration of the web server from the old context to the new context would copy the existing fields *as is* and initialize the new field `siteUrl` with a predefined value. Note that in this case, the object existed before the update and the migration from the new to the old context will never happen in practice[5]. Methods `Context.synchronize{To|From}` are responsible for subsequent updates of the state. In the case of our example, the field `siteUrl` must not be initialized again.

---

[5] This may not always be the case. It is possible for an object to be created in the new context and become reachable for objects in the old context.

3.2   Reified State

From the application point of view, the state of an object will depend on the active context, and objects will have several representations. The transformations need to access both the old and new representations of an object. This requires the old and new representations to be *reified* into distinct objects, before they are passed to the transformations. Also, transformations are never called by the application, but by the run-time itself when necessary upon state read or write. Transformations run outside of any context.

Messages cannot be sent to contextual objects from within a transformation, as the system would not be able to decide what the "contextual" class of the object is in the absence of any context. This implies that certain objects must be primitive: they have a unique state in the system and are not subject to contextual variations. This is notably the case for the reified state, but also for contexts themselves. Immutable objects (string, numbers, *etc.*) are also considered to be primitive so that they can be used within transformations.

The reified state of an object can reference other contextual objects, however. If one has to query the state of such a dependent object from within a transformation, one would need first to obtain the reification of its state in either the old or new context.

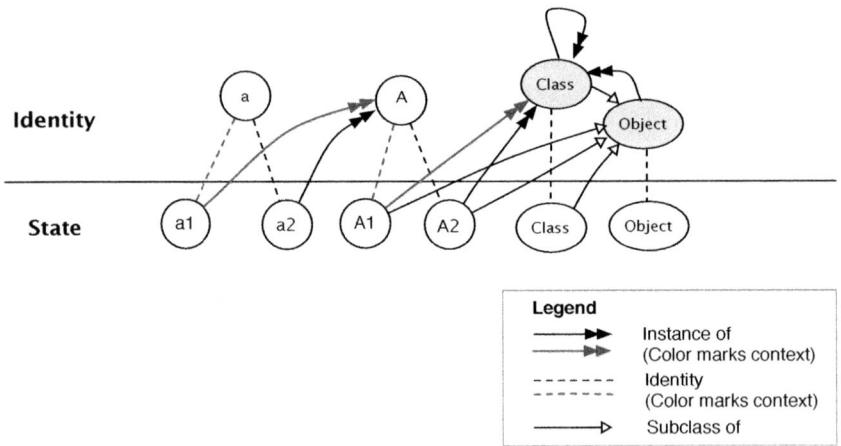

Fig. 4. Conceptual view of contextual objects and classes. `Object` and `Class` are primitive. Object `a` is contextual. Object `A` is a first-class class that is also contextual. The red path illustrates a reification: if the state of `a` is reified in the first context, one obtains `a1`, which is an instance of `A1`.

3.3   First-Class Classes

Classes are first-class in our model. They are contextual objects as well and a contextual class might have two versions, as depicted in Figure 4.

Conceptually, each contextual state is an instance of a contextual class, for example, the contextual state `a1` is an instance of the contextual class `A`. In practice, when the state is reified, the object that is obtained is not an instance of the contextual class, but of the reification of the contextual class: if the contextual state a1 is reified, one obtains a primitive object that is an instance of A1.

When an object is migrated, a specific version of its state is reified and passed as a parameter to migrate{To|From}. The method must return the new version of its reified state, e.g., migrate a1, which is an instance of A1, to a2, which is an instance of A2. The class can change only during migration. Indeed, methods synchronize{From|to} take as arguments the old reified state and the new reified state, but are not able to change the class they correspond to.

Classes are migrated similarly to regular objects. A specific version of the class is reified and passed as parameter to migrate{To|From}. The method must return the new version of the class, e.g., migrate A1 which is an instance of Class to A2 which is also an instance of Class. Note that Class is a primitive in the system.

Classes are peculiar in that they can be resolved via a name, unlike "regular" objects. Contexts are responsible for class name resolution and must implement the method Context.resolveClass(String) which must return a specific version, e.g., in Figure 4 "A" might resolve either to A1 or A2. The way classes are migrated must correspond to the way classes are resolved for the system to be consistent.

3.4   Spawning Thread

A thread can have one *active* context at a time. A predefined context exists, called the *Root*, which is the default context after startup. The runtime must be extended with a mechanism to query the active context, and also to specify a new context when a new thread is spawned. If none is specified, the thread will inherit the context of its parent thread.

4   Implementation

We report on the implementation of Theseus in Pharo Smalltalk. In contrast to our earlier work, this implementation does not require changes to the virtual machine. A unique aspect of our implementation is that it does not rely on proxies or wrappers, which do not properly support self-reference, do not support adding or changing public method signature, and break reflection [24,20].

During an incremental update, a contextual object corresponds concretely to two objects in memory, one per context. Figure 5 depicts such a setting. To maintain the illusion that the old and new representations of an object have the same identity, we adapt the references when necessary: for instance, if b1 is assigned to a field of a1 in the old context, this results in b2 being assigned to the corresponding field of a2 in the newest context.

Objects are migrated lazily, and can be either flagged as "clean" or "dirty". Dirty objects are out-of-date, and need to be synchronized upon the next access. Figure 5 shows the effect of an access to the dirty representation b2, which triggers the migration of the representation c2 it references directly. After the synchronization, the two representations b1 and b2 of object b are clean. Subsequent writes to either representation would however result in the other one to

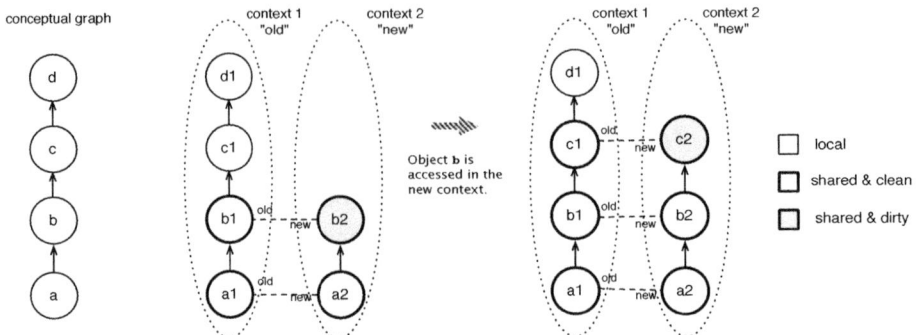

Fig. 5. The arrows between the four objects a,b,c,d represent references via a field. The objects exist in two contexts. Shared objects have one representation per context, which can be either "clean" or "dirty". Objects are migrated lazily. When object b is accessed in the new context for the first time, the representation b2 is synchronized. Since b refers to c, this triggers the migration of c and the representation c2 is created, originally considered "dirty". An access to c in the new context would create the representation d2, *etc.* Dashed lines represent relationships visible only to the implementation, not the application.

be flagged as dirty. In the case of Figure 5, if b2 is modified, b1 would be marked as dirty.

We use bytecode rewriting to alter accesses to state and the way classes are resolved. Concretely, an extra check is added before each state read and state write to determine whether the object is shared between contexts. If it is, and the object is "dirty", it is synchronized and then marked as "clean". In case of state writes, the other representation is also invalidated and flagged as "dirty".

When the old context can be garbage-collected, we must ensure that all objects reachable from the new context have been migrated. In the case of Figure 5, the system would force the migration of d1 before garbage collection. If the graph of reachable objects is big, this operation can be relatively long, but can be conducted in background with low priority.

Concurrency. We assume that the subject program already correctly synchronizes concurrent reads and writes to thread-shared entities. Indeed, developers should neither make assumptions about the atomicity of read and write operations, nor about the visibility of side-effects between threads. Reads and writes are not atomic and concurrent accesses might trigger concurrent transformations.

Let us consider the web server of section 2. Field numRequests is synchronized with a lock, but port is not, as the value never changes after object creation. It is possible that numRequests is written and port is read concurrently. Two concurrent transformations might overlap and the new value of the field numRequests might be overwritten with the previous one. To ensure that the behavior of the original program is not altered, methods synchronize{To|From} take an additional parameter field in the full interface (not shown in subsection 3.1). This way, transformations can update fields selectively. There is also a per-field dirty flag.

When an object becomes shared, it is migrated. The migration `migrate{To|-From}` must however apply to the object as a whole (i.e. all its fields), as we cannot "partially" instantiate a representation. Also, a "forced" migration might happen due to the garbage collection of an old context, and despite a properly synchronized original program, concurrent migrations might occur. To resolve this situation, the migration of an object must be exclusive. Before a migration starts, it checks that the object was not migrated in the meantime. If this is the case it either (i) falls back to a `synchronize{To|From}` (normal migration) or (ii) is skipped (forced migration). Changes to the flag that indicates whether an object is shared, must not be cached by the CPU and must update the main memory (this is always the case in Pharo, but it would require a `volatile` declaration in Java).

State Relocation. Transformations can be more complex than one-to-one mappings. For instance, instead of keeping track of the number of requests in `num-Requests` using a primitive numeric type, the developer might introduce and use a class `Counter` for better encapsulation[6]. During the transformation, the actual count would be "relocated" from the web server object to the counter object that is now used. However, in this case, when the counter is incremented, the old representation of the web server with field `numRequests` needs to be invalidated. So far we have assumed that a write would invalidate only the representation of the object written to, which is not the case any longer. To support such transformations, the full interface enables custom invalidation on a per-field basis with `Context.invalidate{To|From}(Object oldState,Object newState,String field)`.

Further Details. We used a custom compiler to rewrite the bytecode of contextual classes. Primitive classes (see subsection 3.2) do not require any bytecode rewriting. In our scheme, contextual objects must have one representation per context, even if they are structurally equivalent. This applies to classes as well (see subsection 3.3). In Smalltalk, two instances of the same metaclass cannot be created, so we need to clone the metaclass as well. Closures are first-class in Smalltak. They encode offsets of bytecode in the `CompiledMethod` they reference. They are treated analogously to other objects. After migration, they reference the newest version of the corresponding `CompiledMethod`. The active context is stored in a thread-local variable and we add a new method to fork a closure in a specific context, e.g.,`[ ... ] forkWith: aContext`. When a closure is forked, it becomes a shared contextual object and is migrated. As the program proceeds, objects referenced by the closure are migrated lazily when accessed. Contexts hold only weak references to their ancestor and implement the method `Object>>#finalize`, which forces the migration of all reachable objects before the context becomes eligible for garbage collection. The class `Semaphore` is treated as primitive so that objects can be synchronized correctly. The `Object` class cannot be modified easily. To keep track of the necessary information we need about

---

[6] This would be the refactoring "Replace Data Value with Object". See
http://www.refactoring.com/

Request	B(ms)	T(ms)	# Read		# Write		# Reachable		Migrated
			Shared	Local	Shared	Local	Shared	Local	
1st request	30	60	-	128923	-	14674	-	-	-
2nd request	30	127	14535	130172	21	17901	1292	2781	585
3rd request	30	77	14547	120991	34	15539	1293	3311	588

Fig. 6. Time for three successive requests, one before the update, and two after the update. T=Theseus, B=Baseline. Migrated=cumulative number of migrated objects.

objects, we maintain a dictionary that maps objects to their extra information. Clearly, this level of indirection would need to be optimized in a full implementation.

5   Validation

Evolution. We conducted a first experiment whose goal was to assess whether our model could support long-term evolution, that is, whether it could sustain successive updates. We considered the small web server of section 2, which despite its simplicity cannot be updated easily with global updates. We selected the 4 last versions with effective changes: version 75 introduced chunked data transfer, version 78 fixed a bug in the encoding of URL, version 82 introduced siteUrl, and version 84 fixed a bug in MIME multipart support.

The listening thread that accepts incoming connections was modified to restart itself periodically. Only one update required us to write a custom transformation: the one that introduced the siteUrl field, which we initialized to a default value. We ran the 4 successive dynamic updates, and verified that once it was no longer used, the old context would be garbage-collected. In this way we validated that our implementation was coherent.

Run-time Characteristics. For the second experiment, we picked a typical technology stack with well-known production projects: the Swazoo web server, the Seaside web framework, the Magritte meta-description framework, and the Pier CMS. This corresponds to several thousand classes. We were interested in the run-time characteristics and to assess (1) whether our assumptions about object sharing hold, and (2) what is the performance overhead. As a case study, we considered the default web site of the Pier demo. During maintenance, only few classes change. Most objects are migrated with the identity transformation, and only certain objects require custom transformations. The exact nature of the transformation is not significant. Therefore, for the sake of simplicity, we artificially updated the system and used the identity transformation for all objects.

We were interested to assess the overhead of our implementation in three different cases: (i) with only the old context when no object is shared, (ii) during the incremental update when objects are shared and migrated lazily, and (iii) after objects have been migrated but are still considered shared. To do so, we measured the time for three successive requests: one before the update, for case (i), and two after the update, for cases (ii) and (iii).

The results are presented in Figure 6. The overhead of our implementation is in the best case of factor two. In the worst case when many objects must be migrated, we have a degradation of factor four. We tracked the number of reads and writes to objects shared between contexts, and to objects local to a context. We clearly see that writes are one order of magnitude less frequent than reads. About 500 objects needed to be migrated and only a minority of accesses concern shared objects. The migrated objects and their direct references correspond to about 1300 reachable objects. These 1300 objects reference further about 3000 objects indirectly. These 3000 objects could be reached indirectly from both contexts, but are in practice local to a context. There are fewer than 50 writes to shared objects and we deduce that the code of the extra logic to invalidate representations is negligible (see section 4). In the first request, the system checks if objects are shared, which is never the case. In the third request, the system needs an additional check for dirtiness, which returns always false. This explains the difference between times (i) and (iii).

Our experiment did not simulate the run-time characteristics of a production system, however. We did not account for concurrent requests, which could cause objects to be synchronized back and forth. Further empirical validation is welcome. Also, our implementation is still relatively naive (see section 4). However, even with this implementation we achieve reasonable response time.

These results show that the approach can be made practical and fits well to the characteristics of real-world software.

6   Discussion

Performance. A drawback of our implementation is that shared objects need two representations, even if they are structurally identical and will use the identity transformation. Wrappers would make it possible to keep only one representation in such cases, but pose problems of self-reference, do not support adding or changing method signatures, and break reflection [24,20,22]. The benefit of our implementation is that object representations are really instances of their respective classes and avoid such problems. We plan to improve performance by not synchronizing state on each access, and instead synchronize groups of fields at precise locations, e.g., synchronize all fields a method uses at once at the beginning and end of the method. Lock acquisitions/releases would force the synchronization of pending changes, similarly to *memory barriers* [9]. It could, at least, be done manually for heavily-used system classes. This would preserve concurrent behavior but increase significantly the performance.

Applicability. The impact on development is small. Developers must figure out the "increment" they wish, which results usually in a few well-located changes after which development proceeds as usual. Compared to other dynamic update mechanisms, there must exist a state mapping only for shared entities (not all entities), but the mapping must be bidirectional (not unidirectional). We can navigate the object graph during the transformation which seems to suffice for most evolution in practice [26,17,2]. Daemon threads must be adapted to restart periodically, but it is easy to do given their cyclic nature. Recent works showed that most of the transformation code can be generated automatically [21] and it would be interesting to assess whether we can generalize such results for bidirectional transformations as well.

7   Related Work

A common technique to achieve hot updates is to use redundant hardware [11], possibly using "session affinity" to ensure that the traffic of a given client is always routed to the same server. Our approach is more lightweight and enables the migration of the state shared across contexts, notably persistent objects. Also, an advantage of being reflective is that the software can "patch itself" as soon as patches become available.

A large body of research has tackled the dynamic update of applications. Systems supporting *immediate and global dynamic updates* have been devised with various levels of safety and practicality. Dynamic languages other than Smalltalk belong naturally to this category; they are very practical but not safe. Dynamic AOP and meta-object protocols also fit into this category. Systems of this kind have been devised for Java [6,20,15,10,3,28,23], with various levels of flexibility (a good comparison can be found in [10]). To be type-safe, HotSwap [6] imposes restrictions and only method bodies can be updated. The most recent approaches [28,23] are more flexible but can still lead to run-time errors if changes impact active methods. Most of these approaches rely on bytecode transformation [20,15,10,3,23] and do not address concurrency.

Several approaches have tackled the problem of safety by relying on temporal *update points* when it is safe to globally update the application. Such systems have been devised for C [11,19], and Java [26,17]. Update points might be hard to reach, especially in multi-threaded applications [18,26], and this compromises the timely installation of updates.

Some mechanisms diverge from a global update and enable different versions of the code or entities to coexist. In the most simple scheme, old entities are simply not migrated at all and only new entities use the updated type definition [13], or this burden might be left to the developer who must request the migration explicitly [8]. The granularity of the update for such approaches is the object; it is hard to guarantee *version consistency* and to ensure that mutually compatible versions of objects will always be used. When leveraged, transactions [2,22] provide version consistency but impede mutations of shared entities. Contexts enable mutations of shared entities and can be long-lived, thanks to the use of bidirectional transformations. With asynchronous communication between objects, the update of an object can wait until dependent objects have been upgraded in order to remain type-safe [14].

To the best of our knowledge, only three approaches rely on bidirectional transformations to ease dynamic updates. POLUS is a dynamic updating system for C [4] which maintains coherence between versions by running synchronizations on writes. We synchronize lazily on read, operate at the level of objects, and take garbage collection into account. Duggan [7] formalized a type system that adapts objects back and forth: when the run-time version tag of an object doesn't match the version expected statically, the system converts the object with an adapter. We do not rely on static typing but on dynamic scoping with first-class contexts, we address garbage collection, concurrency, and provide a working implementation. Oracle enables a table to have two versions that are kept consistent thanks to bidirectional "cross-edition triggers" [5].

Schema evolution addresses the update of persistent object stores, which closely relates to dynamic updates. To cope with the volume of data, migrations should happen lazily. To be type-safe, objects should be migrated in a valid order (e.g., points of a rectangle must be migrated before the rectangle itself) [2,22]. Our approach migrates objects lazily, and avoids the problem of ordering by keeping both versions as long as necessary.

Class loaders [16] allow classes to be loaded dynamically in Java. Types seen within a class loader never change, which ensures type safety and version consistency, similarly to our notion of context. Two versions of a class loaded by two different class loaders are different types, which makes sharing objects between class loaders complicated. This is unlike our approach which supports the migration of classes and objects between contexts.

Context-oriented programming [12] enables fine-grained variations based on dynamic attributes, e.g., dynamically activated "layers". It focuses on behavioral changes with multi-dimensional dispatch, and does not address changing the structure and state of objects as is necessary for dynamic updates. There exist many mechanisms to scope changes statically, e.g., Classboxes [1], but they are not used to adapt software at run-time.

8 Conclusion

Existing approaches to dynamically update software systems entail trade-offs in terms of safety, practicality, and timeliness. We propose a novel, incremental approach to dynamic software updates. During an incremental update, clients might see different versions of the system, which avoids the need for the system to reach a quiescent, global update point.

Each version of the system is reified into a first-class context. Existing objects are gradually migrated to the new context, and objects that are shared between old and new contexts are kept consistent with the help of bidirectional transformations. Our validation with real-world systems indicates that only a fraction of accesses concern such objects.

In two experiments we have demonstrated that our current implementation is practical and flexible, with reasonable overhead. This work opens up several research directions: exploring different granularity of increments, providing developer tools to leverage contexts, and improving further the performance.

Acknowledgments. We gratefully acknowledge the financial support of the Swiss National Science Foundation for the project "Synchronizing Models and Code" (SNF Project No. 200020-131827, Oct. 2010 - Sept. 2012).

References

1. Bergel, A.: Classboxes — Controlling Visibility of Class Extensions. Ph.D. thesis, University of Bern (November 2005)
2. Boyapati, C., Liskov, B., Shrira, L., Moh, C.H., Richman, S.: Lazy modular upgrades in persistent object stores. SIGPLAN Not. 38(11), 403–417 (2003)
3. Cech Previtali, S., Gross, T.R.: Aspect-based dynamic software updating: a model and its empirical evaluation. In: Proceedings of the Tenth International Conference on Aspect-Oriented Software Development, AOSD 2011, pp. 105–116. ACM, New York (2011)
4. Chen, H., Yu, J., Hang, C., Zang, B., Yew, P.C.: Dynamic software updating using a relaxed consistency model. IEEE Trans. Software Eng. 37(5), 679–694 (2011)
5. Choi, A.: Online application upgrade using edition-based redefinition. In: Proceedings of the 2nd International Workshop on Hot Topics in Software Upgrades, HotSWUp 2009, pp. 4:1–4:5. ACM, New York (2009)
6. Dmitriev, M.: Towards flexible and safe technology for runtime evolution of Java language applications. In: Proceedings of the Workshop on Engineering Complex Object-Oriented Systems for Evolution, in association with OOPSLA 2001 (October 2001)
7. Duggan, D.: Type-based hot swapping of running modules. In: Intl. Conf. on Functional Programming, pp. 62–73 (2001)
8. Gemstone/s programming guide (2007)
9. Gharachorloo, K.: Memory consistency models for shared-memory multiprocessors. Tech. rep., DEC (1995)
10. Gregersen, A.R., Jørgensen, B.N.: Dynamic update of Java applications — balancing change flexibility vs programming transparency. J. Softw. Maint. Evol. 21, 81–112 (2009)
11. Hicks, M., Nettles, S.: Dynamic software updating. ACM Transactions on Programming Languages and Systems 27(6), 1049–1096 (2005)
12. Hirschfeld, R., Costanza, P., Nierstrasz, O.: Context-oriented programming. Journal of Object Technology 7(3) (March 2008)
13. Hjálmtýsson, G., Gray, R.: Dynamic C++ classes: a lightweight mechanism to update code in a running program. In: Proceedings of the annual conference on USENIX Annual Technical Conference, ATEC 1998, p. 6. USENIX Association, Berkeley (1998)
14. Johnsen, E.B., Kyas, M., Yu, I.C.: Dynamic Classes: Modular Asynchronous Evolution of Distributed Concurrent Objects. In: Cavalcanti, A., Dams, D.R. (eds.) FM 2009. LNCS, vol. 5850, pp. 596–611. Springer, Heidelberg (2009)
15. Kabanov, J.: Jrebel tool demo. Electron. Notes Theor. Comput. Sci. 264, 51–57 (2011)
16. Liang, S., Bracha, G.: Dynamic class loading in the Java virtual machine. In: Proceedings of OOPSLA 1998. ACM SIGPLAN Notices, pp. 36–44 (1998)
17. Malabarba, S., Pandey, R., Gragg, J., Barr, E., Barnes, J.F.: Runtime Support for Type-Safe Dynamic Java Classes. In: Bertino, E. (ed.) ECOOP 2000. LNCS, vol. 1850, pp. 337–361. Springer, Heidelberg (2000)

18. Neamtiu, I., Hicks, M.: Safe and timely updates to multi-threaded programs. In: Proceedings of the 2009 ACM SIGPLAN Conference on Programming Language Design and Implementation, PLDI 2009, pp. 13–24. ACM, New York (2009)
19. Neamtiu, I., Hicks, M., Stoyle, G., Oriol, M.: Practical dynamic software updating for C. In: Proceedings of the 2006 ACM SIGPLAN Conference on Programming Language Design and Implementation, PLDI 2006, pp. 72–83. ACM, New York (2006)
20. Orso, A., Rao, A., Harrold, M.J.: A Technique for Dynamic Updating of Java Software. In: IEEE International Conference on Software Maintenance, p. 0649+ (2002)
21. Piccioni, M., Oriol, M., Meyer, B., Schneider, T.: An ide-based, integrated solution to schema evolution of object-oriented software. In: ASE, pp. 650–654 (2009)
22. Pina, L., Cachopo, J.: Dustm - dynamic software upgrades using software transactional memory. Tech. rep., INESC-ID (2011)
23. Pukall, M., Kästner, C., Cazzola, W., Götz, S., Grebhahn, A., Schröter, R., Saake, G.: Flexible dynamic software updates of java applications: Tool support and case study. Tech. Rep. 04, School of Computer Science, University of Magdeburg (2011)
24. Pukall, M., Kästner, C., Saake, G.: Towards unanticipated runtime adaptation of java applications. In: APSEC 2008: Proceedings of the 2008 15th Asia-Pacific Software Engineering Conference, pp. 85–92. IEEE Computer Society, Washington, DC (2008)
25. Rivard, F.: Smalltalk: a reflective language. In: Proceedings of REFLECTION 1996, pp. 21–38 (April 1996)
26. Subramanian, S., Hicks, M., McKinley, K.S.: Dynamic software updates: a VM-centric approach. In: Proceedings of the 2009 ACM SIGPLAN Conference on Programming Language Design and Implementation, PLDI 2009, pp. 1–12. ACM, New York (2009)
27. Wernli, E., Gurtner, D., Nierstrasz, O.: Using first-class contexts to realize dynamic software updates. In: Proceedings of International Workshop on Smalltalk Technologies (IWST 2011), pp. 21–31 (2011), http://esug.org/data/ESUG2011/IWST/Proceedings.pdf
28. Würthinger, T., Wimmer, C., Stadler, L.: Unrestricted and safe dynamic code evolution for java. Science of Computer Programming (July 2011)

Elucidative Development
for Model-Based Documentation*

Claas Wilke, Andreas Bartho, Julia Schroeter, Sven Karol, and Uwe Aßmann

Institut für Software- und Multimediatechnik
Technische Universität Dresden
D-01062, Dresden, Germany
{claas.wilke,andreas.bartho,julia.schroeter,
sven.karol,uwe.assmann}@tu-dresden.de

Abstract. Documentation is an essential activity in software development, for source code as well as modelling artefacts. Typically, documentation is created and maintained manually which leads to inconsistencies as documented artefacts like source code or models evolve during development. Existing approaches like literate/elucidative programming or literate modelling address these problems by deriving documentation from software development artefacts or vice versa. However, these approaches restrict themselves to a certain kind of artefact and to a certain phase of the software development life-cycle. In this paper, we propose elucidative development as a generalisation of these approaches supporting heterogeneous kinds of artefacts as well as the analysis, design and implementation phases of the software development life-cycle. Elucidative development links source code and model artefacts into documentation and thus, maintains and updates their presentation semi-automatically. We present DEFT as an integrated development environment for elucidative development. We show, how DEFT can be applied to language specifications like the UML specification and help to avoid inconsistencies caused by maintenance and evolution of such a specification.

Keywords: Elucidative programming, literate programming, literate modelling, automated documentation, automated specification, UML.

1 Introduction

To ensure comprehensibility and reusability, documentation is essential in the software development process. Source code belonging to frameworks that shall be reused by other developers need to be documented, as developers have to understand how to instantiate its classes or to invoke its operations. Besides, development models intended for reuse or explanatory reasons have to be documented as well. Finally, modelling languages or frequently used metamodels need to be documented (typically as specifications) to explain their concepts and intensions.

---

* An extended version of this paper has been published as a technical report [1].

C.A. Furia and S. Nanz (Eds.): TOOLS Europe 2012, LNCS 7304, pp. 320–335, 2012.
© Springer-Verlag Berlin Heidelberg 2012

Today, documentation is mostly created and maintained manually. Textual documents are maintained using text processing software, code listing and diagrams are created and pasted into these documents manually. This leads to problems, once documented software or development artefacts evolve: The documentation needs to be maintained and artefact changes have to be reflected in the documentation. Manual maintenance can cause inconsistencies, as sections requiring a revision could be overlooked. Furthermore, it is possible that not all occurrences of evolved artefacts are updated in the documentation, leading to inconsistencies and contradictions. A good example for a documentation with many inconsistencies caused by evolution and maintenance is the Unified Modeling Language (UML) specification [2], which does not document a tool or a framework but a modelling language used by a large community of software developers. Since its first revision, the UML specification documents have been maintained manually, and as a matter of fact, current versions contain many errors and contradictions [3–8].

To solve these kinds of problems, approaches such as literate programming (LP) [9], literate modelling (LM) [10] and elucidative programming (EP) [11] emphasise a documentation-centric style of programming or modelling. However, they only partially cover the software life-cycle restricting themselves to source code documentation during the implementation phase or the documentation of UML diagrams during the early stages of software analysis. Furthermore, to support documentation in model-driven software development (MDSD) processes, a holistic approach would have to consider documentation of artefacts from textual and graphical domain-specific modelling languages (DSMLs), metamodels and general purpose modelling languages, which is not the case for the current approaches. In this paper, we propose *elucidative development (ED)* as a holistic approach to create and maintain documentation, which covers multiple phases of the software development life-cycle and also supports documentation in MDSD processes. In fact, ED is a generalisation of LP, LM and EP. Furthermore, we present the Development Environment For Tutorials (DEFT), a tool supporting ED. We show how documentation can be created and maintained with DEFT and apply ED to a short excerpt from the UML specification to show, how inconsistencies in evolving specifications can be avoided.

The remainder of this paper is structured as follows. First, we introduce ED and DEFT in Sect. 2. In Sect. 3, we present an excerpt from the UML superstructure as a usage example for ED and show, how DEFT can be used to maintain its evolution. Afterwards, we discuss our approach in Sect. 4 and present related work in Sect. 5. Finally, we conclude the paper and give an outlook for future work in Sect. 6.

2   From Literate Programming to Elucidative Development

In this section we introduce ED as a paradigm for documenting arbitrary software and model artefacts consistently. ED is a generalisation of the EP paradigm, proposed by Nørmark [12], which itself is a variant of LP introduced by Knuth [9].

Both, EP and LP put strong emphasis on supporting developers in writing and maintaining program source code and its documentation in parallel during the implementation phase of the software life-cycle. In the following, we briefly introduce LP, EP and LM—a further variant of LP for documenting UML analysis models. Afterwards, we discuss the ED approach and compare it to the aforementioned documentation approaches. Subsequently, we present DEFT,[1] an Eclipse-based tool with ED support.

2.1   Literate Programming and Related Documentation Approaches

LP is an integrated approach for writing documentation and programming within the same file format. Code and text are intertwined in the same document by embedding the source code into the documentation files. Hence, programming takes place in the documentation environment, e.g., a TEX [13] editor. Consequently, before the program can be executed or the final documentation is rendered, pre-compilers (called weave and tangle) have to extract printable TEX documentation and compilable source code from the documentation files. This way, LP completely avoids inconsistencies between source code and code listings in the rendered documentation. However, LP has drawbacks in large software projects: The program is scattered across the documentation files and every code detail has to be described textually. As a result, the program is fragmented and intertwined with pieces of text which makes it harder to understand its real structure for average programmers who expect programs to be organised along a certain structure determined by the concepts of the programming language.

EP tries to overcome these problems by strictly separating documentation and source code artefacts. The connection between them is maintained within an integrated elucidative programming environment. As a result, programming language semantics such as name analysis can be reused for consistency checks in the documentation files. Furthermore, the granularity of the documentation is adjusted to its actual purpose, e.g., abstract interface descriptions as well as complete source code descriptions are possible. In comparison to LP, consistency between code listings and the actual program code is ensured by adding so-called relations between locations in the documentation and elements of the source code. The entirety of documentation, source code, and relations between those two is called an *elucidative program* [11]. If the source code evolves, the final documentation can be regenerated. It is possible to identify inconsistencies to some extent, e.g., relations which refer to removed or renamed source code.

The LM [10] approach applies concepts of LP to high-level UML analysis models. The main focus of LM lies in improving the communication between developers, requirements engineers and other stakeholders who are not educated in UML and, thus, have difficulties in interpreting UML diagrams. Similar to LP, models and documentation are intertwined within the same document – the *literate model*. However, recent efforts also move LM in the direction of separating documentation and the documented artefacts: The *Literate Modelling*

---

[1] http://deftproject.org/

Table 1. Comparison of different advanced documentation approaches

	documentation format	artefact support	artefact location	tool support	operations	software dev. phases
literate programming (LP)	typesetting language (e.g. TEX)	homogenous (source code)	integrated	pre-compiler (e.g. CWEB [13])	weave, tangle	implementation
elucidative programming (EP)	typesetting language	homogenous (source code)	separate	elucidative IDE (e.g. Java Elucidator [15])	embed	implementation
literate modelling (LM)	WYSIWYG format	homogenous (UML diagrams)	separate	literate model editor (e.g. LiMonE [14])	embed	analysis
elucidative development (ED)	WYSIWYG format or typesetting language	heterogeneous (models, source code, XML . . .)	separate	elucidative development environment (e.g. DEFT [16])	hot update, transconsistency	analysis, design, implementation

Editor (LiMonE) [14] implementation keeps both separate and combines textual model documentation with Object Constraint Language (OCL) consistency constraints derived from natural language descriptions.

The first three rows of Tab. 1 contrast LP, EP, and LM with each other. As an essence, it can be seen that each of them is restricted to a single phase in the software life-cycle and to a single type of artefact, i.e., source code in a certain (implementation-dependent) programming language or artefacts in a certain modelling language.

2.2   Elucidative Development

ED generalises the aforementioned documentation approaches in two ways (cf. last line of Tab. 1). First, it covers the analysis, development and implementation phases in software development. Hence, programmers, designers and other stakeholders can share their views on the system at different levels of abstraction. Second, ED provides a conceptual grounding for the documentation of heterogeneous kinds of software artefacts, e.g., formalised requirements specifications, models, or source code. This is essential for model-driven software development processes, where many different metamodel-based languages are used to implement a system by transformation and code generation. As a consequence, an *elucidative development environment (EDE)* has the following basic requirements which go beyond the requirements known from EP, LP and LM tools:

Support for model transformations. Different kinds of languages require different kinds of transformations to prepare artefacts to be displayed in a documentation file. This includes model-to-model transformations (e.g., operations to filter elements not being included in the documentation), model-to-text transformations (e.g., deriving textual artefact representations) and model-to-image transformations (e.g., converting a diagram into an image).

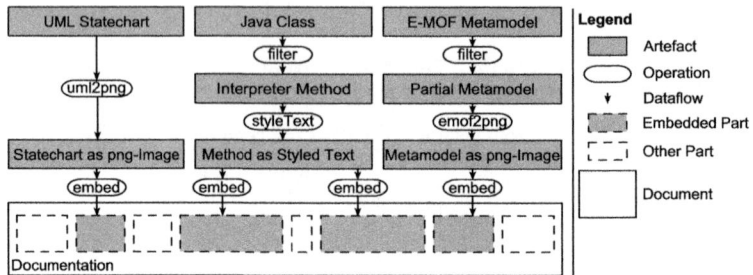

Fig. 1. Dataflow diagram of an ED document

Composition of model transformations. The aforementioned transformations need to be composable to produce images or code listings that integrate with the surrounding hand-written text and other parts in the documentation file. Valid compositions are determined by the types of input and output ports of the participating transformations. Consequently, the compositional relation of transformations, data and the documentation text form a directed bigraph, which represents the documents architecture [17]. Fig. 1 shows the architecture of an hypothetic ED document. Assume a project that implements an interpreter for a DSML in Java. The corresponding Java source code is extracted from a Java class model and transformed into a styled code listing which is finally embedded in the documentation file. To support the documentation, a statechart image is generated from a UML statechart diagram. The statechart specification originates from the design phase. Finally, the documentation includes parts from the metamodel specification of the DSML which are relevant for documenting the interpreter.

Hot update and immediate invalidation. As the documented system artefacts and the documentation itself evolve, frequent updates have to be triggered over time. ED documents are *active documents* [17]. An active document triggers an update operation as soon as a change in a source artefact is observed. Due to its explicit architecture, the document (or the EDE, respectively) is aware of all places where artefact representations to be recomputed occur. Since the required transformations may contain complex computations, the corresponding invalid parts of the document are marked until the recomputation is finished and the document becomes consistent again. In [17], this kind of update is called a *hot update* while an active document with hot update is called a *transconsistent* document. *Transconsistency* is closely related to the terms *transclusion* and *transclude*, which both originate from the early hypertext systems [18]. Nelson defines *transclusion* as "the same content knowable in more than one place" [19].

In the following, we introduce our tool DEFT. DEFT supports the features discussed above to a large extent and, thus, is a good candidate for supporting an ED processes.

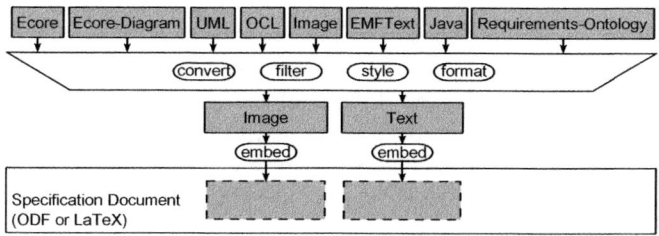

Fig. 2. Supported artefacts and operations in DEFT

2.3   The Development Environment for Tutorials (DEFT)

An EDE supports developers in creating and maintaining elucidative documentations. It also provides automatic notifications and further support for hot updates
of the included source artefacts once the documented concepts evolve. DEFT is
an implementation of such an EDE. It was originally designed to keep the documentation of whole software systems and tutorials up to date. As we show in this
paper, it is also feasible for writing and maintaining large language specification
documents.

Out of the box, DEFT supports the documentation of artefacts that occur
in usual software development or MDSD, such as Java source files and Eclipse
Modeling Framework (EMF) artefacts (cf. Fig. 2, top). Furthermore, the integration of DEFT with EMF allows users to document arbitrary languages based
on Ecore, which is an Essential MOF (EMOF) implementation for Java. Consequently, DEFT supports the documentation of the UML metamodel based
on EMF. For textual modelling, DEFT is integrated with EMFText [20] such
that support for EMFText-based languages is available. OCL constraints can
be documented by using the EMFText-based OCL implementation of Dresden
OCL [21]. For graphical modelling, the Ecore diagram editors of the EMF are
supported. The integration of UML models and diagrams is current work in
progress. As documentation formats, DEFT supports LaTeX and Open Document
Format (ODF) documents (cf. Fig. 2, bottom).[2] A documentation file produced
with DEFT can contain manually written parts like continuous text, as well as
transcluded elements like code listings or images. These elements can be derived
from all the input formats described above and can be converted or formatted
before embedded into the specification document (cf. Fig. 2, center). For example, OCL constraints can be transformed into code listings, UML diagrams can
be rendered as images, or enumerations can be generated from UML metamodel
elements (e.g., class properties and operations). If a modification of an artefact
requires a modification of a transcluded element in the documentation, DEFT
updates the artefact representation automatically. The user interface of DEFT is

---

[2] These formats have been selected for as they are open an broadly used. Of course,
similar formats, e.g., Office Open XML (docx) could be supported as well.

divided in multiple areas[3]. A *project explorer* presents documentation chapters, source artefacts, and their relations. The largest part of the screen is covered by the *writing area*, where the documentation text can be edited. Relations to artefacts can be added to the document using a wizard. By default, DEFT does not display the relations directly. Instead, the computed representation is transcluded. Finally, DEFT provides a *task view* which tells the author where changes in the source artefacts took place, where the documentation has been updated and, thus, where proofreading is necessary.

3   The UML Use Case for Elucidative Development

To demonstrate the advantages of ED in contrast to other documentation approaches, we decided to use an excerpt from the UML 2 specification. In this section, we first identify different kinds of consistency problems and give examples for them within the current UML standard. Afterwards, we apply ED to the example and show, how ED can avoid the current inconsistency problems of the UML specification.

3.1   Inconsistencies in UML 2.4.1

Since its first specification, the UML has been extended and revised multiple times. A major change in the UML was the specification of UML 2.0 in 2005 which contained many new concepts. However, further revisions of UML 2 added many inconsistencies to the specification document. As a small example, we compare Sect. 7.3.37 of the UML 2.4.1 specification [22, p. 108–110] with the same section of the UML 2.0 specification document [23, p. 103–105]. It specifies the class Package within the UML Kernel package as shown in Fig. 3. Changes between UML 2.0 and UML 2.4.1 are highlighted, as well as inconsistencies that have not been revised, yet. The example section contains a short description of the Package class, its inheritance relationships, attributes, associations, constraints, additional operations, and semantics.[4]

The major changes of the example section are located within the *Attributes* and the *Associations* subsections, as shown in Fig. 3, [A]. A new attribute URI is introduced. The association ownedMember is renamed to packagedElement. This association and the ownedType association are marked as derived, which is indicated by a leading backslash. Furthermore, the package association is removed. References to the renamed element are revised as well (e.g., the subsets relationship from nestedPackage to ownedMember). However, these references are sources of potential errors as the complete specification has to be inspected to check whether other references to the modified element exist that must be updated as well. For example, the renaming of the ownedMember association leads to an inconsistency within the *Additional Operations* subsection where an OCL

---

[3] A screenshot will be presented in Sect. 3.2, in context of the case study.

[4] For complexity reasons, the graphical notation, presentation options, and examples following in the specification are not considered as part of our example.

7.3.37 Package (from Kernel)

A package is used to group elements, and provides a namespace for the grouped elements.

Generalizations

• "Namespace (from Kernel)" on page 95
• "PackageableElement (from Kernel)" on page 105

Description

A package is a namespace for its members, and may contain other packages. Only packageable elements can be owned members of a package. By virtue of being a namespace, a package can import either individual members of other packages, or all the members of other packages.

In addition a package can be merged with other packages.

Attributes

No additional attributes

Associations

• /nestedPackage: Package [*]   References the owned members that are Packages. Subsets *Package::ownedMember*

• /ownedMember: PackageableElement [*]   Specifies the members that are owned by this Package. Redefines *Namespace::ownedMember*

• /ownedType: Type [*]   References the owned members that are Types. Subsets *Package::ownedMember*

• package: Package [0..1]   References the owning package of a package. Subsets *NamedElement::namespace*

• packageMerge: Package [*]   References the PackageMerges that are owned by this Package. Subsets *Element::ownedElement*

• nestingPackage: Package [0..1]   References the Package that owns this Package. Subsets *NamedElement::namespace*

A

Constraints

[1] If an element that is owned by a package has visibility, it is public or private.
self.ownedElements->forAll(e | e.visibility->notEmpty() **implies** e.visibility =#public **or** e.visibility =#private)

Additional Operations

[1] The query mustBeOwned() indicates whether elements of this type must have an owner.
Package::mustBeOwned() : Boolean
mustBeOwned = false

C

[2] The query visibleMembers() defines which members of a Package can be accessed outside it.
Package::visibleMembers() : Set(PackageableElement)
visibleMembers = member->select(m | self.makesVisible(m))

C

[3] The query makesVisible() defines whether a Package makes an element visible outside itself. Elements with no visibility and elements with public visibility are made visible.
Package::makesVisible(el: Namespaces::NamedElement) : Boolean
pre: self.member->includes(el)
makesVisible =

C

-- case: the element is in the package itself
(ownedMember->includes(el)) **or**
-- case: it is imported individually with public visibility
(elementImport->select(ei|ei.importedElement =#public)->collect(ei|ei.importedElement->includes(el)) **or**
-- case: it is imported in a package with public visibility
(packageImport->select(pi|pi.visibility =#public)->collect(pi|pi.importedPackage.member->includes(el))->notEmpty())

B

Semantics

A package is a namespace and is also a packageable element that can be contained in other packages.

The elements that can be referred to using non-qualified names within a package are owned elements, imported elements, and elements in enclosing (outer) namespaces. Owned and imported elements may each have a visibility that determines whether they are available outside the package.

A package owns its owned members, with the implication that if a package is removed from a model, so are the elements owned by the package.

The public contents of a package are always accessible outside the package through the use of qualified names.

Legend: A ▭ Changes performed between UML 2.0 and 2.4.1
B ▭ Semantic error in OCL expression introduced by a metamodel modification between UML 2.0 and 2.4.1
C ▭ Syntactic and semantic error in OCL expression, not revised in UML 2.4.1

Fig. 3. Excerpt from UML 2.0 and its modification until UML 2.4.1 (cf. [23, p. 103f])

expression references this association (cf. Fig. 3, [B]). This is not surprising since obviously the OCL expressions used within the UML specification have not been revised since their original definition in UML 2.0 and have been specified without checking their syntax and static semantics [8]. Thus, the expressions contain various syntactic and semantic inconsistencies (cf. Fig. 3, [C]). Summarising, we identified four kinds of problems[5] occurring during specification maintenance:

(P1) Textual Representation: Modification of elements (e.g., rename, remove, insert) specified in the language, entails the update of enumerations in the specification containing those elements. For example, the renaming of the association `ownedMember` must be performed in the *Associations* subsection. Neglecting this leads to inconsistent documents.

(P2) Continuous Text: Missing updates of continuous text that documents and clarifies specification elements. For instance, if the class `Package` is renamed, the introduction of the section and the *Description* subsection need to be revised accordingly as they describe the `Package` class.

(P3) Graphical Representation: The concepts of UML are specified graphically as class diagrams. Thus, if any property or association of the `Package` class is modified, all diagrams containing this class must be updated as well. For example, the specification contains the *Fig. 7.14* documenting the `Package` class and its relations [23, p. 31] that must be revised after modifications of this class.

(P4) External References: Other content referring to the specified model elements (e.g., the OCL expressions) must be updated and modified as well. This is a task that is obviously too complicated to be performed manually, as the UML specification contains many inconsistency problems of this category [8].

3.2   UML Language Specification with DEFT

In this section, we show how DEFT supports ED exemplified by the UML specification excerpt presented above. The example is realised using the EMF-based UML metamodel of Eclipse Eclipse Model Development Tools (MDT). For the specification of derived operations and OCL well-formedeness rules (WFRs) we use Dresden OCL. Finally, a diagram representation of the `Package` class and its relations to other classes is created using the graphical Ecore editor of EMF.

For the UML example we transclude diagrams and OCL files in a specification document. This includes the selection which parts (e.g., which lines from an OCL file) shall be presented in the document. That way, almost all sections from the given example can be transcluded into the document (cf. Fig. 4). The introductory paragraph is derived from an annotated comment of the `Package` class. The *Generalizations*, *Attributes*, and *Associations* sections are taken from the `Package` class and its relations to other classes. The content of those sections

---

[5] Three out of the four problem kinds exist within our small example.

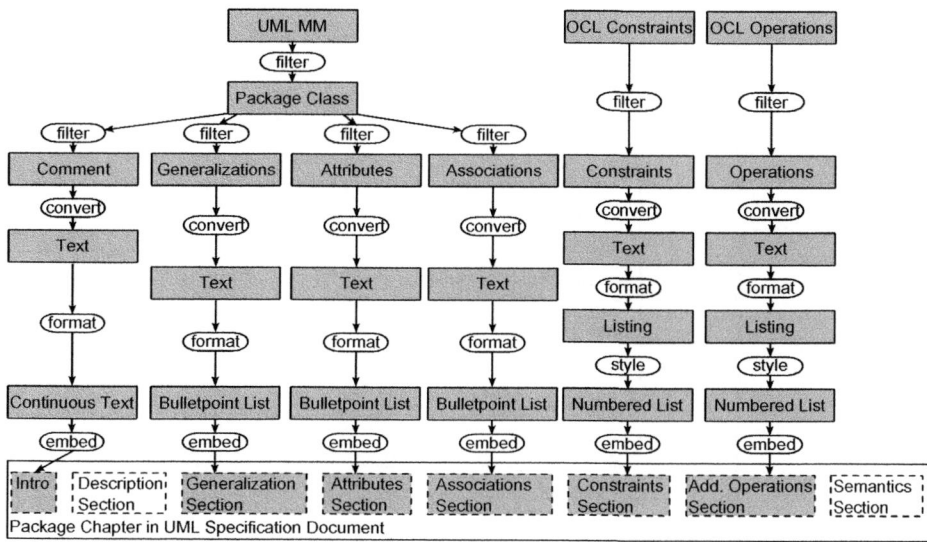

Fig. 4. Transclusion graph for an elucidative UML specification

is directly derived from the metamodel and formatted using rendering templates. The *Constraints* and *Additional Operations* sections are transcluded from the linked OCL files. Only the sections *Descriptions* and *Semantics* are not present in the artefacts and must therefore be written directly into the document.

Fig. 5 shows a snippet of the elucidative UML specfication in DEFT according to the transclusion graph in Fig. 4. On the left side of the screen the project content is shown in the *project explorer*. It presents chapters, source artefacts like the UML metamodel and OCL constraints, and their relations side by side. The actual specification document is displayed in the *writing area* and can be edited using OpenOffice. As visualised in Fig. 5, the artefact representations in the documentation file are transcluded from the artefacts added to the project explorer.

To solve the identified problems (P1) to (P4), model artefacts and the specification document have to be modified concurrently. DEFT supports the author with the revision of the specification. If a referenced model element changes, DEFT immediately updates the corresponding elements in the documentation and notifies the author. The changes are displayed in the *task view* (cf. Fig. 5), which helps to keep track of the changed specification parts.

(P1) problems can be avoided by transcluding textual model descriptions. If the models are modified, DEFT will update the descriptions automatically. (P2) problems can be handled in a similar way. Words relating to names or content of the UML metamodel (e.g., `package` or `namespace` in Fig. 3) are transcluded as well, such that after a renaming, the specification is automatically updated and the new names appear in the document. However, if the changes are more complex or the semantics of the model changes, manual updates guided by DEFT

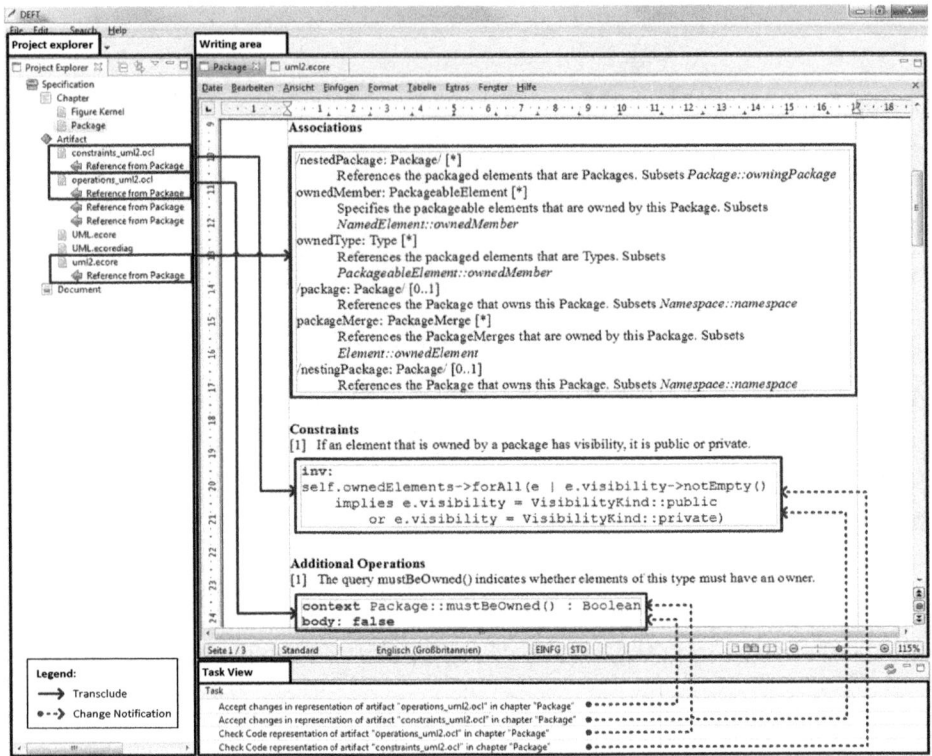

Fig. 5. Screenshot of the specification document in DEFT

hints might be necessary. (P3) problems are also solved automatically. The outdated graphical representation will be replaced by the current version of the diagram. Finally, (P4) problems can be avoided if the OCL constraints are reparsed after metamodel modifications and it is checked whether they are still consistent w.r.t. their static semantics. Possible modifications are immediately reflected in the specification.

Maintenance of the specification is expected to be rerun in multiple iterations. After each modification of the specified metamodel the documentation can be revised semi-automatically using DEFT. A revised specification can be released and the next maintenance cycle can be performed. This iterative process, using small changes and fast iterations helps to avoid inconsistencies as each modification of the metamodel or related artefacts is immediately displayed in the specification via hot update.

4   Discussion

After presenting ED and applying it to an excerpt of the UML specification we now discuss the resulting benefits. In our opinion ED can help to achieve more consistent language documentation and more formal specifications in MDSD processes. As our results from earlier work demonstrated, almost every second OCL constraint of the UML 2.4.1 specification contains errors that are avoidable by applying ED [8]. A simple integration of model-based techniques and OCL parsing into the specification process is sufficient to solve problems as syntactical and type checking errors (about 61.6% of all inconsistencies identified in [8]). Besides, the use of transclusion avoids inconsistencies due to overlooked modifications caused evolution of the UML metamodel (another 22.1% of all inconsistencies identified in [8]). Furthermore, ED allows short maintenance iterations as the maintenance of source artefacts and the specification are intertwined. Thus, requested changes are realised and newly revised specifications can be released quickly and regularly. Another advantage of using source artefacts during the specification process is that models can be shipped together with the specification. For example, the specified UML metamodel and parsable OCL files can be provided.

However, creating an initial documentation using DEFT can at first be time-consuming and more complicated than using a non-elucidative process, since the transclusion relations have to be marked-up and configured. However, we argue that ED pays off when the documentation (or the system) evolves. Besides, for documents like the UML specification—where similar sections occur for all the different classes defined in the standard—a script could help to generate a first version of the documentation containing similar information transcluded from all the different artefacts. Such a script would have to be written once, generating the content for all metaclasses, whereas otherwise, the same structure would have to be created manually again and again.

The UML specification process could also be enhanced using a standard template engine. However, instead applying ED with DEFT has several advantages. First, the only purpose of DEFT is creating and maintaining large documentation files in an author-oriented way. Hence, it offers more appropriate abstractions and a WYSIWYG editor while a template engine is more like a simple programming language and requires a certain amount of extra learning effort. Second, a template engine is not aware of the involved artefact relations, thus there is no support for hot update. Regeneration has to be triggered manually and involves the whole documentation, in the case of the UML specification this is time-consuming. Third, it is more difficult to identify changes that need to be proofread by humans. Finding differences between new and previous versions requires to run a diff tool. With standard diff tools, this is cumbersome to examine.

5   Related Work

In this section we discuss tools that are related to DEFT and applicable for maintaining documentations and specifications. Furthermore, we present work discussing the soundness of the UML specification and quality of WFRs within this specification.

Documentation in MDSD processes. Besides DEFT, other tools for documentation in MDSD processes exist. *Topcased*[6] is an open-source tool for model-driven development. It is based on the modelling capabilities of the Eclipse MDT but comes together with its own editors for graphical UML modelling and OCL editing support. As part of the tool suite, Topcased Gendoc allows the generation of textual documentations for UML models. Templates consisting of explanatory descriptions of the modelled concepts can be defined, including queries against UML models to derive explanatory figures and diagrams. It is possible to generate reports similar to the documents maintained with DEFT. However, Topcased Gendoc uses a completely generative approach to create model documentations and, thus, suffers from the shortcomings for generative approaches as discussed in Sect. 4. The Eclipse-based tool suite *Business Intelligence Reporting Tools (BIRT)* can be used to generate business reports from data maintained in databases.[7] It uses a template-based approach for the generation of textual reports, including tables and charts derived from the documented data. Although BIRT allows the creation and maintenance of documents, its major focus is on the generation of database reports and not on the documentation of modelling artefacts, such as EMF models. Furthermore, similar to Topcased Gendoc, BIRT only supports a model-based an no elucidative documentation process. *Intent*[8] is a recent documentation project inspired by LP. Documentation is created and maintained in a textual DSML that can express textual documentation as well as EMF-based artefacts (e.g., EMF model elements). The described artefacts and the documentation are derived from this description.[9] Besides models, Intent also supports other artefacts expressible using EMF (e.g., source code). The *LiMonE* [14] tool uses natural language processing for improving documentation consistency. For example, a sentence like *"A Class can have multiple Operations"* can be transformed into an OCL query that checks that the association between the classes Class and Operation has the right multiplicity in the UML metamodel. By combining DEFT and LiMonE, the elucidative process outlined in this paper could be further improved, as consistency checks on explanatory descriptions within the UML specification would be possible. Theoretically, even hints could be derived to inform the user which sentences within the specification have to be modified in which way to update the descriptions w.r.t. the modified metamodel.

Consistency of UML Specifications. A lot of related work with focuses on consistency of the UML specification exits. One of the most well-known publications in this domain is an article by Henderson-Sellors [4] that documents the result of a panel discussion of a group of modelling experts documenting their impressions of UML 2.0. Although the article addresses various kinds of problems in UML, these descriptions include the necessity of future revisions to improve the specification and the finding that many definitions are scattered throughout the specification.

---

[6] http://www.topcased.org/
[7] http://www.eclipse.org/birt/
[8] http://eclipse.org/intent/
[9] According to http://wiki.eclipse.org/Intent/Architecture, visited in March 2012.

In [3] Selic defines a basis for a formal description of the runtime semantics of UML 2.0. Although the paper focuses on the semantics definition, it also documents that semantics of UML concepts is scattered throughout the complete specification and different statements even contradict, which leads to inconsistent semantics definitions and statements such as that UML has "no semantics". Again, this work can be considered a motivation that the UML specification requires techniques such as ED. Other authors focus on the consistency of OCL rules within the UML specification and also on co-refactoring (or co-evolution) of OCL rules and their constrained (meta)model. Some of these works are outlined below. In 2003, Fuentes et al. [6] investigated the consistency of OCL rules within the UML 1.5 specification. They identified about 450 errors they categorised into non-accessible elements, empty names and other errors, including about 150 errors w.r.t. inconsistencies between the rules and the UML metamodel. Besides the identification of 450 errors Fuentes et al. also investigated inconsistencies between the given OCL rules and their textual documentation. In 2004, Bauerdick et al. investigated OCL WFRs specified within the UML 2.0 superstructure [7] and detected more than 350 errors within these OCL rules. In an earlier work we investigated the consistency of constraints specified within the UML 2.3 specification using OCL [8]. We identified about 320 errors within 442 OCL constraints. About 26% of all investigated OCL rules contained errors w.r.t. consistency between the rules and the evolved UML metamodel. Marković et al. formalised first refactorings of UML class diagrams that affect related OCL constraints and proposed Query/View/Transformation (QVT) rules for OCL co-refactorings [24]. Further work in this area based on existing Eclipse tools was done by Hassam et al. [25]. These results could be used to further improve our approach w.r.t. guidance for semi-automated OCL co-evolution which could help to keep the OCL WFRs and operation body definitions consistent to the UML metamodel.

6 Conclusion

In this paper we presented the *elucidative development* approach as a more versatile variant of *literate programming*. ED supports the documentation of source code, model artefacts, language specifications, and DSMLs. In ED source artefacts, such as metamodels and OCL constraints, are transformed and transcluded into documentation files via hot update. As a use case, we investigated an excerpt from the UML specification and identified inconsistency problems of different kinds resulting from manual specification maintenance. As demonstrated, these problems can be prevented by using an elucidative IDE such as DEFT.

For future work, further case studies in industrial scenarios are planned to explore the scalability of DEFT and ED. Besides, support for describing variants of the same specification would be a valuable add-on for ED, since a different group of readers may require different levels of abstraction with regard to the full specification. For instance, to ease the understanding a specification usually needs to be more abstract for a business audience, than for technical experts.

In [26], we proposed to use *feature models* [27] to model and generate variants from *document families* based on ODF and OpenOffice document formats. Since DEFT also supports ODF, an integration of both approaches would be feasible in the future. Also, a combination with the LiMonE approach seems promising, especially by using feature models to capture semi-structured text content of specifications. However, these ideas are still in an early state of evaluation. Furthermore, ED could be combined with other techniques for co-evolution. For example, co-evolution of UML models and OCL constraints that allows the propagation of model modifications to their OCL rules would be an interesting task. First works in this domain [24, 25] could provide a basis for such an integration. Finally, the usability of DEFT and ED could be improved by adding round-trip support. That allows editing transcluded model representations in the documentation and propagating changes back to the model.

Acknowledgement. The authors would like to thank the unknown reviewers for their valuable comments that helped to improve the paper. This research has been co-funded by the European Social Fund and Federal State of Saxony within the project ZESSY #080951806, by the European Social Fund, Federal State of Saxony and SAP AG within project #080949335, by the Collaborative Research Center 912 (HAEC), funded by DFG, and by the Federal Ministry of Education and Research within the project CoolSoftware #FKZ13N10782.

References

1. Wilke, C., Bartho, A., Schroeter, J., Karol, S., Aßmann, U.: Extended Version of Elucidative Development for Model-Based Documentation and Language Specification. Technical Report TUD-FI12-01-Januar 2012, TU Dresden (2012)
2. Object Management Group (OMG) Unified Modeling Language. Online available specification, http://www.omg.org/spec/UML/
3. Selic, B.: On the Semantic Foundations of Standard UML 2.0. In: Bernardo, M., Corradini, F. (eds.) SFM-RT 2004. LNCS, vol. 3185, pp. 181–199. Springer, Heidelberg (2004)
4. Henderson-Sellers, B.: UML – The Good, the Bad or the Ugly? Perspectives from a panel of experts. Software and Systems Modeling 4, 4–13 (2005)
5. Richters, M., Gogolla, M.: Validating UML Models and OCL Constraints. In: Evans, A., Caskurlu, B., Selic, B. (eds.) UML 2000. LNCS, vol. 1939, pp. 265–277. Springer, Heidelberg (2000)
6. Fuentes, J., Quintana, V., Llorens, J., Génova, G., Prieto-Díaz, R.: Errors in the UML metamodel? ACM SIGSOFT Software Engineering Notes 28(6) (2003)
7. Bauerdick, H., Gogolla, M., Gutsche, F.: Detecting OCL Traps in the UML 2.0 Superstructure: An Experience Report. In: Baar, T., Strohmeier, A., Moreira, A., Mellor, S.J. (eds.) UML 2004. LNCS, vol. 3273, pp. 188–196. Springer, Heidelberg (2004)
8. Wilke, C., Demuth, B.: UML is still inconsistent! How to improve OCL Constraints in the UML 2.3 Superstructure. In: Proceedings of the Workshop on OCL and Textual Modelling (OCL 2011). Electronic Communications of the EASST, vol. 44 (2011)

9. Knuth, D.E.: Literate Programming. The Computer Journal 27(2), 97–111 (1984)
10. Arlow, J., Emmerich, W., Quinn, J.A.: Literate Modelling — Capturing Business Knowledge with the UML. In: Bézivin, J., Muller, P.-A. (eds.) UML 1998. LNCS, vol. 1618, pp. 189–199. Springer, Heidelberg (1999)
11. Nørmark, K.: Elucidative programming. Nordic Journal of Computing 7, 87–105 (2000)
12. Nørmark, K.: Requirements for an Elucidative Programming Environment. In: Proceedings of the 8th International Workshop on Program Comprehension, IWPC 2000, pp. 119–128. IEEE Computer Society, Washington, DC (2000)
13. Knuth, D.E., Levy, S.: The CWEB System of Structured Documentation: Version 3.0, 1st edn. Addison-Wesley Longman Publishing Co. Inc. (1994)
14. Schulze, G.: Synchronization of UML Models and Narrative Text using Model Constraints and Natural Language Processing. Master's thesis, University of Innsbruck (2011)
15. Nørmark, K., Andersen, M., Christensen, C., Kumar, V., Staun-Pedersen, S., Sørensen, K.: Elucidative programming in Java. In: Proceedings of IPCC/SIGDOC 2000, pp. 483–495. IEEE Educational Activities Department (2000)
16. Bartho, A.: Creating and maintaining tutorials with DEFT. In: IEEE 17th International Conference on Program Comprehension (ICPC 2009), pp. 309–310. IEEE (2009)
17. Aßmann, U.: Architectural styles for active documents. Science of Computer Programming - Spec. Issue on New Software Composition Concepts 56, 79–98 (2005)
18. Nelson, T.H.: Complex information processing: a file structure for the complex, the changing and the indeterminate. In: Proceedings of the 1965 20th National Conference, pp. 84–100. ACM, New York (1965)
19. Nelson, T.H.: Literary Machines, 3rd edn. Mindful Press (1981)
20. Heidenreich, F., Johannes, J., Karol, S., Seifert, M., Wende, C.: Derivation and Refinement of Textual Syntax for Models. In: Paige, R.F., Hartman, A., Rensink, A. (eds.) ECMDA-FA 2009. LNCS, vol. 5562, pp. 114–129. Springer, Heidelberg (2009)
21. Heidenreich, F., Johannes, J., Karol, S., Seifert, M., Thiele, M., Wende, C., Wilke, C.: Integrating OCL and Textual Modelling Languages. In: Dingel, J., Solberg, A. (eds.) MoDELS 2010. LNCS, vol. 6627, pp. 349–363. Springer, Heidelberg (2011)
22. Object Management Group (OMG) Unified Modeling Language: Superstructure Version 2.4.1. Online available specification (August 2011)
23. Object Management Group (OMG) Unified Modeling Language: Superstructure Version 2.0. Online available specification (August 2005)
24. Marković, S., Baar, T.: Refactoring OCL Annotated UML Class Diagrams. In: Briand, L.C., Williams, C. (eds.) MoDELS 2005. LNCS, vol. 3713, pp. 280–294. Springer, Heidelberg (2005)
25. Hassam, K., Sadou, S., Le Gloahec, V., Fleurquin, R.: Assistance System for OCL Constraints Adaptation During Metamodel Evolution. In: Proceedings of 15th European Conference on Software Maintenance and Reengineering (CSMR 2011), pp. 151–160. Conference Publishing Services, CPS (2011)
26. Karol, S., Heinzerling, M., Heidenreich, F., Aßmann, U.: Using feature models for creating families of documents. In: Proceedings of the 10th ACM Symposium on Document Engineering, DocEng 2010, pp. 259–262. ACM, New York (2010)
27. Kang, K., Cohen, S., Hess, J., Nowak, W., Peterson, S.: Feature-oriented Domain Analysis (FODA) Feasibility Study. Technical Report CMU/SEI-90-TR-21, Software Engineering Institute, Pittsburgh, PA (1990)

Viewpoint Co-evolution through Coarse-Grained Changes and Coupled Transformations

Manuel Wimmer, Nathalie Moreno, and Antonio Vallecillo

Universidad de Málaga, Spain
{mw,moreno,av}@lcc.uma.es

Abstract. Multi-viewpoint modeling is an effective technique to deal with the ever-growing complexity of large-scale systems. The evolution of multi-viewpoint system specifications is currently accomplished in terms of fine-grained atomic changes. Apart from being a very low-level and cumbersome strategy, it is also quite unnatural to system modelers, who think of model evolution in terms of coarse-grained high-level changes. In order to bridge this gap, we propose an approach to formally express and manipulate viewpoint changes in a high-level fashion, by structuring atomic changes into coarse-grained composite ones. These can also be used to formally define reconciling operations to adapt dependent views, using *coupled* transformations. We introduce a modeling language based on graph transformations and Maude for expressing both, the coarse-grained changes and the coupled transformations that propagate them to reestablish global consistency. We demonstrate the applicability of the approach by its application in the context of RM-ODP.

1 Introduction

Large-scale heterogeneous systems are inherently much more complex to design, develop, and maintain than classical, homogeneous, centralized systems. One way to cope with such complexity is by dividing the design activity according to several areas of concerns, or *viewpoints*, each one focusing on a specific aspect of the system and allowing different stakeholders to observe the system from different perspectives [18].

Although separately specified, developed, and maintained to simplify reasoning about the complete system specifications, viewpoints are not completely independent: elements in each viewpoint need to be related to elements in the other viewpoints to ensure consistency and completeness of the global specifications. Such relationships are normally specified by means of *correspondences*, which are statements that permit some items in each viewpoint to be identified as related to items in the other viewpoints. Prominent examples that advocate such architectural decomposition are the Reference Model of Open Distributed Processing (RM-ODP) [17], the Model-Driven Web Engineering (MDWE) initiative [26] or UML [27], which provide different diagrams to represent different aspects of a system.

In this paper we are concerned with the evolution of multi-viewpoint specifications. As any other software artefact, they evolve over time due to a variety of reasons: changes in the requirements, errors in the design, evolution in the underlying technology, modifications in the system configuration, hardware or network connections to improve performance, etc. In general, dealing with model evolution is not easy, and the situation

C.A. Furia and S. Nanz (Eds.): TOOLS Europe 2012, LNCS 7304, pp. 336–352, 2012.

is even worse in case of multi-viewpoint system specifications: this implies not only consistent single-view evolution but also consistent multi-view evolution. A change in a view may imply changes in the rest of the views, or in the set of correspondences, which need to be synchronized to restore consistency.

A large number of approaches address the problem of multi-viewpoint integration and synchronization (e.g., cf. [7,10,32,37]). Due to the low-level of detail at which model changes are identified, represented, and handled by them, in terms of fine-grained atomic changes, most of these approaches become quite unnatural to system modelers, who think of model evolution in terms of coarse-grained high-level changes. Furthermore, tools supporting model evolution neither support detecting changes at this level of abstraction, nor do they permit propagating these kinds of changes through the correspondences. Therefore, everything needs to be done at the level of basic atomic changes, such as adding and removing elements or modifying their values. Thus, the semantic of the coarse-grained changes is lost which again may hamper the reconciliation of models, e.g., information is lost which should be preserved.

In order to bridge this gap, we propose an approach to formally express and manipulate viewpoint changes at a higher level of abstraction, by structuring fine-grained changes into coarse-grained ones that represent the conceptual units by which domain experts think and reason about the changes. They can also be used to formally define reconciling operations to adapt dependent views, using *coupled* transformations. For this purpose, we introduce a modeling language based on graph transformations and Maude for expressing both the coarse-grained changes and the coupled transformations that propagate them between viewpoints. Although our proposal has been designed to be generally applicable to any multi-viewpoint specification framework, in this paper we demonstrate the applicability of the approach by its application in the context of RM-ODP [17], the ISO/IEC and ITU-T standard architectural framework for multi-viewpoint specification of open distributed systems. RM-ODP provides five complementary viewpoints: *enterprise, information, computational, engineering*, and *technology* that allow to observe the environment from different perspectives.

2   Motivating Example

In order to illustrate our proposal we will use here a simple example of a multi-view specification in the context of the RM-ODP (Fig. 1-top). It models a banking application, which manages accounts owned by customers. Users can access banking services through Branches or ATMs. Some operations should be authorized by regional head offices, and several databases store the customers information, account, and the own bank organization. This can be seen as a three-layer architecture, where branches and ATMs provide the interfaces and basic banking operations to users, the headquarters provide the main business logic, and the databases store the system data.

The *Computational Viewpoint* (CV) focuses on the functionality of the system and its software architecture, which is described in terms of components (computational objects) and connectors (that can be either simple primitive bindings or more complex binding objects). The *Engineering Viewpoint* (NV) deals with how the functional components (basic engineering objects, or BEOs) are distributed in nodes (separated computing places) and connected via channels. Fig. 1 shows these two views, using the UML Profiles defined by the UML4ODP standard notation [16]. The other three viewpoints described by ODP (Information, Enterprise, and Technology) have not been included here for simplicity.

The elements of these two models are related through correspondences, which are expressed here using UML dependencies. Correspondences are shown in Fig. 1 using thicker dashed lines. They relate computational objects and bindings with the corresponding engineering objects and channels in the NV.

Evolution Scenarios in ODP. Let us think of a revised version of the Bank IT system specification, shown in Fig. 1-bottom. It contains three main changes: (1) computational objects Branch and ATM have been merged; (2) the primitive binding between HeadOffice and DBManager computational objects has been substituted by a binding object with more functionality (to add more powerful security mechanisms), and (3) the replica manager Dup in the NV has been moved from node Site4 to Site5.

Describing the changes at this level of detail is the way in which we normally reason about any system specification. Existing model difference tools calculate a very large number of atomic changes that need to be applied to the individual model elements. Understanding and manipulating those changes to, e.g., reason about the evolution of the system specifications or to propagate the (atomic) changes from one view to the rest, becomes quite a complex and brittle task. Quoting the well-known saying: "you can't see the forest for the trees."

In order to address this problem, we need to have a mechanism for representing and manipulating changes in models at a higher level of abstraction. We do that by structuring atomic changes into coarse-grained changes, which are closer to the way in which domain experts think about viewpoint evolution. Of course, the higher the abstraction level, the more *domain-specific* they get. This is because of the semantics they convey. In general, high-level composite operations depend on the specific domain. Each one defines a set of operations which reflect the kinds of changes commonly used in such a domain. For example, when dealing with software architectures two usual changes are to split a component into several and to merge several components into one. They imply a set of many atomic changes due to all the arrangements that need to be done with their ports, their connections with other components, etc. But conceptually they are just two changes.

In the following sections, the evolution of the Bank IT system specification is used to describe how composite changes are (a) represented; (b) identified and constructed from the set of individual atomic changes that existing model difference tools detect; and (c) propagated from one viewpoint to others by using Maude.

3 Formalizing Viewpoints in Maude

Maude [6] is a high-level language, a high-performance interpreter and compiler that supports rewriting logic based specification and programming of systems. Because of its efficient rewriting engine and complete analysis toolkit, Maude turns out to be an

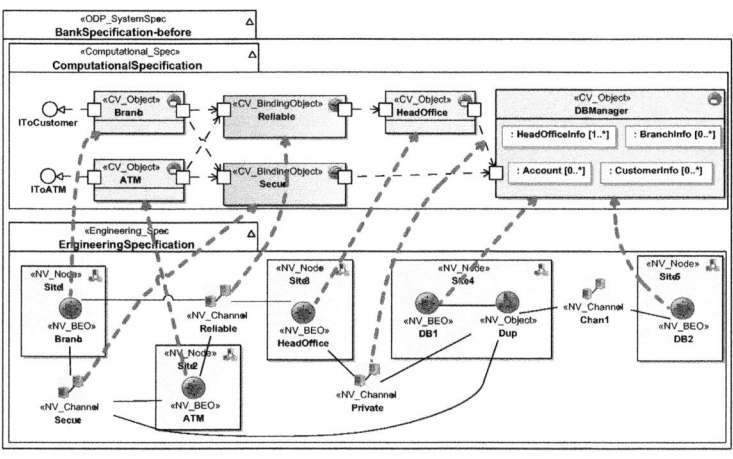

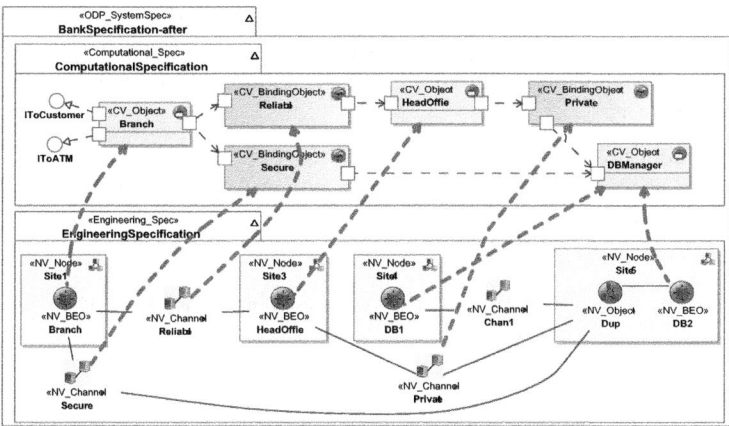

Fig. 1. Bank IT system specification expressed in ODP: Initial (top) and revised (bottom) models

excellent tool to specify and analyze many kinds of systems, at the appropriate level of abstraction. One of the benefits of using Maude is that its specifications are executable, since the rewrite rules that describe the behaviour of the system can be used to simulate it. The syntax for conditional rules is **crl** [l] : $t => t'$ if $Cond$, with l the rule label, t the left-hand side (LHS) of the rule, t' the right-hand side (RHS), and $Cond$ its condition.

Maude supports the specification of concurrent object-oriented systems in terms of object-oriented modules, which specify the system classes and their behaviour. Maude objects are structures of the form $< o : c \mid a_1 : v_1, ..., a_n : v_n >$, where o is the object identifier (of Sort Oid), c is the class the object belongs to, a_i are attribute identifiers and v_i their corresponding current values. The current state of the object-oriented system, which is called a *configuration*, has the structure of a multiset made up of objects that evolves as dictated by the rewriting rules. Predefined sort Configuration represents configurations of Maude objects, with none as the empty configuration.

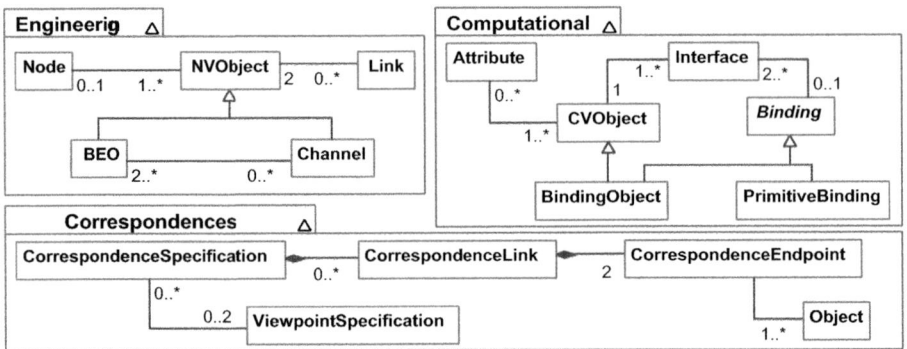

Fig. 2. Basic metamodels for CV, NV and Correspondences

In Maude, metamodels can be seen as object-oriented modules, which contain the specification of the metamodel classes. Thus, attributes can be represented as Maude attributes and references between metaclasses can be also represented as attributes, by means of sets of Maude object identifiers (Oid's). In this regard, depending on the multiplicity, we can use:

- a single identifier if the multiplicity is [1]
- a Maybe{Oid} which is either an identifier or a null value, for representing a [0 − 1] multiplicity or
- a Set{Oid} for multiplicity [∗]

The following listing describes the CV metamodel shown in Fig. 2 as a Maude object-oriented module:

```
(omod ODP is
protecting QID INT BOOL SET{Oid} CONVERSION .
--- Computational Viewpoint
class CVObject | interface : Set{Oid}, attribute : Set{Oid} .
class Attribute | cVObject : Set{Oid} .
class Interface | binding : Maybe{Oid}, cVObject : Oid .
class Binding | interface : Set{Oid} .
class PrimitiveBinding .
class BindingObject .
subclasses BindingObject PrimitiveBinding < Binding .
subclass BindingObject < CVObject .
endom) .
```

In the same way, a model that conforms to this metamodel can be represented in Maude by a configuration of Maude objects. Since objects may have attribute values and links, they are encoded as values of Maude objects' attributes. The configuration of Maude objects shown below represents an extract of the Bank specification model w.r.t. the CV specification illustrated in Fig. 1. It models two CVObjects, Branch and HeadOffice, linked by the BindingObject Reliable and two Bindings.

```
< 'Branch : CVObject | interface : ( 'IC1 , 'IC2 ) >
< 'HeadOffice : CVObject | interface : ( 'IC3 , 'IC4 ) >
< 'Reliable : BindingObject | interface : ( 'IC5 , 'IC6 ) >
< 'BC1 : Binding | interface : ( 'IC2 , 'IC5 ) >
< 'BC2 : Binding | interface : ( 'IC6 , 'IC3 ) >
```

4   Change Detection: From Fine- to Coarse-Grained Changes

Two kinds of approaches to change detection may be distinguished, namely, *model comparison* and *change tracking*. In a perfect world, we would assume to have a complete change log produced by the model manipulation tools automatically. However, current modeling editors are often not equipped with a change recorder. Furthermore, models can be edited with different tools and on different levels, e.g., within graphical or textual modeling editors, using UML and DSM tools, using the models' XML-based serializations, or by applying automatic model transformations. Model comparison is a generic approach to decouple the change log computation from the actual model manipulation.

In the context of this paper, we employ a two-phase *model comparison* approach. In the first phase, fine-grained changes are computed based on object identifier equivalences. For this phase, we build on our previous work presented in [30]. In the second phase, the fine-grained changes are analyzed to find coarse-grained changes between the two model versions. Furthermore, coarse-grained changes can also be composed into even coarser ones. In the following, we demonstrate both phases with the help of our running example.

4.1   Phase 1: Detecting Fine-Grained Changes

The first phase of the change detection consists of two sequential steps. The first step is to find the corresponding elements in the initial model and revised model based on matching rules. From the match result, differences are derived in the second step based on differencing rules.

Step 1: Matching. In the context of this paper, we use object identifiers to find the corresponding elements. A match is reported for each pair of objects having the same identifier assigned in the initial model and in the revised model. If such a pair is found, a match object is created which links the two objects. Of course, more sophisticated match rules based on name and structure similarities may be applied [30].

The following listing formalizes the previously explained match strategy. First, classes for representing MatchModels and Matches are introduced which are instantiated by the subsequent equation match. This equation is executed as long as objects with same identifier are found in the initial and the revised version of the model. Please note that both models are represented as *configurations* in Maude. Thus, the match operation is defined for two configurations (representing the initial and the revised model) and returns a match model which is again a configuration.

```
(omod Match is
 class MatchModel .
 class Match | initEl : Oid, revEl : Oid .
 subclass MatchModel < Configuration .
 vars INITIAL, REVISED, MATCH : Configuration .

 op match : Configuration Configuration -> MatchModel .
 eq match(< O : C1 | ATTS1 > INITIAL, < O : C2 | ATTS2 > REVISED)
 = < M : Match | initEl : O, revEl : O > match(INITIAL, REVISED) .
 eq match(INITIAL, REVISED) = none [owise] .
```

Example. When the match operation is executed for a subset of our running example considering only the elements involved in the EnrichBinding change, matches are generated for the CVObjects, but the Binding in the initial model as well as the BindingObject and its Bindings in the revised model remain unmatched.

Step 2: Differencing. Based on the match model, the difference detection is performed. In the following, we introduce fine-grained change types and how instances of them may be detected. The following listing shows the supported fine-grained change types as Maude classes.

```
(omod fDiff is
 class DiffElement .
 class Addition | elem : Oid .
 class Deletion | elem : Oid .
 class Update | elm1 : Oid, elm2 : Oid, feature : String .
 subclass Addition, Deletion, Update < DiffElement .
endom)
```

Diff Calculation. Classes Addition, Deletion, and Update are instantiated by equations. These equations are built based on the following change detection rules explained in natural language: (a) If a model element of the initial model is not matched then it generates a deletion; (b) If a model element of the revised model is not matched then it generates an addition; (c) If a model element of the initial model is matched to an element of the revised model then they are compared for each feature the values of both model elements. Just when their values are different, an update is generated.

Diff Representation. For representing changes in a more convenient way, we rewrite the produced diff elements which are typed by generic change types (cf. classes Addition, Deletion, and Update) to metamodel-specific changes. Although, such differences are specific for a given metamodel, the difference metamodel is automatically derivable from the modeling language metamodel by using a dedicated transformation [4]. Instead of stating in the change model that an object has been added and more information about this change has to be queried by navigating to the objects in the revised and initial models, we aim for presenting more information about a change directly in the difference model (diff model) by having metamodel specific change types.

The design rationale for choosing this change representation is based on the assumption that metamodel-specific change types allow for a more concise formulation of programs analyzing the fine-grained changes—so to speak to provide an intuitive programming interface. Such programs are actually needed for finding coarse-grained changes in a set of fine-grained changes as well as for change propagation. Besides usability, also performance of dependent programs may be enhanced by this kind of representation.

Example. The differencing rules explained above allow to derive the following difference model for EnrichBinding change excerpt of the running example. By starting from the previously calculated matches, we end up with four fine-grained differences: DELBinding, ADDBindingObject, ADDBinding, ADDBinding.

```
Maude> rewrite < 'M1 : Match | iniEl : 'Branch, revEl : 'Branch >
                < 'M2 : Match | iniEl : 'DBManager, revEl : 'DBManager >
 result @Object: < 'D1 : DELBinding | element : 'B1 >
 < 'A1 : ADDBindingObject | element : 'Reliable >
 < 'A2 : ADDBinding | element : 'B2 >
 < 'A3 : ADDBinding | element : 'B3 >
```

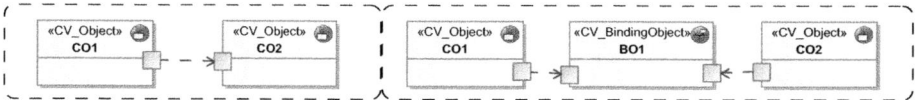

Fig. 3. Evolution pattern for the EnrichBinding change

4.2   Phase 2: Detecting Coarse-Grained Changes

Additional rules have to be formulated to structure fine-grained changes into coarse-grained changes. The development of such rules should be done in the language of the modelers. Because, in contrast to fine-grained changes which have simple and generic contracts, coarse-grained changes may comprise complex contracts. Thus, we sketch in the following subsection coarse-grained changes based on graph transformations patterns stating the situation before a coarse-grained change is applied, i.e., the pre-condition, as well as showing the effect of the coarse-grained change, i.e, the post-condition. These graph transformation patterns act as blueprints for the implementation of the detection rules for coarse-grained changes in Maude.

Sketching coarse-grained Changes. For sketching coarse-grained changes, we use *evolution patterns* which are based on graph transformation patterns using the concrete syntax of modeling languages. The pattern shown in Fig. 3 visualizes the EnrichBinding change in the concrete notation of ODP. The LHS of the pattern represents the situation before the change is executed and the RHS is showing the situation after the change has been applied. Thus, the semantic of the patterns is equivalent to standard graph trans-formation patterns. If an element resides on the LHS as well as on the RHS (i.e., the same variable name is used on the LHS and on the RHS), then it stays in the model. If an element only resides in the LHS and not in the RHS, it is deleted. Finally, if an element only resides in the RHS and not in the LHS, it is created. However, the operational semantics of such evolution patterns are different to standard graph transformation approaches. The evolution pattern is not executed by finding a match of the LHS in a model to rewrite it as given by the RHS to produce a new model version. Instead the evolution pattern is used to derive a program which detects the application of the described change. The detection is done by analyzing the initial and the revised model as well as the fine-grained changes between them.

Encoding detection rules in Maude. The detection rules for finding the evolution patterns are implemented in Maude based on the Maude operation called evolution, which has as input parameter a triple of models: (a) model before the change, (b) the model after the change, and (c) the difference model describing the fine-grained changes. The output is again a model which covers all coarse-grained changes happened between the initial and the revised model.

Based on the notion of the evolution operation and sketched evolution patterns, e.g., cf. Fig. 3, a Maude rule may be developed which searches for the application of the change. The main mechanism is to match for the set of fine-grained changes which make up the coarse-grained change. Each change type is represented by its own class which is instantiated by an accompanying rule.

```
(omod cDiff is
op model : Configuration -> Model[ctor] .
op evolution : Model Model Model -> Model .
class EnrichBinding | binding : Oid, bindingObject : Oid .
rl [EnrichBinding] :
   evolution (
     model( < C01 : CVObject | > < C02 : CVObject | >
       < B1 : Binding | source : C01, target : C02 > INITIAL ),
     model( < D1 : DELBinding | element : B1 >
       < A1 : ADDBindingObject | element : B01 >
       < A2 : ADDBinding | element : B2 >
       < A3 : ADDBinding | element : B3 > DIFF ),
     model( < C01 : CVObject | > < C02 : CVObject | >
       < B01 : CVBindingObject | >
       < B2 : CVBinding | source : C01, target : B01 >
       < B3 : CVBinding | source : C02, target : B01 > REVISED ) )
=> evolution (
     model( < C01 : CVObject | > < C02 : CVObject | >
       < B1 : Binding | source : C01, target : C02 > INITIAL ),
     model( < EB1 : EnrichBinding | binding : B1, bindingObject : B01 > DIFF ),
     model( < C01 : CVObject | > < C02 : CVObject | >
       < B01 : BindingObject | >
       < B2 : Binding | source : C01, target : B01 >
       < B3 : Binding | source : C02, target : B01 > REVISED ) ) .
endom )
```

Example. For detecting EnrichBinding changes, the Maude rule is shown in the above listing. The LHS of the rule is searching for matches of the evolution pattern of Fig. 3 by matching it on the initial, diff, and revised models. If a match is found, the atomic differences in the diff model are consumed and the coarse grained change EnrichBinding is instantiated instead, linking to the deleted binding in the initial model and to the introduced binding object in the revised model. By using this rule, the atomic differences computed by **Phase 1** can be reduced to just one EnrichBinding change. This result is further processed for change propagation in order to reflect the coarse-grained change of one view in depending views which is explained in the next section.

5   Change Propagation by Coupled Transformations

After coarse-grained changes in one viewpoint have been detected, they have to be propagated to dependent viewpoints. For this purpose, we follow the idea of *coupled transformations*—a term originally coined by Ralf Lämmel [22]. In particular, we aim for asymmetric reconciliation of viewpoints by exploiting explicit correspondence links between viewpoints.

The schema on the RHS illustrates the notion of coupled transformations interpreted in the context of viewpoint synchronization. An *initiator change*, by executing t_1 on the viewpoint VP_{a_v1}, produces a new version VP_{a_v2}. For retaining consistency between the dependent viewpoint VP_{b_v1} and VP_{a_v2}, the reconciling transformation t_2 has to be executed on VP_{b_v1}. Furthermore, to consider the modifications in the two viewpoints, another reconciling transformation t_3 has to be executed on the correspondence model CM_{ab_v1}.

$$
\begin{array}{ccc}
VP_{b\_v1} & \xrightarrow{(t_2)} & VP_{b\_v2} \\
\uparrow & & \uparrow \\
| & & | \\
CM_{ab\_v1} & \xrightarrow{(t_3)} & CM_{ab\_v2} \\
| & & | \\
\downarrow & & \downarrow \\
VP_{a\_v1} & \xrightarrow{(t_1)} & VP_{a\_v2}
\end{array}
$$

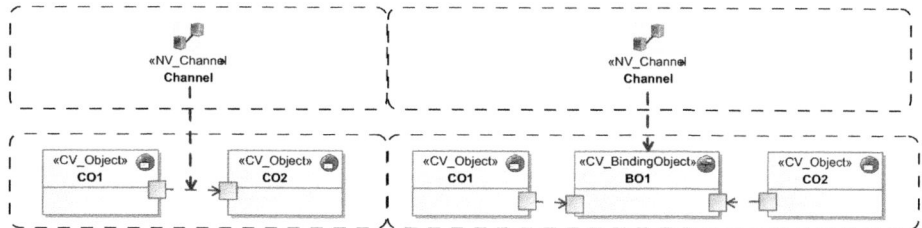

Fig. 4. Co-Evolution pattern for the EnrichBinding change

The execution of the initiator transformation is independent, meaning that it does not dependent on matches of other rules to compute its own matches. In contrast, the matches of reconciling transformations are based on the matches of the initiator transformations to consider the proper set of elements in dependent viewpoints which have to be adapted. To identify this proper set of elements, the correspondences between elements involved in the initiator change and elements of dependent viewpoints are the key information.

In the following, a high-level notation is introduced for coupling transformations which represents coarse-grained changes on different viewpoints. The notation extends the evolution patterns for coupling different evolution patterns to model *co-evolution patterns*. Subsequently, it is shown how co-evolution patterns are implemented in Maude.

5.1   Sketching Coupled Transformations

Co-evolution patterns, e.g., as shown in Fig. 4, comprise the following structure. First the initiator transformation (t_1) has to be specified. This is done by reusing an already evolution pattern which describes the change as discussed in the previous section. Having the initiator transformation as a basis, we may define new or reuse existing evolution patterns for describing reconciliator transformations (t_2 and t_3). For determining the exact matches of the reconciliator transformations, links between elements of the different patterns are used. In case of modeling languages offering explicit correspondence models, these links are expressed by additional correspondence models interlinking elements of two evolution patterns.

Example. For the EnrichBinding change, we may reuse the evolution pattern of Fig. 3 as the initiator transformation for defining the co-evolution pattern. Bindings in the CV are linked to Channels in the NV via correspondences. So when a Binding is deleted—this is actually the case when an EnrichBinding transformation is executed—there remain correspondences linking to missing elements in the CV. Thus, reconciliator changes are necessary to reestablish a link to proper CV elements. In case of EnrichBinding, the correspondences from Channels have to be relinked from missing Bindings to newly introduced BindingObjects. This reconciliation is specified in the co-evolution pattern of Fig. 4 by modeling another transformation for the correspondence model (middle layer). However, for finding the correspondences to adapt,

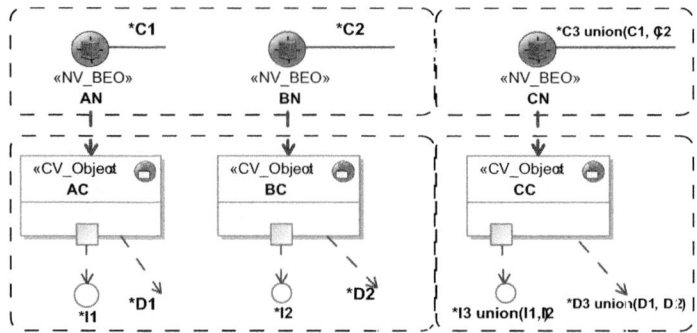

Fig. 5. Co-Evolution pattern for the MergeComponent change

the Channels of the NV are needed. Therefore another layer is introduced on top. No change in the NV is necessary, so one Channel is shown in the LHS and in the RHS to find the proper set of correspondences to relink.

A more complex example concerning the reconciliation of multi-viewpoints is the MergeComponent change. When it is detected in the CV, not only the correspondences, but also the NV has to be modified. This also involves to have sets of elements in the evolution patterns which are marked in our notation by the star operator. For instance, as sketched in Fig. 5, if two CVObjects named AC and BC are merged in a final CVObject CC, the union of their interfaces and bindings (cf. union(I1,I2) and union(D1,D2)) are required for CC. Similarly, when two BEOs are merged to reflect the change also in the NV, the union of their links to channels has to be build as well (cf. union(C1,C2) in Fig. 5).

5.2 Encoding Coupled Transformations in Maude

We describe the co-evolution of multi-viewpoints in Maude as an operation named multievolution that when applied to a particular configuration of viewpoints, produces a new configuration of them as a result.

```
(omod Reconciliator is ...
op multievolution : Configuration Configuration Configuration -> Configuration .
... endom)
```

Although more than one viewpoint may evolve at the same time, for the sake of simplicity, we assume here that there is only one base view that initializes the change. Thus, for each initiator change type, we use a Maude rule to trigger the evolution of other viewpoints related to the changed viewpoint. Of course, changes in one viewpoint will require the definition of several rules—one rule for each of the viewpoints that might be affected by the change—which describe how the system must continue to evolve in order to reach a reconciliation state between all viewpoints. The following listing sketches the general form of a propagation rule.

```
rl [nameRule] :
 multievolution( --- detection of the initiator change
   evolution ( --- V2: dependent viewpoint
     model( V2-BEFORE ), model( V2-REST ), model( V3-AFTER ) ),
   evolution ( --- correspondences
     model( CORR-BEFORE ), model( CORR-REST ), model( CORR-AFTER ) ),
   evolution ( --- V1: viewpoint originating the change
     model( V1-BEFORE ), model( V1-REST ), model( V1-AFTER ) )
 ) =>
 multievolution( --- execution of the reconciliation change
   evolution ( --- V2: dependent viewpoint evolves
     model( V2-BEFORE ), model( V2'-REST ), model( V3'-AFTER ) ),
   evolution ( --- correspondences evolve
     model( CORR-BEFORE ), model( CORR-REST' ), model( CORR-AFTER' ) ),
   evolution ( --- V1: viewpoint originating the change
     model( V1-BEFORE ), model( V1-REST ), model( V1-AFTER ) )
 ) .
```

The LHS of the rule contains the evolution models for the initiator and the related viewpoint and the correspondences relating them. For the viewpoint initiating the evolution, the composite operation representing the initiator change has to be identified. In this way, the RHS contains the effect of propagating the change to the other viewpoints and to the correspondences, again defined in terms of the high-level composite operations.

Example. Let us consider the Maude rule for propagating the EnrichBinding change from CV to NV. As mentioned before, the NV needs no adaptation, but the correspondences may have to be updated. Thus, the following rule matches for an occurrence of the EnrichBinding change that has not been propagated yet, using the third evolution pattern in the LHS. The first and the second evolution patterns are used to find the elements that are involved in the reconciliation. Thus, the LHS has to find the correspondence which link a channel with the enriched binding. In the RHS, the first and the third evolution patterns are equivalent to the LHS patterns, but the second evolution pattern is not. It takes care of relinking the correspondence to the created BindingObject.

```
rl [EnrichBinding2NV] :
multievolution(
 evolution ( --- engineering viewpoint
     model( < Chan : Channel | > ENG-BEFORE ),
     model( ENG-REST ),
     model( < Chan : Channel | > ENG-AFTER ) ),
 evolution ( --- correspondences
     model( < C1 : Correspondence | source : B1, target : Chan > CORR-BEFORE ),
     model( CORR-REST ),
     model( < C1 : Correspondence | source : B1, target : Chan > CORR-AFTER ) ),
 evolution ( --- computational viewpoint originates the change
     model( < C01 : CVObject | > < C02 : CVObject | >
     < B1 : Binding | source : C01, target : C02 > INITIAL-REST ),
     model( < EB1 : EnrichBinding | binding : B1, bindingObject : B01, propagated-
         ↪NV : false > DIFF-REST ),
     model( < C01 : CVObject | > < C02 : CVObject | >
     < B01 : BindingObject | > ... REVISED-REST ) )
) =>
multievolution(
 evolution ( --- engineering viewpoint same as in LHS ),
 evolution ( --- correspondences are updated
     model( < C1 : Correspondence | source : B1, target : Chan > CORR-BEFORE ),
     model( CORR-REST ),
     model( < C1 : Correspondence | source : B01, target : Chan > CORR-AFTER ) ),
 evolution ( --- computational viewpoint same as in LHS
             --- except < EB1 : EnrichBinding | propagated-NV : true >  )
) .
```

Let us now consider the Maude rule[1] for propagating the MergeComponent change. The third evolution pattern of the LHS matches for MergeComponent change in the CV that has not been propagated, yet. If a match is found, the NV and the correspondences start to evolve as the RHS of the rule dictates. Since each computational object that is not a binding object corresponds to a set of one or more basic engineering objects (and any channels which connect them), the coarse-grained MergeComponent operator causes that the Branch and ATM BEOs in the NV must also be merged. Finally, in order to preserve the system correspondences, the rule throws a final reconciliator evolution in the correspondences model to reestablish proper links between the new elements generated in the CV and the NV models. The reader should note that, at this point, a similar rule will also be required to define the effects of the MergeBEO composite operator in the entire system specification that we omit here for the sake of simplicity.

```
rl [MergeComponent2NV] :
multievolution(
 evolution ( --- engineering viewpoint
    model( < AN : BEO | > < BN : BEO | > ENG-BEFORE ),
    model( ENG-REST ),
    model( < AN : BEO | > < BN : BEO | > ENG-AFTER ) ),
 evolution ( --- correspondences
    model( < C1 : Correspondence | source : AC, target : AN >
           < C2 : Correspondence | source : BC, target : BN > CORR-BEFORE ),
    model( CORR-REST ),
    model( < C1 : Correspondence | source : AC, target : AN >
           < C2 : Correspondence | source : BC, target : BN > CORR-AFTER ) ),
 evolution ( --- computational viewpoint originating the change
    model( < AC : CVObject | > < BC : CVObject | > COMP-BEFORE ),
    model( < MC : MergeComponent | target : CC, source1 : AC, source2 : BC,
           ↪propagated-NV : false > COMP-REST ),
    model( < CC : CVObject | > COMP-AFTER ) )
) =>
multievolution(
 evolution ( --- engineering viewpoint
    model( < AN : BEO | > < BN : BEO | > ENG-BEFORE ),
    model( < XN : MergeBEO | target : CN, source1 : AN, source2 : BN, propagated-
           ↪TV : false > ENG-REST ),
    model( < CN : BEO | > ENG-AFTER ) ),
 evolution ( --- correspondences
    model( < C1 : Correspondence | source : AC, target : AN >
           < C2 : Correspondence | source : BC, target : BN > CORR-BEFORE ),
    model( CORR-REST ) , --- replaces both correspondences by a new one
    model( < C3 : Correspondence | source : CC, target : CN > CORR-AFTER ) )
 evolution ( --- computational viewpoint same as in LHS
           --- except < MC : MergeComponent | propagated-NV : true > )
) .
```

6   Related Work

Multi-Viewpoint Integration and Synchronization. A large number of approaches address the problem of multi-viewpoint integration and synchronization [7]. We have works on synchronizing artifacts in software engineering, mostly influenced by original works on multi-view consistency [11,13] using a generic representation of modifications and relying on users to write code to handle each type of modification in each type of view. This idea influenced later efforts on model synchronization

---

[1] Building the union of the links (cf. union(C1,C2) in Fig. 5) requires an additional rule for filtering reflexive links as well as duplicates which is not shown for sake of simplicity.

frameworks in general [19,20] and in particular bi-directional model transformations [33,37]. Other approaches use so-called correspondence rules for synchronizing models in the contexts of RM-ODP and MDWE [3,10,32]. More theoretical works propose to use different kind of lenses [8,9,12,15].

All these approaches have in common that they consider only atomic changes when reconciling models. Thus, the goal of the reconciliation is to change the models in a way that they satisfy again the given constraints. However, when structuring the changes to composite changes, more appropriate reconciled models may be found. The reason for this is that the semantics of the changes, modeling languages, and modeling domains are considered instead of reasoning with generic atomic changes for generic model elements. For example, when merging two elements into one may be represented by three atomic changes, namely deleting both elements and adding a new element which represents the two merged elements. When considering each atomic change in isolation, depending elements in other views may be deleted and a new element may be added if we have a one-to-one correspondence to fulfill between the views. However, the information of the deleted elements is lost. By using our approach, we are able to specify the rules for the reconciliation without information loss by merging also dependent elements in the other views instead of deleting them. The only work we are aware of allowing to propagate more complex changes is [29], however, in this approach it is required to record the initiator changes during model editing.

Metamodel/Model and Model/Instances Co-evolution. This involves synchronization between models of different abstraction levels [34]. In the general case, semantics-preserving transformations must be developed manually, based on the understanding of the semantic intent of the change. Several dedicated languages for metamodel/model co-evolution have been recently developed for specifying semantic-preserving transformations [5,14,25,31]. Most related to our approach is [36], where the composition of atomic differences to composite differences is discussed for Ecore-based metamodels. Having composite differences between metamodel versions is considered to be the prerequisite for finding the appropriate co-evolution for the model level. However, the propagation of the composite changes to the instances has not been presented. Our approach is generic in the sense that also metamodel/model co-evolution may be supported. In particular, the coupling between the metamodel changes and model changes is similar as the coupling of changes between different views.

Coarse-grained changes for models. Most existing approaches for defining coarse-grained changes focus solely on model refactorings. The work in [35] defined a set of UML refactorings on the conceptual level by expressing pre- and post-conditions in OCL, and [2] presented a refactoring browser for UML supporting the automatic execution of pre-defined UML refactorings. While these two approaches focus on pre-defined refactorings only, other approaches [21,28,38] allow the introduction of user-defined refactorings by using dedicated textual languages. A similar idea is followed in [1,24] but instead of textual languages, graph transformations are used to describe refactorings. However, the proposed approaches cover mostly single-view evolution and focus on the implementation of semi-automatically executable refactorings. Only some first ideas for tackling consistency between different views in the context of coarse-grained changes have been presented. For instance, [23] proposed to refactor UML class diagrams, also adapting attached OCL constraints.

7   Conclusions and Future Work

We have presented an approach for expressing, executing, and synchronizing viewpoint changes at a high-level of abstraction. We structure atomic changes into coarse-grained changes that represent the conceptual units that domain experts are used to, and are coupled for propagating the semantics of one change in one viewpoint into related viewpoints. A major strength of our approach comes from the use of Maude and its expressive power. Although coarse-grained changes and coupled transformations have been used in previous works, the composition of fine-grained changes into coarse-grained changes for viewpoint synchronization using coupled transformation is novel and represents an alternative to constraint-based model synchronization.

As future work, we want to investigate a hybrid synchronization approach by using in the first phase the presented approach for propagating coarse-grained changes and in the second phase a constraint-based approach for propagating atomic changes which could not be composed into coarse-grained changes. In addition, applying the approach to other modeling domains will provide us extensive feedback. These experiences will be used to establish a model synchronization benchmark based on real-life scenarios coming from different application domains.

Acknowledgements. This work has been partially funded by the Austrian Science Fund (FWF) under grant J 3159-N23, and by Spanish Research Project TIN2011-23795.

References

1. Biermann, E., Ehrig, K., Köhler, C., Kuhns, G., Taentzer, G., Weiss, E.: Graphical Definition of In-Place Transformations in the Eclipse Modeling Framework. In: Wang, J., Whittle, J., Harel, D., Reggio, G. (eds.) MoDELS 2006. LNCS, vol. 4199, pp. 425–439. Springer, Heidelberg (2006)
2. Boger, M., Sturm, T., Fragemann, P.: Refactoring Browser for UML. In: Aksit, M., Awasthi, P., Unland, R. (eds.) NODe 2002. LNCS, vol. 2591, pp. 366–377. Springer, Heidelberg (2003)
3. Cicchetti, A., Ruscio, D.D.: Decoupling Web Application Concerns through Weaving Operations. Science of Computer Programming 70(1), 62–86 (2008)
4. Cicchetti, A., Ruscio, D.D., Pierantonio, A.: A metamodel independent approach to difference representation. Journal of Object Technology 6(9), 165–185 (2007)
5. Cicchetti, A., Di Ruscio, D., Pierantonio, A.: Managing Dependent Changes in Coupled Evolution. In: Paige, R.F. (ed.) ICMT 2009. LNCS, vol. 5563, pp. 35–51. Springer, Heidelberg (2009)
6. Clavel, M., Durán, F., Eker, S., Lincoln, P., Martí-Oliet, N., Meseguer, J., Talcott, C.: All About Maude - A High-Performance Logical Framework. LNCS, vol. 4350. Springer, Heidelberg (2007)

7. Diskin, Z., Xiong, Y., Czarnecki, K.: Specifying Overlaps of Heterogeneous Models for Global Consistency Checking. In: Dingel, J., Solberg, A. (eds.) MoDELS 2010. LNCS, vol. 6627, pp. 165–179. Springer, Heidelberg (2011)
8. Diskin, Z., Xiong, Y., Czarnecki, K.: From State- to Delta-Based Bidirectional Model Transformations: the Asymmetric Case. JOT 10(6), 1–25 (2011)
9. Diskin, Z., Xiong, Y., Czarnecki, K., Ehrig, H., Hermann, F., Orejas, F.: From State- to Delta-Based Bidirectional Model Transformations: The Symmetric Case. In: Whittle, J., Clark, T., Kühne, T. (eds.) MoDELS 2011. LNCS, vol. 6981, pp. 304–318. Springer, Heidelberg (2011)
10. Eramo, R., Pierantonio, A., Romero, J.R., Vallecillo, A.: Change management in multi-viewpoint systems using ASP. In: WODPEC 2008. IEEE (2008)
11. Finkelstein, A., Gabbay, D.M., Hunter, A., Kramer, J., Nuseibeh, B.: Inconsistency Handling in Multi-perspective Specifications. In: Sommerville, I., Paul, M. (eds.) ESEC 1993. LNCS, vol. 717, pp. 84–99. Springer, Heidelberg (1993)
12. Foster, J.N., Pilkiewicz, A., Pierce, B.C.: Quotient lenses. In: ICFP 2008, pp. 383–396. ACM (2008)
13. Grundy, J., Hosking, J., Mugridge, W.B.: Inconsistency Management for Multiple-view Software Development Environments. IEEE Trans. Softw. Eng. 24(11), 960–981 (1998)
14. Herrmannsdoerfer, M., Benz, S., Jüergens, E.: COPE - Automating Coupled Evolution of Metamodels and Models. In: Drossopoulou, S. (ed.) ECOOP 2009. LNCS, vol. 5653, pp. 52–76. Springer, Heidelberg (2009)
15. Hofmann, M., Pierce, B.C., Wagner, D.: Symmetric lenses. In: POPL 2011, pp. 371–384. ACM (2011)
16. ISO/IEC: Information technology – Open distributed processing – Use of UML for ODP system specifications (2009), iSO/IEC19793, ITU-T X.906
17. ISO/IEC: RM-ODP. Reference Model for Open Distributed Processing (2010), iSO/IEC 10746-1 to 10746-4, ITU-T Recs. X.901 to X.904
18. ISO/IEC 42010: Systems and software engineering – Architectural description (2008)
19. Ivkovic, I., Kontogiannis, K.: Tracing Evolution Changes of Software Artifacts through Model Synchronization. In: ICSM 2004, pp. 252–261 (2004)
20. Johann, S., Egyed, A.: Instant and Incremental Transformation of Models. In: ASE 2004, pp. 362–365. IEEE (2004)
21. Kolovos, D.S., Paige, R.F., Polack, F., Rose, L.M.: Update Transformations in the Small with the Epsilon Wizard Language. JOT 6(9), 53–69 (2007)
22. Lämmel, R.: Coupled Software Transformations (Extended Abstract). In: First International Workshop on Software Evolution Transformations (2004)
23. Markovic, S., Baar, T.: Refactoring OCL annotated UML class diagrams. SoSym 7(1), 25–47 (2008)
24. Mens, T.: On the Use of Graph Transformations for Model Refactoring. In: Lämmel, R., Saraiva, J., Visser, J. (eds.) GTTSE 2005. LNCS, vol. 4143, pp. 219–257. Springer, Heidelberg (2006)
25. Meyers, B., Wimmer, M., Cicchetti, A., Sprinkle, J.: A generic in-place transformation-based approach to structured model co-evolution. In: MPM 2010 (2010)
26. Moreno, N., Romero, J.R., Vallecillo, A.: An Overview of Model-Driven Web Engineering and the MDA. In: Web Engineering: Modelling and Implementing Web Applications, pp. 353–382. Springer (2007)
27. OMG: Unified Modeling Language (UML) 2.3. Object Management Group, Inc. (2010)
28. Porres, I.: Rule-based Update Transformations and their Application to Model Refactorings. SoSym 4(4), 368–385 (2005)
29. Ráth, I., Varró, G., Varró, D.: Change-Driven Model Transformations. In: Schürr, A., Selic, B. (eds.) MoDELS 2009. LNCS, vol. 5795, pp. 342–356. Springer, Heidelberg (2009)

30. Rivera, J.E., Vallecillo, A.: Representing and Operating with Model Differences. In: Paige, R.F., Meyer, B. (eds.) TOOLS EUROPE 2008. LNBIP, vol. 11, pp. 141–160. Springer, Heidelberg (2008)

31. Rose, L.M., Kolovos, D.S., Paige, R.F., Polack, F.A.C.: Model Migration with Epsilon Flock. In: Tratt, L., Gogolla, M. (eds.) ICMT 2010. LNCS, vol. 6142, pp. 184–198. Springer, Heidelberg (2010)

32. Ruiz-Gonzalez, D., Koch, N., Kroiss, C., Romero, J.R., Vallecillo, A.: Viewpoint synchronization of UWE models. In: MDWE 2009, pp. 46–60 (2009)

33. Song, H., Huang, G., Chauvel, F., Zhang, W., Sun, Y., Shao, W., Mei, H.: Instant and Incremental QVT Transformation for Runtime Models. In: Whittle, J., Clark, T., Kühne, T. (eds.) MoDELS 2011. LNCS, vol. 6981, pp. 273–288. Springer, Heidelberg (2011)

34. Sprinkle, J., Karsai, G.: A domain-specific visual language for domain model evolution. J. Vis. Lang. Comput. 15(3-4), 291–307 (2004)

35. Sunyé, G., Pollet, D., Le Traon, Y., Jézéquel, J.-M.: Refactoring UML Models. In: Gogolla, M., Kobryn, C. (eds.) UML 2001. LNCS, vol. 2185, pp. 134–148. Springer, Heidelberg (2001)

36. Vermolen, S., Wachsmuth, G., Visser, E.: Reconstructing complex metamodel evolution. In: SLE 2011. Springer (2012)

37. Xiong, Y., Liu, D., Hu, Z., Zhao, H., Takeichi, M., Mei, H.: Towards automatic Model Synchronization from Model Transformations. In: ASE 2007, pp. 164–173. ACM (2007)

38. Zhang, J., Lin, Y., Gray, J.: Generic and Domain-Specific Model Refactoring using a Model Transformation Engine. In: Model-driven Software Development—Research and Practice in Software Engineering, pp. 199–217. Springer (2005)

Turbo DiSL: Partial Evaluation for High-Level Bytecode Instrumentation

Yudi Zheng[1], Danilo Ansaloni[2], Lukas Marek[3], Andreas Sewe[4], Walter Binder[2], Alex Villazón[5], Petr Tuma[3], Zhengwei Qi[1], and Mira Mezini[4]

[1] Shanghai Scalable Computing Lab, Shanghai Jiao Tong University, China
{zheng.yudi,qizhwei}@sjtu.edu.cn
[2] Faculty of Informatics, University of Lugano, Switzerland
{danilo.ansaloni,walter.binder}@usi.ch
[3] Faculty of Mathematics and Physics, Charles University, Czech Republic
{lukas.marek,petr.tuma}@d3s.mff.cuni.cz
[4] Technische Universität Darmstadt, Germany
andreas.sewe@cased.de, mezini@informatik.tu-darmstadt.de
[5] Universidad Privada Boliviana, Bolivia
avillazon@upb.edu

Abstract. Bytecode instrumentation is a key technique for the implementation of dynamic program analysis tools such as profilers and debuggers. Traditionally, bytecode instrumentation has been supported by low-level bytecode engineering libraries that are difficult to use. Recently, the domain-specific aspect language DiSL has been proposed to provide high-level abstractions for the rapid development of efficient bytecode instrumentations. While DiSL supports user-defined expressions that are evaluated at weave-time, the DiSL programming model requires these expressions to be implemented in separate classes, thus increasing code size and impairing code readability and maintenance. In addition, the DiSL weaver may produce a significant amount of dead code, which may impair some optimizations performed by the runtime. In this paper we introduce Turbo, a novel partial evaluator for DiSL, which processes the generated instrumentation code, performs constant propagation, conditional reduction, and pattern-based code simplification, and executes pure methods at weave-time. With Turbo, it is often unnecessary to wrap expressions for evaluation at weave-time in separate classes, thus simplifying the programming model. We present Turbo's partial evaluation algorithm and illustrate its benefits with several case studies. We evaluate the impact of Turbo on weave-time performance and on runtime performance of the instrumented application.

Keywords: Bytecode instrumentation, aspect-oriented programming, domain-specific languages, partial evaluation, Java Virtual Machine.

1 Introduction

Dynamic program analysis tools support numerous software engineering tasks, including profiling, debugging, and reverse engineering. Prevailing techniques for

C.A. Furia and S. Nanz (Eds.): TOOLS Europe 2012, LNCS 7304, pp. 353–368, 2012.

building dynamic analysis tools are based on low-level abstractions that make tool development tedious, error-prone, and expensive. In the context of managed languages, bytecode instrumentation is a widely used implementation technique for dynamic analysis tools. For example, the Java Virtual Machine (JVM) supports bytecode instrumentation through a native code interface and there are many low-level libraries and frameworks for manipulating bytecode (e.g., ASM, BCEL, gnu.bytecode, Javassist, Serp, ShrikeBT, Soot).

The domain-specific language DiSL [8] offers high-level abstractions to enable rapid development of efficient dynamic analysis tools for the JVM. DiSL succeeds in reconciling a high level of abstraction for tool development, expressiveness, and efficiency of the resulting tools. DiSL is an aspect language based on a pointcut/advice mechanism [7]. The benefit of using aspects for dynamic program analysis stems from the convenient model offered by join points (representing specific points in the execution of a program), pointcuts (denoting a set of join points of interest), and advice (code to be executed whenever a join point of interest is reached) [13]. A dynamic analysis aspect is concise and is easier to define, tune and extend, compared to an equivalent implementation based on low-level bytecode instrumentation techniques [8].

DiSL supports the weave-time evaluation of custom conditionals to decide whether join points are woven, as long as these conditionals only depend on static context information of the join point in question. This feature is key to avoiding the repeated evaluation of such conditionals within advice at runtime. Alas, the user needs to factor out the code that is to be evaluated at weave-time from the advice. This complicates the DiSL programming model, as extra classes and methods need to be introduced, and in some cases advice needs to be split up into several pieces for which the weaving order has to be explicitly specified.

From the user's point of view, it would be much more convenient to simply write conditionals within advice code and rely on the DiSL weaver to optimize the code and to move as much computation as possible from runtime to weave-time. However, the DiSL weaver as presented previously [8] does not perform any optimization of the woven advice. It may even generate a significant amount of dead code that may hinder certain optimizations of the runtime.[1]

In this paper we introduce Turbo, a new partial evaluator that is plugged into the DiSL weaver to optimize woven advice. Turbo performs constant propagation and executes pure methods (i.e., methods that are free of side effects and compute the same result when invoked multiple times with the same arguments) at weave-time; it also removes dead code. Thanks to Turbo, the DiSL programmer usually does not need to take care of factoring out expressions to be evaluated at weave-time. Instead, such expressions are simply embedded in advice code. Turbo will detect them and evaluate them at weave-time. In particular, Turbo guarantees that conditionals that only depend on static context information will always be

---

[1] For example, the just-in-time compilers of some recent JVMs base inlining decisions on the size of methods; if the weaver inserts a lot of dead code, the woven method may not be eligible for inlining (a very effective compiler optimization) anymore.

evaluated at weave-time. Furthermore, the DiSL user may annotate methods that are pure such that Turbo may execute them at weave-time. Turbo is also aware of many pure methods in the standard Java class library (e.g., methods in `java.lang.Integer` or `java.lang.String`).

The original, scientific contributions of this paper are twofold:

1. We introduce Turbo, a partial evaluator for DiSL [8]. While partial evaluation has been explored by others, Turbo is unique in simplifying the programming model for the development of instrumentation-based dynamic analyses.
2. We present four case studies to illustrate the benefits of Turbo. With one of these case studies, we evaluate the performance impact of Turbo both on weave-time and on runtime of the woven application.

Section 2 gives an overview of DiSL. Section 3 introduces Turbo, our new partial evaluator for DiSL. Section 4 illustrates how Turbo simplifies the DiSL programming model in four case studies, before Sect. 5 explores the performance impact of Turbo. Section 6 discusses related work and Sect. 7 concludes.

2   Background: DiSL Overview

Below we give an overview of some language constructs supported by DiSL, limiting the discussion to the features used in this paper. We will show the DiSL language constructs with concrete examples in Sect. 4. We refer the reader to our comprehensive description of the DiSL language [8] for further information.

Join point model. DiSL has an *open join point model* in which any region of bytecodes can be used as a join point. Pointcuts are expressed with *markers* that select bytecode regions. DiSL provides an extensible library of such markers including ones for selecting whole method bodies, basic blocks, single bytecodes, and exception handlers. DiSL relies on *guards* to further restrict the join points selected by a marker. Guards are predicate methods free of side-effects that are executed at weave-time which have access to static context information.

Advice. Advice in DiSL are expressed in the form of code *snippets*. Snippets are void methods that are instantiated by the weaver and that take annotations indicating whether they are to be woven before or after a join point. In contrast to mainstream AOP languages such as AspectJ, DiSL does not support around advice (synthetic local variables [8] mitigate this limitation).

Context information. Snippets and guards have access to complete static context information (i.e., static reflective join point information). To this end, snippets and guards can take an arbitrary number of static context references as arguments. Methods in static context classes return constants: primitive values, strings, or class literals. DiSL provides an extensible library of static context classes. Snippets have also access to complete dynamic context information, including local variables and the operand stack. Dynamic context information is provided through an interface type; snippets may take an argument of that type to access dynamic context information.

When a snippet is selected to be woven at a join point, it is first instantiated with respect to the context of the join point. The DiSL weaver first replaces invocations of static context methods with the corresponding constants. That is, static context method invocations in the snippet are pseudo-method calls that are substituted with concrete constants. This step in the weaving process introduces constants into the snippet; thus, the opportunity to optimize the code with partial evaluation arises. Dynamic context method invocations in the snippet are also pseudo-method calls that are replaced with bytecode sequences to access local variables respectively to copy operands from the stack. The partial evaluator Turbo described below is invoked after the removal of static context method calls but before the removal of the dynamic context method calls.

3   Turbo: Partial Evaluator for DiSL

Turbo is a new on-the-fly partial evaluator integrated with the most recent version of the DiSL weaver. If enabled, Turbo performs code optimizations during the process of snippet instantiation. As discussed in Sect. 2, the DiSL weaver instantiates snippets by replacing invocations of static context methods with bytecodes that load the corresponding constants. Turbo can perform any computation in snippets that depends only on constants and does not produce any side effects at weave-time, thus avoiding repetitive runtime computations. To reduce the weaving overhead, Turbo is designed to be simple but efficient, aiming at simplifying the DiSL programming model.

Turbo partial evaluation is divided into three major steps that can be iterated until no further optimization is possible: (1) constant propagation, (2) conditional reduction, and (3) pattern-based code simplification. Turbo guarantees that any intermediate result in the process of partial evaluation represents valid bytecode without any change in the semantics with respect to the initial bytecode. Consequently, it is easily possible to adjust the trade-off between the quality of the partially evaluated bytecode and the time spent in optimization. For example, the DiSL programmer may specify an upper limit on the number of iterations performed by Turbo on each snippet, so as to limit the performance impact of Turbo on weave-time.

If Turbo is iterated until no further optimizations are possible, it guarantees that any bytecode within conditionals that are statically known to evaluate to false (i.e., that only depend on computation with constants and on invocations of pure methods) will be discarded. Such conditionals may even enclose snippet code that results in bytecode which would fail the JVM's bytecode verification when instantiated; as the unreachable snippet code is discarded by Turbo, this otherwise unverifiable bytecode can neither cause a weave-time error nor a verification error when the instrumented class is linked. In Sect. 4.3 we will show an example where this property of Turbo is useful, as it allows the programmer to access potentially illegal positions on the operand stack when enclosed by an appropriate static context information check.

Below we explain each step in the partial evaluation algorithm.

Constant propagation. The constant interpreter performs constant propagation on the input snippet. It symbolically executes the bytecodes in the control-flow graph by transforming an input frame (which represents the local variables and the operand stack) into an output frame according to the bytecodes' semantics. For each bytecode, Turbo stores a frame containing the constant status of each local variable and stack operand before executing it. If a bytecode is reachable through multiple execution paths, Turbo merges the input frames. This operation will replace a constant with a dedicated value indicating that the local variable respectively stack operand is not constant or not the same constant for all merged input frames. Our implementation of the constant interpreter is based on the symbolic analyzer provided by ASM, a Java bytecode manipulation framework. This is a sensible implementation choice, since DiSL's weaver is itself ASM-based.

Besides symbolically executing bytecodes, Turbo also executes pure methods at weave-time, thus enabling constant propagation across pure method calls. To this end, the DiSL programmer must annotate such methods with @Pure and ensure that the annotated methods indeed have no side effects and that their output does not change for subsequent invocations with the same arguments. Moreover, the methods have to be static with parameters of primitive (resp. wrapper) types or strings. Out-of-the-box, Turbo also supports the removal of calls to pure methods in the Java class library (e.g., string operations).

Figure 1a presents the algorithm of constant propagation implemented by Turbo. It uses the auxiliary operations defined in Fig. 1b.

Conditional reduction. After constant propagation, some branch instructions can be resolved to either if(true) or if(false). Turbo discards the branch that is not taken and replaces the branch bytecode with a number of **pop** bytecodes corresponding to the number of operands that would be consumed by the branch bytecode. This code transformation ensures that the snippet code remains valid. After all branch bytecodes have been processed, Turbo removes inaccessible basic blocks from the control-flow graph.

Pattern-based code simplification. After each iteration, Turbo eliminates superfluous code matching one of several different patterns, such as jumping to the next instruction. Another code pattern optimized by Turbo is the sequence of **pop** bytecodes introduced by conditional reduction. For each **pop** bytecode, Turbo finds out the source bytecodes that push the operand. If all those bytecodes are free of side effects, Turbo removes both the **pop** bytecode and its source bytecodes; for each bytecode thus removed, Turbo inserts **pop** bytecodes corresponding to the number of stack operands that would be consumed by the removed source bytecode.

Input   : An instruction list Φ
Output   : $\cup_{instr \in \Phi} instr.frame$
Initially :
  $Q :=$ **new** Queue();
  Q.enqueue($\langle$first instruction of Φ, **new** Frame()$\rangle$);
Iteration:
  while $Q \neq \emptyset$ **do**
      $\langle instr, input \rangle := Q$.dequeue();
      $changed :=$ **false**;
      if $instr.frame =$ **null then**
          $instr.frame := input$.clone();
          $changed :=$ **true**;
      else
          for $i := 0$ **to** $input.size - 1$ **do**
             if $input$.get(i) $\neq instr.frame$.get(i) **then**
                $instr.frame$.set($i, \hat{c}$);
                $changed :=$ **true**;

          end
      if $changed$ **then**
          $output := input$.clone();
          switch instruction pattern of $instr$ **do**
             case Load_constant: $c \rightarrow dst, c \in C$
                $output$.set(dst, c);
             case Data_transfer: $src \rightarrow dst$
                $v := input$.get(src);
                $output$.set(dst, v);
             case Data_processing: $(op)srcs \rightarrow dst$
                if $\forall src \in srcs : input$.get($src$) $\in C$ **then**
                    $v := instr$.process($\cup_{src \in srcs} input$.get($src$));
                    $output$.set(dst, v);
                else
                    $output$.set($dst, \hat{c}$);

             case Invocation: $call\ f(srcs) \rightarrow dst$
                if $\forall src \in srcs : input$.get($src$) $\in C$ **and** f is pure **then**
                    $v := instr$.invoke($f, \cup_{src \in srcs} input$.get($src$));
                    $output$.set(dst, v);
                else
                    $output$.set($dst, \hat{c}$);

             otherwise if $instr$ rewrites dst **then** $output$.set($dst, \hat{c}$);
          endsw
          $\forall next \in instr.next : Q$.enqueue($\langle next, output \rangle$);

  end

Fig. 1a. Turbo's algorithm for constant propagation. Auxiliary procedures used are shown in Fig. 1b (Notation: C denotes the set of constants (e.g., 0, 1.0, null), $\hat{c} \notin C$ denotes a dedicated non-constant value.)

class Queue
    dequeue(): Return and remove the first tuple from the queue;
    enqueue($\langle instruction, frame \rangle$):
        Insert the tuple $\langle instruction, frame \rangle$ at the end of the queue;

class Frame
    Frame(): Initially all elements are assigned the non-constant value $\hat{c}$;
    clone(): Return a copy of this frame;
    get(*position*): Return the element at the specified *position* in the frame;
    set(*position, value*):
        Replace the element at the specified *position* in the frame with *value*;

class Instruction
    frame: constant status of each local variable or stack operand before evaluation;
    next: union of possible next instructions;
    invoke(*method, set*$\langle argument \rangle$): Execute *method*;
    process(*set*$\langle operand \rangle$):
        Symbolically execute the instruction according to its semantics;

Fig. 1b. Auxiliary procedures used by Turbo's algorithm for constant propagation

4 Case Studies

Below we discuss four case studies comparing real-world dynamic analyses using plain DiSL with equivalent versions using Turbo DiSL. They illustrate how Turbo simplifies the programming of efficient dynamic analysis tools.

4.1 Case Study 1: Configurable Instrumentation

Dynamic analyses often require some external configuration to bypass part of their behaviors. When analyzing method calls, e.g., one might be interested in the arguments passed or the execution time of the call. But since not all information is always needed, it is desirable to configure the analysis accordingly to avoid unnecessary overhead.

A straightforward implementation of such a configurable analysis is shown in Fig. 2a. The snippet is woven in at the beginning of each method body; its code will be executed upon each method entry. All configurable cases are coded as conditionals within this single snippet. Alas, the configuration is evaluated at runtime each time the snippet is invoked.[2]

Now, if the boolean methods `profileArgs()` and `profileTime()` always return the same constant value, one would prefer to evaluate the conditionals within the snippet once at weave-time instead of evaluating them upon each method call. In plain DiSL (i.e., without Turbo), the programmer may resort to guards [8] to factor out the code to be evaluated at weave-time, as illustrated in

---

[2] The JVM's just-in-time compiler may be able to remove some of this overhead.

```
public class MethodAnalysis {
  @Before(marker = BodyMarker.class)
  static void onMethodEntry() {
    if (Configuration.profileArgs()) { ... /* profile method arguments */ }
    if (Configuration.profileTime()) { ... /* profile current wall time */ }
  }
}
```

Fig. 2a. Skeleton implementation of a configurable analysis

```
public class MethodAnalysis {
  @Before(marker = BodyMarker.class, order = 1, guard = ArgsGuard.class)
  static void onMethodEntryArgs() { ... /* profile method arguments */ }

  @Before(marker = BodyMarker.class, order = 0, guard = TimeGuard.class)
  static void onMethodEntryTime() { ... /* profile current wall time */ }
}

public class ArgsGuard {
  @GuardMethod
  static boolean evalGuard() { return Configuration.profileArgs(); }
}

public class TimeGuard {
  @GuardMethod
  static boolean evalGuard() { return Configuration.profileTime(); }
}
```

Fig. 2b. Configurable analysis implemented with guards

Fig. 2b. However, the resulting code is more complicated and verbose, as the programmer has to implement two snippets, two guards, and to supply additional information to the snippet annotation to fix the weaving order.

With Turbo, it is not necessary to use guards to reduce runtime overhead; the code can be implemented exactly as shown in Fig. 2a above. If the methods `profileArgs()` and `profileTime()` in class `Configuration` are annotated with `@Pure`, Turbo will evaluate these methods at weave-time and remove any dead code when weaving the snippet. Consequently, the snippet code can stay simple with all the benefits of weave-time evaluation. As another benefit, the reduction in code size achieved by Turbo helps avoid overlong methods that would violate constraints of the JVM.

4.2   Case Study 2: Tracking Monitor Ownership

In the JVM, each object has an associated monitor. As contention for monitor ownership limits application's scalability, a dynamic analysis to track ownership can assist in finding performance bottlenecks in multi-threaded Java programs.

A thread gains ownership of a monitor either explicitly by entering a **synchronized** block (i.e., by executing **monitorenter** at the bytecode level), or implicitly by entering a **synchronized** method. In the latter case, it is the

```
public class MonitorOwnershipAnalysis {
  @Before(marker = BodyMarker.class, guard = SynchronizedClassMethodGuard.class)
  static void acquireMonitorForClass(MethodStaticContext msc, ClassContext cc) {
    Object assocObj = cc.asClass(msc.thisClassName());
    ... /* track ownership */
  }

  @Before(marker = BodyMarker.class, guard = SynchronizedInstanceMethodGuard.class)
  static void acquireMonitorForInstance(DynamicContext dc) {
    Object assocObj = dc.getThis();
    ... /* track ownership */
  }
}

public class SynchronizedClassMethodGuard {
  @GuardMethod
  static boolean isApplicable(MethodStaticContext msc) {
    return msc.isMethodSynchronized() && msc.isMethodStatic();
  }
}

public class SynchronizedInstanceMethodGuard {
  @GuardMethod
  static boolean isApplicable(MethodStaticContext msc) {
    return msc.isMethodSynchronized() && !msc.isMethodStatic();
  }
}
```

Fig. 3a. Analysis to track monitor ownership using guards

```
public class MonitorOwnershipAnalysis {
  @Before(marker = BodyMarker.class)
  static void acquireMonitor(DynamicContext dc, MethodStaticContext msc,
                             ClassContext cc) {
    if (msc.isMethodSynchronized()) {
      Object assocObj =
        msc.isMethodStatic() ? cc.asClass(msc.thisClassName()) : dc.getThis();
      ... /* track ownership */
    }
  }
}
```

Fig. 3b. Analysis to track monitor ownership relying on partial evaluation

monitor of the receiver object (`this`) that is acquired for instance methods and the monitor of the corresponding instance of `java.lang.Class` for class (static) methods. Which object and hence which monitor is meant is statically known.

With plain DiSL, however, this distinction needs to be expressed through guards, leading to the both duplicated and hard-to-read code shown in Fig. 3a. Said code is not only verbose but also makes it hard to see that the two cases (`acquireMonitorForClass`/`ForInstance`) complement each other. With Turbo's partial evaluation, the above code can be written in a single snippet using straightforward conditionals as shown in Fig. 3b.

```
public class FieldAccessAnalysis {
  @Before(marker = BytecodeMarker.class, args = "getfield")
  static void onFieldRead(FieldAccStaticContext fasc, MethodStaticContext msc,
                          DynamicContext dc) {
    String methodID = msc.thisMethodFullName();
    String fieldID = fasc.thisFieldID();
    Object ownerObj = dc.getStackValue(0, Object.class);
    ... /* profile field read */
  }


  @Before(marker = BytecodeMarker.class, args = "putfield")
  static void onFieldWrite(FieldAccStaticContext fasc, MethodStaticContext msc,
                           DynamicContext dc) {
    String methodID = msc.thisMethodFullName();
    String fieldID = fasc.thisFieldID();
    Object ownerObj = dc.getStackValue(1, Object.class);
    ... /* profile field write */
  }
}
```

Fig. 4a. Field access analysis with code duplication

```
public class FieldAccessAnalysis {
  @Before(marker = BytecodeMarker.class, args = "getfield,putfield")
  static void onFieldAcc(FieldAccStaticContext fasc, MethodStaticContext msc,
                         DynamicContext dc) {
    String methodID = msc.thisMethodFullName();
    String fieldID = fasc.thisFieldID();
    int stackDistance = (fasc.getOpcode() == Opcodes.GETFIELD) ? 0 : 1;
    Object ownerObj = dc.getStackValue(stackDistance, Object.class);
    ... /* profile field access (read or write) */
  }
}
```

Fig. 4b. Field access analysis relying on partial evaluation

4.3   Case Study 3: Field Access Analysis

Figure 4a shows an instrumentation to profile any access to instance fields. The first snippet is woven before each read access (**getfield**) while the second snippet is woven before each write access (**putfield**). In the former case, the owner object resides on top of the operand stack, whereas in the latter case it is the second topmost stack operand.

Without partial evaluation, it is impossible to combine the two snippets by choosing the stack location to access based on the opcode. As the first argument for the pseudo-method getStackValue must be a constant, the snippet would include two branches to access the stack position zero respectively one; for each woven join point, one of the branches would constitute dead code. Moreover, that dead branch would possibly access an illegal position on the operand stack, resulting in bytecode that would fail verification[3]. With partial evaluation, such code duplication is unnecessary; a single snippet with a conditional suffices as

---

[3] The DiSL weaver may generate warnings if bytecode is generated that would fail load-time verification.

```
public class ExecutionTraceProfiler {
  @Before(marker = BasicBlockMarker.class, order = 1, guard = ClassInitGuard.class)
  static void onClassInit(MethodStaticContext msc) {
    ... /* profile class initialization */
  }

  @Before(marker = BasicBlockMarker.class, order = 0)
  static void onBB(CustomBasicBlockStaticContext cbbsc) {
    String bbID = cbbsc.thisBBID();
    ... /* profile basic block entry */
  }
}

public class CustomBasicBlockStaticContext extends BasicBlockStaticContext {
  public String thisBBID() {
    String methodFullName = staticContextData.getClassNode().name
      + "." + staticContextData.getMethodNode().name;
    return methodFullName + ":" + String.valueOf(getBBindex());
  }
}

public class ClassInitGuard {
  @GuardMethod
  static boolean evalGuard(BasicBlockStaticContext bbsc, MethodStaticContext msc) {
    return (bbsc.getBBindex() == 0) && msc.thisMethodName().equals("<clinit>");
  }
}
```

Fig. 5a. Execution trace profiler using a custom static context class and a guard

```
public class ExecutionTraceProfiler {
  @Before(marker = BasicBlockMarker.class)
  static void onBB(BasicBlockStaticContext bbsc, MethodStaticContext msc) {
    if (bbsc.getBBindex() == 0 && msc.thisMethodName().equals("<clinit>")) {
      ... /* profile class initialization */
    }
    String bbID = msc.thisMethodFullName() + ":" + String.valueOf(bbsc.getBBindex());
    ... /* profile basic block entry */
  }
}
```

Fig. 5b. Execution trace profiler relying on partial evaluation

shown in Fig. 4b. Turbo guarantees that this conditional is evaluated at weave-time (since it only depends on constant data) and that only the proper constant is propagated to the pseudo-method `getStackValue`.

4.4   Case Study 4: Execution Trace Profiling

Figure 5a shows a profiler that traces each executed basic block of code, identified by a unique string comprising the fully qualified method name (package, class, method, signature) and a basic block ID (an integer value that is unique within the scope of a method body). In addition, the execution of the first basic block in each class initializer (method `<clinit>` at the bytecode level) is specially tracked by the profiler. The DiSL code in Fig. 5a is complicated; it comprises two snippets and requires both a custom static context and a guard. The static context ensures that the special basic block identifiers are built at weave-time, while the guard identifies the first basic block of class initializers. The snippet order guarantees that the special profiling of the first basic block in a static initializer happens before the normal basic block profiling.

Figure 5b shows a naïve single-snippet implementation with a conditional; the basic block ID is built within the snippet code. While this implementation is sound, it incurs excessive runtime overhead, since the conditional is evaluated and the identifier is built at runtime for each woven join point, i.e., for each basic block in the base program. However, with partial evaluation, the woven bytecode for both versions of the profiler will be the same, as the conditional depends on static information only and the string operations are pure. Hence, Turbo evaluates these parts of the snippet code at weave-time. In the next section, we will explore weave-time and runtime performance of both versions of the profiler.

5   Performance Evaluation

We use the execution trace profiler of the fourth case study for our performance evaluation, because it intercepts the highest number of join points, both statically at weave-time and dynamically at runtime. That is, the impact of partial evaluation on weave-time performance and the impact of code quality on runtime performance is most pronounced in this case study.

The base programs are benchmarks from the DaCapo suite (release 9.12).[4] We exclude tradebeans and tradesoap because of a well-known issue with a hardcoded timeout[5], which prevents their use together with expensive instrumentation. All measurements were conducted on a 3.0 GHz Intel Core 2 Quad Q9650 with 8 GB RAM running Ubuntu GNU/Linux 10.04 64-bit with kernel 2.6.35. We use Oracle's JDK 1.6.0_30 Hotspot Server VM (64-bit) with a 7 GB heap and DiSL pre-release version 0.9 with complete bytecode coverage, i.e., with a completely woven Java class library [8].

We evaluate three versions of the execution trace profiler: (1) the naïve implementation shown in Fig. 5b *without Turbo*, which serves as a baseline for the comparison; (2) the manually optimized implementation shown in Fig. 5a (without Turbo), henceforth called "DiSL optimized"; and (3) the naïve implementation of Fig. 5b *with Turbo*, called "Turbo DiSL". Moreover, we consider three performance metrics: (a) the weave-time, i.e., the time to weave all classes loaded during a single benchmark iteration; (b) the startup time, i.e., the process time from creation to the termination of the first benchmark iteration; and (c) the steady-state execution time, i.e., the median of the execution times of 15 benchmark iterations within the same JVM process.

For each metric, Fig. 6 illustrates the speedup of "DiSL optimized" and "Turbo DiSL" relative to the baseline. The gray marks refer to the individual

---

[4] See http://www.dacapobench.org/.

[5] See http://sourceforge.net/tracker/?group_id=172498 (artifact ID 2955469).

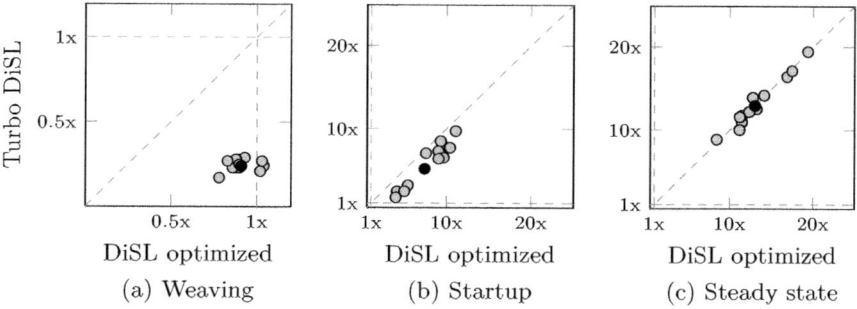

Fig. 6. Speedup factor relative to the naïve implementation without Turbo for the considered DaCapo benchmarks (values below 1x indicate slowdowns)

benchmarks, while the black marks refer to the geometric mean of all speedup factors. When the speedup factor is below 1x, it indicates a slowdown. The diagonal line indicates data points for which the performance of "DiSL optimized" and "Turbo DiSL" is the same.

Regarding weave-time, Fig. 6(a), the baseline is generally faster than both the "DiSL optimized" and "Turbo DiSL" versions, because for the baseline, Turbo is deactivated and there is no guard to be evaluated at weave-time. However, in a few benchmarks "DiSL optimized" outperforms the baseline because the reduced complexity of the inlined snippet code outweighs the cost of guard evaluation. On average, "DiSL optimized" is only 10% slower than the baseline, while the use of Turbo increases weave-time by a factor of 4.2. This result clearly shows the drawback of partial evaluation, a considerable increase in weave-time.

Regarding startup performance, Fig. 6(b), "DiSL optimized" outperforms the baseline by a factor of 7.4, and "Turbo DiSL" outperforms the baseline by a factor of 5.18. Interestingly, a single benchmark iteration (which includes weave-time) is sufficient to achieve a significant speedup by partial evaluation. The manually tuned version is faster still, as it does not significantly increase weave-time.

Regarding steady-state performance, Fig. 6(c), "DiSL optimized" and "Turbo DiSL" reach the same high speedup of about 13x. This result highlights the strengths of Turbo; high steady-state performance is achieved without having to write complicated, manually tuned code. The fact that "Turbo DiSL" significantly outperforms the baseline clearly shows that the just-in-time compiler of the JVM is not able to perform the same kind of optimizations as Turbo.

6   Related Work

Partial evaluation (also called program specialization) enables aggressive inter-procedural constant propagation, constant folding, and control-flow simplifications [6]. An online partial evaluator makes decisions about what to specialize during the specialization process, while an offline partial evaluator makes all the decisions before specialization. Hybrid Partial Evaluation (HPE) [12] combines both approaches by letting the programmer guide the specialization process through annotations, e.g., to indicate which objects are to be instantiated at compile time. This is similar to Turbo's annotations used to guide the partial evaluation, without which not all optimization decisions can be made in an offline-fashion. Thus, Turbo can be considered to follow a hybrid approach, too.

Some approaches to partial evaluation are based on translating the source program into another programming language that provides more powerful specialization mechanisms. For example, Albert et al. use partial evaluation to automatically generate specialized programs by transforming Java bytecode into Prolog to apply powerful constraint logic programming [1]. The Prolog code is then interpreted by the CiaoPP abstract interpreter [5]. While this approach allows for powerful interpretative partial evaluation, it only handles a subset of Java that lacks exception handling, multi-threading, and reflection. In contrast, Turbo's partial evaluator is less powerful, but does not have such limitations.

AspectJ [7] is a language often used for the kind of bytecode instrumentation tasks DiSL is designed for. The standard AspectJ compiler (ajc) already performs partial evaluation of the aspects' pointcuts, which are akin to DiSL's markers, scopes, and guards. It does not, however, partially evaluate the aspects' advice, which are akin to DiSL's snippets. Masuhara et al. describe this approach in terms of a semantics-based compilation model [9]. This model follows an interpretative approach to compilation, based on partially evaluating the AOP interpreter itself (written in Scheme) to remove unnecessary pointcut tests. In contrast to Turbo, advice code is not partially evaluated, but rather the partial evaluator verifies if the advice should be inserted in compiled code or not.

Pesto [2] is a declarative language to describe specialization of object-oriented programs. Pesto generates all context and configuration information needed to use the JSpec offline Java partial evaluator [11], which then generates residual code in AspectJ. Like Turbo, Pesto uses guards to select specialized code when invariants are satisfied. The approach is based on the observation that partial evaluation of an object-oriented program creates new code with dependencies that cross-cut the class hierarchy. Thus, the methods generated by a given specialization can be encapsulated into a separate aspect. Whereas Turbo uses partial evaluation to optimize the execution of advice code, Pesto performs specialization of the base program using AspectJ aspects, which unfortunately do not benefit from optimizations at the advice level.

Spoon [10] is a framework for program transformation and static analysis in Java, which reifies the program with respect to a meta-model. This allows for direct access and modification of its structure at compile-time and enables template-based AOP; similar to DiSL, users can insert code, e.g., before or after a method body. Spoon, however, uses source code-level transformations. This limits its applicability for dynamic analysis, as neither basic blocks analysis nor efficient access to context information are possible. For constant propagation, dead-code elimination, and access to static context for template instantiation, Spoon provides a meta-model partial evaluation facility. Whereas Turbo performs partial evaluation of advice code, Spoon's partial evaluator specializes the meta-model; partial evaluation returns specialized models rather than code.

While Spoon reifies the entire program with respect to a meta-model, the ALIA4J approach [3] to language implementation stipulates a common meta-model only for so-called advanced dispatching, during which one or more actions are selected depending on the current runtime context, and subsequently executed. Many, but not all bytecode instrumentation tasks possible with DiSL also fit this model. During language implementation, ALIA4J's concepts like actions, predicates, and contexts can be refined to realize the desired language semantics, e.g., by implementing the semantics based on interpretation or code generation [4]. In the latter case, the code generator is exposed to additional static information which often allows for partial evaluation of a refined concept. Unlike in Turbo, this requires manual analysis by the language implementer.

7   Conclusion

We presented Turbo, a new partial evaluator for the domain-specific aspect language DiSL [8] that targets the development of dynamic program analysis tools based on bytecode instrumentation. Turbo is designed as an optional component that is activated by the DiSL weaver during the instantiation of snippets, after static context information has been resolved. Turbo propagates constants, reduces conditionals, evaluates pure methods with constant input data, simplifies certain code patterns, and performs dead-code elimination.

The most significant benefit of Turbo is that it simplifies the DiSL programming model, as we illustrated with four case studies. The DiSL programmer does not need to factor out code to be evaluated at weave-time, but can rely on Turbo to automatically detect and optimize such code. While it is always possible to program efficient instrumentations using DiSL constructs such as guards and custom static context classes, the equivalent code relying on Turbo is generally more concise and easier to write, understand, and maintain.

Our performance evaluation confirms that a simple DiSL instrumentation optimized by Turbo can reach the same steady-state performance as a complicated, manually tuned instrumentation, at the expense of an increase in weave-time, i.e., lower startup performance. Turbo ideally supports rapid prototyping of dynamic analyses in DiSL; the programmer need not care about factoring out parts that can be evaluated at weave-time. If the analysis is applied only a few times (e.g., during workload characterization) or is applied to long-running base programs, the increase in weave-time is usually not an issue. If fast weaving is essential, for example in the case of frequently used profilers, the DiSL programmer may prefer to refactor the code using guards and custom static context classes; still, Turbo is valuable during development to explore the possible steady-state performance of an optimized analysis before implementing it by hand.

Acknowledgments.   The research presented here was conducted while L. Marek was with the University of Lugano. It was supported by the

Scientific Exchange Programme NMS–CH (project code 10.165), by a Sino-Swiss Science and Technology Cooperation (SSSTC) Institutional Partnership (project no. IP04–092010), by the Swiss National Science Foundation (project CRSII2_136225), by the National Natural Science Foundation of China (project no. 61073151), by the Science and Technology Commission of Shanghai Municipality (project no. 11530700500), by the Czech Science Foundation (project GACR P202/10/J042), as well as by CASED (www.cased.de).

References

1. Albert, E., Gómez-Zamalloa, M., Hubert, L., Puebla, G.: Verification of Java Bytecode Using Analysis and Transformation of Logic Programs. In: Hanus, M. (ed.) PADL 2007. LNCS, vol. 4354, pp. 124–139. Springer, Heidelberg (2006)
2. Andersen, H.M., Schultz, U.P.: Declarative specialization for object-oriented-program specialization. In: Proceedings of the Symposium on Partial Evaluation and Program Manipulation, pp. 27–38 (2004)
3. Bockisch, C., Sewe, A., Mezini, M., Akşit, M.: An Overview of ALIA4J: An Execution Model for Advanced-Dispatching Languages. In: Bishop, J., Vallecillo, A. (eds.) TOOLS 2011. LNCS, vol. 6705, pp. 131–146. Springer, Heidelberg (2011)
4. Bockisch, C., Sewe, A., Zandberg, M.: ALIA4J's [(just-in-time) compile-time] MOP for advanced dispatching. In: Proceedings of the 5th Workshop on Virtual Machines and Intermediate Languages, pp. 309–316 (2011)
5. Hermenegildo, M.V., Puebla, G., Bueno, F., López-García, P.: Integrated program debugging, verification, and optimization using abstract interpretation (and the Ciao system preprocessor). Science of Computer Programming 58(1-2), 115–140 (2005)
6. Jones, N.D., Gomard, C.K., Sestoft, P.: Partial Evaluation and Automatic Program Generation. Prentice Hall (1993)
7. Kiczales, G., Hilsdale, E., Hugunin, J., Kersten, M., Palm, J., Griswold, W.G.: An Overview of AspectJ. In: Lee, S.H. (ed.) ECOOP 2001. LNCS, vol. 2072, pp. 327–353. Springer, Heidelberg (2001)
8. Marek, L., Villazón, A., Zheng, Y., Ansaloni, D., Binder, W., Qi, Z.: DiSL: a domain-specific language for bytecode instrumentation. In: Proceedings of Modularity: aosd, vol. 12, pp. 239–250 (2012)
9. Masuhara, H., Kiczales, G., Dutchyn, C.: A Compilation and Optimization Model for Aspect-Oriented Programs. In: Hedin, G. (ed.) CC 2003. LNCS, vol. 2622, pp. 46–60. Springer, Heidelberg (2003)
10. Pawlak, R., Noguera, C., Petitprez, N.: Spoon: Program Analysis and Transformation in Java. Rapport, INRIA (2007), http://hal.inria.fr/inria-00071366/en/
11. Schultz, U.P., Lawall, J.L., Consel, C.: Automatic Program Specialization for Java. Transactions on Programming Languages and Systems 25(4), 452–499 (2003)
12. Shali, A., Cook, W.R.: Hybrid partial evaluation. In: Proceedings of the 26th Conference on Object-Oriented Programming, Systems, Languages, and Applications, pp. 375–390 (2011)
13. Tanter, E., Moret, P., Binder, W., Ansaloni, D.: Composition of dynamic analysis aspects. In: Proceedings of the 9th International Conference on Generative Programming and Component Engineering, pp. 113–122 (2010)

Author Index

GPSR Compliance

The European Union's (EU) General Product Safety Regulation (GPSR) is a set of rules that requires consumer products to be safe and our obligations to ensure this.

If you have any concerns about our products, you can contact us on ProductSafety@springernature.com

In case Publisher is established outside the EU, the EU authorized representative is:

Springer Nature Customer Service Center GmbH
Europaplatz 3
69115 Heidelberg, Germany

Batch number: 09478804

Printed by Printforce, the Netherlands